CAMBRIDGE GREEK

CAESAR
BELLUM GALLICUM

BOOK VII

EDITED BY

CHRISTOPHER B. KREBS
Stanford University

CAMBRIDGE
UNIVERSITY PRESS

Shaftesbury Road, Cambridge CB2 8EA, United Kingdom

One Liberty Plaza, 20th Floor, New York, NY 10006, USA

477 Williamstown Road, Port Melbourne, VIC 3207, Australia

314–321, 3rd Floor, Plot 3, Splendor Forum, Jasola District Centre,
New Delhi – 110025, India

103 Penang Road, #05–06/07, Visioncrest Commercial, Singapore 238467

Cambridge University Press is part of Cambridge University Press & Assessment,
a department of the University of Cambridge.

We share the University's mission to contribute to society through the pursuit of
education, learning and research at the highest international levels of excellence.

www.cambridge.org
Information on this title: www.cambridge.org/9781009177122
DOI: 10.1017/9781009177139

First published 2023

A catalogue record for this publication is available from the British Library.

ISBN 978-1-009-17712-2 Hardback
ISBN 978-1-009-17714-6 Paperback

In my heart, as a blessing

∗∗∗

Julio-Bodo Guido, Josephine Tove,
and Maria Luisa

CONTENTS

ILLUSTRATIONS

PREFACE AND ACKNOWLEDGMENTS

In a different corner of the world, in the library of the *Institut für Klassische Altertumskunde*, Robert Coleman warned that "writing a commentary [was] both a chastening and an instructive experience. Once the work [was] finished, one [felt] very nearly equipped to begin the task properly." I have found occasion, while working on this commentary, to recall these words from his preface to *Vergil's Eclogues* (1977: viii), their meaning increasingly more personal than when I first encountered them during my student days at the Christiana Albertina in Kiel; but I should like to add "exciting" and "fraught" to characterize my own experience.

Writing this commentary has been "chastening" and "instructive" for all the obvious reasons: Caesar's text, in a foreign language, reflects a culture that is never nearly as close as it is foreign (to adapt Uvo Hölscher's oft-repeated characterization of Greco-Roman antiquity as *das nächste Fremde*) and that has reached us in no more than fragments to boot. Further and sometimes quite different meanings of a word, a phrase, a paragraph most likely lurk there somewhere out of earshot. There is ever more to investigate, to learn, to say – and so the specter of Zeno's turtle turns its head, always just about out of reach for breathless Achilles.

But even though (or rather because) the pursuit of understanding so often leads uphill, it is also both deeply human – with exegesis requiring many of the same qualities as empathetic listening – and exciting in the way of Sherlock Holmes' keen investigations: to find out (or come closer to hearing) what was *really* said some 2,000 years ago! Was there not, I wondered, more to Caesar, whose literary expertise Cicero equivocally sought (*QFr.* 2.15), and his text than what we were taught as high-school students, when we encountered him as the general, politician, and, above all, involuntary teacher of Latin? As this commentary will detail, the man of letters has indeed left his imprint on every page of the *Bellum Gallicum*; and to detect and contextualize those features has provided Holmesian excitement. But it has been tempered with that rue we feel when reading Vergil's beautiful line on Turnus' sorrowful death, cruelly representative of the countless victims Roman imperialism would claim (*Aen.* 12.952): *uitaque cum gemitu fugit indignata sub umbras.* To understand and appreciate the *Gallic War* as a literary text is the duty of the historian and literary critic; to remember the lives lost and brutalized during the war in Gaul is the responsibility of us all.

As these reflections may indicate, it has been quite an endeavor, and I am deeply thankful for the support and encouragement that I have received over the years. First and foremost, I should like to acknowledge the mentorship and friendship of Christina Kraus as well as Tony Woodman: Their respective impact on the field of Roman historiography has been profound, and so it has been on this commentary, which each accompanied from start to finish, unfailingly, unflaggingly, with comments on every draft, help with any questions, and general cheer: thank you both. Philip Hardie and Stephen Oakley, as eminent editors of the "Green and Yellow" series, were just as assiduous and generous and helped to make this a better book. Amongst my readers of chunks and ready respondents were Brandon Bark, Cynthia Damon, Andrew Fitzpatrick, Luca Grillo, Melissa Haynes, Sabine Hornung, Bob Kaster, Bob Morstein-Marx, Cal Oltrogge, Dan-el Padilla Peralta, Michel Reddé, and Guichard Vincent. Thanks of a different kind I owe to those institutions and individuals that invited me to discuss with their students and faculty sections of the commentary in progress: Anne Kolb at the University of Zürich (who also kindly showed me around a number of archaeological sites, including those at Lac de Neuchâtel), Dennis Pausch at the TU Dresden, the late Rex Stem at UC Davis, and the department of classics at Princeton; and to Emory University, Whitman College, and Princeton University for the honors of delivering the third Annual Benario Lecture, the Forty-third Skotheim Lecture, and the Prentice Lecture, respectively. Andrew Fitzpatrick and Colin Haselgrove enabled me to learn from a group of characteristically enthusiastic archaeologists, when they invited me to give the opening address at their 2017 conference on "Julius Caesar's Battle for Gaul: New Archaeological Perspectives" at Oxford University: it remains a memorable experience. For fellowships that allowed for pursuit and progress in *relative* (see below) quiet I am grateful to the Loeb Classical Library Foundation and the Stanford Humanities Center. Michael Sharp and his team at Cambridge University Press have shown their customary interest, kindness, and forbearance, especially during the final stretch, when the pandemic wreaked havoc on the lives of many and made it all more difficult for everyone.

The final words are reserved for my family, who have variously but consistently delayed and complicated the completion of this project – for which I am more grateful than I can say except that in the dark of night, you shine the light.

Christopher B. Krebs
Stanford University

ABBREVIATIONS AND REFERENCES BY AUTHOR'S NAME ALONE (EXCLUDING STANDARD COMMENTARIES)

Caesar is abbreviated as C., Labienus (in 57–62) as L., Vercingetorix as V. References to the *BG* normally omit the title.

C.E.L.	F. Buecheler, *Carmina epigraphica Latina*, Leipzig [2] 1895
CG	T. R. Holmes, *Conquest of Gaul*, Oxford [2] 1911
CIL	*Corpus Inscriptionum Latinarum*, Berlin 1863–
C-L	J.-P. Chausserie-Laprée, *L'expression narrative chez les historiens latins*, Paris 1969
DKM	*C. Iuli Caesaris Commentarii de bello Gallico*. Hrsg. u. mit Erläuterungen versehen v. F. Kraner, W. Dittenberger, Zürich 1961 (20th ed. prepared by H. Meusel)
DLG	X. Delamarre, *Dictionnaire de la langue gauloise*, Paris [2] 2003
Edwards	H.J. Edwards. *Caesar. Gallic War*. Cambridge 1917
E-M	A. Meillet and A. Ernout, *Dictionnaire étymologique de la langue latine: Histoire des mots*, Paris 2001 (orig. 1932)
FLP	E. Courtney, *The Fragmentary Latin Poets*, Oxford [2] 2003
FRHist	T. J. Cornell (ed.), *The Fragments of the Roman Historians*, Oxford 2013
Gelzer	M. Gelzer, *Caesar, Politician and Statesman*. Cambridge 1985
G-L	B. L. Gildersleeve and G. Lodge, *Latin Grammar*, Wauconda [3] 1997
GPN	E. E. Evans, *Gaulish Personal Names*, Oxford 1967
HLR	H. Lausberg, *Handbook of Literary Rhetoric: a Foundation for Literary Study*, trans. by M. T. Bliss, A. Jansen, D. E. Orton; ed. by D. E. Orton and R. Dean Anderson, Leiden & Boston 1998
H-S	J. B. Hofmann and A. Szantyr, *Lateinische Syntax und Stilistik*, Munich 1965

ILA	*Inscriptions latines d'Aquitaine*, Bordeaux 1994–
ILS	*Inscriptiones Latinae Selectae*, Berlin 1892–1916
K-H	R. Kühner, *Ausführliche Grammatik der lateinischen Sprache*, Band 1, neu bearbeitet v. Fr. Holzweissig, Hanover 1982 (orig. 1912)
K-S	R. Kühner, *Ausführliche Grammatik der lateinischen Sprache*, Band 2, neu bearbeitet v. K. Stegmann, Hanover 1982 (orig. 1914)
LSJ	H. G. Liddell and R. Scott, *A Greek-English Lexicon*, 9th ed. rev. by H. S. Jones, Oxford 1940
Meusel	H. Meusel, *Lexicon Caesarianum*, Berlin 1887–93
M-P	R. Menge and S. Preuss, *Lexicon Caesarianum*, Hildesheim 1972 (orig. 1890)
MRR	T. R. S. Broughton, *The Magistrates of the Roman Republic*. Vols. I–II, New York 1951–60
M-W	R. H. Martin and A. J. Woodman, *Tacitus: Annals Book IV*, Cambridge [2] 1999
N-H	R. G. M. Nisbet and M. Hubbard, *A Commentary on Horace*, Vol. 1 *Odes I*, Vol. 2 *Odes II*, Oxford 1970, 197
NLS	E. C. Woodcock, *A New Latin Syntax*, London 1959
N-R	R. G. M. Nisbet and N. Rudd, *A Commentary on Horace, Odes Book III*, Oxford 2004
Odelman	E. Odelman, *Étude sur quelques reflets du style administratif chez César*, Stockholm (Diss.) 1972
OLD	*Oxford Latin Dictionary*, ed. by P. G. W. Glare, Oxford 1982
OLS	H. Pinkster, *Oxford Latin Syntax, Vol. 1 The Simple Clause, Vol. 2 The Complex Sentence and Discourse*, Oxford 2015 and 2021[1]
ORF	E. Malcovati, *Oratorum Romanorum fragmenta*, Turin 1976–1979 (4th ed.)
Otto	A. Otto, *Die Sprichwörter und sprichwörtlichen Redensarten der Römer*, Darmstadt 1968 (orig. 1890)
Rambaud	M. Rambaud, *L'art de la déformation historique dans les Commentaires de César*, Paris [2] 1966

---

[1] The syntactical part of the commentary was completed when the first volume appeared; references to the *OLS* are therefore less numerous than they would have been otherwise.

RE	A. Pauly, G. Wissowa *et al.* (eds.), *Realencyclopädie der classischen Altertumswissenschaft*, Stuttgart 1894–1980
Riggsby	A. Riggsby, *Caesar in Gaul and Rome. War in Words*, Austin 2006
Schneider	C. *Iuli Caesaris Commentarii de bello Gallico*, rec. et ill. C. E. C. Schneider, Halis 1855
SEG	*Supplementum Epigraphicum Graecum*, Amsterdam 1923
TGF	E. Nègre, *Toponymie générale de la France*, Geneva 1990
TLL	*Thesaurus Linguae Latinae*, Leipzig 1900–
VL	J. Hellegouarc'h, *Le vocabulaire latin des relations et des partis politiques sous la république*, Paris 1963
Wills	J. Wills, *Repetition in Latin Poetry*, Oxford 1996
W-M	A. J. Woodman and R. H. Martin, *The Annals of Tacitus Book 3*, Cambridge 1996

INTRODUCTION

1 JULIUS CAESAR, MAN OF LETTERS

After the dictator's visit in December 45, Cicero exclaimed: "That a guest of mine could be so onerous and yet not disagreeable" (*o hospitem mihi tam grauem ἀμεταμέλητον, Att.* 13.52). No wonder: Gaius Iulius Caesar (C.) and he had "talked about nothing serious but literary matters aplenty" (σπουδαῖον οὐδὲν in *sermone,* φιλόλογα *multa*); their political differences went unremarked. Decades later, Lucan acknowledged C.'s wide-ranging interests when he had him request a didactic poem on Egypt (10.177–79); and Pliny the Elder would remark on his "intellectual excellence capable of comprehending everything under the sky" (*sublimitatem omnium capacem quae caelo continentur, HN* 7.91–92) – while expressing reservations about his conquests (*tantam ... humani generis iniuriam*).[1]

These three testimonia – among others – attest to C.'s literary and intellectual interests and contributions, which, generally speaking, have received less attention than his far more problematic military and political exploits in Gaul and Italy.[2] The fragmentary state of his letters, poems, speeches, linguistic treatise, and other writings has not failed to compound this negligence;[3] and the preoccupation with the "politician and statesman" (as Matthias Gelzer titled his influential biography), often tinged with a historically insensitive Napoleonic admiration, has also affected the reception of his extant works on the Gallic and the civil wars (henceforth *BG* and *BC*).[4] Until rather recently, both were read with predominantly historical, linguistic, and didactic interests, the *BG* especially enjoying the standings of a "citadel of *classical* Latinity" and sole contemporary source on the war in Gaul.[5] What care was spent on them as *arti*facts went into revealing their rhetorical distortion of events for the

---

[1] On Cicero's use of φιλόλογος, see Kuch 1965: 60–72. On Lucan's *Cesare "scienziato,"* cf. Berti 2000: 161–64, 212–14 (and Krebs 2018d: 93–94).

[2] On C.'s intellectual interests, see Fantham 2009, Schiesaro 2010. I use "Gaul" throughout in reference to *Gallia omnis* (p. 11); "*Gallic War*" refers to C.'s written account, the "war in Gaul" to the campaign.

[3] Cf. e.g. Meier 1996: 485 on C.'s "achievements in war and politics"; tellingly, *De analogia* receives but one sentence (313). But see Poli 1993, Grillo-Krebs 2018.

[4] For Mommsen's glorification of C. (and his influence on e.g. Gelzer), see Christ 1994: 134–54, 166–83; Bringmann's review points to the "Napoleonerfahrung" as a factor in C.'s ideation (1997: 254). Adcock 1932 and esp. Strasburger 1938 and 1968 (with Balsdon's review) cut C. down to size.

[5] Frese 1900: 3 (my italics). I translate most non-English-language quotations (except in the footnotes).

1

sake of C.'s "propagandistic" aims: what Michel Rambaud called *"l'art de la déformation historique"* (pp. 24–25).[6] Meanwhile, their literary features – their use of the historiographical tradition, engagement with Greek and Roman literature, and intersections with contemporary discourses – drew much less scrutiny.

Ironically, it is the latter, literary, perspective that characterizes the first remarks on the qualities of the *BG*. Brutus, in the eponymous dialogue, first praises C.'s orations (*uehementer probantur*), and then, in taut transition (via repetition of *probare*), turns to his *commentarii … rerum suarum*, or rather, as their full and non-tendentious title most likely ran, *Caesaris commentarii rerum gestarum belli Gallici*.[7] Cicero, in much-discussed words, is quick to rejoin (*Brut.* 262):

> ualde quidem … probandos; nudi enim sunt, recti et uenusti, omni ornatu orationis tamquam ueste detracta. sed dum uoluit alios habere parata, unde sumerent qui uellent scribere historiam, ineptis gratum fortasse fecit, qui uolent illa calamistris inurere: sanos quidem homines a scribendo deterruit; nihil est enim in historia pura et inlustri breuitate dulcius.

> Yes, indeed, … they are most praiseworthy; for they are naked, upright, and charming, with all rhetorical ornament stripped away just like a garment. But while he wanted to provide the material to others who wanted to write history, he perhaps gratified the fools who will want to scorch them with curling irons; sensible men, however, he has certainly scared away from writing. For there is nothing in history sweeter than pure and lucid brevity.

That Cicero read the *BG* through a rhetorical and historiographical lens has often been forgotten over his – personal, polysemous, and insidious – claim that there was nothing to be seen.[8] C. himself may have begged to differ with Cicero when they discussed φιλόλογα, just as he had many a time before;[9] but most of his modern readers did not. The Siren song had cast its spell once more.[10]

---

[6] Rambaud 1966 (2nd ed.); see Krebs 2018a: 29–31 on "propaganda."

[7] On the misquoted title (p. 26), cf. Krebs 2017: 211.

[8] For discussion of Cicero's words (too rarely read alongside Cic. *Att.* 2.1.1–2), cf. Kraus 2005: 111–12; Garcea 2012: 49–81. They apply to the *BG* alone (Kelsey 1903: 223).

[9] On *De analogia* as a response to *De oratore*, see Garcea 2012: 78–124; on their epigrammatic banter, Marciniak 2008, and on C.'s use of Cicero's favorite dialogue, Krebs 2018c. Cf. *Index*, s.v. "Cicero."

[10] On the difficulties of a non-Ciceronian reading of the Republic's literary scene, see Levene 2005.

There have always been dissenting voices, of course, and read from a literary point of view Rambaud's monumental 1953 study abounds with insights.[11] It was not until the 1990s, however, and in the wake of the so-called historiographical turn in the study of ancient historians more generally – i.e. the modern critics' re-focus on historical texts as literary artifacts – that they grew louder.[12] The oft-cited 1998 collection *Julius Caesar as artful reporter* may still have shown the traditional preoccupations (e.g. with "propaganda"); but the programmatic title, narratological and stylistic analyses, and the occasional aside on e.g. "Thucydidean touches in C.'s *Commentaries*" suggested another and – in its last consequence – different look at the Roman author.[13] A series of articles and monographs followed that elucidated literary and other original aspects of his work, freeing it from the confines of "the world-conquering *school* text," as Christina Kraus phrased it in an iconoclastic discussion.[14] The man of letters, whose literary criticism Cicero sought (*QFr.* 2.15.5), was finally beginning to receive his due.

To appreciate C. as a writer and the seventh book of his *BG* (henceforth *VII*) within its "horizon of expectations" and especially in its historiographical aspects is the foremost goal of this commentary, the first in over a century (pp. 57–58). It attempts a contextualized reading of C.'s work through the eyes of a contemporary Roman reader, who was trained in rhetoric, versed in Greek and Roman literature, and familiar with the same political and cultural conventions and discourses as its author.[15] However approximative such a reading, it reveals much in these *commentarii* – and nowhere more so than in *VII* – that rewards careful attention, including a dramatized narrative, (sustained) intertextual borrowings and allusions, (in)direct speeches telling of Rome's second-greatest speaker (Quint. 10.1.114) and word- and sound-play telling of the leading linguist (cf. Gell. *NA* 1.10.4), not to mention technical *ekphraseis* that lack parallels

---

[11] Feller 1929 read the *BG* as "kunstmäßige Geschichtsschreibung," Oppermann 1974 surveyed "literary aspects."
[12] As provoked by Wiseman 1979 and Woodman 1988. Feldherr 2009b: 6–8 reflects on the "changes in thinking about historiography."
[13] Welch-Powell 1998 (with Riggsby's review). Powell 1998: 121 suggests "Thucydidean touches."
[14] Kraus 2005: 112 (my italics); partly anticipated by Hall 1998. Pascucci 1973: 502 elegantly speaks of "la (s)fortuna di Cesare." Anglophone monographs include Batstone-Damon 2006, Riggsby 2006, Grillo 2012.
[15] And thus to narrow "die desolate Diskrepanz zwischen Autorabsicht und Rezeptionsverhalten" (Lohman 1990: 58). I take Jauss' 1970 concept to include all the political, cultural, and literary assumptions a contemporary reader such as Cicero would have brought to his reading of C.'s *commentarii*. The historical contextualization will make it necessary to go beyond the contemporary perspective (p. 18).

in the Roman republic. All these aspects are part and parcel of Greek and Roman historiography; they contribute – often in evocative fashion – their share to the amphibian nature of C.'s *commentarii rerum gestarum* as more than "notes" but still less than "history" (p. 31, 3a). If these features were to be classified under any one title, it might as well be *la formation historique*.[16]

None of this is to gloss over the immense suffering that the conquest inflicted and the *commentarii* mention so casually, suggesting their author's "total callousness [and] indifference to human life and suffering," as Ernst Badian put it (1990: 31). Nor is it to deny the fundamentally political nature of the *commentarii* with their advertising C.'s leadership and accomplishments as well as – in the *BC* – peaceful intentions; or to suggest that they not be read critically as a historical source. In fact, *VII* monumentalizes C. as the perfect Roman general and his troops as representatives of *Romanitas* (pp. 45–50), and it repeatedly makes "visible" its author's plotting hand at the expense of historical accuracy (pp. 42–43), while offering many more opportunities for historical scrutiny, given its three verified siege-sites (including the archaeological evidence of the fortifications at Alise-Sainte-Reine). But it is to restate that there is an often-underappreciated literary quality to C.'s text; and it is that quality that my reading hopes to bring out. It will come at a price: Critognatus will appear to be no more than the product of C.'s lively literary imagination (77n.); and whatever Vercingetorix's historical role, whatever he said or did – his words and deeds in *VII* are no more than historiographical commonplaces.[17] There is nothing to suggest that C. bothered to find out (an unlikely scenario to begin with); this applies to the Gallic side in general, and even the Roman side is subjected to C.'s "schematic composition" (p. 41). As with so many other historical texts from antiquity, the historiographical reading of *VII* reveals its narrow limitations as a historical source.

2 THE WAR IN GAUL

"The subjugation of the west" was how Theodor Mommsen, in his *Roman History*, entitled C.'s war in Gaul, deeming it an event of "world-historic" proportion.[18] This title stands out in its sober accuracy. It rightly avoids "Gaul" – a Roman, especially Caesarian invention – which, however, Mommsen could not avoid in his discussion (and neither can I), as C.'s words and deeds made it a fact of history (pp. 11–12); and "subjugation" plainly calls

---

[16] Rambaud 1977 (reviewing Mutschler 1975) anticipates my use of the phrase.
[17] Cf. Lendon 2017: 41 on how "ancient battle descriptions turn out to be mummified by convention."
[18] Mommsen 1895: 4; cf. Thorne 2018: 311–13.

it as it was, viz. a brutal, imperialistic war (cf. 1.5n. *libertatem*), waged for economic, military, and personal gains, with radical consequences for C. and Rome and above all the Gauls (pp. 13–14). As such a war of conquest it fitted in with contemporary Roman practice and aligned well with Rome's ideology, as Vergil would define it three decades later (*Aen.* 6.851–53, trans. Fairclough): *tu regere imperio populos, Romane, memento | (hae tibi erunt artes), pacique imponere morem, | parcere subiectis et debellare superbos* ("you, Roman, be sure to rule the world (be these your arts), to crown peace with justice, to spare the vanquished and to crush the proud").[19] C. was careful, it is true, to motivate his aggressive interventions in accordance with the notion of the *bellum iustum* (cf. Riggsby 157–89), especially early on; and occasionally, some Romans felt distress over his treatment of the enemy. But by and large, the promagistrate's aggressive victories were celebrated in Rome, as his three unprecedented *supplicationes* (90.7n.) evince.[20]

It may be overstating the case to speak of C. as "the most consistent representative of the Republic [who] waged the last great war of pillage"; but in its meanness this characterization serves as a realistic corrective to that trans- and ultimately ahistorical perspective that views the conquest through its later consequences, misconceiving of the war as the ultimately beneficial *mission civilisatrice* and C. as the Hegelian agent of the "Spirit of the world" (as Mommsen did, his sober title notwithstanding, not to mention others).[21] It would not be necessary, perhaps, to differentiate quite so decidedly between the two perspectives (as readings from the ahistorical vantage point have receded lately), were it not that the *Gallic War* itself engenders the latter, so curiously removed from its "Sitz im Leben" as it is (p. 25). The oft-remarked lapidary monumentality of the *Gallic War* favored the long typical ahistorical interpretation of the war in Gaul. It is especially regrettable, then, that C.'s narrative is virtually the only contemporary source; for large stretches, the difference between the war in Gaul and the *Gallic War* collapses, as the latter *is* (for us) in effect the former. Just how limiting this evidentiary situation is appears from a comparison

[19] Raaflaub 2018: 22–23.
[20] On C.'s motivating his early interventions, cf. 1.11.3–6 with Cic. *Rep.* 3.35; Collins 1952: 20–38 aggregates many relevant passages in attempting to *dis*prove their significance. Cato's criticism is discussed below (p. 26), Pliny's mentioned above (p. 1); cf. Strasburger 1968: 22–23.
[21] "... konsequenster Vertreter ... letzten großen Raubkrieg" (Will 1992: 250), following Badian's "the greatest brigand" (1968: 89). Contrast Mommsen's talk of Rome as a "pioneer of a higher culture" and the war's "influences [upon] the destinies of the world" (1895: 4; p. 1, fn.4). For an historicizing reading of "C. and the pirates," see Osgood 2010. Batstone-Damon discuss the *BC* "in its contemporary literary and historical context" (2006: 7).

of C.'s sparse and selective representation of Gallic life with the sophisticated lifestyle that archaeologists have unearthed (pp. 12–13).

This first, mostly historical, half of the introduction re-situates the
"timeless" narrative in its historical time (but note the remarks below,
"timeline"). However, it cannot do more than gesture towards a fuller
effort, as it will be confined to providing biographical and historical information as needed for an informed reading of *VII*, beginning with C.'s
obtaining his proconsular provinces.

(2 a) Preliminaries

C. obtained *Gallia cisalpina, Illyricum,* and *Gallia transalpina* under unusual
but telling circumstances. In the spring of 59, the year of his consulship,
the tribune Publius Vatinius (*MRR* 2.190) proposed to the popular assembly that the consul obtain *Gallia cisalpina* and *Illyricum* along with three
legions for the duration of five years until March 1, 54; he was also to
select his *legati*.[22] The motion was unusual (though not unprecedented)
because of its timing and scope, authorizing body, and length of the
appointment; usually, such appointments were made for one or two years
(*annua prouincia*), by decree of the senate (which was also to have a say
regarding the *legati*), and – according to the *lex Sempronia de prouinciis
consularibus* – *before* the consular election.[23] This had, in fact, happened
the year before when the senate decreed *siluae callesque*, "forests and path-
ways" in Italy, as the field of operations for the incoming consuls. That
may have been intended as a slight to C. (Suet. *Iul.* 19.2), whose election
his opponents deemed certain.[24] Yet, supported by his allies M. Licinius
Crassus and Gnaeus Pompeius, C. found a way to bypass the senate, whose
decree was invalidated once the *lex Vatinia* passed the assembly.[25] But the
senate then entrusted C. additionally with *Gallia transalpina* (and one
legion), to be renewed customarily by an annual *senatus consultum*. Its
motivation is unclear, pragmatism most likely, as Badian has shown that
the two Gauls had been assigned to one governor before (the extension of
imperium, i.e. *prorogatio,* was quite common, too).[26] In effect, the combined

---

[22] Suet. *Iul.* 21, Cic. *Vat.* 35–36; Gelzer 1968: 86n.3. Morstein-Marx 2021: 168–
81 offers an up-to-date discussion (with conclusions that differ from the *communis
opinio*). North 2006 surveys the constitutional parameters.
[23] On the *lex,* see Grillo 2015: 20–23. Gruen 1974: 534–43 discusses other
unusual promagistracies.
[24] … *ut prouinciae futuris consulibus minimi negotii, id est siluae callesque, decerner-
entur* (with Rich 1986).
[25] On the coalition of the "three potentates," see Ramsay 2009: 37–45.

Gallo-Illyrian assignment was weighty: "there was to be no other commander on the borders of Italy." If C. desired "a great command" to allow
"his *uirtus* to shine" (*magnum imperium ... uirtus enitescere*, Sall. *BC* 54.4), he
now had it secured – until he be recalled, that is, from either transalpine
Gaul at rather short (one year's) notice or towards the end of the five-
year appointment (whose prolongation he negotiated with Crassus and
Pompey in 56).[27] There is evidence of C.'s opponents undertaking efforts
to that effect as early as 57. This threat of recall may have influenced his
military decisions (so his "rather mysterious" invasion of Britain in 56);[28]
and the wranglings back in Rome inform the *BG* in its smaller and larger
aspects, even though they go mostly unremarked (1.1n.).

The appointment's circumstances were telling not only of the political
situation of the late republic, which witnessed violent domestic conflicts,
rampant manipulations of the constitution (cf. 1.1n. *de Clodii caede*, 6.1n.
uirtute Cn. Pompei), and extraordinary commands such as C.'s in ever greater
numbers, but also of C.'s own political career.[29] The son of Gaius Iulius
Caesar (père) and Aurelia, he was born on July 12, 100, quite possibly in
Rome, into a patrician family that claimed descent from Venus (cf. Badian
2009), as C. himself pronounced at his aunt Julia's funeral in 69 (Suet. *Iul.*
6.1); he had just gained the quaestorship (*MRR* 3.105–6) and therewith
entry to the senate. It was at that prominent occasion that he paraded in
the procession the death masks of Gaius Marius, Julia's late husband, and
their son (Plut. *Caes.* 5.3 [with Pelling]).[30] A *nouus homo*, plebeian hero
in the war against the Cimbri and Teutones (113–101), and seven-time
consul, Marius had fought against the patrician L. Cornelius Sulla and his
coalition during the civil war in the 80s; since he was voted *hostis*, any public commemoration of him was discouraged (if not forbidden). But Marius
remained popular with the Roman people and Plutarch reports how his
imago was received enthusiastically. Whatever C.'s personal reasons to
honor his uncle – whose military example he seems to have heeded as well,
in some respects – most scholars have sided with Plutarch in interpreting
C.'s parade as a political statement.[31] This appears all the more likely given
that his *laudatio funebris* not only evinces the accomplished speaker who
had studied with some of the same teachers as Cicero (Molon of Rhodes

---

[26] Cf. Suet. *Iul.* 22.1 (and Dio 38.8.5), Cic. *Att.* 8.3.3 (and Plut. *Crass.* 14.3).
Badian 1966 (with Ebel 1976: 94, 96–102); the following quotation is on p. 918.
[27] See Grillo 2015: 9–12 on Luca.
[28] Stevens 1947: 5. Further: Stevens 1952 (with Levick 1998); cf. fn. 65.
[29] Meier sums it up with his much-debated "Krise ohne Alternative" (1980: xliii;
Hölkeskamp 2010: 14–17).
[30] On the *imagines*, see Flower 1996: c. 4.
[31] Flower 1996: 124, Canfora 1999: 17; Morstein-Marx 2021: 33–50 is more
skeptical. Cf. Zecchini 2001: 117–21 on Marius' *exemplum*; further below, p. 45.

[Suet. *Iul.* 4.1]) and enjoyed a reputation since his famous prosecution of Cn. Cornelius Dolabella in 77/6; it also bespeaks the consummate politician who emphasizes his *dignitas generis* and performs *pietas* before the Roman people (30.3n. *dignitas*, 17n.) – in short, who draws on his symbolic capital to canvass for higher office.[32] Later expressions of respect (including, a decade plus later, the mention at 1.40.5 *Cimbris et Teutonis a C. Mario pulsis*, and, indirectly 77.12 [n.] *bello Cimbrorum Teutonumque*) are of similar political consequence (cf. Plut. *Caes.* 6.2 with Pelling).

In fact, the political stance in 69 exemplifies C.'s consistent, often rather ostentatious, and career-long demonstration of his "popular" partiality (Krebs 2018a: 38–41). By birth and upbringing, he could have followed in Sulla's footsteps; and his adjutancy on the staff of Sullan officers (p. 9), second marriage (in 67) to the late dictator's grand-daughter Pompeia, and cooperation with the sometime *Sullani* Crassus and Pompey both indicate a lack of ideological rigidity and hint at the political persona he *might* have become (and may have feared becoming; cf. *L. Sullam quem imitaturus non sum*, [Cic.] *Att.* 9.7C.1). But these instances hardly change a "popular" record of measures undertaken throughout his career (and especially his consulship) that targeted the many and lent credibility to Cicero's reservations about C.'s "popular" ways as expressed over twenty years (e.g. *Cat.* 4.9–10, *Prou. cons.* 38, *Phil.* 5.49).[33] Cicero's (and others') characterization of politics as dominated by two ideological camps – here the *optimates*, elitist gatekeepers of the established order; there the *populares*, reformers bent on improving the people's lot – has drawn scrutiny; a further complication arises from the questionable significance of "the" *populus* in the political process, given how few (relative to the mass of citizens) were those ever able to exercise their constitutional powers.[34] But whatever C.'s political beliefs, his appointment by the power of "the" people aligns with his public support of them, which will also find expression in his frequent and flattering mention of them in the *BG* (17.3n. *populi Romani maiestate*); it is especially pronounced in *I* (C. knew his creditor), and all the more striking for the opposite treatment given the senate.[35]

---

[32] Van der Blom 2018: 195–96 on C.'s early speech; Wistrand 1978: 6 on his *dignitas*; Wiseman 1974 on "legendary genealogies." On communication and performance, see Flaig 2003, esp. cc. 3+4, Jehne 2006: 12–13, and Steel-Van der Blom 2013. Hölkeskamp 2010: 107–24 applies Bourdieu's *capital symbolique*.

[33] Gruen 1974: 397–403 discusses the *leges Iuliae agrariae*. Canfora 1999 is an extreme take on C.'s popular politics (cf. Seager's review). Griffin 2009b: 5 summarizes the debate about C.'s political *persona*.

[34] The *locus classicus* for *optimates/populares* is Cic. *Sest.* 96; see Yakobson 2016. Cf. Wiseman 2009: 5–32 on the *populus*, Mouritsen 2017: 55–58 on voter participation. Jehne 2006 surveys the debates.

Given the political circumstances of his appointment and contested consulship, it does not surprise that his departure for his proconsular appointment was complicated by challenges to his legislation, facing which he composed three speeches *In C. Memmium et L. Domitium*, the two praetorian orchestrators (*MRR* 2.194); but even after he had crossed the *pomerium* to take up his *imperium* (with which came immunity), he stayed nearby until Cicero was forced into exile.[35] When he finally left, around 15–20 March 58, he was battle-hardened, campaign-experienced, and well-read (p. 46). He had begun his military career two decades earlier as an officer on the staff of M. Minucius Thermus, a Sullan propraetor of Asia (*MRR* 2.81).[37] Barely 20, he earned the *corona ciuica* saving the life of a fellow soldier during the siege of Mytilene (Suet. *Iul.* 2); the honor, *militum uirtutis insigne clarissimum*, came with considerable privileges, including everyone's rising to their feet when a decorated recipient arrived (Plin. *HN* 16.4–6; Polyb. 6.39.6).[38] C. continued his training in the campaigns against the Cilician pirates: first, in 78, under the leadership of P. Servilius Vatia (*MRR* 2.87), another *Sullanus*, then, in 74, under Marcus Antonius Creticus (*MRR* 2.115–16), the father of the triumvir. It was during the latter campaign that he allegedly demonstrated the determination and speed that would later become his signature (pp. 46–47). But both episodes – the capture and crucifixion of the pirates that had taken him hostage and the repulsion of a military detachment by Mithridates – are implausible, garnished by hindsight, and indicative of the spell of the "Caesar Myth." In fact, as Hermann Strasburger (1938) showed, the life of young C. in flesh and blood was less than extraordinary until his election to *pontifex maximus* in 63 (his gaining every office *suo anno* notwithstanding). Yet following his praetorship in 62 (*MRR* 2.173), during his promagistracy in Spain in 61 and 60 (*MRR* 2.180, 184–5), he won decisive victories over the Lusitanians, earning a triumph (which he forwent to submit his candidacy for the consulship). It is sometimes said that the

---

[35] Krebs 2018a: 38–39. Cf. the support C. received from the *plebs* in the build-up to the civil war (Morstein-Marx 2004: 132). For Roman politicians' sense of debt, see ibid. 258–76.

[36] The legal proceedings: Cic. *Sest.* 40 (with Kaster), Suet. *Iul.* 23.1; Badian 1974 on Gruen 1971. Awaiting Cicero's exile: Cic. *Sest.* 41; cf. Moles 1989 on Plut. *Cic.* 30–32. Date of departure: Shackleton Bailey 1965: 227.

[37] *MRR* 2.76. See Badian 1990: 28 on the *contubernium*; Santangelo 2012 on *Sullanus/i*.

[38] It would render his address of his soldiers as *commilitones* (pp. 49–50) more credible; and it would affect his Roman readers' reception of his (a) criticism of the highborn members on his staff (1.39.2), (b) reverential representation of the common soldier, and (c) appearances in the thick of battle (p. 45).

progression of the *BG* reveals the progress C. made in the art of warfare;
but Gelzer (1968: 63) more plausibly observed that it was in Spain that C.
came into his own as a general.

(2 b) Gaul and the Gauls

Gallus, "(the) Gaul," is the name by which Romans referred to heteroge-
neous groups living (or originating) to the north of the Alps; C. asserts
this of one such group: *qui ipsorum lingua Celtae, nostra Galli appellantur*
(1.1.1).[39] In fact, their primary identity was tribal – as the many names in
the *BG* and inscriptions such as those at Lyon's amphitheatre more than
half a century later testify – even if many of them spoke a Celtic dialect
and shared a related set of religious beliefs and cultural practices.[40]
    The Gauls were on Roman minds in March 60, when the specter of
a war arose (*Gallici belli ... metus*, Cic. *Att.* 1.19.2; 75.3n. *Heluetiis*): The
Aedui, Roman allies, had suffered defeat in the battle of Magetobriga
against a Gallic–Germanic coalition including their longstanding rivals,
the Arverni (1.31.12; 4.1n. *Aruernus*, 5.2n. *Haeduos*, 67.7; Thévenot 1960:
13–19); another group, the Helvetii, were in arms and raiding *Gallia transalpina*. The senate decreed that the consuls take charge of the "two Gauls"
(i.e. *transalpina* and *cisalpina*) and conduct a levy. Two months later, calm
had returned (Cic. *Att.* 1.20.5, 2.1.11). But fewer than two years later yet
again, C. would march against the alleged threat of a Helvetian migration
(1.7.1), reminding his readers towards year's end of the pain Rome had
suffered from the Gauls more recently during the Cimbrian war (*patrum
nostrorum memoria*, 1.12.5).[41]
    Such reminders were all the more effective because of the traumatic
experience of the Gauls' sack of Rome in the early fourth century, which
occurred in the context of the Celtic migrations and their subsequent
settlements in northern Italy. It left a scar on the Roman psyche.[42] Later
invasions and conflicts, such as the Boii's descending on Telamon (about
100 miles north of Rome) in 225, or Rome's defeats in the said Cimbrian

---

[39] McCone 2006 discusses endonym and exonym. C. never uses the former
again.
[40] On the definitions of the Celts, see Cunliffe 2018: 1–52, on the amphitheater
of the three Gauls, Guey-Audin 1964: 46–47. A rare and late instance of an individual identifying with a *Großgruppe* may be *CIL* 7.49 *Iulius Vitalis ... Natione Belga*.
More on Gaul before C.'s arrival in Timpe 1972.
[41] 1.12.6–7 *Tigurini* (with Walser 1998: 58–59; cf. Kaenel 2019); cf. 77.12n.
Cimbrorum Teutonumque.
[42] On the migrations, see Cunliffe 2018: 132–34; on the *metus Gallicus* and
Gallo-Roman interactions, Williams 2001 (esp. cc. 3+4).

war (ca. 113–101) would bring its terrors back to life; and so the terrifying Gaul was easily evoked even in the middle of the first century, when the "Romanization" in *G. cisalpina* had brought its inhabitants close to obtaining Roman citizenship (which C.'s language anticipates [1.1n. *Italiam*]).[43]

G. cisalpina was, at the time of C.'s appointment, one of three territories Romans associated with *Gallia*. Situated in the north of Italy between the Alps and the Apennines, with the Rubicon as its southern border, it traced the beginnings of its Romanization back into the third century. It was joined by *G. transalpina* in southern France, following Roman victories over the Allobroges and Arverni near the confluence of the Rhône and Isère in 121; it did not, however, amount to much more than a passageway to *Hispania* (Cic. *Prou. cons.* 22 *semitam*, with Grillo).[44] Lastly, the Romans also knew of Gallic tribes farther north in regions called *G. comata*.[45]

It was those regions that C. was to conquer and redefine with his army and his pen: *Gallia est omnis diuisa in partes tres, quarum unam incolunt Belgae, aliam Aquitani, tertiam qui ipsorum lingua Celtae, nostra Galli appellantur* (1.1.1).[46] C.'s imperialistic concept of *Gallia omnis* marks the first major contribution to Rome's borealistic discourse, i.e. its writing about northern Europe out of political motive rather than ethno-geographic curiosity.[47] It prioritizes the unity of the territory with its natural boundaries, viz. the Atlantic, the Northern Sea, the Rhine, and the Alps, Cévennes, and Pyrenees (partly specified in 1.1.5–7); and it disregards blatantly the diversity of its three populations (not to mention their individual tribes), which C. fully acknowledges: *hi omnes lingua, institutis, legibus inter se differunt* (1.1.2).[48] It is named – by way of a synecdoche – after the Roman name of its largest, central group (which frequently results in uncertainty over the precise meaning of *Gallia* [4.1n. *Galliae*]).[49] As a corollary of

---

[43] The "trousered giants," Badian 1966: 907; cf. Johnston 2018: 82n.5. For critical comments on "Romanization," see Barrett 1997.

[44] Ebel 1976.

[45] Catull. 29.3, Cic. *Phil.* 8.27, *CIL* XI (add.) 7553; cf. Hirt. 8.24.3; Hering 1954/5: 310. Cicero would speak of *G. ultima* in reference to C.'s conquests (e.g. *Phil.* 2.48).

[46] On the reorganization of Gaul, cf. the literature in Krebs 2006: 113n.10; on its technical underpinnings, Krebs 2018d: 96–102. It has been debated to what extent C.'s internal divisions correspond to realities (Fichtl 2013). On Aquitania: 31.5n.

[47] More on the dynamics of *Borealism* in Krebs 2010, Johnston 2019.

[48] Cf. Pliny's perplexity at *HN* 4.42: *Gallia ... uno nomine appellata in tria populorum genera diuiditur.*

this reorganization of northern Europe, the Rhine became an ethnic borderline, to the east of which C. located the *Germani* as a separate ethnos living in the territory he called – once again by way of synecdoche – *Germania* (65.4n. *Rhenum*). And once again, his willfulness appears in all desirable clarity from the acknowledged existence of *Germani cisrhenani*, sc. five *Germanic* tribes that live in his *Gallia* (2.40.10, 6.32.1). By the end of his campaigns, C. had ventured into *Germania* and *Britannia* on two occasions each; but he had conquered the peoples and their territories defined as *Gallia omnis* at the beginning of his *BG*.[50] Under Augustus, it would be organized into three provinces, which joined G. *Narbonensis* (formerly *Transalpina*): G. *Aquitania*, G. *Lugdunensis*, and G. *Belgica* (the three latter often referred to as *tres Galliae*). With modifications, this arrangement largely instituted C.'s tripartition; the latter's Gaul became historical fact.[51]

As for the Iron Age societies living in Gaul until the time of C.'s conquest in the late La Tène period, they appear to have been mostly oligarchic, occasionally monarchic (3.2n. *ciuitates*, 4.1n. *regnum*); C. himself would appoint Rome-friendly leaders as so-called client kings (e.g. 5.25, 76.1–2n.).[52] It is unclear whether the political elites gathered regularly at a *totius Galliae concilium* (63.5n.), not to mention its other modalities. C. does assert regularized meetings for the religious elites (the Druids; 6.13.10 *certo anni tempore … in loco consecrato*; cf. 2.1n. *Carnutes*, 3.1n. *Gutuatro*); but here, too, details are murky. Alliances and client relations existed between societies (75.2 *clientibus*; Ralston 2019: 21) and with Rome (so the *Haedui, fratres consanguineique*, 1.33.2; cf. 5.2n.). The social, cultural, and economic life – regional variation notwithstanding – was far more sophisticated than any reader of the *BG* could imagine (p. 23). The ceramic and metallic productions and artistry were vigorous and refined (Guillaumet 1996; cf. 22.2n. *cuniculorum*; 11.9n. *praedam*). Trade was brisk (not for nothing do *mercatores* enjoy pride of place at 1.1.3) and reached – along an elaborate network of rivers and roads – far-flung corners both in Britain and the Mediterranean: in around 100, some

---

[49] C.'s geographic terminology is generally inconsistent; cf. 1.7.2 *prouinciae toti quam maximum potest militum numerum imperat (erat omnino in Gallia ulteriore legio una)*, 1.1n. *prouincia*, 1.2n. *transalpinam*.

[50] It is possible, perhaps probable, that 1.1 was added to the *commentarii* at a later stage (p. 28).

[51] Drinkwater 1983 (esp. pp. 19–53).

[52] La Tène, the cultural period stretching from the fifth into the first century, is named after the type of site discovered in 1857 near lake Neuchâtel (Olivier 2019: 286–89). See Ralston 2019 on Celtic life, Arbabe 2013 on *Vie Politique et Institutions en Gaule*.

20,000 liters of wine seem to have arrived every year in the *oppidum* of Corent alone.[53] The coinage included both coins of lower value and limited local distribution as well as higher value coinage in line with Mediterranean standards; those found at Alesia exemplify military circulation (Haselgrove 2019: 242). Names in coin legends have been related to eight of the Gallic leaders C. mentions.[54] Much economic and political power had moved from the farmsteads (14.5 *uicos atque aedificia*) to complex major settlements typically in elevated positions and known by C.'s designation as *oppida* (4.2n.). Many of them included as part of their fortifications an elaborate "stone-faced and timber-laced" rampart, one type of which, the *murus Gallicus*, C. describes of Avaricum (23n.).[55] They appear to have been built decades before C.'s arrival. His praise of their aesthetics and efficacy should not be reduced to the purpose of self-aggrandizement; it may rather be the inadvertent testimony to the highly developed culture his Roman troops were fighting.

(2 c) The campaigns

Rome's generals took pride in conquest: L. Furius Philus (*cos.* 136 [*MRR* 1.486]) states in a second-century setting that the phrase *finis imperii propagauit* appeared on their monuments (Cic. *Rep.* 3.34); a century later, an inscription celebrated Pompey for "extend[ing] the empire's borders to reach the borders of the world" (τὰ ὅρια τῆς ἡγεμονίας τοῖς ὅροις τῆς γῆς προσβιβάσας, Diod. 40.4).[56] C. was not to be outdone. Whatever his specific intentions when he secured his appointments, and whether or not he left Rome determined to conquer it all,[57] "he acted positively, early, and with full force" (Thorne 2007: 36) right away and did not stop until he had conquered *Gallia omnis*, completing the "greatest single extension of the Roman Empire" (Sherwin-White 1957: 36) and foraying farther even into *Germania* and *Britannia* (cf. 65.4n. *Rhenum*). When he departed a decade later, he had secured three *supplicationes* (90.7n.), ruthless wealth that made him Rome's richest man (as late as 62 he may have depended

[53] On Corent's (36–56n.) wine, cf. Poux 2012: 134; on Gallic roads, Chevallier 1997, Bruant 2017.
[54] Cf. Nieto-Pelletier 2004: 20–23. Correspondences include Commius (76.1–2n.), Litaviccus (37.1n.), Lucterius (5.1n.), and V. (p. 51, n. 211), but not 88.4n. Sedullus (Colbert de Beaulieu 1962).
[55] The quotation is from Ralston 2019: 31. For the dating, cf. Krausz 2019: 167.
[56] Cf. Brunt 1978: 163, Harris 1979: 125; on the "economic motive," Badian 1968: 16–29.
[57] Seager 2003: 19–22; Thorne 2007: 27; cf. Woolf 2019: 12. On C. in Illyricum (mentioned at 3.7, 5.1), Džino 2010: 80–98.

on Crassus to underwrite his debts), and a brutally efficient army ready to fight for him in the civil war. Contrariwise, *Gallia omnis* had lost a quarter of its population, its lands and homes had been burned, and temples, treasuries, and resources plundered (28.5n. *numero*, 11.9n. *praedam*).[58] The triumph in 46 and execution of its prize captive Vercingetorix (89.4n. *Vercingetorix deditur*) emblematize both aspects, if inadequately.[59]

The Gallic campaign began with C.'s arrival at Geneva by 28 [25 (Jul.)] March 58, having hurried there at near impossible speed; and it ended when he crossed the Rubicon in January 49 [December 50 (Jul.)].[60] Its rhythm was seasonal: Typically, campaigns were limited to the "summer" (35.1n. *aestatis*), whereupon the troops wintered in Gaul (1.54.2; 90.3n. *hiberna*), while C. performed administrative duties, mostly from Ravenna (1.1n. *conuentus*). Three phases can be identified (Will 1992: 87–90): From 58 until 56, C. first defeated the Helvetii and Ariovistus (1.30.1, 53.1–3), then waged the Belgian campaign, which he celebrated preemptively with <u>omni</u> *Gallia pacata* (2.35.1; the senate granted a *supplicatio* of an unprecedented fifteen days, surpassing Pompey's ten days in 63 [2.35.4; Cic. *Prou. cons.* 25–27]). C. started to worry more earnestly about a recall (Gelzer 1968: 117–19) and negotiated an extension of his appointment with Crassus and Pompey in Luca; when he returned to Gaul late in May (at the earliest), he was to be victorious in Aquitania (3.27.1). He now had conquered virtually "all Gaul," as he reiterates (3.28.1, with greater plausibility; but cf. 1.1n. *Quieta Gallia*). However, instead of consolidating his conquest, he turned to *Germania* (4.16.1) and *Britannia* (4.20.1), possibly wishing to suggest that work remained (Stevens 1952: 13). That year of adventures earned him another *supplicatio* (twenty days long [4.38.5]), even though he had massacred the Tencteri and Usipetes, while detaining their ambassadors in contempt of the *ius legatorum*, causing Cato to suggest that C. be handed over to the *Germani* (Plut. *Caes.* 22.4). Neither expedition succeeded militarily,[61] however, nor did his second, larger campaign across the English channel in 54 (5.1–28; this was also the year when C. used some of his Gallic loot to begin major building projects in Rome).[62] Worse, upon returning to Gaul, he faced the beginnings of a resistance

---

[58] Cf. Powell 1998, Roymans 2019, and Will 1992: 264n.21 (estimates of the Gallic population).

[59] On the quadruple triumph, cf. Gelzer 1968: 286–87. Sympathy for C.'s victims is rarely expressed; Strasburger 1968 (esp. p. 73) was long the notable exception (but cf. Badian [above, p. 4]).

[60] Plut. *Caes.* 17.5; cf. 1.6.4, 7.1–2; Raaflaub-Ramsey 2017: 6–7. I largely follow the latter's chronology (but see below, "timeline").

[61] But both secured him fame (Schadee 2008: 171–75, Krebs 2018d: 103–12).

that would last three years, culminate in 52, and continue into 51, when rumors had C. stripped of his cavalry and surrounded (Cael. [Cic.] *Fam.* 8.1.4; 59.2n. *Bellouaci*). C.'s claims that the uprising of 52 sprang up that year and was quelled by year's end are wrong (nn. on 1–5, 89–90): not before his final year was Rome's position secured.[63]

This third phase began with the assassination of the Rome-friendly king Tasgetius (5.25; cf. 2.1n. *Carnutes*) and attacks by the Eburones and others on Roman camps (5.26.1–2). C. stayed the winter (5.24.8) after the loss of Cotta and Sabinus' fifteen cohorts (5.37): It was one of three major defeats he suffered in Gaul, and he publicly mourned the dead and, in writing *V*, visited all blame on Sabinus.[64] The next year – his troops augmented, in part with Pompey's help (6.1.4; cf. 6.1n. *Pompei*) – C. confronted the continuous recalcitrance of the Carnutes, Senones, and others (6.3.3; cf. 1.4n. *Acconis*), crossed over into *Germania* to cut off its alleged Gallic support (6.9), but mostly hunted Ambiorix, the leader of the Eburones, wanting his people extirpated (6.34.8; cf. 8.24.4–25.1). But the resistance grew, and C. would hardly have left for Ravenna (1n.), had the situation in Rome not demanded it.

The *BG* rarely acknowledges any correlation between Roman politics and Gallic affairs (1.1n.), though many a connection can be discerned, e.g. between the laudatory representation of Crassus *adulescens* and his father's clout in Rome (1.52.7; Ebert 1909: 25), or the legates' greater visibility in *III* and C.'s preoccupation with extending his Gallic command (partly pursued in Luca).[65] But Rome's tumultuous winter of 53/2 finds mention in *VII* (nn. on 1.1–4, 6.1): it is to blame the domestic crisis for its share in the unrest abroad and to excuse C.'s extended absence from Gaul. While it caused C. delay, it cannot have affected developments in Gaul: the chronology in C.'s plot does not hold;[66] nor did V. contribute to the rebellion's alleged "beginnings"; and the *unum consilium totius Galliae* the Gallic leader is credited with later (29.6n.) was essentially in place

---

[62] On the *Forum Iulium* and the *Saepta Iulia*, see Ulrich 1993.

[63] Rambaud 1962: 439, succinctly: "[L]a guerre de libération … commencé en 54."

[64] Suet. *Iul.* 25.2 (cf. 36–56n.). On Sabinus, see Welch 1998: 93–95.

[65] Will 1992: 142–47 enumerates major Roman events during C.'s campaigns.

[66] Under ideal conditions, it would take news from Rome some twenty days to reach Agedincum, where the legions wintered (Raaflaub-Ramsey 2017: 55n.172). It would subsequently have to reach the Gauls farther west (near Cenabum, presumably, adding two days), who would then gather from various locations for meetings and organize the attack on Cenabum; news of that attack would then have to travel some twenty-two days once more to reach C. in Ravenna. The time span between the two *termini post quos* – i.e. the Roman riots and C.'s learning of Pompey's election – is about sixty days; even under ideal conditions, this would

when C. left Ravenna around 9 February, what with the Senonian leader
Drappes and the Atrebatan king Commius attacking Roman camps and
inciting Belgic tribes, and the Aedui a cause for C.'s concern (nn. on
1–5, 5.6 *perfidia*). Rome's longstanding ally may have deserted openly
only subsequently, other tribes may not have joined until later in the year
(cf. 75n.) – but much of *tota Gallia* was in arms early on in 52. Moreover,
the Gallic coalition appears to have pursued a coordinated strategy that
aimed at isolating and starving C.'s troops by cutting off supplies and
scorching the earth (10.1n. *re frumentaria*, 14.2–9), pursuing Rome's allies
(5n.), weakening its cavalry (65.4n.), and adapting guerilla warfare. The
narrative again credits V. with its design, who presents this "novel" strategy in a speech following a series of defeats (14–19n.) – but it is clearly
at work from the start. It played to Gallic strengths (4.8n. *equitatui*), was
employed until the late summer (67n.), and succeeded in starving the
Roman army (20.8 *fama et inopia*) and leading it to the strongholds of
Avaricum, Gergovia, and Alesia (15.6, 34.2–3, 68.1).[67] C.'s narrative suggests that all sieges resulted from Gallic failure and his own initiative;
more probably, the Gauls hoped to overcome C.'s starved forces with their
(near) impenetrable strongholds as bases. In fact, it looks as if the "hammer and anvil" tactic at Alesia (68n.) was merely the delayed realization
of a long-hatched plan.

Even after Avaricum fell in June, C.'s dispatching Labienus with almost
half the army back north was likely partly intended to alleviate the supply
shortage, as was his decision to follow V. to Gergovia (34.2n.). There he
realized that he had to withdraw from Gaul (43.5–6, 53.1), when his pre-
dicament was compounded by the Aedui and their allies' openly joining
the Gallic cause.[68] His attempt at storming the stronghold resulted in
defeat (44–52n.), and once he had withdrawn, reunited with Labienus
(62.10), and recruited additional Germanic cavalry (65.4), he was fleeing back to *prouincia* – much though he attempts to discredit that notion
(66.3n. *fugere*).[69] But then the Gauls – in discontinuation of their strategy, it would seem – sought battle (67n.), which C. won, and the two
sides moved on to Alesia for the showdown. Here, too, C.'s plot strains
credulity, as it is hardly possible for the Gallic relief forces to have been

---

hardly allow for more than ten days for the Gauls to gather, debate, and organize
the attack.
[67] On the Gallic strategy, cf. Deyber 2017: 65–100.
[68] C.'s reiterated decision to abandon Gergovia *before* his defeat smacks of "protesting too much" (other aspects merit skepticism, too [36–56n.]).
[69] The chronology is once more doubtful (65.4n.).

requested, gathered, and welcomed at Alesia within slightly more than thirty days. It is more plausible that V. had requisitioned those forces well in advance and led C. to Alesia (67n.). But, in the end, the Romans built massive fortifications and secured victory in a series of two-fronted engagements.

Following V.'s surrender, C. spared the Aedui and Arverni but distributed the other Gauls as slaves amongst his troops. The different treatments represent his wielding of the standard tools of Roman imperialism: He weakens opposition and consolidates power by managing both intra- and intertribal divisions ("*diuide et impera*"), which he claims to have been endemic prior to his arrival (p. 55).[70] He supports pro-Roman factions and tribes (as early as 1.19–20), selectively granting tax exemption and other benefits (76.1n.), and advances individuals (39.1n. *summam dignitatem*), some to client-kingships (76.1–2n.). He takes hostages to secure compliance (2.2n. *obsidibus*), requisitions supplies and auxiliary troops, especially cavalry (17.2–3; 8.3n. *equitibus*), and does not shrink from brutal punishment of recalcitrance or disloyalty (11.9).

C. then moved into Aeduan territory (there to winter), and sent his legions into quarters. His appointment had come with four legions (1.7.2, 10.3) to which he added – of his own volition – two at the beginning of the first year (1.10.3), and another two the following year (2.2.1); for both levies he received retroactive authorization in 56.[71] In 54, he specifies his army's legionary strength at eight and a half (5.24.2–6; the origin of the five additional cohorts is unknown).[72] When, in 53, he enlisted two legions and borrowed one from Pompey to make up for the loss of 15 cohorts to Ambiorix (6.1), he raised the total to ten (6.44.3), which is the number at his disposal in 52 as well (34.2n. *legiones*). But the following year, Hirtius lists eleven legions (8.24.3, 46.4); the origin of the eleventh legion is also unclear, as are the beginnings of the *legio Alaudae* (cf. 65.1n. *prouincia*). To secure nutrition during winter, local resources were drained; during the campaign season, C. relied on supply chains and foraging (16.3n. *pabulationes frumentationesque*).[73] If Xerxes' troops drank rivers dry (Hdt. 7.20–21), so did C.'s.

---

[70] On "elements of empire," cf. Lintott 1993: 16–109; C.'s "thinking about … foreign relationships," Lendon 2015.
[71] Labisch 1975: 20–21. Gelzer 1968: 123–24, Ramsey 2009: 39.
[72] By C.'s time, a legion counted 4,800 soldiers (Lendon 2005: 225), distributed over ten cohorts, each of which contained three maniples (cf. 47.7n. *manipulares*), each of two centuries (cf. 12.4n. *centurionibus*).

With these dispositions C. insinuates the end of the uprising; but he was to be on the march again in December 52.

Approximate "timeline" of events in 5 2

C. rarely specifies dates in the *BG* and never in *VII* (the dates below are owed to other sources). Equally rare are specifications of routes, distances (3.3 *spatium*), or time spent traveling or resting (11.1 *altero die*, 9.1 *biduum moratus*).[74] In consequence, any historical reconstruction is largely speculative and subject to inaccuracy or worse (except when other sources provide pertinent detail). Just as problematically, any precise reconstruction based on supplementation not only engenders in the reader a misconception of knowledge, but it also forces upon the text a framework that its author had removed (p. 29): C. could have been specific – and on occasion is (e.g. 1.2.6, with Krebs 2018d: 99) – but chose not to be (the contrast with Hirtius quoted below is instructive). A recreation of the war in Gaul with the help of the *Gallic War* is thus doubly fraught.

Then again, as observed above, the *BG* needs to be resituated in its contexts, both Gallic and Roman, and the approximate "timeline" below attempts a compromise: intended to offer a quick overview of the major events, it hews to the information provided in *VII*, while {bracketing} a selection of contextualizing information. I have mostly abstained from speculating about routes and travel times, with the partial exception of the early parts (especially cc. 6–13), as there is greater certainty as to C.'s routes and, more importantly, it seems as though C. wanted his readers to get an impression of the distances and his speed (9n.). Throughout, I have relied on Kurt Raaflaub and John Ramsey's 2017 "chronology"; they are more comfortable than I am specifying dates and other details and should be consulted by those wishing for more than offered below.

The below follows the narrative, except where C.'s plot is at odds with historical circumstances (viz. the early chronology; but skepticism is called for elsewhere, too [*Index*, s.v. "chronology, doubts"]).

---

[73] The logistics involved were staggering (Labisch 1975). On the legionaries' marching, Roman camps, the baggage train, rewards, cf. *Index*, s.vv.

[74] This neglect is akin perhaps to the low quality of the Roman historians' topographical writing (cf. Horsfall 1985).

Roman Date [Julian]	Events	Source
Winter 53	{Commius incites the Belgae; Drappes attacks the legions' supply lines.} The Carnutan coalition plans further attacks.	8.23.3; 8.30.1; 1.2–2.2
Jan. 18 [Dec. 8, 53]	P. Clodius is murdered {outside Rome}.	1.1
ca. Feb. 1 [Dec. 20][75]	The senate passes a *consultum ultimum* authorizing {Pompey} to levy troops.	1.1
	C. is in *G. cisalpina* {Ravenna} when he learns of the murder and the {later} *scu*; he levies troops.	1.1
	{A new phase of the resistance begins with} the killing of Roman citizens in Cenabum. V. joins the uprising from Gergovia.	3–4
	Lucterius marches against the Ruteni, V. against the Bituriges.	5
Intercal. 24[76] [Feb. 5]	{Pompey is elected *consul sine collega* [6.1n. *uirtute*]}	
	C. learns of developments in Gaul and of the return of order in Rome.	6.1
Early March [2nd week of February][77]	He leaves for *G. transalpina*. Having arrived there {probably in Arelate}, he soon after hurries on to Narbo Martius. {The distance from Ravenna to Narbo is ca. 1,030 km [645 mi], which he could have covered in thirteen days. His travel options likely included a fast carriage and a ship sailing along the coast.} {At some point in March (?), the tribunes' law passes concerning C.'s candidacy *in absentia* for the consulship in 48.}	6.2–7.4

[75] Unlike the date of Clodius' murder, this is merely a likely date (Raaflaub-Ramsey 2017: 53n.165).

[76] In 52, an intercalary month of twenty-seven days was inserted (Raaflaub-Ramsey 2017: 53n.162).

[77] C.'s statement in 6.1 is too vague to allow for more than a rough estimate of his departure. The date proposed by Raaflaub-Ramsey 2017: 182, March 1 [Feb. 9], is the earliest possible; in fact, *urbanas res ... commodiorem in statum peruenisse* suggests that C. had let a few more days pass.

Roman Date [Julian]	Events	Source
	In Narbo, C. organizes the defense of the province. He then leaves for the Helvii {possibly Alba Helviorum [7.5n. *Heluios*], ca. 235 km [147 mi] away from Narbo, requiring six days of travel}.	7.4–8.1
	C. and troops cross the Cévennes into Arvernian territory.	8.2–5
	After two days, he leaves for Vienna {which he appears to reach within three days [9.2 *triduo*]}. He then hurries on through Aeduan territory to the Lingones {covering another 300 km [186 mi] in no fewer than four days} to reach his troops {at *castrum Diuionense* [Dijon] or Andematunnum [Langres]}. {Including the crossing of the Cévennes and the journey to Vienna, C. would have traveled about 2,000 km [1,250 mi] by now.} He gathers his full army in one place {probably 10.4n. *Agedincum*}.	9
"Winter," still (10.1n. *hiemis*)	When V. attacks the Boian *oppidum* Gorgobina, C. marches for Vellaunodunum.[78] Reaching it on the second day, he receives it into submission on the fifth. He leaves for Cenabum {on the sixth day, presumably}, which he reaches at nightfall {of the seventh} and takes on the next day. {Most likely leaving the next day,} he then besieges Noviodunum {about 56 km [35 mi] from Cenabum; its surrender marks the third such within a week and a half after C.'s leaving Agedincum}. He leaves immediately for Avaricum {112 km [70mi] away}, reaching it in three days.	10–13
	After a long siege, including the construction of a ramp over twenty-five days, C.'s troops take Avaricum.	14–28

[78] The location of Vellaunodunum is unknown; the distance between Sens (Agedincum) and Orléans (Cenabum) along the Chemin de César is about 120 km [75 mi].

Roman Date [Julian]	Events	Source
June (?)	He rests there, awaiting the beginning of the proper campaign season (32.2n. *prope hieme confecta*).	32.1
	From Avaricum he marches to Decetia {120 km [74 mi] away} to resolve an Aeduan conflict.	33
	Afterwards, C. divides his troops, dispatching Labienus to the Senones and Parisii, while he himself follows V. to Gergovia {ca. 140 km [87 mi] away from Decetia [29–35n.]}, which he reaches five days after crossing the Elaver.	34.4–36.1
	From Gergovia, C. rushes with troops to meet an Aeduan army 25 Roman miles away {37 km [23 mi]}; he returns *ante ortum solis* {i.e. within 24 hours [41.5n.]}.	37–41
	Assaulting Gergovia, C. suffers defeat. He withdraws, reaches the Elaver on the third day, and crosses into Aeduan territory.	44–53
"Corn in the fields"	With the Aedui in open revolt, C. hurries to the Liger, crosses, and enters the territory of the Senones.	54–56
Aug. 1 [Jul. 12]	{Q. Metellus Scipio is elected consul to join Pompey}	*MRR* 2.235
	Labienus, after a few battles, rejoins C. {presumably to Agedincum's south}. {At some point [65.4n.],} C. recruits cavalry from across the Rhine.	57–62, 65.4
	C. {is marching back to G. *transalpina* when he} is attacked by V. After victory, C. follows V. to Alesia, a day's march away from the battle side (68n.).	66–68.2
	After a cavalry engagement and more than thirty days, the Roman troops prevail in a series of two-fronted battles.	69–88
	Following V.'s surrender, C. marches into Aeduan territory, allocates winter camps and stays in Bibracte. He reports to Rome and receives a *supplicatio*.	89–90

Roman Date [Julian]	Events	Source
Dec. 29 [Dec. 3]	{C. leaves Bibracte *pridie Kal. Ianuarias* to campaign against the Bituriges. He returns *die XXXX.*	8.2.1–4.1
Feb. 28 [Jan. 29]	After *dies non amplius decem et octo*, C. marches against the Carnutes, leaving two legions to winter in Cenabum.	8.4.2–6.1
	C. then campaigns against the Bellovaci with four legions.}	8.6.2–23

(2 d) Other "voices"?

As students of the late republic find it difficult to see around Cicero (p. 2), so it is difficult to peer around C. when studying the war in Gaul (Thorne 2018: 304). Of its contemporary accounts – including histories by Q. Aelius Tubero or Tanusius Geminus, epics by Varro Atacinus or M. Furius Bibaculus, or the biographical tradition as represented by Gaius Oppius – only the *BG* has reached us, barring a few fragments; the loss of Asinius Pollio is particularly dire, given his partial eye-witness testimony and critical attitude.[79]

The degree to which these lost sources may be responsible for the non-Caesarian details in later retellings has been much debated.[80] Of these later narratives, the most significant are parts of Plutarch's *Caesar*, Florus' *Epitome*, and Cassius Dio's *Roman History*.[81] Most of their differences from C.'s account are likely caused by error, condensation, or rhetorical elaboration; but, of the more substantial ones (and regarding the seventh year alone), the following may indicate another source: in Plutarch, the appraisal (and detail) of C.'s cavalry victory, the descriptions of the two battle lines at Alesia as unaware of each other, and V.'s surrender.[82] In

---

[79] Zecchini 1978: 188–200 reviews contemporary anti-Caesarian accounts (with questionable conclusions). Livy's *Periochae* (103–08) contain little detail, but their *res a legatis eius … gestas* intrigue (cf. p. 50). See further: Gelzer 1955, Le Bohec 1998: 86–89.

[80] Cf. Thorne 2018: 304–09, Pelling 2011: 42–56 on the "Pollio-tradition," McDougall 1991 on Dio.

[81] Suet. *Iul.* 25 has little to say about the campaign. App. *Gall.* 1.3–5 is truncated, Polyaenus 8.23 fanciful (cf. Zecchini 1978: 203–05), and Eutrop. 6.17 lacks detail. For Orosius' deviations from C. in his *History against the Pagans*, cf. 53.2n. and *Index* (and Zecchini 1978: 123–50); for Frontinus: p. 46.

[82] Cf. nn. on 66–67, 90, and Plut. *Caes.* 27.5 (with Pelling). For other possibly significant differences, cf. nn. on 1–5, 59.1 *Haeduorum defectione.*

Florus, too, the depiction of the surrender is the single most striking variance; then again, it conforms all too well with his rhetoric.[83] Of the various
differences between C. and Cass. Dio, who has received the most attention
as a possible witness to an earlier source, there are his claims that C. was
absent from Gergovia at the defeat (40.38.1, 36–56n.), that thereafter he
rested amongst the Sequani (40.39.1, 67n.), or that V. surrendered hoping to obtain pardon due to their former friendship (ὅτι ἐν φιλίᾳ ποτὲ τῷ
Καίσαρι ἐγεγόνει, 41.1, 89n.).[84] Any review of the later tradition concludes
with the renewed realization of the singular significance of the *BG*. It is an
egregious instance of *histoire écrite par les vainqueurs*.

C.'s influence on modern, archaeological efforts to recover Gallic life
has been similarly profound and problematic:[85] Beginning with his borealistic constructs of "Gaul" and "the" Gauls (p. 10) – occasionally still
exploited to advance the mistaken notion of a Gallic "nation" – and ending with his readers' obedient elevation of Vercingetorix to France's (!)
"premier héros historique" (p. 51), C.'s terms to this day shape our understanding of Gallic society, such as *ciuitas*, *oppidum*, or *murus Gallicus*, not to
mention the instances of *interpretatio Romana* (cf. *Index* s.v.). Fortunately,
the archaeological record – while still scant considering the duration of
Roman campaigning and with significant gaps remaining (Reddé 2019:
110) – has increased over the last decades, and especially so for Bibracte
(which offers many insights into Celtic life) and the three major sites in
VII (Avaricum, Gergovia, and Alesia).[86] It has also grown more independent of *the* written source (Reddé 2008: 280). Where comparison of the
archaeological remains and C.'s account is possible, it has largely confirmed the latter (68–90n.).

3 THE *GALLIC WAR*

Suetonius singles out "eloquence and military affairs" as areas wherein C.
excelled (*Iul.* 55). These were the recognized areas of excellence in Rome
ever since the third century, when Q. Caecilius Metellus in his *laudatio
funebris* praised his father's urge "to be a warrior of the first rank, the best
speaker, the bravest commander, (and) to accomplish the greatest deeds

---

[83] Flor. *Epit.* 1.45; cf. 89n. and *Index*, s.v. Cf. Harmand 1967: 34–41, Guillaumin
1985: 749, Jal 1989: 137.
[84] See Pelling 1982 on Zecchini 1978; McDougall 1991: 638. Cf. *Index*, s.v.
[85] "Caesar's references ... led to ... distortions of the archaeological record,"
Champion 1985: 13; cf. Barrett 1989.
[86] Fitzpatrick-Haselgrove 2019 review the archaeological *status quaestionum*;
Hornung 2016 offers a comprehensive discussion of eastern Gaul.

under his own auspices" (*primarium bellatorem esse, optimum oratorem, fortissimum imperatorem, auspicio suo maximas res geri*, Plin. *HN* 7.139).[87] The *BG* puts both talents on display in singular fashion.

As its title indicates (p. 26), *C. Iuli Caesaris commentarii rerum gestarum belli Gallici* are the record of C.'s *res gestae*, "(military) accomplishments"; the latter included the celebrated passages into Germania and Britannia, culminated in the conquest of all of Gaul, and mostly met with enthusiasm back in Rome.[88] As such a record, they are akin to the epigraphic commemorations that Ennius evokes when he wonders "how great a statue [the Roman people will make] to speak of your (sc. Scipio's) accomplishments (*quantam columnam quae res tuas gestas loquatur, FLP* 30 [with Courtney's note]).[89] At the same time, this record also advertises C.'s rhetorical talents, written by himself as it is; the title alludes to this once more, as "*Caesaris*" specifies the writer and the agent. There were precedents here, too, e.g. in the autobiographical writing of the elite (including Cicero's recent compositions on his consulship); but C.'s closest rival Pompey had employed Theophanes to produce a record of his eastern campaigns. In a society as "permeated ... by competition for prestige and recognition" as Rome's, C. was to outdo Pompey twice over.[90]

It has long been wondered how much the identity of *actor* and *scriptor* compromises the record's accuracy.[91] Leaving aside its many limitations and exclusions, C. undoubtedly (and, within Roman society, predictably) cast himself in the best light.[92] Rambaud has documented the rhetoric; and even if he overstates the case in speaking of "déformation," any reader

----

[87] Similarly in Greek culture (14n.). Metellus adds six qualities; cf. Flower 1996: 136–42.

[88] Aside from the *supplicationes* and triumph, there are literary celebrations (Krebs 2018a: 33–34); even Strasburger 1968: 23 acknowledges "soliden Chauvinismus der Mehrheit." C. himself deemed his conquest his greatest *beneficium* to the Roman people (Knoche 1951: 144). Critical voices: fn. 20.

[89] Knoche 1951: 155n.25 points at Suet. *Iul.* 25.1 *gessit autem nouem annis ... haec*; cf. Cooley 2009 on Aug. *Anc.* 1.1. The *Index*, s.v. "epigraphic conventions," lists parallels between epigraphic conventions and the *BG*.

[90] Flower 1996: 139. On autobiographical writing, cf. Chassignet 2018: 259–62; on Theophanes' role, Cic. *Arch.* 24. Welch 1998: 86 (and Raaflaub 2018: 15–16) emphasizes the difference between C. and Pompey.

[91] Krebs 2018a: 29–31 reviews the debate.

[92] C. reduces actions and actors to what is militarily relevant, including his own mono-dimensional *persona* as general (and, less so, governor). He foregoes mention of booty (11.9n. *praedam*), rarely remarks on the logistics (3.1n. *qui ... praeerat*), religious matters (Rüpke 2018), soldiers' hardship (nn. on 17, 32.1), or camp life (14.2n. *pabulatione*). These restrictions are partly due to the conventions of *res gestae* (Knoche 1951: 144).

of C.'s works had better practice discernment.[93] However, the said rhetoric did not cause any major distortions, apparently (and unsurprisingly, given the traffic of information between Rome and Gaul); moreover, even when C.'s version is demonstrably fictional, as it is at the beginning of *VII* (1–5n.), his plotting need not be politically motivated – it may simply make for a better story. More detrimental to the record's historical value is its abstract and generalized nature (which has made localizing most battle sites a matter of guesswork [67n.]), not to mention its schematism and formulaic phrasing (p. 41).

In the end, however, this record came to be of historic significance, much as the events it narrates. What began as a politically motivated *Gelegenheitsschrift* to represent in Rome the remote doings of its magistrate would, some 1,500 years later, serve as a military manual, an inspiring history, and the emblematic textbook of classical Latin.[94] This transformation is largely owed to C.'s lapidary, limpid, and regularized idiom, which was considerably of his own making. It aimed at being understood by the many – there is sundry evidence that its intended audience was primarily the *populus Romanus* – and at rendering the Roman general in action.[95] In forming his style, C. hewed to Rome's standardized administrative language, as used in the magisterial reports, his primary code model (p. 29). In effect, C.'s writing evokes the Roman state, displaying the magistrate's deeds on behalf of the *res publica* in words highly reminiscent of its administration: The *BG* is a supremely patriotic work that represents a remarkable cohesion of content and form, whose full effect is largely lost on any audience but a Roman. It is ironic, then, that such a thoroughly historical, Roman text was to be elevated to a timeless model of *Latinitas*, which helped to solidify the standing of Latin as a world language.[96]

The desire to reach the many did not, however, prevent C. from composing select episodes with rather different (and specific) audiences

---

[93] Cf. Rambaud's sententious remark (1966: 112): "[d]ès le début, le *Bellum Gallicum* plaide." Cf. Damon 1993, Morstein-Marx 2021: 241–44 on C.'s "strategic writing."

[94] On the need to be present in Rome during his absence, see Krebs 2018a: 31–35. On C. in Renaissance "classrooms," see Grendler 1989: *passim*; on C.'s afterlife in military manuals, Schadee 2018.

[95] Gesche 1976: 78–83 discusses audiences (which have often been conceived too exclusively): the partly hostile, generally well-informed senate is unlikely, local elites across Italy quite possible. For arguments in favor of the *populus*, cf. Krebs 2018a: 38–41 (with lit.); they include C.'s portrayal of the soldiery (pp. 48–49), and both *nostri* and *Caesar* gain significance in this context, too (p. 43). In the light of the reading proposed under 3d, future generals should be included in C.'s envisioned audience.

[96] On the world language, see Waquet 1998, Leonhardt 2013.

in mind: his acknowledgment that Pompey respected their *amici-tia* addressed Pompey primarily (cf. p. 15 on Crassus); the apologetic account of the massacre of the Tencteri and Usipetes in 55 was composed with Cato in mind (and those sharing his criticism); the summary of the Druidic doctrine made use of Cicero's favorite Platonic dialogue in a way only the *Platonis aemulus* could fully appreciate.[97] Incidentally, these are also some of the instances that allow for the re-situation of the *BG* in the curiously excluded politics in Rome (p. 15). Along similar lines, even though the military report was C.'s primary code model, it did not prevent him from turning to Greek and Roman historiography as a second code model or indulging his linguistic, literary, and rhetorical interests (and increasingly so as years and their respective *commentarii* went by); in fact, it would be more surprising if the linguist, poet, and speaker had not left any traces in his *commentarii*. *VII* in particular, with its elaborate use of (and occasional allusion to) episodes in Thucydides and Polybius, provides ample evidence of the importance of this additional code model.

The result is a work *sui generis* (as, again, the title may have indicated): more than "notes," less than "history"; seemingly simple yet highly resonant with the language and ideology of the Roman state, evocatively laced with elements of Greek and Latin historiography, and of a varied audience.

(3 a) Matters of composition

The *BG* covers the events in Gaul from the spring of 58 to December 50: C. recounted seven seasons (58–52); Hirtius added the final two when, soon after C.'s death, he put together the so-called *Corpus Caesarianum* (*CC*).[98] References to the *BG* in the MSS and the *testimonia* vary; yet the original title must have included *commentarii rerum gestarum*, its author's name, and a topical specification: *Caesaris commentarii rerum gestarum belli Gallici*.[99] The clipped *Bellum Gallicum* can be traced back to the fifth century (*Caesar in V. belli Gallici*, Prisc. *Gramm. Lat.* II 352.6 Keil).

---

[97] 6.1.4, 4.4–15 (with Plut. *Caes.* 22.4, Powell 1998: 124–29), 6.13–14 (with Krebs 2018c).

[98] Hirt. 8.*pr.*2. Cf. Suet. *Iul.* 56.1 *reliquit et rerum suarum commentarios Gallici ciuilisque belli Pompeiani. nam Alexandrini Africique et Hispaniensis incertus auctor est.* Both *testimonia* are discussed in Gaertner-Hausburg 2013: 21–30. For a brief discussion of the *Corpus*, see Gaertner 2018.

[99] Kelsey 1905, supplemented by Seel 1977: CIV–CXIII; cf. Mensching 1988: 20–23. Cicero's and Hirtius' discussions presuppose the restored title (Krebs 2017).

As Hirtius acknowledges, C. presented each year in a self-contained *commentarius* (8.48.10).[100] This annalistic nature stands in tension with their arrangement into one narrative, which has provoked inquiry into the circumstances of the writing and dissemination of the *BG* (a longstanding *quaestio Caesariana*): Some, most influentially Theodor Mommsen, believed that C. wrote and published all books in one fell swoop in the winter of 52/51 (or a little later); others argued in favor of serial (and, mostly, annual) composition.[101] In the virtual absence of testimony (Cic. *Brut.* 262 marks a *terminus ante quem*, i.e. 46; Hirt. 8.*pr.*6, 48.10 are of no help), the *BG* itself must be mined for clues, and the debate, wherein the matters of composition and publication have not always been distinguished properly, has continued into recent times – even though Christian Ebert in 1909 made an irrefutable case for C.'s writing year by year. The more important arguments are (excluding stylistic changes): Every *commentarius* is limited to its respective year, and while some foreshadow later events within the same year, none indubitably anticipates events outside its annalistic frame.[102] Earlier *commentarii* contain premature or otherwise problematic pronouncements (e.g. 2.35.1 *omni Gallia pacata*, corrected at 3.7.1 *cum ... Caesar pacatam Galliam existimaret*), while later ones proffer information C. would have included earlier, had he known it then (the *portus Itius* identified at 5.2.3 goes unnamed at 4.23.1).[103] Most significantly, Ebert demonstrates how reading the *commentarii* as annual compositions enables or enriches our understanding of certain aspects: C.'s complimentary individuation of *P. Crassus adulescens* (1.52.7) is astute late in 58 – but in 52 when both father and son were dead (Ebert 1909: 25)? This view also accommodates the appearance of Lucretian language in *V* and C.'s "responses" to *De oratore* in *VI* (and perhaps *V–VII* more generally).[104] None of this is to exclude that C. may have had rhetorical reasons as well for so blatantly maintaining the seriatim impression.

[100] 3.1–6 is the only exception, most likely resulting from annual composition (Ebert 1909: 49–53).
[101] Nipperdey 1847: 3–8. Mommsen 1905: 499. Norden (1920: 87–92) admits serial composition but postulates "complete works" after Alesia. Radin 1918 and Adcock (1956: 77–89) argue for publication in installments. Riggsby (2006: 9–12) surveys the debate. The *BC* poses its own problems: Grillo 2012: 178–80, Gaertner-Hausburg 2013: 189–203.
[102] Nn. on 1.1, 90.3–7. The exception is 1.28.4 (cf. 10.1n. *stipendiariis*), which must be discounted (Ebert 1909: 6–10).
[103] Ebert 1909: 63; cf. Krebs 2018d: 103–12, Creer 2019. It is hardly credible that the praise of the Aedui *pro uetere ac perpetua ... fide* (5.54.4) was written after their defection in 52; cf. 75.3n. *Neruiis*.
[104] Lucretius: 1.2n. *addunt*; Krebs 2013. Fletcher 1968: 884 misidentifies *BC* 3.69.4 as *BG* 3.69.4; this has caused confusion. Cicero: Krebs 2018c; below, p. 30. Rhetorical benefits: Riggsby 2006: 133–55.

The question of publication, meanwhile, is exceedingly speculative. It would seem natural enough, had C. circulated each *commentarius* upon completion: in addition to the obligatory end-of-the-year report for the senate, aimed at a wider public (thus in motivation similar to his decree that the *acta diurna* be published), and perhaps even to be read out loud – if nothing else, this would explain the absence of major revisions.[105] Yet, such readings (or any form of annual circulation) lack contemporary evidence;[106] more importantly, just as C. cannot possibly have envisaged his *Gallia omnis* (1.1) by the end of his first season, so does *VII* show every sign of being intended as the conclusive finale (68–90n.), not to mention the links between the books (2.1.1 *uti supra* [=1.54]; 1.1n. *proficiscitur*).[107] On balance, then, a combination along the lines Karl Barwick and others have suggested seems most credible: C. began the *commentarii* to keep the larger public apprised, then formed a notion of a unitary work (after his appointment was renewed, perhaps), which he concluded with *VII* (while rereading *I* [below, 3c]), revising the whole minimally (and perhaps adding the geography in 1.1), before (re)distributing these "complete works" on his Gallic campaigns some time no sooner than 51 (some edits may have occurred when the *Corpus Caesarianum* was put together).[108] Whether or not C. thought that the battle of Alesia had effectively ended the war, to end the *BG* with the seventh book had the distinct advantage of evoking the first historical monograph in Latin, Coelius Antipater's *belli Punici alterius libri*, an evocation which *bellum Gallicum* in C.'s full title would have corroborated.[109]

In composing a *commentarius* at season's end (cf. 1.1n.), he had various sources and models at his disposal. Most fundamentally, for facts, he would draw on the dispatches that circulated between his *legati* and himself during their wide-ranging operations (e.g. 5.47.4), the communiqués he sent to the senate after major events and by year's end (90.7n.), and a magisterial "logbook"; like other governors, he maintained a "chancellery" (cf. 5.47.2 *litteras publicas*).[110] None of these writings have come

---

[105] Wiseman 1998 suggests readings to the *populus*; cf. also 89n. on enactments of V.'s surrender. On the *acta diurna* (Suet. *Iul.* 20.1), see Barwick 1938: 124–25.

[106] This *argumentum ex silentio*, applied with due consequence – should it not necessitate deferment of the publication until 46, when the *Brutus* appeared?

[107] Kraus 2009: 160. Radin 1918: 291–93 lists other joints.

[108] Barwick 1938: 213, who also reflects on the place of the *BG* in the *CC* (206–15), on which see Gaertner-Hausburg 2013: 21–30, 160–63.

[109] *FRHist* 1.257 (Briscoe), with Krebs 2015: 518–19. Other historical works in seven books lack a similar thematic significance.

[110] See Rambaud 1966: 45–96 and Osgood 2009 on the communiqués; Malitz 1987 on "Die Kanzlei Caesars." Cic. *Fam.* 15.1.1 is illuminating on the reports' frequency. The existence of logbooks appears from C.'s posthumous *commentarii*

down to us (Suetonius still had access to C.'s letters to the senate);[111] but
there exist – especially in Cicero's and Pliny's epistolary corpora, juridical
writings, and inscriptions – other instances of senatorial letters, military
reports, and bureaucratic communications. A synoptic reading of these
reveals a standardized language of the Roman state which: (1) strives for
simplicity, clarity, and precision; (2) relies on standardizations of (a) syntax and (b) phraseology (e.g. an abl. absolute followed by a *cum*-clause
[6.1], 4.1n. *ob eam causam quod*); and (3), regarding the sub-category of
military reporting more particularly, utilizes standard (a) themes and
(b) expository schemes (e.g. nn. on 5.2 *aduentu*, 5.1).[112] The *commentarii*
share an overwhelming number of these features (*Index*, s.v. "administrative style"). In some parts, they so closely adhere to this official register
that there, it has seemed to some in the heydays of *Quellenforschung*, they
reproduce the original communication (88n.); but given C.'s skillful use
of the register throughout – if to varying degrees – such identifications
are hazardous, and it is more likely that he employed the form for rhetorical effect. The same criticism applies to attempts to extract the legates'
reports verbatim from episodes C. had not witnessed himself, even if some
eccentricities in C.'s write-up of one such episode are best explained as
echoes of Labienus' voice (57–62n.).[113]

While jettisoning some features of the official register such as regular
mention of dates, distances, and timespan (Rambaud 1966: 27–29, 61–67;
cf. 24.1n. *diebus*), C. by and large preserved its ring, and its significance
is best captured by what Gian Biagio Conte has elsewhere styled the code
model: a discursive system of generic stipulations and expectations that C.'s
audience was as familiar with as he himself (if Plautus' parody of the milita-
ristic abl. absolute is any indication).[114] The consequences of this adaptation
include: First, the *commentarii* retain an official tone; second, the manifold
events in Gaul are often reduced to fit the standard form (Rambaud 1966:
38); third, details may carry surprising significance (30.4n. *patienda*).

---

et chirographa (e.g. Cic. *Phil.* 2.35 [Bömer 1953: 243n.4]); but there is no need
to postulate their circulating independently (as some have with ref. to Plut. *Caes.*
22.2).

[111] Suet.'s characterization at *Iul.* 56.2 has caused much difficulty; see
McCutcheon 2013: 163.

[112] Norden 1920: 87–92 pointed the way; Fraenkel 1956 focused on military
reports (with Horsfall 1988 on *CIL* VIII 2728). Rambaud 1966: 19–43 is most
comprehensive, Odelman 1972 most detailed on linguistics.

[113] Pollio's criticism – *cum Caesar ... quae per alios erant gesta temere crediderit ...*
(Suet. *Iul.* 56.4) – offered all the encouragement needed. Rambaud 1966: 51–56
lists the episodes (with Rüpke 1992: 217–18).

[114] Conte 2007: 184–210, differentiating it from specific example models.
Plaut. *Pers.* 753–54 (Leeman 1963: 176); below, p. 36.

But just as C. relied on reports and drew on the official register, so he turned to Greek and Roman historians for inspiration (narrative detail and phrasing) and the occasional allusion (cf. 57–62n.).[115] The significance both of historiography as another code model for C. (as advanced, *avant la lettre*, by Gärtner 1975) and of individual historians and episodes is amply apparent in *VII*: while Thucydides serves as example model for the assault on Avaricum (14–28n.) and Alesia (79–88n.), Polybius' influence is pervasive (*Index*, s.v.). Even if some parallels may be owed to the Hannibalic or Scipionic traditions rather than Polybius specifically, their number and specificity is such as to point decisively to the pragmatic historian. This should not surprise: C. would have recognized himself in the latter's ideal historian as a "man of action" (e.g. 12.28.2), fulfilling to a tee his requirements (experience, autopsy, study of sources), and he embraces an idea of history quite close to ἡ πραγματικὴ ἱστορίη; Polybius is C.'s single most important example model.[116]

While the historiographical model and its representatives are of especial importance in *VII*, they appear already in the first *commentarius*: *Gallia est omnis diuisa in partes tres* may recall Thucydides' representation of the Malians (3.92.2; Kraus 2009: 164); indubitably, the extensive background information C. then provides on the Helvetians' migration (1.2–5; cf. 1–5n.) is as foreign to a military report (clearly evoked at 1.7.1) as it is akin to historiography (especially the προκατασκευή [Polyb. 1.13.8–9]; cf. 1–5n.). C.'s writing evolves over the years, as he adds such historiographical elements as direct speeches, ethnographic digressions, and technical ekphrasis; and the appearance of Cicero's *De oratore* in 55 with its discussion of (rhetorical) *exaedificatio* and the plea for *ornamenta* (2.63, 52) may well have provoked him to embrace the historiographical model more fully – but it pervades all books.[117] The full title itself suggests as much, with *res gestae* evoking both a magisterial record and Sempronius Asellio's recent historical work (an allusion to which being all the more suitable in the light of Polybius' importance for both), and *bellum Gallicum* resonating with Antipater's *bellum Poenicum*; it is little surprise, then, that the two contemporary reactions discuss these *commentarii* with *historia* in mind.[118]

[115] Krebs 2021 argues for the retention of the term "source," *from* which C. drew facts or inspiration, and the validity of its difference" from an intertext, *to* which C. refers his readers.

[116] Krebs 2015 offers literature on Polybius and discusses his influence; a comprehensive study of Polybius in the *commentarii* is a desideratum (but see Grillo 2016, Krebs 2021). For other Greek and Roman historians' influences, see Chassignet 2018, Pitcher 2018; *Index*, s.v.

[117] Riggsby 2006: 141–42, with n.49 on earlier positions.

[118] Hirt. 8.*praef*. Cic. *Brut.* 261–62; on both Rüpke 1992: 204–07 offers the most painstaking analysis. On Asellio's *res gestae*, see Krebs 2015 (esp. p. 511); cf. above, p. 24.

The title's most important generic marker, *commentarius*, is also the most difficult to grasp because of the absence of contemporary *commentarii* (or *commentaria*) save the *commentariolum petitionis*, the term's vague significance ("notes," "records") and wide range of referents, and the misleading identification of ὑπόμνημα as its natural Greek equivalent in earlier scholarship; nor has it helped that it has often been studied in isolation.[119] If *commentarius* suggests "records" by an official (as implied by *res gestae*) on a topic of first-hand experience, it accords well with the official register informing C.'s actual text and its limitations to matters of war and administration, while accommodating its more didactic and technical aspects (to serve as a form of handbook, pp. 45–48). But three vexing problems remain: First, while there is evidence of contemporary first-person narratives by officials (e.g. *Scaurus de uita sua: in agrum hostium ueni. pilatim exercitum duxi, FRHist* F7), there is none of another third-person narrative (Marincola 1997: 193–97); but if this suggests that C.'s mostly third-person narrative (pp. 43–44) was anomalous, no one comments thereupon (even if this was the point of Cicero's misquoting the title [p. 2]). Second, recent scholarship has relinquished the notion that *commentarius* implied a lack of stylistic finesse; but Cicero's joking reference to the heavily adorned *commentarium* he had sent Posidonius in Greek as *nostrum illud* "ὑπόμνημα" (*Att.* 2.1.1) and Hirtius' discussion (8.*praef.*4) of *horum elegantia commentariorum* – as if a contradiction in terms – indicate that normally a *commentarius/m* would be expected to lack finesse. Third, both Hirtius and Cicero seem to presuppose that a *commentarius* would serve specifically as a draft for a fully decked-out history (8.*praef.*5, *Brut.* 262); but C. published this "draft," and its generic affinities go beyond history alone, since it may also be developed into a memoir (such as Q. Lutatius Catulus' *liber de consulatu et rebus gestis*), an autobiography (such as M. Aemilius Scaurus' just-quoted *De uita sua*), or a technical treatise (cf. Vitr. *De arch.* 4.*praef.*1).

In sum, however, all three issues may be interpreted as pointing to the genre of history, on which C. demonstrably draws in composing his account. His *commentarii* are a magistrate's report of historical ambition; and as such *sui generis*.[120]

---

[119] But cf. Knoche (1951: 144): "Wesentlich ist ... die nähere Bestimmung des Titels durch ... *rerum gestarum.*" Premerstein 1900 offers much material; Bömer (1953: 211) demonstrates the misidentification with the Greek term. Tellingly, two more recent discussions (Rüpke 1992, Riggsby 2006: 133–55) differ in important points. Batstone-Damon 2006: 8 propose, on etymological grounds, "records" for *commentarii*.

[120] On the *Corpus Caesarianum* as "Gattungsgeschichte *en miniature*," see Rüpke 1992: 201.

(3 b) A style of choice and a functionalist aesthetic[121]

In the midst of a century characterized by heightened linguistic aware-
ness and concerted efforts to standardize a Latin language sprawling in
its orthography (*cum/quom*), morphology (*senatūs/i*), and syntax (*potiri
+ rei/rem/re*), C. made two contributions, both during the Gallic campaigns. In 54, he published *De analogia*. A linguistic treatise, it argued
for *Latinitas*, "correct (and clear) Latin," as a primary stylistic concern
against the florid style advocated by Cicero (*De or.* 3.48); and it presented
a doctrine (*ratio Latine loquendi*, Cic. *Brut.* 253) that favored standardiza-
tion by way of regularization.[122] Secondly, he combined this theory with
"his pure and uncorrupted (language) use" (*Brut.* 261) in writing his
commentarii; their lapidary style emblematizes an unparalleled regularity
and embodies the said tenets of correctness and clarity,[123] which is why
it would ultimately serve as a school text (p. 25). The earliest critics of
the *commentarii* testify to that effect when they extol their *elegantia*, comprising both *Latinitas* and *explanatio* (cf. *Rhet. Her.* 4.17), and intimate
their kinship to the *genus tenue*, "simple style," with its primary functions
of *docere* and *probare* (Cic. *Orat.* 20).[124] To accomplish such regular(ized)
Latinity and perspicuity, C. had to make choices and his own rules; in so
doing, he borrowed from Rome's official register, committed, as it was, to
the selfsame ideals.[125] C.'s language is, first and foremost, the language of
the Roman state, as he himself may acknowledge in his characterization
of it as "the language of a military man" (στρατιωτικοῦ λόγον ἀνδρός, Plut.
Caes. 3.4).[126] However, just as his linguistics strive for regularity but allow
consuetudo (i.e. entrenched practice) its exceptions, other influences on
his style can be discerned: from poetry to barracks lingo, not to mention
instances of inattention.[127] Just as importantly, in his propulsive period
in particular, he elevated steely functionalism to an artform of lasting
consequence.

[121] This section adapts and partly enhances my 2018b contribution, to which I
refer for discussion of C.'s stylistic developments, "classical" status, and additional
bibliography.
[122] See Garcea 2012, Pezzini 2018 for C.'s linguistics.
[123] Willi 2010: 232, 242, Pezzini 2018: 182–83 discuss disagreements with rules
in *De anal.* (cf. 11.5n. *diei*).
[124] Wölfflin 1893: 142–43 offers *testimonia*; Krebs 2018b: 117–18 discusses the
genus tenue.
[125] Cf. Barwick 1951: 155, Hall 1998; Odelman 1972 on his debts to "le style
administratif."
[126] This is not to deny its "sardonic" tone (Pelling ad loc.).
[127] Editors often went against attested readings to make C.'s language "noch
einheitlicher" (Klotz 1917: 272).

C.'s regularization of his **orthography**, **morphology**, and **syntax** appears from his (e.g.): (1) avoidance of geminate "ss" following a diphthong or long vowel (2.1 *causa*, not *caussa* [cf. Quint. 1.7.20]), *os*, *om* as alternatives for *us*, *um*, and (most influentially) "u" instead of "i" as "sonus medius" (15.4 *pulcherrimam*, not *pulcherrumam* [Sall. *Cat.* 50.20]); (2) rejecting the archaic genitive (26.3n. *familiae*), alternative forms such as *qui*, *quis* for *quo*, *quibus*, and (with rare exceptions) the perfect ending "*-ere*" instead of "*-erunt*"; (3) limiting alternative construals to just one (11.9 *oppido potitur*, 76.5 *fiduciae pleni* [both with Krebs 2018b: 114], 60.3n. *imperat*); and (4) mastery of the sequence of tense especially in participial constructions (cf. *OLS* 2.793) and indirect speech (p. 37). Yet, in all these areas, he can be seen to let his attention slip or yield to convention (cf. *Index*, s.v. "Style, irregular uses"): He bows to the conventional inconsistency in the assimilation of prefix vowels (as the MSS suggest; cf. Quint. 1.7.7), allows for syncopation (17.3n. *sustentarint*), uses "*-um*" in certain instances of the genitive plural of the first and second declension (36.7 *duodenum*, 77.12n. *Teutonum*), and randomly retains *esse* in infinitival constructions (1.6n. *rationem esse habendam*), not to mention prepositions in abl. expressions (15.2n. *magno cum dolore*); particularly conspicuous are his inconsistent treatment of the historic present (as either a primary or secondary tense: contrast 1.2 *addunt ... quod uidebatur* to 2.2 *petunt ... ne deserantur*) and the occasional *constructio ad sensum* (5.4n. *qui*).[128]

Among C.'s regularizing choices and penchants, several are in line with the official register, including *causa* following gerund(ive)s and *habere* with the perf. participle (3.1n. *negotiandi causa*, 29.6n. *effectum habere*).[129] It is also the inspiration behind his two overarching (and contradictory) characteristics: economy and expansiveness of expression, each employed for clarity.[130] The **economy of expression** is most evident from C.'s limited lexicon (corresponding to the thematic limitations of the *commentarii*). In line with the stipulations of *elegantia*, viz. to rely on *usitata uerba et propria* (*Rhet. Her.* 4.17; cf. Cic. *De or.* 3.49), and his own doctrine, viz. *uerborum dilectum originem esse eloquentiae* (*De anal.* Frg. 1a), he favors **common words** and limits synonyms. His choices reveal not only the said adherence to the official register (3.1n. *causa*, 4.2n. *existimabant*, 5.4n. *flumen*, 28.4n. *mulieribus*); they also show a fine ear for words too coarse, outdated (5.5n. *ueritos*), or poetic (1.3 *incipiunt*, 1.5 *initium*, 14.4 *aedificiis*, and 17.2

[128] Barwick 1951: 155–61 and Richter 1977: 187–88 list other noteworthy expressions.
[129] For mannerisms such as 1.1n. *cognoscit de*, 1.5n. *initium faciunt*, cf. *Index*, s.v. "style, mannerisms."
[130] Cf. Coleman 2012: 189–92 on these two characteristics.

adhortari instead of *ordiri, principium, aedes,* and *alloqui*).[131] Partly in consequence, C.'s writing abounds in **repetitions** of words, phrases, formulae and sentences (e.g. 8x *oppidum* in 11; 1.1n. *certior factus,* 4.1n. *cuius ... obtinuerat,* 11.7n. *paulo ... egressi*).[132] But he knew to vary if he wanted to (*Index,* s.v. "*uariatio*"), and some repetitions appear purposeful (cf. 5.3n. *legatorum*),[133] be it to highlight the *genus tenue* (as befitting a magistrate's record [p. 32, fn. 124]), be it for rhetorical, narratological, or discursive purpose: so as to (a) connect sentences (90.2n. *imperat*), (b) resume a narrative strand (7.1n. *Lucterius ... missus*), (c) highlight the theme of a paragraph, especially by way of ring composition (19.3n. *parati,* 16.3n. *itineribus*), (d) confirm the accuracy of a prediction or plan (51.1n. *insequentes,* 61.3n.), (e) bring out the similarities between C. and V. (4.3n. *habet dilectum*), or (f) mark a dramatic (often ironic) reversal (28.6n. *excepit;* cf. *Index,* s.v. "irony"); of particular note are "transgressive repetitions," i.e. echoes between the narrator and a historical agent, a form of Genette's metalepsis, esp. when they involve "*mis*iterations" (15.5n. *perangustum*).

Just as C. knew to vary, he knew to include the occasional archaism, poeticism, vulgarism (11.7n. *coeperunt*), Greek or Celtic loanword (cf. 3.1n. *Gutuatro*), or expression of the *sermo castrensis.*[134] His sizable lexicon of **uncommon words** (*Index,* s.v.), including *hapax legomena* (33.1n. *detrimentosum,* 54.2n. *admaturari*), comprises an especially noticeable number of technical terms (e.g. 84.1n. *musculos*); they sometimes serve rhetorical effect (such as *euidentia* [73n.]), more often, as *uerba uere propria,* precision (54.2n. *admaturari*).[135] Precision of sorts can also be detected in his limiting certain expressions in their meaning (4.1n. *potentiae,* 9.1n. *per causam,* 19.2n. *fiducia,* 1.4n. *conciliis*). Some of these choices influenced subsequent writers (11.9n. *desideratis,* 12.5n. *complere,* 73.6n. *praeusti;* p. 55).

On the syntactical plane, C.'s economy is epitomized by his deft handling of the **ablative**: the *BG*'s most frequent case (Kollmann 1977: 48–49, Eden 1962: 101–04), it is occasionally construed in ways that push the envelope (68.3n. *equitatu*), often added to highlight the aspect involved

---

[131] Cf. Krebs 2018b: 124 on *missum facere.* Chance or idiosyncrasy may factor, too (cf. 8.3n. *inopinantibus*).

[132] Cf. Pickering 2003. Pliny's seven instances of *flumen* in *Ep.* 10.61 represent the feature in administrative writing. Cf. *Index,* s.v. (including "local repetition" [Frese 1900: 21; 25.2n. *e regione*]).

[133] Cf. the frequency of totalizing expressions, esp. *omnis,* which is a general characteristic of C.'s "mythic" writing (Batstone 2018: 53) but may on occasion take on an especial rhetorical point (e.g. 4.6n. *omnium*).

[134] Specifically on the *sermo castrensis,* see Mosci Sassi 1983. Cf. fn. 128; Krebs 2018b: 125–26.

[135] Cf. Damon 2015: 109–20 on rare words in C.

in a verb's action (9.1n. *opinione praeceperat*), and frequently strung together in multiples of differing function (81.1).[136] His handling of the **abl. absolute**, a hallmark of the military report and especially in combination with a *cum* clause (1.1n. *Quieta Gallia*; 6.1n.), is similarly conspicuous and partly innovative: his favorite narrative connective (2.1n. *his rebus agitatis*; Chausserie-Laprée 1969: 109–24), he uses its nominal version rather generously, expands it with another clause (17.3n.), employs several of them consecutively (8.1), and often favors it over a more integrated participial construction, occasionally compromising the construction's "absoluteness" (4.1n. *conuocatis suis ... incendit*, 27.1n. *hanc tempestatem*). In the latter case, it bestows greater independence onto the action; more generally, it often allows C. to mirror the sequence of events (2.3) – but habit of mind cannot be excluded either. By inserting the subject of the main clause amidst the ablative absolute, he simplifies the identification of its agent (1.4n. *indictis ... conciliis*; the device found favor with later historians).

The **expansiveness** of expression manifests itself in (a) often near-synonymous pairings (1.3n. *liberius atque audacius*); (b) the scheme known as "theme and variation" (12.3n. *ignosceret ... consuleret*), especially in the form of a general concept followed by its specification;[137] (c) pleonasms, including grammatical ones, such as 1.3 *consilia inire incipiunt*, 4.1 *ob eam causam quod*, 4.7n. [*imperium ...*] *qua oblata potestate*, 64.2 *perfacile ... factu*, and 81.6 *auxilio ... summittebant*;[138] and (d) an abundant use of "determiners" that anticipate a clause (5.5n. *id consilii ... ut*) or, and especially frequently, resume something already stated (e.g. 7.1 *in Rutenos missus eam ciuitatem Aruernis conciliat*); the five instances in c. 1 are not unusual.[139] All four manifestations serve clarity and are paralleled in administrative writing,[140] as is another form of resumption that C. employs frequently, viz. the cross-reference (17.1n. *ut supra diximus*).

This use of determiners points at C.'s **sentence** architecture, which is most fundamentally characterized by the self-contained "narrative unit" expressing a stand-alone thought, frequently with the verb in the final position (as was standard in the administrative style).[141] Such a unit can

---

[136] Such "string" concision (which is also applied, if less frequently, to the genitive [22.1n. *cuiusque modi Gallorum*]) occasionally puts clarity at risk (Fischer 1853: 3–4, Eden 1962: 103–04).

[137] Courtney 1999: 4 identifies it as a feature of archaic (and legal) Latin.

[138] Hellwig 1889 documents C.'s pleonasms (but his definition of "grammatical" is vague). Cf. *Index*, s.v.

[139] On "determiners," see *OLS* 1.969–74. Cf. Eden 1962: 86, Odelman 1972: 152–59, who relates the feature to legal writing.

[140] Cf. Coleman 2012.

constitute a whole sentence: *eae res in Galliam Transalpinam celeriter per-feruntur* (1.2); to align several such "sentence-units," often asyndetically, was a mainstay of the military report, and C. imitates it occasionally (and markedly towards the end of *VII* [79–88n.]).[142] Or else several of them can form a string within a sentence, as when three units, each phrased differently, are linked together in 6.1: *his rebus in Italiam Caesari <u>nuntiatis</u>, | cum iam ILLE urbanas res uirtute Cn. Pompei commodiorem in statum peruenisse <u>intellegeret</u>, | in Transalpinam Galliam <u>profectus est</u>*. C. may organize these narrative units hypotactically (as in 6.1) or paratactically: *ipse imperat reliquis ciuitatibus obsides <u>diemque</u> EI rei constituit* (64.1). Both examples contain the above-mentioned resumptive "determiner," many of which are, in fact, a syntactical consequence of the primacy of the stand-alone unit (Courtney 1999: 3–6); this is particularly apparent in instances of the "compromised" ablative absolute (as discussed above). Quite frequently, at least in *VII*, C. seems at pains to balance the units, be it regarding their lengths, or sound patterns including homoeoteleuton (*Index*, s.v. "isocolon," "sound pattern").[143]

C. typically arranges these units in a "forward-moving," **propulsive** sequence to form what Mignonette Spilman (1932: 202) called the "**cumulative-complex**" sentence, which often preserves the chronological or otherwise logical order and ends with the main clause: *celeriter effecto opere » legionibusque traductis » et loco castris idoneo delecto » reliquas copias reuocauit* (35.5). Its force appears clearly when contrasted with Plautus' parody of the strings of ablative absolutes in military reports, which lacks the said propulsion: *hostibus uictis, ciuibus saluis, re placida, pacibus perfectis, | bello exstincto, re bene gesta, integro exercitu et praesidiis, … (Pers. 753–54)*. The "cumulative-complex" sentence is as different from the Ciceronian period with its suspension of thought as it is typical of much of Roman historiography – and nowhere more so than with C.[144] Indeed, in its perfection and pervasiveness it may be singled out as a hallmark of his style, so often

---

[141] Spilman 1932: 157. I adapt her "narrative unit" to emphasize the constitutive importance of the thought or action comprised in each (cf. Chausserie-Laprée 1969: 129–30; Fraenkel's "*guttatim* style" [on Aesch. *Ag.* 2]). On the verb's position, cf. Krebs 2018b: 119n.27 (C. knew to vary here, too [*Index*, s.v. "word order, verb"]).

[142] Eden 1962: 80. Fraenkel 1956. On C.'s use of asyndeton, cf. *Index*, s.v.

[143] On such sound effects in archaic texts to mark off word groups, see Lindholm 1931: 1–116.

[144] Contrast e.g. Cic. *Cat.* 4.19: *atque haec, non ut uos (qui mihi studio paene praecurritis) excitarem, locutus sum sed ut mea uox (quae debet esse in re publica princeps) officio functa consulari uideretur.* Spilman 1932: 241 and Chausserie-Laprée 1969: 173 document C.'s predominance. Cf. pp. 55–57.

perceived to be "march[ing] along, as orderly as a legion" (Adcock 1956: 71).[145] Its intentional use appears from its suspension when, amidst much typical movement, the narrative lingers over P. Sextius Baculus (2.25).

In its most compelling form, the "cumulative-complex" sentence aggregates a number of circumstances or observations in a series of subordinate clauses, the result of which is reached – by a seeming "pull of necessity" – in the conclusive main clause: *altero die cum ad oppidum Senonum Vellaunodunum uenisset,* | *ne quem post se hostem relinqueret,* | *quo expeditiore re frumentaria uteretur,* » *oppugnare instituit idque biduo circumuallauit* (11.1).[146] C.'s presence at Vellaunodunum and his desire to leave no enemy behind *necessarily* lead to his decision to besiege the *oppidum*. This propulsion and pull of necessity result from the excision of everything not strictly relevant to the action and the careful arrangement of the remaining information through a "rhetoric of stringency"; the price paid is a rather lifeless narrative deprived of much particularity (p. 41).

That C. turns functionality into an aesthetic can also be gleaned from another trademark of his: **indirect "speeches"** number 125 instances in the *BG* and 66 in the *BC*, far outnumbering direct speeches (twelve and thirteen instances).[147] While their origin can be traced back to the official register, C. elevates them to unparalleled sophistication ("le triomphe du style indirect" [Hyart 1954: 171]), turning them into a favored *literary* device: often composed in adherence to the rhetorical system, they serve to enliven the conveyance of information (1.4–8), characterize an actor or ambience (66n.), or recapture the contingency of history (as when V. proposes that all *oppida* not entirely safe be burnt down [14.9] but then concedes an exception [15.5–6]).[148] Their decrease in frequency (the *BG*'s first two books account for the highest percentage) along with the concomitant rise of the more blatantly literary *oratio recta* (absent from *I–III* and *BC* 1) is much less significant than the fact that *VII*, the most

---

[145] It is more common than the other two patterns in historical narratives identified by Chausserie-Laprée (1969: 251–82, 283–336) as sentences consisting of (a) at least two main clauses (each of which is accompanied by a subordinate phrase [e.g. 11.5–6n.]) and (b) a main clause that is succeeded by a subordinate phrase (typically abl. absolutes or participial constructions [e.g. 15.6]).

[146] Fränkel 1933: 171 speaks of the "Caesarische Periode." Cf. Krebs 2018b: 117–23.

[147] C. uses *oratio* irrespective of character and length (Dangel 1995: 95n.1). Grillo 2018 offers charts.

[148] Hyart 1954: 137–50. For its functions, cf. Oppermann 1933: 72–85, Morrison 2006: 13–21, and Pausch 2011: 158–61. Murphy 1949 reveals their "recognizably rhetorical form" (122); cf. my nn. on 1.4–8, 14, 20.3–12, 29, 52, 64, 77, 89.

elaborate *commentarius*, still counts four times as many instances of indirect speech.[149]

C.'s **rhythm** – both inside and outside the speeches – has been characterized as "synthesizing certain aspects of Cicero's style with the rhythms natural to the Latin language" (Oberhelman 2003: 77), in line, it would seem, with his overall approach to the Latin language. Artistic rhythms, comprising the cretic [–◡–] + trochee [–x], cretic or molossus [– – –] + cretic, double trochee, hypodochmiac [–◡–◡x], and their various resolutions, are less frequent and conspicuous than in Cicero's speeches (the traditional benchmark), but more so than in Varro, say.[150] C.'s fine ear can also be detected in his adding or removing words for the sake of isocolon (often combined with homoioteleuton [69.4n. *fastigio*]), choosing a rare synonym for the sake of euphony (29.4n. *obsequentia*), or the instances of sound play (88.2n. *utrimque clamore … clamor*).

Such sound play points to ornamental elements that transcend the functional; they include instances of mimetic word order (16.1n. *Vercingetorix … subsequitur*), telling names and (other) bilingual wordplay, mimetic translation, and erudite glossing (17.3n. *tenuitate*; 77.2n. *Critognati*; 17.1n. *aggerem apparare*; 75.4n. *quae Oceanum attingunt*), adnominatio (19.3n. *propinquitatem … iniquitatem*), congeries (24.5n. *alii … alii … omnis … multitudo*), sententiae (26.4n. *timor … recipit*), and others (*Index*, s.v. "style, ornamental elements"). But even in *VII*, wherein the vocabulary is broader, the historiographical elements more numerous, and the administrative style in some regards less dominant than in the earlier *commentarii*,[151] they are outliers that hardly distract from the narrative, and even then only those as attuned to literary sophistication as the author himself. Until the end, the style *is* – first and foremost – the Roman pro-magistrate, C.

[149] Rasmussen 1963: 130–59 on *oratio recta* (with Maniet's 1965 criticism). The much-discussed "parallel development" (von Albrecht 1997: 332–33) within the two sets of *commentarii* fares poorly under scrutiny; so does Klotz's claim that the changes in (in)direct speech evince the transition from *commentarius* to fully decked-out *historia* (Klotz 1917: col. 259): too vague is our understanding of the *commentarius*.

[150] For these rhythms as "artistic," see Keeline-Kirby 2019: 163–66; id. (187–88) for C. compared with Varro. The commentary notes only those more noticeable instances where rhythmic concerns seem the simplest explanation of a marked word order.

[151] See Gaertner-Hausburg 2013: 44n.7 on C.'s changing vocabulary, their Appendix F, and Krebs 2018b: 117n.24 for the partial waning of the bureaucratic influence. On literary elements, cf. pp. 41–42.

(3c) The narrative of VII: a semi-historical monograph of tragic connotations

C.'s final book is ambiguous in nature. As the finale, it concludes the continuous narrative of the *Gallic War*, the first installment of which it recalls variously.[152] It shares several features with the series: Its beginning and ending conform with the annalistic framework, the former typically linking back to the previous *commentarius* and postulating that peace was established (1.1nn. *quieta Gallia, in Italiam*; 1.4n. *de Acconis morte*);[153] the latter terminating the year just as typically with the legions' distribution into camps – as if to be resumed next spring (Hirtius would have no difficulty picking up the baton [90n.]). It features the same anonymous narrator, who focuses on military affairs, cheers for "our men," and celebrates C. At the same time, *VII* stands apart not only by its length and the elaboration of literary elements but also by its centering *uno in argumento* and *una in persona*, viz. the war for all of Gaul against V. Such unity defines the historical monograph (as Cicero discussed in his "public" letter to Lucceius).[154] It requires a proper overture and closure, the kind which, paradoxically, *VII* also provides: for such are the *bellum subitum* C. devises (1–5n.) and V.'s surrender (89n.).[155] His showcasing his *uirtutes imperatoriae* in the early "Parade Chapters" (6–13n.) – like Horace's parading his poetics in the opening odes – and his throning amidst the massive fortifications in the final section gain significance in this light.[156] *VII* has long been recognized as the most accomplished *commentarius*; its monographic tendencies partly account for it.

[152] C. reread *I* from 58/7 before writing *VII* (cf. p. 27): the opening scenes, incl. their protagonists, resemble one another (1–5n.); a striking number of words recur in *VII* after they figure in *I* only (e.g. 55.3 *coemptum*, 1.3.1 *coemere*), which I have not documented; cf. *Index*, s.v. "ring compositions, *I–VII*."

[153] The annalistic frame and internal division into administrative winters and campaign summers evoke the magistrate's annual report (1.1n. *conuentus*, 90.7n. *litteris*). Yet, by C.'s time, that frame was also an established principle in the annalistic tradition of historical writing (its conventional opening, the naming of the consuls, occurs in *IV*, *V*, and *BC* 3 [Eden 1962: 77]); cf. Rich 2011: 1–3. Just so, the division κατὰ θέρος καὶ χειμῶνα as a structural device was already established by Thucydides (2.1 [with Hornblower]).

[154] Cic. *Fam.* 5.12. Deeming the letter *ualde bella*, he asked Atticus *ut ... sumas* (*Att.* 4.6.4).

[155] Cf. Cic. on the proposed beginning (*a principio ... coniurationis*) and ending (*ad reditum nostrum*) of the said monograph on the Catilinarian conspiracy (5.12.4; Sall. wisely ended instead with Catiline's death [*BC* 61]). In *VI*, C. represents a similar situation dissimilarly (6.1.1 *maiorem Galliae motum exspectans*). On notions of closure and overtures, see Fowler 1997, Dunn-Cole 1992.

[156] C.'s sitting in triumph over all of Gaul *in munitione pro castris* offers an apt conclusion to the entire *BG*, too (89n.). Lowrie 1995: 34n.5 offers literature on the "parade odes."

This monographic unity is strengthened by structural elements. Five leitmotifs run through the book: *libertas*, the freedom of <u>all</u> Gaul (4.4n. *communis libertatis*), is "the main theme of the book" (Murphy 1977: 241) and highlighted by ring composition (1.5, 89.2; cf. Flor. *Epit.* 1.45.21 *ad ius pristinum libertatis*). It is joined by the quintuple challenge to V.'s leadership (4.2, 20, 29, 63.6, 75.1) and C.'s twin worries about supplies and the Aedui (10.1n. *ab re frumentaria*, 90.7n. *frumentariae*, 5.6n. *perfidia*).[157] While these three dominate the first two thirds, the stereotype of the Gallic "hordes" comes to the fore in the final third (21.1n. *omnis multitudo*, 79–88n.). These threads are woven into a narrative comprising three main acts (cf. Flor. *Epit.* 1.45.23 *capita belli*), viz. the sieges of Avaricum, Gergovia, and Alesia, each divided into halves, the first and last being clearly defined set-pieces (14–28n.).[158] They are: (a) preceded by a "prelude" that sets the scene in Gaul (1–5) and follows C.'s efforts to reunite with his legions and confront V. (6–13); (b) separated by *intermezzi* – shorter, quieter narratives that deal with Aeduan affairs, Labienus' battle, and V.'s fateful decision to attack (29–35, 57–62, 63–67); and (c) concluded by an anti-climactic coda (89–90), which is marked off by a speech, as is typical (cf. 15n.).[159] These main acts form a rising tricolon, with V. first proposing a "new" strategy before Avaricum (14.1 *longe alia ratione*), then promising *more* troops from a united Gaul before Gergovia (29.6 *unum consilium totius Galliae*), and finally requisitioning *all* Gauls capable of arms for the battle at Alesia (71.2 *omnesque ... ad bellum*);[160] at least the last two recruitments are chronologically impossible (nn. on 29, 68–90). At its center stands the double reversal of fortune at and after Gergovia, first in V.'s and then in C.'s favor, representing the kind of *temporum uarietates fortunaeque uicissitudines* sure to delight a Roman reader.[161] The *peripeteia(i)* along with the clearly discernible acts, the high calling of *libertas*, and V.'s role as "tragic" protagonist

---

[157] Cf. Gärtner 1975: 88, 96 and Görler 1977: 320 on C.'s twin worries.

[158] Avaricum (14–28), Gergovia (36–56), and Alesia (68–90) contain the preparations (14–19, 36–43, 68–78) and the battle (20–28, 44–56, 79–88). Disagreements about the structure of *VII* have focused on the specific boundaries between acts, internal divisions, and *intermezzi*. My "segmentation" (cf. Fowler 1997: 12–14) follows thematic and narratological criteria; it is certainly open to challenge.

[159] Rambaud 1966: 232–38. Kahn 1971: 251 remarks on C.'s using oratory to highlight turning points (but in selecting 1.6–10, 14, 29, 63, 75, and 89, he overlooks 66 and 77). Cf. nn. on 38, 52.

[160] C.'s limiting his account to three "wrestling bouts" is thus for literary reasons (and explains his forgoing a detailed description of the siege of Noviodunum [12.2], say); in Greek, the third bout signifies the "crowning achievement" (Wheeler 1988: 38). Other *crescendo* elements: nn. on 29.7, 31.4 (V. recruits *sagittarii*), 63, 76.

[161] Cic. *Fam.* 5.12.4. Görler 1977: 319 places the "Hauptperipetie" in c. 56.

have suggested to Arthur Kahn (1971) that C. devised *VII* as a tragedy; one may disagree on specifics, but a tragic resonance is hard to deny, especially if it is accepted that C. casts V. as "perilously proud," a ὑβριστής, before his failed attack (63–68n.). C. had written tragedies before (*Laudes Herculis, Oedipus* [Suet. *Iul.* 56.7]); he would do so again.[162]

Amongst the most consequential *uicissitudines* was the defection of the Aedui, which might have been revealed as soon as the narrator raised the specter of their *perfidia* (5.4); and it should have been revealed then, if nothing but a military communication were intended. Instead, the reader shares C.'s growing suspicion until 54.2 *perfidiam … perspectam* (marked by a ring-compositional repetition).[163] In its military relevance and literary elaboration, this storyline exemplifies the two largely contradictory paradigms of these *commentarii rerum gestarum* (pp. 29–30). On the one hand, the imprint of the military report on *VII* is as easy to discern as on earlier installments: Much of its content is selected for military significance; the topography is viewed "through the commander's eye" before which rivers, woods, and hills appear as obstacles, hiding places, and advantageous heights; and variations on the scheme of information and analysis, decision and action provide regular structure (achieving its own artform, as in c. 10, and inviting the study of "the eye of command" [Kagan 2006: 181–200]).[164] These characteristics combine with the stringent and compulsive style discussed above to represent war as an "exercise of the mind" (Adcock 1956: 50). This rationalization with its emotional distance is attended by the excision of individuating detail, effecting the reiterations of actions, scenes, and entire sequences, which correspond thematically to the repetitive phraseology and now and then suggest the reapplication of a template rather than the thoughtful representation of the repetitiveness of war (let alone intratextual enrichment); one might be inclined to speak of schematic composition.[165] Hirtius remarked on the speed of C.'s writing (8.*praef.*6); it shows, occasionally.

On the other hand, and in contradiction to the military paradigm of straightforward sparsity, *VII* abounds in elaborate *expugnationes urbium* (Tac. *Ann.* 4.32.2), detailed technical ekphraseis, an epic catalogue, and

---

[162] For the *BC*, see Rowe 1967, Mutschler 1975: 52–81, Grillo 2012: 32–36.

[163] C. maintains a similar suspense narrating the Aeduan desertion in *I* (1.15, 1.18.10; Lohmann 1990).

[164] Rambaud 1966: 38 thinks of "l'équivalent des ‹loci communes› de la rhétorique." Cancik 1998: 120 speaks of "[d]ie … mit dem Auge des Feldherrn geprüfte Natur." On C.'s schematization, see Kraus 2009: 165–68.

[165] The moves in 10–13 mirror those in 6–9 (6–13n.). 63(n.) reassembles stock motifs, much in c. 70 rehashes 13.1–2; cf. *Index*, s.v. "schematic composition," and, Damon 2010 on "Déjà vu or déjà lu."

the *BG*'s longest direct speech – in short: literary elements that set it apart (by degree, not category) from the other *commentarii*.[166] By inserting V.'s self-defense and the *murus Gallicus* (20 + 23), C. succeeds in representing in narrative time (seven cc.) the time it took to build the ramp before Avaricum (twenty-five days). Such a correlation of discourse and story is effected repeatedly, and for space just as much: not before c. 13 do readers arrive with C. at Avaricum, whence they move through an Aeduan *intermezzo* (cc. 29–35) to reach Gergovia, thence to Alesia through cc. 54–67.[167] No surprise, then, that *VII* begins with the narrator "following" news from Rome to Gaul (whence then back to Italy [nn. on 1.2, 6.1]). When the Gauls call a war council (1.4–8), it not only introduces the pervasive Gallic focalization, which leads to a (mostly) binary narrative that – often swiftly – pivots from one side to the other; it also represents what Gärtner has called a "reflection," and which, along with the "individual scene" (*Einzelszene*), he identifies as building blocks (*Bauelemente*) of literary historiography.[168] Both "blocks" occur frequently in the *commentarii*, and especially in *VII*, including the heroic self-sacrifice of Marcus Petronius at Gergovia's gate (50n.), which rather famously exemplifies C.'s use of pathos.[169]

The rhetorical purpose of Petronius' scene to distract from C.'s defeat is hard to deny, and for a long time scholars interpreted virtually all literary elements as evidence of C.'s *déformation historique* for political purchase.[170] It is true that several of them not only render the author's plotting hand visible (cf. *Index*, s.v.) but also clash with historical realities. This narrow perspective, however, overlooks that these elements are also part and parcel of *la formation historique* (at least of the Greek and Roman

---

[166] This was recognized a long time ago (e.g. Feller 1929: 3, on "Anklänge an die kunstmäßige Geschichtsschreibung"). The literarization of the earlier *commentarii* has been underestimated.

[167] Cf. *Index*, s.v. "narrative, time/space," and Kraus 2007: 350.

[168] On focalization, including the "deviant" kind (cf. *Index*, s.v.), see Fowler 1990. Gärtner 1975: 63–134; cf. Rambaud's identification of "des éléments étrangers aux techniques du rapport" (1966: 51).

[169] Rambaud 1966: 230–32; he lists other members of Petronius' kin (e.g. Pullo and Vorenus, 5.44), on pp. 244–45 (the anonymous *aquilifer* at 4.25.3–4 could be added).

[170] None more so than Rambaud 1966; cf. his pithy "le pittoresque n'est jamait gratuit" (230; similarly 237). Ogilvie's criticism of two readers of C. as "rather too inclined to look for ulterior motives" (1977: 87) is of wider purview. Recent interpretations that focus on the literary aspects include Kraus 2007, Gerlinger 2008, Gerrish 2013, Grillo 2012 + 2016, Krebs 2016 + 2018.

variety [pp. 3–4); moreover, it often throws a political shadow over C.'s
"visible hand" when the historical inaccuracy – such as the chronological
impossibilities – is more readily explained as the byproduct of an aesthetic
motivation than the product of a political one. It makes little difference,
politically, that V.'s strategy is announced belatedly, or that he is cast as
a ὑβριστής; narratologically, however, the former helps to demarcate a
new "chapter," while the latter offers a historiographical explanation for
V.'s sudden discontinuation of his successful guerilla strategy. Lastly, the
intertextual engagements especially with Thucydides and Polybius, or the
"evocative gestures" towards literary motifs such as the battle address or
teichoscopy, not to mention the playful invention of Critognatus (nn. on
62.2, 88.5, 77) – they all evince how close C. comes in *VII* to a fully formed
example of classical historiography.[171]

In this regard, no single narratological choice is of greater consequence than the twofold separation of the narrator from C. as author,
who is never identified within the narrative, and actor, who is never
referred to other than in the third person (and usually by his cognomen
[1.1n. *Caesar*]).[172] In his narratorial reticence C. differs from Thucydides
and Polybius, who both employ the third person in reference to themselves (intermittently, in Polybius' case) but state their identity.[173] The
closest parallel is Xenophon's *Anabasis*, as it shares both the third-person reference and the anonymity;[174] and just as Xenophon's identity
was well known at C.'s time (Cic. *Diu.* 1.122–23), so was C.'s, apparently,
which suggests that the *commentarii* circulated *suo nomine* (p. 26).[175] But
C.'s narrator does not even admit to being personally involved – the partial exceptions being 5.13.4 and 7.25.2(n.).[176] In all other instances of
the narrator's referring to himself, it is in his capacity as narrator, who
refers to other parts of the narrative, and then he prefers the first-person

---

[171] I speak of "evocative gesture" (cf. *Index*, s.v.) since many of the historiographical features are frequently evoked rather than elaborated.
[172] This led to the problematic designation of the *commentarii* as third-person
narratives (Riggsby 2006: 150). Reijgwart 1993 offers a subtle analysis.
[173] Thuc. 4.104.4, 5.26.5; Polyb. 3.4.13. On their differences, see Marincola
1997: 182–84, 188–92.
[174] Pelling 2013 discusses the differences between Xenophon (whose case is
more complicated because of *Hell.* 3.1.2) and C.
[175] On contemporary identifications as well as later misattributions, see Krebs
2017.
[176] The first-person plural used in both undermines the oft-advanced identification with "C." Riggsby 2006: 150–52 points at differences between narrator and C.
(contrast Pelling 2013: 49–50).

plural (5.6n. *nobis*, 17.1n. *ut supra diximus*).[177] This preference is in harmony with his address of choice of the Roman soldiers as *nos* and *nostri*
(pp. 49–50): however anonymous, the narrator is certainly Roman (just
like his intended audience).[178] While he mostly follows C. (and especially so in the early books), he occasionally and increasingly occupies an
"Olympic" point of view, which allows for the ethnographic, geographic,
and historical digressions, the coordination of several theatres of war, and
the Gallic focalization.[179]

   An author's reference to himself in the third person was not without
precedent in Greek historiography; but it appears unprecedented at
Rome (p. 31). In his choice C. was likely influenced by epigraphic conventions regarding the celebration of accomplishments, wherein the
third person was standard (*Cornelius Scipio Carthagine capta* [*CIL* 625]),
as Andrew Riggsby has documented. This "alignment of 'Caesar' with …
Roman authority" correlates with the authoritative tone of his lapidary
style specified above, as if the *res publica Romana* herself spoke about
C.[180] Practical concerns may have mattered, too: It certainly would have
facilitated public readings (should they have been intended), not to
mention the added advantage of the relentless repetition of his name
(1.1n. *Caesar*).[181] Most importantly, it allowed C. to do what Cicero (and
others) struggled with: *scribere ipsum de se*, while limiting the loss of *fides*
and *auctoritas* known to attend autobiographical writing (Cic. *Fam.*
5.12.8; cf. Plut. *De glor. Athen.* 345e on Xenophon's ploy). The narrator
may occasionally seem to enjoy "privileged knowledge" of C.'s thoughts;
but the overwhelming impression is one of separation, which affords
the personal remove that Greek and Roman historians liked to affect.
Herein, too, in that "manner of the historian," C.'s narrative approx-
imates to history – whatever its undeniable rhetorical (and political)
benefits.[182]

---

[177] Rasmussen 1963: 73–79 observes that such self-references often occur in
particularly "engaging" contexts.
  [178] Cf. Torigian 1998: 50 on C. as "agent of Rome." He does not shed his
Romanness entirely either when focalizing events through Gallic eyes (*Index*, s.v.
"focalization, deviant").
  [179] Görler 1976 proved influential (cf. Reijgwart 1993, Riggsby 2006: 153–54,
and Grillo 2011).
  [180] Batstone-Damon 2006: 146. Riggsby 2006: Appendix B collates "generals'
inscriptions."
  [181] Wiseman 1998: 8. Rambaud 1966: 196; Kollmann 1977: 45 "der Name sollte
ein Begriff werden" (cf. Cic. *Att.* 16.10.1 *Caesariana uti celeritate*).
  [182] The quotations are from Pelling 2013: 47, and Marincola 1997: 198. Cf.
e.g. Sall. *BC* 4.3 … *quod mihi a spe, metu, partibus rei publicae animus liber erat* (with
Ramsey ad loc.). For discussion of "l'objectivité apparente" (Rambaud 1979: 39),

(3 d) Caesar imperator and his "commentarii rerum militarium"

The "Parade Chapters" represent C. as an astute, speedy, tireless, decisive, and courageous general (6–13n.); the final scenes show him – amidst the fortifications he had had the foresight to design – analyzing the battle and orchestrating his troops (85n.), then entering the melee and restoring confidence by his authoritative presence (nn. on 87, 88): the next day, a vanquished V. admits *Fortunae cedendum* (89.2n.). C. thus displays the *uirtutes imperatoriae* Cicero had used in 66 to define the clichéd *summus ac perfectus imperator* (*Leg. Man.* 36), whom, he argued, Pompey embodied: *scientia rei militaris, uirtus, auctoritas, felicitas ... labor in negotiis, fortitudo in periculis, industria in agendo, celeritas in conficiendo, consilium in prouidendo* (28–29).[183] As Cicero portrayed Pompey in order to win him the command of the Mithridatic campaign, so C. portrays himself "to augment [his] reputation" (Rambaud 1966: 245) and do Pompey one better. In either case, readers should proceed cautiously from rhetoric to reality when studying the actual generalship.[184]

To cast himself as a model general (much after Polybius' liking), C. modulates these conventional qualities, as when he highlights his special relationship to his soldiery (pp. 48–50), while also alluding to specific models and rivals, such as, at Alesia, Marius, Scipio (Aemilianus), and Pompey (88.1n. *uestitus*, 77.12n. *Cimbrorum Teutonumque*, 68–78n.).[185] Of particular interest is his calibration of the importance of raw bravery (*uirtus*) *vis-à-vis* strategy and technology (*consilium, scientia*).[186] C. had won the *corona ciuica* as a young man (p. 9). This lent credence to the many (yet often questionable) instances in his *commentarii* where he enters the fray (87.3n. *proelio intersit*; Goldsworthy 1998: 204–10); other writers, including those of the *corpus*, happily expounded on his *uirtus* and *fortitudo* (Plut. *Caes.* 56.2). But he himself asserts "that it behooves a general rather more to win by planning than by fighting" (*consilio ... quam gladio, BC* 1.72.2); his *commentarii* accordingly emphasize *consilium* more than *uirtus* (nn. on 7.3 *consiliis*, 19, 22, 52), present schemes and poliorcetics, and in their style bespeak a rationalistic conception of war (Cancik 1998: 105; p. 41;

---

see further Batstone-Damon 2006: 144–45, and Riggsby 2006: 149–52. Cf. Grillo 2011 and Kraus 2009: 162–63 (for other interpretations).

[183] Cf. Collins 1972: 933, and Combès 1966: 214–19 (on Cicero's impact on definitions of leadership). On the perfect general (*Index*, s.v.), cf. Onas. 1; Rosenstein 1990: 114–52.

[184] On C. as "chef de guerre," see Le Bohec 2001b.

[185] Cf. *Index*, s.vv. Zecchini 2001: 117–36 discusses "Cesare et i suoi modelli." On Hannibal: *Index*, s.v.

[186] Cf. 22.1n. *uirtuti consilia ... occurrebant*; Lendon 1999, Zecchini 2001: 147–57.

9n.). Confirmation comes from Hirtius' remark on his late commander's *scientia suorum consiliorum explicandorum*; and the author of *BAfr.* praises C. as *peritus scientia bellandi* (Hirt. 8.*praef.*7, *BAfr.* 31).

These last two remarks not only indicate C.'s (likely) familiarity with military handbooks;[187] they also invite a reading of the *commentarii* as a contribution to the tradition of "military writings" (τὰ περὶ τῶν στρατηγικῶν ὑπομνήματα, Polyb. 10.44.1).[188] *VII* in particular abounds in poliorcetic blueprints and stratagems: V.'s threat to the province to force C. to vacate Gaul (the ἀντιπερίστασις [51n.]); C.'s counterthreat and mastery of surprise (8n.); V.'s guerilla strategy (14n.) and luring C. into a trap (19); the (counter-)mining (22.2n. *cuniculis*); river crossings (36n.); ambushing (18.1n. *insidiarum*); the use of false reports (38n.); C.'s feigned attack (ψευδέφοδος [45n.]); his dressing up muleteers (45n.); Labienus' pretense of panic (ψευδοπανικά [60.3n. *tumultu*]).[189] By their detail, these episodes instruct as much as illustrate, and it should be remembered that C. is depicted as an instructor of his troops (*BAfr.* 71.1, 72.4, 73.2). Frontinus – who introduces his *Strategemata* as a sourcebook *unde illis* [sc. *imperatoribus*] *excogitandi generandique similia facultas nutriatur* (*Str.* 1.*praef.*1) – would have an easy time: he mentions some fifty episodes of C. in Gaul (nn. on 35.3–5, 45.2, 60; but his direct reliance on the *BG* is dubious [Rosset 1954: 282]).[190]

The distribution of the stratagems between the Gallic and the Roman side, especially the face-off at Avaricum where C. extricates himself from the trap set by his wily opponent (19n.), emphasizes the character of the war between the generals as one of wits (Gärtner 1975: 70–72). In conflicts of that fashion, "quickness of mind" is of paramount importance (18n.); C. (as well as V.) demonstrates it along with its related talents: Time and again, he analyzes a situation (λογισμός, 6n.) or anticipates an event (πρόνοια [9.1n.]);[191] he knows opportunity (*occasio* [44–52n.]) and how to make situational adjustments (49n.). Such speed of mind is ideally and in C.'s case famously paired with speed of action: The soon-to-be proverbial *Caesariana celeritas* (9.4n. *celeritate*) sears through the Gallic and

---

[187] Cf. Sall. *Iug.* 85.11 and esp. Cic. *Fam.* 9.25.1: *summum me ducem litterae tuae reddiderunt: ... Pyrrhi te* (sc. *L. Papirium Paetum*) *libros et Cineae uideo lectitasse.* Cf. Lenoir 1996 (on military writing), Loreto 1993: 242–43 (on C.'s reading list).

[188] On *commentarii* as military manuals, cf. Campbell 1987: 13–28, Rüpke 1992: 210–18.

[189] Cf. Wheeler 1988: 25–49 on the stratagems; cf. fn. 184.

[190] Cf. Zecchini 1978: 201–05 on "la tradizione stratagemmografica." In Polyaenus C. shares the second place for most stratagems listed under a general's name (Wheeler 2010: 37).

[191] Cf. Wheeler 1988 s.v.

Italic landscapes much as the pages of the *commentarii*, and especially so in 6–13[n.].

While speed and boldness were admired, recklessness was not, and Cicero's juxtaposition of "speed" and "diligence" (above) anticipates another aspect of C.'s generalship, i.e. as one "based on as much careful preparation as was possible."[192] To be so bold and fast required what Hubert Canzik has called "the organization of space," above all through military intelligence and logistics.[193] C. extensively uses the former, and his procurement (as e.g. in 1.21–22) and handling of its various kinds are exemplary, as his reconnaissance of the hill by Gergovia reveals (44n.). He is as assiduous in securing supplies (first time at 1.16.1), and nowhere more so than in *VII*, when an unseasonable beginning to the campaign combined with various compounding circumstances to elevate this concern to the highest level (10.1n. *re frumentaria*).

(3 e) Building empire: technical ekphrasis

The *BG* ends with a victory made possible by the fortifications around Alesia (80.1n. *munitionis*, 68–78n.) and secured by the pliable and reliable cohorts; it symbolizes skill, order, and rationality as much as *uirtus* and *disciplina*.[194] A highly suitable ending, it also returns to the beginning of the campaign with its own feat of engineering (1.8.1): *a lacu Lemanno ... ad montem Iuram ... milia passuum XVIIII murum ... fossamque perducit*. This ring-compositional correspondence represents the prevalence of engineering in both *commentarii*: "no other Latin historian includes so many [references to it]," and no republican writer rivals C.'s technical ekphrasis in length or detail (nn. on 11.1 *circumuallauit*, 23, 72–74).[195]

C. may herein reveal his affinity to Polybius yet again; he certainly shares the latter's belief that Rome owed its military success in no small amount to its sense of order and engineering talents.[196] Why else would he narrate how the Helvetii were "astounded" by the speed with which the legions crossed the Arar (1.13.1–2), how the Atuatuci "laughed at" the Romans'

---

[192] Goldsworthy 1998: 197. Suet. *Iul.* 58.1 captures it consummately: *dubium cautior an audentior*.

[193] Suet. *Iul.* 58.1. Cancik 1998: 113. On intelligence: Ezov 1996, Bertrand 1997. Cf. 1.1n. *cognoscit*, 11.8n. *exploratores*, 18.1n. *captiuis*, 44.2n. *perfugis*, 56.4 *per equites*.

[194] On Roman values, cf. Lendon 2005: 310–16, and pp. 49–50.

[195] Kraus 2009: 173. Dodington 1980: 80–85 lists C.'s references, including 3.13, 4.17; *BC* 1.25, 2.9+10.

[196] Gärtner 1975: 92 suggests "Nähe zu Polybius." On Polybius, cf. Erskine 2013: 237–41.

seemingly immovable siege towers – but not for long (2.30.3–31.1), or
how only a bridge across the Rhine was "worthy" of Rome (4.17.1)?[197] But
in celebrating this aspect of *Romanitas*, C. also (and once again) advertises
his *scientia militaris* and consummate generalship (pp. 45–47; 68–90n.),
and his predominance is underlined when (in conventional fashion) he
credits himself rather than the *praefecti fabrum* or the soldiers with the
designing, digging, and building.[198] In reality, just as he would have had
plenty of help, so would his several participations in campaigning over
two decades prior to his Gallic campaign along with his (likely) study of
such technical writers as Aeneas Tacticus or Philo Mechanicus have prepared him plenty.[199]

In addition to the ideological function, C.'s ekphraseis – for which he
drew on other technical writings, especially of the agricultural kind (nn.
on 23, 72–74) – serve a literary and perhaps even educational purpose:
They typically build the object before the reader's eyes, emphasize order,
and prioritize the abstract clarity resulting from generalization over dis-
tractive specifics, thus enabling future generals to turn to them for inspiration. They allow for narrative retardation to increase suspense or align
narrative time with narrated time; their laborious details specify the labor
that the constructions required; and their style represents the same prin-
ciples – order, balance, regularity – that characterize the artifacts.[200] These
descriptions were designed to impress the Roman audience just as the
actual constructions were designed to intimidate the Gallic enemy.[201]

(3 f) Caesar's men

When C. approaches his soldiers at Avaricum offering to abort the long
siege out of concern for them, they refuse out of respect for their accomplishments under his leadership (17.4–5). An emblematic scene, suitably
augmented by Homeric resonances (17n.), it contrasts with the campaign's beginning when C. had to coerce his troops into fighting Ariovistus

---

[197] Cf. Riggsby 2006: 73–83 on C.'s representation of "siegecraft" and the Gauls'
adaptiveness (pp. 52–53).

[198] Cf. 72–74n. Inscriptions reveal the convention: *uiam fecei ... forum aedisque
poplicas h(e)ic fecei* (*CIL* I².638, of P. Popillius); Riggsby 2006: 236n.78 offers more
examples.

[199] "[T]he legions provided also a school of engineering" (Macmullen 1963:
34). Cf. n. 187.

[200] Cf. Scarola 1987 on narratological aspects of the *murus Gallicus*; Brown 2013
on the Rhine bridge.

[201] Cf. Micunco 1995: 101 on the bridge as "un' azione dimostrativa per incutere
timore ... nei Germani," while "un gesto significativo, ... un 'segno' per i Romani."

(1.39–41);[202] ever after, "C. and his soldiers" formed a special union. They crossed mountains (8.2–3), rivers (35n.), and oceans, escaped perdition on their long road to triumph more than once, while killing and violating Gauls in the hundreds of thousands; and they ultimately marched into Italy *ut eius* (sc. *Caesaris*) *existimationem dignitatemque ab inimicis defendant* (*BC* 1.7.7).[203] This union is characterized by, on the one hand, a general who cares for his men (19.5n. *se … cariorem*), shares their labors (24.2n. *Caesar … excubaret*), and continuously communicates his considerations (17.4n. *appellaret*); who teaches and trains them (19.4 *edocet*; *BAfr.* 71.1, 72.4, 73.2) and leads by example (40.4n. *adhortatus … permoueatur*); and who appeals to their competitive spirit, rewards accomplishment (27.2 *eis qui primi … praemia*), and indulges them (11.9n. *praedam*), while punishing them only when necessary (52n.).[204] His leadership has been questioned, but there is no reason to doubt the extraordinary testimony in *BAfr.* 10.3.[205]

What he expects from them in return – aside from loyalty – he asserts after their typical eagerness for battle (19.4n.) resulted in defeat (52.4nn.): *nec minus se ab milite modestiam et continentiam quam uirtutem atque animi magnitudinem desiderare.* In addressing the fundamental tension in the Roman military at large between individual bravery and collective effort, for all his admiration for raw *uirtus* (22.1n. *uirtuti*), C. emphasizes both "subordination" and "discipline." After all, it is their "ethic of restraint" (Lendon 2005: 312) that allows him to conduct his rationalistic style of warfare, to direct and employ the flexible cohort as confidently and smoothly as success required (84.7n.).[206] The integral significance of Roman order is memorably rendered in the "tale of two camps" (Johnston 2018: 85) during the Belgic campaign (2.7–8, 11; 75.1n. *confusa*, 82.3n.); and even more so in the tale of laborious siegeworks and rapid cohort interventions at Alesia.

This "special relationship" between general and devoted soldiery, which C. stresses frequently (cf. especially Curio's declaration *equidem me Caesaris militem dici uolui* [*BC* 2.32.14]), finds its most conspicuous expression in C.'s frequent use of *nostri* in reference to the Roman army (16.3n. *nostris*). However conventional such reference was in historiography, and however

---

[202] On C.'s manipulation of his troops at 1.40.15, see Collins 1952: 119; cf. 17.4–7n.
[203] Vogt's 1960 "Caesar und seine Soldaten" is as fundamental still as it is discomfiting (it appeared in 1940).
[204] His appreciation of his soldiers corresponds to his declarations of "popular" leanings (above, pp. 7–9).
[205] Fuller 1965 was most critical (or rather too critical [Balsdon]).
[206] On C.'s "legion of cohorts," cf. Lendon 2005: 212–33.

inclusive of the Roman audience (cf. Cic. *Arch.* 21–24, especially *nostri illi fortes uiri*; pp. 25–26), in C.'s case it functions foremost as the narrative equivalent to his preferred address of his soldiers in life as <u>commilitones</u>.[207] Both terms express emotional attachment, which is why he continues to employ the possessive in the *BC* of his own men alone (Marincola 1997: 287), and why he famously releases from service a mutinous legion with a simple "*Quirites.*"[208]

C.'s emphasis on the military collective goes hand in hand with sparing individuation (which Cato had famously anticipated [Nep. *Ca.* 3.4, Plin. *HN.* 8.11; *FRHist* T20]); instances are often especially motivated (50n.). This affects his *legati*, too (whose responsibilities in military operations he may have increased at the expense of the *tribuni militum*):[209] They do not receive as much attention in his writing as they might have (as the comparison with the *corpus* underlines), and in the early *commentarii* – excepting the anomalous *III* – even less so than in the latter ones (twelve *legati* are named in *VII*, some repeatedly, almost all remain pale).[210] Then again, they are rarely blamed for lack of success either (as Lucullus' *legati* were [Plut. *Luc.* 19.7, 31.1–3, 35.1]), the most unfortunate exception being Titus Sabinus, whose individuation as a scapegoat for the loss of fifteen cohorts against Ambiorix is complemented by Q. Cicero's portrait as competent leader (5.30, 37, 52.6 *culpa et temeritate legati*; 39–41, 52.4 *Ciceronem ... collaudat*; Rambaud 1966: 297). Rhetorical (and often political) considerations here and elsewhere influence both forms of representation (either to limit distraction from C. or to distract from defeat, as most conspicuously in Curio's case during the civil war [2.23–42]); Titus Labienus (34.2n.), who alone figures in all of the *BG*, is the partial exception (57–62n.). The centurions, on the other hand, receive rather noticeable attention (12.4n. *centurionibus*), especially when cast as "the faithful and brave" kind (Welch 1998: 90).

(3 g) Vercingetorix and the not-so-impulsive Gallic masses

The voluminous modern biographies notwithstanding, little is known of Vercingetorix [V.], and that little, numismatic evidence aside, is mostly

---

[207] *Nec milites eos pro contione, sed blandiore nomine commilitones appellabat* (Suet. *Iul.* 67.2).

[208] The incident became legendary: Suet. *Iul.* 70, Plut. *Caes.* 51, App. *B Civ.* 2.93, Dio 42.53; cf. Tac. *Ann.* 1.42.2. Cf. Chrissanthos 2001.

[209] 5.3n. *legatorum*, 17.8n. *tribunis*. The one named *tribunus* in *VII* is the otherwise unknown M. Aristius (42.5).

[210] "On chercherait en vain ... un thème des legats," Rambaud 1966: 296. Welch 1998: 88 compares Hirtius' treatment.

derived from C. (7.4).[211] The son of the felicitously named Arvernian Celtillus, he was born in the 80s or 70s in or near Gergovia, reclaimed his father's position, and then orchestrated the resistance until surrendering at Alesia. Sadly, as the notes show, much of this information is problematic, as is the non-Caesarian information on V.'s service under C. early on, the details of his surrender, and his death in 46 (20.2n. *regnum*, 89n.), not to mention his alleged role early in the uprising (1–5n.). V.'s elevation to France's "premier héros historique" as emblematized by Aimé Millet's 1865 statue, occurred during the nineteenth century; but it is ultimately a consequence of the "effet de reel" of C.'s narrative, which creates V. according to Roman presuppositions and its author's rhetorical needs.[212] In line with the "great-man" theory of history, he is made *the* face of the historical phenomenon, who – young, talented, born to lead, and fiendish – looks the type: He starts out a factious leader (reminiscent of both Orgetorix and Catiline [4n.]), but then learns and grows (especially after Avaricum [29–35n.]) into the leader of all Gaul to ultimately render C.'s victory more impressive (*et fortitudinem Gallorum Germanorumque miramur quo sit maior C. Caesaris gloria* [Quint. 8.4.20]).[213] He is the product of the borealistic imagination, whose deeds and characteristics are to be seen through Roman eyes; no surprise, then, that after his victory at Gergovia, he appears as a typical ὑβριστής (63–67n.).

In his bellicose agitation, rhetorical (and perhaps idiolectic) prowess, cruel streak, and overconfidence, V. embodies stereotypical Gallic qualities;[214] but in speed, determination, leadership, and strategic thinking he seems to have learnt from Rome (as well he might).[215] The latter aspect manifests itself most clearly in his insistence on discipline: his punishing disobedience, advocacy of self-sacrifice for a greater good, insistence on the laborious construction of camps (nn. on 4.9, 14.10, 29.7 *castra munire*), and refusal of pitched battle (until he did not [63–67n.]). It is not all rhetoric, as the Gallic strategy succeeded in sending C. fleeing to the province (above, pp. 15–16): There is reason to believe that the Gauls' focus on the cavalry and combination of guerilla tactics with the

[211] "[U]n étonnant paradoxe," Le Bohec 1998: 85. The numismatic evidence poses hermeneutical difficulties (Colbert de Beaulieu-Lefèvre 1963: 11n.1, Nieto-Pelletier 2012: 235–36).
[212] Le Gall 1970 (the statue), Nicolet 2009: 414–17 (Napoleon III). Ankersmit 1994: 125–61 discusses Barthes' 1968 concept regarding historiography, and Harmand 1989 offers an "historiographie d'un mythe."
[213] Cf. Diod. Sic. 34/5.33.5 on how "Rome's strength" should be judged "by its apparent superiority over the mighty."
[214] Nn. on 4, 14, 4.10, and 20.7 *uictoria*; cf. p. 52, fn. 221.
[215] Nn. on 4.7 *celeriter*, 4, 14.

scorched-earth strategy bore fruit and that they outmaneuvered C. and
sent him fleeing to the province.[216] But C. highlights V.'s distinctiveness –
nowhere more than when he has him voice Roman stereotypes about
Gauls (20.5n.) – and ultimately draws him as a flawed mirror image of
himself: consistent phraseological echoes (starting with 4.3n. *habet dilectum*, 4.5n. *in fide maneant*), the two leaders' speeches after defeat (29, 52),
and their *pas de deux* of reciprocity in a conflict foremost represented as
a "game of wits" encourage readers to engage in a sustained *synkrisis*.[217]
C. had been challenged before, notably by Ariovistus and Ambiorix; but
V. is the first to lead Gaul united (29.6n.), battle C. for an entire season
(functioning "throughout [the narrative] as a fully articulated second
focal point"), rise and sacrifice himself for *libertas*, and receive a proper
exit dramatis persona.[218] It is in this final book that C. finds his match, his
Hannibal (*Index*, s.v.), and V.'s surrender symbolizes the subjection of
Gallia omnis and thus marks the end of the *Gallic War*.

The representation of the Gallic people follows similar lines. There
is evidence of C.'s at least rudimentary knowledge of Celtic (75.4n.
Aremoricae), unsurprisingly given his decade-long interaction with its
speakers (e.g. 1.19.3).[219] But those interactions had but little bearing upon
"the" Gaul as he emerges from his narrative (more so than from the ethnographic digression [42.2n. *auaritia*]); for that construct aims at rendering
C.'s victory as *convincing* as possible.[220] It is largely arranged from conventional material: C.'s sources would have included Cato, Polybius, Claudius
Quadrigarius, and Posidonius.[221] In its formative background stand two
age-old theories: the anthropo-geographical theory, which relates certain
characteristics of a people to the climate of its habitat, and a sociological
model that posits a correlation between a people's institutionalized lifestyle and its character (the "*nomos* theory"); C. acknowledges them both.[222]

[216] On "Vercingétorix, chef de guerre": Deyber 2017.
[217] E.g. 9n. (on reciprocity); Jervis 2001: 150–88 offers a *synkrisis* of her own.
[218] On V. compared to Indutiomarus, Orgetorix, other Gallic leaders, see
Ferraris 1997, Torigian 1998: 56–58, Jervis 2001: 150–55. The quotation: Kraus
2010a: 44.
[219] Only here does C. mention his reliance on interpreters (5.36.1 of Sabinus).
Sertorius learned the language, or so Plut. *Sert.* 3.2 reports. Adams 2003:184–200
surveys contacts between Latin and Celtic.
[220] Of the digressions (4.1–3: Suebi, 5.12–14: Britons, 6.11–28: Germani and
Galli) only the last one addresses the Gauls.
[221] Jervis 2001: 17–53 reviews Gallic ethnography before C. (emphasizing the
"apparent contradictions"), as does Williams 2001: 68–99; Riggsby 2006: 47–50
discusses methodological problems.
[222] Thomas 2000: 86–98 discusses them with regard to the Ps.-Hippocratic treatise περὶ ἀέρων ὑδάτων τόπων.

The cold and rainy northern climate (24.1nn. *frigore, imbribus*) caused its inhabitants' hot-bloodedness, making them emotional rather than rational (20.5n. *impelleretur*, 42.2n. *generi ... innata*; cf. *sanguine multo ab umoris plenitate caelique refrigerationibus* [Vitr. 6.1.3]). Hence the Gauls are commonly described as impulsive, fickle, faithless, prone to migrate, eager to fight and brag but unable to endure, and easily swayed (cf. *infirmitas Gallorum* [36–43n.]); their effect on Greeks and Romans was magnified by the notion of them as "hordes." C.'s command of the rhetorical operability of these stereotypes is at full display from the start: Double-dealing Orgetorix sways the Helvetii to migrate (*coniurationem ... fecit et ciuitati persuasit*, 1.2.1).[223] His argument bespeaks Gallic braggadocio (*perfacile esse, cum uirtute omnibus praestarent, totius Galliae imperio potiri*). He is helped by circumstances but mostly his audience's character, *homines bellandi cupidi* (1.2.4), who felt confined by natural boundaries *ut et minus late uagarentur et minus facile finitimis bellum inferre possent*. Given their huge numbers (*pro multitudine*) and their warrior reputation (*pro gloria belli*), this was unacceptable. There is smug humor in the comparatives (i.e. "than they would like"), which is amplified when C. specifies the huge size of their small territory: *in longitudinem milia passuum CCXL, in latitudinem CLXXX*, or almost half the size of Italy.[224] C.'s evocation of "the" Gaul from his Roman readers' background knowledge to explain his intervention closely resembles Cicero's evocation of the Gaul in *Pro Fonteio* (especially 30–31, with Vasaly 1993: 193–94). It is this deep cultural grammar that allows his readers to make sense of the Aeduan defection, too (42n.), just as elsewhere it enables them to discern atypical traits.[225]

For C.'s *largely* conventional image reveals particular accentuations and dynamics. First, he rather stresses Gallic *uirtus* (from 1.1.4 to 7.83.4), the Gauls receiving thirty-six attributions, the Romans thirty-one; and if, traditionally, their "primitive courage" (βαρβαρικὴ ἀνδρεία [Arist. *Eth. Eud.* 1229b28]) was tainted by madness and transience (42.1n. *temeritas*), under his pen it appears more resolute than impulsive – of course, both his paean on the determined-unto-death Nervii at 2.27 and the explanatory coda to the surrender of the Venelli (viz. typical Gallic lack of determination [3.19.6]) ultimately differ because they serve different rhetorical needs:[226] the Nervii's surprising (to Roman eyes) resolution

---

[223] There are a telling four instances of *persuadere* (Johnston 2018: 84). Cf. nn. on 4, 1.7 *facile*, 29.6 *cuius ... obsistere*, 20.5 *studium dimicandi*, 21.1 *multitudo*, 1.8 *belli gloriam*; also 1.2 *rumoribus*, 1.3 *impulsi*, 17.7 *perfidia Gallorum*.
[224] Instances of humor in *VII: Index*, s.v.
[225] Cf. Erickson 2002: 603. Johnston 2018: 84n.18 lists instances of ethnic stereotypes elsewhere in the *BG*.
[226] The statistics are from Jervis 2001: 8. Tradition and innovation: Pallavisini 1972. *uirtus* has received much attention (Johnston 2018: 86n.24).

elevates C.'s victory. Just so, the Gauls' determination in their great uprising extols C.'s victory (especially 25, 77.4–5; n. on 79–88); and all the
more as they appear to have learned from the Romans a more disciplined
uirtus and the use of technology (22n.). Whatever the historical truth, the
rhetoric is clear: C.'s near-match V. commanded the soldiery that matched
the Romans – almost.

A second difference arises from C.'s separation of *Gallia* from *Germania*
(pp. 11–12), whose two peoples he differentiates by way of the *nomos*
theory: *Germani multum ab hac* [sc. *Gallica*] *consuetudine differunt* (6.21.1).
This differentiation between "other" and "other other" (Riggsby 2006:
47–72) is foundational (as its early appearance at 1.1.4 indicates).[227]
However threatening the *Galli* (especially in *VII*), they had been exposed
to the influence of *cultus atque humanitas* (1.1.3), and the more so the
closer they lived to Rome (as goes C.'s typically ethnocentric reasoning);
because of that influence, they had fallen from their past excellence and
succumbed increasingly to the *Germani* (76.2n. *pristinae belli laudis recuperandae*).[228] It is this contrast to the *Germani* as uncivilized, indomitable,
and single-minded warriors that throws into relief the Gauls' readiness
for integration, a readiness enhanced by C.'s pervasive application of
Roman terminology to Gallic institutions (a common method known,
by its Tacitean phrase, as *interpretatio Romana*); it provides the ethnographic explanation for C.'s decision to integrate one people in the *orbis
Romanus* but not the other.[229] It is only consequent, if ironical, that it is
the Germanic cavalry that saves the day for C. repeatedly in his final battle
(13.1n. *Germanos equites*).

Lastly, while *libertas* is yet another traditional northern stereotype (a
by-product of hot-bloodedness), and while Romans were ready enough to
acknowledge other peoples' desire "to defend their own safety and liberty"
(Plancus, of the Gauls, to the senate [*apud* Cic. *Fam.* 10.8.6]), C. makes
a special point of recognizing the Gauls' claim to it, and nowhere more
so than in *VII* (1.5n. *libertatem*).[230] It chimes with the several instances of
anti-imperialistic criticism (*Index*, s.v.). While C.'s influence on Sallust and
Tacitus is easy to discern (38.8n. *latrones*), it is much harder to find his

---

[227] On the significance of the *nomos* theory in C.'s ethnography, see Krebs 2010:
205–07, and on degrees of otherness in *BG*, Schadee 2008.
[228] But C.'s "moral map" does not correspond to the valor shown by individual
tribes (Jervis 2001: 61–101).
[229] On C.'s limiting his conquest, see Seager 2003: 30–34. Instances of *interpretatio Romana*: *Index*, s.v.
[230] E.g. Sen. *Dial.* 4.15.4 *feritate liberae gentes*. Seager 2003: 22–26 discusses the
motif in the *BG* (first at 1.17.4), Murphy 1977: 241–42 its prevalence in *VII*.

precedents.[231] Both the recognition and the criticism may express a certain imperialistic unease; but C. makes sure to undermine both sentiments by discrediting the proponents (1.5n. *pollicitationibus ac praemiis*; Gärtner 1975: 70) and elucidating the consequences of a Gallic people left to itself: *in omnibus ciuitatibus atque in omnibus pagis partibusque, sed paene etiam in singulis domibus factiones sunt* (6.11.2). Factionalism, the Gallic societal phenomenon C. singles out, is both an expression of the precarious line between *libertas* and *licentia* and a consequence of the Gallic character; in line with Roman imperialistic reasoning, C.'s presence in Gaul quelled it (32–33n.).[232] The fact that V. *also* united Gaul behind himself (p. 52) is thus yet another aspect of the eleventh-hour scenario.

(3 h) Caesar and no end? A few observations on influence

Immediate reactions to the *BG* are hard to come by;[233] but if the parallels in later authors – as documented in the commentary – are anything to judge by, C.'s influence on Latin literature was greater than is commonly assumed.[234] Of more fundamental significance than such local cases of intertextuality as Sallust's adaptation of "Gergovia" in his battle by the Muluccha (Martin 2001: 398–400), or Tacitus' modelling his father-in-law after C. (Woodman 2014: *Index*, s.v. "Caesar") – but also more difficult to determine – are his contributions to the stock of stereotypes (16.1n. *paludibus siluisque*), the lexicon of the historical (geographical and ethnographical [Bell 1995]) as well as military narratives (4.2n. *fortunam temptandam*, 64.6n. *pagos*, 72.4n. *loricam*), and their style. The difficulties arise from the topical nature of classical historiography, the loss of much literature, and the possibility that Roman army language continued to exert its influence on later authors as it had on C. (23.4n. *contexitur*, 42.6n. *continuo in itinere adorti*).

[231] Cato's oft-cited speech *Pro Rhodiensibus* is different. The classic discussion is Fuchs 1938; cf. Balsdon's 1979 "Bad press for Rome," Oakley on Livy 9.1, and Adler 2011.

[232] Cf. Perl on Tac. *Germ.* 33.2 *hostium discordia*. On the binary division in C.'s account of Gallic society, see Riggsby 2006: 62–63. The classic treatment of *libertas-licentia* is Wirszubski 1950: 7–8.

[233] Cicero's *Gallia* in 56 (*Prou.* 32) is *Gallia omnis*, but not necessarily from the *commentarii* (Krebs 2006: 115–16). Catull. 115.5 is interesting (16.1n. *paludibus siluisque*). Cf. above, 3a, for Cic. *Brut.* and Hirt.

[234] Joseph 2018 and Kraus 2018 offer recent discussions. For parallels in Ammianus, Curtius, Livy, Lucan, Sallust, Tacitus, and Vergil, see *Index* s.vv. Of particular interest are such passages that in their close adherence to C. allow for the choice between competing MS variants (84.4n. *uirtute* [Klotz 1953]). The continuators are a separate issue (Gaertner 2018). On Augustus' *Res Gestae*, see Power 2014: 8n.24.

These complications notwithstanding, pride of place must fall to Livy: Not only does he employ numerous Caesarian expressions, many of which are unparalleled elsewhere (e.g. 5.6n. *pro certo esse ponendum*), some occurring in clusters (e.g. 46.1–2n.); it is also hard to imagine how he could have written 1.36.2 – *dubia uictoria* (80.6n.) *magna utrimque caede* (81.5 *multa utrimque uulnera*) *pugnatum est* (25.1n. *pugnaretur*) – without C.'s influence, and because of the expressions just as much as the stylistic features of the sequential ablative absolutes, impersonal passive, and colometry (Livy 6.24 is another noteworthy example). Livy's subsequent sentence is no less Caesarian in its "cumulative-complex" structure (p. 37): *reductis deinde in castra hostium copiis | datoque spatio Romanis ad comparandum de integro bellum, | Tarquinius equitem maxime suis deesse uiribus ratus | ad Ramnes, Titienses, Luceres – quas centurias Romulus scripserat – addere alias constituit | suoque insignes relinquere nomine.* One begins to see why "the sentence-structure of no two other historians is so alike" (Oakley 1997: 129).

Tacitus, too, read C. carefully, as appears from Sabinus' Thracian campaign (especially *A.* 4.47–51), which amalgamates elements from "Gergovia" and "Alesia." Two passages may exemplify this. Sabinus challenges the Thracians much as C. challenged V. after the latter's success (49.1): *postera die Sabinus* (52.1 *postero die Caesar* [with 27.1n.]) *exercitum aequo loco* (52.2n. *iniquitas loci*) *ostendit, si barbari successu noctis alacres* (76.5n.) *proelium auderent. et postquam ... non degrediebantur* (53.2 *cum Vercingetorix nihilo minus ... descenderet*), *obsidium coepit.* As in Livy's case, there is a Caesarian air about these sentences beyond simple phraseology (and not the least because of the word order). The following sentence also abounds in Caesarian detail and phraseology (e.g. *fossam loricamque contexens* [23.4n. *contexitur*, 72.4n. *loricam*]), as does Tacitus' description of the fight (51.1): *interea barbari cateruis decurrentes nunc ... saxa, praeustas sudes* (73.6n. *praeusti*, 81.4n. *sudibus*), *decisa robora* (73.2 *truncis ... aut ramis abscisis*) *iacere, nunc uirgultis et cratibus et corporibus exanimis complere fossas* (79.4n. *fossam cratibus integunt atque aggere explent*), *quidam pontis et scalas ante fabricati inferre propugnaculis ... miles contra deturbare telis* (86.5nn. *multitudine telorum ... propugnantes deturbant*), *pellere umbonibus, muralia pila* (82.1n. *pilis muralibus*) *... prouoluere.* Some of these details and expressions are used by other pertinent authors (Sallust and Vergil [Woodman ad loc.]), and Tacitus may, of course, have been inspired by Sall. *Hist.* 2.87 as well; but the Sallustian account of Isaura itself draws on C.'s narrative: *dein signo dato praecipiti iam secunda uigilia simul utrimque pugnam occipiunt; magno tumultu primo eminus per obscuram noctem tela in incertum iacientes, post, ubi Romani de industria non tela neque clamorem reddebant, perculsos formidine aut desertam munitionem rati auide in fossas et inde ... per uallum properat. at superstantes tum denique saxa, pila, sudes iacere et multos* *prope egressos comminus plagis aut omni re deturbare; qua repentina formidine pars [in] uallo transfixa, alii super tela sua praecipitati ... ceteris fuga tuta fuit.* Possibly Caesarian features include: the sequential ablatives (71.5 *his datis mandatis, ... secunda uigilia*), the two-sided conflict (88.2 *utrimque clamore sublato*), the differentiation between battling from afar and at close quarters (82.1 *dum longius ... posteaquam propius*; for Sallust's phrasing, cf. 24.4 *eminus iaciebant*), the aberrant missiles at night (81.5 *tenebris ... multa utrimque uulnera*), the triad of missiles (81.2 *fundis, sagittis, lapidibus*), the toppling (86.5n. *deturbant*), the *distributio* (85.5 *alii ... alii ... ab uniuersis*), and, perhaps above all, the cumulative-complex structure with its typical mix of abl. absolutes, participial constructions, and subordinate clauses. In short, some of the seemingly Sallustian features in Tacitus may well in one way or another derive from C. Similar considerations apply to C.'s impact on Vergil's narratives and their respective influence on the later tradition (e.g. 73.6n. *praeusti*).[235]

4 ABOUT THIS COMMENTARY AND ITS TEXT

C.'s *commentarii* are best characterized as politically motivated historical texts written by an eminent man of letters. As specified above (1), the last-mentioned aspect, their literariness, is this commentary's primary concern for two reasons.[236] First, there is now little doubt that ancient histories must principally be appreciated as creative compositions: basic historical facts arranged, expanded, and embellished with the help of techniques and materials from the Greco-Roman rhetorical and literary traditions.[237] Caesar's *commentarii* – not in and of themselves history but akin to it (pp. 41–42) – differ in degree rather than category, which may surprise a modern reader all the more, as C. witnessed much of what he writes about (25.1n. *inspectantibus*). Second, the historical and the linguistic aspects of the *BG* are at the forefront of the two commentaries that have guided readers for over a century: Heinrich Meusel's 1913 text along with a completely revised 17th edition of Friedrich Kraner's and Wilhelm Dittenberger's commentary and T. Rice Holmes' 1914 edition cum commentary.[238] Meusel's expertise in Caesar's *usus scribendi* (as

---

[235] Horsfall's commentaries on Vergil contain much material.

[236] In the light of Ash 2002, it might also be said that this is a commentary on *BG VII*, not the seventh year of the war in Gaul.

[237] Wiseman 1979, Woodman 1988. Champion 2016 reviews the debate; stabs at revisionism have failed.

[238] Kraner published his text cum commentary in 1853 to provide students with "necessary" linguistic and historical information (1855 [2nd ed.]: vi). Dittenberger, in 1867, updated the sixth edition for the same readers with an eye on the "results

emblematized by his *Lexicon Caesarianum*) is rivaled by few, as is Holmes' historical knowledge of the campaigns (as emblematized by his *Caesar's Conquest of Gaul*), and one can still learn from them both, even if some of their information, not to mention their largely positivist confidence in C.'s narrative, require correction in the light of new archaeological, narratological, and linguistic evidence and observations. But one cannot find in them more than a passing remark on the *BG* as a literary work, which, in effect, misrepresents the text.

Part and parcel of the literary commentary is the identification of parallels in other ancient texts, which generally serve several purposes.[239] They may assist in (1) "establishing the text" (8.2n. *discissa niue*), or (2) "comprehending" a difficult phrase (16.1n. *Vercingetorix ... subsequitur*). Elsewhere, they allow for (3) the discernment of "register within the text": of the numerous instances of administrative phrasing, I quote parallels only for those not identified by Eva Odelman (1972; 56.5n. *iter ... facere instituit*). As for poeticisms, colloquialisms, and archaisms (hazardous classifiers), a simple reference to a parallel use here or there does not suffice for such classification; but the distribution of attestations may be telling, and I provide, where possible, a significant sample and contextual information to make the case (26.2n. *silentio noctis*). Parallels, more loosely defined, are also quoted to (4) "contextualize" a passage: The commentary will reveal over and again the paramount importance of the rhetorical tradition; V.'s final plea (89.1[n.]) is a case in point, as it cannot be appreciated without knowledge of the *concessio* (*Rhet.* 1.24). I therefore provide its definition to show how the specifics of V.'s speech meet the rhetorical guidelines. His conclusion "*Fortunae cedendum*" is – as my eclectic references are meant to demonstrate – itself one of the many commonplaces in C.'s text. Their identification is not only another (fifth) traditional purpose of the documentation of parallels, but also particularly pertinent in C.'s case, given the predominant reading of the *BG* as a (mostly factual) report: It certainly seems more likely than not that V. would institute a war council (36.3); but, as the note shows, it is also true that it was *expected* of any competent leader and that, as a literary motif, it is of Homeric pedigree. Last but not least (6), parallels serve to reveal instances of intertextuality (broadly defined as the contact between [normally two] specific texts), ranging from apparently accidental iteration, whereof there exist many between Cicero and Caesar (beginning with

that studies of Caesar ... had yielded" (iii). Meusel thought of his work as a vade mecum, too, but now for "young philologists and teachers" (1968 [21st ed.]: v).

[239] I follow (with modifications) Gibson 2002; the unattributed quotations are from his discussion.

1.3n. *liberius atque audacius*); via reminiscence or adaptation, such as the Lucretian 1.2n. *addunt et affingunt* or the Polybian elements in 57–62n.; to (the most specific and meaningful) allusion, as when C. tests his men before Avaricum in a way that is meant to recall Agamemnon's testing his before Troy (17n.).[240] Under the same category fall such instances of C. providing later authors with phraseology or other detail (pp. 55–57).

I have limited the use of the all-embracing "cf.," just as I have limited cross-references. Much of their lighter weight is shouldered by the indices: With few exceptions, all names are discussed on first occurrence, as identified in the *Index* (which then also accounts for all later instances in *VII*); individual terms (such as *adulescens*) and particularly frequent *syntactica* (such as "verb, position" or "ablative absolute, expanded") are handled similarly. Any "hit-and-run" user (Gibson-Kraus 2002: 8) of this commentary is therefore encouraged to visit the *Index* when the desired explanation could not be found in the section consulted. Relatively few, too, are references to the introductions to individual chapters as well as the general introduction; both of which will give greater depth to the discrete discussions. Much of the material below is rather advanced, perhaps; but I have attempted to provide as much guidance for upper-level undergraduates as space would permit.

The text

The *editio princeps* of Caesar's works as well as the *bella* was published in 1469 in Rome. It was prepared by Giovanni Andrea Bussi.[241] Decades later, in 1513, the first edition from the Aldine Press in Venice appeared, with the text of the *BG* much improved by the work of Giovanni Giocondo.[242] The groundbreaking modern (and first critical) edition appeared in 1847, when Karl Nipperdey grouped the manuscripts into those that contained the *BG* only (called **α**), including the *codex Amstelodamensis* 73, written at Fleury Abbey in the late ninth century; and those that comprised all of the *Corpus Caesarianum* (called **β**), including the *codex Parisinus Latinus* 5764 from the eleventh century.[243] The two groups would seem to derive from one sixth-century manuscript (which already contained *duplas lectiones*

---

[240] The three categories are ideal types; they sit on a rising scale of intentionality (cf. Farrell 2005) and "semantic payoff." Cf. above, fn.115.
[241] On the *fortuna* of C.'s texts, see Brown 1976: 88–97; Damon 2015: 10–14.
[242] Hernández 2009: 225–28 discusses Giocondo's method.
[243] Nipperdey 1847: 37–49. However, several MSS thus classified as **β** (or **α**) appear to have the text of the **α** (or **β**) tradition (e.g. N, L, S contain the *Corpus Caesarianum* but appear to be derived from **α**'s B).

[Hering 1997: xiii]); they split soon after (possibly some time after the seventh century).[244] They differ significantly in their *BG* readings, without either group appearing superior.[245] During the decades following Nipperdey's edition new manuscripts were discovered. Wolfgang Hering therefore undertook a *recensio* of the most important MSS of the *BG* (1963: 7–44) in preparation of his edition for the *Bibliotheca Teubneriana*. It came out in 1987 and is superior both to Otto Seel's 1961 Teubner edition and Renatus Du Pontet's 1900 Oxford Classical Text edition (which is problematic because of its insufficient consideration of the *β* family and the haphazard *apparatus criticus*).[246]

The *sigla* below are Hering's (1997: xviii). I list all those that occur in my *apparatus criticus*, including the derivative MSS that contain accepted corrections. I part from Hering in following Hernández's restitution of **O**, which represents the heavily interpolated codex Oxford, Merton Coll. 307, as it offers support to my reading in 1.1 (and, more generally, contains other valuable readings, some of which can be found in the Aldine edition).[247] I also include the names of all textual critics mentioned in my *apparatus*. The latter is largely "negative" (except where confusion may arise) and limited to alternative readings of significance, which are therefore discussed in the commentary, and to instances where the text differs significantly from the (near) unanimous reading of the MSS (**ω**). My text is based on Hering's but deviates in the instances listed below; it furthermore differs in that (i) the spelling has been regularized (especially regarding assimilation), (ii) the paragraphing (12.1n. *Vercingetorix*) has been modified occasionally, and (iii) the frequency of interpunctuation has been much reduced.

ω   consensus codicum **ABTU** uel trium ex his
α   consensus codicum **AB**
β   consensus codicum **TU**

A   codex Amstelodamensis 73 saec. IX
B   codex Parisinus Latinus 5763 saec. IX
    S   codex Laurentianus Ashburnhamensis 33, saec. X
    N   codex Neapolitanus IV c. 11 saec. XI
    L   codex Louaniensis (sive Musei Britannici Addit. 10084) saec. XII

---

[244] Hering 1963: 95–96.
[245] Winterbottom 1983: 35, Hering 1997: xii–xiii.
[246] The *OCT* was quickly condemned by reviewers (Meusel 1901, Holmes 1901).
[247] Hernández 2009; on previous editors' use of the codex, ibid. 228–32.

T codex Parisinus Latinus 5764 saec. XI
U codex Vaticanus Latinus 3324 saec. XI/XII
R codex Laurentianus Riccardianus 541 saec. X/XI

O codex Oxoniensis Mert. 307 saec. XII

Aldina (editio)
Thomas *Bentley*[248]
Petrus *Ciacconius* Toletanus
*Felicien *De Saulcy*
ed. pr. = *editio princeps*
Carl Wilhelm *Elberling*
Andreas *Frigell*
*Martin Clarentius *Gertz*
Henricus Loriti *Glareanus*
Hand = Ferdinandi Handii
Tursellinus
Heinrich Justus *Heller*
*Alfred *Klotz*
Hermann *Kraffert*

Paullus *Manutius*
Heinrich Meusel
Samuel Friedrich Nathanael *Morus*
Nicasius Ellebodius Casletanus
Carl *Nipperdey*
*Wilhelm Paul
Karl Ernst Christoph *Schneider*
*Rudolf Sydow
Robertus *Stephanus*
Michaelis *Vascosanus*
Leopold *Vielhaber*
*Otto *Wagner*
Johannes Kofod *Whitte*

Conspectus

locus	Hering	Krebs
1.1	caede senatusque	caede de senatusque
3.2	fama	⟨ea⟩ fama
3.2	ubi qu⟨a⟩e	ubi qu⟨a⟩
8.2	discussa	discissa
	labore	sudore
14.10	aestimari debere	aestimari
19.2	generatimque distributi in ciuitates	generatimque distributi [in ciuitates]
20.3	ipsum	ipse
20.4	essent profecti	sint profecti
34.1	iis	his

[248] Meusel's 1893 *Coniecturae Caesarianae* helps identify most of the critics (except for those marked with "*," for whom I provide the information in my bibliography).

locus	Hering	Krebs
38.3	his	ipsis
38.10	in eodem mendacio ... permanet	eodem mendacio ... permouet
40.6	deditionem significare	[deditionem significare]
42.4	inclinatam	proclinatam
45.1	eodem. media nocte	eo de media nocte;
45.9	uitari	euitari
46.1	mille	mille CC
47.3	appropinquarent	appropinquarunt
52.1	temeritatem cupiditatemque militum	temeritatem militum cupiditatemque
52.2	quod ipse	quid ipse
54.2	maturari	admaturari
56.2	‹non› tunc quidem	‹ne› tunc quidem
58.2	confici	confieri
62.2	secundissimorum	secundissumorum
64.2	acie dimicaturum	in acie dimicaturum
72.2	opus	corpus
72.2	posset	possent
75.2	Aulercis, Brannouicibus	Aulercis Brannouicibus
75.3	Aulercis, Cenomanis	Aulercis Cenomanis
75.4	xxx milia	† xxx † milia
77.1	consilio	concilio
80.3	leuis armaturae	[leuis armaturae]
80.5	aut	ac
81.4	ac glandibus	[ac glandibus]
85.4	iniquum	exiguum
90.5	huius anni rebus cognitis	his rebus ex litteris cognitis

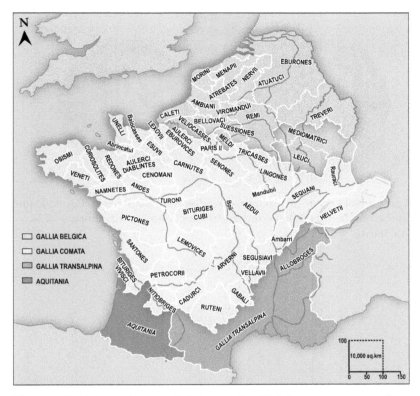

Figure 1 Gaul, its regions, and *ciuitates* (after Fichtl 2013; courtesy of
A. Fitzpatrick and C. Haselgrove).

(a)   (b)

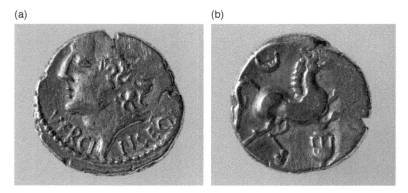

Figure 2 Gold stater of Vercingetorix, discovered at Pionsat, Puy-de-Dôme
(at the musée Alfred-Danicourt at Péronne; photograph courtesy of V.
Guichard).

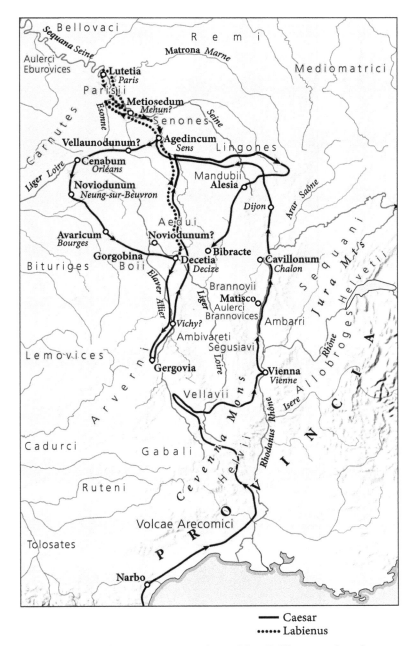

Figure 3 Approximate representation of the Gallic campaigns in 52;
adapted from W.C. Compton, *Caesar's seventh campaign in Gaul, B.C. 52*,
London 1907: 28.

Figure 4 Prototype of the *murus Gallicus* on the site of Bibracte including the new hypothesis of a wooden frame in the façade (Bibracte EPCC, Centre archéologique européen; photograph courtesy of A. Maillier [2022]).

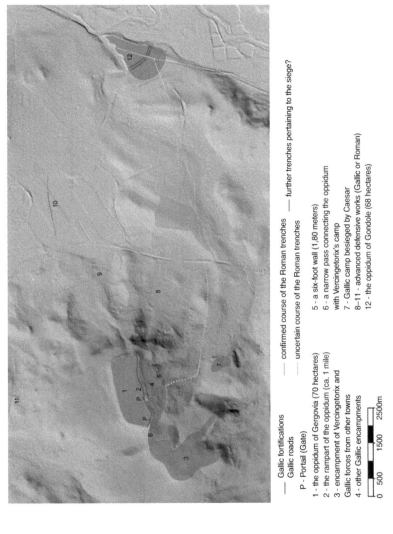

— Gallic fortifications
— Gallic roads
P - Portail (Gate)

— confirmed course of the Roman trenches
.... uncertain course of the Roman trenches

— further trenches pertaining to the siege?

1 - the oppidum of Gergovia (70 hectares)
2 - the rampart of the oppidum (ca. 1 mile)
3 - encampment of Vercingetorix and
Gallic forces from other towns
4 - other Gallic encampments

5 - a six-foot wall (1.80 meters)
6 - a narrow pass connecting the oppidum
with Vercingetorix's camp
7 - Gallic camp besieged by Caesar
8-11 - advanced defensive works (Gallic or Roman)
12 - the oppidum of Gondole (68 hectares)

0 500 1500 2500m

Figure 5 Gergovia, plan of the layout, including the *oppidum* of Gondole (courtesy of Y. Deberge, Inrap.).

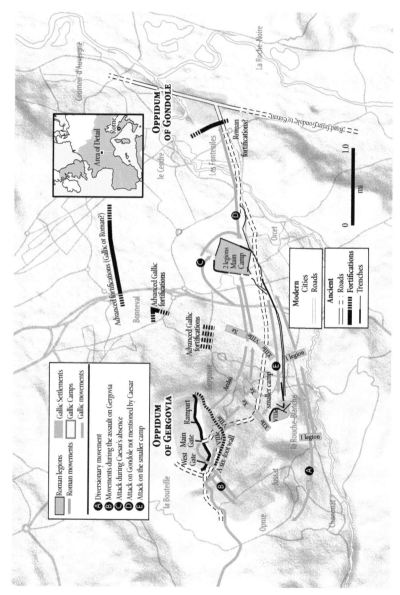

Figure 6 Gergovia, topographical map (courtesy of Y. Deberge, Inrap.).

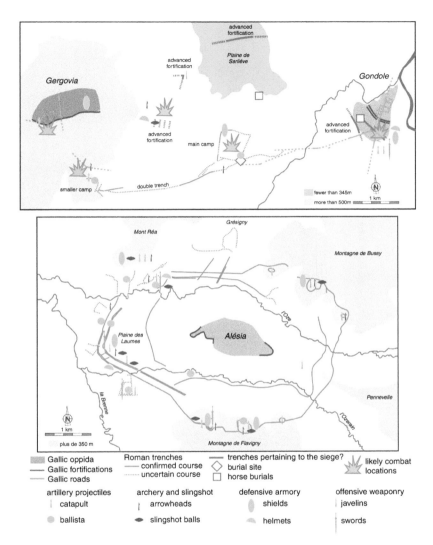

Figure 7 The battles of Gergovia and Alesia (courtesy of Y. Deberge, Inrap.).

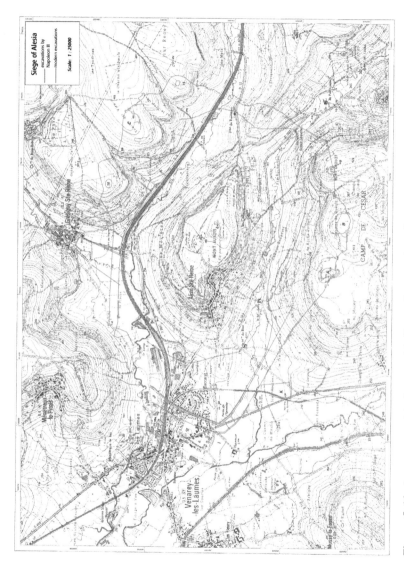

Figure 8 Alesia, topographical map with lines of excavations (courtesy of M. Reddé).

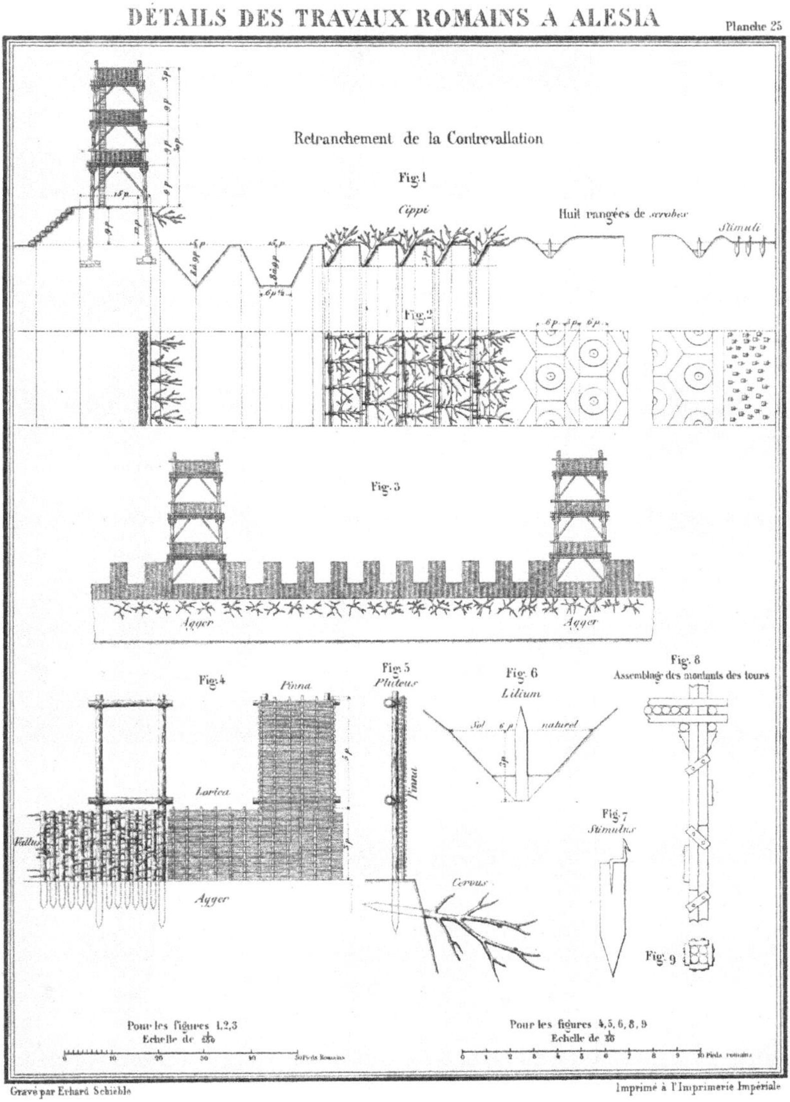

Figure 9 Alesia, the Roman fortifications according to Caesar, as represented on the "Planche 25 de l'Atlas de Napoléon III" (courtesy of M. Reddé).

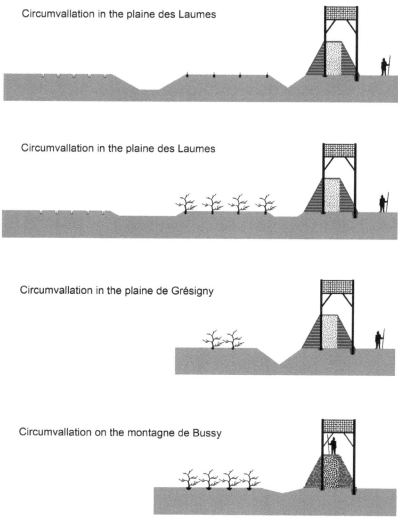

Figure 10 Alesia, a selection of the varied Roman fortifications according to the latest excavations (courtesy of M. Reddé).

C. IVLI CAESARIS
COMMENTARIVS RERVM GESTARVM
BELLI GALLICI SEPTIMVS

C. IVLI CAESARIS
COMMENTARIVS RERVM GESTARVM
BELLI GALLICI SEPTIMVS

Quieta Gallia Caesar, ut constituerat, in Italiam ad conuentus agen- 1
dos proficiscitur. ibi cognoscit de P. Clodii caede de senatusque consulto certior factus, ut omnes iuniores Italiae coniurarent, dilectum
tota prouincia habere instituit. eae res in Galliam Transalpinam 2
celeriter perferuntur. addunt ipsi et affingunt rumoribus Galli
quod res poscere uidebatur: retineri urbano motu Caesarem neque
in tantis dissensionibus ad exercitum uenire posse. hac impulsi 3
occasione qui iam ante se populi Romani imperio subiectos dolerent liberius atque audacius de bello consilia inire incipiunt. indic- 4
tis inter se principes Galliae conciliis siluestribus ac remotis locis
queruntur de Acconis morte; posse hunc casum ad ipsos recidere
demonstrant. miserantur communem Galliae fortunam. omnibus 5
pollicitationibus ac praemiis deposcunt qui belli initium faciant et
sui capitis periculo Galliam in libertatem uindicent. eius in primis 6
rationem esse habendam dicunt, priusquam eorum clandestina
consilia efferantur, ut Caesar ab exercitu intercludatur. id esse fac- 7
ile, quod neque legiones audeant absente imperatore ex hibernis
egredi, neque imperator sine praesidio ad legiones peruenire possit. postremo in acie praestare interfici quam non ueterem belli 8
gloriam libertatemque quam a maioribus acceperint recuperare.

His rebus agitatis profitentur Carnutes se nullum periculum 2
communis salutis causa recusare principesque ex omnibus bellum
facturos pollicentur; et, quoniam in praesentia obsidibus cauere 2
inter se non possint, ne res efferatur, at iure iurando ac fide sanciatur petunt, collatis militaribus signis, quo more eorum grauissima
caerimonia continetur, ne facto initio belli ab reliquis deserantur.
tum collaudatis Carnutibus, dato iure iurando ab omnibus qui 3
aderant, tempore eius rei constituto ab concilio disceditur.

Vbi ea dies uenit, Carnutes Gutuatro et Conconnetodumno 3
ducibus, desperatis hominibus, Cenabum signo dato concurrunt
ciuesque Romanos qui negotiandi causa ibi constiterant, in his

1.1 P. *om.* αT caede de senatusque consulto O de *om.* ω   1.4 consiliis α
1.6 eius *om.* α   2.2 at] aut α ut Tᶜ   3.1 cotuato ω *corr. Nipperdey* (cf. 8.38.3)

Gaium Fufium Citam, honestum equitem Romanum, qui rei frumentariae iussu Caesaris praeerat, interficiunt bonaque eorum
2 diripiunt. celeriter ad omnes Galliae ciuitates ‹ea› fama perfertur.
nam ubi qua maior atque illustrior incidit res, clamore per agros
regionesque significant; hunc alii deinceps excipiunt et proximis
3 tradunt, ut tum accidit. nam quae Cenabi oriente sole gesta essent
ante primam confectam uigiliam in finibus Aruernorum audita
sunt, quod spatium est milium passuum circiter centum sexaginta.

4   Simili ratione ibi Vercingetorix, Celtilli filius, Aruernus, summae
potentiae adulescens, cuius pater principatum Galliae totius obtinuerat et ob eam causam, quod regnum appetebat, a ciuitate erat
2 interfectus, conuocatis suis clientibus facile incendit. cognito eius
consilio ad arma concurritur. prohibetur ab Gobannitione, patruo
suo, reliquisque principibus, qui hanc temptandam fortunam non
3 existimabant; expellitur ex oppido Gergouia. non desistit tamen,
atque in agris habet dilectum egentium ac perditorum. hac coacta
manu, quoscumque adit ex ciuitate ad suam sententiam perducit;
4 hortatur ut communis libertatis causa arma capiant, magnisque
coactis copiis aduersarios suos, a quibus paulo ante erat eiectus,
5 expellit ex ciuitate. rex ab suis appellatur. dimittit quoque uersus
6 legationes; obtestatur ut in fide maneant. celeriter sibi Senones,
Parisios, Pictones, Cadurcos, Turonos, Aulercos, Lemouices, Andes
reliquosque omnes [qui Oceanum attingunt] adiungit: omnium
7 consensu ad eum defertur imperium. qua oblata potestate omnibus his ciuitatibus obsides imperat, certum numerum militum ad
8 se celeriter adduci iubet; armorum quantum quaeque ciuitas domi
quodque ante tempus efficiat constituit; in primis equitatui studet.
9 summae diligentiae summam imperii seueritatem addit; magnitu-
10 dine supplicii dubitantes cogit. nam maiore commisso delicto igni
atque omnibus tormentis necat, leuiore de causa auribus desectis
aut singulis effossis oculis domum remittit, ut sint reliquis documento et magnitudine poenae perterreant alios.

5   His suppliciis celeriter coacto exercitu Lucterium Cadurcum,
summae hominem audaciae, cum parte copiarum in Rutenos mittit;
2 ipse in Bituriges proficiscitur. eius aduentu Bituriges ad Haeduos,
quorum erant in fide, legatos mittunt subsidium rogatum, quo

3.2 ciuitates fama *ω corr. Sydow*   ubi qua *Krebs* ubique α*U* ubi **T** ubi quae *Schneider*

facilius hostium copias sustinere possint. Haedui de consilio lega- 3
torum, quos Caesar ad exercitum reliquerat, copias equitatus peditatusque subsidio Biturigibus mittunt. qui cum ad flumen Ligerim 4
uenissent, quod Bituriges ab Haeduis diuidit, paucos dies ibi morati neque flumen transire ausi domum reuertuntur, legatisque nos- 5
tris renuntiant se Biturigum perfidiam ueritos reuertisse, quibus id
consilii fuisse cognouerint ut, si flumen transissent, una ex parte
ipsi, altera Aruerni se circumsisterent. id eane de causa, quam lega- 6
tis pronuntiauerint, an perfidia adducti fecerint, quod nihil nobis
constat, non uidetur pro certo esse ponendum. Bituriges eorum 7
discessu statim se cum Aruernis coniungunt.

His rebus in Italiam Caesari nuntiatis, cum iam ille urbanas res 6
uirtute Cn. Pompei commodiorem in statum peruenisse intel-
legeret, in Transalpinam Galliam profectus est. eo cum uenisset 2
magna difficultate afficiebatur, qua ratione ad exercitum peruenire posset. nam si legiones in prouinciam arcesseret, se absente in 3
itinere proelio dimicaturas intellegebat; si ipse ad exercitum con- 4
tenderet, ne iis quidem eo tempore qui quieti uiderentur suam
salutem recte committi uidebat.

Interim Lucterius Cadurcus in Rutenos missus eam ciuitatem 7
Aruernis conciliat. progressus in Nitiobroges et Gabalos ab utrisque 2
obsides accipit et magna coacta manu in prouinciam Narbonem
uersus eruptionem facere contendit. qua re nuntiata Caesar 3
omnibus consiliis anteuertendum existimauit, ut Narbonem pro-
ficisceretur. eo cum uenisset timentes confirmat, praesidia in 4
Rutenis prouincialibus, Volcis Arecomicis, Tolosatibus circumque
Narbonem, quae loca hostibus erant finitima, constituit, partem 5
copiarum ex prouincia supplementumque quod ex Italia adduxe-
rat in Heluios, qui fines Aruernorum contingunt, conuenire iubet.

His rebus comparatis, represso iam Lucterio et remoto, quod 8
intrare intra praesidia periculosum putabat, in Heluios proficiscitur. etsi mons Ceuenna, qui Aruernos ab Heluiis discludit, duris- 2
simo tempore anni altissima niue iter impediebat, tamen discissa
niue sex in altitudinem pedum atque ita uiis patefactis summo
militum sudore ad fines Aruernorum peruenit. quibus oppressis 3
inopinantibus, quod se Ceuenna ut muro munitos existimabant

6.4 qui eo tempore pacati *β*   **8.2** discissa] discussa *α*   sudore] labore *β*

ac ne singulari quidem umquam homini eo tempore anni semitae
patuerant, equitibus imperat ut quam latissime possint uagentur et
4 quam maximum hostibus terrorem inferant. celeriter haec fama ac
nuntii‹s› ad Vercingetorigem perferuntur; quem perterriti omnes
Aruerni circumsistunt atque obsecrant ut suis fortunis consulat,
neu se ab hostibus diripi patiatur, praesertim cum uideat omne
5 ad se bellum translatum. quorum ille precibus permotus castra ex
Biturigibus mouet in Aruernos uersus.

9 At Caesar biduum in his locis moratus, quod haec de
Vercingetorige usu uentura opinione praeceperat, per causam
supplementi equitatusque cogendi ab exercitu discedit; Brutum
2 adulescentem his copiis praeficit. hunc monet ut in omnes partes
equites quam latissime peruagentur: daturum se operam ne lon-
3 gius triduo a castris absit. his constitutis rebus, omnibus suis inopinantibus quam maximis potest itineribus Viennam peruenit.
4 ibi nactus recentem equitatum, quem multis ante diebus eo praemiserat,[neque diurno neque nocturno itinere intermisso]per fines
Haeduorum in Lingones contendit, ubi duae legiones hiemabant,
ut, si quid etiam de sua salute ab Haeduis iniretur consilii, celer-
5 itate praecurreret. eo cum peruenisset, ad reliquas legiones mittit priusque omnes in unum locum cogit quam de eius aduentu
6 Aruernis nuntiari posset. hac re cognita Vercingetorix rursus in
Bituriges exercitum reducit atque inde profectus Gorgobinam,
Boiorum oppidum, quos ibi Heluetico proelio uictos Caesar collocauerat Haeduisque attribuerat, oppugnare instituit.

10 Magnam haec res Caesari difficultatem ad consilium capiendum afferebat, si reliquam partem hiemis uno loco legiones contineret, ne [stipendiariis Haeduorum expugnatis] cuncta Gallia
deficeret, quod nullum amicis in eo praesidium uideret positum
esse; si maturius ex hibernis educeret, ne ab re frumentaria duris
2 subuectionibus laboraret. praestare uisum est tamen omnes diffi-
cultates perpeti quam tanta contumelia accepta omnium suorum
3 uoluntates alienare. itaque[cohortatus Haeduos de supportando
commeatu]praemittit ad Boios qui de suo aduentu doceant horten-
turque ut in fide maneant atque hostium impetum magno animo

8.4 ac nuntii **α** nuntii **β** *corr. Manutius*   **9.6** Gorgobinam] gortonam **β** gorgobinam **U** *marg.*

sustineant. duabus Agedinci legionibus atque impedimentis⌈totius   4
exercitu⌋relictis ad Boios proficiscitur.

Altero die cum ad oppidum Senonum Vellaunodunum uenisset,   11
ne quem post se hostem relinqueret, quo expeditiore re frumentaria uteretur, oppugnare instituit eoque biduo ⌈circumuallauit.⌉
tertio die missis ex oppido legatis de deditione arma conferri,   2
iumenta produci, sescentos obsides dari iubet. ea qui conficeret,
C. Trebonium legatum relinquit. ipse, ut quam primum iter con-   3
ficeret, Cenabum Carnutum proficiscitur. qui tum primum allato   4
nuntio de oppugnatione Vellaunoduni, cum longius eam rem duc-
tum iri existimarent, praesidium Cenabi tuendi causa, quod eo
mitterent, comparabant. huc biduo peruenit. castris ante oppidum   5
positis diei tempore exclusus in posterum oppugnationem differt,
quaeque ad eam rem usui sint militibus imperat et, quod oppidum   6
Cenabum pons fluminis Ligeris contingebat, ueritus ne noctu
ex oppido profugerent, duas legiones in armis excubare iubet.
Cenabenses paulo ante mediam noctem silentio ex oppido egressi   7
flumen transire coeperunt. qua re per exploratores nuntiata   8
Caesar legiones ⌈quas expeditas esse iusserat⌋portis incensis⌉ intro-
mittit atque oppido potitur, perpaucis ex hostium numero desideratis quin cuncti caperentur, quod pontis atque itinerum angustiae
multitudini fugam intercluserant. oppidum diripit atque incendit,   9
praedam militibus donat, exercitum Ligerem traducit atque in
Biturigum fines peruenit.

Vercingetorix ubi de Caesaris aduentu cognouit, oppugnatione   12
desistit atque obuiam Caesari proficiscitur. ille oppidum Biturigum   2
positum in uia Nouiodunum oppugnare instituerat. quo ex oppido   3
cum legati ad eum uenissent oratum ut sibi ignosceret suaeque uitae
consuleret, ut celeritate reliquas res conficeret, qua pleraque erat
consecutus, arma conferri, equos produci, obsides dari iubet. parte   4
iam obsidum tradita, cum reliqua administrarentur, centurionibus
et paucis militibus intromissis qui arma iumentaque conquirerent,
equitatus hostium procul uisus est, qui agmen Vercingetorigis
antecesserat. quem simulatque oppidani conspexerunt atque in   5
spem auxili uenerunt, clamore sublato arma capere, portas claudere, murum complere coeperunt. centuriones in oppido cum ex   6

11.1 eoque] idque *a*   11.3 conficeret] faceret *a*

significatione Gallorum noui aliquid ab iis iniri consilii intellex-
issent, gladiis destrictis portas occupauerunt suosque omnes incolumes receperunt.

13 Caesar ex castris equitatum educi iubet proeliumque equestre
committit. laborantibus iam suis Germanos equites circiter CCCC
2 summittit, quos ab initio habere secum instituerat. eorum impetum Galli sustinere non potuerunt atque in fugam coniecti multis
amissis se ad agmen receperunt. quibus profligatis rursus oppidani
perterriti comprehensos eos[quorum opera plebem concitatam
ℛₗₗexistimabant]ad Caesarem perduxerunt seseque ei dediderunt.
3 quibus rebus confectis Caesar ad oppidum Auaricum, quod erat
maximum munitissimumque in finibus Biturigum atque agri fertilissima regione, profectus est, quod eo oppido recepto ciuitatem
Biturigum[se in potestatem redacturum]confidebat.

14 Vercingetorix tot continuis incommodis Vellaunoduni, Cenabi,
2 Nouioduni acceptis suos ad concilium conuocat. docet longe alia
ratione esse bellum gerendum atque antea gestum sit. omnibus
modis huic rei studendum ut pabulatione aut commeatu Romani
3 prohibeantur. id esse facile, quod equitatu ipsi abundent et quod
4 anni tempore subleuentur. pabulum secari non posse; necessario
dispersos hostes ex aedificiis petere: hos omnes cotidie ab equiti-
5 bus deleri posse. praeterea salutis causa rei familiaris commoda
neglegenda: uicos atque aedificia incendi oportere hoc spatio ab
uia quoque uersus quo pabulandi causa adire posse uideantur.
6 harum ipsis rerum copiam suppetere, quod quorum in finibus
7 bellum geratur, eorum opibus subleuentur. Romanos aut inopiam
non laturos aut magno cum periculo longius a castris processuros.
8 neque interesse ipsosne interficiant impedimentisne exuant, qui-
9 bus amissis bellum geri non possit. praeterea oppida incendi oportere[quae non munitione et loci natura ab omni sint periculo tuta]
[ne]suis sint ad detractandam militiam receptacula [neu] Romanis
10 proposita ad copiam commeatus praedamque tollendam. haec si
grauia aut acerba uideantur, multo illa grauius aestimari, liberos,
coniuges in seruitutem abstrahi, ipsos interfici; quae sit necesse
accidere uictis.

14.2 aut] et β   **14.4** deleri] diligi α   **14.9** neu β   **14.10** aestimari *Krebs*
aestimare α aestimari debere β

Omnium consensu hac sententia probata uno die amplius XX **15**
urbes Biturigum incenduntur. hoc idem fit in reliquis ciuitatibus: 2
in omnibus partibus incendia conspiciuntur. quae etsi magno cum
dolore omnes ferebant, tamen hoc sibi solacii proponebant, quod
se⸢prope explorata uictoria⸥celeriter amissa recuperaturos confidebant. deliberatur de Auarico in communi concilio, incendi placeat 3
an defendi. procumbunt omnibus Gallis ad pedes Bituriges: ne 4
pulcherrimam prope totius Galliae urbem, quae et praesidio et
ornamento sit ciuitati, suis manibus succendere cogantur: facile 5
se loci natura defensuros dicunt, quod prope ex omnibus partibus flumine et palude circumdata unum habeat et perangustum
aditum. ⸢datur petentibus uenia⸥dissuadente primo Vercingetorige⸥ 6
post concedente et precibus ipsorum et misericordia uulgi. defensores oppido idonei deliguntur.

Vercingetorix minoribus Caesarem itineribus subsequitur et **16**
locum castris deligit paludibus siluisque munitum ab Auarico
longe milia passuum XVI. ibi per certos exploratores in singula 2
diei tempora quae ad Auaricum gererentur cognoscebat et quid
fieri uellet imperabat. omnes nostras pabulationes frumentation- 3
esque obseruabat dispersosque, cum longius necessario procederent, adoriebatur magnoque incommodo afficiebat, etsi quantum
ratione prouideri poterat ab nostris occurrebatur, ut incertis temporibus diuersisque itineribus iretur.

Castris ad eam partem oppidi positis Caesar, quae intermissa **17**
a flumine et a paludibus aditum, ut supra diximus, angustum
habebat, aggerem apparare, uineas agere, turres duas constituere
coepit. nam circumuallare loci natura prohibebat. de re frumen- 2
taria Boios atque Haeduos adhortari non destitit. quorum alteri,
quod nullo studio agebant, non multum adiuuabant, alteri non
magnis facultatibus, quod ciuitas erat exigua et infirma, celeriter quod habuerunt consumpserunt. summa difficultate rei 3
frumentariae affecto exercitu tenuitate Boiorum, indiligentia
Haeduorum, incendiis aedificiorum, usque eo ut complures dies
frumento milites caruerint et pecore ex longinquioribus uicis
adacto extremam famem sustentarint, nulla tamen uox est ab iis
audita populi Romani maiestate et superioribus uictoriis indigna.

15.4 cogerentur ω *corr. Whitte*   **17.3** sustentarent ω *corr. Whitte*

4 quin etiam Caesar cum in opere singulas legiones appellaret et, si
acerbius inopiam ferrent, se dimissurum oppugnationem diceret,
5 uniuersi ab eo, ne id faceret, petebant: sic se complures annos illo
imperante meruisse ut nullam ignominiam acciperent, nusquam
6 infecta re discederent; hoc se ignominiae laturos loco, si inceptam
7 oppugnationem reliquissent; praestare omnes perferre acerbitates
quam non ciuibus Romanis qui Cenabi perfidia Gallorum interis-
8 sent parentarent. haec eadem centurionibus tribunisque militum
mandabant, ut per eos ad Caesarem deferrentur.

18 Cum iam muro turres appropinquassent, ex captiuis Caesar
cognouit Vercingetorigem consumpto pabulo castra mouisse propius Auaricum atque ipsum cum equitatu expeditisque qui inter
equites proeliari consuessent insidiandi causa eo profectum quo
2 nostros postero die pabulatum uenturos arbitraretur. quibus rebus
cognitis media nocte silentio profectus ad hostium castra mane
3 peruenit. illi celeriter per exploratores aduentu Caesaris cognito
carros impedimentaque sua in artiores siluas abdiderunt, copias
4 omnes in loco edito atque aperto instruxerunt. qua re nuntiata
Caesar celeriter sarcinas conferri, arma expediri iussit.

19 Collis erat leniter ab infimo accliuis. hunc ex omnibus fere partibus palus difficilis atque impedita cingebat non latior pedibus
2 quinquaginta. hoc se colle interruptis pontibus Galli fiducia loci
continebant generatimque distributi [in ciuitates] omnia uada
ac saltus eius paludis certis custodiis obtinebant, sic animo parati
ut, si eam paludem Romani perrumpere conarentur, haesitantes
3 premerent ex loco superiore; ut qui propinquitatem loci uideret
paratos prope aequo Marte ad dimicandum existimaret, qui
iniquitatem condicionis perspiceret inani simulatione sese osten-
4 tare cognosceret. indignantes milites Caesar, quod conspectum
suum hostes perferre possent tantulo spatio interiecto, et signum
proelii exposcentes edocet quanto detrimento et quot uirorum
5 fortium morte necesse sit constare uictoriam. quos cum sic animo
paratos uideat ut nullum pro sua laude periculum recusent, summae se iniquitatis condemnari debere, nisi eorum uitam sua salute
6 habeat cariorem. sic milites consolatus eodem die reducit in castra
reliquaque quae ad oppugnationem pertinebant oppidi administrare instituit.

19.1 leuiter *ω corr. (ex. gr.)* N² **19.2** in ciuitates *del. Morus*

Vercingetorix cum ad suos redisset, proditionis insimulatus, **20**
quod castra propius Romanos mouisset, quod cum omni equitatu
discessisset, quod sine imperio tantas copias reliquisset, quod eius
discessu Romani tanta opportunitate et celeritate uenissent; non **2**
haec omnia fortuito aut sine consilio accidere potuisse; regnum
illum Galliae malle Caesaris concessu quam ipsorum habere beneficio — tali modo accusatus ad haec respondit: quod castra mou- **3**
isset, factum inopia pabuli etiam ipsis hortantibus. quod propius
Romanos accessisset, persuasum loci opportunitate qui se ipse
sine munitione defenderet. equitum uero operam neque in loco **4**
palustri desiderari debuisse et illic fuisse utilem quo sint profecti.
summam imperii se consulto nulli discedentem tradidisse, ne **5**
[h]is multitudinis studio ad dimicandum impelleretur; cui rei
propter animi mollitiem studere omnes uideret, quod diutius laborem ferre non possent. Romani si casu interuenerint, Fortunae, **6**
si alicuius indicio uocati, huic habendam gratiam, quod et paucitatem eorum ex loco superiore cognoscere et uirtutem despicere
potuerint, qui dimicare non ausi turpiter se in castra receperint.
imperium se a Caesare per proditionem nullum desiderare quod **7**
habere uictoria posset, quae iam sit sibi atque omnibus Gallis explorata. quin etiam ipsis remitteret, si sibi magis honorem tribuere
quam ab se salutem accipere uideantur. 'haec ut intellegatis', **8**
inquit, 'a me sincere pronuntiari; audite Romanos milites.' pro- **9**
ducit seruos quos in pabulatione paucis ante diebus exceperat et
fame uinculisque excruciauerat. hi iam ante edocti quae inter- **10**
rogati pronuntiarent, milites se esse legionarios dicunt. fame atque
inopia adductos clam ex castris exisse, si quid frumenti aut pecoris
in agris reperire possent. simili omnem exercitum inopia premi **11**
nec iam uires sufficere cuiusquam nec ferre operis laborem posse.
itaque statuisse imperatorem, si nihil in oppugnatione oppidi
profecisset, triduo exercitum deducere. 'haec', inquit, 'a me', **12**
Vercingetorix, 'beneficia habetis, quem proditionis insimulatis.
cuius opera sine uestro sanguine tantum exercitum uictorem fame
paene consumptum uidetis. quem turpiter se ex hac fuga recipientem ne qua ciuitas suis finibus recipiat a me prouisum est.'

20.3 ipsum *ω corr. Bentley*   **20.4** sint *ω* essent *Klotz*   **20.5** his *ω corr.* A^c
20.7 sit] esset *ω corr. Meusel*   **20.12** hac *om.* α

21   Conclamat omnis multitudo et suo more armis concrepat, quod
       facere in eo consuerunt cuius orationem approbant: summum esse
       Vercingetorigem ducem nec de eius fide dubitandum nec maiore
2   ratione bellum administrari posse. statuunt ut X milia hominum
3   delecta ex omnibus copiis in oppidum summittantur, nec solis
       Biturigibus communem salutem committendam censent, quod
       penes eos, si id oppidum retinuissent, summam uictoriae constare
       intellegebant.
22   Singulari militum nostrorum uirtuti consilia cuiusque modi
       Gallorum occurrebant, ut est summae genus sollertiae atque ad
       omnia imitanda et efficienda quae ab quoque traduntur aptis-
2   simum. nam et laqueis falces auertebant, quas cum destinau-
       erant, tormentis introrsus reducebant et aggerem cuniculis
       subtrahebant, eo scientius quod apud eos magnae sunt ferrariae
3   atque omne genus cuniculorum notum atque usitatum est. totum
       autem murum ex omni parte turribus contabulauerant atque has
4   coriis intexerant. tum crebris diurnis nocturnisque eruptionibus
       aut aggeri ignem inferebant aut milites occupatos in opere adorie-
       bantur, et nostrarum turrium altitudinem, quantum has cotidianus
       agger expresserat, commissis suarum turrium malis adaequabant,
5   et apertos cuniculos praeusta et praeacuta materia et pice ferue-
       facta et maximi ponderis saxis morabantur moenibusque appro-
       pinquare prohibebant.
23   Muri autem omnes Gallici hac fere forma sunt: trabes derec-
       tae perpetuae in longitudinem paribus interuallis, distantes inter
2   se binos pedes, in solo collocantur. hae reuinciuntur introrsus
       et multo aggere uestiuntur; ea autem, quae diximus, interualla
3   grandibus in fronte saxis effarciuntur. his collocatis et coagmen-
       tatis alius insuper ordo additur ut idem illud interuallum seruetur
       neque inter se contingant trabes, sed paribus intermissis spatiis
4   singulae singulis saxis interiectis arte contineantur. sic deinceps
5   omne opus contexitur dum iusta muri altitudo expleatur. hoc cum
       in speciem uarietatemque opus deforme non est alternis trabibus
       ac saxis quae rectis lineis suos ordines seruant, tum ad utilitatem
       et defensionem urbium summam habet opportunitatem, quod
       et ab incendio lapis et ab ariete materia defendit, quae perpetuis

23.2 haere uiciuntur *a* hae reuintiuntur **T** aere uinciuntur **U**

trabibus pedes quadragenos plerumque introrsus reuincta neque
perrumpi neque distrahi potest.

His tot rebus impedita oppugnatione milites cum toto tempore   **24**
‹so›luto frigore et assiduis imbribus tardarentur, tamen continenti
labore omnia haec superauerunt et diebus XXV aggerem latum
pedes CCCXXX, altum pedes LXXX exstruxerunt. cum is murum   2
hostium paene contingeret, et Caesar ad opus consuetudine excubaret militesque hortaretur ne quod omnino tempus ab opere
intermitteretur, paulo ante tertiam uigiliam est animaduersum
fumare aggerem, quem cuniculo hostes succenderant, eodemque   3
tempore toto muro clamore sublato duabus portis ab utroque latere turrium eruptio fiebat. alii faces atque aridam materiam de   4
muro in aggerem eminus iaciebant, picem reliquasque res quibus ignis excitari potest fundebant, ut quo primum occurreretur
aut cui rei ferretur auxilium uix ratio iniri posset. tamen, quod   5
instituto Caesaris semper duae legiones pro castris excubabant
pluresque partitis temporibus erant in opere, celeriter factum est
ut alii eruptionibus resisterent, alii turres reducerent aggeremque
interscinderent, omnis uero ex castris multitudo ad restinguendum concurreret.

Cum in omnibus locis consumpta iam reliqua parte noctis pugna-   **25**
retur semperque hostibus spes uictoriae redintegraretur, eo magis
quod deustos pluteos turrium uidebant nec facile adire apertos ad
auxiliandum animaduertebant, semperque ipsi recentes defessis
succederent omnemque Galliae salutem in illo uestigio temporis
positam arbitrarentur, accidit inspectantibus nobis quod dignum
memoria uisum praetereundum non existimauimus. quidam ante   2
portam oppidi Gallus, qui per manus sebi ac picis traditas glaebas
in ignem e regione turris proiciebat, scorpione ab latere dextro
traiectus exanimatusque concidit. hunc ex proximis unus iacen-   3
tem transgressus eodem illo munere fungebatur. eadem ratione   4
ictu scorpionis exanimato alteri successit tertius et tertio quartus,
nec prius ille est a propugnatoribus uacuus relictus locus quam
restincto aggere atque omni ex parte summotis hostibus finis est
pugnandi factus.

24.1 luto β *om.* α *corr. Wagner*   **24.4** materiem α

26 Omnia experti Galli, quod res nulla successerat, postero die consilium ceperunt ex oppido profugere hortante et iubente
2 Vercingetorige. id silentio noctis conati non magna iactura suorum sese effecturos sperabant, propterea quod neque longe ab oppido castra Vercingetorigis aberant et palus quae perpetua inter-
3 cedebat Romanos ad insequendum tardabat. iamque haec facere noctu apparabant, cum matres familiae repente in publicum procurrerunt flentesque proiectae ad pedes suorum omnibus precibus petierunt ne se et communes liberos hostibus ad supplicium dederent, quos ad capiendam fugam naturae et uirium infirmitas
4 impediret. ubi eos in sententia perstare uiderunt, quod plerumque in summo periculo timor misericordiam non recipit, conclamare
5 et significare de fuga Romanis coeperunt. quo timore perterriti Galli ne ab equitatu Romanorum uiae praeoccuparentur consilio destiterunt.

27 Postero die Caesar promota turri perfectisque operibus quae facere instituerat, magno coorto imbri non inutilem hanc ad capiendum consilium tempestatem arbitratus, quod paulo incautius custodias in muro dispositas uidebat, suos quoque languidius
2 in opere uersari iussit et quid fieri uellet ostendit; legionibusque intra uineas in occulto expeditis cohortatus ut aliquando pro tantis laboribus fructum uictoriae perciperent, iis qui primi murum
3 ascendissent praemia proposuit militibusque signum dedit. illi subito ex omnibus partibus euolauerunt murumque celeriter compleuerunt.

28 Hostes re noua perterriti, muro turribusque deiecti in foro ac locis patentioribus cuneatim constiterunt hoc animo ut, si qua ex
2 parte obuiam contra ueniretur, acie instructa depugnarent. ubi neminem in aequum locum sese demittere sed toto undique muro circumfundi uiderunt, ueriti ne omnino spes fugae tolleretur, abiectis armis ultimas oppidi partes continenti impetu petiuerunt,
3 parsque ibi, cum angusto exitu portarum se ipsi premerent, a militibus, pars iam egressa portis ab equitibus est interfecta. nec fuit
4 quisquam qui praedae studeret. sic et Cenabensi caede et labore operis incitati non aetate confectis, non mulieribus, non infantibus
5 pepercerunt. denique ex omni eo numero, qui fuit circiter milium XL, uix DCCC, qui primo clamore audito se ex oppido eiecerant,
6 incolumes ad Vercingetorigem peruenerunt. quos ille multa iam

nocte silentio ex fuga excepit, ueritus ne qua in castris ex eorum
concursu et misericordia uulgi seditio oriretur, ut procul in uia
dispositis familiaribus suis principibusque ciuitatum disparandos
deducendosque ad suos curaret, quae cuique ciuitati pars castrorum ab initio obuenerat.

Postero die concilio conuocato consolatus cohortatusque est **29**
ne se admodum animo demitterent neue perturbarentur incommodo. non uirtute neque in acie uicisse Romanos, sed artificio **2**
quodam et scientia oppugnationis, cuius rei fuerint ipsi imperiti.
errare, si qui in bello omnes secundos rerum prouentus exspect- **3**
ent. sibi numquam placuisse Auaricum defendi, cuius rei testes **4**
ipsos haberet; sed factum imprudentia Biturigum et nimia obsequentia reliquorum uti hoc incommodum acciperetur. id tamen **5**
se celeriter maioribus commodis sarturum. nam quae ab reliquis **6**
Gallis ciuitates dissentirent, has sua diligentia adiuncturum atque
unum consilium totius Galliae effecturum, cuius consensui ne
orbis quidem terrarum possit obsistere; idque se prope iam effectum habere. interea aequum esse ab iis communis salutis causa **7**
impetrari ut castra munire instituerent, quo facilius repentinos
hostium impetus sustinere possent.

Fuit haec oratio non ingrata Gallis, et maxime quod ipse animo **30**
non defecerat tanto accepto incommodo neque ‹se› in occultum
abdiderat et conspectum multitudinis fugerat, plusque animo **2**
prouidere et praesentire existimabatur, quod re integra primo
incendendum Auaricum, post deserendum censuerat. itaque ut **3**
reliquorum imperatorum res aduersae auctoritatem minuunt, sic
huius ex contrario dignitas incommodo accepto in dies augebatur. simul in spem ueniebant eius affirmatione de reliquis adiun- **4**
gendis ciuitatibus; primumque eo tempore Galli castra munire
instituerunt, et sic sunt animo consternati homines insueti laboris,
ut omnia quae imperarentur sibi patienda existimarent.

Nec minus quam est pollicitus Vercingetorix animo laborabat **31**
ut reliquas ciuitates adiungeret, atque earum principes donis
pollicitationibusque alliciebat. huic rei idoneos homines delige- **2**
bat, quorum quisque aut oratione subdola aut amicitia facillime
capere posset. qui Auarico expugnato refugerant, armandos **3**

29.5 senaturum **A** sanaturum **B**β *corr. Bentley*   **30.1** se *om.* ω *add. editio princeps*

4 uestiendosque curat. simul ut deminutae copiae redintegrarentur, imperat certum numerum militum ciuitatibus, quem et quam ante diem in castra adduci uelit, sagittariosque omnes, quorum erat permagnus numerus in Gallia, conquiri et ad se mitti iubet. his rebus

5 celeriter id quod Auarici deperierat expletur. interim Teutomatus, Ollouiconis filius, rex Nitiobrogum, cuius pater ab senatu nostro amicus erat appellatus, cum magno equitum suorum numero et quos ex Aquitania conduxerat ad eum peruenit.

32 Caesar Auarici complures dies commoratus summamque ibi copiam frumenti et reliqui commeatus nactus exercitum ex lab-

2 ore atque inopia reficit. iam prope hieme confecta cum ipso anni tempore ad gerendum bellum uocaretur et ad hostem proficisci constituisset, siue eum ex paludibus siluisque elicere siue obsidione premere posset, legati ad eum principes Haeduorum ueniunt

3 oratum ut maxime necessario tempore ciuitati subueniat: summo esse in periculo rem, quod, cum singuli magistratus antiquitus creari atque regiam potestatem annuam obtinere consuessent, duo magistratum gerant et se uterque eorum legibus creatum esse

4 dicat. horum esse alterum Conuictolitauem, florentem et illustrem adulescentem, alterum Cotum, antiquissima familia natum atque ipsum hominem summae potentiae et magnae cognationis, cuius

5 frater Valetiacus proximo anno eundem magistratum gesserit. ciuitatem esse omnem in armis; diuisum senatum, diuisum populum, suas cuiusque eorum clientelas. quodsi diutius alatur controuersia, fore uti pars cum parte ciuitatis confligat. id ne accidat, positum in eius diligentia atque auctoritate.

33 Caesar etsi a bello atque hoste discedere detrimentosum esse existimabat, tamen non ignorans quanta ex dissensionibus incommoda oriri consuessent, ne tanta et tam coniuncta populo Romano ciuitas, quam ipse semper aluisset omnibusque rebus ornasset, ad uim atque arma descenderet, atque ea pars quae minus sibi confi-

2 deret auxilia a Vercingetorige arcesseret, huic rei praeuertendum existimauit et, quod legibus Haeduorum eis qui summum magistratum obtinerent excedere ex finibus non liceret, ne quid de iure aut de legibus eorum deminuisse uideretur, ipse in Haeduos proficisci statuit senatumque omnem et quos inter controuersia esset

32.3 annum α

ad se Decetiam euocauit. cum prope omnis ciuitas eo conuenisset 3
doceretur que paucis clam conuocatis alio loco, alio tempore atque
oportuerit fratrem a fratre renuntiatum, cum leges duo‹s› ex una
familia uiuo utroque non solum magistratus creari uetarent, sed
etiam in senatu esse prohiberent, Cotum imperium deponere coe-
git; Conuictolitauem, qui per sacerdotes more ciuitatis intermissis 4
magistratibus esset creatus, potestatem obtinere iussit.

Hoc decreto interposito cohortatus Haeduos ut controuer- **34**
siarum ac dissensionis obliuiscerentur atque omnibus omissis his
rebus huic bello seruirent eaque quae meruissent praemia ab se
deuicta Gallia exspectarent equitatumque omnem et peditum
milia x sibi celeriter mitterent, quae in praesidiis rei frumentariae causa disponeret, exercitum in duas partes diuisit: quattuor 2
legiones in Senones Parisiosque Labieno ducendas dedit, sex ipse
in Aruernos ad oppidum Gergouiam secundum flumen Elauer
duxit; equitatus partem illi attribuit, partem sibi reliquit. qua re 3
cognita Vercingetorix omnibus interruptis eius fluminis pontibus
ab altera fluminis parte iter facere coepit.

Cum uterque utrique in conspectu esset exercitui fereque e **35**
regione castris castra poneret, dispositis exploratoribus, necubi
effecto ponte Romani copias traducerent, erat in magnis Caesari
difficultatibus res ne maiorem aestatis partem flumine impediretur, quod non fere ante autumnum Elauer uado transiri solet.
itaque ne id accideret, siluestri loco castris positis e regione unius 2
eorum pontium quos Vercingetorix rescindendos curauerat, postero die cum duabus legionibus in occulto restitit; reliquas copias 3
cum omnibus impedimentis, ut consueuerat, misit, carptis quibusdam cohortibus, uti numerus legionum constare uideretur. his 4
quam longissime possent progredi iussis, cum iam ex diei tempore
coniecturam caperet in castra peruentum, isdem sublicis, quarum
pars inferior integra remanebat, pontem reficere coepit. celeriter 5
effecto opere legionibusque traductis et loco castris idoneo delecto
reliquas copias reuocauit. Vercingetorix re cognita, ne contra suam 6
uoluntatem dimicare cogeretur, magnis itineribus antecessit.

Caesar ex eo loco quintis castris Gergouiam peruenit equestri- **36**
que eo die proelio leui facto, perspecto urbis situ, quae posita in

---

33.3 duo ω *corr. recc.*   **35.1** uterque utrimque exisset exercitus α
35.3 captis αTᶜU craptis Tˡ *corr.* Rᶜ

altissimo monte omnes aditus difficiles habebat, de oppugnatione
desperauit; de obsessione non prius agendum constituit quam rem
2 frumentariam expedisset. at Vercingetorix castris prope oppidum
in monte positis mediocribus circum se interuallis separatim sin-
gularum ciuitatum copias collocauerat atque omnibus eius iugi collibus occupatis, qua dispici poterat, horribilem speciem praebebat;
3 principesque earum ciuitatum quos sibi ad consilium capiendum
delegerat prima luce cotidie ad se conuenire iubebat, seu quid
4 communicandum, seu quid administrandum uideretur; neque
ullum fere diem intermittebat quin equestri proelio interiectis sagittariis quid in quoque esset animi ac uirtutis suorum periclitare-
5 tur. erat e regione oppidi collis sub ipsis radicibus montis egregie
munitus atque ex omni parte circumcisus; quem si tenerent nostri, et aquae magna parte et pabulatione libera prohibituri hostes
6 uidebantur. sed is locus praesidio ab his non nimis firmo teneba-
7 tur. tamen silentio noctis Caesar ex castris egressus, priusquam subsidio ex oppido ueniri posset, deiecto praesidio, potitus loco duas
ibi legiones collocauit fossamque duplicem duodenum pedum a
maioribus castris ad minora perduxit, ut tuto ab repentino hostium incursu etiam singuli commeare possent.

37　　Dum haec ad Gergouiam geruntur, Conuictolitauis Haeduus,
cui magistratum adiudicatum a Caesare demonstrauimus, sollicitatus ab Aruernis pecunia cum quibusdam adulescentibus colloquitur, quorum erat princeps Litauiccus atque eius fratres, amplissima
2 familia nati adulescentes. cum his praemium communicat hortat-
3 urque eos ut se liberos et imperio natos meminerint: unam esse
Haeduorum ciuitatem quae certissimam Galliae uictoriam distineat; eius auctoritate reliquas contineri; qua traducta locum con-
4 sistendi Romanis in Gallia non fore. esse nonnullo se Caesaris
beneficio affectum, sic tamen ut iustissimam apud eum causam
5 obtinuerit; sed plus communi libertati tribuere. cur enim potius
Haedui de suo iure et de legibus ad Caesarem disceptatorem quam
6 Romani ad Haeduos ueniant? celeriter adulescentibus et oratione
magistratus et praemio deductis, cum se uel principes eius consili
fore profiterentur, ratio perficiendi quaerebatur, quod ciuitatem
temere ad suscipiendum bellum adduci posse non confidebant.

36.1 de oppugnatione desperauit, de obsessione] expugnatione **α**　　　**36.2** despici
ω corr. **S**

placuit uti Litauiccus decem illis milibus quae Caesari ad bellum 7
mitterentur praeficeretur atque ea ducenda curaret, fratresque
eius ad Caesarem praecurrerent. reliqua qua ratione agi placeat
constituunt.

Litauiccus accepto exercitu, cum milia passuum circiter XXX ab **38**
Gergouia abesset, conuocatis subito militibus lacrimans, 'quo proficiscimur', inquit, 'milites? omnis noster equitatus, omnis nobilitas
interiit; principes ciuitatis, Eporedorix et Viridomarus, insimulati 2
proditionis ab Romanis indicta causa interfecti sunt. haec ab ipsis 3
cognoscite qui ex ipsa caede fugerunt. nam ego fratribus atque
omnibus meis propinquis interfectis dolore prohibeor quae gesta
sunt pronuntiare.' producuntur ii quos ille edocuerat quae dici 4
uellet, atque eadem quae Litauiccus pronuntiauerat multitudini
exponunt: multos equites Haeduorum interfectos, quod collocuti 5
cum Aruernis dicerentur; ipsos se inter multitudinem militum
occultasse atque ex media caede fugisse. conclamant Haedui et 6
Litauiccum obsecrant ut sibi consulat. 'quasi uero', inquit ille, 'consilii sit res, ac non necesse sit nobis Gergouiam contendere et cum
Aruernis nosmet coniungere. an dubitamus quin nefario facinore 7
admisso Romani iam ad nos interficiendos concurrant? proinde, si 8
quid in nobis animi est, persequamur eorum mortem qui indignissime interierunt atque hos latrones interficiamus.' ostendit ciues 9
Romanos qui eius praesidii fiducia una erant. continuo magnum
numerum frumenti commeatusque diripit, ipsos crudeliter excruciatos interficit. nuntios tota ciuitate Haeduorum dimittit, eodem 10
mendacio de caede equitum et principum permouet, hortatur ut
simili ratione atque ipse fecerit suas iniurias persequantur.

Eporedorix Haeduus, summo loco natus adulescens et summae **39**
domi potentiae, et una Viridomarus pari aetate et gratia sed genere
dispari, quem Caesar ab Diuiciaco sibi traditum ex humili loco ad
summam dignitatem perduxerat, in equitum numero conuenerant
nominatim ab eo euocati. his erat inter se de principatu contentio, 2
et in illa magistratuum controuersia alter pro Conuictolitaui, alter
pro Coto summis opibus pugnauerat. ex his Eporedorix cognito 3
Litauicci consilio media fere nocte rem ad Caesarem defert. orat
ne patiatur ciuitatem prauis adulescentium consiliis ab amicitia

38.3 ipsis] his *β*   **38.5** multos] omnes *β*   **38.10** in eodem mendacio *β*
permouet **L** permonet **AB**c*β* permanet **B**

populi Romani deficere; quod futurum prouideat, si se tot hominum milia cum hostibus coniunxerint, quorum salutem neque
propinqui neglegere neque ciuitas leui momento aestimare possit.
40   Magna affectus sollicitudine hoc nuntio Caesar, quod semper
Haeduorum ciuitati praecipue indulserat, nulla interposita dubitatione legiones expeditas quattuor equitatumque omnem ex cas-
2   tris educit; nec fuit spatium tali tempore ad contrahenda castra,
3   quod res posita in celeritate uidebatur. C. Fabium legatum cum
legionibus duabus castris praesidio relinquit. fratres Litauicci cum
4   comprehendi iussisset, paulo ante reperit ad hostes fugisse. adhortatus milites ne necessario tempore itineris labore permoueantur, cupidissimis omnibus progressus milia passuum XXV agmen
Haeduorum conspicatur. immisso equitatu iter eorum moratur
atque impedit interdicitque omnibus ne quemquam interficiant.
5   Eporedorigem et Viridomarum, quos illi interfectos existima-
6   bant, inter equites uersari suosque appellare iubet. his cognitis et
Litauicci fraude perspecta Haedui manus tendere [deditionem sig-
7   nificare] et proiectis armis mortem deprecari incipiunt. Litauiccus
cum suis clientibus, quibus more Gallorum nefas est etiam in
extrema fortuna deserere patronos, Gergouiam perfugit.
41   Caesar nuntiis ad ciuitatem Haeduorum missis qui suo beneficio conseruatos docerent quos iure belli interficere potuisset, tribusque horis noctis exercitui ad quietem datis castra ad Gergouiam
2   mouit. medio fere itinere equites a Fabio missi quanto res in periculo fuerit exponunt. summis copiis castra oppugnata demonstrant,
cum crebro integri defessis succederent nostrosque assiduo labore
defatigarent, quibus propter magnitudinem castrorum perpetuo
3   esset isdem in uallo permanendum. multitudine sagittarum atque
omnis generis telorum multos uulneratos; ad haec sustinenda
4   magno usui fuisse tormenta. Fabium discessu eorum duabus
relictis portis obstruere ceteras pluteosque uallo addere et se in
5   posterum diem similem ad casum parare. his rebus cognitis Caesar
summo studio militum ante ortum solis in castra peruenit.
42   Dum haec ad Gergouiam geruntur, Haedui primis nuntiis ab
Litauicco acceptis nullum sibi ad cognoscendum spatium relin-
2   quunt. impellit alios auaritia, alios iracundia et temeritas, quae

39.3 posset ω *corr. Vascosanus*   **40.6** deditionem significare *del. Whitte*
40.7 profugit α

maxime illi hominum generi est innata, ut leuem auditionem
habeant pro re comperta. bona ciuium Romanorum diripiunt, 3
caedes faciunt, in seruitutem abstrahunt. adiuuat rem proclina- 4
tam Conuictolitauis plebemque ad furorem impellit, ut facinore
admisso ad sanitatem reuerti pudeat. M. Aristium, tribunum mil- 5
itum, iter ad legionem facientem fide data ex oppido Cauillono
educunt: idem facere cogunt eos, qui negotiandi causa ibi constiterant. hos continuo <in> itinere adorti omnibus impedimentis 6
exuunt; repugnantes diem noctemque obsident; multis utrimque
interfectis maiorem multitudinem armatorum concitant.

Interim nuntio allato omnes eorum milites in potestate Caesaris **43**
teneri, concurrunt ad Aristium, nihil publico factum consilio
demonstrant. quaestionem de bonis direptis decernunt, Litauicci 2
fratrumque bona publicant, legatos ad Caesarem sui purgandi gratia mittunt. haec faciunt reciperandorum suorum causa. sed con- 3
taminati facinore et capti compendio ex direptis bonis, quod ea res
ad multos pertinebat, et timore poenae exterriti consilia clam de
bello inire incipiunt ciuitatesque reliquas legationibus sollicitant.
quae tametsi Caesar intellegebat, tamen quam mitissime potest 4
legatos appellat: nihil se propter inscientiam leuitatemque uulgi
grauius de ciuitate iudicare neque de sua in Haeduos beneuolentia
deminuere. ipse maiorem Galliae motum exspectans, ne ab omni- 5
bus ciuitatibus circumsisteretur, consilia inibat quemadmodum a
Gergouia discederet ac rursus omnem exercitum contraheret, ne
profectio nata a timore defectionis similisque fugae uideretur.

Haec cogitanti accidere uisa est facultas bene gerendae rei. **44**
nam cum in minora castra operis perspiciendi causa uenisset,
animaduertit collem qui ab hostibus tenebatur nudatum hominibus, qui superioribus diebus uix prae multitudine cerni poterat.
admiratus quaerit ex perfugis causam, quorum magnus ad eum 2
cotidie numerus confluebat: constabat inter omnes – quod iam 3
ipse Caesar per exploratores cognouerat – dorsum esse eius iugi
prope aequum, sed hunc siluestrem et angustum, qua esset aditus
ad alteram partem oppidi; huic loco uehementer illos timere nec 4
iam aliter sentire, uno colle ab Romanis occupato, si alterum ami-
sissent, quin paene circumuallati atque omni exitu et pabulatione

---

42.4 inclinatam U inclitam T¹   42.6 in *suppl. editio princeps*   44.3 hunc silues-
trem] siluestre β   44.4 quin] non dubitari (dubitare T¹) quin β

interclusi uiderentur. ad hunc muniendum omnes a Vercingetorige euocatos.

45 Hac re cognita Caesar mittit complures equitum turmas eo de media nocte; imperat his ut paulo tumultuosius omnibus locis
2 peruagentur. prima luce magnum numerum iumentorum ex castris mulorumque produci deque his stramenta detrahi mulionesque cum cassidibus equitum specie ac simulatione collibus
3 circumuehi iubet. his paucos addit equites qui latius ostentationis causa uagentur. longo circuitu easdem omnes iubet petere
4 regiones. haec procul ex oppido uidebantur, ut erat a Gergouia despectus in castra, neque tanto spatio certi quid esset explorari
5 poterat. legionem unam eodem iugo mittit et paulum progressam
6 inferiore constituit loco siluisque occultat. augetur Gallis suspicio
7 atque omnes illo ad munitionem copiae traducuntur. uacua castra hostium Caesar conspicatus tectis insignibus suorum occultatisque signis militaribus raros milites, ne ex oppido animaduerterentur, ex maioribus castris in minora traducit legatisque, quos singulis
8 legionibus praefecerat, quid fieri uelit ostendit. in primis monet ut contineant milites, ne studio pugnandi aut spe praedae longius
9 progrediantur; quid iniquitas loci habeat incommodi proponit: hoc una celeritate posse euitari; occasionis esse rem, non proelii.
10 his rebus expositis signum dat et ab dextra parte alio ascensu eodem tempore Haeduos mittit.

46 Oppidi murus a planitie atque initio ascensus recta regione, si
2 nullus amfractus intercederet, mille CC passus aberat. quidquid hu[i]c circuitus ad molliendum cliuum accesserat, id spatium
3 itineris augebat. a medio fere colle in longitudinem, ut natura montis ferebat, ex grandibus saxis sex pedum murum quo nostrorum impetum tardarent praeduxerant Galli, atque inferiore omni spatio uacuo relicto superiorem partem collis usque ad
4 murum oppidi densissimis castris compleuerant. milites dato signo celeriter ad munitionem perueniunt eamque transgressi
5 trinis castris potiuntur; ac tanta fuit in castris capiendis celeritas, ut Teutomatus, rex Nitiobrogum, subito in tabernaculo oppressus,

45.1 eo de *dett.*, *Aldina* eodem β eisdem α peruagerentur U uagarentur α
45.2 impedimentorum ω *corr. Ciacconius* **45.9** euitari *Paul* mutari α uitari β
46.1 mille CC **B** mil. CC **A** CC β mille *Klotz* **46.2** huic ω *corr. Vascosanus*
46.3 nostrum ω *corr. recc.*

ut meridie conquieuerat, superiore corporis parte nuda uulnerato equo uix se ex manibus praedantium militum eriperet. Consecutus id quod animo proposuerat, Caesar receptui cani **47** iussit legionisque decimae, quacum erat, continuo signa constiterunt. at reliquarum legionum milites non exaudito sono tubae, 2 quod satis magna ualles intercedebat, tamen a tribunis militum legatisque, ut erat a Caesare praeceptum, retinebantur. sed elati 3 spe celeris uictoriae et hostium fuga superiorumque temporum secundis proeliis nihil adeo arduum sibi existimabant quod non uirtute consequi possent, neque finem prius sequendi fecerunt quam muro oppidi portisque appropinquarunt. tum uero 4 ex omnibus urbis partibus orto clamore, qui longius aberant repentino tumultu perterriti, cum hostem intra portas esse existimarent, sese ex oppido eiecerunt. matres familiae de muro 5 uestem argentumque iactabant et pectore nudo prominentes passis manibus obtestabantur Romanos ut sibi parcerent neu, sicut Auarici fecissent, ne a mulieribus quidem atque infantibus abstinerent; nonnullae de muro per manus demissae sese militibus 6 tradebant. L. Fabius, centurio legionis VIII, quem inter suos eo 7 die dixisse constabat excitari se Auaricensibus praemiis neque commissurum ut prius quisquam murum ascenderet, tres suos nactus manipulares atque ab his subleuatus murum ascendit, eos ipse rursus singulos exceptans in murum extulit.

Interim ii qui ad alteram partem oppidi, ut supra demonstrau- **48** imus, munitionis causa conuenerant, primo exaudito clamore, inde etiam crebris nuntiis incitati oppidum a Romanis teneri, praemissis equitibus magno cursu eo contenderunt. eorum ut quisque 2 primus uenerat, sub muro consistebat suorumque pugnantium numerum augebat. quorum cum magna multitudo conuenisset, 3 matres familiae, quae paulo ante Romanis de muro manus tendebant, suos obtestari et more Gallico passum capillum ostentare liberosque in conspectum proferre coeperunt. erat Romanis nec 4 loco nec numero aequa contentio; simul et cursu et spatio pugnae defatigati non facile recentes atque integros sustinebant.

Caesar cum iniquo loco pugnari hostiumque augeri copias **49** uideret, praemetuens suis ad Titum Sextium legatum, quem

47.3 appropinquarent β   48.3 passum] sparsum β

minoribus castris praesidio reliquerat, misit ut cohortes ex castris celeriter educeret et sub infimo colle ab dextro latere hostium
2 constitueret, ut, si nostros loco depulsos uidisset, quo minus libere
3 hostes insequerentur terreret. ipse paulum ex eo loco cum legione progressus ubi constiterat, euentum pugnae exspectabat.
50 Cum acerrime comminus pugnaretur, hostes loco et numero, nostri uirtute confiderent, subito sunt Haedui uisi ab latere nostris aperto, quos Caesar ab dextra parte alio ascensu manus dis-
2 tinendae causa miserat. hi similitudine armorum uehementer nostros perterruerunt, ac tametsi dextris umeris exsertis animaduertebantur, quod insigne pactum esse consuerat, tamen id ipsum sui fallendi causa milites ab hostibus factum
3 existimabant. eodem tempore Lucius Fabius centurio quique una murum ascenderant circumuenti atque interfecti de muro
4 praecipitabantur. Marcus Petronius, eiusdem legionis centurio, cum portas excidere conatus esset, a multitudine oppressus ac sibi desperans multis iam uulneribus acceptis manipularibus suis, qui illum erant secuti, 'quoniam', inquit, 'me una uobiscum seruare non possum, uestrae quidem certe uitae prospiciam, quos
5 cupiditate gloriae adductus in periculum deduxi. uos data facultate uobis consulite.' simul in medios hostes irrupit duobusque
6 interfectis reliquos a porta paulum summouit. conantibus auxiliari suis 'frustra', inquit, 'meae uitae subuenire conamini, quem iam sanguis uiresque deficiunt. proinde abite, dum est facultas, uosque ad legionem recipite.' ita pugnans post paulo concidit ac suis saluti fuit.
51 Nostri cum undique premerentur, XLVI centurionibus amissis deiecti sunt loco. sed intolerantius Gallos insequentes legio decima tardauit, quae pro subsidio paulo aequiore loco con-
2 stiterat. hanc rursus XIII legionis cohortes exceperunt, quae ex castris minoribus eductae cum Tito Sextio legato locum ceperant
3 superiorem. legiones ubi primum planitiem attigerunt, infestis
4 contra hostes signis constiterunt. Vercingetorix ab radicibus collis suos intra munitiones reduxit. eo die milites sunt paulo minus septingenti desiderati.
52 Postero die Caesar contione aduocata temeritatem militum cupiditatemque reprehendit, quod sibi ipsi iudicauissent quo

50.2 pacatum ω corr. Heller   52.1 cupiditatemque militum α

procedendum aut quid agendum uideretur neque signo recipiendi
dato constitissent neque a tribunis militum legatisque retineri potuissent. exposuit quid iniquitas loci posset, quid ipse ad Auaricum   2
sensisset, cum sine duce et sine equitatu deprehensis hostibus
exploratam uictoriam dimisisset, ne paruum modo detrimentum
in contentione propter iniquitatem loci accideret. quanto opere   3
eorum animi magnitudinem admiraretur, quos non castrorum
munitiones, non altitudo montis, non murus oppidi tardare potuisset, tanto opere licentiam arrogantiamque reprehendere, quod
plus se quam imperatorem de uictoria atque exitu rerum sentire
existimarent. non minus se ab milite modestiam et continentiam   4
quam uirtutem atque animi magnitudinem desiderare.

    Hac habita contione et ad extremum oratione confirmatis militi-   53
bus ne ob hanc causam animo permouerentur neu quod iniquitas
loci attulisset id uirtuti hostium tribuerent, eadem de profectione
cogitans quae ante senserat, legiones ex castris eduxit aciemque
idoneo loco constituit. cum Vercingetorix nihilo minus in aequum   2
locum descenderet, leui facto equestri proelio atque eo secundo
in castra exercitum reduxit. cum hoc idem postero die fecisset,   3
satis ad Gallicam ostentationem minuendam militumque animos
confirmandos factum existimans in Haeduos mouit castra. ne tum   4
quidem insecutis hostibus tertio die ad flumen Elauer ‹reuersus›
pontem refecit eoque exercitum traduxit.

    Ibi a Viridomaro atque Eporedorige Haeduis appellatus discit   54
cum omni equitatu Litauiccum ad sollicitandos Haeduos profectum: opus esse ipsos antecedere ad confirmandam ciuitatem. etsi   2
multis iam rebus perfidiam Haeduorum perspectam habebat atque
eorum discessu admaturari defectionem ciuitatis existimabat,
tamen eos retinendos non censuit ne aut inferre iniuriam uideretur aut dare timoris aliquam suspicionem. discedentibus iis breuiter   3
sua in Haeduos merita exposuit, quos et quam humiles accepisset –
compulsos in oppida, multatos agris, omnibus ereptis sociis,
imposito stipendio, obsidibus summa cum contumelia extortis –
et quam in fortunam quamque in amplitudinem deduxisset, ut   4
non solum in pristinum statum redissent, sed omnium temporum
dignitatem et gratiam antecessisse uiderentur. his datis mandatis
eos ab se dimisit.

52.2 quid ipse ω quod ipse *Vielhaber*   **53.1** extremam orationem α
53.4 reuersus *suppl. Gertz*   **54.2** maturari β   **54.3** sociis] copiis α

55   Nouiodunum erat oppidum Haeduorum ad ripas Ligeris oppor-
 2   tuno loco positum. huc Caesar omnes obsides Galliae, frumentum,
      pecuniam publicam, suorum atque exercitus impedimentorum
 3   magnam partem contulerat; huc magnum numerum equorum
 4   huius belli causa in Italia atque Hispania coemptum miserat. eo
      cum Eporedorix Viridomarusque uenissent et de statu ciuitatis
      cognouissent – Litauiccum Bibracte ab Haeduis receptum (quod
      est oppidum apud eos maximae auctoritatis), Conuictolitauem
      magistratum magnamque partem senatus ad eum conuenisse,
      legatos ad Vercingetorigem de pace et amicitia concilianda
      publice missos – non praetermittendum tantum commodum
 5   existimauerunt. itaque interfectis Nouioduni custodibus quique eo
      negotiandi aut itineris causa conuenerant, pecuniam atque equos
 6   inter se partiti sunt; obsides ciuitatum Bibracte ad magistratum
 7   deducendos curauerunt; oppidum, quod ab se teneri non posse
 8   iudicabant, ne cui esset usui Romanis, incenderunt; frumenti quod
      subito potuerunt nauibus auexerunt, reliquum flumine atque
 9   incendio corruperunt. ipsi ex finitimis regionibus copias cogere,
      praesidia custodiasque ad ripas Ligeris disponere equitatumque
      omnibus locis iniciendi timoris causa ostentare coeperunt, si
      ab re frumentaria Romanos excludere aut adductos inopia
10   in prouinciam expellere possent. quam ad spem multum eos
      adiuuabat quod Liger ex niuibus creuerat, ut omnino uado non
      posse transiri uideretur.

56   Quibus rebus cognitis Caesar maturandum sibi censuit, si esset
      in perficiendis pontibus periclitandum ut, prius quam essent
 2   maiores eo coactae copiae, dimicaret. nam ne commutato consilio
      iter in prouinciam conuerteret – ut nemo ‹ne› tunc quidem nec-
      essario faciendum existimabat – cum infamia atque indignitas rei
      et oppositus mons Ceuenna uiarumque difficultas impediebat,
      tum maxime quod abiuncto Labieno atque iis legionibus quas una
 3   miserat uehementer timebat. itaque admodum magnis diurnis
      nocturnisque itineribus confectis contra omnium opinionem ad
 4   Ligerim uenit, uadoque per equites inuento pro rei necessitate
      opportuno, ut bracchia modo atque umeri ad sustinenda arma

55.5 aut itineris *om.* **α**   **55.9** ex prouintia expellere **α** prouintia excludere
β *corr. Nicasius*   **56.2** ne] ut **ω** *corr. Elberling*   ne² *suppl. Krebs,* non *suppl.*
Ciacconius   nemo tunc] ne metu **α**

liberi ab aqua esse possent, disposito equitatu qui uim fluminis refringeret atque hostibus primo aspectu perturbatis, incolumem exercitum traduxit, frumentumque in agris et pecoris copiam nactus, repleto his rebus exercitu iter in Senones facere instituit. 5

Dum haec apud Caesarem geruntur, Labienus eo supplemento **57** quod nuper ex Italia uenerat relicto Agedinci, ut esset impedimentis praesidio, cum IIII legionibus Lutetiam proficiscitur. id est oppidum Parisiorum positum in insula fluminis Sequanae. cuius 2 aduentu ab hostibus cognito magnae ex finitimis ciuitatibus copiae conuenerunt. summa imperii traditur Camulogeno Aulerco, qui 3 prope confectus aetate tamen propter singularem scientiam rei militaris ad eum est honorem euocatus. is cum animaduertisset 4 perpetuam esse paludem quae influeret in Sequanam atque illum omnem locum magnopere impediret, hic consedit nostrosque transitu prohibere instituit.

Labienus primo uineas agere, cratibus atque aggere paludem **58** explere atque iter munire conabatur. postquam id difficilius 2 confieri animaduertit, silentio e castris tertia uigilia egressus eodem quo uenerat itinere Metiosedum peruenit. id est oppidum 3 Senonum in insula Sequanae positum, ut paulo ante de Lutetia diximus. deprehensis nauibus circiter quinquaginta celeriterque 4 coniunctis atque eo militibus impositis et rei nouitate perterritis oppidanis, quorum magna pars erat ad bellum euocata, sine contentione oppido potitur. refecto ponte quem superioribus 5 diebus hostes resciderant, exercitum traducit et secundo flumine ad Lutetiam iter facere coepit. hostes re cognita ab iis qui 6 Metiosedo profugerant Lutetiam incendi pontesque eius oppidi rescindi iubent. ipsi profecti a palude in ripa Sequanae e regione Lutetiae contra Labieni castra considunt.

Iam Caesar a Gergouia discessisse audiebatur, iam de Haeduorum **59** defectione et secundo Galliae motu rumores afferebantur, Gallique in colloquiis interclusum itinere et Ligeri Caesarem inopia frumenti coactum in prouinciam contendisse confirmabant. Bellouaci autem defectione Haeduorum cognita, qui ante 2 erant per se infideles, manus cogere atque aperte bellum parare coeperunt. tum Labienus tanta rerum commutatione longe aliud 3

58.2 cumfieri **B** confici **Q**^{c} **58.4** deprenssis **A** deprensis **B** impositis] iniectis α

 4 sibi capiendum consilium atque antea senserat intellegebat, neque
    iam ut aliquid acquireret proelioque hostes lacesseret, sed ut
 5 incolumem exercitum Agedincum reduceret cogitabat. namque
    altera ex parte Bellouaci, quae ciuitas in Gallia maximam habet
    opinionem uirtutis, instabant, alteram Camulogenus parato
    atque instructo exercitu tenebat; tum legiones a praesidio atque
 6 impedimentis interclusas maximum flumen distinebat. tantis
    subito difficultatibus obiectis ab animi uirtute auxilium petendum
    uidebat.
60   Itaque sub uesperum consilio conuocato cohortatus ut ea quae
    imperasset diligenter industrieque administrarent, naues quas
    Metiosedo deduxerat singulas equitibus Romanis attribuit, et
    prima confecta uigilia IIII milia passuum secundo flumine silen-
 2 tio progredi ibique se exspectare iubet. quinque cohortes, quas
    minime firmas ad dimicandum esse existimabat, castris praesidio
 3 relinquit; quinque eiusdem legionis reliquas de media nocte cum
    omnibus impedimentis aduerso flumine magno tumultu proficisci
 4 imperat. conquirit etiam lintres: has magno sonitu remorum
    incitatas in eandem partem mittit. ipse post paulo silentio egressus
    cum tribus legionibus eum locum petit quo naues appelli iusserat.
61   Eo cum esset uentum, exploratores hostium ut omni flumi-
    nis parte erant dispositi, inopinantes, quod magna erat subito
 2 coorta tempestas, a nostris opprimuntur; exercitus equitatusque
    equitibus Romanis administrantibus, quos ei negotio praefecerat,
 3 celeriter transmittitur. uno fere tempore sub lucem hostibus
    nuntiatur   in   castris   Romanorum   praeter   consuetudinem
    tumultuari et magnum ire agmen aduerso flumine sonitumque
    remorum in eadem parte exaudiri et paulo infra milites nauibus
 4 transportari. quibus rebus auditis, quod existimabant tribus locis
    transire legiones atque omnes perturbatos defectione Haeduorum
 5 fugam parare, suas quoque copias in tres partes distribuerunt. nam
    praesidio e regione castrorum relicto et parua manu Metiosedum
    uersus missa, quae tantum progrederetur quantum naues
    processissent, reliquas copias contra Labienum duxerunt.
62   Prima luce et nostri omnes erant transportati et hostium acies
 2 cernebatur. Labienus milites cohortatus ut suae pristinae uirtutis

et tot secundissumorum proeliorum retinerent memoriam atque
ipsum Caesarem, cuius ductu saepenumero hostes superassent,
praesentem adesse existimarent, dat signum proelii. primo 3
concursu ab dextro cornu, ubi septima legio constiterat, hostes
pelluntur atque in fugam coiciuntur; ab sinistro, quem locum 4
duodecima legio tenebat, cum primi ordines hostium transfixi
pilis concidissent, tamen acerrime reliqui resistebant, nec dabat
suspicionem fugae quisquam. ipse dux hostium Camulogenus 5
suis aderat atque eos cohortabatur. at incerto etiamnunc exitu 6
uictoriae, cum a septima legione tribunis esset nuntiatum quae
in sinistro cornu gererentur, post tergum hostium legionem
ostenderunt signaque intulerunt. ne eo quidem tempore quisquam 7
loco cessit, sed circumuenti omnes interfectique sunt. eandem 8
fortunam tulit Camulogenus. at ii qui praesidio contra castra
Labieni erant relicti, cum proelium commissum audissent, subsidio
suis ierunt collemque ceperunt, neque nostrorum militum
uictorum impetum sustinere potuerunt. sic, cum suis fugientibus 9
permixti, quos non siluae montesque texerunt, ab equitatu sunt
interfecti. hoc negotio confecto Labienus reuertitur Agedincum, 10
ubi impedimenta totius exercitus relicta erant: inde cum omnibus
copiis ad Caesarem peruenit.

    Defectione Haeduorum cognita bellum augetur. legationes **63**
in omnes partes circummittuntur: quantum gratia, auctoritate, 2
pecunia ualent, ad sollicitandas ciuitates nituntur. nacti obsides 3
quos Caesar apud eos deposuerat, horum supplicio dubitantes
territant. petunt a Vercingetorige Haedui ut ad se ueniat 4
rationesque belli gerendi communicet. re impetrata contendunt 5
ut ipsis summa imperi tradatur. re in controuersiam deducta
totius Galliae concilium Bibracte indicitur. eodem conueniunt 6
undique frequentes. multitudinis suffragiis res permittitur: ad
unum omnes Vercingetorigem probant imperatorem. ab hoc 7
concilio Remi, Lingones, Treueri afuerunt: illi, quod amicitiam
Romanorum sequebantur; Treueri, quod aberant longius et ab
Germanis premebantur, quae fuit causa quare toto abessent
bello et neutris auxilia mitterent. magno dolore Haedui ferunt 8
se deiectos principatu, queruntur fortunae commutationem et

62.2 secundissimorum α   **62.6** a septima legione] VII legionis β

Caesaris indulgentiam in se requirunt, neque tamen suscepto bello
9 suum consilium ab reliquis separare audent. inuiti summae spei
adulescentes Eporedorix et Viridomarus Vercingetorigi parent.
64 Ille imperat reliquis ciuitatibus obsides. denique ei rei constituit diem. huc omnes equites, XV milia numero, celeriter con-
2 uenire iubet. peditatu quem antea habuerit se fore contentum
dicit, neque fortunam temptaturum aut in acie dimicaturum, sed,
quoniam abundet equitatu, perfacile esse factu frumentationibus
3 pabulationibusque Romanos prohibere; aequo modo animo
sua ipsi frumenta corrumpant aedificiaque incendant, qua rei
familiaris iactura perpetuum imperium libertatemque se consequi
4 uideant. his constitutis rebus Haeduis Segusiauisque, qui sunt
finitimi [ei] prouinciae, decem milia peditum imperat. huc addit
5 equites octingentos. his praeficit fratrem Eporedorigis bellumque
6 inferre Allobrogibus iubet. altera ex parte Gabalos proximosque
pagos Aruernorum in Heluios, item Rutenos Cadurcosque ad fines
7 Volcarum Are‹co›micorum depopulandos mittit. nihilo minus
clandestinis nuntiis legationibusque Allobroges sollicitat, quorum
8 mentes nondum ab superiore bello resedisse sperabat. horum
principibus pecunias, ciuitati autem imperium totius prouinciae
pollicetur.
65 Ad hos omnes casus prouisa erant praesidia cohortium dua-
2 rum XX ad omnes partes opponebantur. Heluii sua sponte cum
finitimis proelio congressi pelluntur et Gaio Valerio Donotauro,
Caburi filio, principe ciuitatis, compluribusque aliis interfectis
3 intra oppida ac muros compelluntur. Allobroges crebris ad
Rhodanum dispositis praesidiis magna cum cura et diligentia
4 suos fines tuentur. Caesar quod hostes equitatu superiores esse
intellegebat et interclusis omnibus itineribus nulla re ex prouincia
atque Italia subleuari poterat, trans Rhenum in Germaniam mittit
ad eas ciuitates quas superioribus annis pacauerat, equitesque
ab his arcessit et leuis armaturae pedites qui inter eos proeliari
5 consuerant. eorum aduentu, quod minus idoneis equis utebantur,
a tribunis militum reliquisque [sed et] equitibus Romanis atque
euocatis equos sumit Germanisque distribuit.

64.1 ille] ipse **α**   **64.2** in acie] acie **β**   **64.4** ei **ω** *del. Stephanus*   **65.5** sed et
(sedent **B**¹) **ω** *del.* **Q**

Interea dum haec geruntur, hostium copiae ex Aruernis equi- **66**
tesque qui toti Galliae erant imperati conueniunt. magno horum 2
coacto numero, cum Caesar in Sequanos per extremos Lingonum
fines iter faceret, quo facilius subsidium prouinciae ferri posset, circiter milia passuum decem ab Romanis trinis castris Vercingetorix
consedit conuocatisque ad concilium praefectis equitum uenisse
tempus uictoriae demonstrat: fugere in prouinciam Romanos 3
Galliaque excedere. id sibi ad praesentem obtinendam libertatem 4
satis esse; ad reliqui temporis pacem atque otium parum profici:
maioribus enim coactis copiis reuersuros neque finem bellandi
facturos. proinde ⟨in⟩ agmine impeditos adoriantur. si pedites suis 5
auxilium ferant atque in eo morentur, iter confici non posse; si,
id quod magis futurum confidat, relictis impedimentis suae saluti
consulant, et usu rerum necessariarum et dignitate spoliatum
iri. nam de equitibus hostium, quin nemo eorum progredi modo 6
extra agmen audeat, ne ipsos quidem debere dubitare. id quo
maiore faciant animo, copias se omnes pro castris habiturum et
terrori hostibus futurum. conclamant equites sanctissimo iure 7
iurando confirmari oportere, ne tecto recipiatur, ne ad liberos,
ad parentes, ad uxorem aditum habeat, qui non bis per agmen
hostium perequitarit.

Probata re atque omnibus iure iurando adactis postero die in tres **67**
partes distributo equitatu duae se acies ab duobus lateribus ostendunt, una a primo agmine iter impedire coepit. qua re nuntiata 2
Caesar suum quoque equitatum tripertito diuisum contra hostem
ire iubet. pugnatur una omnibus in partibus. consistit agmen; 3
impedimenta inter legiones recipiuntur. si qua in parte nostri 4
laborare aut grauius premi uidebantur, eo signa inferri Caesar
aciemque conuerti iubebat; quae res et hostes ad insequendum
tardabat et nostros spe auxili confirmabat. tandem Germani 5
ab dextro latere summum iugum nacti hostes loco depellunt
fugientesque usque ad flumen ubi Vercingetorix cum pedestribus
copiis consederat persequuntur compluresque interficiunt. qua re 6
animaduersa reliqui ne circumuenirentur ueriti se fugae mandant.
omnibus locis fit caedes. tres nobilissimi Haedui capti ad Caesarem 7
perducuntur: Cotus, praefectus equitum, qui controuersiam cum

66.4 in *suppl. codd. recc.*   **66.6** ne ... debere] et ... non debere **α**

Conuictolitaui proximis comitiis habuerat, et Cauarillus, qui post
defectionem Litauicci pedestribus copiis praefuerat, et Eporedorix,
quo duce ante aduentum Caesaris Haedui cum Sequanis bello
contenderant.

68   Fugato omni equitatu Vercingetorix copias suas, ut pro castris
collocauerat, reduxit protinusque Alesiam (quod est oppidum
Mandubiorum) iter facere coepit celeriterque impedimenta ex cas-
2   tris educi et se subsequi iussit. Caesar impedimentis in proximum
collem deductis duabusque legionibus praesidio relictis secutus
hostes quantum diei tempus est passum, circiter tribus milibus ex
nouissimo agmine interfectis altero die ad Alesiam castra fecit.
3   perspecto urbis situ perterritisque hostibus, quod equitatu, qua
maxime parte exercitus confidebant, erant pulsi, adhortatus ad
laborem milites Alesiam circumuallare instituit.

69   Ipsum erat oppidum in colle summo, admodum edito loco, ut
2   nisi obsidione expugnari non posse uideretur. cuius collis radi-
3   ces duo duabus ex partibus flumina subluebant. ante id oppidum
4   planities circiter m. p. III in longitudinem patebat. reliquis ex
omnibus partibus colles mediocri interiecto spatio pari altitudinis
5   fastigio oppidum cingebant. sub muro, quae pars collis ad
orientem solem spectabat, hunc omnem locum copiae Gallorum
compleuerant fossamque et maceriam sex in altitudinem pedum
6   praeduxerant. eius munitionis quae ab Romanis instituebatur
7   circuitus X milia passuum tenebat. castra opportunis locis erant
posita ibique castella XXIII facta, quibus in castellis interdiu stationes ponebantur, ne qua subito eruptio fieret; haec eadem noctu
excubitoribus ac firmis praesidiis tenebantur.

70   Opere instituto fit equestre proelium in ea planitie quam
intermissam collibus tria milia passuum in longitudinem patere
supra demonstrauimus. summa ui ab utrisque contenditur.
2   laborantibus nostris Caesar Germanos summittit legionesque
pro castris constituit, ne qua subito irruptio ab hostium peditatu
3   fiat. praesidio legionum addito nostris animus augetur: hostes in
fugam coniecti se ipsi multitudine impediunt atque angustioribus
4   portis relictis coartantur. Germani acrius usque ad munitiones
5   persequuntur. fit magna caedes: nonnulli relictis equis fossam

69.6 X milia] XI milia α

transire et maceriam transcendere conantur. paulum legiones
Caesar quas pro uallo constituerat promoueri iubet. non minus 6
qui intra munitiones erant perturbantur. Galli ueniri ad se
confestim existimantes 'ad arma' conclamant; nonnulli perterriti
in oppidum irrumpunt. Vercingetorix iubet portas claudi, ne castra 7
nudentur. multis interfectis, compluribus equis captis Germani
sese recipiunt.

Vercingetorix priusquam munitiones ab Romanis perfici- 71
antur, consilium capit omnem ab se equitatum noctu dimittere. discedentibus mandat ut suam quisque eorum ciuitatem 2
adeat omnesque qui per aetatem arma ferre possint ad bellum
cogant. sua in illos merita proponit obtestaturque ut suae salutis 3
rationem habeant neu se optime de communi libertate meritum
hostibus in cruciatum dedant. quod si indiligentiores fuerint, milia
hominum delecta LXXX una secum interitura demonstrat. ratione 4
inita frumentum se exigue dierum XXX habere, sed paulo etiam
longius tolerari posse parcendo. his datis mandatis, qua erat nos- 5
trum opus intermissum, secunda uigilia silentio equitatum dimittit. frumentum omne ad se referri iubet; capitis poenam iis qui non 6
paruerint constituit. pecus, cuius magna erat copia a Mandubiis 7
compulsa, uiritim distribuit; frumentum parce et paulatim metiri
instituit. copias omnes quas pro oppido collocauerat in oppidum 8
recipit. his rationibus auxilia Galliae exspectare et bellum parat 9
administrare.

Quibus rebus cognitis ex perfugis et captiuis Caesar haec gen- 72
era munitionis instituit. fossam pedum XX derectis lateribus duxit,
ut eius fossae solum tantumdem pateret quantum summae fossae labra distarent. reliquas omnes munitiones ab ea fossa pedes 2
quadringentos reduxit, id hoc consilio, [quoniam tantum esset
necessario spatium complexus nec facile totum corpus corona
militum cingeretur,[ne de improuiso aut noctu ad munitiones
hostium multitudo aduolaret aut interdiu tela in nostros operi
destinatos conicere possent. hoc intermisso spatio, duas fossas 3
quindecim pedes latas, eadem altitudine perduxit; quarum
interiorem campestribus ac demissis locis aqua ex flumine deriuata
compleuit. post eas aggerem ac uallum XII pedum exstruxit. 4

72.2 corpus] opus T possent] posset β

huic loricam pinnasque adiecit grandibus ceruis eminentibus
ad commissuras pluteorum atque aggeris qui ascensum hostium
tardarent, et turres toto opere circumdedit, quae pedes LXXX
inter se distarent.

73   Erat eodem tempore et materiari et frumentari et tantas munitiones fieri necesse deminutis nostris copiis, quae longius a castris
progrediebantur; ac nonnumquam opera nostra Galli temptare
atque eruptionem ex oppido pluribus portis summa ui facere con-
2   abantur. quare ad haec rursus opera addendum Caesar putauit,
quo minore numero militum munitiones defendi possent. itaque
truncis arborum aut admodum firmis ramis abscisis atque horum
delibratis ac praeacutis cacuminibus perpetuae fossae quinos
3   pedes altae ducebantur. huc illi stipites demissi et ab infimo
4   reuincti, ne reuelli possent, ab ramis eminebant. quini erant
ordines coniuncti inter se atque implicati; quo qui intrauerant
5   se ipsi acutissimis uallis induebant. hos cippos appellabant. ante
hos obliquis ordinibus in quincuncem dispositis scrobes tres in
altitudinem pedes fodiebantur paulatim angustiore ad infimum
6   fastigio. huc teretes stipites feminis crassitudine ab summo
praeacuti et praeusti demittebantur, ita ut non amplius digitis
7   quattuor ex terra eminerent; simul confirmandi et stabiliendi
causa singuli ab infimo solo pedes terra exculcabantur, reliqua
pars scrobis ad occultandas insidias uiminibus ac uirgultis
8   integebatur. huius generis octoni ordines ducti ternos inter se
9   pedes distabant. id ex similitudine floris lilium appellabant. ante
haec taleae pedem longae ferreis hamis infixis totae in terram
infodiebantur mediocribusque intermissis spatiis omnibus locis
disserebantur; quos stimulos nominabant.

74   His rebus perfectis regiones secutus quam potuit aequissimas
pro loci natura XIIII milia passuum complexus pares eiusdem generis munitiones, diuersas ab his, contra exteriorem hostem perfecit, ut ne magna quidem multitudine, si ita accidat eius discessu,
2   munitionum praesidia circumfundi possent. ⟨ne⟩ aut⟨em⟩ cum
periculo ex castris egredi cogatur, dierum XXX pabulum frumentumque habere omnes conuectum iubet.

74.2 ⟨ne⟩ aut⟨em⟩] aut αT ut **U** corr. Hand

Dum haec apud Alesiam geruntur, Galli concilio principum **75**
indicto non omnes eos qui arma ferre possent, ut censuit
Vercingetorix, conuocandos statuunt, sed certum numerum
cuique ciuitati imperandum, ne tanta multitudine confusa nec
moderari nec discernere suos nec frumentandi rationem habere
possent. imperant Haeduis atque eorum clientibus, Segusiauis, **2**
Ambiuaretis, Aulercis Brannouicibus, Blannouiis, milia XXXV;
parem numerum Aruernis adiunctis Eleutetis, Cadurcis, Gabalis,
Vellauiis, qui sub imperio Aruernorum esse consuerunt; Sequanis, **3**
Senonibus, Biturigibus, Santonis, Rutenis, Carnutibus duo-
dena milia; Bellouacis decem; totidem Lemouicibus; octona
Pictonibus et Turonis et Parisiis et Heluetiis; Suessionibus,
Ambianis, Mediomatricis, Petrocoriis, Neruiis, Morinis,
Nitiobrogibus quina milia; Aulercis Cenomanis totidem;
Atrebatibus IIII; Veliocassi‹bu›s, Lexouiis et Aulercis Eburouicibus
terna; Rauracis et Bois † XXX † milia uniuersis ciuitatibus quae **4**
Oceanum attingunt quaeque eorum consuetudine Ar‹e›moricae
appellantur, quo sunt in numero Coriosolites, Redones, Ambibarii,
Caletes, Osismi, Veneti, † Lemouices †, Venelli. ex his Bellouaci **5**
suum numerum non contulerunt, quod se suo nomine atque
arbitrio cum Romanis bellum gesturos dicebant neque cuiusquam
imperio obtemperaturos; rogati tamen ab Commio pro eius
hospitio duo milia miserunt.

Huius opera Commii, ut antea demonstrauimus, fideli atque **76**
utili superioribus annis erat usus in Britannia Caesar. quibus ille
pro meritis ciuitatem eius immunem esse iusserat, iura legesque
reddiderat atque ipsi Morinos attribuerat. tamen tanta uniuersae **2**
Galliae consensio fuit libertatis uindicandae et pristinae belli
laudis recuperandae, ut neque beneficiis neque amicitiae
memoria mouerentur omnesque et animo et opibus in id bellum
incumberent. coactis equitum milibus VIII et peditum circiter **3**
CCL haec in Haeduorum finibus recensebantur numerusque
inibatur, praefecti constituebantur. Commio Atrebati, Viridomaro **4**
et Eporedorigi Haeduis, Vercassiuellauno Aruerno, consobrino
Vercingetorigis, summa imperii traditur. his delecti ex ciuitatibus

5 attribuuntur, quorum consilio bellum administraretur. omnes
6 alacres et fiduciae pleni ad Alesiam proficiscuntur, neque erat
omnium quisquam qui adspectum modo tantae multitudinis
sustineri posse arbitraretur, praesertim ancipiti proelio, cum
ex oppido eruptione pugnaretur, foris tantae copiae equitatus
peditatusque cernerentur.

77   At ii qui Alesiae obsidebantur, praeterita die qua auxilia suorum exspectauerant, consumpto omni frumento, inscii quid in
Haeduis gereretur, concilio coacto de exitu suarum fortunarum
2 consultabant, apud quos uariis dictis sententiis, quarum pars deditionem, pars, dum uires suppeterent, eruptionem censebat, non
praetereunda oratio Critognati uidetur propter eius singularem
3 ac nefariam crudelitatem. hic summo in Aruernis ortus loco et
magnae habitus auctoritatis, 'nihil', inquit, 'de eorum sententia
dicturus sum qui turpissimam seruitutem deditionis nomine
appellant, neque hos habendos ciuium loco neque ad concilium
4 adhibendos censeo. cum his mihi res sit qui eruptionem probant;
quorum in consilio omnium uestrum consensu pristinae residere
5 uirtutis memoria uidetur. animi est ista mollitia, non uirtus, paulisper inopiam ferre non posse. qui se ultro morti offerant faci-
6 lius reperiuntur quam qui dolorem patienter ferant. atque ego
hanc sententiam probarem (tantum apud me dignitas potest), si
7 nullam praeterquam uitae nostrae iacturam fieri uiderem, sed in
consilio capiendo omnem Galliam respiciamus, quam ad nostrum
8 auxilium concitauimus. quid enim hominum milibus LXXX
uno loco interfectis propinquis consanguineisque nostris animi
fore existimatis, si paene in ipsis cadaueribus proelio decertare
9 cogentur? nolite hos uestro auxilio exspoliare qui uestrae salutis
causa suum periculum neglexerunt, nec stultitia ac temeritate
uestra aut animi imbecillitate omnem Galliam prosternere et
10 perpetuae seruituti addicere. an, quod ad diem non uenerunt,
de eorum fide constantiaque dubitatis? quid ergo? Romanos in
illis ulterioribus munitionibus animine causa cotidie exerceri
11 putatis? si illorum nuntiis confirmari non potestis omni aditu
praesaepto, his utimini testibus appropinquare eorum aduentum;
12 cuius rei timore exterriti diem noctemque in opere uersantur. quid

77.1 concilii **B** consilio **A**   **77.8** quid enim] quid in **α** quid **β** *corr. Frigell*

ergo mei consili est? facere quod nostri maiores nequaquam
pari bello Cimbrorum Teutonumque fecerunt: qui in oppida
compulsi ac simili inopia subacti eorum corporibus qui aetate ad
bellum inutiles uidebantur uitam tolerauerunt, neque se hostibus
tradiderunt. cuius rei si exemplum non haberemus, tamen libertatis 13
causa institui et posteris prodi pulcherrimum iudicarem. nam 14
quid illi simile bello fuit? depopulata Gallia Cimbri magnaque
illata calamitate finibus quidem nostris aliquando excesserunt
atque alias terras petiuerunt; iura, leges, agros, libertatem nobis
reliquerunt. Romani uero quid petunt aliud aut quid uolunt, nisi 15
inuidia adducti quos fama nobiles potentesque bello cognouerunt,
horum in agris ciuitatibusque considere atque his aeternam
iniungere seruitutem? neque enim umquam alia condicione
bella gesserunt. quodsi ea quae in longinquis nationibus geruntur 16
ignoratis, respicite finitimam Galliam, quae in prouinciam redacta
iure et legibus commutatis securibus subiecta perpetua premitur
seruitute.'

Sententiis dictis constituunt ut ii qui ualetudine aut aetate **78**
inutiles sint bello oppido excedant; atque omnia prius experiantur
quam ad [e]Critognati sententia‹m› descendant. illo tamen potius 2
utendum consilio, si res cogat atque auxilia morentur, quam aut
deditionis aut pacis subeundam condicionem. Mandubii, qui eos 3
oppido receperant, cum liberis atque uxoribus exire coguntur. hi
cum ad munitiones Romanorum accessissent, flentes omnibus precibus orabant ut se in seruitutem receptos cibo iuuarent. at Caesar 4
dispositis in uallo custodibus recipi prohibebat.

Interea Commius reliquique duces quibus summa imperii per- **79**
missa erat cum omnibus copiis ad Alesiam perueniunt et colle
exteriore occupato non longius mille passibus a nostris munitionibus considunt. postero die equitatu ex castris educto omnem 2
eam planitiem quam in longitudinem milia passuum III patere
demonstrauimus, complent pedestresque copias paulum ab eo
loco abditas in locis superioribus constituunt. erat ex oppido Alesia 3
despectus in campum. concurritur his auxiliis uisis; fit gratulatio
inter eos, atque omnium animi ad laetitiam excitantur. itaque 4
productis copiis ante oppidum considunt et proximam fossam
cratibus integunt atque aggere explent seque ad eruptionem atque
omnes casus comparant.

AA+PC

80   Caesar [omni exercitu ad utramque partem munitionis disposito
     ut, si usus ueniat, suum quisque locum teneat et nouerit] equitatum
2   ex castris educi et proelium committi iubet. erat ex omnibus castris
     quae summum undique iugum tenebant despectus, atque omnes
3   milites intenti pugnae prouentum exspectabant. Galli inter equites
     raros sagittarios expeditosque [leuis armaturae] interiecerant qui
     suis cedentibus auxilio succurrerent et nostrorum equitum impet-
     us sustinerent, ab his complures de improuiso uulnerati proelio
4   excedebant. cum suos pugna superiores esse Galli confiderent et
     nostros multitudine premi uiderent, ex omnibus partibus et ii qui
     munitionibus continebantur et ii qui ad auxilium conuenerant
5   clamore et ululatu suorum animos confirmabant. quod in con-
     spectu omnium res gerebatur neque recte ac turpiter factum cel-
     ari poterat, utrosque et laudis cupiditas et timor ignominiae ad
6   uirtutem excitabat. cum a meridie prope ad solis occasum dubia
     uictoria pugnaretur, Germani una in parte confertis turmis in
7   hostes impetum fecerunt eosque propulerunt; quibus in fugam
8   coniectis sagittarii circumuenti interfectique sunt. item ex reliquis
     partibus nostri cedentes usque ad castra insecuti sui colligendi
9   facultatem non dederunt. at ii qui ab Alesia processerant maesti
     prope uictoria desperata se in oppidum receperunt.
81   Uno die intermisso Galli atque hoc spatio magno cratium, scala-
     rum, harpagonum numero effecto media nocte silentio ex castris
2   egressi ad campestres munitiones accedunt. subito clamore sub-
     lato [qua significatione qui in oppido obsidebantur de suo aduen-
     tu cognoscere possent,] crates proicere, fundis, sagittis, lapidibus
     nostros de uallo proturbare reliquaque quae ad oppugnationem
3   pertinent parant administrare. eodem tempore clamore exaudito
4   dat tuba signum suis Vercingetorix atque ex oppido educit. nostri,
     ut superioribus diebus suus cuique erat locus attributus, ad
     munitiones accedunt; fundis, librilibus sudibusque quas in opere
5   disposuerant [ac glandibus] Gallos proterrent. prospectu tenebris
     adempto multa utrimque uulnera accipiuntur. complura tormentis
6   tela coniciuntur. at Marcus Antonius et Gaius Trebonius legati,
     quibus hae partes ad defendendum obuenerant, qua ex parte

---

80.1 munitionum **α**   **80.2** omnes milites intenti] omnium militum intenti animi **β** prouentum pugnae **β**   **80.3** leuis armaturae *secl. Krebs*   **80.5** ac] aut **U**
81.4 ac glandibus *secl. Krebs*

nostros premi intellexerant, his auxilio ex ulterioribus castellis
deductos summittebant.

Dum longius a munitione aberant Galli, plus multitudine telorum **82**
proficiebant; posteaquam propius successerunt, aut se ipsi stimulis
inopinantes induebant aut in scrobes delati transfodiebantur aut ex
[uallo ac turribus] traiecti pilis muralibus interibant. multis undique 2
uulneribus acceptis nulla munitione perrupta, cum lux appeteret,
ueriti ne ab latere aperto ex superioribus castris eruptione
circumuenirentur, se ad suos receperunt. at interiores, dum ea 3
quae a Vercingetorige ad eruptionem praeparata erant proferunt,
priores fossas explent, diutius in his rebus administrandis
morati prius suos discessisse cognouerunt, quam munitionibus
appropinquarent. ita re infecta in oppidum reuerterunt.

Bis magno cum detrimento repulsi Galli quid agant con- **83**
sulunt. locorum peritos adhibent: ex his superiorum castrorum
situs munitionesque cognoscunt. erat a septentrionibus collis, 2
quem propter magnitudinem circuitus opere circumplecti non
potuerant nostri, necessarioque paene iniquo loco et leniter
decliui castra fecerant. haec Gaius Antistius Reginus et Gaius 3
Caninius Rebilus legati cum duabus legionibus obtinebant. cognitis 4
per exploratores regionibus duces hostium LX milia ex omni
numero deligunt earum ciuitatum, quae maximam uirtutis
opinionem habebant. quid quoque pacto agi placeat occulte 5
inter se constituunt; adeundi tempus definiunt cum meridie‹s›
esse uideatur. his copiis Vercassiuellaunum Aruernum, unum ex 6
quattuor ducibus, propinquum Vercingetorigis, praeficiunt. ille 7
ex castris prima uigilia egressus prope confecto sub lucem itinere
post montem se occultauit militesque ex nocturno labore sese
reficere iussit. cum iam meridies appropinquare uideretur, ad ea 8
castra quae supra demonstrauimus contendit; eodemque tempore
equitatus ad campestres munitiones accedere et reliquae copiae
pro castris sese ostendere coeperunt.

Vercingetorix ex arce Alesiae suos conspicatus ex oppido egre- **84**
ditur; crates, longurios, musculos, falces reliquaque quae eruptionis causa parauerat profert. pugnatur uno tempore omnibus locis, 2
atque omnia temptantur: quae minime uisa pars firma est, huc

82.3 praeparata erant] praeparauerant *ω corr. Aldina*   **83.5** meridie *ω corr. edd.*

3 concurritur. Romanorum manus tantis munitionibus distinetur nec
4 facile pluribus locis occurrit. multum ad terrendos nostros ualet
   clamor, qui post tergum pugnantibus existit; quod suum periculum
5 in aliena uident uirtute constare; omnia enim plerumque quae
   absunt uehementius hominum mentes perturbant.

85 Caesar idoneum locum nactus quid quaque ex parte geratur
2 cognoscit; laborantibus summittit. utrisque ad animum occurrit
3 unum esse illud tempus quo maxime contendi conueniat: Galli
   nisi perfregerint munitiones, de omni salute desperant; Romani
4 si rem obtinuerint, finem laborum omnium exspectant. maxime
   ad superiores munitiones laboratur, quo Vercassiuellaunum
   missum demonstrauimus. exiguum loci ad decliuitatem fastigium
5 magnum habet momentum. alii tela coniciunt, alii testudine facta
6 subeunt; defatigatis inuicem integri succedunt. agger ab uniuersis
   in munitionem coniectus et ascensum dat Gallis et ea quae in terra
   occultauerant Romani contegit; nec iam arma nostris nec uires
   suppetunt.

86 His rebus cognitis Caesar Labienum cum cohortibus sex subsi-
2 dio laborantibus mittit. imperat, si sustinere non possit, deductis
3 cohortibus eruptione pugnet; id nisi necessario ne faciat. ipse
   adit reliquos, cohortatur ne labori succumbant; omnium
   superiorum dimicationum fructum in eo die atque hora docet
4 consistere. interiores desperatis campestribus locis propter
   magnitudinem munitionum loca praerupta atque ex ascensu
5 temptant; huc ea quae parauerant conferunt. multitudine telorum
   ex turribus propugnantes deturbant, aggere et cratibus fossas
   explent, falcibus uallum ac loricam rescindunt.

87 Mittit primum Brutum adulescentem cum cohortibus Caesar,
   post cum aliis Gaium Fabium legatum; postremo ipse, cum uehe-
2 mentius pugnaretur, integros subsidio adducit. restituto proelio
   ac repulsis hostibus eo quo Labienum miserat contendit. cohortes
   IIII ex proximo castello deducit, equitum partem se sequi, partem circumire exteriores munitiones et a tergo hostes adoriri
3 iubet. Labienus postquam neque aggeres neque fossae uim
   hostium sustinere poterant, coactis una de XL cohortibus quas ex
   proximis praesidiis deductas fors obtulit, Caesarem per nuntios

84.4 uirtute] salute *α*   **85.4** exiguum] iniquum *a*   **86.4** atque *om. a*

facit certiorem quid faciendum existimet. accelerat Caesar ut
proelio intersit.
Eius aduentu ex colore uestitus cognito, quo insigni in proe- **88**
liis uti consueuerat, turmisque equitum et cohortibus uisis quas
se sequi iusserat, ut de locis superioribus haec decliuia et deuexa
cernebantur, hostes proelium committunt. utrimque clam-**2**
ore sublato excipit rursus ex uallo atque omnibus munitionibus clamor. nostri omissis pilis gladiis rem gerunt. repente post **3**
tergum equitatus cernitur. cohortes aliae appropinquant. hostes
terga uertunt; fugientibus equites occurrunt: fit magna caedes.
Sedullus, dux et princeps Lemouicum, occiditur. Vercassiuellaunus **4**
Aruernus uiuus in fuga comprehenditur. signa militaria LXXIIII
ad Caesarem referuntur. pauci ex tanto numero se incolumes in
castra recipiunt. conspicati ex oppido caedem et fugam suorum **5**
desperata salute copias a munitionibus reducunt. fit protinus hac **6**
re audita ex castris Gallorum fuga. quod nisi crebris subsidiis ac
totius diei labore milites essent defessi, omnes hostium copiae
deleri potuissent. de media nocte missus equitatus nouissimum **7**
agmen consequitur: magnus numerus capitur atque interficitur;
reliqui ex fuga in ciuitates discedunt.
Postero die Vercingetorix concilio conuocato id bellum se sus- **89**
cepisse non suarum necessitatum sed communis libertatis causa
demonstrat, et quoniam sit Fortunae cedendum, ad utramque rem **2**
se illis offerre, seu morte sua Romanis satisfacere seu uiuum tradere
uelint. mittuntur de his rebus ad Caesarem legati. iubet arma tradi, **3**
principes produci. ipse in munitione pro castris consedit: eo duces **4**
producuntur. Vercingetorix deditur, arma proiciuntur. reseruatis **5**
Haeduis atque Aruernis, si per eos ciuitates recuperare posset,
ex reliquis captiuis toti exercitui capita singula praedae nomine
distribuit.
His rebus confectis in Haeduos proficiscitur; ciuitatem **90**
recipit. eo legati ab Aruernis missi: quae imperaret se facturos **2**
pollicentur. imperat magnum numerum obsidum. [legiones in **3**
hiberna mittit.] captiuorum circiter XX milia Haeduis Aruernisque

---

88.3 emissis β   88.4 asedullus α : sedulius β *corr. de Saulcy*   89.2 fortunae sit β
90.3 legiones … mittit *post* reddit *transposuit Kraffert, ante* captiuorum *habet* ω

4 reddit. ‹legiones in hiberna mittit.› Titum Labienum duabus cum
legionibus et equitatu in Sequanos proficisci iubet; huic Marcum
5 Sempronium Rutilum attribuit. Gaium Fabium legatum et Lucium
Minucium Basilum cum legionibus duabus in Remis collocat
6 ne quam a finitimis Bellouacis calamitatem accipiant, Gaium
Antistium Reginum in Ambiuaretos, Titum Sextium in Bituriges,
Gaium Caninium Rebilum in Rutenos cum singulis legionibus
7 mittit. Quintum Tullium Ciceronem et Publium Sulpicium
Cauilloni et Matiscone in Haeduis ad Ararim rei frumentariae
8 causa collocat. ipse Bibracte hiemare constituit. his rebus ex litteris
cognitis Romae dierum XX supplicatio redditur.

90.8 his rebus ex litteris *Krebs* his litteris **α** huius anni rebus **β** his rebus litteris
Aldina

COMMENTARY

1–5 THE RESISTANCE "BEGINS"

The resistance "begins" when the Carnutes – after meetings with nearby tribes triggered by events in Rome – raid Cenabum. News reaches Gergovia, where V. seizes control and strategizes to confine C. in northern Italy, threaten *Gallia transalpina*, and check the Aedui. There was, normally, no warfare in winter (Deyber 2009: 95–98); so, the events forced C.'s hand (nn. on 6, 10.1).

The first chapters set the scene, a common technique in historiography, esp. visible in Polybius' προκατασκευή, "preparatory introduction"; other *commentarii* begin similarly (*IV*, *BC* 1), but the parallels with *I* are particularly pronounced (*Introd.* 3c): C. is away from Gaul (1n. *Gallia*), his arrival delayed until readers have learnt of the trouble brewing (partly because of one man's regal aspirations (4.1n. *ob ... interfectus*); worse, the Aedui cannot be trusted (5.6n. *eane ... adducti*). The dramatic narrative – partly composed from the reports of C.'s *legati* (cf. 5.3; Rambaud 53; *Introd.* 3a) – is problematic: first, the chronology founders (1n.); then, we know that (a) the Carnutes and allies <u>continued</u> their fight from the year(s) before (nn. on 1.4 *Acconis*, 2.1 *Carnutes*; Plut. *Caes.* 25.2; Jullian 1977: 88–90), (b) Commius galvanized the Belgae during the same winter (Hirt, 8.23.3; cf. 76.1–2n.), and (c) Drapes attacked the supply lines of the wintering legions (Hirt. 8.30.1; 5n.). C.'s "déformation" generates a *bellum subitum* and thus a proper opening with an exculpatory bend (Rambaud 301–04; *Introd.* 3c), and it establishes V. as "the face of the resistance" early on (4n.). But his plotting hand is visible: V.'s stepping onto the scene is forced (nn. on 3.3, 4.1 *simili ratione*; Florus and Cassius Dio would smooth it out [*Epit.* 3.10.21; 40.33.1]); and his standing is clearly enhanced by the tribes C. lists as recruited by him, when they must have participated in the *concilia* already (where C. glosses them over [4.6n.]). The Carnutes' disappearance from *VII* is odd, too (2.1n. *Carnutes*); and if the likely location of the *concilia* and the mention of *Gutuater* indicate the participation of the druids (1.4n. *siluestribus*, 3.1n. *Gutuatro*; cf. 6.13.5 *fere de omnibus controuersiis ... constituunt*), their presence is also omitted (which would, however, cohere with C.'s general taciturnity in religious matters [Rüpke 2018: 61–63]).

Roman slogans color the account (2.1 *communis salus*, 4.6 *omnium consensu*), incl. incriminatory terms and motifs associated with Catiline and Clodius (1.1): The intention "to free" Gaul (1.5 *in libertatem uindicent*), the cynical promotion of *libertas* (4.4), a "following" of *egentes ac perditi* (4.3), recklessness and desperation (5.1n. *audaciae*, 3.1 *desperatis*) all intimate that the Gallic uprising was "born of *perfidia*, brigandage and revolutionary fervor" (Barlow 1998: 153). Hirt. 8.1 is modelled after this paragraph.

1 News of events in Rome incites Gauls to hold a war council. C. is in northern Italy, likely Ravenna (Cic. *Att.* 7.1.4 [with Shackleton Bailey], Flor. *Epit.* 1.45.22).

The dramatized (nn. on §§2–8, 4–8, §4 *siluestribus*) plot is historically implausible: time constraints alone necessitate that the Gauls conspired *long before* news of Clodius' death could have arrived (*CG* 736; *Introd.* 2c [fn.66]; C. himself may let on: *liberius atque audacius*, i.e. than before). But this plot combines with an intimation of hesitancy (nn. on *inire incipiunt, conciliis, omnibus ... praemiis, deposcunt*; 2.1 *agitatis*) to corroborate his assertion of *quieta Gallia* and blame events at home for troubles abroad. The *concilia* probably took place in Carnutan territory (§4n. *locis*); all legions wintered farther east (§1.2n. *exercitum*), which may bespeak C.'s lack of foresight and account for his temporary bewilderment (§6.2n. *magna difficultate*).

1.1 C. appropriates language from the *scu* to justify his levies (*caede, dilectum ... habere*). Roman politics is rarely acknowledged as a factor in *BG* (1.39.2, 44.12, 6.1, 7.6.1); yet its significance is pervasive (Maier 1978). **Quieta Gallia**: a hallmark of military reports, the abl. absolute is uncommonly frequent and varied in C. (Gotoff 1984: 9–11, Adams 2005: 74–75). The claim itself is typical of the rhetoric of Roman imperialism (Pelling 2011: 219; cf. 65.4n. *pacauerat*) and appears variously (2.35.1, 3.7.1, 28.1, 5.58.7; cf. Hirt. 8.1.1); it also justifies C.'s absence (Adcock 1956: 43). In fact, Cic.'s statement in 56, *nationes* (sc. *Gallicae*) ... *nondum satis firma pace deuinctae*, remained valid even after 52 (*Prou. cons.* 19; *Introd.* 2c). *Gallia* is placed similarly prominently in *I*, perhaps intentionally. **Caesar**, except for *BC* 3.1.1, refers to himself by his cognomen (which Luc. 3.135–40 may parody), and mostly in the third person (*Introd.* 3c). The second most frequent substantive in the *commentarii*, it begins 10 percent of all chapters, and appears predominantly in the nominative (Kollmann 1977). **ut constituerat** echoes 6.44.3 *ut instituerat*. Such parentheses often highlight C.'s intentionality and foresight (9.1n. *opinione praeceperat*). **in Italiam ... proficiscitur**: formulaic, it here links back to the previous book (6.44.3 *in Italiam ad conuentus agendos profectus est*; cf. 1.54.3); similarly 2.1.1, 3.1.1. As a compositional technique, such linking can be traced back to Hom. *Il.* (9.713 + 10.2). C. considers *G. cisalpina/citerior* as part of *Italia*, hence: *iuniores Italiae ... dilectum tota prouincia* (cf. 65.4). He thus anticipates its enfranchisement in 49 (Gruen 1974: 410n.16; on "Italia," cf. Williams

2001: 127–37). C. normally (5.1.1 *consuerat*) spent winters in northern Italy on administrative duty but also "to pay attention to affairs in Rome" (Plut. *Caes.* 20.1; cf. Cass. Dio 40.32.5); in 54, 52, and 51, however, he wintered in Gaul (5.53.3, 7.90.7, 8.46.6, 49.1). **ad conuentus agendos** "to hold the assizes (*OLD conuentus* 4)." *ad* + gerundive phrase is typical administrative language (Coleman 2012: 194). A governor was expected *aestiuos mensis ... rei militari dare, hibernos iuris dictioni* (Cic. *Att.* 5.14.2; cf. 8.46.5; Lintott 1993: 50–59). **ibi**: adverbs in initial sentence position (*ibi*: 9.4, 16.2, 54.1) are a characteristic of simple, "popular narrative" (esp. if repeated [59.3–5 *tum ... tum*]; Adams 2016: 9). **cognoscit de**: C. often construes transitive verbs with *de* (12.1, 26.4, 55.4, 81.2). A verb's initial position generally serves emphasis, here of a dramatic development (Marouzeau 1938: 49–82); cf. nn. on 2.1 *profitentur*, 4.2 *prohibetur*, 67.2 *pugnatur*. A courier service kept C. *au courant* wherever he went (Cic. *QFr.* 2.13.3, 3.1.8, 7.6; Maier 1978: 82–83). **P. Clodii caede**: C.'s quoting from the *senatus consultum* (*P. Clodi caedem*, Asc. *Mil.* 44) explains *caedes*, which he does not normally use of individuals. It also supports the poorly attested initial (which the context requires anyway [cf. Adams 1978: 146]); cf. §4n. *morte*, 3.1n. *Citam*. P. Clodius (*RE* 48) Pulcher, who had emblazoned his agitations with *libertas* (4.4n.), was killed on 8 Dec. To rein in unrest, the senate passed the said *consultum ultimum* (Tatum 1999: 214–46). His death receives emphasis, as its position recalls consular year-names (4.1.1, 5.1.1), rather similar to Cic.'s argument that it marked a new era (*Mil.* 78, 98). C. had not severed his various ties with Clodius even after the Bona Dea scandal (Tatum 1999: 62–86). **de senatusque**: the preposition is preferable on semantic grounds ("[informed] of" rather than "by"). For the position of *-que*, cf. e.g. Cic. *De or.* 1.2 *inter nosque, Fin.* 1.3 *in reque*. **certior factus**, "informed" (*OLD certus* 12b), is an idiomatic expression of wide distribution but predominant in military narratives; it occurs 48x in *CC*. **ut** introduces an indirect command or else explicates the content of the *scu* (G-L 546n.2, 557). **iuniores** "men ... of military age" (*OLD*), ranging from 17 to 46. **coniurarent** "to be sworn in all at once" (*OLD* 1a; the meaning occurs only here in *CC*). Normally, recruits took the *sacramentum* individually; the *coniuratio*, Servius explains (*Aen.* 2.157, 7.612–14; Rüpke 1990: 70–75), *fit in tumultu, id est Italico bello et Gallico, quando uicinum urbis periculum singulos iurare non patitur*. In its other meaning, "to conspire," the verb casts a suggestive shadow over the Gallic meeting (§4). **dilectum tota prouincia habere**: the expression is formulaic (*BC* 1.2.2, 2.18.1, 6.3, 6.8, 9.4), but here echoes the *scu* that authorized Pompey (!) *ut ... dilectus ... tota Italia haberet*, Asc. 35, perhaps to suggest the legality of C.'s action (then again, C. had recruited legions of his own volition before [1.10.2,

2.2.1; Gelzer 123–24]). Since the *dilectus* required recruits to swear the *sacramentum* individually (Brunt 1971: 625–44), it sits oddly with *coniurare* (similarly Livy 41.5.4); cf. 7.5n. *supplementum.* **tota prouincia** = *G. cisalpina.*

1.2–8 C. dramatizes the background information in historiographical fashion (Gärtner 1975: 95n.84 lists all instances in *VII*). For the commonplace entanglement of domestic and foreign affairs, cf. Plancus' fear *ne ... gentes* [sc. *Gallicae*] *nostra mala suam putent occasionem,* [Cic.] *Fam.* 10.4.4. **eae**: demonstrative and relative connectives are a hallmark of C.'s style; the former dominate early Latin (Courtney 1999: 7). **transalpinam** refers to the territory of C.'s conquest in contrast to its only other instance in *CC* at 6.1[n.]. C.'s confusing geography: *Introd.* 2b. **addunt ... adfingunt**: this alliterative double recurs at Lucr. 5.164; cf. nn. on 16.3 *incertis*, 30.2 *prouidere*, 49.1 *praemetuens* (Krebs 2013). **ipsi ... Galli**: epithet and noun are distributed over both phrases (cf. Knox on Ov. *Her.* 1.92 *auidas ... manus*); sim. 14.9[n.] *sint ... proposita*, 20.2 *malle ... habere*, 20.6 *interuenerint ... gratiam.* **rumoribus** "by rumors" rather than "to (these) rumors"; C. often comments on Gallic rumormongering (4.5.1–3, 6.20.1–2, 7.59.1; *Introd.* 3g). Too little is known of the verse *rumoresque serunt uarios et multa requirunt* attributed to Bibaculus' *Ann. Belli Gallici* (*FLP* 195–200). **quod ... uidebatur**: parenthetical. The Gauls, reputed speakers (4n.), add "what is appropriate" (τὰ δέοντα, Thuc. 1.22.1); rhetoricians discuss this practice under *amplificatio* (*HLR* 400–09). **retineri ... uenire posse**: a chiastic arrangement. **Caesarem**: in a form of *coniunctio* (*Rhet. Her.* 4.38), C. often places the subject of two infinitives in the middle. **urbano** "Roman," first here in C. **in tantis dissensionibus** "because of (*OLD in* 40a–b) such fierce disagreements"; *tantus* "often takes its coloring from the noun it modifies" (Tarrant on Verg. *Aen.* 12.72). **exercitum**: two legions wintered amidst the Lingones, six among the Senones (4.6n.) at Agedincum (10.4n.), and two farther north-east at the western border of the Treveri (6.44.3; not the Hermeskeil fortress, in all likelihood [Hornung 2019: 215]).

1.3 hac impulsi occasione: this disjunctive word order is esp. frequent with demonstratives and quantitative terms. With two exceptions (*BC* 2.38.3, 3.40.4), C. reserves *impellere* for his enemies' impetuous behavior. It here alludes to the Gauls' stereotypical volatility, their obeying "passion rather than reasoning" (θυμῷ μᾶλλον ἢ λογισμῷ, Polyb. 2.35.3); cf. 20.5, 42.2. **se populi Romani imperio subiectos dolerent**: cf. Aug. *Anc.* 1.1 *orbem terrarum imperio populi Romani subiecit.* Genitive attributes generally precede their noun when contrastive or emphatic (Adams 1976: 80). Like other Roman leaders (*Introd.* 3g), C. acknowledges the resistance, most markedly at 3.10.3 and 5.7.8. The theme, missing from *VI* alone, culminates in *VII* (1.5+8, 4.4, 37.2+4, 64.3, 66.4, 71.3, 76.2, 77.13+14, 89.1), where it is frequently counterpointed by the moral discrediting of its proponents (3.1n. *desperatis*). **dolerent**: subj. of cause or character (G-L 626R; 631). C. mentions their pain twice more (*queruntur, miserantur*). **liberius atque audacius**: *atque* (*ac*) is C.'s favored connective for comparatives/ superlatives (Ringe 1880: 12). This pair appears in 1.18.2, is prefigured in Cic. *Rosc. Am.* 31 *audacter libereque*, and modified at *BC* 1.59.2 *minus libere, minus audacter*, cf. 5.1n. *audacia*. On the frequency of pairs in C. as a characteristic shared with the legal discourse, see Krebs 2018b: 120–21. **inire incipiunt** is a common pleonasm (Landgraf on Cic. *Rosc. Am.* 26 *primo ... coeperunt*), which recurs at 43.3. It may suggest hesitation (but cf. also 26.4n. *coeperunt*).

1.4–8 A miniature deliberative speech sets out "the motifs and beliefs which led the Gauls to rebel" (Murphy 1949: 123): The *exordium* mentions the troubles (*queruntur, miserantur*), a commonplace to make an audience well disposed (*Rhet. Her.* 1.8); the aim is put forth (*propositio*: *Galliam ... uindicare*), its feasibility demonstrated (*confirmatio*: *eius in primis ... facile esse*); the conclusion, affective more than recapitulatory (*HLR* 432), employs other commonplaces (*Rhet. Her.* 3.9 *uirtutem nullo tempore relinquendam*) and arouses pity (*Rhet. Her.* 2.50) by comparing their ancestors' glory with their own. The pain of the Aedui in 63.8 is presented in similar textbook fashion.

1.4 indictis ... principes Galliae conciliis: *concilium* and *consilium* are often confused in the MSS (*TLL* 4.45.14–23). Here *conciliis* (β) is preferable to *consiliis* (α), as C. reserves *concilium* for Gallic war councils (an influential choice [Bell 1995: 762]), *consilium* for Roman ones. He regularly encloses the subject to clarify the agent of the abl. absolute (DKM *ad* 2.11.2). The plural *concilia* may serve emphasis (H-S §25; cf. Clark on Cic. *Mil.* 17 *maiorum*) or else indicate several gatherings (perhaps hinting at hesitation); but the following (and 2.3 *concilio*) suggests one (final) meeting. A Gallic *concilium armatum* itself marked *initium belli* (5.56.2; Livy 21.20.1). Cf. 63.5n. *indicitur*. **inter se** is in its natural second position (19.1n. *hoc se*) but depends on *queruntur* more than *indictis* (cf. 24.5n. *omnis ... multitudo*). **principes** "chief men" (*OLD* 3a). As with all Roman terms applied to Gallic society (*interpretatio Romana* [*Introd.* 3g]), greater specificity is elusive (Lamoine 2003: 189n.10; Arnold 1995). **siluestribus ... locis**: woods are a stereotypical feature of the north (Nenninger 2001: 87–110; cf. 16.1n. *siluis*). The atmosphere is suitably sinister (cf. Hardie on Verg. *Aen.* 9.381–83). The Carnutes would have hosted the council: they "volunteered" to take the lead, attacked their town Cenabum, and

hosted the Druids' annual meetings (nn. on 2.1, 3.1; 6.13.8–10, 8.5.2).
Acconis morte: contrast §1 *caede* (on C.'s vocabulary of killing, see Opelt
1980; cf. §8n. *interfici*, 4.10n. *necat*). A leader of the Senones, he had
rebelled in 53 (6.4.1, 44.2). His name (*GPN* 297–98) may have reminded
educated Romans of ἄκκώ, "a bugbear" (LSJ). Names and their meanings
greatly interested ancient writers and readers, even bilingually (W-M on
Tac. *Ann.* 3.75.1); cf. *Index*, s.v. "names, telling." **posse**: emphatic position.
hunc = *huius* (sc. *Acconis*); cf. 4.2n. *hanc*. **casum ... recidere**: the *figura
etymologica* has a hint of grandiloquence (N-H on Hor. *Carm.* 2.10.11);
recidere, "rebound on" (*OLD* 2), occurs only here in C. **demonstrant. miserantur**: a chiastic arrangement.

1.5 communem Galliae fortunam: many writers prefer this arrangement,
when "a genitive depend[s] on a noun which is qualified by an adjective"
(Adams 1976: 80); but in *VII* exceptions are many. **omnibus** "all possible"
(*OLD* 6b). **pollicitationibus ac praemiis**: alliterative pairs are frequent in
Latin (Wölfflin 1977: 225–52, Courtney 1999: 3). This one is common in
C. and recurs slightly varied at 31.1. It is the first of many suggestions of
bribery (*Index*, s.v.; Plut. *Caes.* 25.3 "lots of money" may be extrapolated
from this); it undermines the Gauls' moral credibility just before they
invoke *libertas*. **deposcunt** "they demanded emphatically" (*OLD* 1a; only
here in *BG*). The prefix *de-* may express "thoroughness or completeness"
(*OLD* s.v.); cf. 31.4n. *deperierat*. The verb, in combination with the preceding expression, smacks of desperation. **sui capitis periculo** "at the risk of
their own lives." "Anteposition is the rule when the possessive adjective
is semantically prominent" (*OLS* 2.1072). The metonymic use of *caput* is
esp. common in legal contexts (cf. 71.6). The abl. is modal (G-L 399; cf.
DKM on 6.44.1) or of attendant circumstances (*NLS* §47, K-S 410–11),
the singular generic. **in libertatem uindicent**: the expression, "to free ...
from oppressive rule" (*OLD uindico* 3b; cf. 76.2), was used to claim as free
a slave (3a); it played a central role in Rome's factional rhetoric (Cic. *Brut.*
212, Aug. *Anc.* 1.1 with Cooley; Wirszubski 1950: 103–04). Its rhetorical
handiness appears in Hirt. 8.1.2. *libertas*, "independence from Rome,"
occurs 11x in *VII* (4x in *I–VI*): the dominant leitmotif (*Introd.* 3c), it rings
the narrative (89.1) and marks *VII* as the final book.

1.6 eius anticipates the *ut*-clause (K-S 625). **rationem esse habendam**: in
gerundival infinitives C. normally omits *esse* (DKM *ad* 1.7.4). **priusquam**:
C. (and "old Latin" [K-S II 366]) favors *priusquam* over *antequam* (only
BC 1.2.2, 3.11.1). **eorum** = *sua*. The temporal clause depends on the
ut-clause; in such a "double dependence," non-reflexive pronouns are
common (K-S 611). **clandestina consilia**: *clandestinus* recurs once in C. at

64.7. The collocation is attested in L. Crass. *Frg. Cic. Orat.* 223, Sis. *FRHist* F111, then 5x (esp. Livy) after C. The word reflects C.'s view (hardly the Gauls').

1.7 C.'s deliberation at 6.3–4 will echo the Gauls' reasoning. **id esse facile** recurs at 14.3. "*esse*" often follows an emphatic or focusing word, including demonstratives (Adams 1994a: 27). Rhetorical handbooks recommend emphasizing how "easily done" are the actions proposed (ῥάδια πραχθῆναι, *Rhet. Alex.* 1421b26). But it dooms the Gauls, as "easily" in contexts as this one regularly flags impending failure in historiography and C. (beginning at 1.2.2, 3.6; Pitcher 2018: 242–43). Moreover, merely the first of many empty promises, it contributes to the Gauls' "caractère caricatural" as naïve blusterers (14.3, 15.5, 19.3n. *inani simulatione*, 55.10, 64.2; Dangel 1995: 99). **neque legiones ... neque imperator**: the two-cola reprise *Caesar ab exercitu* in inverted order (as is typical [14.3n. *quod*]). **hibernis**: 1.2n. *exercitum.* The archaeological record of C.'s winter bases is scant (Fitzpatrick-Haselgrove 2019: xix); on the practice, see Dobson 2013. **peruenire possit**: the Gallic confidence is asserted so that C. can prove them wrong later (9.5n. *peruenisset*).

1.8 postremo ... interfici is a commonplace (Hdt. 9.17, Sall. *Cat.* 20.9 with Vretska); C. will rephrase it at *BC* 2.30.2. *interficere* is his commonest word of killing (cf. 1.4n. *morte*). **praestare** "to be preferable" (*OLD* 4). **quam ... recuperare**: 3.8.4 *ut in ea libertate quam a maioribus acceperint permanere ... malint.* The appeal to ancestral achievements is another commonplace (cf. 77.12): Sall. *Iug.* 31.17 *uos pro libertate quam ab illis* (sc. *maioribus*) *accepistis ...* (adapted from Thuc. 2.62.3), Verg. *Aen.* 10.282 *patrum laudes* (with Harrison). **gloriam libertatemque quam**: the relative regularly connects with one of the nouns only (K-S 16b).

2 The Gauls decide on war. The Carnutes, after "hesitation" (perhaps reflected in the meandering sentence), "volunteer" to lead (rather, they were in charge all along [cf. 1–5n.]).

The vocabulary and symbolism are sacral (cf. Cic. *Nat. D.* 1.13 *quid de ... sanctitate, caerimoniis, fide, iure iurando, ... existimandum sit – haec enim omnia ad hanc de dis inmortalibus quaestionem referenda sunt*), perhaps suitably so given the Carnutes' religious role (§1n. *Carnutes*). The gathered standards symbolize Gallic unity, which is highlighted by *communis salus* and corroborated by the repetition of the prefix *cum-* (*collatis, continetur, collaudatis, constituto, concilio*; cf. 4.2n. *ex-*).

2.1 His rebus agitatis: resumptive abl. absolutes are a hallmark of C.'s style (cf. 1.1n. *Quieta*); they seamlessly integrate discourse into the narrative

(C-L 71–86). *agitare* = "discuss" (*OLD* 18a, only here in C.), with a hint of frequency (cf. 1n.). **profitentur**: verbs governing an inf. often precede it. *profitentur* forms a chiasmus with *pollicentur*; the pairing is frequent (*TLL* 10.2.1715.35–36). **Carnutes**: situated in the heart of Gaul (6.13.10) in and around Loir-et-Cher (where Chartres is named after them [*TGF* 153]), with Cenabum (3.1) as a center, they hosted the Druids' annual meeting (6.13.8–10). C. made the Rome-friendly Tasgetius king, whose murder in 54 initiated their uprising (2.35.3, 5.25.3, 6.2.3); they will disappear after Cenabum, but continue their resistance the following year (8.31.4). Their etymology (< *carnon*, "trumpet" [*DLG* 106]; cf. κάρνον, LSJ) makes them fitting war leaders. **se** "[... that] *they* [would ...]"; its position is emphatic (contrast 4.6n. *celeriter sibi*). **nullum ... causa recusare**: *nullus*, "none at all," is more emphatic than *non* (K-S 824A.5); it forms a litotes (again 19.5, similarly *BC* 3.26.1) and a slight antithesis (with *communis*). *recusare* is derived from *causa* (E-M "*causa*"); their juxtaposition highlights the *figura etymologica* (cf. 1.4n. *recidere*). **communis salutis**: 2x in *V*, 3x in *VII* (21.3, 29.7; cf. 25.1, 85.3). The appeal is commonplace (e.g. Thuc. 6.80.2 τὴν τε κοινὴν ὠφελίαν τῇ Σικελίᾳ φυλάξαι), the phrase a favorite of Cic.'s (*Cat.* 1.12, 4.15; Winkler 1995: 16–35). Along with reff. to *communis fortuna/libertas* (nn. on 1.5, 4.4), it emphasizes that this battle was about *Gallia omnis* (4.6n. *omnium*). **principes** = *primi*; with *ex* only here in *CC*. **pollicentur**: C. forgoes *promittere*, the preferred verb in legal texts. The semantic difference Serv. proposes ("we promise [*pollicemur*] voluntarily but give assurance [*promittimus*]," on Verg. *Aen.* 1.237) may account for this choice (Odelman 1985).

2.2 "and since ... they could not give one another surety (*OLD cauere* 8) by means of hostages ..., they asked that it at least be sanctioned by a solemn oath before the assembled standards ... that they not be abandoned ...." **in praesentia** "for the moment"; *praesentia* may be the abl. of the noun or the acc. of *praesens* (*OLD* 16b). **obsidibus**: hostages commonly served to secure treaties (Perl on Tac. *Germ.* 8.1; Allen 2006: 77), and C. routinely demands them after victories (11.2); V. will request them of other Gallic tribes (4.7). **possint**: subjunctive of indir. speech. C. avoids *(ne)queo*, as do administrative texts (Odelman 23–24). **ne ... efferatur**: *ne* here introduces a final clause (not an object clause after *cauere*), with *efferatur* recalling 1.6 *efferantur*. A hostage exchange would reveal their plan. **at** "at least," similar to the "apodotic *at*" (McKeown on Ovid *Am.* 1 *epigr.* 4) at 1.43.9, 5.29.7, 5.30.3 (with Landgraf 1899 [*Philologus* 58]), 6.40.2; cf. K-S II 83.4. The variants are either impossible (*aut*) or simplistic (*ut*). **iure ... fide** "a solemn oath"; a frequent hendiadys. The pledge is expressed in *ne ... deserantur*. On Gallic oaths (again at 66.5), see Rawlings 1998: 182–84, and, on C.'s manipulation of *iusiurandum*, Grillo 2012: 63–67. **sanciatur:** an independent subj. (G-L 546R2; DKM on 1.20.5 *rogat* collect other instances, incl. 86.2 *pugnet*). **collatis … signis** is "standard 'technical' language of military narrative" (Horsfall on Verg. *Aen.* 11.517). Gallic standards were sacred (Deyber 2009: 132–36), just like the Roman legionary eagles – *propria legionum numina* – by which oaths were sworn, too (Tac. *Ann.* 2.17.2 with Goodyear; Watson 1969: 127–31). **quo more** "in which custom" (with the appositional noun inserted in its rel. clause [cf. 28.6n. *quae … pars*]) rather than "in which according to their custom." C. (unlike Cic.) often expands the abl. absolute with dependent clauses (Gotoff 1984: 9). Variations of this phrase are common in ethnographic contexts (W-M on Tac. *Ann.* 3.43.2). **grauissima** "most venerable" (*OLD* 13). **caerimonia** occurs only here in *CC* (and in a speech quoted at Suet. *Iul.* 6); it connotes sanctity (Roloff 1952: 110–14). **facto initio belli** repeats 1.5 *belli initium faciant*.

2.3 A typical cumulative-complex sentence, wherein each asyndetic abl. absolute expresses a consecutive action. The imbalance between the subordinate constructions and the pithy main clause is typical, too, the former enumerating circumstances or arguments, the latter expressing the consequence (Fränkel 1933; *Introd.* 3b). **collaudatis** "praised from all sides." **eius rei** = *belli faciendi*. **disceditur** "they parted, each their way." The impersonal passive, a feature of military bulletins (Fraenkel 1956: 189–94), is another characteristic of C.'s style (25.1n. *pugnaretur*, 60.1n. *uentum*); it demotes the agent (Pinkster 1992).

3 The Carnutes attack Cenabum, killing Roman inhabitants; news thereof reaches the Arverni by "shouts down the lane." The attack on C.'s supplies, as implied by the assassination of Cita, suggests that the Gauls planned to starve the Roman army all along (Krausz 2015: 7; *Introd.* 2c).
    The massacre would have reminded readers of similar calamities, incl. *Iugurthae scelus* (Sall. *Iug.* 27.2, with Paul) in 112 or Mithridates' scheme in 88, when *quidquid ciuium Romanorum in Asia fuit … trucidatum est* (Livy *Epit.* 78; cf. App. *Mith.* 22). The episode's emotive force is counterpointed by its plainspokenness (cf. 89n.), in marked contrast with the last paragraph's atmosphere (2n.).

3.1 Ubi ea dies uenit: a legal expression (*CIL* I² 583; Fraenkel 1916: 32), it recurs at 1.8.3. *dies* (*f.*) normally signifies the beginning or end of a period of time by which something is to occur, *dies* (*m.*) an individual day (Fraenkel 1916: 30–31). **Gutuatro et Conconnetodumno**: the MSS offer *Cotuato*; but Hirt. 8.38.3, referring to this passage, speaks of one leader, *Gutuatrum*. Meanwhile, as a title of religious office, *Gutuater* is attested epigraphically

(Le Bohec 2001a, *DLG* 184–85), and most edd. print the above. But were there two leaders or one, the Gutuater Conconnetodumnus, whose title was mistaken for a name (by C. or a scribe)? Uncertainties notwithstanding, this passage has played an important role in efforts to maintain Druidic participation in the rebellion (Goudineau 2003, Le Bohec 2005). **desperatis hominibus:** the adj. serves Cic. to denunciate Catiline's followers, e.g. *Cat.* 2.10 *desperatorum hominum flagitiosi greges. homo* (rather than *uir* [19.4n.]) is typically used of bad characters (Landgraf on Cic. *Rosc. Am.* 51 *uiri … homines*). C. further defames the Gallic rebels at 1.5n. *praemiis*, 4.1n. *regnum*, 4.3n. *egentium ac perditorum*, 4.4n. *libertatis*, 4.10n. **Cenabum:** Romans would have noticed that the *res frumentaria* was supervised in *Cenabum*. Located on the bank of the Loire (on the site of Orléans), it was ideally placed to turn over grain coming from the plains of La Beauce and the Limagne d'Auvergne (Debal 1983: 91–99). It was forced to accommodate C.'s troops the following year (Hirt. 8.5; cf. 90.3n.). **negotiandi causa** is frequent in legal texts, with which C. also shares his preferences for the gerund(ive) + *causa* and *causa* over *gratia* (Odelman 55, 97–107; 43.2n.). *negotiatores* (and *negotiari*) normally refer to those in finance (Kneissl 1983: 74–75). Cic. *Font.* 5.11 asserts that in Gaul all business ran through Roman hands. **C. Fufium Citam:** C. varies his form of address; including all *tria nomina* was formal (Klotz 1910: 205–12; cf. Adams 1978: 145–66, Shackleton Bailey 1992: 3–8). He typically singles out individuals for emotive/dramatic purpose (cf. 25.2, 46.5, 47.7, 50.4, 65.2, 75.5, 77, 88.4): Cita (to whom Cic. *Flac.* 46 may refer [*RE* "Fufius" 12]) personalizes the loss; he may also be mentioned for his name's peculiar resonance with the speed of events (§2 *celeriter*). **honestum** often refers to the governing class, esp. the *ordo equester*, while connoting "moral value" (*VL* 462–64); it contrasts with *desperatis*. **qui … praeerat:** a rare remark on the actual organization of provisions (Labisch 1975: 115–21). On *horrea*, see Rickman 1971: 213–70. **interficiunt … diripiunt:** a sadly frequent (38.9, 42.3) pairing.

3.2 ciuitates are territorial entities that C. applies to socio-political groups, "tribes," and territories, "states" (Ralston 2019: 20). The *BG* contains about sixty of them (Fichtl 2013: 291); cf. 64.6n. *pagos*. ‹**ea**› **fama perfertur:** a formula (5.39.1, 53.1, 2, *BC* 3.102.8; cf. 7.8.4, *BC* 3.7.3, 8.5.1). *fama* is in the nominative; the conjecture is Sydow's (1898: 17; with *ea* = *huius rei* [cf. 4.3n. *hanc*]). *fama* was the proverbial manifestation of speed (e.g. Verg. *Aen.* 4.174 *fama, malum qua non aliud uelocius ullum*). **ubi qu‹a›:** most MSS offer *ubique*, which would be unparalleled as an alternative to *ubicumque* (cf. *OLD* s.v. 3). But Schneider's *qu‹a›e* suffers shortcomings, too, most significantly C.'s using *quă* (rather than *quae*) as the fem. of the indef. adj. (DKM *ad* 5.27.5); no better solution has been found, but because of C.'s *usus* I print *qu‹a›*. **maior ... res**: a "verbal hyperbaton," an artistic flourish that C. uses more frequently in his later books (Adams 1971: 1, 6). It adds focus/emphasis, and is therefore especially common with adj. of quantity. **maior atque inlustrior**: attested in Cic. *Verr.* 4.97; cf. Nep. *Eum.* 1.1. **clamore ... significant**: Diod. Sic. 19.17.7 reports this of the Persians (cf. Riepl 1913: 52–54). C. is similarly impressed with the Gauls' messaging at 5.53.1. **per agros regionesque** "across fields and (whole) regions." **ut tum accidit** is formulaic (cf. *BC* 1.80.1, 2.4.3, 3.68.1; *BAlex.* 18.2); Preiswerk 1945: 223 lists Greek precedents. *accidit* varies *incidit*.

3.3 The story moves along with the message, and the narrative detail of the speedy messaging relieves C. of explaining the precise political circumstances (Rambaud 207; cf. 4.1n. *simili*; 1–5n.). **quae ... gesta essent ... audita sunt** is a rather common blend of a determinative relative clause (hence the specific plural *audita sunt*) and an indirect question (hence the subjunctive *gesta essent*); Bräunlich 1918: 66–68. **oriente sole**: around 8 o'clock. **ante ... uigiliam**: the night watch – "*uigiliae* is an abstract noun used to denote the activity of the *uigiles*" (Oakley on Livy 8.8.1, *addendum*) – commenced with sun set and ended with sun rise; it was divided into four parts with the help of the water clock (Veg. 3.8.17, with Milner; cf. Cupcea 2017). The first night watch would have ended around 9 o'clock. **Aruernorum**: a Celtic people in (eponymic) Auvergne to the south of Cenabum, they dominated the lands from the Pyreneans to the ocean and the Rhine in the second century (Strabo 4.2.3; Jullian coined "l'empire Arverne" [Fichtl 2013: 294]); they then suffered defeat from Rome in 121 (1.45.2; Livy *Per.* 61; Gelzer 1955: 982). Their influence diminished, they battled the Aedui for dominance until C.'s arrival (1.31; 5.2n. *Aeduos*); peculiarly, they have been absent from the *BG* until now. The archaeological record is documented in Mennessier-Jouannet-Deberge 2007. **quod spatium est**: 28.6n. *quae ... pars*, 14.2n. *ratione esse*.

4 Amongst his Arverni, V. incites clients and outcasts to join the uprising; then, having overcome internal opposition, he takes charge of the resistance.

The "face of the resistance" (*Introd.* 3g) is introduced forcedly (§1 *simili ratione*; 1–5n.) but momentously with a mini-biography (a historiographical feature: Sall. *Cat.* 5, Livy 21.1.4, Amm. Marc. 16.7.4–10), a mini-catalogue of the coalition improbably claimed to be of his making (§6n.), and his initial measures as commander, which in speed, severity, and circumspection set the tone for his leadership; much of it is rendered, suggestively, *imperatoria breuitate* (cf. 5.1n.). In his belligerence and eloquence (§1n. *incendit*) he embodies the two skills that Romans thought Gauls generally pursued (*rem militarem et argute loqui* [Cato *FRHist* F33;

cf. Williams 2001: 79–84]). His biography and rise to power are conventional, too, as comparisons with Xen. *Ages.* (esp. 1.2–8) or Hannibal reveal (nn. on *adulescens*, §§2, 10); but V. also recalls Orgetorix (Torigian 1998: 56–58) and Rome's tribulations under Catiline and Clodius (nn. on *potentiae, clientibus, egentium, libertatis*; Barlow 1998: 152–57, Seager 2003: 29); these resonances tarnish him as do his acclamation (§5n. *rex*) and possibly cruel streak (§10n.). If he had served under C. (Cass. Dio 40.41; perhaps presupposed at 20.1; cf. 89n.), C.'s silence is noteworthy (cf. 76.1n.).

4.1 Simili ratione: similar to "by the same token," it loosely links V.'s activities to those of the Carnutan leaders. **Vercingetorix** signifies "great king of warriors" (*GPN* 121–22, discarding the thesis that it was [also] a title). *-rix*, "king" (*DLG* 260–61), would have reminded Romans of its cognate *rex* (§5n.); Florus' remark (*Epit.* 1.45.21) on how the name was formed *quasi ad terrorem* perhaps alludes to its eerie, growly syllable Ve(r)-, as in Ve(d)iouis, or *uae*; cf. also *<r littera . . .> inritata canes quam homo quam planius dicit* (Lucil. Fr. 4 [Warmington]). **Celtilli ... adulescens**: a standard introduction, typical of epigraphy (e.g. *T(itus) P(ompeius) T(iti) f(ilius) Tromentina*, *AE* 1935, 5) and paralleled in biographies (*Hannibal, Hamilcaris filius, Carthaginiensis*, Nep. *Hann.* 1); it is largely formulaic (1.3.4, 47.4, 7.31.5, 83.6; contrast 65.2). C.'s biographical "annotations [on Gauls] could ... have been written about Romans [just] as easily" (Seager 2003: 26; cf. 32.4, 37.1, 39.1). **Celtilli**: in "patronymic expressions" the gen. normally precedes (Adams 1976: 75). Paternal ancestry is regularly specified in (Celtic) inscriptions (Lambert 1994: 30–32). V.'s father is not mentioned elsewhere, but his name is (*CIL* XIII 5260); it would have evoked *Celtae* (1.1.1). **summae potentiae** recurs at 32.4 and 39.1 in *CC*: a local repetition. C. limits *potentia* to his enemies, upholding its difference from *potestas* (§7) as personal, not constitutional, power (*VL* 242; Krebs 2018b: 127). Amongst Gauls, it rested on *ambacti clientesque* (6.15.2; Polyb. 2.17.12, Diod. Sic. 5.29.2). **adulescens** spans from late boyhood to the late 30s (Le Bohec 1998: 96–97); "youth" is also conventional for characters like V. (cf. Xen. *Ages.* 1.6, when Agesilaos was over 40; Polyb. 3.15.6): both circumstances preclude speculation on his age. *adulescens* may connote inexperience and rashness (*BC* 2.38.2 *adiuuat adulescentia*, Cic. *Phil.* 5.47 *adulescentiae temeritatem*); only two instances in *VII* do not allow for these (9.1n.). **cuius ... obtinuerat** is a formula common in military reports and C. (Odelman 167–68). The statement contradicts information at 2.4.7. **principatum** "the chief position in the state" (*OLD* 2.2; 2.1n. *principes*); unlike *regnum*, a positive term (*VL* 340). **Galliae** is typically ambiguous, referring to *Celtica* or *Gallia omnis* (Stevens 1980, Schadee 2008: 159–61). **ob ... interfectus**: Celtillus' career resembles

Orgetorix's (1.2.1–4.4); its mention casts a shadow over V. (§5 *rex*). **ob ... quod** is pleonastic like 26.2n. *propterea quod*, characteristic of administrative writing, and most frequent in the early *commentarii* (Odelman 139–42). **regnum** is applied to anti-Roman leaders and those predating C.'s invasion (Barlow 1998: 143). C. mines the aversion the term provoked in Romans (*nomen ... Romae intolerabile*, Livy 27.19.4), who would also have associated *regnum affectare*, long deemed a crime (Rawson 1975). Before C.'s campaigns, oligarchies seem to have dominated in Gaul; C. (re)instituted leaders to exert control (Arbabe 2013: 309–12). **interfectus** suggests a legal execution unlike §10n. *necat.* **conuocatis ... clientibus**: C. often uses the abl. absolute instead of an integrated construction (*conuocatos ... clientes*; Eden 1962: 104–06). He is the first to apply *cliens* to foreigners (Bell 1995: 762), thereby inviting comparison with Rome (1–5n.). **incendit**: sc. *eos*, inferred from the abl. absolute (cf. 27.1n. *hanc*). Imagery of fire often describes speakers arousing an audience (Fantham 1972: 152–54); it is the first flash of V.'s rhetorical talent (cf. 14n.).

4.2 The theme of internal opposition is conventional (Livy 21.3.2–6, of Hannibal); but it here exemplifies the factionalism that C. identified in Gallic society (below, *patruo*) and that, by his time, often took an anti- vs. pro-Roman form. It also introduces the leitmotif of challenges to V.'s leadership (*Introd.* 3c). **cognito ... concurritur**: the referents of the abl. absolute and the main clause (in isocolon) are V.'s opponents, as C. uses *concurrere* of reactions only. **ad arma**: 70.6n. **prohibetur ... expellitur**: the initial position conveys concessive force, reinforced by *tamen*. **Gobannitione**: the name is attested epigraphically (*GPN* 350). **patruo suo**: the noun, only here in *CC*, highlights Gallic factionalism *paene etiam in singulis domibus* (6.11.2). Such familial divisions are a commonplace in *BG*, e.g. 1.20.6 of Diviciacus and Dumnorix (Riggsby 62–64; cf. Perl *ad* Tac. *Germ.* 33.2). **hanc** = *eius rei* (K-S 64.5). **fortunam temptandam** recurs at 64.2. Not attested prior to C. (6x), the phrase recurs in Sallust, Livy, Lucan. The passive periphrastic with *uerba sentiendi* is a characteristic of administrative writing (Odelman 109–14). For "*temptare* of dangerous ventures," cf. N-R on Hor. *Carm.* 3.4.29–31; 84.2n. **existimabant. expellitur ex**: the repetition of the prefix/preposition emphasizes the point; Plautus' use of *e(x)-* and *ab(s)-* (*Most.* 1–8) shows the potential in such cumulative use (cf. Cic. *Cat.* 1.12 *sin ... exieris, exhaurietur ex urbe*; Kenney on Lucr. 3.16–17; below, *attingunt*). C. prefers *existimare* to *arbitrari*, both to *putare*, as do administrative writers (Odelman 17–23). **oppido**: C. applies *oppidum* imprecisely to settlements of a certain sophistication that are typically protected by an elevated location and/or fortification (nn. on 15.1 *urbes*, 14.9 *munitione*, 36.1 *altissimo*; Collis 1984: 16–20). Archaeologists employ C.'s term of

Celtic settlements of the late La Tène culture (Woolf 1993: 224–26; cf.
Moore 2017). **Gergouia**: 36n. Strabo 4.2.3 specifies it as V.'s birthplace,
possibly inferred from here.

4.3 habet dilectum recalls C.'s action (1.1); it is the first of many phraseological parallels (nn. on §§5 *ut ... maneant*, 6 *celeriter; Introd.* 3g). It is
undercut by the recruits' character. **egentium ac perditorum**: Cic. applies
both words to the followers of Catiline and Clodius (*Dom.* 58, *Att.* 10.8.6;
cf. 1–5n.). **manu** "gang" (*OLD* 22b); frequent in civil war contexts (*VL*
61). **ad ... perducit**: C. remarks on V.'s rhetoric again.

4.4 ut ... capiant: sim. Cic. *Rab. Post.* 27 *qui tum arma pro communi libertate
ceperunt* (again *Phil.* 10.8). **communis libertatis**: recurs at 37.5, 71.3, 89.2;
cf. 1.5n. *in libertatem*, 2.1n. *salus*. The plea is undermined by the expulsion
of V.'s opponents and his acclamation, as *libertas* and *regnum* were antithet-
ical (cf. Livy 1.60.1 *liberatorem urbis laeta castra accepere, exactique inde liberi
regis*); this suggests mere rhetoric to Romans who knew of *libertatis simu-
lacrum* (Cic. *Dom.* 110, 116; cf. Tac. *Hist.* 4.73.3 *libertas et speciosa nomina
praetexuntur*). **aduersarios** "personal opponents," only here in *BG*. **eiectus
expellit**: varies §3 *expellitur*. Quadruple alliteration on -e appears 4x in *VII*,
25x in all of C. (cf. 18.1n. *cognouit*, 25.1n. *animaduertebant*).

4.5–7 V. does as leaders do: "straightaway [Darius] sent messengers to
the various cities and ordered that they ready a force, assigning each the
supply of ...," Hdt. 7.1.2. **rex** is applied to fourteen mostly anti-Roman
chieftains (cf. §1n. *regnum*). In Oros. 6.11.7 V. is king; his name suggested as much. **suis**: sc. *clientibus*. The possessive is commonly used of
troops (9.3n.), but may here emphasize the factionalism. **quoque uersus**
"in every direction" (*OLD quoqueuersus*). **obtestatur**: not before *VII* (exc.
4.25.3β), where it occurs 4x of Gauls only. **ut in fide maneant** recurs at
10.3 (C.'s voice). *fides* continues the language of clientship (cf. Cic. *Rosc.
Am.* 106 *in Chrysogoni fidem et clientelam; VL* 32–35) and alludes to Gallic
fickleness (cf. Cic. *Part. or.* 9 *fides est firma opinio; 1.3n. impulsi*).

4.6 A mini-catalogue of tribes from *Gallia Celtica*, presented in disorient-
ing fashion (cf. 75n.), conjures up the forces; all except the Andes recur
at 75. With V. the resistance comes into its own, or so it seems: Almost all
tribes neighbored the Carnutes, some were allies of the Aedui, the rivals
of the Arverni; these tribes must have joined right at the *concilium* (1.4;
cf. *Introd.* 2c). Given Roman trade (3.1), it is unclear whether the names
were as unfamiliar as Cic. *Prou. cons.* 33 suggests. **celeriter sibi ... adiungit**:
adverbs often "host" pronouns, esp. when needing intensification (Adams
1994b: 139–40); cf. 19.2n. *hoc se*. This is the first of many references to
V.'s speed (4.7, 5.1, 8.4, 29.5, 31.4, 64.1), who rivals C. (cf. 9.4n. *celeritate*).

Senones: strong and respected (5.54.2), they inhabited the regions of Yvonne and Seine et Marne (around eponymous Sens [*DLG* 270]), to the north of the Aedui, their patrons (6.4.2). At first cooperative (2.2.3), they had rebelled over an imposed king and lead the resistance in 53 (cf. 1.2n. *exercitum*) – each time with the Carnutes, their westerly neighbors. **Parisios**: close allies of the neighboring Senones, whose earlier rebellion they had shunned (6.4.4–5); C. had moved the *concilium Gallorum* to their chief town, Lutetia (57.1n.). **Pictones**: west of the Carnutes and "next to the ocean" (Strabo 4.2.2), they lived around Deux-Sèvres, with Lemonum as chief town (8.26.1). They were *pacati* in 56 (3.11.5). Their name lives on in Poitiers (*TGF* 156). **Cadurcos**: neighbors and clients of the Arverni in the region of Tarn-et-Garonne, with Uxellodunum as chief town (75.2; 8.34). The reason for their (dis)placement between the Pictones and Turones is unclear. Cahors is named after them (*DLG* 304). **Turonos**: in eponymic Touraine (*TGF* 158), surrounded by the Carnutes, Pictones, and Andes (with whom they are also associated at 2.35.3; Tac. *Ann.* 3.41.1). **Aulercos**: a collective name for tribes north of the Turoni and Carnutes, around Sarthe. Subjected in 57, they had risen again in 56 (2.34, 3.29.3); cf. 75.2n. **Lemouices**: north-eastern neighbors of the Arverni in the eponymic region of Limousin (*DLG* 199); cf. 88.4n. *Sedullus*. **Andes**: northern neighbors of the Pictones in Maine-et-Loire (where Angers is named after them [*DLG* 112]). They disappear until 8.26.2. **reliquosque**: C. is fond of the summary *reliquus* + *que* (8x in *VII* alone); it here allows him to delay the tribes' names, mentioned already at 2.34.1, until his climactic catalogue (75.4n. *Armoricae*). **qui Oceanum attingunt**: similarly at 2.34.1 and 75.2. *attingere* is a technical term (*OLD* 4), of which C. is fond. **attingunt adiungit**: the repetition of the prefix *ad-* stresses V.'s contribution (below, *adduci*). **omnium consensu**: formulaic; it recurs at 15.1, 77.4. The polyptoton of *omnis* (generally favored by Roman authors [Wills 224–25]) emphasizes the movement's size and unity (cf. Cic. *Dom.* 26 *omnes iam di atque homines ... bonis omnibus, totius Italiae ...*; 68–90n.). V. has grown from an Arvernian *dux partium* to a Gallic *princeps ciuitatum*, whose *auctoritas* will continue to depend on *consensus* (cf. 15.6, 20.7, 30, 63, 89.2; *VL* 358). **imperium**: with the "command" (Richardson 2008: 92–94) comes *coercitio*, the power to enforce it (§§9–10).

4.7 qua oblata potestate: a variation of *itinera duo, quibus itineribus* (1.6.1; 12.3n. *quo ex oppido*; cf. Verg. *Aen.* 7.477 *speculata* [sc. Allecto] *locum, quo litore ...* [with Horsfall]). *potestas* (not §1n. *potentia*, as his power is *now* constitutional) is treated as synonymous with *imperium* (again 33.4; contrast 4.16.4, *BC* 2.32.9). **imperat ... iubet ... constituit**: the asyndetic tricolon renders V.'s quick actions, underlined by the repeated **celeriter**.

4.8 will be rephrased at 31.4. **armorum quantum quaeque**: the order results from the enclitic nature of *quisque*. **quantum ... quodque**: on two questions (*quodque = et quod*) predicated on one verb, cf. K-S II 497.4. Such pairings have an administrative ring, cf. Plin. *Ep.* 10.92 *quid et quatenus* (with Coleman 2012: 215).

4.9 in primis equitatui studet: cf. Pericles' plea that the Athenians "ready their fleet, wherein lay their power" (τὸ ναυτικόν, ᾗπερ ἰσχύουσιν, ἐξαρτύεσθαι, Thuc. 2.13.2). Several of V.'s coins depict a horse or chariot (fig. 2b; Colbert de Beaulieu 1962). For fourth-declension nouns, C. recommended dative singular endings in "-u" (*De anal.* F24); the *commentarii* do not bear this out. **summae diligentiae imperii summam seueritatem**: the epigrammatic verdict is adorned by alliteration and diacope (cf. Cic. *De or.* 1.6 *summos homines ac summis ingeniis praeditos*); its tone may be gauged from Cato's admonition of Cicero (*Fam.* 15.6): *seueritatem diligentiamque sociis et rei publicae praesta*. *diligentia* signifies "scrupulous attention" to responsibilities (*VL* 251–52; 65.3n.); *imperii seueritas* (only here in C.), which the punishments exemplify, is deemed a necessity, *sine qua administrari ciuitas non potest* (Cic. *Off.* 1.88; cf. Cic. *Cat.* 2.3 with Dyck, Livy 5.26.8). But a general "must be ... not so lenient as to be despised, nor so severe as to be hated...," Onas. 2.2 (cf. Frontin. *Str.* 4.1.2, Suet. *Iul.* 75; §10n. *leuiore*), and while C. reserves *crudelitas* for Critognatus (77.2n.), §10 may suggest as much. **dubitantes**: present participles serve as nouns almost exclusively when a noun is unavailable (G-L 437; Adams 1973b: 121; cf. 15.6n. *petentibus*, 86.5n. *propugnantes*). By punishing *dubitantes*, V. appears overly severe; cf. Cic. *Leg.* 3.6: *magistratus nec oboedientem et noxium ciuem multa uinculis uerberibusue coherceto*.

4.10 Though the Roman army perfected "discipline by terror" (Erskine 2013: 242; Phang 2008: 120–29 surveys the measures), C.'s description condemns V.'s punitive excess, playing on the stereotype of barbaric cruelty (Kremer 1994: 183, Le Bohec 1998: 109). However, following the surrender of Uxellodunum, *exemplo supplicii deterrendos reliquos existimauit* (sc. C.). *itaque omnibus qui arma tulerant manus praecidit* (8.44.2); Hirtius deemed the charge of *crudelitas naturae* too plausible to gloss over (cf. 28.4–5n.). **igni ... tormentis**: 6.19.3 *igni atque omnibus tormentis excruciatas* [sc. *uxores*] *interficiunt*. V. will torture again (20.9). For other references to torture in *BG* (incl. 38.9), see Riggsby 64n.45; on fire, cf. Cic. *Verr.* 2.5.163, Tac. *Ann.* 15.57.1 with Koestermann. **necat**: sc. *eos* (inferred from the abl. absolute). C. reserves *necare* for executions (an original meaning), all of which have a note of cruelty (Opelt 1980: 111–12). **leuiore de causa** "concerning slighter cases." The adjective's front position lends it greater emphasis (W-M on Tac. *Ann.* 3.16.1), which highlights the disproportion: *cauendum est … ne maior poena quam culpa sit*, Cic. *Off.* 1.89. **auribus desectis … effossis oculis**: a close parallel is Sulla's infamous execution of M. Marius Gratidianus *cruribus bracchiisque fractis, auribus praesectis et oculis effossis* (Livy *epit.* 88; cf. Luc. 2.183–85 with Fantham on 2.173–93). *desecare* occurs only here in *BG*; *effodere* is a quasi-technical term for an eye's violent removal (*TLL* 5.2.196.40–66). **reliquis documento**: cf. Livy 5.51.8 *tantum poenarum … dedimus ut terrarum orbi documento essemus*. **magnitudine poenae** reiterates *magnitudine supplicii*. The apotropaic purpose is often thematized in classical literature (Plat. *Prt.* 324b; Cic. *Rosc. Am.* 70 *ut … magnitudine poenae a maleficio summouerentur*; *BC* 3.8.3 [similarly phrased]).

5 To bar C. and weaken his position in Gaul, V. adapts a composite strategy (cf. Plut. *Caes.* 26.1): he dispatches Lucterius to the Ruteni to threaten *prouincia* (§1n.) and himself leads another contingent to the Bituriges, thereby (a) beginning his campaign for the Aedui, and (b) hoping to secure the space between the Arverni and their northern confederates as well as access to C.'s legions (1.2n. *exercitum*). The Bituriges might have resisted (§2n. *facilius*) but fall quickly when the Aedui fail to intervene (which introduces the Aeduan leitmotif). C. glosses over the attacks by Drappes, who would join Lucterius, and Commius (1–5n.); these may account for Labienus' invisibility until later (*CG* 134; cf. 34.2n.).

5.1 *exercitum in hiberna … deducendum Quinto fratri dabam; ipse me Laodiceam recipiebam* (Cic. *Att.* 5.20.4): "actions of subordinates" followed by "actions of the general" is a standard scheme in military writing (Rambaud 40). The form confirms V.'s standing as *imperator* (4n.), as does his counterattack on Roman territory, an acknowledged strategy (the ἀντιπερίστασις; cf. Xen. *Ages.* 1.8 on Agesilaus' "attacking, in turn, (ἀντιδιαβῆναι) the Persians," Frontin. *Str.* 1.8). C. would soon counter (7n.). **celeriter**: 4.6n. **exercitu**: 4.3 *manu*, 4.4 *copiis* – the changing terminology reflects V.'s changed status and military strength. **Lucterium**: he is celebrated on coins found in the territory of the Arverni and Cadurci (*GPN* 363). He vanishes quickly from *VII* but returns the following year (8.1; 8.32, 44.4–6). **summae hominem audaciae**: *BC* 3.104.2 *singulari hominem audacia*; the word order is frequent (DKM *ad* 6.14.3). Generally, descriptive genitives and ablatives are not attached to names but generic nouns in apposition (H-S 119γ; *NLS* §§72[6], 84–85; 43[6], 83; contrast 39.1). A stock-in-trade in denunciations of *populares*, *audacia* was embodied for Cicero by Clodius and his following *hominum cum egestate tum audacia perditorum* (*Sest.* 85; Wirszubski 1961: 15n.18). *summa audacia* also characterizes Dumnorix (1.18.3). **Rutenos**: located to the south of the Massif Central in Tarn and l'Aveyron, they were former vassals of the Arverni. After their joint defeat by Rome in 121, part of their territory fell to the *prouincia*

(7.4 *prouinciales*; cf. 1.45.2); their silver mines were of special interest
(Strabo 4.2.3). Their name lives on in Rodez (*TGF* 156). **ipse** commonly
refers to the commander in military reporting (above, "*ipse me*"); C. is particularly fond of the use, normally of himself (below, §6.4). It will become
common in Roman historiography (M-W on Tac. *Ann*. 4.24.3). **Bituriges**:
once a dominant Celtic tribe (Livy 5.34.1), now in fealty to the Aedui,
they lived north of the Arverni (around eponymic Berry [*DLG* 76]), with
Avaricum as main town (13.3n.). They continued their resistance the following year (8.2.2).

5.2 eius aduentu: complemented ablatives of fourth-declension nouns
may be temporal and carry a causal connotation (K-S 356); they are frequent in C. References to a general's arrival are a standard feature of military reporting and of historiographical narratives (3x in Cic. *Fam*. 15.2;
9.5n.). **Haeduos**: the name is attested as *Aedui, Haedui*, and *Hedui* in the
MSS, other texts, and inscriptions (Glück 1857: 9–13); the proper Celtic
form is "aidu-" (*DLG*, s.v.), but Romans typically adapted the diphthong
"ai" to "ae" and added an aspiration (cf. the ridicule in Catull. 84.1),
which is the spelling commonly accepted for the Latin text (whereas in
English *Aedui* is more common). A preeminent people, the Aedui inhabited the territory of Bourgogne (Barrall *et al*. 2002: 275–92 offers specifics), with Bibracte being their "largest and wealthiest town" (1.23.1;
55.4n.). Roman allies since at least the second century (Flor. *Epit*. 1.37;
Dobesch 2001: 755–62), they were the sole Gauls to become *fratres consanguineique* of the Romans, perhaps because of an alleged shared descent
from Troy (1.33.2; Cic. *Att*. 1.19.2; Tac. *Ann*. 11.25.2; Braund 1980). In
inner-Gallic struggles, they had been defeated by the Sequani and Arverni
in the Battle of Magetobriga (1.31, 6.12, 7.67.7), when their appeal for
help in Rome in 61 had been ignored, most likely by C. himself (Brunt
1978: 180); but the latter restored them to eminence (54.3n. *sua ... merita*), and they remained his special concern (40.1n. *praecipue indulserat*),
even if they caused him difficulties in 58, 54, and especially in 52, when
their unreliability constitutes a leitmotif (1.11, 16, 5.6; *Introd*. 3c). C.
relied on their cavalry (65.4n.). **quorum erant in fide**: similarly at 6.4.2.
esse often "attach[es] to the relative" (Adams 1994a: 44). 1.18.6 mentions
familial ties between the tribes. **facilius**: the comparative suggests that the
Bituriges did not require the help of the Aedui (cf. *statim*, below, §5.7).
sustinere: 10.3n. *sustineant*.

5.3 de consilio "on the advice" (*OLD de* 2c; G-L 408N3). **legatorum**
repeats *legatos* but now signifying "deputies" (cf. Varro *Ling*. 5.87: *legati ...
quorum opera consilioque uteretur peregre magistratus quiue nuntii senatus aut
populi essent*). Such repetitions are variously classified in ancient rhetoric

(e.g. *reflexio, distinctio* [*HLR* 657–63]). They are frequent in C. (and classical literature generally [Seyffert-Müller on Cic. *Amic.* 40 *turpis*; Pickering 2003]) and rarely as blatantly significant as 19.5n. *iniquitatis*. C. enhanced the role of the *legati* at the expense of the *tribuni* (17.8n.); he defines their role at *BC* 3.51.4 as *omnia agere ad praescriptum* (cf. Parker 1958: 52–54; Thomasson 1991: 9–12, 17–22). **ad exercitum:** probably the troops wintering among the *Lingones* (1.2n.). C. usually uses *apud* with "stationary" verbs and *ad* with "mobile" verbs (DKM 5.53.3). **subsidio** is a pred. dative (*NLS* §68i).

5.4 qui: a *constructio ad sensum*, with *qui* referring to *copias equitatus peditatusque* (K-S 21; contrast 3.20.4). **flumen Ligerim:** C. prefers *flumen* over *fluuius* and *amnis* in line with the administrative style (Odelman 50). A likely location is near Decize (Thévenot 1960: 49–50; 33.2n.).

5.5 ueritos reuertisse: the echo may emphasize the fear (cf. 4.1n. *Vercingetorix*). C. avoids *metuere* (not *metus*, 56.2; Krebs 2018b: 124). **id consilii ... ut:** the partitive gen. is idiomatic (K-S 431 Anm.10). *id* is a typical placeholder for the *ut* clause (G-L 557). **cognouerint** instead of *cognouissent* (a frequent change [DKM *ad* 1.7.3]). **una ... altera:** between the Bituriges in the north, and the Aedui in the south. **una ex parte:** 4.1on. *leuiore de causa.* **ipsi** = the Bituriges. **se** = *Haeduos* (indirect reflexivity).

5.6 eane ... an ... adducti: the abl. is coordinated with a part. (*inconcinnitas* [20.7n. *proditionem*). The "loaded alternative" (Whitehead 1979) allows the narrator to cast doubt on the Aedui; they had caused worry in *I* as well (1.3.4; *Introd.* 3c). **perfidia** emphatically repeats §5 *perfidiam*, introducing C.'s worry about his ally; cf. 17.7n. **pronuntiauerint:** the subjunctive results from mood attraction (G-L 508, 4). **nobis:** C.'s narrator often refers to himself in the first-person plural (Riggsby 150–55; 17.1n. *diximus*; *Introd.* 3c). **pro certo esse ponendum** ends on a cretic-spondee. Suspension of judgment over uncertainty is a historiographic commonplace (Perl on Tac. *Germ.* 3.3). This expression found favor with Livy (10.9.12, 23.6.8).

5.7 statim suggests they intended to join V. all along.

6–13 EXEMPLARY LEADERSHIP IN A "WAR OF MOVEMENTS": FROM RAVENNA TO AVARICUM

C. has to protect the province and reunite with his legions. Leaving Italy (Ravenna, after 9 Feb. [nn. on 6.1, §1 *uirtute*]), he hurries to Narbo to repel Lucterius (7.2n. *Narbonem*) and from there back to the Helvii (7.5n. *Heluios*) to cross the Cévennes and on through the territory of the Vellavi for the Arverni (8.2n. *ad fines Aruernorum*; possible routes: *CG*

134–36). He thus forces V. to relinquish his station among the Bituriges to protect his people (8.5), which clears C.'s path: rushing eastward to Vienne, he heads north through Aeduan territory to the Lingones, there to reunite with two of his legions (at *castrum Diuionense* [Dijon] or Andematunnum [Langres]; Raaflaub-Ramsey 2017: 57). He gathers all legions at Agedincum (10.4n.). After more than 2,200 km (1,370 mi) covered in probably less than two months (cf. *Introd.* 2c, *Timeline*) at breakneck speed (9.4n. *celeritate*), C. has thwarted the Gauls' attempts to bar him from his troops. The narrative's intended effect can be gleaned from Florus' laconic words: *ante in media Gallia fuit quam ab ultima timeretur* (*Epit.* 3.10.22; cf. 2.3.1 for a similar feat).

The next moves in this "guerre de movement" (Deyber 2017: 81) partly replay the first sequence: V. challenges the Aedui again by attacking their clients, the Boii (9.6n.), putting C. in another bind (10n.). But the latter extricates himself, hurrying unexpectedly (perhaps [11n.]) in a westerly, then southerly direction through the territories of the Senones and Carnutes, instigators of the uprising, before arriving among the Bituriges, recently defected neighbors of the Arverni – razing three towns along the way. The renewed threat to his people causes V. to come to their aid once more (12.1n.). After weeks of maneuvering, the two leaders finally engage, bringing this narrative theme to a conclusion (*Introd.* 3c). Victorious, C. moves in a southwardly direction on Avaricum (13.3).

The narrative, which in arrangement and phrasing resembles 1.7 (nn. on 6.1 *nuntiatis*, 7.2 *in prouinciam*, 8.3 *quam maximum*, 9.3 *itineribus*), celebrates C.'s leadership: He cares about Rome, its province, and allies (6.1, 7.3, 10.1–2), and avenges, *more Romano*, rebels and deserters (11.3n. *Cenabum*; cf. 1.12.5–6, 17.7n. *parentarent*); he displays the *uirtutes imperatoriae* (Cic. *Leg. Man.* 29; *Introd.* 3d), esp. acumen, daring, and speed, each of which particularly developed in a "parade chapter" (nn. on 10, 8, 9); and he outsmarts V. twice by way of an ἀντιπερίστασις (5.1n.) and beats him in his chosen combat arms, the cavalry (13.1n. *Germanos*). The most exciting part, the crossing of the Cévennes, is suitably evocative of Hannibal's overcoming the Alps (8n.).

6 When Rome seems sufficiently safe, C. leaves for Gaul with his newly recruited troops (cf. 7.5) but stalls in *prouincia*.

Just as Roman news travelled north to set off the narrative of Gallic events (1.2 *eae res*), so news from Gaul now arrives in *Italia*, causing another change of focalization (with §1 *his rebus* summing up developments in 1–5). Other features link this chapter back to the first one, marking it as introductory to a new phase: *in Italiam* is repeated, *urbanae res* echoes 1.2 *urbano motu* just as *ad exercitum peruenire posset* echoes 1.7

ad legiones peruenire posset; and after mostly dramatic presents, the static imperfect dominates. C. begins a typical demonstration of his *scientia suorum consiliorum explicandorum* (10n.), which normally results in decisive action; here, however, it is aborted amidst the dilemma (§§3–4n.), with C. apparently at a loss (until 7.3).

6.1 Similar statements occur at 1.7.1 (esp. close), 2.2.1–2, 3.9.1–2, 4.6.1, 5.2.1 (absent from *VI*, as C. had remained with his troops). Parallels in Cic.'s letter to the senate (*Fam.* 15.4.2 *cum in prouinciam ... uenissem*, §3; *Att.* 5.20.2) identify them as standard elements of official reporting (*Introd.* 3a), with which C. also shares his favored combination of abl. absolute + *cum*-clause (Rambaud 34–5). **His rebus ... nuntiatis**: a common transition formula in C. (*VII*: 7.3, 11.7, 18.4, 67.2; once at *BAfr.* 21.3). As "a narrative gesture [it is] akin to a historian's citing his sources" (Kraus 2007: 351). Cf. 10.1n. *magnam ... difficultatem*. **Italiam**: 1.1n. **Caesari ... ille** is slightly pleonastic (contrast 1.4 *principes*, 7.2 *Caesar*) and testifies to C.'s *guttatim* style. **urbanas res** = "Roman affairs." C. is seen caring about Rome (he worried about it, too [*Introd.* 2c]). **uirtute Cn. Pompei** may signify "thanks to" rather than "by the resolution of Pompey" (*OLD uirtus* 7, 1). Either way, Gnaeus Pompeius (*RE* 31) Magnus was commonly associated with *uirtus* (McDonnell 2006: 313–15), other sources acknowledge his role (Asc. *Mil.* 34–41, App. *B Civ.* 2.24–25; Gruen 1974: 453–55), and his relationship with C. was strong – no need to read it other than complimentary (Welch 1998: 102n.66). Tumults in Rome continued despite the *scu* (1.1n.), and Pompey was elected *consul sine collega* around 5 Feb. [Jul.] (Raaflaub-Ramsey 2017: 54). C. mentions Pompey once more in *BG* (6.1). **commodiorem in statum** "in a more favorable state"; cf. 4.10n. *leuiore de causa*. **Transalpinam** here (unlike 1.1) refers to the Roman province, as §3 specifies.

6.2–4 Detailing his difficulty, C. has the reader wonder *how* he will prevail: "The question [with ancient historians] is seldom 'What will happen?' but 'How will it happen?' ... [It involves a] suspense of anticipation" (Luce 1971: 295). He also has his audience participate in his reasoning (cf. *Introd.* 3d). **eo cum uenisset** is a frequent transition formula (C-L 98–99; *VII*: 7.4, 9.5, 55.4, 61.1). **difficultate ... qua ratione**: a virtually unparalleled construction (*TLL* 5.1.1096.21–23). Although it is commonplace to emphasize the difficulties a general faced (cf. Polyb. 3.50.1, 102.2), it occurs noticeably often in *VII* (10.1, 17.3, 35.1, 59.6; cf. *Introd.* 3g). C.'s frequent use of *ratio* (16.2 *quantum ratione prouideri*, 21.1, 63.3) bespeaks his intellectualistic approach to war (cf. 7.3n. *consiliis*). **exercitum**: 1.2n. **peruenire** echoes *peruenisse*, differing in meaning (cf. 5.1n. *legatorum*); the echo reasserts the dependency of C.'s Gallic moves on Roman affairs.

6.3–4 C. ponders his situation in two hypothetical scenarios, neither good, the latter inverting the former: a dilemma (cf. the figure *complexio in qua, utrum concesseris, reprehenditur,* Cic. *Inu. rhet.* 1.45). Multiple hypotheticals are typical of the legal discourse (*lex xii tab.* 3.4 *si uolet suo uiuito. ni suo uiuit [qui eum uinctum habebit] libras farris endo dies dato;* Hyart 1954: 159), and frequent in C. (starting at 1.13.3–4; *VII*: 10.1, 20.6, 66.5). C.'s phrasing echoes the Gauls' thoughts at 1.7. **prouinciam** = *G. transalpinam.* **se ... proelio**: a typical string of ablatives. **dimicaturas** "they would have to fight"; the fut. may have "potential sense" (K-S 142.2). The "colloquial" omission of the subj. in the acc. (Landgraf on Cic. *Rosc. Am.* 59 *quaesisse*) is common in C.

6.4 iis hints at the Aedui, whose territory lay en route to C.:'s legions (9.4). **eo tempore** "given the current situation"; but in the sense of "at that time" it warns of the Aedui's later desertion. It oscillates between the main clause and the relative clause; a difficulty that the reading in β removes. **salutem recte committi** "it would be right to entrust [his] safety." *salutem committere* is common, but Cic. would use it, discussing *fidi homines* (*Off.* 2.33), in a similar context: *ita fides habetur, ut nulla sit in iis fraudis iniuriaeque suspicio. itaque his salutem nostram ... rectissime committi arbitramur.*

7 News of Lucterius' threat – quite possibly greater even than C. lets on (5n.) – reaches C. He rushes to Narbo to fortify the provincial defenses (*G. transalpina* was one of the territories assigned him, so he was right to worry [*Introd.* 2a]).

Resuming the reflections from the previous section (6.3–4), the narrative develops the typical sequence of action, report, and reaction (cf. 61n.). In rushing to protect his province, C. shows himself a laudable magistrate: ... *magistratus imperatoresque ex hac una re maximam laudem capere studebant, si prouincias, si socios aequitate et fide defendissent* (Cic. *Off.* 2.26; cf. Cic. *QFr.* 1.1.27 *utilitati salutique seruire*; Lintott 1993: 43–69, Morrell 2017: 5–8).

7.1 Interim marks the transition to concomitant events (C-L 24–39; similarly at 31.5, 43.1, 48.1, 66.1 *interea dum,* 79.1). C. favors *interim* over *interea*; but in *VII* they are even. **in Rutenos**: contrary to Lucterius' likely route, C. fronts the tribe that partly belonged to the province in order to heighten the danger. **missus** resumes 6.1 *mittit;* similarly 8.3+4 *terrorem inferant ... perterriti,* 18.1+2, 23.1+3, 35.4–5 *reficere ... effecto,* 88.3 *terga uertunt. fugientibus* (cf. 54.3n. *discedentibus*). To resume a verb by its participle is a common form of repetition (Wills 311–17), traceable to Hom. *Il.* 1.595. It is a hallmark of Hdt. (7.208.3 ἐμάνθανε. μαθών) and frequently attested among republican historians (Cato *FRHist* F76 *circumueniuntur, circumuenti*). For the inversion, cf. 20.12n. *recipiat.* **eam** = *Rutenorum;* a typical resumptive use (6.1n. *Caesari ... ille*).

7.2–5 The polyptoton of *prouincia* highlights the movements. **Nitiobroges** are attested on a contemporaneous torque (*ILA* vol. 118: 9). They lived along the Garonne (in Agen), abutting *prouincia* to the northwest of the Ruteni. Honored as *amici*, they still joined V. (nn. on 31.5, 75.3). **Gabalos:** living to the northwest of the Cévennes (in the eponymous Gévaudan region [*TGF* 656]), they neighbored the Ruteni as well as the Arverni (their patrons, 75.2n.). **ab utrisque** is plural, as both parties consist of many. **manu:** 4.3n. **in prouinciam:** a threat to the province propelled C. into action at 1.7.1, too. **Narbonem uersus** "in the direction of Narbo." A Roman colony in the province, Cic. *Font.* 13 describes it as *specula populi Romani ac propugnaculum istis ipsis nationibus oppositum*. C. repeatedly remarks on its risky proximity to Gaul (§4–5n.). **eruptionem facere:** C. is fond of periphrastic expressions with *facere*. They are common in Latin literature; but Cic.'s snarky question for Anthony: *quid est porro facere contumeliam? quis sic loquitur?* (*Phil.* 3.22 [with Adams 2016: 135]), may suggest that it belonged to a lower register. *eruptio = incursio* is unparalleled until the third century (*TLL* 5.2.847.13).

7.3 qua re nuntiata: 6.1n. **consiliis:** the frequency of references to *consilium/a* (157x [M-P]), especially C.'s own, is indicative of the store he sets by planning and, *ipso facto*, his intellectualistic approach to war; cf. nn. on 6.2 *ratione*, 10; *Introd.* 3d. **anteuertendum existimauit:** sim. 1.38.1 *praecauendum Caesar existimabat*, 33.1 *praeuertendum. anteuertere* occurs only here in *CC* and in the rarest meaning of "to give priority to [sc. marching to Narbo over all other plans]," attested once before C. (Plaut. *Bacch.* 526), then not again until the third century (*TLL* 2.162.19–25). C. favors a gerundive + inf. depending on a verb of thinking, as does the official register (Odelman 109–14; 87.5n.).

7.4–5 The clipped and mostly asyndetic *narratio*, suggestive of *imperatoria breuitas*, amplifies C.'s actions (63.1–4n.). C. had already in 58 and 56 strengthened key points in *prouincia* against Gallic threats (1.8, 3.20). **eo cum uenisset:** 6.2n. **timentes confirmat** contrasts with V.'s *dubitantes cogit* (4.9). **confirmat … constituit … conuenire:** an alliterative rising tricolon of increasing complexity. **praesidia:** specified at 65.1. **prouincialibus:** only here in C. Cf. 5.1n. *Rutenos.* **Volcis Arecomicis:** the Volcae migrated repeatedly from east of the Rhine (6.24.2); one group, internally divided into Arecomici and Tectosages, settled in the territory hemmed in by the Rhône, Cévennes, Garonne, and Pyrenees, with the Arecomici to the northeast of the Tectosages. Strabo (4.1.12) attributes Narbo to them; but this passage has been read as contradictory. **Tolosatibus:** the inhabitants of Tolosa (Toulouse) or, more broadly, a powerful group of the Volcae Tectosages centered there (Plin. *HN* 3.4.37). They were famous for their wealth (Strabo 4.1.13; cf. 1.10.2). **circumque** "in the vicinity of" (*OLD* 5). **quae loca**: in apposition (28.6n. *quae … pars*) to all locations previously mentioned metonymically (cf. 10.1n. *uideret*).

7.5 ex prouincia: prepositional phrases quite commonly function as adjectives (cf. Cic. *De or.* 1.1 *in otio cum dignitate*, 1.3 *tempus omne post consulatum*). The *prouincia* (= G. *transalpina*) contrasts to *ex Italia* (= G. *cisalpina*). **supplementumque**: the noun (first here in C.) refers to the reinforcements recruited at 1.1. They fell short of a legion, as 34.2 reveals. **Heluios**: situated between the Rhône and the Cévennes (in Ardèche), they neighbored the Gabali and Vellauii, Aruerni and Segusiaui – all of whom joined the rebellion – and came under attack later. C. probably sent his troops to Alba Heluiorum (Alba-la-Romaine; cf. Dupraz 2004: 220–22), the region's major settlement, which a northbound road connected with Vienne (9.3). **qui … contingunt**: preciser geographical information is provided in 8.2.

8 The attack on the province rebutted (which V. will renew [64]), C. follows his troops to the Helvii, traverses the Cévennes, and marches on Arvernian territory, thus threatening V.'s homeland in turn (cf. 5.1n).

   C. offers masterclasses in the art of surprise and the counterthreat (§3n. *oppressis*, §2n. *fines Aruernorum*; *Introd.* 3d) and models his "unprecedented" (§3n. *ne … umquam*) conquest of the Cévennes after Hannibal's ascent of the Alps, esp. in Polybius' version. His styling them a "bulwark" flags the model, as that imagery, applied to the Alps, was a mainstay in the Hannibalic tradition (§3n. *muro munitos*). Both narratives stress the wintery conditions, the mountainous inaccessibility, the enemy's surprise, and end with identical outcomes (nn. on *discissa niue, singulari, oppressis inopinantibus, ut … consulat*). C.'s feat impressed: the Cévennes are the only mountain range Lucan mentions in his catalogue of Gallic tribes (1.435), and Florus celebrates C.'s crossing as *felicissima temeritas* (*Epit.* 1.45; cf. Plut. 25.3–4 with Pelling).

8.1 The syntax is typical (2.3n.), the alliterations noteworthy (*r-r-r-i-i-p-p-p*). **His … comparatis**: sim. at 1.6.4, 5.4.1, *BC* 2.1.4. **Lucterio**: 1.5n. *Caesarem* (its middle position). **intrare intra praesidia** "to enter into fortified territory"; *intrare intra* is attested once before C. and not again until the fourth century (Plaut. *Men.* 416; *TLL* 7.2.57.50–55). The metonymical sense of *praesidium* is also exceedingly rare (*TLL* 10.2.892.17–18).

8.2 The ideal general was expected to master difficult terrain (e.g. Frontin. *Str.* 1.4.7, 3.9.3) and to prevail over an inimical nature (cf. Tac. *Agr.* 33.2 *paene aduersus ipsam rerum naturam*, with Woodman). C. made a point of conquering natural limits, most famously the Rhine (4.17–19; cf. Rambaud 224, Micunco 1995: 107–09, Krebs 2008); further instances of

his overcoming natural obstacles include 35, 55.9–10. C. does not indulge
in a full *regionis descriptio* (Cic. *De or.* 2.63), and his account appears
restrained when compared with similar ones elsewhere (e.g. Livy 21.36.7,
37.4–5; cf. Polybius' criticism at 3.48); this is perhaps owed to the conventions of the *commentarius* (*Introd.* 3a). **etsi:** *(tam)etsi* appears 24x in *BG*, 22
of which are associated with C. or his leaders, indicating superior judgment and will (Batstone 1990). **Ceuenna:** the Cévennes. **qui ... discludit:**
background information in a rel. clause was a feature of military reporting
(Rambaud 31–32); cf. 68.1, 80.1. *discludere* (once more in *CC* [4.17.7])
may have a Lucretian ring; cf. 5.438 *discludere mundum* (with Macrob. *Sat.*
6.4.11 on Verg. *Ecl.* 6.35); 1.2n. **addunt. durissimo tempore anni:** Cic. *Att.*
10.11.4 dreads sailing *duro tempore anni*; *BC* 3.25.3; cf. Hirt. 8.6.1 *tempore
anni difficillimo.* The superl. only here in C. **altissima niue:** *altus* is ambiguous, cf. 1.2.3 *flumine ... altissimo ... monte Iura altissimo*; N-H on Hor. *Carm.*
1.9.1. Within the panegyrical tradition, the perils of snow serve *amplificatio*
(Woodman on Vell. *Pat.* 2.105.3); they had recently featured in writings
on the Mithridatic campaigns (Plut. *Luc.* 32.1–2). **discissa ... patefactis:** a
chiasmus. **discissa niue:** the expression lacks a parallel (*TLL* 5.1.1315.30),
nor does C. use *discindere* elsewhere. *discutere*, meanwhile, occurs elsewhere
in C. (*BC* 2.9.4) and in conjunction with *nix* repeatedly elsewhere (*ueter-
emque iugis nutantibus Alpes | discussere niuem*, Luc. 1.553–54). β's *discissa*
is therefore more difficult than α's *discussa*, and it receives support from
Polyb. 3.55.6, where Hannibal "cut through ... the snow," διαμησάμενος
τὴν ... χιόνα. **sex in altitudinem pedum:** expressions with *in* = "in reference
to" (*OLD* 17), a fixture in technical texts, are frequent in C. (23.1, 69.5,
73.5). The snowpack need not be exaggerated (cf. *Rev. des études anciennes*
12 [1910] 85). **summo ... sudore** is *apo koinou* with the abl. absolutes and
finite verb. *sudor*, "effort" (*OLD* 2), occurs only here in *CC*; but it has an
epic tone (N-H on Hor. *Carm.* 1.15.9 *quantus ... sudor*), forms, in conjunction with *sanguis*, a proverb (Otto 1708), and adds an alliteration to
a highly alliterative context (*dd, aa, ii*). It thus seems preferable to *summo
labore* (4.2.2, *BC* 1.62.1), even if Polyb. 3.55.6 μετὰ πολλῆς ταλαιπωρίας,
lends it support. **ad fines Arvernorum peruenit:** after the descent, C.
entered the territory of the Vellavii en route to the Arverni (hence *ad*, not
in). Cass. Dio 40.33.2 spells out the implication: "by attacking the Arverni
in turn (ἀντεμβαλὼν [*Introd.* 3d]), he forced the enemy to return home."

8.3 oppressis inopinantibus: at Polyb. 3.61.9, the Romans are "confronted
with this unexpected (παραδόξου) event [i.e. Hannibal's arrival across the
Alps] ... and confounded (διαταραχθέντες)" – but such emphatic doublings
are common (4.4.5, 7.61.1; Cic. *Fam.* 15.12.2 *necopinatus et improuisus*). C.
"objected to *nec* before a vowel" (Clark on Cic. *Mil.* 29 [citing Landgraf];

cf. 35.1n. *necubi*) and consequently avoids *necopinans* (*-atus*); but he avoids *inopinatu*, too, and is the first to use *inopinans* (*TLL* 7.1.1748.65; 11x; not in *CC*). It is a commonplace to contrast the expectation that an obstacle cannot be overcome with the protagonist's successful overcoming (e.g. Xen. *An.* 1.4.18), just as it is characteristic of successful generals and C. in particular to catch an enemy unawares (*OLD opprimere* 7; again 46.5, 61.1), often by speed (as early as 1.13.1; cf. *BAlex.* 30.1; Frontin. *Str.* 3.1.2, Veg. 3.26 *subita conterrent hostes*). **ut muro munitos**: an etymological play, as *murus* was related to *munire* (Varro *Ling.* 5.141). As a description of the Alps it is clichéd: Cato *FRHist.* F150 *Alpes ... muri uice tuebantur Italiam* (with Cornell); Polyb. 3.54.2 ἀκροπόλεως ... τῆς ὅλης Ἰταλίας, "a stronghold ... of all of Italy"; more recently: Cic. *Prou. cons.* 34 *Alpibus Italiam munierat natura*. **ne ... quidem umquam**: "*ne-quidem* straddles the emphatic word or group" (G-L 448N2; but hardly more than two words). C. presents himself as *primus inuentor*, a topos (N-H on Hor. *Carm.* 1.3.12) traceable to Cassius Hemina among Roman historians (*FRHist* 1.223). Its significance in Roman politics appears from the inscriptions in honor of Duilius' naval victory, which mention his being *primus* four times (*CIL* 1.2), or of Hirrus' accomplishments, introduced by: *quod neque conatus quisquanst neque [post audebit] noscite rem, ut famaa facta feramus uirei* (*CIL* i²/2.2662, with Courtney 1995: 15). **singulari**: *singularis* normally means "excellent" in C. (cf. 77.2), rarely "individual" (*OLD* 4, 2), here possibly both: "not even a remarkable man on his own." Polyb. 3.47.9 discusses historians who stress how the Alps "could not be crossed easily even by unencumbered foot soldiers," μηδὲ πεζοὺς εὐζώνους εὐχερῶς ἂν διελθεῖν. **semitae** "narrow paths," a meaning elucidated by the (mistaken) etymology reported in Varro (*Ling.* 5.35): "where [the going] was narrow (*anguste*), it was called – as if from "halfway" (*semiter*) – *semita*." It resonates with *singulari* and contrasts with *uiae* (above; cf. Mart. 7.61.4 *quae fuerat semita, facta uia est*). **patuerant** reprises, with due emphasis, *patefactis* (cf. 20.12n. *recipiat*). **equitibus**: the cavalry consisted of auxiliary troops, most importantly from the Aedui (1.15.1 *equitatumque ... ex omni prouincia et Haeduis atque eorum sociis coactum*); he also levied troops from newly subjected Gallic tribes (4.6.5, 6.4.6; a Roman practice [Dixon-Southern 1992: 22]) and others (5.26.3 *Hispanis equitibus emissis*), and at some point from Germanic tribes quite possibly out of distrust (13.1n. *Germanos*). In fact, the Aeduan cavalry would play a role at Gergovia (50.1–3n.). **quam latissime possint ... quam maximum**: 9.3n. *quam maximis potest.* **terrorem**: C. shared the Roman belief in "the power of fear" (Lendon 2015: 7–9).

8.4 celeriter: 4.6n. **haec fama ac nuntii‹s›**: α's text is possible. But the demonstrative is harsh (the instances DKM list at 4.24.4 *eadem alacritate ac studio* do not quite match), nominatives and ablatives are commonly confused, and *BC* 2.37.2 *res secundae in Africam nuntiis ac litteris perfere-bantur* supports Manutius' conjecture. That *fama* outpaces all is a com-monplace (3.2n. *fama*); the word order intimates as much. **perterriti**: a word much favored in *CC* (esp. the part. perf.); C. prefers it to *terrere* 4:1 (cf. *TLL* 10.1.1782.19–43). His vocabulary of fear is limited compared with other Roman historians (Travilian 2013). **omne ad se bellum**: unem-phatic pronouns often follow "adjectives of quantity and size" (Adams 1994b: 125; cf. 4.6n. *celeriter sibi*); *omne* reprises *omnes* emphatically. **ut suis fortunis consulat**: an instance of indir. reflexivity (as is *se*). Polyb. 3.61.9 has the Romans ask of Tiberius "to come to the aid of their state," βοηθεῖν τοῖς ἰδίοις πράγμασιν.

8.5 quorum ille precibus permotus: relative pronouns frequently "host" nominative pronouns (Adams 1994b: 144; cf. 5.2n. *quorum erant*); but the order also mirrors *circumsistunt* advantageously. In line with contem-poraneous practice, C. prefers *permotus* (and *commotus*) to *motus* (*TLL* 10.1.1567.41–44). This is not the last time V. will yield to emotional appeal (cf. 15.6; *Introd.* 3g). **mouet** echoes *permotus*, the action being ele-gantly linked to its motivation.

9 With V. back among the Aruerni and thus out of his way, C. leaves Brutus in charge of his troops (a loose end [§2n.]), pretending to wish to fetch more troops; but, unbeknownst to all, he hurries to Vienne, whence north to his legions. V. moves his troops back to the Bituriges and on to the Boii (Thévenot 1960: 35–40 details the movements).

C. offers a masterclass in warfare "as an exercise of the mind" (Adcock 1956: 52; cf. Loreto 1993: 308–35; *Introd.* 3d): He outwits his opponent, whose moves he anticipates (nn. on §1 *quod … opinione praeceperat*, 10), always appearing two steps ahead (as underpinned by the recurrent pre-fix *prae- ceperat, miserat, curreret*); he moves with such speed – its effect enhanced by specifications of the brief durations (§§ 1 *biduum*, 2 *triduo*; cf. 11n.) and reiterated mention of forced marches (§§ 3, 4) – as to outpace even rumors of his arrival (nn. on §§4 *celeritate*, 5 *aduentu*); and he exe-cutes his designs under the cover of secrecy and deception, therein, too, the consummate general (nn. on §§ 1 *per causam, ut peruagentur*, 3–5). There is triumphant exuberance in the phrasing (*usu uentura opinione praeceperat, celeritate praecurreret, priusque nuntiari … posset*) – echoing relief?

9.1 At marks a change of subject with more or less contrastive force (Goodyear on Tac. *Ann.* 1.49.1; but his comment on C. lacks nuance); it is frequent in C. (and *BAlex.*). **biduum … moratus**: a variously modified formula (incl. 5.4, 82.4), often used in transition (so at 32.1). It was a fixture of military reports (Cic. *Fam.* 15.2.3, 4.6; *BAfr.* 2.3 with Wölfflin-Miodoński; Rambaud 27–28) and military narratives more generally; cf. the equally formulaic ἐνταῦθα ἔμεινεν ἡμέρας ἑπτά, "there he remained for seven days," Xen. *An.* 1.2.6. **in his locis:** "*loco* and *locis*, esp. when used with adjectives, usually omit *in*" (G-L 385N1); but it is quite frequent in *CC*, incl. 20.4, 25.1, 79.2. **quod haec ... opinione praeceperat** "for he had anticipated (*OLD praecipere* 4) this [development]"; the parenthetical expression emphasizes C.'s planning (cf. 16.3n. *ratione prouidere*). C. generally favors abls. of respect that highlight the part of the person involved in the verb's action (cf. 19.3n. *animo*); but here *opinione* also contrasts with *usu* and *inopinantes* (§3). *opinione praecipere* recurs in Livy 35.35.5. **de,** "regarding," indicates "the subject of speech, thought ... [or] other action" (*OLD* 12). **usu uentura** "would in fact occur"; this idiomatic use of *usus* (*OLD* 8a) occurs only here in C. **per causam** signifies a pretext (only here in *BG*; cf. *BAlex.* 49.1 *per causam ... speciosam*; *OLD causa* 5). C. would have feared spies. **Brutum adulescentem:** Decimus Iunius (*RE* 55a) Brutus had joined C. at the beginning of his proconsulship (cf. 3.11.5). He would receive a critical post at Alesia (87n.), fight for C. during the civil war (*BC* 1.56.1–58.4), but then join the conspirators. He is almost always identified as *adulescens*, possibly to differentiate him from his father M. I. Brutus; certainly, no tendentious undertone can be discerned (3.11.5, 3.14.3, 7.87.1; *TLL* 1.795.36–37; 4.1n.). **his copiis:** the troops that had accompanied C. across the Cévennes.

9.2 We do not hear of Brutus until c. 87 (C. may have left him and part of the troops behind as additional protection for *prouincia* [Jullian 1977: 132]); a loose end like 11.2n. *Trebonium.* **in omnes ... latissime ... peruagentur:** the pleonasm is used *affirmationis gratia* (Quint. 8.3.54; cf. Sandys on Dem. 54.30 ἐκκρούων); *peruagentur* first here in C. (cf. 45.1n.). The tactic serves as a diversion from the actual plan. **quam latissimi** repeats 8.3.

9.3–5 Among the criteria of a successful military operation, Polyb. 9.13 lists "secrecy" and "knowledge of routes by day and night (τὰς ἡμερησίους καὶ νυκτερινὰς πορείας) and their distances," not least to ensure speed; its completion would redound to the credit of the general's planning (Polyb. 10.9.2). Such secrecy becomes a commonplace: Xen. *An.* 1.3.1, *Ages.* 6; Polyb. 10.6.7; Frontin. *Str.* 1.1; Onas. 9.22. **his constitutis rebus** is a transition formula that C. favors (10x, incl. 64.4), others not so much. **suis inopinantibus:** C. uses the third person of "his men" (*OLD suus* 6) less frequently than the first (16.3n.); cf. 8.3n. *inopinantes.* **quam maximis potest itineribus:** identical at 1.7.1 and once outside C. (Cic. *Fam.* 15.4.7, intimating its military provenance); without *posse* in Hirt. 8.50.1, Sall. *Hist.* 4.59, Tac. *Hist.* 4.24.1. Both are variations on the formulaic *magnis (maioribus, maximis) itineribus*, wherein *iter* regularly signifies "(a day's) march" (*TLL* 7.2.540.29–46). One of C.'s poetic attempts is not improperly entitled *Iter*. C. varies 8.3 *quam … maximum*, reallocating *potest*. **Viennam**: in *prouincia* (viz. the territory of the Allobroges), it straddles the Rhône; mod. Vienne and Saint-Romain-en-Gal and Sainte-Colombe.

9.4 nactus: a favorite word with C. (Odelman 1985: 84–85). **recentem** "newly arrived" rather than "fresh" (*OLD* 1b, 2b), as the contrast to "many days before" in the following rel. clause emphasizes C.'s speed. **quem … praemiserat**: most likely, part of C.'s cavalry accompanied him across the Cévennes (8.3), part was dispatched to Vienne. **multis ante diebus**: a common anastrophe. **eo**: 6.1n. *Caesari … ille*. **diurno … intermisso**: similarly 56.5; cf. also 1.38.7, *BC* 3.13.1. **Lingones**: eastern neighbors of the Aedui and the Senones, with Andematunum (Langres) as their capital, they were loyal to Rome from the beginning of the campaign until the end (1.40.11, 8.11.2; Cass. Dio 40.38.3 may suggest tensions). **hiemabant**: 1.2n. *exercitum*. **si quid etiam** = *etiamsi quid*; cf. 6.43.3 *si qui etiam in praesentia se occultassent, tamen* … and *TLL* 5.2.934.75–935.30 for further instances. **quid … consilii**: the separation of *quis/quid* (and neuter pronouns generally) from a partitive genitive is frequent and can be traced back to Cato (Ahlberg 1911: 89); but the degree here is noteworthy (sim. 77.8; 4.13.3). **Haeduis**: for C.'s suspicion of them, cf. 5n. **iniretur**: an impersonal passive. **celeritate praecurreret**: another instance of emphatic pleonasm. *celeritas in conficiendo* was a *uirtus imperatoria* (Cic. *Leg. Man.* 29; Combès 1966: 288–98), famously associated with Pompey, Scipio Africanus, and Alexander. It became a proverbial characteristic of C.'s campaign style that awed his contemporaries (Cic. *Att.* 16.10.1 *aiunt enim eum Caesariana uti celeritate*; *Att.* 16.10.1, 7.22.1; Woodman on Vell. Pat. 2.41.1) and later found expression in Lucan's lightning (1.151–57). It is a hallmark of C.'s self-portrait (starting 1.13; Rambaud 251–54; Gerlinger 2008: 159–76), whose withholding of geographic specificity augments the impression. But the *commentarii* also show that speed requires circumspection (cf. 47.3; *Introd.* 3d [fn. 192]); and they contain many references to *celeritas* of an enemy (4.6n. *celeriter*; Grillo 2012: 14–36).

9.5 eo cum peruenisset: 6.2n. **reliquas legiones**: the six legions at Agedincum and the two among the Treueri (1.2n. *exercitum*). **mittit** "to send someone" (*OLD* 16), elliptical. **omnes in unum**: a common and variously proverbial antithesis (cf. Verg. *Aen.* 2.65 *crimine ab uno disce omnes*, with Horsfall; Cic. *Att.* 2.19.3 *una uox omnium*; Otto 358), recurring at 15.5, 29.6, 63.6, 67.3, 84.2. C. gathered his legions in his main winter camp at Agedincum (as 10.4 suggests). **quam … posset**: "[a]fter Historical Tenses the Subjunctive is almost invariable when the action does not, or is not to, take place," G-L 577. **de ... nuntiari** occurs only here in *CC* (cf. 1.1n. *cognoscit de*). **aduentu**: conforming to tradition (cf. Thuc. 7.42.3; Cic. *Leg. Man.* 13, 30), C. dramatizes arrivals, esp. his own. They are promised or anticipated, mark *peripeteiai* (88.1n.), and epitomize speed, which is here too great to allow for advance notice: a commonplace that can be traced back to Hdt. 1.79, where Cyrus marches so swiftly, he is "himself the herald of his arrival (αὐτὸς ἄγγελος)"; cf. Tac. *Ann.* 2.39.4 *relinquebat famam aut praeueniebat, Ann.* 15.4.1 *ut famam sui praeiret.* C. also employs this topos at 5.39.1, 6.30.2; *BC* 3.7.2, 36.1.3: all mention *fama* (3.2n.), which we should associate here, too (as suggested by *fama ac nuntiis*). Other instances of C.'s *aduentus* in *VII*: 10.3, 12.1, 18.3, 67.7, 88.1; the continuators celebrated them, too (Hirt. 8.3.1; the panegyrical tradition: Oakley on Livy 10.11.4).

9.6 hac re cognita: a common transition formula in *CC* (*VII*: 18.2, 34.3, 41.5, 45.1, 56.1, 72.1; C-L 73); much rarer elsewhere. **rursus ... reducit** "[V.]" in turn (*OLD rursus* 4) led [his army] back"; but *rursus* might also signify repetition (*OLD* 3), in which case: "led ... back *again*." **atque inde**: a paratactic formula frequently used by C. (and *BAlex.*) instead of *unde.* **Gorgobinam, Boiorum oppidum**: even if, strictly speaking, this is the dir. obj. of *oppugnare* rather than an acc. of direction with *profectus* (as the latter should require *ad* in the apposition [cf. G-L 337R2]), a Latin speaker would have associated it with both verbs. Thévenot's localization of the *oppidum* at Sancerre has found favor (1960: 27–61; Krausz 2015: 19). He also argues that its original name was "Gortona"; but most edd. opt for Gorgobina as (slightly) favored by the MSS. The Celtic Boii originated in central Europe but migrated and settled variously (cf. eponymous Bohemia and Bologna [*DLG* 82]): they fought the Romans in the third century, and Plautus could pun on their name at *Capt.* 888 (Williams 2001: 211–12; 17.3n.); later on they fought C. in the Helvetian war (1.5.3; Thévenot 1960: 27–43, 52). **quos ... attribuerat**: in 58, C. "gave them as a present to the Aedui" (Jullian 1977: 136; cf. 1.28.5, 10.1n. *stipendiariis*). This is their first reappearance since then. *attribuere*, "to put under the political jurisdiction of" is a technical term (*OLD* 5b). **oppugnare instituit** recurs at 11.1, 12.2; *BC* 3.9.2. Just as *constituere, instituere* appears in military formulae to express decisions (Rambaud 33–34): 19.6, 56.5, 68.3. The siege has met with skepticism in the light of the Boian anti-Roman actions later (10.3; 17.3; 75.4; Krausz 2015: 20).

10 Forced to either leave his winter quarters prematurely and risk supply shortages or abandon an ally and hazard the loyalty of others, C. sets out for the beleaguered Boii (cf. 12n.), thus acting as a true representative of *Romanitas* (§§1–2n.).

The chapter, which echoes cc. 6+7 (cf. 6–13n.), lucidly exemplifies
C.'s scheme of analysis – decision – action: Gallic moves cause difficulty
(§1 *magnam ... difficultatem ... afferebat*, 6.2 *magna difficultate afficiebatur* –
descriptive imperfects), the nature of which is spelled out in two parallel
conditionals (nn. on §1 *quod ... esse*, 6.3–4). C. forms a decision (§2 *uisum
est*; 7.4 *existimauit* – resultative perfects) in emotive language (*omnes diffi-
cultates*; nn. on *perpeti, tanta contumelia, suorum*), which he enacts (§§3–4
praemittit, proficiscitur; 7.4 *confirmat* – dramatic presents). The pattern of
time is finely spun (cf. Mack 1978: 48 on Verg.), contributing to the air
of swift decisiveness.

Like cc. 6+7, it also offers a demonstration of C.'s *scientia suorum consiliorum explicandorum*, which, next to *celeritas*, is his most emphasized quality (Hirt. 8 *praef.*7; Rambaud 250–52; *Introd.* 3d). These demonstrations
correspond to the ancients' esteem for military planning (Moore 2013):
Polybius deplored generals who expressed surprise when outmaneuvered
(10.32.12); Cicero knew to praise Pompey's *consilium in prouidendo* and
consilii celeritas (*Leg. Man.* 29, 30); and Frontinus hoped that studying
consilii ... et prouidentiae exempla would help readers to devise their own
stratagems (*Str.* 1.*praef.*1).

10.1–2 C. here (33.1–2, 54.2, and elsewhere, e.g. 1.33.2; cf. Hirt. 8.6.2,
BAlex. 34; Cic. *Prou. cons.* 25 *in gremio imperii*, *Fam.* 15.4.1, Livy 21.19.10,
Tac. *Ann.* 15.1.3) alludes to the Roman *patrocinium orbis terrae* (Cic. *Off.*
2.27), viz. the notion "that the *maiestas* of Rome involved her in an obliga-
tion to protect her allies ... [T]his view is difficult to substantiate in official
pronouncements [but common among] certain Roman writers" (Paul *ad*
Sall. *Iug.* 14.7; cf. Lavan 2013: 176–210).

10.1 C. describes his conundrum in the form of another *complexio* (6.3–
4n.). The year before, he had marched against the Neruii *nondum hieme
confecta* but then returned with his legions into winter camps (6.3).
Magnam ... difficultatem ... afferebat: the wording at *BC* 3.51.6 and
Amm. Marc. 21.13.7 is close. While the hyperbaton is emphatic, the con-
voluted order is functional – it forms an immediately intelligible self-sufficient unit – and frequent in C. (below, 20.7 *imperium ... nullum*; DKM *ad*
5.11.8 *maiores ... copiae*; cf. 25.4n. *omnis ... multitudo*). The difficulty (cf.
6.2n.) is detailed by alternative *ne*-clauses (K-S II 254.3), each headed by
a conditional clause. **ad consilium capiendum**: *consilium capere* occurs 30x
in C. (8x in *CC*); cf. 7.3n. *consiliis*. **reliquam partem hiemis**: roughly the
period from mid-March into late May (cf. 32.2n. *hieme confecta*). **stipendiariis Haeduorum**: sc. the Boii, cf. 9.6. This appears to contradict the information given at 1.28.4 (cf. 75.4n. *Bois*; *Introd.* 3a). **expugnatis**: the *uerbum
proprium* for "storm[ing] troops in a fortified position" (*OLD* 1b; contrast

9.6 *oppugnare*). **cuncta Gallia**: the expression occurs only here in *CC* (*G. omnis/tota* is preferred). *cunctus* is a sophisticated and official synonym of *omnis*, frequent in epic and historiography (Adams 1973a: 129–31). It may have a Ciceronian tone, as *Italia cuncta* was "a major motif ... in all the speeches [Cic.] delivered after his return from exile" (Kaster *ad* Cic. *Sest.* 25). **nullum ... praesidium**: another self-sufficient unit. The language casts C. as *patronus* and the Boii as *clientes*; cf. Cic. *De or.* 1.184 *praesidium clientibus atque opem amicis*; *VL* 172–74. **amicis** "(of foreign rulers, states, *etc.*) having friendly relations with one's state" (*OLD* 2b; cf. 31.5n.), i.e. the Boii or the Aedui. The dat. depends on *praesidium*. **uideret**: sc. *Gallia*, a common metonymy (*Gallia pro Gallis*). **maturius**: forms derived from *matur-* appear regularly in military reporting (Cic. *Fam.* 15.2.1 *maturius ... uenire*; Galba [Cic.] *Fam.* 10.30.1). But here it resonates, by its common meaning of "ripe" (*OLD* 1), with *res frumentaria*. **educeret**: either used absolutely (*OLD* 1b; common enough but unparalleled in C.) or with *legiones* (as supplied from above). **ab re frumentaria ... laboraret** "he would suffer hardship over supplies." *BC* 3.9.5 is phrased similarly, and the rare *laborare ab* may recur at *BAfr.* 5 (cf. *TLL* 7.2.804.64–65). A general had to ensure his men's "safety and possession of what they needed" (Xen. *Mem.* 3.2), and C. knew that insufficient supplies undermined a general's authority and *saepius ... penuria quam pugna consumit exercitum* (Veg. 3.3; cf. Xen. *Cyr.* 1.6.9, 18, 6.2.25–40). He mentions his concern for provisions frequently, but esp. in this campaign (14.2–4, 17.3, 18.1n. *pabulo*, 20.10, 36.1, 55.9, 90.7n. *frumentariae*), when Drappes' interception, Cita's death, and his allies' reluctance compounded the issue (nn. on 3.1, 5, 10.2 *commeatu*; cf. *Introd.* 3c; Goldsworthy 1998: 202–04). **duris subuectionibus** breaks the parallelism: it is semantically but not syntactically parallel to the causal clause *quod ... esse. duris* = "hard to deal with" (*OLD* 9), because of the weather conditions (cf. 8.2 *durissimo tempore*). *subuectio* is rare (and only here in *CC*).

10.2 praestare ... perpeti is clichéd (cf. 2.31.6, 7.1.8 [with n. on *praestare*], 17.7, *BC* 2.30.2). **omnes ... perpeti**: varies the formulaic *omnia perpeti* (*BC* 3.9.5; cf. Shackleton Bailey, *Propertiana* 291). C.'s soldiers will echo the sentiment (17.7n.). The compound emphasizes endurance "to the full/ end." **contumelia** "affront" (*OLD*) is stronger than *iniuria*, as it involves an attack on *dignitas* (Livy 26.29.8 *quanto maiorem iniuriam, immo contumeliam*; *VL* 405). **suorum**: in reference to allied Gauls only here in C. (cf. 13.1n. *suis*). It heightens the emotionality, even if it may include C.'s legionaries, as eager as him to protect their reputation. *suus* also makes for a pointed antithesis with *alienare*. **uoluntates** "goodwill" (*OLD* 10b).

10.3 itaque: the realization of what should be done (*praestare uisum*) is typically followed by a description of what was done, which is frequently introduced by *itaque* (35.2, 55.5, 56.3, 73.2; Rambaud 35). **cohortatus ... de**: the construction (cf. 1.1n. *cognoscit de*) is attested at Cic. *Red. pop.* 11. **supportando commeatu**: a frequent collocation in *CC*, rare elsewhere (*TLL* 3.1824.18–20); the verb is technical, the noun signifies the "obtaining of supplies, provisions" (*OLD* 4b). **praemittit**: sc. *eos* (as inferred from the rel. clause). **qui ... sustineant** forms a chiasmus (*de suo aduentu* + verb || verb + *ut*). **hortenturque** echoes *cohortatus* for urgency. **ut in fide maneant**: already at 4.5; the formulaic phrase is esp. common in Livy (*TLL* 6.1.675.33–39). The Boii's questionable loyalty: 9.6n. *oppugnare*. **maneant ... sustineant**: a marked homoioteleuton (cf. *HLR* 725–28). **atque** "and, more particularly" (*OLD* 8). **impetum ... sustineant**: like the Greek historians, C. centers his "grammar of battle descriptions" on physical metaphors, such as 59.5 *instare*, 51.1n. *premere*, and 87.3 *uis*; but unlike them, he "tends to envisage the fundamental mechanics of battle not as the pushing of a weight [i.e. of the phalanx] but as the crash of one moving force, an *impetus*, against a stationary one," which must "sustain" it (Lendon 1999: 281, 285–90).

10.4 Agedinci: the chief town of the Senones (who bestowed on it its modern name Sens [*DLG* 270]), located at the intersection of two thoroughfares (Chevallier 1997: 211, 216). **impedimentis ... relictis**: the expression occurs 9x in C. (1x in *BAlex.*). Heavy baggage was routinely left behind before an attack (55.2n.). **ad Boios**: C. headed *towards* (*OLD ad* 3) them but did not reach them.

11 Leaving Agedincum to bring relief to the Boii in the east (a loose end [12n.]), C. circles in a westerly direction via Vellaunodunum to Cenabum, both stormed by his troops.

C.'s route surprises, and all the more given his careful justifications (§1 *ne ... relinqueret*, §3 *quam primum*; cf. 12.2 *positum in uia*). But he may have followed roads from Agedincum to Cenabum and Avaricum (Chevallier 1997: 89), not to mention his need of a bridge (§6); and his audience did not possess sufficient grasp of Gallic geography anyway. It further surprises that the attack on Cenabum is the only unmotivated one, when revenge was ready at hand (but is reserved for later instead [28.4]).

The narrative emphasizes C.'s speed again, which overwhelms the Gauls (§4n. *longius*): He specifies the brief time span each step required (*altero die, tertio die, biduo*), which culminate in the seizure of Cenabum the night of his arrival; and he omits all ekphrastic detail of the siegecraft that would slow down his account, typically aligning narrative and narrated time.

11.1 Altero die "the next day"; a rare synonym for *postero die* (Durand 1930), it occurs first here in *BG* (then 68.2, thrice in *BC*; cf. 27.1n.). **oppidum:** 8x in this paragraph, a frequency suggestive of the series of rapid captures. **Vellaunodunum:** its precise location is uncertain, Château-Landon a possibility (Goudineau 1998: 178–79). **ne ... relinqueret, quo ... uteretur:** cf. Hannibal's similar reasoning that, having seized Saguntum, "he could march on safely, with no enemy left behind at his rear (οὐδὲν ἀπολιπὼν ὄπισθεν πολέμιον), and that he would then abound in supplies (εὐπορήσειν ... χορηγιῶν, Polyb. 3.17.6–7)." **quo** "so that thereby" (*OLD* 3). **expeditiore** "more readily available" (cf. *OLD* 4). **eoque biduo** "within two days [of the beginning of the siege]," an idiomatic expression (cf. *BC* 1.41.1, 87.4; *BAlex.* 9.3; K-S 356–57). *eo* (instead of *eius* by enallage [cf. *TLL* 7.2.470.26–28]) loosely resumes *oppugnare instituit*; α's *idque* simplifies matters. **circumuallauit:** sc. *oppidum*; first here in C. The circumvallation is an "encirclement designed to ensure the complete investment of a target" (Davies 2006: 63). It was a common feature of Rome's siegecraft at C.'s time (Campbell 2019: 246; cf. nn. on 36, 72–74). There are over 100 references to engineering in the *commentarii*, 16 in *VII* alone (Dodington 1980: 80–85; cf. *Introd.* 3e).

11.2 de deditione may be construed with *legatis* or independently (*TLL* 5.1.74.37–39). Roman treatment of an enemy depended on whether and when they received the *deditio*; cf. 2.32.1; 8.44; Cic. *Off.* 1.35, Livy 1.38; Timpe 1972, Gilliver 1996. **arma ... dari:** a rising tricolon. C. evokes the language of the *deditio in fidem* (Livy 1.38.1–2 with Ogilvie; cf. Krebs 2018b: 124). To stipulate the surrender of weapons and hostages was common (cf. the bronze tablet of Alcántara [Nörr 1989: 21–22], Livy 28.34.7; 89.4). **sescentos obsides:** C. often stints on specific numbers; here he provides a standardized figure (12x, 1x *CC*), which often means "many" (Usener 1903: 353; cf. Scheidel 1996: 224 on "multiples of thirty"). **C. Trebonium:** he had, as *tribunus plebis* (*MRR* 2.217), secured the provinces of Spain and Syria for Pompey and Crassus in 55. With C. subsequently, he acquitted himself well into the civil wars but joined the assassins (*RE* "Trebonius" 6). He disappears until 81.6 (another loose end [Rambaud 64–65]; cf. 9n.). **legatum relinquit:** 40.3n.

11.3 ipse ... proficiscitur: similarly in 5.1 (of V.). **conficeret:** the repetition may have caused α's *faceret*; but such repetitions are frequent, and "to conclude his journey" makes better sense. *iter conficere* belongs to the military register and is frequent in *CC* (cf. 34.3n. *iter facere*). **Carnutum:** this possessive gen. with towns or territories (6.3.4 *Luteciam Parisiorum*) may shade into a chorographic genitive (G-L 362N2), as in 1.10.5 *in fines Vocontiorum ulterioris prouinciae*.

11.4 qui tum primum allato nuntio "and they, as soon as news reached them." The *TLL* lists parallels for *primum* + participle, e.g. *ueniens*, in the sense of *ubi primum uenit* (10.2.1367.38–45; cf. *BC* 3.106.4). **oppugnatione** echoes *oppugnare*, tightening the narrative. **longius … existimarent:** a reasonable expectation (cf. Polyb. 1.17.9 "the siege promising to be long," Livy 34.34.2 *res tam lenta quam ipsi scitis oppugnatio urbium*); it sets C.'s *celeritas bellandi* in relief (cf. 8.3n. *inopinantibus*). **eam rem** = *oppugnationem*, exemplifying C.'s use of *res* where a pronoun would suffice (Lebreton 1901: 30–33); cf. 4.7n. *potestate*. **tuendi causa:** the phrase has been doubted, as (a) it is unclear why news of an attack on Vellaunodunum should motivate the dispatch of troops to Cenabum, and (b) *quod eo mitterent* is redundant (but not so without the dubious phrase). Neither objection is decisive, however, and the narrative moves on to Cenabum. **comparabant** "they began assembling"; the inchoative aspect (G-L 233) contrasts with *peruenit*. **huc biduo peruenit:** the terse sentence contrasts with its lengthy forerunner, marking C.'s speedy arrival. The repetition of §1 *biduo* highlights the rapid, brief intervals.

11.5–6 Three main clauses, each containing a subordinate clause, each linked by *-que, et*, form a typical "phrase à relance" (*Introd.* 3b). **castris … positis:** the typical temporary camp consisted of a ditch, a rampart, and a parapet (Ps.-Hyg. *Mun. castr.* 49, with Luttwak 2016: 60–63). "[A] fine-tuned instrument of war," it would normally be set up every day (cf. 2.20.2; Polyb. 6.31.12–14, Frontin. *Str.* 4.7.2, Veg. 1.21; Dobson 2013). It symbolized Rome and its conquest: *uidemus populum Romanum orbem subegisse terrarum … disciplina castrorum* (Veg. 1.1; cf. Polyb. 6.42; Goldsworthy 1996: 111–13; 30.4n. *laboris*). **diei tempore:** the first of four instances in *VII* (16.2, 35.5, 68.3), but not elsewhere in C. (but 4x *CC*); a local repetition. C. advocates the genitive singular endings *die* and *specie* at *De anal.* F26; but the MSS do not bear this out. **exclusus:** a witty word choice, as C. is not so much "shut out" (*OLD* 1) from the town as "prevented" (*OLD* 3) by the time of day. **in posterum** sc. *diem.* **quaeque … sint:** C. frequently employs *-que* to connect sentences, esp. when it introduces an action naturally pursuant to the preceding statement (K-S II 13). The subjunctive signifies an indir. question (cf. *OLD imperare* 4e; so 16.2, 31.4), or a rel. clause either generic or in virtual indir. speech (or both; cf. *BC* 2.40.2). *quae ad* + acc. (often gerundive) *usui sint/sunt* is formulaic in military situations.

11.6 contingebat: south of the river lay the Bituriges' territory. **excubare** "to keep watch out in the open" (*OLD* 1a+c); cf. Cic. *Diu.* 1.112 *ut urbem et tecta linquerent armatique* (sc. *Lacedaemonii*) *in agro excubarent*. First here in Latin literature; cf. 69.7n. *excubitoribus*.

11.7 C.'s anticipation (*ueritus*) forestalls the Gauls' escape. **paulo ante mediam noctem silentio ex oppido egressi**: first instance of a "local formula" that C. reemploys at 36.7, 58.2, 60.1+4, 81.1, and Sall. *Iug.* 106.4 and Livy 24.40.11 adapt. *silentium* occurs first here in C. and recurs, in juxtaposition with *nox*, at 18.2, 26.2, 28.6, 36.7, 81.1 (*BAlex.* 61.2). It contributes to *euidentia* (*HLR* §§ 810–19; Kraus 2010b: 259–61). **transire coeperunt**: *coepisse* + inf. occurs 13x in *VII*, a "constant use … especially characteristic of what might be called popular/informal/naive narrative" (Adams 2016: 126). Cf. 26.4n. *conclamare … coeperunt.*

11.8 qua … nuntiata: 7.3n. **exploratores**: military writers stress the importance of reconnaissance (Veg. 3.6, Onas. 6.7). Suet. *Iul.* 58 praises C. in this regard; in fact, the *commentarii* mention *exploratores* some 25x. Likely Gallic or Germanic auxiliaries, they often operated at a great distance (Austin-Rankov 1995: 42–54, 95–102). **expeditas** "ready for action" (*OLD* 1), i.e. free of *impedimenta* and *sarcinae* (cf. 18.1n. *expeditis*). **portis incensis**: the gates were weak points; *cauetur … ne portae subiectis ignibus exurantur* (Veg. 3.4). **perpaucis … quin cuncti caperentur** "very few … were missing from an otherwise complete capture." The appended abl. absolute substitutes for *neque multum afuit*. Adjectives with *per-*, extremely rare in poetry, are "characteristic of the polite, urbane language of Cicero's dialogues and letters" (Powell on Cic. *Sen.* 3 *perstudiosum*). C. employs them moderately (*Index*, s.v. "*per-*"). He is fond of *quin*, which he uses similarly loosely at 44.3; in connection with *desiderare* it is unparalleled (and overlooked in the *TLL*). *capere* is frequent in military inscriptions (Riggsby 196–97). **quod … angustiae … intercluserant**: a commonplace; cf. Livy 10.5.10 *haerent fugientes in angustiis portarum* (with Oakley). It recurs at Avaricum (28.3).

11.9 The brutal destruction of Cenabum (cf. 28.4–5n.), narrated *imperatoria breuitate*, is both punishment and determent (cf. Walbank 1974: 14–15; Levithan 2013: 205–27). **diripit atque incendit** is a sadly "conventional pair … in … logical order" (Kraus on Livy 6.4.9), wherein *diripere* signifies looting, raping, and killing (Ziolkowski 1993). **praedam donat**: the *praeda* included goods and inhabitants (6.3.2 *magno pecoris atque hominum numero capto atque ea praeda militibus concessa*; 89.5). The *locus classicus* for how the Romans distributed loot is Polyb. 10.16.2–17.5. Soldiers expected a share to supplement their salary (Paul *ad* Sall. *Iug.* 41.7 *praedas*; Keppie 1998: 54–55; cf. 28.4n. *praedae*). For them to receive all was exceptional and certain to raise morale (cf. *BAlex.* 42.3). C. never mentions the wealth plundered from Gaul (Catull. 29.1–4, Suet. *Iul.* 54.2 *urbes diruit saepius ob praedam quam ob delictum*, Plut. *Caes.* 20.3; Morstein-Marx 2021: 616–21 details the profits); it secured loyalty in the civil war (Suet. *Iul.* 38.1). For the Romans' reputation of a "liking for loot," cf. Balsdon 1979: 172–76.

12 V. learns of C.'s approach and departs from Gorgobina to confront him amongst the Bituriges; C. thus accomplishes (but does not remark upon) what he set out to do (10.4n. *ad Boios*), and without entering Boian territory even. When V.'s vanguard appears before Noviodunum, its inhabitants resume fighting.

V.'s encounter with C. marks a turning point, suitably dramatized by his cavalry's arrival in the dusty distance (§4n. *equitatus*). It brings the first major plotline to an end.

12.1 Vercingetorix ubi: C. normally places a subject common to both main and subordinate clause before the conjunction; exceptions occur (14.10, 20.6, 32.5). The chapter divisions are not authorial (they go back to Jungermann's 1606 edition); yet it seems significant that V. opens six chapters (14, 16, 20, 71, 84; cf. 64, 89), as it is a unique concentration, which testifies to his preeminence (*Introd.* 3g). More on such headings in narratives of swiftly changing focalization in C-L 18–21, Luce 1971: 285–87. **oppugnatione**: sc. *Gorgobinae* (9.6). **obuiam**: first here in C.

12.2 ille "denotes that which is more remote from the speaker" (G-L 307); the focalization is still V.'s. **Nouiodunum**, the Celtic equivalent of "Newtown" (*DLG* 155, 236), is attested of several fortifications, whereof the *BG* mentions three (2.12; 7.55n.). This *oppidum* has been located at Neung-sur-Beuvron (Delétang 2008: 17–24). **in uia**: its position justifies C.'s decision to besiege it despite his hurry. **oppugnare instituerat** repeats 9.6n. (of V.) and resonates with *oppugnatione desistit*; a typical parallel between C. and V. (*Introd.* 3g).

12.3 A typical Caesarian period. The friendly advance of town representatives is a topos in narratives of surrender, as are "open gates" (below, §12.5): Sall. *Iug.* 46.5 *ex oppidis … procedebant parati … omnia quae imperarentur facere* (adapted in Livy 6.25.7), Dion. Hal. *Ant. Rom.* 8.14.1–2. **quo ex oppido**: the repetition of the antecedent is a common feature of administrative writing (Odelman 148–52), a provenance also suggested by the kind of words repeated (*dies, locus, iter*). Its frequency decreases across the *commentarii* (*VII*: 4.7n. *potestate*, 69.2, 69.7). **ad eum**: *is* regularly continues *ille* (K-S 626). **oratum ut sibi ignosceret** recurs at *BAlex.* 67.1. *sibi* and *suae* are indir. reflexives (referring to the *legati*). **ignosceret … consuleret**: a particularly clear instance of *interpretatio* (*Rhet. Her.* 4.28), often called "theme and variation," i.e. the "combination of two adjacent expressions apparently conveying the same idea, so that the second appears as a variation" (Conte 1993: 209); frequent in *VII. consulere* = "to give thought to" (*OLD* 6b); but effectively = *parcere.* **ut celeritate ... conficeret ... erat consecutus:** C. highlights his most eminent characteristic (9.4n. *celeritate*). *erat consecutus* varies *conficeret.* **arma ... dari** repeats 11.2n. Such repetitions in proximity are common (Eden 1962: 86; 69.7n. *ne ... fieret*).

12.4 iam: a marker of temporal transition (C-L 497–517); only *III* counts as many instances as *VII.* **obsidum:** the close repetition of *obsides* tightens the narrative (cf. 90.2n. *imperat*). **centurionibus:** at C.'s time, a centurion led a *centuria*, a division roughly eighty men strong, six of which formed a *cohors.* The centurions enjoy C.'s special attention – amidst the Venetian crisis, *Caesar ... processit centurionibusque <u>nominatim</u> appellatis reliquos cohortatus milites* (2.25.2) – and often appear to "fight against all the odds to win [his notice]" (Welch 1998: 90; cf. Brown 1999: 356; nn. on 147.7, 50.4–6). They were reputedly violent; hence Tacitus' reference to them as *ea uetustissima militaribus odiis materies* (*Ann.* 1.32.1). In general, see Dobson 1974: 393–95. **equitatus ... antecesserat:** the appearance of cavalry in the distance is a topos, vividly represented by the shape-shifting cloud at Xen. *An.* 1.8.8–9 (cf. Polyaenus 8.23.6, Veg. 3.5).

12.5–6 C. faced a similar change of heart among the Aduatuci (2.33). The narrative, a series of stock motifs in short sequence, renders the unexpected turn by *simul atque ... atque,* a rapid tricolon, and *noui ... consilii.* **simul atque ... atque:** this coordination occurs only here in *CC* and twice in Lucr. (3.211, 4.319). **in spem ... uenerunt:** C. favors the idiom (M-P 1250.25–35). **clamore sublato:** a stock motif (28.5, 47.3, 48.1, 80.4, 81.3, 84.4) in a formulaic phrase (*VII:* 24.3, 81.2, 88.2). C. knew of the effectiveness of *clamoris horror* (Veg. 3.18): *et hostes terreri et suos incitari* (*BC* 3.92.4–5; cf. Plut. *Cat. Mai.* 1.7). **portas claudere:** closed gates symbolize enmity (esp. 3.17.3, *BC* 1.34.4 *Massilienses portas Caesari clauserant*), open gates amity (esp. 2.32.4). The motif is commonplace; cf. Hdt. 5.104.2, Thuc. 2.2.2, 3.65.3, and esp. 4.85.4: "I am surprised at being shut out from your gates that I do not meet with a welcome from you"; Livy will favor it. **murum complere** "to man (*OLD complere* 6) the wall." This technical use is here first attested; it recurs at 27.3 and 69.5, Verg. *Aen.* 9.39 *Teucri portas et moenia complent,* then predominantly in historical texts (*TLL* 3.20.92.68–82).

12.6 centuriones in oppido "the centurions inside the town" (cf. 7.5n. *ex prouincia*). **ex significatione** "on account of (the Gauls') reaction"; cf. *OLD significatio* 2. **noui ... consilii:** both word order (cf. Cic. *Att.* 1.13.6 *noui tibi quidnam scribam?*) and hyperbaton emphasize the sudden change; the shrill assonance heightens the sense of danger. **ab iis** is typically resumptive (6.1n. *Caesari ... ille*). **gladiis destrictis:** a common motif and phrase (1.25.3, *BC* 1.46.1, 47.1, 75.3; Oakley on Livy 7.16.5). On late-republican *gladii*, see Bishop-Coulston 2006: 54–56. **receperunt** "they pulled out" (*OLD* 11).

13 In their first skirmish, C. defeats V. thanks to his tactical deployment of the Germanic cavalry that he had recruited providently (§1nn. *laborantibus ... summittit, instituerat*). Noviodunum re-surrenders, marking the third surrender in just over a week after C.'s breaking winter camp (10.4): a rapid succession eerily anticipatory of his later capturing Italian cities (Cic. *Fam.* 16.12.2). The battle description (§§1–2), which evokes the military bulletin, is typically schematic, formulaic, and propulsive.

13.1 Cavalry engagements were standard initial gambits (36.1, 53.2, 70.1; Cagniart 1992). **ex castris equitatum educi:** a formula, frequent in C. (incl. 40.1, 79.2, 80.1), once elsewhere (*BAfr.* 38.3). **laborantibus ... summittit** recurs at 70.2, 85.1, 86.1; it is a commonplace (and similarly phrased at Sall. *Iug.* 98.1, Livy 22.28.11, Curt. 9.1.15). *laborare* is technical *de eis qui mala fortuna pugnant* (*TLL* 7.2.807.49; *VII:* 67.4, 85.1, 86.1; cf. 86.3n. *labori*); *summittere* = "to send (relief or reinforcement)," *OLD* 5. The struggling forces were Gallic auxiliaries (cf. Calgacus' indignation over *Britannorum plerosque* amongst Roman troops [Tac. *Agr.* 32.2]). The timely deployment of reserves was deemed crucial (Veg. 3.17); C. offers a masterclass at 87.1. **suis:** 9.3n. **Germanos equites ... quos ab initio ... instituerat:** *initio* probably refers to the beginning of this campaign season. This is the first mention of a Germanic escort (possibly originating the emperor's *Germani corporis custodes* [Speidel 1994: 12–13]). C. expresses reservations about his Gallic cavalry early on (1.42.5; cf. 8.3n. *equitibus*); he was well-advised to seek relief elsewhere, esp. in this seventh year (65.4n.), and Germanic cavalry were reputed fierce (4.12). C. would recruit more later (65.4), and they would repeatedly save his day (67, 70, 80; Campi 1996). His success is all the greater, as V. decided to focus on the cavalry (4.9n. *equitatui*). Cf. 65.4n. *Germaniam.* **CCCC:** a stylized number. Romans favored multiples of four (Scheidel 1996: 224; cf. 11.2n. *sescentos*). **secum habere** refers to an escort; cf. *BC* 1.75.2 *quos suae custodiae causa habere consuerat*, 2.40.1 *quos ... circum se habere*; Speidel 1994: 164n.1. **instituerat** highlights C.'s foresight.

13.2 offers an instance of "theme and variation." **atque:** 10.3n. **in fugam coniecti** is a Caesarian mannerism (9x + *BAfr.* 17.1, 66.1); rare elsewhere. **amissis:** in its meaning "to die," the verb belongs to the military register (*TLL* 1.1931.82–32.85). C. uses it only here of Gallic losses. **rursus** "in turn" rather than "for a second time" (cf. 9.6n.). **oppidani ...**

dediderunt: the surrender of ringleaders was common practice and commonplace; cf. Hdt. 9.86, Polyb. 3.8.8, *BC* 1.20; 89.2. **plebem concitatam** "the common people (*OLD* 2) had been incited"; both terms are common of Rome's civil strife (cf. *TLL* 4.67.37–63; 1–5n.). **ad Caesarem perduxerunt** "they brought [them] before Caesar" (*OLD perducere* 1b, possibly with an administrative ring); again 67.7. **sese:** C. employs *sese* for emphasis (Klotz 1910: 223–39) in contrast to his syntactical recommendation at *De anal.* F29 (of doubtful authenticity [Garcea ad loc.]).

13.3 To move on a major stronghold after several successes (cf. 14.1 *tot incommodis*) is typical; cf. Tac. *Ann.* 14.23.1 *Corbulo post deleta Artaxata utendum recenti terrore ratus ad occupanda Tigranocerta, quibus excisis metum hostium intenderet* ... **quibus rebus confectis:** a frequent transition formula in C. (and *BAlex.* 56.5; again at 90.1). **maximum munitissimumque:** the alliterative superlatives elevate Avaricum to a major site, as required by the *urbs-capta* motif, wherein the assertion of a city's greatness highlights the reversal of its fortune (Polyb. 2.56.6; Arist. *Pol.* 13.4; Rossi 2003: 30–40; nn. on 15.1 *urbes*, 15.4–5). **atque agri fertilissima regione** "and, what is more, (*OLD atque* 1) situated in a most fertile area": *situm erat* can be inferred from *erat* (cf. *OLD sum* 3, 11). *agri* is either a gen. of reference (G-L 374) signifying "grain(fields)" and specifying *fertilissima* (cf. Livy 28.37.8 *insulam ... fertilem agro*); or a chorographic gen. (11.3n. *Carnutum*) meaning "territory" and depending on *regione* (viz. "district in the territory"). **eo oppido recepto** = *si id oppidum recepisset.* **in potestatem redacturum** "would bring (back) under [his] power," an administrative formula (*OLD redigere* 10a+b; again at 77.16); here, the connotation "to bring back" (*OLD* 2) applies, too.

14–28 SIEGING IN THE RAIN: AVARICUM

The battle over Avaricum, the *BG*'s first major siege, is a self-contained "set piece" (Gärtner 1975: 1–7, 74–77; 68–90n.). Its beginning and end are marked by a speech (14, 29), the ring-compositional repetition of *misericordia uulgi* (15.6, 28.6), and the fact that, just as capable men leave <u>for</u> the *oppidum* (15.6), so few escape <u>from</u> it (28.6). It is "built" around the construction of the assault ramp (17.1n. *aggerem*), a demonstration of Rome's technological power (like the siegeworks before Alesia), and comprises two parts: a "prelude" (14–19n.) and an elaboration of the *urbs-capta* motif (20–28n.), the latter being introduced by yet another speech and the dispatch of additional defenders (20, 21).

The episode is dramatized: ending after a month with Avaricum's inevitable fall due to C.'s inspiration (27n.), its "suspense of anticipation"

(6.2–4n.) is heightened by retarding elements that help align narrative and narrated time (esp. 23; cf. 24.1n. *diebus xxv*). It is enlivened by (in)-direct speech, dialogues between the two leaders and their soldiers, autopsy, and vivid detail (*euidentia*), and amplified by specific allusions, some to Troy (nn. on 17, 20–28, 23; cf. Paul 1982: 147–48). It elevates V. as a capable and farsighted leader (nn. on 14, 15, 21), who narrowly fails to trick C. in an emblematic battle of wits (18–19); and it advertises C.'s leadership and his soldiers' *Romanitas* (nn. on 17, 19, 27). In the end, it exemplifies what Vegetius later captured (*Mil.* 1.1): *populum Romanum orbem subegisse terrarum ... armorum exercitio, disciplina castrorum usuque militiae.*

Avaricum (Bourges) was situated in the region of Centre-Val de Loire on top of a hill (cf. 36.1n. *monte*) at the confluence of the Auron and Yèvre. A commercial center with access to several waterways and roads, it served as the capital of the Bituriges. Inhabitants are said to have numbered in the ten-thousands (28.5n.), which the archaeological evidence renders doubtful (Krausz-Ralston 2009). See further Troadec 2006.

14–19 A "new" strategy and an "exception"

From Noviodunum C. marches to Avaricum (13.3). Meanwhile, V. addresses his men, proposing a new strategy. It is approved, and Gallic settlements are lit up near and far, except for Avaricum, which the Gauls decide to defend. V. then follows after C. to Avaricum. When a battle opportunity seems to arise, the Roman siege is briefly suspended.

C.'s plotting reveals his hand: whatever the exact location of Noviodunum, Avaricum cannot have been more than two days away, as a mere 60 miles separated it from Cenabum, Noviodunum lay "on the way" (12.1), and a road facilitated movements (Chevallier 1997: 89). In consequence, the Gallic events detailed in cc. 14–15 cannot have unfolded in such a brief period (V.'s following C. "by shorter stages" [16.1n.] seems odd, too; Cass. Dio 40.34 differs, interestingly). Upon closer inspection, even the strategy *change* is hard to believe, as is Avaricum's exception due to V.'s erroneous concession (cf. *Introd.* 2c). But as improbable as the narrative is historically, so effective is it dramaturgically: A few skirmishes (14.1n. *incommodis*) lead to a debate, wherein V. steps up to make his first major speech in favor of a change of strategy; as this new phase consists largely in the battle over Avaricum, it is given prominence by yet another debate (15n.).

14 V. proposes to the assembled Gauls that they avoid pitched battles; they should instead scorch the earth and harass and starve the Roman troops.

It is a commonplace in Greek and Roman life and literature that a leader be "a speaker of words and doer of deeds" (Hom. *Il.* 9.443; *Introd.*

3), which applies to V. all the more readily, given Roman assumptions about Gallic talents (4n.). Partly due to this leadership ideal, speeches featured prominently in ancient literature ever since the Homeric poems (whence they entered the historiographical tradition [Strasburger 1972: 38–39]). The ancient historians habitually made them up, rewriting them even when an original was at hand (Tac. *Ann.* 11.24 with Malloch 339–41; Marincola 2007b).

C. composed this speech for V. to present to his Roman audience the Gallic strategy. He largely draws on the formulaic language and generic thought proffered in rhetorical handbooks and historical narratives (to be rehashed in 63). The two complimentary strategies are frequently discussed by ancient historians, and the parallels with Pericles' reasoning quoted below are *exempli gratia* (Thuc. 1.140–44; cf. Hdt. 4.120, Sall. *Iug.* 55, and Aen. Tact. 8 [with Whitehead]; Cadiou 2013). In fact, the Romans themselves famously employed this strategy under Q. Fabius Maximus *Cunctator*, and Livy 22.11.5–7 reports his edict (of questionable authenticity [Erdkamp 1992]) in similar fashion: *ut, quibus oppida castellaque immunita* (§9 oppida ... non munitione ... tuta) *essent, ut ii commigrarent in loca tuta, ex agris quoque demigrarent omnes regionis eius qua iturus Hannibal esset* (§5 hoc spatio ... quo ... adire) *tectis prius incensis ac frugibus corruptis ne cuius rei copia esset* (§9 ne ... ad copiam tollendam).

The speech is of the deliberative kind (cf. 1.4–8n.), more particularly, a *contio* (52.1n.). Its *exordium* summarily names the issue (*bellum*) and emphasizes the necessity of a novel approach (*alia ratione*) – a move recommended for making an audience *attentus* (*Rhet. Her.* 1.7). It segues into the *propositio*: to cut the Romans off from supplies (*prohibeantur*). The *confirmatio* (*id esse facile*) demonstrates the viability of the proposal and elaborates on the necessity of sacrifice with the help of a commonplace (§5n.). The affective *peroratio* (*haec si grauia...*) adumbrates the bleak alternative (another commonplace [§10n.]): death and slavery. There are several linguistic idiosyncrasies that may in sum intimate idiolect (nn. on *ad concilium conuocat, abundent, deleri, ipsosne, abstrahi*; cf. nn. on 20, 29.5 *sarturum*; Marincola 2007b: 129).

14.1 tot ... acceptis: the abl. absolute retrieves (1.4n. *indictis*) the sites of defeat in a swift, asyndetic, and chronological tricolon. **continuis** "consecutive" (*TLL* 4.726.58–727.18); but the more typical meaning "continuous" (*OLD* 1) would fit the exaggerative rhetoric (*tot*). **incommodis ... acceptis** "having suffered (*OLD* 8) ... setbacks (*OLD* 2b)." The expression is freq. in C. (and *BAlex.*) but otherwise unattested (*detrimentum* or *calamitas* [90.4n.] are typically used). **ad concilium conuocat** varies *concilium* (or 77.1n. *consilium*) *conuocare*. It recurs at 66.3 (again of V.), then once more at Livy 36.28.8.

14.2 To determine a war's character was a crucial part of warfare (Frontin. *Str.* 1.3 *de constituendo statu belli*). The verb *docet* and the focus on *ratione* mark this as a speech on strategy. In Roman military thought, one school cautioned against pitched battle (cf. Asel. *FRHist* F6, Val. Max. 7.2.2, Veg. 3.9); another school considered anything but battle inglorious (Livy 42.47.5 with Lendon 2005: 193–211; cf. Cic. *Pis.* 62 *nullo certo hoste* with Nisbet). **docet**: a technical term for a rhetorical strategy that appeals to the intellect (*HLR* 257; cf. 19.4n. *edocet*; Dangel 1995: 99 differs). **longe alia ratione** is used identically at 3.28.1 (similar in content, too, as is 59.3n. *aliud ... consilium*); Sall. *Iug.* 54.5–7 appears to adapt this passage. On the importance of a general's ability to modify his plan: Polyb. 9.9, Onas. 1.7. **esse** focuses *ratione* (Adams 1994a: 34). **huic rei**: 1.6n. *eius.* **pabulatione aut commeatu** "foraging and supplies." *pabulatio* is a military term unattested before C. (Mosci Sassi 1983: 115; cf. Hirt. 8.7.7). "Collecting fodder" constituted, along with *aquatio, lignatio,* and *frumentatio,* a daily chore (Fischer 1914: 13). In β *aut* is replaced by the simpler *et* (cf. 16.3 *pabulationes frumentationesque,* 64.2); but *aut* may in meaning "approximate '*et uicissim, modo ... modo, et ... et, partim ... partim*'" (Goodyear on Tac. *Ann.* 1.8.2).

14.3–9 The *argumentatio* is tripartite, with *praeterea* introducing the second and third part (a Lucretian mannerism [*TLL* 10.2.1006.15–17]). The measures proposed grow more painful (the tricolon rises analogously). **id esse facile**: 1.7n. **quod ... quod**: the anaphora introduces two parallel cola, whose content is elaborated in inverted order, as is typical of content lists and their elaboration (1.1.1–3; Cic. *Quinct.* 1.1 *gratia et eloquentia*; Hor. *Carm.* 3.4.64 *Delius et Patareus*; Verg. *Aen.* 1.1 *arma uirumque*; Kraus 1994: 22n.92). **equitatu ... abundent**: the unusual expression recurs at 64.2, *BAfr.* 5; Flor. *Epit.* 2.47 may bespeak C.'s influence. **quod anni tempore subleuentur**: this was presumably the reason why the Gauls intensified their resistance in the middle of winter (*Introd.* 2c).

14.4 hostes of Romans is common; but might it not have struck Roman readers much as Screwtape's referring to God as "the Enemy" strikes C. S. Lewis' Christian readers? **deleri**: *deligi* (*diligi*) is the *lectio difficilior*; but no instance of a related metaphorical use is attested (*TLL* 5.1.452.32–38). Then again, it may have been intended to reflect V.'s idiolect (cf. 29.5n. *sarturum*).

14.5 V.'s argument is captured in Cic. *Off.* 2.74: *si salui esse uelint necessitati esse parendum.* Both vary a commonplace defined as *nullo dolore cogi ut ab officio recedatur* (*Rhet. Her.* 3.5). **salutis causa**: cf. 2.1n. **uicos atque aedificia incendi**: a frequent phrase in C. (Odelman 179–81). **hoc spatio**: an abl. of measure specifying the distance from the path rather than an abl. of place (K-S 81c, 79 esp. c); the demonstrative anticipates the rel. clause. **quoque uersus**: 4.5n. **pabulandi causa**: Gell. identifies *pabulari* as well as *copiari, lignari,* and *aquari* as *uerba castrensia* (17.2.9; Krebs 2018b: 125; 73.1n. *materiari*). **posse uideantur**: a standard clausula (resolved cretic + trochee).

14.6 harum ipsis: 8.5n. *quorum ille.* **copiam … opibus … inopiam**: all three are etymologically related, and wordplay on *copia – inopia* is particularly common (Pub. *Sent.* M 69 *mala est inopia, ex copia quae nascitur*). Here the antonyms capture the contrary situations; cf. Pericles' emphasis on Spartan "poverty" (πενία) when war requires "abundance" (περιουσία), which the Athenians possess (Thuc. 1.141.4–5, 143.3–4). *inopia* recurs 4x (17.4, 20.3, 10, 11), a "thematic repetition" that 32.1 *ex inopia* concludes. **subleuentur** repeats §3, emphasizing the existence of several helpful factors.

14.7 inopiam non laturos "they would not endure the lack," with common ellipsis of *esse* (G-L 209). But V. underestimates the Romans (17.4–6). **magno periculo**: foraging troops were a recommended military target (Veg. 3.6; cf. 36.5–7n.).

14.8 ipsosne … impedimentisne: C. typically construes indirect disjunctive questions with *-ne/utrum … an*; simple *an* (15.3n.) and *-ne … -ne* each occur but once. **interficiant … exuant**: a commonplace in military reasoning (*aut inopia aut superuentibus aut terrore melius est hostem domare quam proelio*, Veg. 3.26). C. himself would prefer starving the Numantines to killing them (App. *Hisp.* 87; cf. Frontin. *Str.* 4.7.1 *fame potius quam ferro*).

14.9 oppida: in addition to *aedificia* and *uici,* larger settlements were to be burnt, too. The Helvetii had proceeded similarly systematically (1.5.2). **incendi**: the passive glosses over the touchiest point that they would have to set fire themselves (15.4n. *suis*). Pericles feared that the Athenians would not be up to "laying waste to [their property] *themselves*" (Thuc. 1.143.5). **munitione … loci natura**: such combinatorial fortification seems to have been the standard in Gaul (Audouze-Büchsenschütz 1992: 88), and C. often applies these two criteria (69n.). They were, however, also a standard feature of military writing: e.g. Polyb. 6.42.2, Curt. 9.1.14, and esp. Veg. 4.1: *urbes atque castella aut natura muniuntur aut manu aut utroque.* The language is formulaic and administrative (Odelman 174–75). *loci natura* is a Caesarian mannerism (*VII*: 15.5, 17.1, 74.1). **ab omni sint periculo**: forms of *esse* often follow "adjectives of quantity and size" (Adams 1994a: 19–24). Cf. 36.1n. *additus difficiles.* **ne … neu**: the standard form to coordinate two negative final clauses (K-S II 211b). **sint**: for the attraction of the auxiliary to a word of emphasis (here *suis* in contrast to

Romanis), cf. K-S 603 Anm. 7. **ad detractandam militiam** "to refuse military service" (Ogilvie on Livy 2.43.4, identifying it as "the technical expression for the offence"; *TLL* 5.1.835.26–31). *detractare* appears only here in *CC*. In expressing his worry that they might take flight, V. may hint at the Gauls' stereotypical fickleness (20.5n.). **receptacula** "refuge, shelter" (*OLD* 2), only here and *BC* 2.8.1. The notion of an *oppidum/ urbs* as *fugae receptaculum* becomes a cliché in Livy (6.22.2 with Kraus); it reappears in Curt. (e.g. 5.9.8) and, slightly varied, Tac. *Ann.* 14.29.3. **proposita** is usually understood as verbal (*OLD* 7 "to hold out [as a prospect or possibility]"), with *sint* inferred from the preceding colon (cf. 1.2n. *ipsi Galli*). But might it not be a noun corresponding to *receptacula?* **ad … tollendam**: this would happen to Avaricum (32.1).

14.10 The *peroratio* employs a commonplace recommended for emotional appeal (*Rhet. Her.* 2.50): *misericordia commouebitur … si quid nostris parentibus, liberis, ceteris necessariis casurum sit propter nostras calamitates aperiemur.* The specific threats are typical aspects of the *urbs-capta* motif (beginning with Hom. *Il.* 9.590–94) – just as they were among the brutal realities of warfare (as suffered by the people of Cenabum [11.9]; cf. Paul on Sall. *Iug.* 91.6 *oppidum incensum*). **haec … illa**: *haec* resumes, *illa* looks forward (K-S 624 Anm. 9), viz. to the infinitives. V. concedes the loss involved, a rhetorical move known as *concessio*: *cum aliquid etiam iniquum uidemur <u>causae fiducia</u> pati* (Quint. 2.9.51; *HLR* 856). **grauia aut acerba**: combinations of these two adjs. are frequent, but the corrective *aut* ("or rather," *OLD* 6b) is rare (but cf. Sall. *Cat.* 51.23 [Caesar's speech]). Pericles advised "not to fight the Peloponnesians out of anger over [lost property]," Thuc. 1.143.5. **grauia … grauius**: the intensifying polyptoton – a form of repetition that "makes plain words pointed" (Wills 227; cf. 235–36) – highlights the alternatives. The contrast between loss of property and human life is a commonplace (Thuc. 1.143.5, Verg. *Aen.* 12.765 [with Tarrant]). The adverb instead of the gen. of value or cost may be used with verbs of rating (G-L 379, K-S 86 Anm. 5). **aestimari**: both MSS readings partially retain the original. α's *aestimare* suggests the absence of a modal verb, and β's *aestimari debere* suggests the passive infinitive (on which, however, cf. Damon 2015: 103n.3); *debere* may have resulted from dittography (*liberos*). **liberos, coniuges**: the *asyndeton bimembre* is rare in C. It gives full weight to both groups (cf. Nägelsbach's "schroffe Kraft" [1904: 704]; Adams 2016: 81–84). This is also the only instance of the literary term *coniunx*. C. prefers *uxor* (66.7, 78.4), as do administrators (Odelman 43–44). His rare mentions of women are listed in Bellemore 2016: 888–90; cf. Phang 2004, Milnor 2009. **in seruitutem abstrahi**: again at 42.3 (C.'s voice); otherwise unparalleled. **quae … uictis**: cf. Onas. 38.4

"nothing makes men so brave as the fear of what ills they will suffer if they surrender (εἴξαντες)." The weighty participle, its force conditional, is kept until last (cf. Cic. *Dom.* 98 *quae capta urbe accidunt uictis*), forming another resolved cretic + trochee.

15 The Gauls implement their "new" strategy, then make a fateful exception.

C.'s improbable claim (14–19n.) that the fate of Avaricum was debated only *after* twenty-some locations had been burned is dramaturgically effective (and the alleged second debate the clearest example of C.'s employing speeches/debates as a narrative device [*Introd.* 3c]). The drama is heightened by the Bituriges' *conquestio*, the rhetorical embellishment of the *oppidum* (§4–5n.), and the ironic reversal (§6n. *idonei*).

15.1 Omnium consensu: 4.6n. Four (out of five) instances of *omnis* bespeak the universal determination. **sententia probata:** an instance of *interpretatio Romana*, as the noun is the technical term for a senatorial recommendation (cf. *sententiam rogare/dicere* [77.2]; *OLD sententia* 3, *VL* 116–20), and the verb is used in the same context to express formal approval (Cic. *Cat.* 1.21). For other instances of the collocation (again at 77.6) in the senatorial context, cf. Cic. *Prou. cons.* 36, Tac. *Ann.* 14.18.3. The Gauls' orderly reaction – contrast 21.1 *conclamat* – may conform with V.'s rational presentation (14.2n. *docet*). **uno** "only one" (again at 15.5); cf. Kenney on Lucr. 3.143 *ad numen ... momenque* for the occasional need to add "only" "to bring out the full sense." It stands in antithesis to the many settlements. **amplius:** following *amplius* (*plus, minus*), *quam* is often omitted (G-L 296R4, K-S II 471); but cf. 19.1n. *latior.* **urbes:** only in *VII* does C. use *urbs* of Gallic settlements, including Avaricum (15.4), Gergovia (36.1, 47.4), and Alesia (68.3). While these are also called *oppida* (15.6, 36.2, 47.3), the grander term is employed for the same reason Servius detected in Anna's use (Verg. *Aen.* 4.40): *ad terrorem* "*urbes*" *posuit: nam in mapalibus habitabant;* cf. Cic. *Fam.* 15.4.9 *Eranam autem, quae fuit non uici instar sed urbis.*

15.2 conspiciuntur: cf. 6.43.2 *aedificia quae quisque conspexerat incendebantur.* C. uses *conspicere* when several objects are seen at the same time. **magno cum dolore** but 63.8 *magno dolore.* "The Ablative of Manner ... is used ... with or without *cum* when it has an Adjective or its equivalent" (G-L 399). **hoc sibi solacii:** 19.2n. *hoc se*; 9.4n. *quid ... consilii.* **proponebant** "they bore in mind" (*OLD* 5c). **explorata** "certain" (*OLD* 1), in conjunction with *uictoria* 5x in *BG* and mostly of impetuous Gauls, whose confidence is then belied; an instance of the Gauls' *tragische Stilisierung* (3.18.8, 5.43.3, 7.20.7, 52.2; Gärtner 1975: 98; cf. 1.6n. *facile*, 19.2n. *fiducia*). Their confidence, here all the more surprising given their recent defeats, may reflect V.'s inspirational leadership.

15.3 incendi = *incendine*. The first interrogative particle of the disjunctive question is frequently omitted by other authors, but only this once by C. This is the third polyptotic instance of *incendere*, highlighting the Gauls' determination.

15.4–5 The plea is a typical *conquestio*, i.e. *oratio auditorum misericordiam captans* (Cic. *Inu. rhet.* 1.106): starting with a supplicatory gesture (*procumbunt*), it attempts to move the audience by appealing to its emotions, provoking pity (§6 *misericordia*). The grand style (*genus grande*) is usually associated with this strategy (Quint. 12.10.59), here possibly intimated by the superlative, repeated exaggerations and emphases, antithesis, hendiadys, and the colorful verb in the passive. Rhetoric shines through the city encomium, too, which should discuss "the position of the city" (θέσιν πόλεως) and its characteristics "with regards to both pleasure and utility" (καὶ πρὸς ἡδονὴν καὶ ὠφέλειαν, Men. Rhet. 346.26–351.19; below on *praesidio*). This tradition explains the parallels in Cicero's description of Syracuse (*Verr.* 4.117, with Quint. 3.7.26–27): *urbem Syracusas maximam esse Graecarum, pulcherrimam omnium saepe audistis. … nam et situ est cum munito tum ex omni aditu uel terra uel mari praeclaro ad aspectum, et portus habet.* **procumbunt**: gestures were an integral part of rhetoric (Cic. *De or.* 3.213–27). This standard gesture (Naiden 2006: 49) intended to induce compassion (*Rhet. Her.* 4.34). It is repeatedly attributed to the Gauls (1.27.2, 31.2: 7.26.3; cf. *BC* 2.12–13). **ne** introduces either a negated imperative in indirect speech or a complementary final sentence as if preceded by a verb of requesting (G-L 652, 546). **pulcherrimam prope totius Galliae urbem**: by speaking of *tota Gallia*, the Bituriges make *their* city a concern for *all* Gauls (cf. *communi concilio*). The position of *prope* suggests that it qualifies *totius*; cf. 33.3. On *pulcherrimus*: Introd. p. 33. **et praesidio et ornamento**: commonplaces in city encomia (Men. Rhet. 350.11–13 καὶ ἀντὶ κόσμου … καὶ εἰς ἀσφάλειαν). **suis**: the possessive adds emphasis (G-L 312; *OLS* 2.1072). **succendere** "to set alight (below, at the base)" (*OLD* 1). **cogantur**: the change from consensus (above, 15.1) to compulsion is startling.

15.5 facile is emphatic by position; cf. 1.7n. *facile*. **defensuros**: sc. *urbem*, the object (/subject) of the previous clause (/following *quod*-clause). **flumine**: the Yèvre. **circumdata**: sc. *urbs*. **unum habeat et perangustum aditum** "had really only one (accentuated by verbal hyperbaton [3.2n. *maior … res*; cf. 37.3n. *unam esse*]) and moreover (*OLD et* 1) exceedingly narrow point of access"; cf. Plut. *Crass.* 9.1 ἐν ὄρει μίαν ἔχοντι καὶ χαλεπὴν καὶ στενὴν ἄνοδον, "on a hill which had only one ascent, and a narrow and difficult one to boot"; Sall. *Iug.* 92.5 *uno perangusto aditu* (which may echo our passage). This colon specifies the general description preceding it (cf. Courtney 1999: 5). It effectively renders the Bituriges' emotional investment, which also appears in their exaggerating the narrowness: *perangustum* (cf. 11.9n. *perpaucis*) occurs only here in *CC* and will be corrected by the authorial 17.1 *angustum*. C. enjoys such *mis*iterations (and esp. when they involve metalepsis), beginning with 1.1.4 *Heluetii … reliquos Gallos uirtute praecedunt* and 1.2.2 *cum uirtute omnibus praestarent* (Orgetorix speaking [Torigian 1998: 60]); instances in *VII* include: 20.8n. *milites*, 47.4n. *intra portas*, 52.1n. *cupiditatem*, 66.3n. *fugere*; cf. 31.1n. *donis*, 29.2n.

15.6 datur petentibus uenia: sim. at 6.4.3. C. often omits resumptive pronouns (*iis*, sc. *Biturigibus*; cf. Livy 32.15.3 *uenia iis petentibus datur*) with pres. participles, which thus shade into substantives. **dissuadente … concedente**: a slight chiasmus, centered around V. who yields to pity instead of reason (8.5n. *precibus permotus*). **ipsorum** = *Biturigum*. **misericordia uulgi**: this second ablative, in a polysyndeton (*HLR* 686), is strictly parallel to the first; this makes it likely that *uulgi* is a subjective genitive, as is the case in its second occurrence (28.6). C. uses *uulgus* always in reference to the common people or general public and sometimes with a derogatory tone (43.4 *inscientiam leuitatemque uulgi*). Here it serves to discredit the decision, as does *misericordia*, known to thwart proper judgment (Quint. 5.pr.1). **defensores oppido idonei**: the chapter ends stating that the Gauls do the opposite of what they had started out to do. *idonei*, as seen through Gauls' eyes, is tainted with dramatic irony, given readers' hindsight.

16 V. follows C. and from his camp near Avaricum harasses the legions, enacting his strategy's second part (14n.). In consequence, "the many setbacks" the Gauls suffered (14.1 *tot … incommodis*) are remedied by a *magnum incommodum* (§3) inflicted on the Romans. Verbal correspondences between C.'s narrative and V.'s promises underline the latter's consistency (§3nn. ~ 14.4+7). The "battle of wits" theme is noticeably developed (§3).

16.1 Vercingetorix minoribus Caesarem itineribus subsequitur "V. immediately followed after C. by shorter stages" (Edwards). A commonplace of military reports (cf. Brut. [Cic.] *Fam.* 11.13.2 *biduo me Antonius antecessit, itinera fecit multo maiora fugiens quam ego sequens*), here of difficult phrasing. It is paralleled at *BC* 3.102.1, where the context specifies *minoribus itineribus* as "with shorter marches" (i.e. than the cavalry); so here also: V. followed C. but more slowly (cf. 14–19n. on the chronological inconsistencies). The imbricated word order mimics the chase; the sound effect: 77.16n. **locum castris deligit**: a general's essential skill, attributed to e.g. Cyrus, Alexander, Hannibal, and C. (Xen. *Cyr.* 6.1.23, Livy 9.17.15 [with Oakley], Frontin. *Str.* 2.3; 35.5, where the formulaic phrase recurs). **paludibus siluisque munitum**: for the verbal hyperbaton (*locum … deligit … munitum*), cf. 3.2n. *maior … res*. For similarly fortified sites, cf. 5.21.2,

6.5.4 (and 8.7.4), and for discussion of a campsite's topography, Veg.
2.22, 3.8, 4.1, Ps.-Hyg. *Mun. castr.* 57 (with Lenoir). C. mentions *siluae
paludesque* 7x in *BG*, a frequency that helped to establish it as a cliche
of northern Europe (perhaps beginning with Catull. 115.5; Livy 34.48.1,
Vell. Pat. 2.119.2, Pomp. 3.29, Tac. *Agr.* 26.2 [with Woodman], *Germ.* 5.1
[sc. *Germania*] *aut siluis horrida aut paludibus foeda*, Flor. *Epit.* 1.108; cf.
[Cic.] *Fam.* 10.30.2 *angustias paludis et siluarum*; Östenberg 2017). Polyb.
3.71.2 remarks how "the Romans were suspicious of wooden locations
(πρὸς μὲν τοὺς ὑλώδεις τόπους ὑπόπτως εἶχον)," as they often hid an ambush
(esp. 5.19; cf. 1.4n. *siluestribus*). **longe** "at a distance [of …]" (*OLD* 2c).

16.2 certos "regular" (*OLD* 1). **exploratores**: V. makes ample use of scouts,
like C. (11.8n.). **in … tempora** "for (*OLD in* 5c) every moment of the day."
ad "near," "(spec.) outside the walls of" (*OLD* 13). **quid fieri uellet imperabat**: an administrative formula, common in C. (27.1, 45.8; Odelman
170–73); cf. 45.8–10n. The imperfect indicates iteration.

16.3 Cf. Polyb. 1.17.10 where the Romans "went about collecting
grain more vehemently than they ought to (ἐκθυμότερον τοῦ δέοντος)";
the Carthaginians "observed how they were scattered about the land
(κατιδόντες … ἐσκεδασμένους κατὰ τῆς χώρας), marched out and attacked
the foragers (τοῖς σιτολογοῦσιν)." Cf. 14.7n. *magno periculo*. **pabulationes
frumentationesque** recurs at 64.2; cf. 74.2, Hirt. 8.7.8. *frumentatio* =
"corn-collecting" is a technical term first attested in C. (*TLL* 6.1.1408.69;
14.2n. *pabulatio*). **dispersosque**: sc. *nostros*, to be inferred from *nostras*.
The participle echoes V.'s prediction (14.4). **cum … procederent** "whenever they …." Iterative clauses normally require the indicative, but there
are exceptions (K-S 182.8), here possibly caused by the causal connotation ("since they"). **longius procederent** echoes 14.7 *longius … processuros*.
necessario: echoes 14.4. **incommodo** "with harm" (*OLD* 1); cf. nn. 14.1,
16. **ratione prouideri**: cf. Cic. *Diu.* 2.16 *medicus morbum ingrauescentem
ratione prouidet, insidias imperator* …. C. mentions his *consilium in prouidendo*
again (10n.); he may add *ratione* (9.1n. *opinione praeceperat*) in response to
V.'s 14.1 *ratione*. References to the *prouidentia ducis* (Tac. *Hist.* 2.19.1) are
many in the Roman historians, but cf. esp. Tac. *Hist.* 5.17.2 [*Ciuilem*] *quae
prouideri astu ducis oportuerit prouidisse*; cf. 30.2n. **ab nostris**: "historians frequently used the first-person plural when referring to the Roman state,
… soldiers, or … citizens …" (Cornell on Cato *FRHist* F20). This form
of reference "fosters a sense … of intimacy [and] common achievement"
in the reader (Marincola 1997: 212); but it also expresses C.'s special
bond with his men (*Introd.* 3f). **occurrebatur** is used metaphorically ("to
counteract," *OLD* 6) in a context of physical movement. **ut … iretur** "by

going ...." The *ut*-clause explains the *ratio* (G-L 557). **incertis ... itineribus**: cf. Lucr. 2.127 *incerto tempore ferme* | *incertisque locis* (*TLL* 7.1.878.10–12). *itineribus* resumes §1 *itineribus*, highlighting by way of ring composition the paragraph's theme (sim. 20.1+12 *proditionis insimulatus*, 25.1+4 [49.1+2] *pugnaretur ... pugnandi*, 71.5n. *mandatis*). Cf. Thuc. 2.9.1+6 ξυμμάχους ... ξυμμαχία (with Rusten on 2.61.4), Lucil. 20–22 *concilio ... concilio*, Cic. *Rosc. Am.* 83 *fides ... fides*, and McKeown on Ovid *Am.* 1.5.26 *medii ... dies*. By contrast, the following paragraph opens with 17.1 *castris ... positis*.

17 With Avaricum protected from a blockade, the legions build an assault ramp (§1n. *aggerem*). Despite C.'s efforts (§2n. *non destitit*), they suffer hunger; but when offered withdrawal, they refuse out of piety, duty, and devotion.

Sieging forces suffered depravations frequently (Roth 1999: 317–19; §3n. *caruerint*); they became an historiographical topos: *inopia obsidentibus quam obsessis ... grauior* (Vell. Pat. 2.51.3 with Woodman; cf. Cass. Dio 40.34.2). C.'s acknowledgement thereof allows him to advertise his leadership (cf. 16.3n. *nostris*, 19n.) and celebrate his troops. When he "tests" them as Agamemnon famously had (Hom. *Il.* 2.72–74; §4–7n.), they rise to the challenge, demonstrating Roman virtues: in mastering their hunger (§3n. *famem*), they exemplify *patientia*, i.e. *rerum ... difficilium uoluntaria ac diuturna perpessio* (Cic. *Inu. rhet.* 2.163; Kaster 2002); in recognizing their duties to guard their reputation (§5n. *ignominiam*) and avenge those Romans killed in Cenabum, they express *pietas* (§7n. *parentarent*); they possess what Horace would celebrate as *uirtus repulsae nesciens sordidae* (*Carm.* 3.2.13). Livy (5.5–6) has Appius Claudius declare that perseverance in the siege of Veii was the litmus test of *uirtus, patientia*, and, ultimately, *Romanitas*: C.'s soldiers passed it.

17.1 C. employs standard devices of Roman siegecraft; cf. Sall. *Iug.* 76.3 *uineas agere, aggerem iacere ... impositis turribus*, Tac. *Hist.* 3.20, Veg. 4.15; Levithan 2013: esp. 128–30. **Castris positis**: south-east of the town (Krausz-Ralston 2009: 149–50). **intermissa a flumine** "left unoccupied (*OLD* 4) by the river." **aditum ... angustum**: the hyperbaton is wittily incongruous with its content ("narrowness"; contrast Arat. 84 where Ophiuchus straddles, "with both feet, the huge beast [ποσσὶν ... μέγα θηρίον ἀμφοτέροισιν]") and provokes comparison with 15.5n. *perangustum*. **ut supra diximus**: cf. 15.5n. *perangustum*. C.'s many cross-references (10x in *VII*) and preference for *supra* over *ante* are paralleled in the administrative style (Odelman 168–70). Of the four versions he employs, the 1st pers. pl. is the most common, as it allows for his identification with his Roman readers (Kollmann 1977: 54–55; cf. 5.6n. *nobis*). **aggerem apparare** is a singular expression (and *apparare* is not used by C. before). Its sound play imitates Thuc. 2.75.1 χῶμα ἔχουν (Krebs 2018c: 518n.6; 20–28n.). Ramps were a common (though not typical) measure in ancient warfare (Davies 2006: 97–116; Campbell 2019: 247–54); four more occur in *BG* (2.12, 2.30, 3.21, 8.41). This one (reconstructed in Wimmel 1974; further discussed in Krausz-Ralston 2009) dominates the Avaricum episode: 18.1, 22.4, 24, 27.1. **uineas** "shelters," "made of wood … [and] covered with raw and freshly flayed hides and fire-blankets" (Veg. 4.15). **agere** resonates with *aggerem*. Both C. and Sall. playfully juxtapose the two terms (2.12.5; *Iug.* 32.4, 76.3 [above]); less conspicuous wordplay (*adnominatio*) is at play here, too (as in 58.1, *BC* 2.1.1; *BHisp.* 7.2). **turres** were "constructed from beams and planks, … thoroughly armored with raw hides and fire-blankets … Their width increase[d] in proportion to their height" (Veg. 4.17; cf. *BC* 2.9; Vitr. 10.13.3–5; Marsden 1969: 116–63). Their effect on Gallic observers: 2.30–31. **circumuallare:** 11.1n. Contrast 69.1n. *obsidione expugnari*. **loci natura:** 14.9n.

17.2–3 The two tribes are discussed as follows: *Boios, Haeduos – alteri* (Haedui), *alteri* (Boii) – *Boiorum, Haeduorum*. Every block is thus tightly "linked to the preceding one" (Courtney 1999: 7); cf. 14.3n. *quod … quod*. **de re frumentaria** "as for the grain supply"; 9.1n. *de*. **non destitit:** the litotes emphasizes C.'s effort and exculpates him (cf. 10.1n. *frumentaria*; §3n.). **alteri … alteri:** when C. uses these distributives to resume two nouns, he inverts their order 5x, maintains it 2x (*pace* DKM on 5.27.9; four instances are unclear); cf. Courtney 1999: 7 on "the chiastic way of thinking … [as] equally natural [as the parallelistic way]." The two sentences are parallel; the second is longer (a variation of BEHAGHEL's law of increasing terms). **nullo studio:** C. complains about his foremost ally's negligence as early as in his first year (1.16.5; cf. 5.2n. *Haeduos*). **non magnis facultatibus** "of limited resources," an abl. of quality (G-L 400). **exigua et infirma:** cf. Veg. 3.21.6 *exigui numero et infirmi uiribus*. **habuerunt:** the perfect (instead of the descriptive imperfect) simply focuses on the event's past tense (K-S I 128).

17.3 A typical string of abls. highlights the numerous exculpatory causes; equally typical is the expanded abl. absolute (2.2n. *quo more*). **tenuitate Boiorum** "because of the slender weakness of the Boii." *tenuitas* occurs only here in *CC* to allow for bilingual wordplay: the Celtic name was "connected … with *bos*" (Kraus 2009: 164; cf. 9.6n. *Boiorum*), and the expression might suggest an image of slender cows. **indiligentia:** in *CC* only here and (probably) *BC* 3.8.3; cf. 9.4n. *diligentiae*. **aedificiorum:** by adding the abundant noun, C. effects a rising tricolon (cf. Courtney 1999: 9) and homoioteleuton in all its parts. **caruerint**: the perfect (rather than imperfect) subjunctive emphasizes the final outcome (G-L 513). C.'s soldiers repeatedly suffered shortages, none worse than at Ilerda and Dyrrachium (*BC* 1.48–52, 3.47 [where Avaricum is recalled]). **pecore**: for a discussion of meat (*secundum ... inopiae subsidium, BC* 1.48.6) as part of the Roman soldier's diet, see Roth 1999: 27–32. **famem sustentārint**: a rare expression (*TLL* 6.230.12). C. uses syncopated forms liberally, adhering to convention (Cic. *Orat.* 157 *et plenum uerbum recte dici et imminutum usitate*). The endurance of hunger was a prized military virtue (cf. Sall. *Cat.* 5.3 *patiens inediae* [with Vretska], Hor. *Carm.* 3.2.1 *angustam amice pauperiem pati*), esp. in combination with strenuous labor (Sall. *Iug.* 85.33 *eodem tempore inopiam et laborem tolerare*). **nulla ... indigna**: the Roman soldiers' words match their deeds and character; cf. Cic. *Off.* 3.1: *magnifica uero uox et magno uiro ac sapiente digna.* **nulla tamen uox**: the emphatic *nulla*, accentuated by *tamen* (K-S II 99 Anm.), stands in antithesis to *summa, complures*, and *extremam.* **populi Romani maiestate**: a common phrase, but only here in C. It would have brought to mind the *lex maiestatis*, which allowed for prosecution *si quis ... male gesta re publica maiestatem populi Romani minuisset* (Tac. *Ann.* 1.72.2 [with Goodyear on 72.2–74.6]; cf. Cic. *Inu. rhet.* 2.53). *maiestas* signifies "greatness" that inspires "a sense of obedience, reverence, and awe" in those subjected (Lind 1979: 52–56; *VL* 316–20). **maiestate ... uictoriis**: the two abls. form an isocolon. **indigna** is emphasized by hyperbaton; with *uictoriis* it forms a creticus + molossus. It occurs once more in C. in a similar context (5.35.5); cf. 30.3n. *dignitas.*

17.4–7 Agamemnon was disappointed when his soldiers accepted his offer to abandon the "unfinished task" and "flee" back home, even though an "unfinished war" spelled "disgrace" (Hom. *Il.* 2.137–38 ἔργον ... ἀκράαντον, cf. *infecta re*, 140 φεύγωμεν, cf. *discederent*; 119–21 αἰσχρὸν ... ἄπρηκτον πόλεμον πολεμίζειν, cf. *ignominiae ... loco ... inceptam oppugnationem*); not so C. (who has here and elsewhere [nn. on 47.3 *elati*, 54, 67.4 *spe*, 84.4] been credited with psychological astuteness [Vogt 1960: 96–98, Lendon 1999: 295–304]). **in opere** "at work" (*OLD* 2) rather than "at the earthwork" (*OLD* 1c). **appellaret**: 19.4n. *edocet.* **acerbius inopiam ferre**: C.'s question pointedly recalls V.'s mistaken prediction (14.7n. *laturos*). The Gallic leader underestimated the legionaries' endurance. **petebant**: the imperfect expresses iteration (cf. *singulas legiones*).

17.5 sic ... parentarent: indirect speech "often comes in without any formal notice" (G-L 649N2; *NLS §265*), adding liveliness and emphasis. It captures the soldiers' passion (nn. on *nullam ... nusquam, ignominiae, omnes ... acerbitas*), whose sentiment recalls Polyb.'s praise of Romans as ready "to endure all in order to secure a reputation for courage in their fatherland" (6.52.11). **complures annos**: in comparison, a famine lasting *complures dies* hardly mattered. **meruisse:** sc. *stipendia,* "to serve" (*OLD* 2b). **nullam** resonates with §3 *nulla.* **ignominiam:** first here in *BG* (then similarly at 80.4). Shame is a frequent motivation in historiography, esp. in Livy (Oakley 2005: 21). **nusquam ... discederent:** such expressions render "a categorical denial" (Schmalz 1907).

17.6 hŏc: 1.6n. *eius.* **ignominiae laturos loco:** the repetition of *ignominiam* tightens the narrative (cf. 90.2n. *imperat*). *loco* ("by way of," *OLD* 18c) is rarely combined with *ferre* (frequently with *habere* [77.3]), and in collocation with *ignominia* occurs in Pub. *Sent.* L1 *loco ignominiae est apud indignum dignitas.* **inceptam** varies *infecta.*

17.7 The soldiers' memory (and C.'s [28.4]) is partial: they avenged the murders by razing Cenabum (11.8–9). *memoria* repeatedly serves motivation in C. (beginning with 1.7.4, including 47.3). **praestare omnes perferre acerbitates:** identical in Cic. *Cat.* 4.1, echoing 10.2nn. The verbal hyperbaton (3.2n. *maior ... res*) aptly emphasizes *omnes* and *acerbitates.* With the noun (first here in C.) the soldiers "respond" to C.'s §4 *acerbius ferre.* **perfidia Gallorum:** four of *BG*'s six instances of *perfidia* occur in *VII*; of Gallic treachery C. speaks only here (Riggsby 231n.41). A stereotype especially associated with the Carthaginians (Livy 21.4.9 *perfidia plus quam Punica*; Otto 291), it is frequently attributed to the Gauls, too (Cic. *Prov. cons.* 33 [with Grillo on *infidis*]). The Romans, by contrast, claimed *fides* as a national characteristic (Verg. *Aen.* 6.878 *prisca fides* [with Horsfall]; Cic. *Off.* 1.39). C. highlights the perfidy to justify preemptively the destruction of Avaricum soon to follow (4.14.3 *perfidia* equally precedes another massacre [4.14.5]). May it also matter that perfidy played a role in the fall of Troy (N-R on Hor. *Carm.* 3.3.21–22)? **quam ... parentarent:** the subjunctive occasionally replaces the second infinitive construction in such comparative clauses (10.2; K-S II 302). The verb (only here in *CC*) signifies "to avenge" (*TLL* 10.1.371.9); its sacrificial connotations possibly suggest that the victims would be sacrifices to the deceased (cf. Verg. *Aen.* 10.517–20 [with Harrison]). To avenge an injury was deemed an act of *pietas* (5.52.6 *expiato incommodo;* cf. Aug. *Anc.* 2 [with Cooley], 34.3 *pietatis caussa* [with Brunt-Moore]).

17.8 tribunisque militum: junior officers, mostly of equestrian rank, in part elected by the people, in part by the commander (Suolahti 1955: 35–57; cf. 5.3n. *legatorum*).

18 C. learns of Gallic plans to ambush (§1n. *insidiarum*) his foraging troops and moves quickly to turn the tables. But when he arrives at the Gauls' camp, they are ready to counter.

This is the first of three *occasiones* in *VII* (27.1, 44.1), whose narration here also serves retardation (cf. nn. on 23, 26; 14–28). Their proper use was a topic of discussion (Polyb. 9.12.3; 27n.), "quick-wittedness" (ἀγχίνοια, *consilii celeritas* [Cic. *Leg. Man.* 29, 30]; Wheeler 1988: 46) was deemed essential; C. passes the test over and again (19.3n.). The lucidly ordered narrative bespeaks his analytical approach: two longer periods (1+3) detail the circumstances in typically propulsive fashion; each is followed by short sentences that begin with resumptive abl. absolutes and tell of the swift and necessary actions. All are marked by clausulae (creticus + spondee [1+2], spondee + spondee [3+4]).

18.1 Cum ... appropinquassent: the *agger* (17.1) has been heightened and extended across the ground towards Avaricum and with it its towers on top. Cf. 17.3n. *sustentarint*. **ex captiuis Caesar cognouit**: triple alliteration on "c" occurs over 100x in *CC*; it is just as frequent elsewhere (Gaertner on Ov. *Pont.* 1.3.55; cf. 25.1n. *adire ... animaduertebant*). C. often acts on the information of captives and deserters (again at 72.1; Ezov 1996: 71–72). They were an important but risky source of intelligence, not least because it was a common stratagem to have them provide misinformation (as C. himself does at 3.18.1–4; Frontin. *Str.* 1.8.5, 3.6.4; Menge 1905 suspected that V. had done so here). It was therefore recommended that their intelligence be vetted (cf. 8.8.1 *consentientibus pluribus*, *BC* 2.39.1; Austin-Rankov 1995: 67–73). **consumpto pabulo**: this will be confirmed by V. (20.3 *inopia pabuli*). *pabulum* and cognates occur 12x in *VII* (2x in other books), a frequency indicative of the particularly dire supply problems (10.1n. *re frumentaria*). **expeditis** "light-armed troops"; a technical term (*TLL* 5.2.1622.32, 1623.84). **qui ... consuessent**: C. describes this *genus pugnae* at 1.48.5–7 and 4.2.3–4 (attributed to the *Germani*, as again in 7.65.4; 8.13.2, 36.2; cf. Perl on Tac. *Germ.* 6.3). It was a common tactic that C. himself would use (cf. Thuc. 5.57 on ἄμιπποι among the Boeotians, Val. Max. 2.3.3 on the Romans; *BC* 3.75.5 + 84.3 [with Carter]). Of the Gauls, C. mentions it here for the first time, then again 36.4 and 80.3. **insidiarum causa**: *insidiae* is the technical term for ambushing (Wheeler 1988: 85), which was a common component of military schemes (cf. 45.5, 79.2, 83.7; Frontin. *Str.* 2.5 *de insidiis*). **quo nostros ... arbitraretur**: subj. in indir. speech. V.'s information gathering is mentioned in 16.3.

18.2 varies the formula in 11.7n. The string of abls. (of various functions) is typical, too (6.3n.). **quibus rebus cognitis**: 9.6n. *hac re cognita*; *cognitis* resumes *cognouit* (cf. 7.1n. *missus*). **mane** is defined as the time *secundum diluculum* (Censorinus, *DN.* 24).

18.3 celeriter qualifies both *cognito* and *abdiderunt.* V. receives C.'s main characteristic again (4.6n.). **exploratores**: 16.2n. **aduentu ... cognito**: a Caesarian mannerism, it recurs at 57.2, 88.1, and, slightly varied, 12.1, 81.2. Sall. may have picked it up (*Iug.* 87.4, 97.4, 101.6). **carros impedimentaque sua** "their wagons and baggage train." The pair combines "the name of a class and a conspicuous member of it" (Eden *ad* Verg. *Aen.* 8.436); similarly at 1.26.1, 4.14.4, *BC* 1.51.1 (speaking of the Gauls' habitually campaigning with heavy baggage trains [cf. Hirt. 8.14.2]); cf. 1.24.4, 26.3. Like many other words for horse and carriage in Rome (Landgraf on Cic. *Rosc. Am.* 19 *cisiis*), *carrus* is a Gallic term (*DLG* 107). It is first attested in Sisenna *FRHist* F85 *impedimenta collocant omnia, construunt carros*, and brings ethnographic authenticity to the standard military move. **in artiores siluas**: they either moved from the woods' edge (6.10.5, 30.3) deeper into it, or the woods were "rather dense" (cf. K-S II 475–76). The baggage train is usually set up securely before battle (1.24.3, 4.19.2, and below). **abdiderunt ... instruxerunt**: an adversative asyndeton contrasting *impedimenta* to *copiae* and suggesting speedy preparations; cf. 79.2n. *abditas.* **in loco edito atque aperto**: the *collis* in 19.1. C. alerts his readers to a potentially disadvantageous situation.

18.4 Now C. acts *celeriter*, as rendered by asyndeton once again. **sarcinas conferri**: in addition to weapons, the legionaries carried packs that included clothing, equipment (e.g. for cooking), tools (e.g. for trenching), and rations (Roth 1999: 71–77; cf. 71.4n. *triginta dierum*). They were heavy (Veg. 1.19 speaks of 60 Roman pounds [ca. 20 kg]) and put fighting soldiers at a disadvantage (2.17.2; 3.24.3; *BAfr.* 75). To deposit them before battle became a stock motif (Oakley on Livy 8.11.11 *sarcinis ... coniectis*). **arma expediri**: to ready the weapons involved removing the shield's protective cover (2.21.5; *OLD expedire* 5; Bishop-Coulston 2006: 40, 46–47).

19 Surveying the topography (§1), C. perceives its dangers (§§ 2–3; *palus* occurs 3x); he shares his analysis with his battle-eager soldiers (§§ 4–5) and succeeds in persuading them in consolatory fashion (§6n. *consolatus*) to return to the siege.

There is a long history of conflicts between impetuous legionaries and their generals trying to maintain order and obtain advantageous circumstances for battle (Lendon 2005: 163–232; below, §4n.). Within that history, C. appears artful and careful: He demonstrates superior

topographical understanding (as expected of great generals [§3n.]),
which he highlights variously but esp. by wordplay on *aequus* (§3n. *aequo*,
§5n. *iniquitatis*); and he leads his soldiery by reason (§4n. *edocet*), when
other leaders such as Scipio or Aemilius Paullus had <u>tricked</u> their troops
into obedience (Polyb. 10.2.12, Livy 44.36.1–37.4). The chapter forms a
diptych with c. 17, as both show C. interacting with his troops. V.'s manipulation of his men (c. 20) should be read against this background.

19.1 In ancient rhetoric the description of places is discussed under
euidentia, "vivid depiction" (*HLR* 819). It here serves to slow the narrative,
heighten the suspense (cf. Bömer on Ov. *Met.* 3.28), and prepare for C.'s
analysis. **Collis erat**: C. favors the *est locus* formula to introduce a new episode or circumstance (*transitio* [*HLR* 288]): e.g. 1.12.1 *flumen est*, 2.9.1
palus erat, and 55.1, 69.1, 79.3, 83.2. The formula is at home in poetry
(Hom. *Il.* 13.332, Enn. *Ann.* 23; van Dam on Stat. *Silu.* 2.2.1–3) and historiography (Thuc. 1.24.1, Livy 7.26.2 [with Oakley]). **leniter ab infimo
accliuis** "gently sloping upwards from its base," cf. 2.29.3 *leniter accliuis*,
3.19.1 *locus ... paulatim ab imo accliuis*, 83.2 *leniter decliui*; Livy 6.24.2 *lenis
ab tergo cliuus erat*. **fere** regularly follows the word it qualifies (G-L 677R).
difficilis atque impedita "difficult to pass"; the latter term specifies the
former (cf. Wooten on Dem. *Phil.* 1.3.18–19 καλῶς καὶ προσηκόντως). C.
plays on the stem *-ped-* (*expediri, impedita, pedibus*), which is not uncommon
(Livy 6.13.5, Tac. *Ann.* 1.50.2–3); cf. Xen. *An.* 2.5.18 (on πόρος). **latior
pedibus quinquaginta**: C. prefers the abl. of degree after "*plus, amplius,
longius, minus*," though measurements are more usually provided in the
construction used at 15.1n. *amplius*. **cingebat**: its position between two
isocola might mirror the topography.

19.2 hoc se colle: unstressed pronouns regularly stand in the second
position of a sentence or colon (known as Wackernagel's law; refined
by Fraenkel 1964, Agbayani-Golston 2016). They tend to follow certain
"hosts," too, including demonstratives (Adams 1994b: 110–12, 122–24).
fiducia loci "trusting in the strength of their position." C. does not use
fiducia before; it signifies misplaced confidence throughout (38.9, 76.5;
also in *BC* [Mutschler 1975: 64–66]). **continebant ... obtinebant**: both
verbs share the same root (cf. 43.5n. *profectio*) and form a homoioteleuton. **generatimque [in ciuitates] distributi** "arranged according to peoples." "*in ciuitates*" is an interpolated gloss: *generatim* stands by itself in all
other Caesarian instances (1.51.2; *BC* 2.21.1, 3.32.1); and left by itself,
the two main clauses are nearly isocolic (twenty-three and twenty-five syl-
lables), a balance enhanced by their resonant verbs. The arrangement by
"kin" was believed to foster courage (Onas. 24; as a literary motif it can
be traced back to Hom. *Il.* 2.362–68). V. will adhere to it also later (36.2).

uada ac saltus "fords and passes," the latter suggesting forests (mentioned at 18.3). **eius paludis ... eam paludem**: both the repetition (§1 *palus*; serving thematic emphasis [11.1n. *oppidum*]) and the use of the "determiner" are typical. **animo parati**: this abl. of respect (9.1n. *opinione*) recurs 9x in *VII*, highlighting the level of determination on both sides (cf. 30.1n. *animo*), as does the thematic repetition of *parati*. **haesitantes premerent** "[to] harass them [with missiles] when they got stuck"; cf. *BC* 1.45.3+6 *ex loco superiore nostros premebant ... ut nullum frustra telum in eos mitteretur* (with 51.1n. *premerentur*, 85.5n. *tela*). **haesitare** (*OLD* 1) occurs only here in *CC*.

19.3 *amplius prodest locus saepe quam uirtus* (Veg. 3.26). A general should therefore possess topographical understanding (Polyb. 9.13.6, 14.2) and secure a favorable position or else withdraw (cf. 5.49–51; Goldsworthy 1998: 204–06). It became a panegyrical commonplace to celebrate how "[a leader] discovered [an enemy's] traps and ambushes through prudent circumspection (διὰ φρόνησιν) (Men. Rhet. 373.23–24 [Russell-Wilson]). C. demonstrates his "circumspection" in two balanced clauses in adversative asyndeton: They are built around the contrasting sound play (paronomasia [*adnominatio*]) of *propinquitatem* (separated <u>only</u> by the marshes, cf. *tantulo*) and *iniquitatem* (separated by the <u>marshes</u>); the former is highlighted by alliteration of "p," the latter by assonance of "i" and the playful contrast with *aequo* (below). There is the further distinction between *uideret*, "(just) see," and *perspiceret*, "discern" (cf. Xen. *Hier.* 2.5 διὰ τῆς γνώμης ... θεᾶσθαι κάλλιον ἢ διὰ τῶν ὀφθαλμῶν, "to perceive more clearly by reasoning than seeing"); it illustrates the concept of the coup d'œil. The imperfect subjunctives express potential past conditions ("if anyone were to see ..."; *NLS* §199, K-S II 396–98). **ut** "to the effect that" (*OLD* 39). The consecutive clause states the implications of the whole situation. **paratos**: sc. *eos esse*. **prope aequo Marte** "in an almost equal fight," but the meaning of *aequus* = "level" is present, too. The metonymical use of Ἄρης and *Mars* is frequent (Gross 1911: 366–75), but C. uses it only this once (Hirt. 8.19.2 *pari Marte*; cf. Rüpke 2018 on his reticence about gods). This collocation recurs at Verg. *Aen.* 7.540, Livy 9.44.8 (with Oakley). **iniquitatem**: the noun (‹ *in* + *aequus* + *tas*) resonates with *aequo*, thus highlighting the discrepancy between the appearance of equal conditions and the reality of an "unequal advantage" (*OLD* 2; but *OLD* 1 "unevenness of terrain" is present, too; cf. below on *iniquitatis*). **inani simulatione** "in a hollow pretense" (of readiness for battle); a pleonasm, cf. *BAlex.* 74.4 *Caesar irridebat inanem ostentationem*. Gauls were stereotypically portrayed as blusterers lacking stamina (Oakley on Livy 7.10.8 *agitatio uana*; cf. 1.7n. *facile*). **sese ostentare** "show off their military strength" (*OLD* 2b); cf. 83.8 *sese ostendere*.

19.4 C.'s soldiers are keen on battle and often hard to control, as events at Gergovia would demonstrate too clearly (e.g. 1.15.2, 3.19.2, 6.8.3; *BC* 1.64.2–3, 71.2–3, 3.51.4; *BAlex.* 22; *B. Afric.* 82; *BHisp.* 30; 47n.). It is a commonplace attributed to the Roman soldiery generally (Livy 7.16.5 [with Oakley], Tac. *Agr.* 27), which appears grounded in reality (cf. Cic. *Fam.* 10.30.2 *contineri neque legio Martia neque cohortes praetoriae potuerunt*; Frontin. *Str.* 1.10 on *quemadmodum intempestiua postulatio pugnae inhibeatur*). The sentence is noticeably chiastic, suggests C.'s close bond with his soldiers in the forceful juxtaposition "*milites Caesar*," and manages, with a few touches, to evoke the soldiers' emotional complaints (*indignantes, exposcentes, tantulo*). **indignantes … exposcentes**: both verbs (first here in C.) form a chiasmus. The former resonates with 17.3 *nulla uox … indigna* and recalls the attitude the soldiers expressed there; the latter signifies urgent desire (*poscunt qui simpliciter petunt, exposcunt qui desiderant*, Isid. *Diff.* 1.438). **conspectum … perferre**: an insult, *nam primi in omnibus proeliis oculi uincuntur* (Tac. *Germ.* 43.4); cf. 1.39.1 *ne uultum quidem atque aciem oculorum … ferre*. The soldiers' fearful sight (again at 76.6) is a commonplace: Eur. *Heracl.* 687 "no enemy will bear to look at me," οὐδεὶς ἐμ᾽ ἐχθρῶν προσβλέπων ἀνέξεται, Xen. *An.* 1.2.18, Tac. *Ann.* 3.45.1 with M-W, and Veg. 3.12 *infirmiores sunt quorum mentes ipse confundit aspectus*. Cf. the metaphors associated with viewing as wounding (Bartsch 2006: 145–52); 53.2n. on the psychology of offering battle. **tantulo**: diminutives are generally rare in C. (Pascucci 1973: 493; perhaps because of their vulgarity), *tantulus* not so much (4x in *BG*). Here it sounds like what soldiers would say (a "quotation"). **spatio interiecto**: C. favors the expression (6x + 3x *BAfr.*), which recurs 23.3, 69.4. Tac. will favor it, too. **edocet**: 14.2n. *docet*. Whenever C. uses the verb, the intensifying force of the prefix *e(x)* - can be heard (i.e. "to inform thoroughly"). C. can often be observed communicating with his troops (Vogt 1960: 96–98; cf. *BHisp.* 30 *locum definire*). **quanto detrimento et quot uirorum fortium morte**: "theme and variation"; the "lives lost" specify the "loss" (83.1n. *detrimento*), *et* = "and, more precisely" (cf. *OLD* 11). *uiri fortissimi* was a possible address of soldiers (Dickey 2002: 290). **constare** "to cost" (*OLD* 11). **uictoriam**: following the list of heavy losses and delayed until the sentence's end (completing a double cretic), "victory" surprises at first (a figure called παρὰ προσδοκίαν [Cic. *Fam.* 7.32.2]; cf. Mankin on Cic. *De or.* 3.207 *improuisum*); but only to impress upon the reader the more forcefully that C. possesses that "inability to doubt (…) victory" (Goldsworthy 1998: 201) expected of a Roman general (cf. 1.37.4 *minus facile resisti*, 62.6n. *exitu uictoriae*). The same confidence in the mouth of a Gaul, however, suggests braggadocio (20.7n. *uictoria … explorata*, 37.3 *certissimam … uictoriam*).

19.5 sic animo paratos echoes §2 (of the Gauls). **nullum ... periculum**: 10.1n. *nullum ... praesidium.* The pronominal adj. and the hyperbaton add emphasis. **summae se ... cariorem**: *se* focuses *summae* (Adams 1994b: 135). A general should avoid unnecessary dangers (cf. Livy 8.16.8 *Coruus ... labore militum potius quam periculo peragere inceptum uoluit*), and C. shows great diligence *in singulis militibus conseruandis* (6.34.3, 7.52.3; cf. 5.52; *BC* 3.90.2). He will also have known, however, that "people gladly obey whom they believe to take care of their interests more prudently than themselves" (Xen. *Cyr.* 1.6.21). **iniquitatis** pointedly echoes §3 *iniquitatem*: C. would be guilty of "unfairness" (*OLD* 3), if he allowed his soldiers to fight under conditions of "unequal advantage" (*OLD* 2). This repetition (cf. 5.3n. *legatorum*) seems all the more intentional given the soldiers' misperception of the almost "equal advantage" (*aequo Marte*). **condemnari**: in *CC* only here and [Cic.] *Att.* 10.8b.1. **uitam sua salute** is the reading offered by the MSS. C. clearly varies the contrast expressed above in *pro sua laude periculum*, and *salute* (instead of e.g. *gloria* or *dignitate*) has caused difficulty. But it makes good sense in this emotional section, as C. amplifies his attachment to his men: seeing their devotion, how could he rank their lives lower than his "wellbeing" even (let alone the expected "standing"). **cariorem** is highlighted by verbal hyperbaton (15.5n. *habeat*), final position, and a clausula (choriambus + double trochee). It suggests an emotional connection (cf. *suos quisque habet caros*, Caes. *Anticato* [Prisc. *GL* 2.227]).

19.6 consolatus identifies the address as a *consolatio*, defined as *ad omnem animi motum ... mitigatio* (Cic. *De or.* 3.118; Kassel 1958: 40–49; 29.1n.). It bespeaks his sympathies for his soldiers, eager for battle, again (cf. 22.1n. *uirtuti*, 52n.). **reliquaque ... pertinebat ... administrare instituit**: the phrase belongs to the bureaucratic register (cf. Cic. *Fam.* 15.1 *parare ea quae ad exercitum quaeque ad rem militarem pertinerent*; Coleman 2012: 211 on *pertinere ad*). It is common in C. (incl. 81.2). On *reliquaque quae*: 4.6n.

20–28 The sack of the "city"

A Homeric heritage, *expugnationes urbium* are the stuff of great history (Tac. *Ann.* 4.32.1), and their "vivid depiction" is a historiographical hallmark, for which a set of commonplaces was at the historian's disposal (ἐνάργεια, *euidentia* [*HLR* §810]; Paul 1982, Rossi 2004: 17–53). Quintilian's disquisition of the *urbs-capta* motif identifies several such commonplaces (8.3.68–69): *apparebunt effusae per domus ac templa flammae et ruentium tectorum fragor et ex diuersis clamoribus unus quidam sonus,* *aliorum <u>fuga</u> incerta, <u>alii</u> extremo complexu suorum cohaerentes et <u>infantium</u> <u>feminarumque</u> <u>ploratus</u> et male usque in illum diem seruati fato <u>senes</u>: tum illa profanorum sacrorumque direptio, efferentium <u>praedas</u> repetentiumque discursus* ... C. includes: 24.2–4 *fumare aggerem* ... *faces*, 24.4 *alii*, 26.3–4 *precibus petiuerunt* ... *conclamare*, 28.3 *fugae*, 28.4 *aetate confectis* ... *mulieribus* ... *infantibus*, 28.4 *praedae*, and 26.3 *repente*. He will do so again at Gergovia, Alesia, and Massilia (*Index*, s.v. "*urbs capta*," *BC* 2.1–16; at Sall. *Cat.* 51.9 he ridicules the topos). His reliance on the historiographical tradition is complemented specifically by an adaptation of Thucydides' siege of Plataea (22n.); and he might in turn have inspired Sallust's siege of Thala (*Iug.* 75–77; Martin 2001: 395–98). He himself looks back to Avaricum at 47.5+7, 52.2, and *BC* 3.47.5. His "visible hand" arranges "quiet" scenes in alternation with combat scenes (20–21, 23, 26; 22, 24–25, 27–28; 14–28n.), but fails to smooth out the Gauls' sudden change of heart and inexplicable negligence in the rain (26, 27).

C. and his troops possess everything military writers such as Onasander deemed necessary for a siege (40.1): "courage among the soldiers (στρατιωτῶν ἀνδρίαν, 22.1 *militum nostrorum uirtuti*), intelligence in the person of the general (στρατηγικὴν ἐπίνοιαν, 27.1 *consilium*), and war machinery (μηχανημάτων παρασκευήν, cf. esp. 17.1n.)."

20 Unexpectedly accused of perfidy, V. defends himself. The opposition dramatizes Gallic fickleness and the instability of V.'s power (1.3n. *impulsi*, 4.2n.); and it signals the kind of division deemed particularly detrimental during a siege (Whitehead 2002: 27–33). C.'s audience would have categorized V.'s speech under *genus iudiciale* (§3 *accusatus*), whereof there are three more instances (1.20; 44; 2.14; Murphy 1949: 123 adds 1.31). It employs Roman heterostereotypes (§5), follows rhetorical rules closely (§§3–12n.), and confirms V.'s standing as an orator (with occasional hints at his idiolect [nn. on §5, *casu* ... *uocati, Fortunae, per proditionem* ... *uictoria*; cf. 14n.]), while revealing him as treacherous (§§8–9n.) and overbearing (§§7n. *uictoria*, 11n.). The ring-compositional expression *proditionis insimulare* (§1n.) marks the beginning and end of this episode, to which Polybius (3.62.2–6) supplies details: For to rally his troops, Hannibal produced prisoners readied (παρασκευαζόμενος πρὸς τὸ μέλλον, §10 *iam ante edocti*) by torture (§9n. *fame*). After their single combats he spelled out the significance and asked his troops to "see vividly" what lay in store for them (ἐναργῶς θεασάμενοι, §12n. *haec* ... *beneficia*; *uidetis*).

20.1–3 The sentence affects an oral character by its crisp clauses marked by anaphora and homoioteleuton (*quod* ... *uenissent*), repeated resumptions (*haec omnia, tali modo* ... *ad haec*), and anacoluthon (*tali modo*).

proditionis insimulatus is a dangling nominative (K-S II 586.3). *insimulare* occurs only in *VII* (and only in this phrase [20.12, 38.2]; a "local repetition"); the expression recurs once elsewhere (Sall. *Hist.* 2.20). **quod ... uenissent:** four anaphoric clauses (cf. 1.19.1, 43.4; *BC* 1.71; 2.21; Wills 398–400), each marked by homoioteleuton, specify the incriminatory evidence. **discessu:** 5.2n. *aduentu.* **tanta opportunitate** "with such felicitous timing."

20.2 The conclusion is presented in *oratio obliqua.* It follows naturally on the implied verb of saying in *insimulatus.* **fortuito aut sine consilio:** "theme and variation," here involving affirmation and negation (a Demosthenian favorite [*Phil.* 1.9.1–6 with Wooten]). *aut* is corrective. **regnum illum Galliae malle ... habere** "No, he preferred to obtain the kingship of Gaul," an adversative asyndeton; for the distribution of *malle* and *habere,* cf. 1.2n. *ipsi ... Galli.* The charge of collusion is commonplace (cf. Xen. *Ages.* 8.3; Gell. *NA* 4.18.3). Here it is the climax of the accusation (and perhaps an intimation of V.'s acquaintance with C. [*Introd.* 3f]); its intended effect can be gauged from how Dumnorix incited the Aedui by making the same claim (5.6.2). V. had been declared *rex* already – but only by his followers (4.5); he will stay clear of the dangerous term (7n. *imperium*). **concessu:** the noun (only here in C.) is almost solely attested in this formulaic ablative; cf. esp. Cic. *Fam.* 4.6.3 *illius concessu et beneficio.* **habere beneficio** forms a resolved cretic-anapest. *beneficium* is well chosen, as it is a standard term for an office granted by the people (*TLL* 2.1885.23–63; cf. *BC* 1.9.2, with Krebs 2018a: 75).

20.3–12 Omitting an *exordium,* V. begins with the *argumentatio:* its first part, the *reprehensio* (§§3–7), shows his adversaries' *argumentatio* to be *uitiosa* (*Rhet. Her.* 2.31), since they misused circumstances that *could* indicate treacherous intent as if they *did* (*Rhet. Her.* 2.39). He refutes every point in order, marking each by initial position (*quod castra ... quod propius ... equitum ... summam ... Romani ... imperium;* Oppermann 1933: 81–82; 12.1n. *Vercingetorix*). In its second part, the *confirmatio* (§§8–11), he produces witnesses. In the *peroratio* (§12), he contrasts what he has achieved *for* them with how he is treated *by* them, concluding with an *epiphonema* (*HLR* §879) and a promise of what they could expect from his foresight. V.'s riposte brims with confidence: he breaks the first charge into two (*castra ... propius*), escalates his opponents' rhetoric (*Fortunae, remitteret*), reappropriates their words (*opportunitate, beneficia*), and taunts them with a paradox (§6n. *indicio*). But C. undercuts it with irony and sarcasm (nn. on *uictoria ... explorata, honorem ... salutem, sincere, milites ... seruos,* 21.1 *fide*). **tali modo accusatus:** the expression resumes (and varies) *incusatus* after the list of incriminatory evidence; the result is an anacoluthon (cf. 3.22.4). **ad haec:** the redundancy is not uncommon (Eden 1962: 106). **quod** "as for the fact that" (K-S II 270–71). **persuasum** = *id sibi persuasum esse*. The pronouns are omitted to achieve parallelism with *factum* (cf. 17.3n. *aedificorum*); ellipsis of *esse* is frequent with the perf. inf. **loci opportunitate** takes up §1 *tanta opportunitate*, but with a change in meaning (cf. 5.3n. *legatorum*). **qui se ipse:** the *personificatio* of *locus* adds emphasis. The MSS read *ipsum*; Bentley emended to *ipse*, since *sine munitione* (cf. 14.9n.) clarifies that the place *alone* provides defense (cf. 6.37.5 *aditūs locus ipse per se munitioque defendit*). The subject carries the stress, not the object (K-S I 631–32).

20.4 uero marks the transition to a further point (*OLD* 6); it is usually postpositive. **neque ... et** "while not (*OLD* 8) ... at the same time." **sint profecti:** the sequence of tense requires *essent*. But the absolute use of the perfect in reference to where they actually went (cf. Andrewes 1937: 115) is both easy to justify and the more difficult reading.

20.5 Contrast the circumspect general Aeneas, who leaves men in charge for the time of his absence, or C. himself (9.1–3; Verg. *Aen.* 9.171–73 with Hardie; Nisbet 1995). The sound effects may suggest an idiolect: *summam imperi se consulto nulli discedentem tradidisse, ne is multitudinis studio ad dimicandum impelleretur*. **summam imperii** "supreme command," a standard expression. **nulli** = *nemini*, which C. does not use (except at *BC* 1.85.12). **is** resumes *nulli*. **multitudinis ... impelleretur:** the gen. is subjective. "Crowds" are stereotypically fickle (Otto 378, "uulgus"): besides Homer's archetypal scene (*Il.* 2.142–49), cf. esp. Demosthenes' beautiful rendering of the people as "the most unstable and fickle thing of all, like a restless wave of the sea (ὥσπερ ἐν θαλάττῃ κῦμ' ἀκατάστατον [19.136])," and Tac. *Ann.* 1.29.3 and *Hist.* 1.32.1 (with Damon) for two Roman *loci classici*. But fickleness was also an attribute of the Gauls (1.3n. *impulsi*), as was their temperamental *studium bellandi* (3.17.4; below, 7.30.4; Strabo 4.4.2 "the entire people ... is war-crazy, temperamental and quick to fight [ἀρειμάνιόν ἐστι καὶ θυμικόν τε καὶ ταχὺ πρὸς μάχην]') and their lack of endurance. **cui rei** = *dimicationi* (cf. 11.4n. *eam rem*). **propter animi mollitiem ... laborem ferre non possent:** cf. Polyb. 3.79.4 "the Celts' softness and aversion to labor (μαλακίας καὶ φυγοπονίας)." *animi mollities*, "softness of mind" (connoting "effeminacy" [Edwards 1993: 63–97]), recurs at 77.5 *animi ... mollitia* (*mollities/a* [*TLL* 8.1383.12–15] occurs nowhere else in *CC*). V. utters another Greek and Roman stereotype (τὴν ... Γαλατικὴν ἀθεσίαν, Polyb. 2.32.8 [with Walbank]; Johnston 2018: 83–84). It accords with the climatic typology (*Introd.* 3f) and is often combined with the equally stereotypical "impulsive strength" (Polyb.

2.33.2, Livy 7.12.11 *omnis in impetu uis*). By telling contrast, the Romans will prevail 24.1n. *continenti labore.* **studere omnes:** cf. *multitudinis studio.* A common resumption (Wills 327–28), less pronounced than *quos luctu adficeret lugere non sineret* (Cic. *Pis.* 18) or *pro patria mori: mors et fugacem ...* (Hor. *Carm.* 3.2.13–14).

20.6 V. adapts the *argumentatio per complexionem* (6.3–4n.). The tense switches to a primary sequence, engendering greater vividness (Oppermann 1933: 82). **casu ... uocati:** the abl. and the part. are semantically but not syntactically parallel, a lack of congruity known as *inconcinnitas* (cf. below, *per proditionem*). **interuenerint ... habendam gratiam:** both predicates are *apo koinou* (a common form of brachylogy, K-S II 555). **Fortunae:** C. may never mean anything other than *casus* or *felicitas* by *fortuna* (Bömer 1966, Pizzani 1993: 175–81; cf. 87.3n. *fors obtulit*); but V. here (and 89.1n.) certainly evokes *dea Fortuna* in parallel to the alleged informer, with the latter using *indicio* just as the goddess uses *casu.* V. thus one-ups his opponents, who denied that it could all have happened *fortuito.* **alicuius indicio:** the full form of the indefinite pronoun after *si* is used "when there is stress" (G-L 315.1). V. flirts with paradox: the traitor should receive thanks. **uirtutem despicere:** the verb is used figuratively ("to despise," *OLD* 2) in a context suitable to its literal meaning ("to look down on," *OLD* 1). To the Roman reader, this is contradicted by 17.6; not to mention the ultimate Gallic defeat at Avaricum. **paucitatem:** it is a commonplace to comment on an opponent's inferior numbers (Livy 6.13.1 with Oakley, 6.18.5 with Kraus; Dion. Hal. 9.70.1); cf. 48.4n. *numero.* **turpiter ... receperint** echoes the Roman soldiers' sentiment at 19.4. This is C.'s first use of the adverb. The technical phrase (minus the adverb) occurs 19x in C. (12x *CC*).

20.7 imperium ... nullum: the hyperbaton encloses the important points of the charge (similarly e.g. 1.18.3 *magna ... gratia*, 3.12.5 *summa ... difficultas*); it also delays V.'s rebuttal, the more emphatic for its use of *nullum* (similarly 1.7.3). V. is understandably careful to choose *imperium* over *regnum* (4.1n.). **per proditionem ... uictoria:** the variation of a prepositional acc. with an instrumental abl. is a typical form of *inconcinnitas* (von Albrecht 1989 74, 84), frequent in Sallust and Tacitus, but rare in C. The second instance may bespeak V.'s idiolect. **uictoria ... explorata:** 15.2n. here as there premature, bespeaks braggadocio (1.7n. *facile*, 19.4n. *uictoriam*), and undermines the speaker's credibility (cf. below, *milites*; *BC* 3.71.4, with Batstone-Damon 106–09). **remitteret:** sc. *imperium.* The subjunctive, supported by all major MSS, is difficult, and several edd. print the infinitive, rendered more likely even by *quin etiam* (*OLD* 3a), as it is frequently used to introduce an emphatic statement. But the subjunctive may be defended as expressing an indignant question or jussive ("Let me then return …," *OLD*, s.v. *quin* 1; K-S I 201), with *etiam* adding emphasis (*OLD* 4). The offer may reflect the precarious position C. claims Gallic leaders occupied *vis-à-vis* their people (cf. 5.27.3); then again, Curio's similar offer (*BC* 2.32) hints at its rhetorical nature. **honorem … salutem**: V. plays on the same antithesis as C. (19.5n.). There may be a Roman sense of irony in having the Gallic leader speak of *salus* when Gauls have just turned their homeland into a wasteland. **uideantur** = *sibi uideantur* (*OLD* 21).

20.8–9 A general may parade weak prisoners before his soldiers to inspire confidence (Xen. *Ages.* 1.28, Onas. 14.2). V. introduces them as *milites*, the authorial voice discredits them as *serui* (cf. 38.8 *latrones … ciues*; *Rhet. Her.* 2.9 *abs testibus*). The contradiction once more alerts readers to the *color* in V.'s speech (cf. 29.2n. *imperiti*); it also casts doubt on the alleged soldiers' condition. C. repeatedly employs the "discreditable witness" to invalidate a likely true damning fact as rumor (66.3n. *fugere*; cf. 5.29.1 *Caesarem arbitrari* [sc. *Gallos*] *profectum in Italiam*). **haec ut intelligatis … pronuntiari**: V.'s introduction resembles the customary Greek formula, as used by e.g. Dem. 54.9: ὡς οὖν ταῦτ' ἀληθῆ λέγω, τούτων ὑμῖν τοὺς μάρτυρας παρέξομαι, "to prove that I speak truthfully, I shall present witnesses to you"; cf. O'Connell 2017: 86–90. Separated by "inquit," the first three words would be perceived as a jussive (cf. *CIL* I².584.41 *id uti facere liceat*, with Courtney 1995: 10); *audite* is thus a second paratactic command. The change into direct speech is a common device among Greek and Roman historians (K-G II 595.5, K-S II 548 Anm.5), serves dramatization (Dion. Hal. *Thuc.* 37), and is often employed to draw especial attention to what is said (Walsh 1954: 110); so here, when V. is about to lie. **sincere** "truly," only here in *CC* to emphasize the bold lie (Corbeill 2018: 235–36); cf. Cic. *Mil.* 29 *dicam enim aperte*, said when "the advocate ventures on his boldest fiction" (Clark ad loc.).

20.9 producit "he produced." There is wordplay here and §10 *pronuntiare*, as both verbs may be used of actors (*TLL* 10.2.1633.62–1634.9; 10.2.1926.50–27.10). **exceperat** "he had intercepted"; military terminology (Landgraf on Cic. *Rosc. Am.* 151). **fame uinculisque excruciauerat**: cf. Cic. *Leg. Man.* 11 *uinculis ac uerberibus atque omni supplicio excruciatum*. C.'s pairing is rare; but Polybius has Hannibal produce maltreated prisoners (κακῶς διετίθετο), who "carried heavy chains and were in the grip of hunger" (δεσμοὺς εἶχον βαρεῖς καὶ τῷ λιμῷ συνέσχηντο). Both *seueritas* (4.10n.) and *prouidentia* are in character. It may be persnickety to wonder how V. anticipated his trial days in advance.

20.10 iam ante edocti: Litaviccus will use the same ploy (38.4–5). The doubling of adverbs underpins the forward planning. It was common practice to prepare witnesses for their testimony in court (Quint. 5.7.11). **pronuntiarent** repeats §8 *pronuntiari* to emphasize how the slaves' speech validates V.'s. **fame atque inopia adductos**: a frequent pairing (but Amm. Marc. 25 index *fame et inopia suorum adductus* is particularly close). **si** "to see if" (*OLD* 11).

20.11 V.'s prediction will be disproved, as the Romans will prevail *continenti labore* (24.1n.). **simili ... inopia**: a noun-adjective coupling frequently encloses the subject (DKM *ad* 6.41.2); but here it shows the troops pressed (*premi*) by scarcity. **uires sufficere**: the expression recurs in Livy 3.6.9, 27.13.13, Verg. *Aen.* 12.912. The verb occurs only here in *CC.* Cf. 85.6n. *uires suppetunt.* **operis** "of the siege work." **posse**: its subject is *quemquam* (inferred from *cuiusquam* [cf. 89.3n. *iubet*]). **oppugnatione oppidi** is a common jingle.

20.12 haec, inquit, a me echoes §8, perhaps ironically, given C.'s identification of the "slaves." **haec ... insimulatis**: two parallel isocola contrast *beneficia* with *proditionis*, highlighting the injustice. V.'s point may be gathered from *Rhet. Alex.* 1422a37–9 (Mirhady): "Just as it is just to punish those who have done something wrong, it is also fitting to reciprocate benefactors." Cic. (*Rep.* 1.4.3) identifies *iniurias clarissimis uiris ab ingratis impositas ciuibus* as a rhetorical commonplace. **a me** is emphatically set off. **beneficia** repeats §3 *beneficio*, but with a pointed change of meaning (19.5n. *iniquitatis*): these tangible (*haec*) military benefits (*OLD* 2) contrast with a vague kingship "by the [people's] favor" (*OLD* 3). **sine uestro sanguine**: bloodless victory is a motif in Roman historiography; cf. 3.24.2 *sine ... uulnere uictoria potiri*, *BC* 3.84.6, Tac. *Agr.* 35.2 (with Woodman). V. voices a Roman concern; he also echoes C. (19.5). **tantum exercitum uictorem**: verbal nouns (cf. *OLD uictor* 3a) are often used as adjectives. The contradiction between *tantum exercitum* and §6 *paucitas* is rhetorically motivated: leaders portray an enemy as pitiable before battle, but formidable upon defeat. **consumptum** "prostrated" (*OLD* 3), may be wordplay, since their "exhaustion" is due to the "exhaustion" of their supplies (*OLD* 6; cf. 17.2). **turpiter ... recipientem** echoes §6 *turpiter ... receperint*, suggesting that just as the Romans withdrew to their camp, they should soon withdraw from Gaul. **se ex hac fuga recipientem** "when they retreat in the said flight." The prepositional phrase specifies the form of retreat (K-S I 506), the demonstrative resumes the "flight" mentioned by the witnesses (cf. 5.17.5 *ex hac fuga*). **recipiat**: the Roman refugees (*OLD recipere* 12) will not find refuge (*OLD* 1). For poetic instances of the resumption of a participle by

its verb (cf. 7.1n. *missus*), see Wills 325–27. **prouisum est** highlights V.'s
prouidentia by its contrast with *uidetis* (cf. 19.3n.): the Gauls merely see
what lies before them, their leader anticipates.

21 The Gauls confirm V. in, to Roman ears, excessive and double-edged
language (*summum … ducem, fide, maiore ratione*). They appear impulsive
once more (a characteristic that may also make them particularly suscep-
tible to rhetorical persuasion, 4.1n. *incendit*) and stereotypically barbaric
(§1n. *suo more*), what with their multitude, raucous clamoring, rattling of
arms, and petty jealousy.

21.1 Ancient historians typically comment on a speech's reception, as
did already Homer (e.g. *Il.* 2.394 "Thus [Nestor] spoke, whereupon the
Argives shouted loudly [Ἀργεῖοι δὲ μέγ' ἴαχον]"). **Conclamat omnis multitudo … concrepat quod … consuerunt**: the *quod*-clause refers to the
Gauls' *general* practice, hence the plural verb. Raucous clamor is an ethnographic stereotype of northern barbarians (Oakley on Livy 7.8.10), which
C. renders beautifully: *conclamat*, "shouted their approval from all sides"
(*TLL* 4.70.68–69; 2.3n. *collaudatis*), forms with *concrepat* a *cyclos* (*epana-
lepsis*) that represents the noise on all sides (cf. 88.2n. *utrimque clamore …
clamor*). The multitudinous bustle, the archetypal rendering of which
is in Hom. *Il.* 2.209–10 (with strong sound effects), is corroborated by
the repetition of the prefix *con-*, for which, cf. below and Verg. *G.* 3.360
concrescunt subitae currenti in flumine crustae. **omnis multitudo**: Romans
dreaded the *Galli* (and *Germani*) as huge hordes; cf. 1.2.6, Cic. *Prou. cons.*
34 *Gallorum immanitati multitudinique*, Livy 5.34.2 *frugum hominumque fer-
tilis* (sc. *Gallia*); Brunt 1978: 178–83, Kremer 1994: 28–29. This association may be evoked every time C. speaks of *multi(tudo)* with regard to the
Gauls; it will become a leitmotif in the final third (*Introd.* 3c). **suo more
armis concrepat**: the onomatopoetic verb occurs only here in *CC* and, in
conjunction with *armis*, only once before in Sisenna *FRHist* F91 *conglobati
et collecti concrepant armis* (with Krebs 2014); then in Livy 6.24.1. The habit
is often attributed to the Gauls (Livy 7.26.1 with Oakley), but Romans
knew of it as well (Plut. *Mar.* 22.3; Cowan 2007: 115), which is at odds
with *suo more* (2.2n.); but the latter is intended to distance the Gauls. The
armatum concilium is a stereotype of uncivilized societies more generally
(Perl on Tac. *Germ.* 11.2). **approbant**: only here in *CC*. V. will be confirmed as leader twice more (30, 63). **summum esse … ducem**: the indir.
speech follows naturally on *conclamat*. The hyperbaton spans the colon
(20.7n.); *esse* highlights *summum* further (14.9n. *omni sint*). **fide** "loyalty"
(*OLD* 8); but its connotation of "honesty" (*OLD* 6) adds a cynical tone,
given V.'s staging (20.8n. *sincere*). **maiore ratione** "with greater exercise

of reason (*OLD* 7a)." This might have sounded preposterous to Romans who thought that northern "barbarians" lacked *ratio*; cf. Tac. *Hist.* 4.13.2 on Julius Ciuilis *ultra quam barbaris solitum ingenio sollers*.

21.2 in oppidum = *Auaricum*. But surely they would have served a better purpose on the outside (Krausz-Ralston 2009: 149)?

21.3 solis ... communem: a frequent antithesis. **communem salutem**: 2.1n. **penes**: only here in *BG*. **summam uictoriae** "the whole issue (*OLD summa* 5b) of victory"; cf. Tarrant on Verg. *Aen.* 12.572. Does *uictoriae* rather than *belli* allude to Gallic overconfidence (the former recurs only at *BC* 1.82.3 and Veg. 3.1.2, the latter is frequent)? On *uictoria* vs. *salus*, cf. 85.3n. *salute*.

22 C. returns to his siege description (17), as prepared for by the references to *oppidum* in 21.2–3. In detailing the Gallic countermeasures, he adapts Thucydides' account of the siege of Plataea (2.75–77): nn. on §§1 *imitanda*, 2 *laqueis ... auertebant, aggerem ... subtrahebant*, 3 *turribus contabulauerant, coriis intexerant*, 4 *et ... adaequabant*, 17.1 *aggerem apparare*, 24.1 *diebus xxv* (Krebs 2016). These details serve to show the Gauls as technicians of warfare, overall much improved from earlier years (e.g. 2.6.2; Riggsby 73–105; Deyber 2009: 371–84 offers a historical contextualization). Their skills receive the most attention in *VII*, making "the Gaul" "more Roman" and formidable (nn. on §1 *consilia, imitanda*; 23; cf. Sen. *Dial.* 4.11.4, Quint. 8.4.20). The imperfects express repetitive efforts.

22.1 uirtuti consilia ... occurrebant: the clause is built so as to visualize the personified nouns' collision (cf. 16.3n. *occurrebatur*). The rhetorical antithesis will soon be undermined, then inverted (25.2–4, 29.2); but it bespeaks C.'s residual admiration for raw *uirtus* over *consilium* ("contrivance," often "cunning"; nn. on 29.2, 47.7, 50.1 *loco ... uirtute*), although he knew and states that *consilium* ("intelligence," or "strategy") complements and even outranks *uirtus* (*Introd.* 3d). He thus evinces the conflicting attitudes prevalent in Rome about these traditional components of warfare, archetypically embodied by Ajax and Odysseus in their controversy over Achilles' arms (Horsfall on Verg. *Aen.* 2.390 *dolus an uirtus*; Lendon 1999). While the Gauls are credited with *uirtus* early on (1.28.5; Rawlings 1998: 178–79), they are attributed *consilium* only much later (5.34.1). **nostri milites** instead of *nostri*; again at 62.8. **cuiusque modi Gallorum**: C. does not mind attributing two genitives to one noun; again at 35.2, 41.3, 55.1 (cf. DKM *ad* 1.30.2). **ut ... aptissimum**: in content and style very similar is *BAlex.* 3.1 *ea sollertia efficiebant ut nostri illorum opera imitati uiderentur*. **ut est ... genus** "as might be expected of a people"; the

comparative *ut* has a causal connotation (*OLD* 21). In such explanatory
sentences *"esse"* often follows *ut* (45.4, 47.2; Dahl 1882: 94–95). **genus
sollertiae atque ... aptissimum**: C. often coordinates a gen. (or abl.) of
quality with a descriptive adj. *sollertia* occurs first here in C. **genus** = *gens*
(*OLD* 3). **ad ... imitanda ... traduntur ... aptissimum**: the Gauls repeatedly
adapt "new" practices, esp. in *VII* (3.23.5–6, 5.42; nn. on 14.2, 18.1n.
qui ... consuessent, 30.4; Riggsby 103–05; cf. Kraus on Livy 6.32.7 for foreigners fighting like Romans; Deyber 2009: 435–37 looks at Roman borrowings). Cf. Polyb.'s praise of the Romans (6.25.11): "for they are as
good as anyone at adopting fashions and striving for what is best." Given
Thucydides' presence, however, one could read *imitari* and *tradere* as C.'s
signposting (Krebs 2018c: 518n.5) his engagement with his predecessor.

22.2 Cf. Veg. 4.8 *oppugnantium machinis per alias machinas consueuit obsisti.*
et ... auertebant ... et ... subtrahebant: the polysyndeton, chiasmus, and
homoioteleuton make this a carefully wrought sentence; cf. 24.4n. *alii.*
laqueis falces auertebant: cf. Thuc. 2.76.4 ἃς βρόχους τε περιβάλλοντες
ἀνέκλων, "which [siege engines] they caught with nooses and turned
aside"; a standard practice (Veg. 4.23), similarly described at Sisenna
FRHist F126, App. *Pun.* 16. *laqueus* occurs only here in *CC*. A *falx* was a
"beam with an iron hook attached atop" (Veg. 4.14; cf. 3.14.5–6). **quas
cum destinauerant** "and each time they fastened (*OLD* 1) them." **tormentis**: if "ropes" (*OLD* 1), their mention in addition to *laquei* surprises; nor
would it explain how the (heavy) *falces* were pulled inside. Schneider
ad loc. therefore suggested *tormenta* = "windlasses," citing in support
instances wherein *tormentum* loosely signifies *machina*. **introrsus**: rare in
C. but twice more below, 23.2, 5 (a "local" repetition). **aggerem cuniculis
subtrahebant** "through tunnels they dragged away the soil from under
[the ramp]." *aggerem subtrahere*, which occurs only here in Latin literature,
is C.'s translation of Thuc. 2.76.2 (ὑπόνομον ... ὀρύξαντες) ὑφεῖλκον ... τὸν
χοῦν. C. mentions *cuniculi* once at 3.21.3; all other instances occur in *VII*
(22.5, 24.2). (Counter)mining during a siege was standard procedure
(Aen. Tact. 37, Veg. 4.20; Wheeler 1988: 61). **scientius**: the comparative
only here in *CC*. He had earlier credited Gauls with *scientia rei militaris*
(3.8.1, 23.5); cf. 57.3n. **ferrariae** "iron-mines." A modern survey of the
evidence is offered in *RACF* 31 (1992), 57–73. **usitatum**: only here in *CC*.

22.3 murum ... turribus contabulauerant "they had furnished the wall ...
with a superstructure of turrets" (Edwards); another detail C. shares with
Thuc. (2.74.5), though cf. Veg. 4.19. C.'s expression likely signifies that
the Gauls erected turrets on top of the wall, thus adding another level
(*OLD contabulo* 1); cf. 22.5n. *commissis ... malis.* **coriis intexerant**: this is the

first time C. mentions hides, which, often soaked, "covered" constructions
against fire (Thuc. 2.75.5, Veg. 4.17). The textile metaphor (Horsfall
on Verg. *Aen.* 2.16 *intexunt*) is continued below at 23.2 *uestiuntur*, 23.4
contexitur.

22.4 tum "in addition" (*OLD* 9). **eruptionibus**: sallies were a standard feature of sieges (Veg. 4.28) and a commonplace of their descriptions (nn.
on 24, 69.7). **aggeri ignem**: the mound typically rested on a timber structure (as described in Thuc. 2.75.2; Krausz 2019: 33–35). **occupatos …
adoriebantur**: rather than *milites in opere occupatos* (2.19.8, *BC* 1.28.2), as
in opere qualifies both part. and verb. *occupatus* = "engrossed in" (*OLD* 9).
quantum … expresserat: cf. Thuc. 2.75.6. The daily growing ramp (*agger*
refers to the added part) raises (*OLD exprimere* 3) the towers. **commissis …
malis** "by connecting (*OLD* 4) the beams of their towers." Holmes (ad
loc.) interpreted this to mean that the *mali* were "the four uprights, one at
each angle [of each tower], … [whose] tops … projected above the highest storey [and] were connected by planking so as to form a new storey."

22.5 apertos cuniculos: this is the only time C. mentions Roman *cuniculi*. Their understanding poses difficulties: Hough 1940 (endorsed by
Campbell 2019: 253) suggested that they were the *uineae* (17.1n.) that
provided protection to the soldiers working on the *agger*, as they were
"open at both ends"; Wimmel 1974: 20–30 differs. **praeusta et praeacuta**:
73.6n. **materia** "timber" (*OLD* 1). For its use along with pitch (*pix* first here
in C.) and stones in a city's defense, cf. Veg. 4.8; *BC* 2.2. Its morphology:
24.4n. **moenibusque**: 70.6n. *arma*. Its semantic difference from *murus* is
defined in Fest. p. 145 a, 27 *moenia muri et cetera muniendae urbis gratia facta.*

23 The ekphrasis of the *murus Gallicus* naturally follows the mention of
moenia; it documents now, in *VII*, the sophistication of Rome's enemy,
while also serving retardation (22.1n. *consilia*; 24.1nn. *impedita, diebus
XXV*; on ekphrasis and persuasion, see Webb 2016: 131–66). Further
motivation may derive from a similar description in Thucydides' Plataean
siege (3.21.1–4; cf. 22n.) and the long memory of Ἴλιον … εὐτείχεον (e.g.
Hom. *Il.* 2.113; cf. §2n. *hae reuinciuntur*). It is typical of C. in its detail
(cf. 3.13, 4.17, 7.72–74; *BC* 1.25, 2.9–10; *Introd.* 3d) and presentation
not of "a static picture … but rather … the actions taken to build it"
(Dodington 1980: 11; this was a recommended form of ἔκφρασις [Theon,
Prog. 118]). It is informed by architectural theory, as soon after formu-
lated by Vitruvius (cf. Scarola 1987: 195–203): The latter's request (*De
arch.* 1.3.2) *ut habeatur ratio firmitatis, utilitatis, uenustatis* is met (§5); C.'s
accounting for dimensions seems to address the *ordinatio* (roughly, "measured arrangement"), his vertical layering builds an *erecta frontis imago*,

and his eye clearly appreciates *eurythmia* (roughly, "the pleasing harmony between the several parts" [*De arch.* 1.2]). The tightness of the construction (*reuinciuntur, arte, reuincta*) is further underpinned by the reiteration of the prefix *co(n)-*.

Dozens of such *muri* have been excavated, but not at Bourges (Büchsenschütz-Ralston 2014; Krausz-Ralston 2009). Their construction largely matches C.'s description (fig. 4; Dehn 1960: 46); but there existed a second type (§1n. *Muri*).

23.1 Muri … omnes: the *murus Gallicus* was not the only type; there was the Pfostenschlitzmauer, too (Ralston 2006: 56–57). **hac fere forma**: an introductory formula; cf. 3.13.1 *naues ad hunc modum factae*, 4.17.3, 72.1; *BC* 1.255, 2.8.3; Polyb. 6.27.1 ἔστι δὴ τὸ γένος αὐτῶν τῆς στρατοπεδείας τοιόνδε, "the manner of their camp is as follows." **trabes … collocantur** "beams are placed on the ground at equal intervals, two feet apart, throughout the length of the wall and at a right angle to it"; cf. *BC* 2.10.2 *duae primum trabes in solo aeque longae distantes inter se pedes IIII collocantur*. **derectae** "at right angles" (*OLD* 2); cf. 72.1. **perpetuae** "placed at regular intervals throughout" (*OLD* 1b; cf. *BC* 1.21.3). **in longitudinem** "lengthwise" (*OLD* 1c), sc. *muri*.

23.2 hae reuinciuntur: *aere* (‹ *aes*) enjoys partial MS support, would explain how the beams were fastened (cf. below, §5n. *reuincta*), and might even evoke Troy's *murus aeneus* (Hor. *Carm.* 3.3.65 with N-R). But the demonstrative is necessary, and the hiatic and cacophonous -*ae ae*- unparalleled, which renders *hae aere reuinciuntur* unlikely; cf. Litwan 2011. **introrsus** "on the inside" (*OLD* 2); 22.2n. **aggere uestiuntur** "are covered with rubble for protection (*OLD uestire* 2c)"; cf. 22.3n. *intexerant*. **grandibus … saxis**: the "front" (of the expression) is certainly "large"; cf. 24.5n. *omnis … multitudo*. **effarciuntur**: an extremely rare verb, signifying "to fill full" (*OLD*); only here in *CC*.

23.3 collocatis et coagmentis: both verbs are frequently found in one another's vicinity only in Vitr. (e.g. 2.8.7). The latter verb ("joined together") occurs only here in *CC*. Cf. 7.1n. *missus* (on *collocatis* resuming *collocantur*). **idem illud interuallum** "the same interval as [mentioned] above" (§1). **neque … trabes**: they touch neither vertically nor horizontally. **intermissis spatiis**: a Caesarian mannerism (11x), hardly elsewhere; again 72.3, 73.9. **singulae singulis … contineantur** "each [beam] is tightly held in place by single stones placed in-between," mimetic in order and with a polyptotic *geminatio* (32.5n. *pars cum parte*).

23.4 sic deinceps "on in the same manner." **contexitur**: C. likes the textile metaphor (22.3n. *intexerant*) in engineering contexts. Tac. *Ann.* 4.49.1

fossam loricamque contexens may bespeak his influence, even if the verb's uses in *BAfr.* 47.5 and Veg. (e.g. 4.14) suggest military language.

23.5 Given the wall's indestructible nature, the reader wonders *how* C. will prevail (cf. 6.2–4n.). **hoc ... opus**: another noteworthy hyperbaton. **in speciem uarietatemque** "with regard to (*OLD in* 17) its varied appearance"; a hendiadys. **cum ... tum**: proceeding from the general, less important to the specific and more important (K-S II 350); the same criteria are applied to Avaricum (15.4n.). **quae ... seruant** "which maintain, in straight lines, each its proper order." **ad utilitatem et defensionem** "in point of (*OLD ad* 37) the defensive efficiency"; another hendiadys. *ad* varies *in*. **et ... et**: strictly parallel. **materia**: 22.5n. **defendit**: sc. *murum*. **quae ... reuincta** "which [timber] was tied together on the inside by regularly placed beams, generally forty feet long." These *perpetuae trabes* ran in the direction of the wall and connected the *trabes* mentioned above (§1). **pedes quadragenos plerumque**: the acc. of extent characterizes the *trabes*. *plerumque* is here postpositive.

24 When the Romans are completing the ramp, the Gauls set it alight and sally forth, just as they were expected to (cf. Livy 5.7.2; for the equally typical timing, Veg. 4.18). The conventional scene highlights Roman endurance (*continenti labore*) and the commander's vigilance and foresight (*consuetudine, instituto*), who, after momentary confusion, regains control, as the orderly final sentence shows (*alii ... alii ... multitudo*); this impresses all the more, as the dark of night often caused chaos (81.5; Thuc. 7.44, Onas. 41; cf. 80.6n. *solis occasum*).

24.1 His tot rebus: the countermeasures and the *murus Gallicus* (22, 23). **impedita oppugnatione**: similarly 3.12.2. The digression on the wall certainly conjures a sense of impediment. **toto tempore ‹so›luto frigore**: β's *luto* may be a gloss; if not, it can be defended (Pinkster 1969: 265–66). But Wagner's emendation nicely balances the two circumstances (cf. 17.3n. *aedificiorum*), and *frigus soluere*, while not attested before Stat. (*TLL* 6.1.1337.45–47), occurs in a similar context in C.'s reader Amm. Marc. 19.8.1. The first abl. is of time within which (G-L 393R2). Rhymes with nouns in *–or, oris* are popular: e.g. Plaut. *Pseud.* 695 *scis amorem, scis laborem*, Cic. *Cael.* 42 *non odore ullo, non tactu, non sapore*, Cat. 63.37–38 *oculos sopor operit;* | *... rabidus furor animi*; cf. 40.4, 81.3 (where the quantities differ). The cold is a common northern attribute: Tac. *Germ.* 16.2 *rigorem frigorum.* **assiduis imbribus**: once before C. at Lucr. 5.338. Rain was commonly associated with the northern sphere, too: *caelum crebris imbribus ... foedum* (Tac. *Agr.* 12.3). **tardarentur**: it bespeaks the difficulties C. faced fighting V. that *VII* counts twice as many instances of *tardare* as any other book; cf. 65.4n.

interclusis itineribus. **continenti labore**: the collocation recurs *BC* 3.63.4, 97.4. More than a virtue, *labor* defined *Romanitas*: *disce, puer, uirtutem ex me uerumque laborem* (Verg. *Aen.* 12.435; Combès 1966: 256–58, Lau 1975: 26–32, 87–116). A sought-after quality of general and soldier alike (Luc. 9.588 *monstrat* [sc. *Cato*] *tolerare labores* with Wick), it distinguished Rome's military and built its empire: Cic. *Cat.* 4.19 *laboribus fundatum imperium*, Livy 9.19.9 *iam in opere quis par Romano miles? quis ad tolerandum laborem melior?* Within the *BG*, it sets legionaries apart from their Gallic counterparts (cf. 20.5n. *laborem*, 20.11n.). C. tellingly emphasizes this trait in a speech (*apud* Gell. 13.3.5): *equidem mihi uideor pro nostra necessitate non labore ... defuisse.* **superauerunt**: the notion that effort wins, varied at *BC* 3.26.3, is frequent in Roman thought and famously expressed at Verg. *G.* 1.145 *labor omnia uicit* (Lau 1975: 246–53, 466n.37). **diebus XXV**: C. rarely specifies the time needed for major constructions (a regular feature of military reporting, cf. Cic. *Fam.* 2.10.3, 15.4.10) but may do so here to invite comparison with the Peloponnesian ramp at Plataea (Thuc. 2.75.3). By mentioning the work's beginning at 17.1 and conclusion here, he correlates discourse time to story time (*Introd.* 3c). **latum pedes CCCXXX, altum pedes LXXX**: the accusatives are of extent (G-L 335R1). *latum* has been questioned, as it suggests width when the specified dimension is more likely to have been the length of the perpendicular ramp (Krausz 2019). The size of the construction is plausible (Krausz-Ralston 2009: 153–55); the ramp at Massilia was as high (*BC* 2.1.4).

24.2 consuetudine = *ex consuetudine*, as in 6.27.5 (with DKM); a modal ablative, as are 1.6 *periculo*, §5 *instituto.* **excubaret**: soldiers appreciated leaders who shared their hardship (*qui* [Cato] *nuda fusus harena excubat*, Luc. 9.881–83 with Wick, Verg. *Aen.* 10.217 with Harrison) and those who were with them where the action was (Xen. *Cyr.* 1.6.8 boils it down to προνοεῖν καὶ φιλοπονεῖν, "to look ahead and love labor"; Onas. 40.2); cf. 87.1n. *ipse ... adducit.* **omnino** "at all" (*OLD* 3a "with negatives"). **ab opere intermitteretur** "[not] to take a break from working"; with change of meaning of §1 *opus* (cf. 5.3n. *legatorum*). **tertiam uigiliam**: this would have been around midnight (cf. 3.3n.). **fumare**: only here in *CC.* **cuniculo**: 22.2n. **succenderant**: 15.4n. The inflammable materials: 22.4n. *aggeri ignem.*

24.3 eodemque ... portis: a typical string of abls. **toto muro**: abl. with *totus* mostly omit *in* (GL 388). **clamore sublato**: 12.5n. **turrium**: sc. *Romanarum*, near the wall. **eruptio fiebat** first occurs in Sisenna *FRHist* F75 *neque porta neque ullum foramen erat, qua posset eruptio fieri.* C. is fond of it (incl. 7.2, 69.7, 73.1; Krebs 2014: 211), as is *CC. eruptio* is the milit. technical term for "sortie" (*TLL* 5.2.846.63–47.21); the imperfect is conative.

24.4 alii "others" (*OLD* 4), in contrast to those fighting. To break a battle scene into units to present a description "not of a whole but in parts" (Quint. 9.2.40) is essential to *euidentia* and frequent in historiography; cf. below, 28.3, 75[n.], 85.5. **faces:** only here in *CC.* **aridam materiam:** Curt. 5.5.7 *ipsi aridam materiem in incendium iacere* is close. C. seems to have favored *materia* over *materies* (attested here and 4.17.8); but inconsistency is possible. **picem … potest:** cf. Veg. 4.8.1 *bitumen sulphur picem liquidam oleum, quod incendiarium uocant, ad exurendas hostium machinas.* **quibus ignis excitari potest:** for the circumlocution, cf. Tac. *Ann.* 15.38.2 *id mercimonium inerat, quo flamma alitur* (with Ash). Lucr. 6.309 *uis excitet ignem* is the only instance of *ignis excitari* before C. **quo … occurreretur aut … ferretur** "where first to run to confront [the enemy] or, rather, which situation to alleviate"; similarly 3.4.2 *eo occurrere et auxilium ferre.* The pass. is impersonal, *aut* is corrective, and the pregnant construction of *occurrere* combines "running to" and "fighting against." **ratio iniri** "to reason" (*OLD ratio* 4); cf. 16.3n. *occurrebatur.*

24.5 instituto "according to his practice." **pluresque … in opere** "and even more (than two) were at work (at the ramp) in shifts." **partitis temporibus** recurs in Livy 22.27.6. The passive meaning may have been facilitated by the coexistence of *partire* (*TLL* 10.1.522.6–27); but C. uses other deponent verbs passively (DKM *ad* 1.11.4 *depopulatis*; Adams 2016: 46–47 surveys the phenomenon). **alii … alii … omnis … multitudo:** a *congeries*, more specifically, *distributio* (*HLR* §§667, 675), serving *euidentia*; similarly Livy 35.25.6. **interscinderent:** a rare word. The gap stopped the fire from consuming the whole ramp. **omnis … multitudo:** sim. 2.12.4. The position of *ex castris* seems noticeable; but it qualifies both *multitudo* (7.5n. *ex prouincia*) and *concurreret* (cf. Cic. *De or.* 1.13 *praemiis ad perdiscendum amplioribus commoueri*) and is frequent in C. (DKM *ad* 2.12.4; cf. 10.1n. *Magnam … difficultatem*). **uero:** 20.4n. It here (as often) has climactic force; or else it may contrast this group with the one nearer the town (K-S II 80.4–5). **restinguendum:** sc. *ignem*; first here in C.

25 The siege's climax (*omnibus locis, semperque, omnem salutem*) is a vivid episode not atypical of C. (Ramage 2003; Brown 2004: 292n.1). It contains an *aristeia* (Feller 1929: 38–41; Lendon 1999: 278n.14 lists instances in republican historians) that, while upending the *uirtus-consilium* antithesis at 22.1, highlights Gallic valor, and all the more forcefully for the series of nameless fearless deaths: it is an epic scene without the epic hero (nn. on *propugnatoribus, exanimatus*), wherein Romans would have recognized the sober attitude to death they idealized (§2n.); the language is historiographical and elevated (nn. on *inspectantibus nobis, dignum memoria, semperque, adire, uestigio, quidam, per manus, hunc … transgressus, finis*). Claudius

Quadrigarius' *aristeia* of Manlius Torquatus against a formidable Gaul supplies details (*FRHist* F6); the most noticeable are: *Gallus quidam* (quidam
... Gallus) ... *maxime proelio commoto atque utrisque summo studio pugnantibus*
(the climactic moment) ... *pugnae facta pausa est* (finis est pugnandi factus) ... *exercitu inspectante* (inspectantibus nobis) ... *scuto proiecto* ... *hominem iterum deiecit* ... *humerum dextrum* (glebas ... proiciebat: scorpione ab
latere dextro traiectus).

25.1 in omnibus locis ... pugnaretur: marks the climax (cf. 67.2, 84.2; Livy
5.21.13). C. is particularly fond of the imper. pass. of *pugnare* (Pinkster
1992: 165–66, 170–71; 2.3n. *disceditur*). **consumpta ... noctis**: sim. 5.31.4
consumitur uigiliis reliqua pars noctis. **semperque ... semperque**: rhetorical
repetition of *semper* is quite common (esp. in Cic.), anaphoric *semperque*
less so. **spes uictoriae**: identical at 3.26.4, 7.47.3; *BC* 3.82.2 (*BHisp.* 22.7).
The expression becomes frequent in historiography, wherein the "prospect of victory" is a common motif, too. **deustos** "burned down," only
here in C. **pluteos** "screens of wood or wickerwork" (*OLD* 1), first mention
in C. They differed in form and function (Veg. 4.15.5 with Milner, Vitr.
10.15.1+5, cf. nn. on 41.4, 72.4), some were moveable, some fixed (*BC*
2.9.6, 1.25.9). These were most likely mantlets screening the soldiers who
moved the towers (Holmes ad loc., Lambertz in *RE* s.v.). **nec facile adire
apertos ... animaduertebant** "they realized that [the Romans,] exposed
to attack, could not easily (*nec* = *et non*) approach to bring help"; *aper-
tus* = "exposed" is common in the military register (*TLL* 2.221.45–53). A
similarly pronounced quintuple alliteration occurs 2.32.4 *aggerisque altitudinem acervi armorum adaequarent* and *BC* 1.26.4 *illo auctore atque agente
ab armis*. Skutsch's cautionary words on Enn. *Ann.* 104 *O Tite tute Tati tibi
tanta tyranne tulisti* apply: "it is not easy to say whether Ennius ... meant to
achieve a special effect." **recentes defessis succederent**: *succedere* in the
sense of military relief is idiomatic (*OLD* 4b), the whole phrase formulaic
(41.2, 5.16.4 *integrique et recentes defatigatis succederent*, *BC* 3.94.2; cf. 1.5n.
deposcunt), the motifs commonplace (48.4, 86.6). Typically, the besieged
were the ones worn out *opere, uigiliis, uolneribus, quae semper eosdem urgebant*
(Livy 6.3.3); which is why Aen. Tact. 38.1 recommends that "the fighting
force of the city ... be divided into three parts, so that there may always be
one part in action, another off duty, and the third preparing for action:
thus the troops will always be fresh." **omnemque ... salutem**: for the significance of *salus* in this context (in contrast to *uictoriae*, above), cf. 85.2n.
salute. **uestigio temporis** "in this very moment." A rare expression slightly
varied at *BC* 2.26.2 (cf. also Cic. *Cael.* 55, *Pis.* 21). There may be wordplay,
as *in uestigio* means "in the same position." **accidit ... existimauimus**: a
commonplace of ancient historiography; cf. Xen. *An.* 1.5.8 ἔνθα δὴ μέρος τι

τῆς εὐταξίας ἦν θεάσασθαι, "and then it was possible to observe an example of discipline." **inspectantibus nobis** = *inspectante me* ("the only parts of this verb used by Cicero and Caesar," Nisbet on Cic. *Pis.* 9), as the authorial *existimauimus* (= *existimaui*) suggests: "while I looked on in astonishment" (cf. Clark on Cic. *Mil.* 101 *inspectantibus*). It is one of two instances of the narrator identifying with someone present (5.13.4; *BC* 3.17.1 is close; cf. 5.6n. *nobis*). While C. was present at many events (Grillo 2011), as Hirt. 8 *praef.* 8 implies, he rarely stresses autopsy (Marincola 1997: 63–86). It serves suspense, lends greater weight to the following description, and prepares for the following *demonstratio* (which will make the reader *see* [cf. 63.1n. *augetur*]). **dignum memoria uisum praetereundum non existimauimus:** *uideri* is often used redundantly in expressions of personal opinion (H-S 797b). The phrasing is formulaic; cf. Plut. *Cam.* 21.2 οὐκ ἄξιον ἦν ἀμνημόνευτον παρελθεῖν, "it did not deserve to be passed over in silence." The *uita memoriae* was an integral function of ancient historiography ever since Hdt. *Hist.* 1.1; it fell to the historian to decide what should be remembered (Thuc. 1.1.1 ἀξιολογώτατον; Xen. *Symp.* 1.1 ἀξιομνημόνευτα; Sall. *Cat.* 4.2 with Vretska; Marincola 1997: 34–43). For the generic implications, cf. Krebs 2017. *praetereundum* is similarly used at 77.2.

25.2–4 The *propugnatores* demonstrate the *doloris mortisque contemptio* that was the essence of *uirtus* (Cic. *Tusc.* 2.41–43); they are in spirit Mezentius' kin (Verg. *Aen.* 10.907): *iuguloque haud inscius accipit ensem.* **quidam ... Gallus:** the indefinite highlights "an outstanding example of its kind" (*OLD* 2). The word order is mimetic. **per manus sebi ac picis traditas glaebas** "lumps of grease and pitch ... passed on from hand to hand." The proverbial expression *per manus tradere* (Ogilvie on Livy 5.51.4) recurs 47.7, *BC* 1.68.2. The word order is mimetic. **glaebas:** only here in *CC.* **e regione turris** "directly opposite (cf. *OLD* 2b) the tower." *e regione* (first here in C.), recurs 35.1+2, 36.5, 58.6, 61.5 (*BC* 1.25.6 and *CC*); a "local" repetition (Frese 1900: 21). **scorpione:** a small arrow-hurling catapult (Marsden 1971: 188); in C. only here and 25.3. On the Roman penchant to name military equipment for animals, see McGushin on Sall. *Hist.* 2.106. On their demoralizing effect: 41.3n. *tormenta.* Cf. 44.3n. **traiectus exanimatusque concidit** pithily renders the sequence of events. It has an epic ring: cf. e.g. Hom. *Il.* 4.501–04 where Odysseus' spear "passed through [Democoon's] forehead" (διὰ κροτάφοιο πέρησεν), who then "fell to the ground with a thud" (δούπησεν δὲ πεσών). *exanimo*, "to kill," darkly resonates with its original meaning of "to empty of air" (*OLD* 2+1); it, too, comes with Homeric connotations, e.g. *Il.* 20.471–72 τὸν δὲ σκότος ὄσσε κάλυψε | θυμοῦ δευόμενον, "darkness shrouded his eyes, deprived of his breath."

25.3 hunc … transgressus: the double hyperbaton produces a mimetic order. The imagery (and valor) is reminiscent of the *Neruii* fighting *ut ex tumulo* (2.27.4). Other acknowledgements of outstanding Gallic virtue include: 1.26.2, 2.10.2, 33.4, 7.62.7. **ex proximis unus**: only twice elsewhere (Frontin. *Str.* 4.7, Flor. *Epit.* 2.17).

25.4 ictu scorpionis exanimato repeats §2, thus rendering the repetitiveness of the action. **tertius et tertio**: a polyptotic *reduplicatio*. **propugnatoribus**: the prefix's literal meaning is activated by the Gallic defenders' position <u>ante</u> *portam*. Valiant gate-guarding is an epic topos traceable back to Hom. *Il.* 12.127–50; cf. Hardie on Verg. *Aen.* 9.672–755. **ille … locus**: 24.5n. *omnis … multitudo* (word order). **restincto aggere**: as they set out to do 24.5. **finis est pugnandi factus**: the double hyperbaton generates a molossus-spondee. Periphrastic *finem facere* occurs 11x in C. (+ 4x *CC*). *pugnandi* resumes §1 *pugnaretur*, thus highlighting the theme of the paragraph (cf. 16.3n. *itineribus*); again at 49.1+2.

26 The Gauls now plan to escape but the women wail (a standard detail of the *urbs-capta* motif [nn. on §§3–4, 3 *flentes*]); the plan is abandoned. This vignette, marked off by ring composition (§§1+5n. *consilium*), in its despondency contrasts darkly with the death-defying determination just seen (25.4; cf. 3n.), and foreshadows the Gallic defeat (Rambaud 207); its suddenness may also dramatize Gallic fickleness (cf. 21n.). Several rare or poetic expressions elevate the tone (nn. on *hortante et iubente, silentio noctis, apparabant, praeoccuparent*), as does the plangent p-alliteration in §3.

26.1 Omnia experti: identical at 4.4.4; cf. 78.1n. *omnia … experiantur*, 81.2. C. is fond of *omnia* in dramatic battle scenes (2.20.1 *omnia uno tempore erant agenda*, 5.33.1+3+5, 34.1). **res nulla** commonly substitutes for *nihil* (Adams 2016: 103–04; again at 65.4). **hortante et iubente**: the pairing is anticipated at Enn. *Ann.* 432 *iubet horiturque* (cf. Cato *FRHist* F76.6 *imperes horterisque*) before C. It forms an "appendix sentence," "suggest[ing] the language of officialdom" (N-R on Hor. *Carm.* 3.5.3–4); it later becomes a characteristic of Tacitus. *et* = "and then" (*OLD* 16).

26.2 id is *apo koinou* with *conati* and *effecturos*. **silentio noctis**: a poetic expression (repeated at 36.7), attested in Turp. 52 and Lucr. 4.453. But it may be Ennian (as the presence of *hortante et iubente* could also suggest): *qui quidem silentio noctis, ut ait Ennius, "… fauent faucibus russis …,"* Cic. *Diu.* 2.57 (with Pease). The motif: 11.7n. **conati** = *conatos*; for a similarly "alogical attraction" (K-S II 584 A3), cf. 5.39.4 *adepti*. **non magna iactura**: identical at Cic. *Clu.* 23. **propterea quod**: 4.1n. *ob … quod*. This particular expression occurs 15x in *I* but only this once in *VII*. **neque … et**: 20.4n. The negation applies to the adverb (25.1n. *nec facile*). **castra**

Vercingetorigis: 16.1. **palus ... intercedebat**: between Avaricum and V.'s camp. *palus perpetua*: 57.4, 6.5.4; once elsewhere (Luc. 6.344). **ad insequendum tardabat** "hindered them in their hostile pursuit (*OLD* 2)." Verbs of hindering may construe with *ad* (G-L 432R).

26.3–4 This scene will be reprised at Gergovia (47.5–6n.); both are – along with the third scene at 2.13.3 – rhetorical in nature (Bellemore 2016). **iamque**: a temporal transition word common in Verg. and esp. Livy (C-L 514–16); it is frequently followed by *cum inuersum* (*TLL* 7.1.109.56–81). **matres familiae**: again 47.5; an instance of *interpretatio Romana*. C. favors the regular gen. sg. over archaic (*familias*) and plural forms (*familiarum*). **repente**: C. prefers *subito* (45x) to *repente* (9x) 5:1 but *repentinus* (29x) to *subitus* (4x) 7:1. Emphasis on suddenness (27.3, 50.1, 81.2, 88.3) is a commonplace in siege descriptions, e.g. Livy 6.8.6+7, 31.18.6, 38.7.7. **in publicum** "into the streets" (*OLD* 5). **flentesque ... pedes**: 15.4n. *procumbunt*, 38.1n. *lacrimans*. Agitated women, a standard feature of the *urbs-capta*-motif ever since Hom. *Il.* 9.590–94, will recur at 47.5, 48.3, 78.3; cf. 1.51.3, *BC* 2.4.3; 14.10n. *coniuges*. **omnibus precibus petierunt**: sim. at 78.3 (also 5.6.3; cf. *BAfr.* 91); a formulaic expression for urgent requests (Landgraf on Cic. *Rosc. Am.* 11 *quaeso*). **communes liberos**: these words express "an emotional appeal to the ancient notion that children 'cement' a marriage" (W-M on Tac. *Ann.* 3.34.6); cf. 48.3n. *liberos*. **ad supplicium dederent**: once before C. at Cic. *Clu.* 181. **quos**: women and children. **ad fugam capiendam**: an unusual expression, first here in C. (rare afterwards [*TLL* 6.1.1469.73–75]). **infirmitas impediret**: on *impedire ad* (*BC* 1.62.2; 3.76.4), cf. 26.2n *tardabat*. Women and children did occasionally join in the flight: 1.26.5 + 1.29.2; Livy 8.37.8 (with Oakley).

26.4 perstare: only here in C. **timor ... recipit** "fear knows no pity," a gnomic statement (as are 84.5 and 89.1), hence the present (G-L 227) and the generalizing *plerumque*. There are at least ten *sententiae* in *BG* (Preiswerk 1945). They were deemed stylistic elements of great distinction (*Rhet. Her.* 4.24–25, esp. *multum afferent ornamenti*), and, according to Cicero, no speaker was *sententiis aut acutior aut crebrior* than C. (Suet. *Iul.* 55). **conclamare ... coeperunt**: *coepisse* often "marks actions spread over some time" (Courtney 1999: 147; Adams 2016: 126–27). **significare de** "to indicate by physical signs" or "to indicate (by means of speech)" (*OLD* 1, 4); in the latter case it forms a hendiadys with *conclamare*. For its use with *de* (only here in *CC*), cf. 1.1n. *cognoscit*.

26.5 quo timore perterriti ... ne: the fear caused by the women's behavior (*quo timore = cuius rei timore* [K-S I 64.5]) is further specified by the *ne*-clause. Expressions of fright are often doubled (Landgraf on Cic.

Rosc. Am. 5 *terror ... formido*); cf. 43.3, 77.11. C. is fond of this particular doubling (6x). **praeoccuparentur**: the verb first here in C. and just once before (Plaut. *Mostell.* 1061). **consilio destiterunt** contrasts with § 1 *consilium ceperunt* in ring composition (cf. 16.3n. *itineribus*). The expression recurs at *BC* 3.21.5.

27 C. identifies the pouring rain as an opportunity (§1n. *non inutilem*; cf. Polyaenus 8.23.8) to assault the weather-wearied defenders. He has his own troops pretend that they, too, slacken off; but once secretly assembled, they storm the city walls.

It was a commonplace that "opportunity rules all human affairs, but those of war especially" (Polyb. 9.15; cf. Veg. 3.26). A general was expected to read a situation (cf. Vell. Pat. 2.106.3 *obseruantia temporum*; 19.3n.) and to seize an opportunity (cf. Frontin. *Str.* 1.4 *Iphicrates ... cum incidisset frigidior solito dies et ob hoc nemini suspectus, delegit firmissimos quosque ...*). C. repeatedly shows he knew how to (cf. nn. on 18, 36.5–7), and he came to enjoy a reputation for the right moment (Suet. *Iul.* 60 *ex occasione*, Plut. *Caes.* 26.3 μάλιστα δὲ καιρῷ [with Pelling]). He devotes attention to the theme at Gergovia (44–52n.) and may here dwell on his handling of an *occasio* to counterbalance the disastrous outcome there.

In typical Caesarian fashion, a period of participial constructions and subordinate clauses organizes information, reasoning, and decision (Brown 2004: 305), followed by a terse statement on the necessary and swift action (*subito, euolauerunt, celeriter*). There are noticeable rhythms, double trochees (*arbitratus, dispositas uidebat, expeditis*) and a double cretic (*militibusque signum dedit*), and the indirect speech carries an emotional tone (*aliquando, pro tantis laboribus, fructum uictoriae*); cf. Gärtner 1975: 75–77, von Albrecht 1989: 59–68.

27.1 A typical string of ablatives. **Postero die** occurs 63x in C. (29x *CC*), and frequently as a transition formula (*VII*: 29.1, 52.1, 79.2, 89.1; C-L 32–34). This is the siege's 27th day. **turri**: its number surprises (17.1 *turres duas*); the other tower presumably collapsed or burned down. **perfectisque ... facere**: the verbs' shared root highlights the pointed semantic difference. **quae ... instituerat**: 1.1n. *ut constituerat*. **coorto imbri**: C. prefers *cooriri* to *oriri* with weather conditions. **non inutilem**: rain is typically a cause to cease battle (Kraus on Livy 6.8.7 *imber*; cf. above, 24.1); the litotes is therefore particularly apt, as it invokes the normal expectation (Marouzeau 1970: 258). However, some military writers deemed nighttime, storms, and festivals opportune moments "to approach the wall" (Philo, *Bel.* 8.D4; cf. Woodman on Tac. *Ann.* 4.50.4 *nox*). **hanc** resumes the rain mentioned in the abl. absolute, the independence of which is thus compromised; a common occurrence in C. (Lebreton 1901: 8–10;

cf. 4.1n. *conuocatis ... clientibus*). **suos**: 13.1n. **incautius ... languidius**: neither comparative is attested before C. Their parallelism reinforces each.
custodias in muro dispositas: similarly at 55.9, *BC* 2.19.3 (*BAlex*. 13.1).
custodia is the preferred term for guards atop a wall (Fischer 1914: 169–
71); cf. 3.3n. *uigiliam*, 69.7. *murus* occurs thrice in this section ("thematic repetition"). **in opere uersari** recurs at 77.11; nowhere else. **quid
fieri uellet**: 16.2n.

27.2 C.'s brief address is reminiscent of a battle harangue (as *cohortatus*
suggests [29.1n. *cohortatus*]): 2.21.1–3; cf. 29[n.], 62.2, 86.3. **legionibusque ... expeditis cohortatus**: 4.1n. *conuocatis ... clientibus*. **aliquando**, "now
at last" (*OLD* 5), is a variation on the "here and now" commonplace of
the *cohortatio* (86.3n. *in ... hora*). **pro tantis laboribus**: Catull. 31.11 *pro
laboribus tantis*. Mention of labors is another commonplace of the *cohortatio*: Polyb. 3.111.9 "now free yourselves from your toils (ἀπαλλαγέντες δὲ
τῶν νῦν πόνων) ... and you will be the masters"; again at 86.3[n.] *omnium
... dimicationum*. **fructum uictoriae** could be a circumlocution for *praedam*;
but a gen. of specification seems more likely (G-L 361; *NLS* §72.5). The
metaphor, which recurs at 86.3, is anticipated in Cic. *Verr.* 6.77; Livy
36.24.7 *miles ... aliquo tandem loco fructum uictoriae sentiret* may owe it to
C. (esp. in light of 69.2–4n.). Other instances of this commonplace can
be found in Albertus 1908: 61–63. **eis qui primi ... ascendissent praemia
proposuit**: cf. Polyb. 10.11.6 "[Scipio Africanus] promised gold crowns
(χρυσοῦς στεφάνους) to those first to climb the wall along with the customary awards for conspicuous bravery." Such incentives were common
Greek (Philo, *Bel.* D9.3–5) and Roman practice; within the latter, the
corona muralis (= χρυσὸς ... στέφανος) enjoys special recognition (Polyb.
6.39.5; Sall. *Cat.* 7.6; Gell. 5.6.16). But here it would seem likely (and
47.7 indeed suggests) that C. tendered additional rewards (surveyed in
Maxfield 1981). *ascendissent* corresponds to *ascenderint* in dir. speech. For
this usage of the pluperfect, cf. the tense in the apodosis of a past counterfactual in *oratio obliqua* (G-L 597.3).

27.3 subito ... euolauerunt: 3.28.3 is similar. C.'s use of *euolare* of swift
movement in war is unprecedented and rare later (*TLL* 5.2.1065.84–
1066.10). **compleuerunt**: 12.5n.

28 In what reads like an anticlimax (by comparison with 26), C. describes
how the Gauls are caught by surprise (for the third time: 8.3, 11.4) and
panic. A massacre ensues, all elements of which are commonplaces of
the *urbs-capta* motif (cf. 20–28n.); the grim casualty figures bring this first
major "act" to an end (§5n. *numero*; *Introd.* 3c). V. reenters the scene in his
role as exceptional leader, when he cares for the survivors (§6n.).

28.1 A typically propulsive sentence. **re noua perterriti**: again at *BC* 1.65.1. On the element of surprise (*OLD nouus* 4), cf. 8.3n. *inopinantibus*. **locis patentioribus**: on open spaces in towns as points of assembly, see Hornblower on Thuc. 2.2.4 θέμενοι; however, assembling there is also a "historiographical cliché" (W-M on Tac. *Ann.* 3.45.2). **cuneatim** "in combat (or perhaps: wedge) formation," a rare adverb attested here for the first (and in *CC* only) time. Military writers apply the noun *cuneus* both generally to soldiers in combat formation (cf. *acie instructa*) and specifically to a "wedge" formation (Perl *ad* Tac. *Germ.* 6.4). C. standardized the term for Gallic battle formations (Bell 1995: 764–65). **obuiam contra ueniretur** "[if] the enemy [impersonal passive] came up against them." The two adverbs signify position (in front) and direction (against); they are sometimes used pleonastically, too (Horsfall on Verg. *Aen.* 11.504 *ire obuia contra*). **depugnarent** "to fight to the end" (cf. 1.5n. *deposcunt*); only here in C. (5x in *CC*).

28.2 sed toto undique muro circumfundi "but that they were [all] spread out everywhere along the whole wall." *BC* 3.74.2 makes the antithesis explicit: *ut nemo ... imperium desideraret et sibi quisque ... imponeret labores*; *omnes* (*uel sim.*) is here omitted. The pleonasm renders the hopelessness of their situation. **spes fugae tolleretur**: the collocation of the two nouns is frequent (*TLL* 6.1.1469.2–3) but recurs only once in *CC* at 1.25.1. **abiectis armis**: a commonplace in formulaic language (N-H on Hor. *Carm.* 2.7.10 *relicta*). **continenti impetu**: C. normally uses *continuus* with *dies* (M-P 244; but cf. 14.1); this makes α's *continenti* preferable to β's *continuo*.

28.3 parsque ... pars: 24.5n. *alii*; 11.5n. *quaeque*. **angusto ... portarum**: the crowding and self-hindering in gateways is a cliché (Oakley on Livy 10.5.10); cf. 70.3. **se ipsi premerent**: C. often uses *se ipsi* instead of *inter se* to express reciprocity (DKM ad loc., K-S I 617 Anm.10). **nec fuit quisquam** "and there was no one (*nec = et non*)"; the focalization abruptly changes. **praedae**: cf. *BC* 3.97.1 for a general's fear *ne in praeda occupati* (sc. *milites*) *reliqui negotii gerendi facultatem dimitterent*. Military writers and historians abound in examples of soldiers who, "excited about the loot," fell prey to a regrouping enemy (Onas. 10.7; Aen. Tact. 16.5–7), left their position, or took unnecessary risks (45.8). This was undoubtedly a frequent occurrence in real battle; but C.'s comment may also be motivated by his knowledge of "plundering" as an element of the *urbs-capta* motif (20–28n.); as such it can be traced back to Homer (*Il.* 6.68).

28.4–5 Military handbooks advise against atrocities in captured towns, as they would make the surrender of others less likely (Onas. 38). Rome prided itself on the *uetustissimus mos uictis parcendi* (Livy 33.12.7; cf. Verg.

Aen. 6.853 *parcere subiectis*); but it did not shrink from massacre if deemed necessary, as Polyb. 10.15.4–6 observes (cf. Aug. *Anc.* 3, Tac. *Ann.* 2.21.2). C. proceeded accordingly: He cultivated a reputation for leniency but was ready to wield brutality for punishment or intimidation (*BC* 3.80–81, Hirt. 8.41.1 [cf. 4.10n.], Cass. Dio 41.51.4; cf. Collins 1972: 933–37 on the not-so-lenient general, Powell 1998 on massacres). Here C. feels the need to justify the bloodbath (17.7n. *perfidia*; next n.), which was worse than V.'s dire prediction (14.10); but he may also have hoped to make an example of it (cf. Thévenot 1960: 60). At Massilia (*BC* 2.13), C. worries that something similar might happen. **et Cenabensi caede et labore operis incitati**: the first part of this excuse is specious, as Cenabum had already been avenged (3.1, 11.9). *incitati* underpins that legionaries acted out of affect, just as they would at Gergovia (47.3n. *elati*). Incensed soldiery is a common motif: Xen. *An.* 1.2.26 "they plundered the city ... in their anger over the loss of their fellow soldiers," *BC* 2.13.3 *permoti milites et defectionis odio ... et diutino labore*; Livy 9.13.3 (with Oakley). **non aetate ... non infantibus**: triple anaphora (as in 52.3) in a slightly falling asyndetic tricolon, from old age to infancy. The differentiation between these groups was a standard feature of the *urbs-capta* motif (Quint. 8.3.68). *infans* occurs once more in *CC* (47.5). **mulieribus**: C. favors *mulier* (the generally preferred term when there is "emphasis on the sex of a woman" [Adams 1972: 242]) over *femina* in line with the practice in administrative writing (Odelman 47).

28.5 denique "in the end" (*OLD* 1). **ex omni eo numero ... vix DCCC**: peculiarly (cf. 78.1n. *inutiles*), Appian reports the same number of survivors following Hannibal's siege of Petilia (*Hann.* 29). Casualty figures often bring closure to narratives of war (1.29.3, 4.15.3). They are paralleled in triumphal inscriptions (Wiseman 1985: 3–10; Östenberg 2009: 40, 59–60, 72) and, quite possibly, on placards brandished during triumphal processions (Plut. *Pomp.* 45 with Heftner on γράμμασι). It is then unsurprising that C. frequently exaggerates them (even though there seems to have been a law that threatened commanders *qui aut hostium occisorum in proelio aut amissorum ciuium falsum numerum litteris senatui ausi essent referre* [Val. Max. 2.8.1]), as with regard to the 430,000 Germanic casualties at 4.15.3 (Rambaud 179–86, Henige 1998); many such figures are stylized, too (13.2n. *CCCC*). Ancient sources calculate that the war in Gaul caused the death of one million Gauls, with another million enslaved (Plin. *HN* 7.92, Plut. *Caes.* 15.5). **se ex oppido eiecerant**: the phrase recurs 47.4, (5.21.5), *BAlex.* 19.5, Livy 28.3.11.

28.6 By gathering survivors, V. begins his textbook conduct after defeat (cf. Veg. 3.24 [quoted in 29–35n.]). **quos ... ex fuga excepit**: 6.35.6

multos ex fuga dispersos excipiunt. ex fuga = "in (their) flight" (20.12n.), or = "immediately after (their) flight" (*OLD ex* 10); it is frequent in C. (17x, incl. 88.7), *CC* (11x), and Livy (19x), rare elsewhere. **multa iam nocte** can be approximated, with the help of Censorinus, *DN* 24, as the time after you retired to bed and before midnight *(deinde concubium; exinde intempesta id est multa nox; tunc ad mediam noctem dicitur)*. **excepit:** there is sarcasm in C.'s repeating and modifying V.'s words (20.9n.), as the latter now suffered what he had predicted for C. **qua ... seditio:** a common hyperbaton with indefinites. **ex** "in consequence of" (*OLD* 18). **misericordia uulgi:** 15.6n. **disparandos** "to separate off" (*OLD* 1), fairly rare and only here in *CC*. **ut ... curaret** "and so he made sure"; the epexegetical *ut* clause stands in apposition to "*ueritus ne ...*" (*OLD ut* 39). **procul in uia** "at some distance along the road" (Edwards). **ad suos:** the reflexive is used in reference to the logical subject, i.e. the persons at "the center of the thought" (*NLS* §36 [i]). **quae ... pars ... obuenerat** "to the part of the camp each tribe had obtained right at the beginning." The antecedent *partem*, which stands in apposition to *suos*, is enclosed in the rel. clause (K-S II 313.4).

29–35 AVARICUM'S AFTERMATH

After Avaricum's fall, V. takes care of his troops, recruits more, and enlarges his alliance (29–31). Meanwhile, C. stays on to refresh his men and determine what to do (32.2n. *siue*). Approached by Aeduan emissaries requesting help, he leaves for Decetia (33n.), about 74 miles east of Avaricum and across the Elaver (Allier), to decide their domestic issue. Once there, he divides his troops (34.2n.), dispatching Labienus to the north, while marching himself south along the river's right bank, with V. moving in step (Raaflaub-Ramsey 2017: 58 assume C. returned to Avaricum; this is at odds with C.'s narrative [cf. Thévenot 1962]). Crossing with difficulty, he reaches Gergovia after some 150 (185) miles.

In C.'s telling, the Aeduan worry (5n.) resurfaces after Avaricum's dramatic end, which is thus neatly separated from the ensuing battle over Gergovia by an embedded quieter narrative (cf. De Jong 2014: 34–37; *Introd.* 3c): this allows him to pause the narrative proper, align narrated and narrative time, and resume the Aeduan leitmotif with due attention, soon to be the storyline in the "second act" (36–43n.). Another speech marks this chapter (29n.), and renewed war efforts follow once again (cf. 14n.) – but with a sense of escalation: for the first time, V.'s Gauls build proper fortifications, are joined by archers, and augmented by peoples from *Aquitania*. Both the repetition of narrative elements and problematic claims of amplification (29.7n. *instituerent*, 31.5n. *conduxerat*) reveal

C.'s plotting hand; there are chronological problems, too (whereof C. seems aware [29.6n. *idque … habere*]).

V.'s portrait as general is elaborated, as he does what was expected of a textbook leader after defeat (Veg. 3.24): *colligendi sunt superstites bello* (28.6n.), *erigendi adhortationibus congruis* (29n.) *et armorum instauratione refouendi* (31.3). *tunc noui dilectus, noua quaeruntur auxilia …* (31.4). He is praised for his foresight especially, perhaps to make it more noticeable that the resourceful C. outwits him once again (35n.). But the latter's primary role in this section is as exemplary governor (33n.).

29 After a defeat a general should deliver "an encouraging speech [to] give [his soldiers'] souls strength again" (Onas. 1.13; cf. Thuc. 6.72, Xen. *An.* 3.1.39–42). Generically, such speeches belong with the pre- or in-battle address (nn. on 27.2, 62.2, 86.3), which is an essential component in ancient historiography and the Homeric poems (Cic. *De or.* 66; Lendon 2017b: 145–54; Keitel 1987). Strangely, it lacks a consistent name (*cohortatio/-or* dominates in Latin: cf. *BC* 3.90.1 *exercitum cum militari more ad pugnam cohortaretur*; Cato *FRHist* 97, Nep. *Han.* 11.1) and a proper place within the rhetorical system (Quint. 10.1.47, tellingly: *de laudibus exhortationibus consolationibus taceam*; cf. Zoido 2007).

V. combines his *cohortatio* with a *consolatio* (19.6n. *consolatus*), mixes in an apologetic remark (§4), but foregoes lamentation – as well he should, as "it was not the orator's business ‹to cause› to weep those whom he was exhorting to fight" (Men. Rhet. 418.19–21 [Russell-Wilson]). His *argumentatio* (§§2–6) offers an analysis of the defeat and a plan to move forward; it makes much use of commonplaces but may also bespeak more specific debts (nn. §§1–2, *consolatus cohortatusque, animo demitterent, perturbarentur incommode*; cf. 31.1n. *animo laborabat*; Albertus 1908: 46–93). C.'s own *cohortatio* after Gergovia will invite comparison (52n.); other instances include 1.40, *BC* 2.32, 3.86–91.

29.1–2 strikingly resembles Polyb. 10.6.1–2 (of Scipio): "Having gathered his troops, he encouraged them not to be downcast by the recent disaster. For it was not by valor that the Carthaginians had overcome the Romans, not ever, but by the treachery of the Celtiberians" (συνηθροισμένων τῶν δυνάμεων παρεκάλει μὴ καταπεπλῆχθαι τὴν προγεγενημένην περιπέτειαν. οὐ γὰρ ταῖς ἀρεταῖς ἡττῆσθαι Ῥωμαίους ὑπὸ Καρχηδονίων οὐδέποτε, τῇ δὲ προδοσίᾳ τῇ Κελτιβήρων).

29.1 is largely formulaic (cf. 14.1, 52.1 [esp.], 60.1, 89.1). **Postero die:** 27.1n. **concilio conuocato consolatus cohortatusque:** the verbs, whose obj. (sc. *conuocatos*) is to be extrapolated from the abl. absolute (4.1n. *conuocatis*), signal the speech's functions (cf. Utard 2004: 135 on such markers in C.); they often occur together, so in Thuc. 7.76.1 "[Nikias] encouraged and consoled (ἐθάρσυνέ τε καὶ παρεμυθεῖτο)." The repetition of the prefix *cum* emphasizes unity (2n.); for the quadruple alliteration, cf. 4.4n. *eiectus*. **ne se admodum animo demitterent** "not to lose heart altogether (*OLD admodum* 2b)"; cf. 9.1n. *opinione praeceperat*. Loss of heart is a natural consequence (cf. Thuc. 7.76.1 ἀθυμοῦν, Xen. *An.* 3.1.40). No less natural is V.'s appeal: "hold on to hope (ἐλπίδα χρὴ ἔχειν)," Thuc. 7.77.1; "do not be disheartened (μηδὲν ἀθυμήσητε)," Xen. *An.* 5.4.19. **neue perturbarentur incommodo**: "theme and variation." C. never uses *turbare* (2x in *CC*). The four instances of *incommodum* in 29–30 constitute "thematic repetition." Thuc. 7.76 similarly moves from mood (ἀθυμοῦν) to event (ἐν μεγάλῃ μεταβολῇ).

29.2 V.'s *argumentatio* begins with a "response" to C. (22.1) that reassigns bravery to the Gauls and cunning to the Romans; to C.'s audience, he thus appears the crafty speaker yet again (20.8–9n.). His excuse for the loss is typical (cf. Thuc. 6.72.3, Polyb. 10.6.2 [above]); but instances modeled on this passage incl. *BAlex.* 12.1 *non uirtute propugnatorum sed scientia classiariorum se uictos*, Tac. *Agr.* 27.2 *non uirtute se uictos, sed occasione et arte ducis* (similarly rebutting a Roman claim to *uirtus* [27.1]). **non uirtute ... oppugnationis**: the antithetic parts are strictly parallel. **neque** = *et non* (25.1n.). **uicisse Romanos**: the painful fact (constituting a common clausula [*creticus* + *trochaeus*]) is hidden in the middle; cf. Quint. 9.4.29: *si in media parte sententiae latet, transire intentionem et obscurari circumiacentibus solet*. **artificio quodam et scientia oppugnationis** "by craft, of sorts, and knowledge of siege operations" (other shades of meaning are possible). The pair (cf. 19.1n. *difficilis atque impedita*) recurs at *BC* 1.58.2. **cuius rei** "wherein," with *rei* resuming the whole notion (G-L 614R2, again §4). **imperiti**: V. echoes the Roman opinion of their primitive warfare (22n.); but C. had just described the Gauls' countermeasures as conducted 22.1 *scientius*, which undermines V.'s claim.

29.3 The rhetorical tradition had a place in consolations for "philosophical reflection ... on human nature" (Men. Rhet. 414.2). C. may have hoped that his readers would remember V.'s lesson on vicissitude after Gergovia (Rambaud 172). **errare ... exspectent**: the emphatic *errare* follows smoothly on *imperiti*. The statement is a commonplace (cf. Livy 30.30.20 *nusquam minus quam in bello euentus respondent*). **si qui** "whoever" (*OLD quis²* 1a); the subject of *errare*. **omnes** "nothing but"; cf. e.g. Livy 5.14.2 *patricios omnes ... tribunos militum ... creauere*. **secundos rerum prouentus**: *prouentus* occurs first here in C. (but *TLL* 10.2.2313.16–17 *legitur inde a Caes.* may be misleading in the light of Val. Max. 8.1.abs.3).

At 80.2n. it is synonymous with *euentus*, at *BC* 2.38.2 with *successus*; here *secundos* adds emphasis to the latter meaning. *rerum* is a redundant gen. of reference indicating "the physical world" (*OLD* 4). **exspectent** instead of *exspectarent*.

29.4 The assertion of consistency is a commonplace; but Pericles' assertion at Thuc. 2.61.2 is particularly memorable: "I am the same and unchanged" (καὶ ἐγὼ μὲν ὁ αὐτός εἰμι καὶ οὐκ ἐξίσταμαι). **sibi numquam:** emphatically phrased (cf. 2.1n. *se*) to highlight the contrast with the others; true, too (cf. 15.6). **factum:** 20.3n. *persuasum*; it introduces *uti.* **imprudentia Biturigum:** 15.4–5. **obsequentia:** a virtually unparalleled synonym of *obsequium* (*TLL* 9.180.41–48), used for the sake of assonance; cf. Cic. *Mil.* 76 *in longinquos, in propinquos* (instead of *uicinos* [Clark ad loc.]). **uti** was the standard form in legal texts. C. uses it instead of *ut* more often than other contemporary authors (esp. in *I*; Odelman 64–73). **hoc**, rather than *illud*, preserves the speaker's proximity to the event. **incommodum acciperetur:** 14.1n.

29.5 V. switches from the past to the future, just as Onas. 36.3–4 recommends that the general's speech prepare for the next engagement, aiming at "rectifying the defeat." V. had once already remedied *incommoda* by inflicting *incommoda* in turn (16n.). **commodis:** the antonym (to *incommodum*) underscores the reversal; cf. Xen. *An.* 3.1.40+41 "how dispiritedly they came ... they will be much more spirited (ὡς ἀθύμως μὲν ἦλθον ... πολὺ εὐθυμότεροι ἔσονται)." **sarturum:** the MSS read *sanaturum* (sometimes misspelled *senaturum*), which is possible, as *sanare* is (i) frequently employed metaphorically (esp. by Cic.); (ii) attested with *incommodum* (Sen. *Tranq.* 9.3); and (iii) used elsewhere in C. In this passage, however, the medical metaphor would intrude discordantly (yet C. may have wished to hint at V.'s idiolect [cf. 14.4n. *deleri*]). Bentley's conjecture, meanwhile, rests on several parallels, e.g. 6.1.3, *BC* 3.73.5 *acceptum incommodum uirtute sarciretur*; and the figurative use of *sarcire* "repair" is so common as to be unnoticeable (Livy 9.23.13 *damna uestra, milites, ... praeda sarcientur*).

29.6 An adaptation decorates V.'s statue at Alise-Sainte-Reine: "La Gaule unie, formant une seule nation, animée d'un même esprit, peut défier l'univers." Much of Gaul *did* fight together in 52 and with one purpose (*Introd.* 2c). As a literary motif the call to unity first occurs in Hom. *Il.* 2.379–80. Romans would have perceived the threat in *cuius ... obsistere*. **quae ... ciuitates:** the rel. clause typically includes the antecedent when the main clause follows (K-S II 309–10). **ab reliquis Gallis:** those resisting Rome. **adiuncturum:** sc. *sibi*; 14.7n. *laturos* (*esse*). He had done so already (4.6). **unum consilium totius Galliae** "one single (*OLD unus* 6) course of

action (*OLD consilium* 5) for a wholesome Gaul (cf. 4.1n.)." Cf. Cic. *Rep.*
1.41 *omnis ciuitas ... consilio quodam regenda est ut diuturna sit*, and 9.5n.
omnes in unum. **consensui** resonates with *consilium* (a paronomasia) and
contrasts with *dissentirent.* **ne orbis quidem terrarum**: 8.3n. *ne ... quidem.*
obsistere: only here in C. (and *BHisp.* 42) to create sound play with *orbis*
(cf. above, *obsequentia*). **idque ... effectum habere** "and what is more
(*OLD -que*¹ 11), he had almost brought this to pass already"; *effectum habere*
resumes *effecturum* (cf. 7.1n. *missus*). The combination of a part. pass. with
habere (*teneri*) is characteristic of administrative texts and frequent in C.
(Odelman 120–30). Given the distances involved and the time required
for V.'s efforts, C. wisely added this reassurance to reduce the chronological implausibility.

29.7 V. appeals to their sympathy (*aequum, communis salutis*), a standard
function of the *peroratio* (*HLR* 436–39). He is courteous and circuitous –
he could have said: *castra munirent*; this may reflect his precarious command (20.7n. *remitteret*) or C.'s wit (30.4n. *consternati*). **aequum**: a criterion
for proper action as advocated in a deliberative speech (Quint. 3.8.43;
cf. *HLR* §375). **communis salutis**: 2.1n. **ut ... instituerent** "that it should
be obtained from them that they start fortifying the camp." C. mentions
Gallic camps as early as 1.15.1, their adaptation of Roman camp fortification at 5.42.1–2; in *VII*, too, Gallic camps have been mentioned several
times already. But the claim serves both to elevate V. (Nestor had famously
advised defensive fieldworks [Hom. *Il.* 7.336–43]) – and to heighten the
drama (29–35n.): now the Gauls overcome their laziness to become more
Roman (30.4n. *insueti laboris*, 22.1n. *consilia*; Riggsby 122). Then again,
"a standard remedy for defeat was to toughen the troops with toil" (Rives
1999: 129). **quo** = *ut eo.*

30 For the third time a speech by V. is well received (15.1, 21.1), and he
is praised for qualities deemed essential in a leader: determination (esp.
after defeat) and foresight (§2n. *animo prouidere*; the repetition of *animo*
is thematic). The loss at Avaricum had in fact "vindicated" him (§2; Kahn
1971: 251). His increased standing (as measured in two Roman values:
dignitas and *auctoritas*) is thus not as surprising as C. makes it out to be
(§3). But this emphasis on the paradox agrees with his ironic comment on
how the Gauls *now at last* fortify their camps (§4nn. *consternati, patienda*).
The three doublings in their reasoning (*abdiderat ... fugerat, prouidere et
praesentire, primo ... post*) hint at their fervor.

30.1–2 The sentence comprises two parallel parts connected by *plusque*
(11.5–6n.); the first causal clause is divided into isocola. **fuit**: C. rarely
places the copula in first position (DKM ad loc.), but twice more in

VII: 37.4, 48.4. **non ingrata**: the litotes hints at the opposite expectation (27.1n. *non inutilem*), adding emphasis. **et maxime quod** = *praesertim cum*, as in 5.45.1; *BC* 3.37.3; cf. 32.2n. *ut maxime*. **animo non defecerat**: V. follows his advice (29.1n. *ne … animo demitterent*; cf. 31.1n. *animo laborabat*). By appearing optimistic he meets another requirement of the perfect general; cf. Xen. *Ages.* 11.2, Onas. 13.1, and *BAfr.* 10 of C. himself: *neque quicquam solacium … neque auxilium … nisi in ipsius imperatoris uultu uigore mirabilique hilaritate.* **accepto incommodo** resumes 29.4 *incommodum acciperetur* (cf. 7.1n. *missus*; 29.1n. *incommodo*). **neque se in occultum abdiderat … fugerat**: sc. out of shame; cf. Livy 9.6.9 *super maerorem pudor quidam fugere … coetus hominum cogebat.* This instance of "theme and variation" proceeds once more from the general to the specific; the first half is pleonastic (cf. 9.2n. *in omnes partes … peruagentur*), the second half suggests both "to see" and "to be seen". ‹**se**›: haplography caused its omission.

30.2 On the reason of V.'s increased standing, cf. Cic. *Off.* 2.33 *iis fidem habemus quos plus intellegere quam nos … et futura prospicere credimus.* **animo prouidere et praesentire**: Lucr. 5.1343 *animo praesentire atque uidere* (with 1.2n. *addunt*); on *animo* (in meaning differing from §1 *animo*, cf. 5.3n. *legatorum*), cf. 9.1n. *opinione praeceperat.* Foresight characterized both political and military leadership (Cic. *Rep.* 1.45.2 *prospicere … magni cuiusdam ciuis … est*; 16.2n. *ratione prouideri*). Themistocles enjoyed a particular reputation, as he had advocated the abandonment of Athens during the Persian Wars (Thuc. 1.138.3, Nep. *Themist.* 2–3). **re integra** "when the matter was still open (*OLD* 2)"; but there is a sense also of "intact." **primo … post**: 15.6, 26.1.

30.3 ut … sic: the comparative sense frequently shades into the concessive (G-L 482.4). **ut … minuunt**: the same notion at 1.40.12, *BC* 2.31.3. **reliquorum imperatorum** stands in antithesis to *huius* and applies to both *res* and *auctoritatem*. **auctoritatem**: a fundamentally Roman term, "impossible to translate" (Cass. Dio 55.3.5). It signifies influence rather than institutional power (*Anc.* 34.3 *auctoritate omnibus praestiti, potestatis autem nihilo amplius habui* [Galinsky 1996: 10–20]), which, given V.'s precarious *potestas* (20.9n. *remitteret*), is particularly important to him. It requires goodwill, ideally *consensus* among the subordinates (*Anc.* 34.1 *per consensum uniuersorum*), a notion present in this context, too: 30.1 *non ingrata*, 29.6 *consensui*; and etymologically related to *augere* (E-M 57), it is often linked to *dignitas* (Cic. *Inu. rhet.* 2.166) as its "expression" (Balsdon 1960: 45), which is why *dignitas … augebatur* would appear but natural to a Roman. A cardinal characteristic of the *summus imperator* (Cic. *Leg. Man.* 28), it *normally* correlates with victories (*Anc.* 3–4 [Ramage 1987: 38–54]). **ex contrario** "on the contrary." **dignitas** "standing"; literally "worthiness" (‹*dignus*›), due to birth or accomplishment. It comprises objective and subjective aspects, such as office and comportment, and is etymologically connected to *decet* (E-M 166–67), which here suggests that V.'s *dignitas* increased, because the Gauls thought that he behaved or spoke "properly" (*ut illum deceret*). C. held a longstanding claim to it: *sibi semper primam fuisse dignitatem* (*BC* 1.9.2; cf. 1.43.8, 4.17.1, 56.2n. *indignitas*; cf. Morstein-Marx 2000). See further *VL* 388–415, Thome 2000: 117–34. **incommodo accepto** reiterates §1n.

30.4 simul "at the same time"; C. freq. employs the sentence-initial adverb in transition (M-P 1234.51–35.51; incl. 31.4, 48.4, 50.5, 73.7). **in spem ueniebant**: 12.5n. **de ... ciuitatibus** is *apo koinou* with *in spem ueniebant* and *affirmatione* (cf. also 9.1n.). It echoes V.'s promise (29.6), evincing his persuasive powers. **castra ... instituerant**: 29.7n. **animo consternati**: 29.1n. The verb (only here in C.) surprises, as it returns to the Gauls' state of mind *before* V.'s speech. But C. sacrifices logic to wit (below, *patienda*; 29.7n.): it took a "stunning" defeat to have Gauls do what Romans did anyway, viz. to fortify their camp. **insueti laboris** "not used to (this kind of) work"; it has concessive force. C. alludes to the stereotype (20.5n. *mollitiem*); but camp fortification was also deemed essentially Roman (*certissima Romani imperii custos, seuera castrorum disciplina* [Val. Max. 6.1.11]; cf. 11.5n.). **omnia quae imperarentur sibi patienda**: *imperata facere* (*uel sim.*) is a military phrase; cf. Tac. *Ann.* 1.6.3 *nuntianti centurioni, ut mos militiae, factum esse quod imperasset*; Miodoński-Wölfflin *ad BAfr.* 6.7, Odelman 179–80; cf. 90.2n. To Roman ears, both the context and singular substitution of *patienda* for *facienda* give it a wittily ironic tone.

31 V. delivers on his promises. In replenishing his troops – his primary concern, as the repetitions of *numerus* intimate – he sends C. the very message the latter had sent the Gauls the year before (6.1): having lost one-and-a-half legions, he saw to rapid restitution so that the enemy understand *ut si quid esset in bello detrimenti acceptum non modo id breui tempore sarciri, sed etiam maioribus augeri copiis posset ... quid populi Romani disciplina atque opes possent*. To enlarge his Gallic coalition, V. resorts to familiar (and, by C.'s pen, discreditable) measures (nn. on *donis ... alliciebat, huic ... deligebat, oratione subdola*).

31.1 To act according to one's proposals was a topic of praise: *neque minus in rebus gerendis promptus quam excogitandis erat* (Nep. *Themist.* 1.4). It can be traced back to the Homeric poems, e.g. *Il.* 14.44 "I fear [Hector] may fulfill his mighty word (τελέσῃ ἔπος)." **nec minus quam**: sim. 52.4. In tone affirmative (K-S II 481–82), it emphasizes the first part over

the second. **animo laborabat** "he worked zealously (*OLD animus* 8d)."
V. leads by example. The description stands in marked contrast to 30.4
animo consternati and *insueti laboris*; the former contrast is reminiscent of
Thuc. 7.76 where Nikias acts "spiritedly (ὑπὸ προθυμίας)" in the face of
"his dispirited troops (τὸ στράτευμα ἀθυμοῦν)." **reliquas ciuitates adiungeret** repeats 30.4, 29.6; cf. 16n. **donis pollicitationibusque alliciebat**: the
pairing varies 1.5n. *pollicitationibus ac praemiis*; it recurs in Suet. *Dom.* 2.2.
allicere has an illicit tone (*allicit ... dictum a uerbo "lacit," id est decipit*, Paul.
Fest. p. 27); it occurs once more in *CC* at 5.55.3 *magnis praemiis ... allicere*;
cf. Livy 1.47.7 *allicere donis iuuenes*. This latest instance of bribery – of
which, Jullian 1909: 456 thought, the gold coins carrying V.'s name gave
evidence – cynically specifies the *diligentia* V. had promised to exert in
enlisting the remaining Gauls (29.6; cf. 15.5n. *perangustum*).

31.2 huic rei idoneos ... deligebat: the dative is *apo koinou*. For the same
measure similarly phrased, cf. 15.6. **subdola**: only here in *CC*. **capere** "to
win over" (*OLD* 19), sc. §1 *principes*. The verb frequently combines with
oratione, but with *amicitia* only once (Nep. *Dat.* 11.5 *simulata captus est amicitia*). The combination of two different things, rare in C. (again at 56.2),
will be typical of Tac. (*Ann.* 1.68.5 *ira et dies* with Goodyear).

31.3 qui ... refugerant ... curat: 28.6. The relative clause serves as the
main verb's object (instead of *eos*), as is common (DKM ad loc.). **refugerant**: used absolutely; but the obj. is easily inferred from the abl. absolute.
The prefix *re-* may indicate "back to V."

31.4 deminutae copiae: again 73.1, then once more in Livy 39.20.9. **imperat
certum numerum ... quem ... uelit**: similarly 4.7–8; cf. 4.8n. *quodque*. C.
uses a construction frequent in Greek and colloquial Latin, wherein the
object of the subordinate clause is moved into the main clause (prolepsis
[K-G II 579 A.3, H-S 471]). **sagittariosque**: C. has not mentioned Gallic
archers before; and the complicated archaeological evidence (Poux 2008:
360–65) might suggest that military archery became common only in the
course of the Roman conquest. But they are mentioned now to amplify
the stakes (29–35n.). **permagnus** occurs only here in C. (cf. 15.5n. *perangustum*). **conquiri** "to be gathered from everywhere"; cf. 2.3n. *collaudatis*
and *BAlex.* 1 *tormenta undique conquiri et frumentum mitti* (echoing this passage). **celeriter**: fulfils the promise at 29.5. **quod ... deperierat** "the great
loss" (Paul. Fest. p. 70 *"deperire" significat "ualde perire"*). The verb highlights V.'s achievement in replenishing depleted ranks.

31.5 Teutomatus Ollouiconis ... appellatus: a formulaic introduction
(4.1n. *Celtilli ... adulescens*; cf. 4.12.3). Otherwise unknown, Teutomatus

is singled out for his later role (46.5). The *Nitiobroges* were said to join
V. at 7.2. **senatu:** whereas *populus Romanus* frequents all books of the
BG (except the third), totaling eighty instances, *senatus* is mostly passed
over (sixteen instances); this may be indicative of C.'s generally different treatment of the two political entities (Krebs 2018b: 73–74). **amicus
erat appellatus:** *amicus* (or *socius* [*atque amicus*]) and *appellare* are technical terms in Rome's foreign policy (Sands 1908: 10–48; Cursi 2013);
this formula occurs 5x in C. (not in *CC*). *amicitia* meant little "except
when it suited Rome" (Badian 1958: 60); Ariovistus had had to learn that
(1.35.2). C. identifies two more Gallic kings as *amici* (1.3.4, 4.12.4). **et
quos … conduxerat:** sc. *et (cum) eis quos* (cf. 31.3n. *qui*); no such recruitment was previously mentioned. **Aquitania** constitutes the southwesterly
part of C.'s *Gallia omnis* as defined at 1.1.7 (where the name is attested
for the first time [*TLL* 2.379.81]). Since the Aquitani were largely Iberian
rather than Celtic (and of a non-Indo-European language, as C. himself
admits), their inclusion in *Gallia* was for geographical reasons only (cf.
Introd. 2b; Coffyn 1986).

32 While his army recovers, and C. is unsure what to do (§2n. *siue*), he
is approached by an Aeduan delegation with news of domestic discord
(effectively rendered by polyptoton [§5n. *pars … parte*]): Two men claim
election to their highest office (32.3); the people are divided; C. is asked
for help.

The affair represents the kind of *internae discordiae* that served Romans
to justify and exercise their rule (cf. 6.15.1; Tac. *Hist.* 4.74.3; *Introd.* 2c),
even though it may well have resulted from conflicting pro-Roman and
anti-Roman sentiments (Thévenot 1960: 59). C.'s account evokes Roman
politics through emphasis on his own experience, the application of *senatus* and *populus* to the Aedui, the failure of a smooth constitutional transition of power, and parallels with passages in Cicero's *De republica* that
address pertinent Roman themes (nn. on 33.1 *non ignorans*, 32.5 *senatum,
populum*, 33.4 *intermissis magistratibus*, 32.3+5, 33.3 *imperium … obtinere*;
Pelling 2011: 267).

The plea develops the *propositio* (§2 *subueniat*) into a lucidly structured
(§3n. *esse*), tripartite *narratio* that doubles as *argumentatio* (cf. Quint.
4.2.79; *HLR* 348); it concludes (§5n. *quodsi*) by way of ring composition
with another appeal (*in eius diligentia*). Cf. 39n.

32.1 C. rarely mentions resting his troops (41.1 *tribus horis*); it here highlights what harrowing situation they had escaped. If his resting enabled
V.'s regrouping (31.4), the disjointed narrative disguises that (Rambaud
104). **complures dies commoratus** slightly varies the formula at 9.1n.

(Cic. *De or.* 1.82 anticipates this variation). C. normally prefers the simple over the compound verb (35:5) but here deviates to reinforce the notion of a lengthier stay (*OLD commorari* 2). **copiam ... ex labore atque inopia**: the etymological play renders the reversal of fortune; *inopia* recalls 17.4 (especially) and concludes the "thematic repetition" (14.6n. *inopiam*). C.'s troops had mastered what Marius proudly claimed for himself (Sall. *Iug.* 85.33): *eodem tempore inopiam et laborem tolerare*; cf. 17n. *ex* = "from" (*TLL* 5.2.1089.57–76). **frumenti et reliqui commeatus** varies 38.9n. *frumentum commeatumque*; sim. at 3.3.1, 8.7.7.

32.2 iam in initial position prepares for something unexpected (C-L 497–517; cf. 26.3, 59.1, 85.6). **hieme confecta**: "winter" signifies "the season unsuitable for campaigning," which was normally limited to the time when "fodder could ... be found in fields and woods" (Raaflaub-Ramsey 2017: 56, dating the end to "around early June"). **cum ipso anni tempore ... uocaretur**: an unusual expression ("he was summoned," *OLD uocare* 7b); cf. Livy 28.15.12 *fessos ... nox imberque ad necessariam quietem uocabat*. **proficisci constituisset**: formulaic (9.6n. *instituit*). **siue ... siue ... posset**: 20.10n. *si*. C.'s indetermination may reveal that he did not know what to do (we do not learn of his march on Gergovia until 34.2). **ex paludibus siluisque elicere** may allude to V.'s guerilla warfare specifically (14[n.]); but the location is commonplace (16.1n. *paludibus siluisque*). **obsidione premere**: possibly poetic (Enn. *Ann.* 1.25 *obsidio* (< *obsidium*) *magnus Titanus premebat*, Verg. *Aen.* 8.646 *urbem obsidione premebat*); again at *BC* 3.9.4. C. prefers *obsidio* to *obsessio* 13:3 (2:2 in *CC*). **ut maxime necessario tempore** "that now, if ever, in this time of greatest need." For *ut maxime*, cf. *OLD maxime* 5b, and the "habit of the jurists, who reinforce various conjunctions with the adverb" (Coleman 2012: 219). For *maxime necessario*, cf. *BC* 3.112.7 *loca maxime necessaria* (*BAlex.* 71 *res magis necessarias*). On *necessario tempore*: 40.4n.

32.3 The description of the supreme office resembles the interpretation of the consulship Cicero provides as _potestatem_ ... *tempore dumtaxat* _annuam_, *genere ipso ac iure* _regiam_ (*Rep.* 2.56; cf. Livy 2.1.7–8 with Ogilvie). **summo esse**: 21.1n. *esse* recurs twice in the same position (a "positional pattern" [Wills 415–18]), providing structure and punctuation. **esse in periculo rem**: C. favors the expression (5x). **singuli magistratus**: C. identifies the highest Aeduan magistrate as Vergobretus at 1.16.5 (where, however, the text attests to two men in office [Barlow 1998: 166n.16]); cf. Lamoine 2006. **antiquitus** is a Caesarian favorite (11x; not in *CC*). **annuam** rather than *annum* (α), since the former is used by C. at 1.16.5 and Cic. and Livy in the related contexts cited above, and its corruption to *annum* is more

likely than the inverse. **se**: 2.1n. **eorum** resumes *duo*. **legibus** "lawfully."
creatum is the first of three "thematic repetitions."

32.4 Conuictolitauem: the otherwise unattested name (*GPN* 77–78) suggests various unpleasant words, viz. *conuicium, lis* (*litis*), *uis* (esp. in the
nominative); cf. 1.4n. *Acconis*. It will be echoed in 37.1 *Litauiccus*. **florentem et illustrem** "vigorous and illustrious" is unparalleled. *florens* is commonly used of statesmen (Clark on Cic. *Mil.* 21); but in collocation with
adulescens it emphasizes energy (cf. Catull. 64.251 *florens uolitabat Iacchus*;
TLL 6.921.48–63). *illustris* suggests fame (cf. Verg. *Aen.* 7.79 *inlustrem
fama fatisque*). **Cotum**: The Celtic name (attested elsewhere [*GPN* 342])
to a speaker of Greek suggests κότος, "grudge, rancor." **summae potentiae
et magnae cognationis**: another unparalleled pairing, wherein the latter
part ("of most powerful connections") specifies the former (4.1n. *summae
potentiae*); cf. 19.1n. *impedita*. **Valetiacus**: otherwise unattested, the name
suggests strength (*ualet*, to Latin and Celtic speakers alike [*GPN* 269]).

32.5 The Aeduan report resembles Tubero's political analysis in Cic. *Rep.*
1.31.3: *non quaerit cur in una re publica duo <u>senatus</u> et duo paene iam <u>populi</u>
sint? nam ... mors Tiberii Gracchi ... <u>diuisit</u> populum unum in duas <u>partes</u>*. **senatum**: frequently used of foreign peoples (*interpretatio Romana*). **diuisum**:
the emphatic anaphora is suggestive of the speakers' emotional state.
populum: C. uses *populus* exclusively of the Roman people except 1.3.7,
6.13.6, here, *BC* 3.3.2. **suas cuiusque eorum clientelas** "each of them had
his own following." The word order is natural (cf. 71.2): the possessive
is fronted for emphasis (1.5n. *sui*), *quisque* is enclitic, and the partitive
follows its "host." *quisque* is used instead of *uterque*, which "should not be
imitated" (*Antibarbarus* 669; but it recurs at *BC* 3.112.10). The language
bespeaks factionalism (cf. 4.1n. *clientibus*, 4.5nn. *suis, patruo suo*). **quod si**
"if, then." The adverbially used relative indicates a close connection to the
preceding sentence (K-S II 321.1). *quod si* introduces a conclusion of sorts
(N-H on Hor. *Carm.* 1.1.41; again at 77.16). **alatur controuersia**: figurative
use of *alere* is common (*honos alit artes*), but this expression is singular; cf.
33.1n. **pars cum parte** "one faction with the other," Livy 6.27.6 *partem a
parte*. This kind of polyptoton ("substantival parataxis") is employed to
express reciprocity; it is frequent in Latin and Greek (Landgraf 1888:
180, N-R on Hor. *Carm.* 3.1.9–16 *uiro uir*, Wills 191–206; Oakley on Livy
7.10.10 *scuto scutum*). Further instances in *VII*: 33.3 *fratrem a fratre*, 35.1
uterque utrique, castris castra (23.3 *singulae singulis* lacks the reciprocity).
pars/partes is often applied to political groups (so above; Oakley on Livy
9.46.13). **diligentia atque auctoritate**: the two nouns enjoy frequent company in Cic. (but just once in this turn of phrase [*Verr.* 2.3.154]). This is

only the third time that C. is attributed *auctoritas* (after 1.31.16, 33.1); it will be reclaimed by the Aeduans (37.3n.). Rome frequently effected appointments in client states: Cic. *Att.* 5.20.6 (with Shackleton Bailey on *Att.* 5.18), Aug. *Anc.* 27, 33, Tac. *Ann.* 2.1; Lintott 1993: 45-46, 59.

33 C. ponders his situation, then decides to intervene. Out of respect for Aeduan custom, he moves to Decetia, where he confirms the legally elected Convictolitavis.

By detailing the inconveniences incurred, C. highlights the significance of the Aedui. Moreover, in rushing to their aid again (cf. 10.1-2n.), while accepting additional complications to respect their institutions (§2n. *ne quid ... uideretur*), and in selecting the constitutional candidate, he demonstrates exemplary gubernatorial conduct *aequitate et fide* (Cic. *Off.* 2.27). In short, it was not his fault that the Aedui deserted (and under Convictolitavis' leadership to boot [37]). However, Thévenot 1962 has argued that C.'s choice of §3n. *Decetiam* is best explained by his intention to threaten Bibracte and move his troops to the north (Labienus [34.2]) and south (himself) for a two-pronged attack.

33.1-2 C. has his audience participate in his reasoning (cf. 10.1n.). The complex period represents the complexity of the situation: Of its three main clauses, the first is preceded by a string of subordinate clauses that weigh the circumstances (*etsi ... tamen non ignorans*) and detail the consequences (*ne ... descenderet, atque ... arcesseret*); they result, with the pull of necessity, in the first conclusive main verb (*praeuertendum existimauit*). It is followed by additional concerns (*quod ... non liceret, ne ... uideretur*) which similarly result in the concrete actions specified in the main clauses (*et ... statuit senatumque ... euocauit*). **Caesar etsi** is a "narrative gesture" by which C. represents himself as "a man of complex thought" (Batstone 1990: 350); cf. 8.2n. **bello atque hoste**: a common pairing (*TLL* 2.1854.33-39; *BC* 3.3.1). **detrimentosum** is *hapax legomenon*. Adjectives ending in *-osus* are highly descriptive; those derived from abstract nouns (such as *detrimentum*) originally appertained to colloquial Latin (Knox 1986). **non ignorans ... ex dissensionibus ... consuessent** is, not the least because of the emphatic litotes, suggestive of the situation at Rome (1.2 *in tantis dissensionibus*; §4n. *intermissis*); might it be read as addressing Pompey? Cf. 25.5n. *ex castris.* **ne ... arcesseret**: the fear clause either follows epexegetically on *incommoda* or specifies the situation C. hoped to forestall (with *praeuertere* approaching *prohibere*). **tanta et tam coniuncta**: doubled demonstratives (a form of *congeries* [*HLR* 406]) are particularly common in Cic. (Nägelsbach 1905: §92.2); this one recurs at *BC* 2.20.1. **quam aluisset ... ornasset**: an instance of "theme and variation." The former expression, wherein *alere,* "to promote the interests of" (*OLD* 6b), repeats 32.5 *alatur* (with change of meaning), emphasizes time, the latter circumstances. **uim atque arma** "armed violence," a common hendiadys but only here in *CC.* **ea pars … arcesseret**: a reasonable fear, as recruitments of external aid are a recurrent theme in ancient history as well as historical writing, not the least C.'s own (e.g. 1.31.3–4). **sibi** is directly reflexive.

33.2 huic rei resumes the preceding thoughts (29.2n. *cuius rei*). **praeuertendum** "had to be forestalled" (*OLD* 3), occurring only here in *CC*; cf. 7.3n. *anteuertendum.* **excedere … non liceret**: various Roman officials were (once) not supposed to leave Rome or Italy either, including the *pontifex maximus,* at least until the departure of P. Licinius Crassus for Asia in 131 (Vanggaard 1988: 100n.6). **ne … uideretur**: C. displays the kind of *modestia apud socios* Tac. praises in Augustus (*Ann.* 1.9.5 with Goodyear). C. was guided by expediency, not scruples, as his different treatment of Dumnorix's concerns indicates (5.6.3–4; cf. 1.50–51). **de iure aut de legibus** "from their rights or from their laws." *Rhet. Her.* 2.13 captures the semantic difference in this common pairing (again at 37.5, 76.1, 77.14+16): *lege ius est id, quod populi iussu sanctum est …, consuetudine ius est id, quod sine lege aeque ac si legitimum sit, usitatum est* (cf. Isid. *Etym.* 5.3.1). Disrespecting their laws might be construed as undermining their sovereignty (77.16n.). **quos inter**: C. rarely employs anastrophe (6.36.2; *BC* 3.6.6, 105.6 [both questionable]); if it has an archaic ring (H-S 216), it would be in tune with the legalistic context. **Decetiam**: the *oppidum* (Decize in Nièvre) lay at a road junction that allowed for speedy access to the Aeduan capital Bibracte farther east, and easy troop movements both to the north and south along the river (*It. Ant.* 367, 460; Thévenot 1962; 5.4n. *Ligerim*).

33.3 docereturque governs the acc. with the inf. The subject is C. **oportuerit**: the perf. tense is retained from *oportuit* in dir. speech. The verb falls into the legal register; most frequent in *I,* it gradually yields to *debere* (Odelman 24–35). **fratrem a fratre renuntiatum**: sc. *Cotum a Valetiaco.* This common polyptoton (5.14.4 *fratres cum fratribus,* Verg. *Aen.* 10.600 *fratrem ne desere frater,* Wills 205–06) recalls *pars cum parte* (32.5n.). The juxtaposition with the technical term *renuntiare,* "to declare elected" (cf. *OLD* 4), highlighted by the sound pattern, is incongruous and bespeaks the illegitimacy. **uiuo utroque**: the abl. absolute is compromised (27.1n. *hanc*), as *duos* and *utroque* share the same referents. **uetarent … prohiberent**: a frequent variation (e.g. Cic. *Leg. agr.* 2.72 *referre in aerarium* (sc. pecuniam) *lex uetat, exigi prohibet*). **imperium deponere … potestatem obtinere** is once again paralleled in Cic. *Rep.* 2.23 *ut quisquam inueterata potestate aut ad deponendum imperium tardior esset aut ad optinendum munitior* (32n.).

33.4 per sacerdotes: *per* + acc. expresses "person through whom," whereas *a(b)* + abl. expresses "the agent or doer" (G-L 401); but the difference is not always upheld (K-S I 378). C. does not use "*druides*" outside of the digression in *VI.* **intermissis magistratibus** "whenever the office is in abeyance." The interpretation has caused problems (and the election of the supreme druid at 6.13.9 provides no clarification). Given that the Roman transfer of power had failed in 52 so that an *interrex* held the *comitia* when Pompey was elected consul (6.1n.), it is likely that C. had the *interrex* at the back of his mind (*CG* 528–29). If so, *magistratibus* refers to the office of the Vergobretus (the plural signifying iteration [cf. 32.3n. *singuli magistratus*]), not magistrates in general; and *intermittere* signifies a breakdown in the regular succession that forced the *sacerdotes* to step in (not an institutionalized intermission during which they voted).

34 C. encourages the Aedui to apply themselves to the war, promising §1n. *praemia*, and he requests additional troops to protect the grain supply. He then suddenly (§2n.) entrusts Labienus with four legions to campaign farther north (57–62n.), while he himself moves on Gergovia. But V. blocks him.

34.1 Hoc decreto interposito "having made that decision between them" (Edwards); a legal expression (*TLL* 5.1.153.1–11). **controuersiarum ac dissensionis** "contentious disagreements"; the hendiadys recurs at Apul. *Met.* 9.27. C. previously used the terms separately (32.5, 33.1+2); cf. Plaut. *Poen.* 159–62 *nequam dare … dare malum … habebit et nequam et malum.* **his rebus** resumes, in typical fashion (29.2n. *cuius rei*), what was just mentioned. **huic bello seruirent** "they should devote themselves (*OLD seruire* 3b) to the war at hand"; a singular expression. *huic* is retained from *oratio recta* (for liveliness). **eaque … praemia … deuicta Gallia exspectarent** "and they should look forward to (receiving) from him the rewards they had earned, once Gaul was fully conquered." *deuincere* (its prefix emphatic [1.5n. *deposcunt*]) occurs first here in C. The promise does not differ from V.'s "bribes" (31.1n. *alliciebat*). **quae … disponeret** "that he might put them in various garrisons to protect the corn-supply" (Edwards); cf. 10.1n. *ab re frumentaria* (it remained a concern despite 32.1n. *copiam*).

34.2 The juxtaposition of supply concerns and Labienus' order to take four legions up north (a strategic mistake, it has seemed to some [Thévenot 1960: 61]) may intimate that the latter was intended to alleviate the former. **quattuor legiones … sex**: Labienus' legions included the 7th and 12th (62.4+6). C. provides the same total of ten legions the year before (6.44.2); it seems unlikely that he had eleven already (Hirt.

8.24.3, 46.4; *Introd.* 2c). The uncertainty is compounded by the rarity with which C. identifies legions (47.1n. *decimae*) and various unspecified "recruitments" (1.1n. *dilectum*; 65.1n. *prouincia*). **Labieno**: Titus Labienus served C. as *legatus pro praetore* from 58 (first mention: 1.10.3) until 50, distinguished himself repeatedly (57–62n.; Welch 1998: 98–102), and was consequently put in charge of *Gallia Cisalpina* in 50 (Hirt. 8.52.2). But he joined Pompey's side at the beginning of the civil war (Cic. *Att.* 7.12.4–5, 13.1; Wylie 1989; 62.2n. *adesse*). He died at Munda in 45 (*BHisp.* 31.9, App. *BCiu.* 2.435). **ad oppidum Gergouiam**: C. does not motivate his march on Gergovia (32.2n. *siue*). **Elauer** "Allier." **reliquit** "he left remaining" (*OLD* 13).

34.3 V. "turned the river into a bulwark at his front (πρόβλημα ποιησαμένου ... ποταμὸν) ... and made its crossing dangerous," just as Hannibal had (Polyb. 3.14.5), any apt general would (cf. Plancus' choice *flumen oppositum ut haberem, in quo mora transitus esset,* [Cic.] *Fam.* 10.23.2), and military writers recommended (Aen. Tact. 8.3). The problem will recur (56, 57.4, 59.5). **qua re cognita**: 9.6n. **ab altera parte ... coepit**: cf. Xen. *An.* 4.3.17 "as [the Greeks] moved [along the river], the enemy companies ... moved along opposite them (ἀντιπαρῇσαν αἱ τάξεις)." Local expressions with *a(b)/ex* focus more on where something comes from than where it is, and often even when the directional meaning appears less suitable (*NLS* §41.4). **iter facere coepit**: 9x in *CC* (*VII*: 58.1, 68.1); 11.3n.

35 Blocked by the Allier, C. divides his troops, hides two legions, rebuilds a bridge – all unbeknownst to V. Having reunited with the other legions, he follows V. to Gergovia.

River crossings were notoriously difficult: *in transitu fluuiorum grauis molestia neglegentibus frequenter emergit* (Veg. 3.7.1). The maneuver consequently receives regular attention (Frontin. *Str.* 1.5; Campbell 2012: 160–99), not least from C. himself (as early as 1.12–13). It here requires him to employ his talents as a "maker of stratagems" (*Introd.* 3d; §§3–5n.), which, in combination with his engineering skills, enables C. to outwit V. again (cf. 9). The narrative emphasizes their head-to-head maneuvers (§1nn.).

35.1 "When both armies were in sight of each other and [each] set up camp roughly opposite to [the other's] camp, with scouts posted all over to prevent the Romans from building a bridge and crossing [the river] anywhere, C.'s situation was one of great difficulty." The MSS offer two versions, whereof α does not make much sense; β is merely choppy. **uterque utrique** is a polyptotic *geminatio* (again *BAlex.* 4.1; cf. 32.5n. *pars cum parte*). Strictly speaking illogical ("both to both"), the expression was formed in analogy with *uter utri* (Landgraf 1888: 170–71). **fereque e regione**: 25.2n. **castris castra**: another polyptotic *geminatio* (cf. Landgraf 1888: 177); it recurs 5x in C. (7x in *CC*). It reinforces *uterque utrique*, mimics the camps' being *in conspectu*, and, in combination with *ponere*, circumscribes the Greek mot juste ἀντιστρατοπεδεύειν (which Polyaenus uses). **dispositis exploratoribus**: viz. by V. (16.2n. *exploratores*). **necubi** "lest … anywhere"; once more in *CC* at *BC* 2.33.1; cf. 8.3n. *inopinantibus*. **erat … impediretur**: the entire sentence is similar to 10.1nn. *magnam difficultatem … contineret*. C. admits to facing difficulty for the third time. **aestatis**: sc. campaign season (cf. 32.2n. *hieme*). **fere … solet**: a common pleonasm (*TLL* 6.1.499.57–66). **uado transiri** recurs at 55.10 (also at 1.6.1, *BC* 3.30.4).

35.2 ne id accideret repeats 32.5. **e regione** repeats §1. **unius eorum pontium**: exceptionally instead of *unius ex eis pontibus* (K-S I 426); the multiple genitives: 22.1n. *cuiusque*. **(pontes) … rescindendos**: 5x in C. (not in *CC*); its afterlife is limited to the historiographical tradition.

35.3–5 C.'s scheme (cf. Polyaenus 8.23.9) had been used by others (incl. Xen. *An.* 4.3.20 [Frontin. *Str.* 1.4.10]); Labienus would employ it, too (60). **ut consueuerat**: sc. when he marched (in contrast to 10.4n. *impedimentis relictis*). **carptis quibusdam cohortibus** "having selected (*OLD carpere* 4) a certain number (*OLD quidam* 4b) of cohorts." The barely attested *carptis* makes good sense; cf. Cic. *Clu.* 129 … *carpes* (sc. *homines*) *ut uelis et paucos ex multis ad ignominiam sortiere?* C. did not retain two full legions but assembled cohorts from all six legions so that to V.'s scouts, who judged by the number of *aquiliferi*, all legions appeared to be leaving.

35.4 quam longissime possent: 9.3n. *quam … itineribus*. **iam** "already." **ex diei tempore** "judging from (cf. *OLD ex* 14c) the time of day." **coniecturam**: first here in C. **peruentum**: 61.1n. *uentum*. **isdem sublicis** "the original piles."

35.5 A typical propulsive string of abl. absolutes. **celeriter** tightens the string of actions, as it applies to them all (hence its position). **effecto opere** varies §4 *pontem reficere* (cf. 7.1n. *missus*); the change of prefix is pointed. **loco … delecto**: 16.1n. In the Roman army, it normally fell to the *metator* (*mensor*) to scout out and measure campsites (Cic. *Phil.* 11.12, Frontin. *Str.* 2.7.12, Veg. 2.7; Austin-Rankov 1995: 114). **legiones reuocauit**: the marching involved must have been considerable (cf. 40.4n. *milia passuum xxv*).

35.6 re cognita: the absence of a demonstrative/relative is unusual but paralleled at 58.6, 63.5. The formula: 9.6n. **ne … cogerentur**: cf. 14.2–9n.

on V.'s avoidance of pitched battle. C. gives the impression that he is in charge still; but it is more likely V. who drew C. to Gergovia (*Introd.* 2c). **magnis itineribus**: 9.3n. **antecessit**: sc. *Caesarem.*

36–56 THE DEFEAT

Of the three *aduersi casus* C. suffered in Gaul, only Gergovia occurred on his watch, which has redounded to V.'s credit (Suet. *Iul.* 25; Gelzer 1955: 993; Deyber 2017: 94; Cass. Dio's claim at 40.36.5, 38.1 of C.'s absence is unlikely). Such a reverse would have been hard to silence (cf. *crebri et non belli de eo rumores* that reach Caelius from Gaul in 51 [Cic. *Fam.* 8.1]). But Romans were not shy of acknowledging defeat (cf. *Romanus populus ... superatus proeliis saepe est multis, bello uero numquam, in quo sunt omnia* [Lucil. 708–09 (Warmington)]); and all the less, if it could be (a) integrated into a grander narrative of ultimate victory (Clark 2014: 10–11; Rich 2012; cf. Polyb. 6.52.6, and, for the aesthetic appeal, Cic. *Fam.* 5.12 *nihil ... aptius ad delectationem lectoris quam temporum uarietates fortunaeque uicissitudines*), and (b) spun so as to cast the general in the best possible light. C. does both: Gergovia is followed by Alesia; and while he acknowledges the former's gravity (51.4; *BC* 3.73.6 *detrimentum ... ad Gergouiam*), he limits its significance and his responsibility (Choitz 2011), disavowing, once too often, his intention to storm the *oppidum* (36.1n. *oppugnatione*), blaming the topography, his soldiers' temerity, and the fickle Aedui (nn. on 52.2 *iniquitas*, 52.3 *magnitudinem*, 43.5 *circumsisteretur*; Stevens 1952: 16–18), and distracting from the grievous outcome by a dramatic vignette and the mere mention, in passing, of the number of the fallen (nn. on 50, 51.4 *septingenti*). He also disguises his flight – ultimately back to *prouincia* (Le Bohec 1998: 115) – as a regrouping decided on long before any military engagement had occurred (43.5, 53.1n. *cogitans*; cf. 56.2n. *commutato*, 66.3n. *fugere*; Rambaud 172). That Gergovia is a prime case of *déformation historique* (Rambaud, s.v.) is corroborated by the archaeological discovery of the vicinal settlements of Gondole and Corent (figs. 5-7), unacknowledged in the narrative, although C.'s main camp was situated fewer than two miles from the former and right by its thoroughfare (Deberge *et al.* 2014: 45); C. appears to have attacked Gondole, too. There is good reason to believe that C. made an "erreur stratégique" (Deyber 2017: 88), or, rather, that V. tricked him into this trap by his hometown (*Introd.* 2c); there is similarly good reason to doubt C.'s timeline of the Aeduan desertion, which seems plotted for dramatic effect rather than historical accuracy (nn. on 44–53, 53–56; *Introd.* 3c). Gergovia itself has been located four miles to the south(east) of Clermont-Ferrand on an oblong plateau (Kagan 2006: 158).

The episode, which concludes with the Aedui's full and open revolt and C.'s crossing the Loire (53–56n.), is marked off by 36.1 *Gergouiam peruenit* and, less specifically, 57.1 *dum haec apud Caesarem geruntur*. It stands in counterpoint to "Avaricum," notwithstanding the shared binary structure of a prelude (including a Caesarian absence) followed by the assault and several other common features (nn. on 36.1 *aditus*, 38, 45, 47): for whereas "Avaricum" (and "Alesia" [68–90n.]) rises towards the final assault in a steady *crescendo*, "Gergovia" is characterized by sudden disharmonies, and "both [its] physical and emotional focuses ... are markedly diffused" (Kraus 2010a: 49). Its air of jittery purposelessness is partly owed to the two plot lines it entwines: here the concern caused by the flighty Aedui (nn. on 36–43, 53–56), there C.'s unsure presence at Gergovia (36.1n. *oppugnatione*; similarly, in the *BC*, "Massilia" [with Kraus 2007] contrasts with "Curio" [with Batstone-Damon 2006: 98–101]). Intentional or not, it aptly captures C.'s precarious situation. It inspired Sall. *Iug.* 92–94 (Martin 2001: 398–400).

36–43 (Not) at Gergovia

This first half is tellingly demarcated by C.'s decisions first to neither storm nor besiege Gergovia, then not to stay at all (36.1 + 43.5; 36.5–7n.): it tells of his "trying to get away from the area, not [of] its capture" (Kraus 2010a: 47). No sooner has he established his troops than he is called away again, as his Aeduan auxiliaries are about to desert (37–40). During C.'s absence (and surely not by coincidence), his camps come under attack; disaster is narrowly averted by C.'s speedy return (41.5). Having briefly experienced conflict on all sides (43.5n. *circumsisteretur*), and with Aeduan unrest on the rise (42–43), orderly retreat seems most advisable – or so C. says.

Within C.'s entwined narrative, the gradual Aeduan defection is of primary concern (Kraus 2010a: 47–58; Thévenot 1960: 64–72, offers a salutary counternarrative). It combines typical motifs of possibly exculpatory intention: at first it appears an isolated, financially motivated aberration of elite young men (38n.). They then dupe their people, who reveal what C. elsewhere expounds as the *infirmitas Gallorum ... quod sunt in consiliis capiendis mobiles et nouis plerumque rebus student* (4.5.1); they cannot but enter on schemes, *quorum* (sc. *consiliorum*) *eos in uestigio paenitere necesse est*. One wonders how plausible this would have struck a Roman reader, especially as it stands at odds with C.'s lasting suspicion of his ally (5.6n. *perfidia*), not to mention the chronological problems (37n.). But it ensues from Rome's longstanding support of the tribe (40.1 *quod ... indulserat*) and prepares the ground for C.'s lenient treatment of them later (89.5 *reseruatis Haeduis*).

There are striking parallels with an episode in Appian's account (*Hisp.* 94) of Scipio's siege of Numantia (on whose possibly Polybian source C. models his siege of Alesia [68–90n.]): when Scipio "learnt at the eighth hour" (ὀγδόης ὥρας πυθόμενος; cf. 39.3 *media fere nocte*) that "young men" (οἱ ... νέοι; cf. 37.1 *adulescentibus*) were plotting against him in Lutia some "300 stades away from Numantia" (τριακοσίους σταδίους ἀφεστῶσα ἀπὸ Νομαντίνων; cf. 38.1 *cum milia passuum circiter XXX ab Gergouia abesset*), he "left at once with a numerous unencumbered force" (ἐξήλαυνεν αὐτίκα σὺν εὐζώνοις ὅτι πλείστοις; cf. 40.1 *nulla interposita dubitatione legiones expeditas ... educit*). Upon his arrival, Scipio punished the 400 leaders by cutting off their hands (as C. would after Uxellodunum [8.44.2]), then "rushed back again all the way to arrive in his camp with sunrise" (διαδραμὼν αὖθις ἅμ' ἔῳ τῆς ἐπιούσης παρῆν ἐς τὸ στρατόπεδον; cf. 41.5 *ante ortum solis in castra peruenit*).

36 When C. arrives at Gergovia on the fifth day of marching (probably since crossing the bridge [§1n. *loco*]), he finds V. already ensconced to its south-west, with his troops arrayed on its southern slope and surrounding hills, and generally in control (§§ 2–4n.). C.'s topographical analysis and strategy follow the textbook (cf. Philo, *Bel.* 8.D72, 84–85; nn. on *aditus difficiles*, *obsessione*, §§ 5–7): since the settlement is difficult of access, he opts for a siege with the stated intention of restricting the Gauls' access to food and water. To that purpose he sets up two camps: the major one on the *Plateau de la Serre d'Orcet* to the south-east of Gergovia (and right by its thoroughfare to Gondole [36–43n.]); then another, smaller one on a hill farther west called *La Roche Blanche*, connecting both with a double trench. He thereby limits V.'s access to the basin and the Auzon river. Archaeological results have confirmed the fundamentals of C.'s description, but also revealed its selectiveness: Deberge *et al.* 2000, Deberge *et al.* 2014 survey the latest findings; much information can be accessed at www.gergovie.net/site-de-gergovie.

36.1 C. will proceed similarly at Alesia (68.3–69.1). **ex eo loco** likely refers to 35.5 *loco ... delecto* (rather than 33.2 *Decetia*). **quintis castris** "in five days' march." In this sense, *castra* occurs first here (then frequently in the historians [*TLL* 3.563.24–30]). **equestrique ... facto** recurs at 53.2. The adjective is fronted due to the implicit contrast with a "full" engagement. **perspecto urbis situ** recurs at 68.3. C.'s use of *perspicere* in military contexts is paralleled in *CC* but rare elsewhere (*TLL* 10.1.1740.31–45); *situs* is technical (Woodman on Tac. *Agr.* 10.1). For the general's task of surveying, cf. e.g. Polyb. 8.13.3, Livy 9.28.5 *dictator urbis situ circumspecto*, and 19.3n. **in altissimo monte omnes aditus difficiles**: the extended sound pattern may emphasize the reason for the difficulty. The description "captures quickly

[Gergovia's] extraordinarily defensible position" (Kagan 2006: 158), as the *Plateau de Gergovie* rises 1,000 feet above the terrain, its bluff gradient amplifying the effect. Generally, *oppida* were found on hilltops at the time, before they moved into the valleys after Rome's conquest (Collis 1984: 78; cf. 55.4n. *Bibracte*). To an astute reader, a "settlement strong on all sides (πόλιν ... ἰσχυρὰν ... πάντοθεν, Philo, *Bel.* 8.D72)" required a skillful approach: not for nothing did Cato emphasize in his speech on his triumph *asperrimus atque arduissimus aditus* (*ORF* 19); cf. also Hor.'s witty *quae tua uirtus, | expugnabis: et est* (sc. *Maecenas*) *qui uinci possit eoque | difficiles aditus primos habet* (*Sat.* 1.9.55–57). Access to Avaricum was an issue, too (15.5). **oppugnatione ... obsessione**: Livy 31.46.11 captures their semantic difference (not always upheld [*TLL* 9.2.799.83–800.4]): *plusque in obsidione et in operibus quam in oppugnatione celeri spei*. In such contrasts, *oppugnatio* is preferred to *expugnatio*. The first of several disavowals, it may well add up to "protesting too much" (Rambaud 172; 44–56n.). **de ... agendum** stands in an anaphoric parallelism to *de ... desperauit*. **non prius ... quam rem frumentariam expedisset** "not ... until he had procured ...," a future perfect in direct speech (60.1n. *imperasset*). *rem frumentariam expedire* recurs thrice in *BC*, then Fronto *Ep.* 3.9. C.'s concern about supplies continues (10.1n.).

36.2–4 The typically cumulative sentence (its subject fronted for immediate contrast with C.) comprises three falling cola that demonstrate V.'s measures. "The plateau is directly accessible only from its south face" (Kagan 2006: 158). **in monte**: sc. the Plateau de Gergovie. **mediocribus ... interuallis**: mimetic order. *Rhet. Her.* 3.19 offers an approximation: *interualla locorum mediocria placet esse, fere paulo plus aut minus pedum tricenum*. The phrase recurs at 73.9, *BAlex.* 30.5; not elsewhere. **separatim ... collocauerat**: there is no tension between the adverb and the compound verb, which is a standard expression used of contingents in military texts (*TLL* 3.1635.80–1636.65). If anything, the prefix suggests "on all sides" (2.3n. *collaudatis*). The triple alliteration: 18.1n. V.'s troop distribution: 19.2n. *generatim.* **eius iugi** likely refers to the whole range, including the *Plateau de Gergovie* (hence the resumptive *eius*) and the heights of Risolles, Puy de Jussat, and Roche-Blanche. **qua dispici poterat** "as far as one could see." *dispicere,* "to look in several directions" (*OLD* 1; cf. Lucr. 6.648 *cunctas in partes dispiciendum*), is preferable to the vacuous *despici*, even if it occurs only here in *CC*. It alludes to the enemy's *multitudo* (21.1n.) and succinctly prepares for the **horribilem** (possibly only here in *CC* [5.14.3 β]) **speciem**, itself a topos: 19.4n. *conspectum ... ferre.*

36.3 principes ... ad consilium capiendum delegerat: the *figura etymologica* (Isid. *Etym.* 9.3.21 *princeps ... quod primus capiat*; Beikircher 1996) may highlight the leaders' role. A general was expected to consult with trusted leaders (Onas. 3.2); this would seem all the more natural for V. *adulescens* (4.1), whom it behooved *deligere optimos et probatissimos quorum consilio atque auctoritate nitatur* (Cic. *Off.* 1.122). The *consilium* was standard Roman practice (cf. the Asculum inscription [*ILS* 8888], Clark on Cic. *Mil.* 65 *sententia*; Johnston 2008). As a literary motif, the βουλή μεγαθύμων γερόντων, "the great-hearted elders' council," can be traced back to Hom. *Il.* 2.52. **earum ciuitatum**: the pronoun resumes §2 *ciuitatum* (cf. 12.2n. *quo ex oppido*). **prima luce**: C. favors the expression (18x [incl. 45.2, 62.1]; 4x in *CC*). **seu ... seu**: 20.10n. *si*.

36.4 neque ... diem intermittebat quin "and he hardly let a day go by without (11.8n. *quin*)." The same idiom occurs in Ter. *Ad.* 293, Cic. *Att.* 7.15.1, 8.12.1. **equestri proelio ... periclitaretur**: *Caesar ... equestribus proeliis quid hostis uirtute posset et quid nostri auderent periclitabatur* (2.8.2; sim. *BAlex.* 13.4; 13.1n.). A general knew to test and train his troops after defeat (29.7n. *instituerent*); C. would soon do it, too (53). **sagittariis interiectis**: a detail reiterated at 80.3. Cato in *De re mil.* emphasized the impact made by archers mixed in with the centuries (Veg. 1.15). V. had requested archers at 31.4. **quid in quoque esset animi ac uirtutis suorum** "what spirit and courage (Lendon 1999: 304 discusses the difference) there was in each of his men"; an interlaced hyperbaton (but cf. 9.4n. *consilii*).

36.5–7 C. spots an opportunity, reasons, acts (27n.). To starve an enemy was a common offensive strategy: C. would adopt it repeatedly in the civil war, and he is said to have preferred overcoming an enemy *fame potius quam ferro* (Frontin. *Str.* 4.7.1; cf. Veg. 3.26). Here he follows standard procedure, as handbooks recommended the "fortification of a strong place next to the city" and subsequent "installation of reliable guards there to prevent anything ... from being brought in (Philo, *Bel.* 8.D84–85)"; cf. Tac. *Ann.* 6.34.1 ... *infensare pabula; ac saepe in modum obsidii stationibus cingebat*. **erat ... collis**: 19.1n. **e regione**: 25.2n. **collis**: sc. *la Roche Blanche* (Deberge *et al.* 2014: 5–12). **sub ... radicibus montis** "down at the very (*OLD ipse* 8) foot (*OLD radix* 4b) of the mountain." **egregie munitus**: a standard military phrase (Odelman 175). **circumcisus** "sheer on all sides" (*OLD* 1); only here in *CC* and generally rare in this sense, but twice in Cic. (*Verr.* 4.107 *Henna ... ab omni aditu circumcisa atque directa*; *Rep.* 2.11).

36.6 praesidio ab his non nimis firmo: *nimis* only here in C. The negation emphasizes the contrary expectation (cf. 27.1n. *non inutilem*). The word order: 24.5n. *multitudo*.

36.7 Short, cumulative cola render the speed of action. For C.'s description and intention, cf. Polyb. 9.41.7–9: "From the covered way between the siege towers a double trench was brought up to the city wall between its towers ... [There were additional] tunnels ... to protect those going [to the siege works] from the camp and those returning from the works [to the camps] from being wounded by missiles from the town." Hillsides were recommended campsites (Ps.-Hygin. *Castr.* 56). **tamen** "just the same" (*OLD* 4), i.e. despite the garrison. **silentio ... egressus**: 11.7n. **priusquam ... posset** "before any help (5.3n. *subsidio*) could come (61.1n. *uentum*) from the city." **collocauit** matches V.'s §2 *collocauerat*. **fossam ... perduxit**: the verb may be technical (Malloch on Tac. *Ann.* 11.20.2); 72.3. Despite heavy erosion, there is evidence of trenches (Deberge *et al.* 2014: 11–13). **duodenum pedum** "of twelve feet each," the standard width (Veg. 1.24). Generally, unspecified measurements of ditches refer to width as the most significant dimension (cf. 2.12.2 *oppidum ... propter latitudinem fossae murique altitudinem ... expugnare non potuit,* with DKM). The distributive is employed "whenever repetition is involved" (G-L 187). **repentino ... incursu**: military phraseology (Heubner on Tac. *Hist.* 3.9.1).

37 Amongst the Aedui, Convictolitavis succumbs to Arvernian bribes, though newly confirmed in office by C. himself (§4n. *obtinuerit*; cf. Thévenot 1960: 64); he thus joins the list of Caesarian protégés that deserted him (76.1–2n.). With anti-imperialistic rhetoric (§5), soon to be amplified (38.8n. *latrones*), he incites a few fellow Aedui to engineer their tribe's defection in a typical conspiratorial setting (cf. Pagán 2005: 7–24), possibly reminiscent of Orgetorix's machinations (*regni cupiditate inductus coniurationem nobilitatis fecit et ciuitati persuasit ut ...,* 1.2.1). C. here begins distorting the defection as an, at first, isolated and poorly motivated elite aberration (nn. on 36–43, 39.1 *summo*, 43.1 *nihil ... consilio*): the initial bribe is mentioned thrice, as is the young ("rash") age of the conspirators, who, essentially of one family, manipulate their people (nn. on §1 *pecunia, adulescentibus, familia,* §6 *temere*). It seems doubtful that all of this could have happened during the few days since C.'s arrival at Gergovia (§1 *dum ... geruntur*).

37.1 Dum ... geruntur: a transition formula (C-L 101–05), linking theaters of war; it is most frequent in *VII* (42.1, 57.1, 66.1, 75.1). **cui ... demonstrauimus**: 33.4; cf. 17.1n. *ut supra diximus.* **adiudicatum**: the technical term (*TLL* 1.702.25–26) occurs only here in C. **sollicitatus ... pecunia** "incited by money." C. repeats the "bribe" (§§2 *praemium,* 6 *praemio*); cf. 1.5n. The expression recurs in Curt. 3.5.15, 4.11.18. **quibusdam** (35.3n.) may suggest that C. chooses not to name them (K-S 642.5). **adulescentibus**: 4.1n. Stressed thrice more (below, §6, 39.3). **erat ... Litauiccus atque eius fratres**: in C. the predicate "almost without exception" (DKM) agrees with the subject closest by. The name, attested numismatically and epigraphically (*GPN* 217, 360–62), while of uncertain etymology, may have suggested *lis, litis,* "quarrel"; it echoes *Conuictolitauis* (32.4n.). **amplissima familia,** "of greatly distinguished family," an expression favored by Cic. (*Rep.* 2.12, *Parad.* 5.36, *Phil.* 13.12); cf. 4.12.4 *amplissimo genere natus* (and 6.15.2).

37.2 When Dumnorix died, he shouted *liberum se liberaeque esse ciuitatis* (5.7.8). **praemium communicat hortaturque eos** forms a chiasmus. **imperio natos** "meant to rule"; N-H on Hor. *Carm.* 1.27.1; cf. Cic. *Cael.* 59 *natum huic imperio,* Sall. *Iug.* 31.11 *uos, Quirites, in imperio nati ... seruitutem toleratis?* Cf. 1.5n. *libertatem,* 5.2n. *Haeduos.* **meminerint** suggests "*mementote*" in *oratio recta,* a suitably earnest tense commonly used in directives and decrees (Verg. *Aen.* 6.851 *tu regere imperio populos, Romane, memento*).

37.3–6 Unlike earlier indirect speeches, this one lacks structure, which, along with the exclamatory sentences and three cacophonous consonances (*locum consistendi,* §6n. *ciuitatem, reliqua qua*), suggests agitation (cf. Men. Rhet. 413.12–14 [Russell-Wilson] on the absence of structure "due to the speaker's giving the impression of being not himself but distracted by emotion"). **unam ... quae** "there was but one obstacle to the absolutely certain Gallic victory: the Aeduan nation" (untrue, as 63.7 shows). C. is fond of such singularizing statements, wherein enclitic *esse* (14.2n.) adds emphasis: 15.5, 85.2; 3.5.2, 5.29.6, 6.32.1; *BC* 3.10.7; Cic. *Mil.* 2 *unum genus est aduersum* with Clark. **certissimam ... uictoriam:** while *certa uictoria* is common, the superlative is unparalleled; it continues Gallic braggadocio (1.7n. *facile*). **distineat** signifies "to delay," while elegantly intimating the reason for the delay ("to hold or keep apart," *OLD* 1). **eius auctoritate reliquas contineri** "it was by its authority that the others (Aeduan allies, most likely [64.1n.]) were held in check." **locum consistendi:** just as V. had promised at 20.12.

37.4 esse ... affectum "it was true that ...," as suggested by the word order (cf. Cic. *Prou. cons.* 27 *sum Cn. Pompei uirtutem ... admiratus*) and *tamen.* **sic ... obtinuerit** "but only insofar as he had won (*OLD* 10) a fully legitimate case (sc. his disputed magistracy [33.3–4]) before him." **beneficio** casts C. (and Rome) as patron and Convictolitavis (and the Aedui) as *cliens;* cf. *TLL* 2.1886.20–66, 10.1n. *praesidium,* 41.1n. *beneficio;* Lavan 2013: 176–210 [though C.'s case seems misrepresented]). **communi libertati** repeats 4.4n. and resonates with §2 *liberos.* The conflict between *beneficium* and *libertas* will recur at 76.2. The appeal is undermined once again by C.'s speaking of bribery.

37.5 Cic. *Off.* 2.69 helps to understand Convictolitavis' resentment: *at qui se locupletes, honoratos, beatos putant, ii ne obligari quidem beneficio uolunt ... patrocinio uero se usos aut clientes appellari mortis instar putant.* **cur enim ...**

ueniant "for why should they come ...," with the particle and present tense evoking the actual discussion (Dangel 1995: 107). The general question extrapolates from Convictolitavis' specific *causa*. Ariovistus had expressed a similar sentiment (1.34.2). **de suo iure ... legibus**: 33.2n. The possessive owes its emphatic position to the antithesis with Rome. **disceptatorem** "arbiter"; the technical term, common in Roman interstate arbitration, only here in *CC* (cf. Hirt. 8.55.2 *spes ... disceptandi*; *TLL* 5.1.1292.73–83).

37.6 C. differentiates between the elite and the people, attributing the initial defection to the former (a commonplace he employs as early as 1.2.1); cf. 43.1n. *nihil*. **celeriter**, "all too quickly" (a meaning suggested by its position), combines with *adulescentibus* to suggest *temeritas*. **deductis** "induced" (*OLD* 11b). **principes ... profiterentur**: 2.1 *principes ... pollicentur*. **ciuitatem temere**: Romans were sensitive to the consonance of contiguous words (Quint. 9.4.41). Ancient critics consider homophony unfortunate, with Serv. famously criticizing Verg. *Aen.* 2.27 (6.88) *Dorica castra* as *mala compositio*. But, as Hor. puts it disarmingly (*Ars P.* 347; Korpanty 1997: 331): *sunt delicta tamen, quibus ignouisse uelimus*. Homophony is consequently common enough and mostly without poetic effect (van Dam on Stat. *Silu.* 2.1.48–49; Woodman on Tac. *Agr.* 1.1 *antiquitus usitatum*; Cic. is outright fond of *necesse esse*). Most instances in *VII* (iterations of 11.1 *expeditiore re*, 17.4 *appellaret et*, 24.4 *aggerem eminus*, 33.1 *ipse semper*, 36.1 *altissimo monte*, 38.9n. *magnum numerum*; cf. 77.16n. *securibus subiecta*) belong to this category. But the three instances in this speech are noticeably frequent and perhaps suggestive of agitation. The adverb, in effect ironical, expresses the opinion of C. (who will soon reaffirm *temeritas* as a Gallic trait [42.2n.]). **adduci** pointedly varies *deductis* (cf. 43.5n. *profectio*).

37.7 decem ... mitterentur: 34.1 (to which *illis* refers). **reliquā quā ... constituunt** "As for all else, they decided how it had best be conducted"; possibly proleptic (31.4n. *imperat certum numerum ... quem ... uelit*). The slight pleonasm (*placeat constituunt*) recurs at 83.5. *placeat* varies *placuit*.

38 Litaviccus' "false report" (ψευδαγγελία, Xen. *Cav.* 5.8; *Introd.* 3d) arouses the cavalry with textbook cases of the *indignatio* and the emotional appeal, a speaker's most powerful tool (Quint. 4.3.15, 6.2.1).

To rouse in his audience the desired emotion the speaker should experience it himself (*nec incendit nisi ignis*, Quint. 6.2.28); he should create verbal images (*imagines rerum ... ut ... praesentes habere uideamur*, 6.2.29) and use inflammatory speech (*rebus indignis asperis inuidiosis addens uim oratio*, 6.2.24). In his dramatic performance (nn. on §§1–3, 6-8), Litaviccus shares his images with his audience (§§2–3), sheds (their) tears, and employs incendiary language and schemes, including false witnesses. V.

had done the same (20.8–11), and there exist verbal echoes, too (nn. on §§2 *insimulati*, 3, 4, 9 *excruciatos*); but this bespeaks C.'s schematic composition rather than the insinuation that both were devious orators (Rasmussen 1963: 40, 42). Cassius Dio 40.37 elaborates on this episode.

38.1–3 The dramatic opening (*quo*), repetitions of "murder" (*interiit, interfecti, ex caede, interfectis*), and totalizing *omnis* (3x) combine with the keening *ī* sounds to emote pathos, culminating in an *aposiopesis* of sorts. **lacrimans**: a standard means in appeals to pity (*siccis agentis oculis lacrimas dabit* [sc. *auditor*]?, Quint. 6.2.27). On Roman tears, see N-H on Hor. *Carm.* 1.3.18 *occulis*, Rey 2015. **quo proficiscimur**: Plaut. *Curc.* 1 *quo ted hoc noctis dicam proficisci foras*. This abrupt address of great urgency – the question expressing surprise, not curiosity (cf. Serv. *Aen.* 1.615 *admirantis est … non interrogantis*) – sets the dramatic tone (cf. the tragedians Watson lists for Hor. *Epod.* 7.1 *quo, quo, scelesti, ruitis*). The 1st person pl. is more affective than the 2nd. **equitatus** probably (§5 *equites* certainly) refers to the social category; an instance of *interpretatio Romana*.

38.2 Both characters receive more information in c. 39. **Eporedorix**: The Celtic name (possibly "leader of horsemen" [*GPN* 92]) is epigraphically attested; but if to a Greek speaker it suggests ἐπορέγομαι, "to strive, yearn for," he will behave accordingly (cf. 1.4n. *Acconis*, 39n.). He differs from the Aeduan leader at 67.7. **Viridomarus**: this "young man" (*uiridis-mas*), whose Celtic name is variously attested (*GPN* 125), owed his standing to Diuiciacus (and C.) but ultimately joined V. (39.1, 76.4). **insimulati proditionis**: 20.1n. The first parallel with V.'s speech. **ab Romanis**: in middle position signaling their two actions. **indicta causa** "their case unheard"; a technical expression (*TLL* 7.1.1164.7–11), *indictus* only here in *CC*. Cf. §7n. *nefario*.

38.3 Cf. 20.8. **ipsis … ipsa**: emphatic polyptoton; hence α *ipsis* is preferable to β *his*. **dolore prohibeor … pronuntiare**: an "emotive aposiopesis" (*HLR* 887–88) of sorts; overcome by emotion he cannot finish his speech. It is a common artifice (cf. Cic. *Mil.* 105 *neque enim prae lacrimis iam loqui possumus*, with Clark).

38.4 is modelled on 20.9–10nn. *producit, edocti*. As there, *producere* and *pronuntiare* suggest a dramatic performance. **pronuntiauerat** "he had rehearsed," in meaning different from §3 *pronuntiare*.

38.5 multos equites: less totalizing than §1 *omnis … equitatus*, which caused the adjustment in β. **collocuti**: the recall of 37.1 *colloquitur* ironically alerts the reader to Litaviccus' *actual* conspiring. **ex media caede** echoes §3 *ex ipsa caede*.

38.6–8 Litaviccus continues galvanizing his audience with sarcasm, a rhetorical question, loaded language (*nefario, indignissime, latrones*), and repetition of "murder." **conclamant:** 21.1n. It forms a chiasmus with *obsecrant.* **obsecrant ut sibi consulat:** 8.4; *sibi = Haeduis.* **quasi uero consilii sit res** "as if indeed (an ironic introduction, *OLD uero* 2) this were a matter of counsel" (Edwards). Litaviccus' *consilii* sarcastically responds to the soldiers' (cognate) *consulat* (cf. Wills 327, 20.12n. *beneficia*). The commonplace (*audendum … non consultandum* [Livy 22.53.6]) can be traced back to Homer (e.g. *Il.* 20.211). **nosmet** the emphatic pronoun (only here in C.) befits the emotional context.

38.7 an, without a prior question, serves to introduce rhetorical questions that strongly suggest acceptance of the omitted first part (G-L 457.1); its fervor appears from Juvenal's frequent use. **nefario facinore** is memorably employed by Cato *ORF* 59 *tuum nefarium facinus peiore facinore operire postulas … decem capita libera interficis, … indicta causa* (whose argumentative logic Litaviccus shares as well); then quite frequent in Cicero. **interficiendos:** the shared etymology with *facinus* suggests that one crime begets another.

38.8 proinde is regularly used to introduce the conclusion of a speech; it here comes with exhortative connotations ("so then," *OLD* 3a). **si quid … animi:** 9.4n. *quid … consilii.* A commonplace appeal to courage, as e.g. Ps.-Quint. *Decl. min.* 349.11 *si quid in me fuerit fortis animi …, faciam* indicates. **indignissime:** the superlative only here in *CC.* **hos latrones** "these robbers here." This may be the first instance of the anti-imperialist damnation of Romans as robbers. The motif recurs: Sall. *Hist.* 4.69.22 *latrones gentium*; Tac. *Agr.* 30.4 *raptores orbis*; Horace has Hannibal pointedly speak of *lupi rapaces* (*Carm.* 4.4.50); Tac. mentions a "well named" Curtius Lupus (*Ann.* 4.27.2, with Woodman). Cf. 77n. **ciues Romanos** replays the contradiction between agent and narrator at 20.8–9n.

38.9 eius praesidii fiducia: sc. *Litauicci*; 19.2n. *fiducia.* **continuo:** a "local repetition" (42.6, 47.1). **magnum numerum frumenti commeatusque:** a conventional pair of probably military origin; frequent among Roman historians, it occurs, in this exact formula, 7x in C. and twice in Livy (23.27.1, 29.36.1); cf. 32.1n. C. is fond of *magnus numerus* (29x; 9x in *CC*), esp. in the sonorous accusative (cf. 81.1 *harpagonum numerum*; 37.6n. *ciuitatem temere*). **diripit … interficit:** 3.1n. *interficiunt … diripiunt.* **crudeliter excruciatos:** the adv. occurs once elsewhere in *BG* (1.31.12; cf. 77.2n. *crudelitatem*), then 4x in *BC.* Cf. 20.9 *excruciauerat.*

38.10 There is tension again between the Gallic viewpoint (*caede, iniurias*) and the Roman one (*mendacio*). **mendacio:** first here in C. **permouet** sits well with "*hortatur*," and alludes nicely to the primary function of the speech (*mouere*, cf. 63.1n. *augetur*). Its object is inferred from *Haeduorum* (cf. 10.1n. *educeret*). **suas iniurias persequantur** "that they seek requital (*OLD persequi* 3) for the wrongs suffered." The possessive serves instead of an objective genitive (G-L 304.2n.2); "Romans ... understood that foreigners often regarded Roman actions as *superbia* and *iniuriae* against them" (Lendon 2015: 11). *persequantur* recalls §8 *persequamur* (corroborating *simili ratione*).

39 C. continues his account of the Aedui as a riven society (*his erat ... contentio*), his exemplary care for them (nn. on 33, 40), and his personal disappointments: of the two men Litaviccus claimed dead, it is not C.'s protégé who reports the affair but Eporedorix, possibly to improve his standing (as his name may suggest [38.2n.]); his account matches C.'s narrative (§3). But in the end, he, too, will desert C. (55.4, 76.4). The chronology of events challenges belief once more (40.4n. *milia passuum*).

39.1 summo loco natus ... potentiae is formulaic, cf. Plut. *Cat. Mai.* 3.1 "a man of the highest birth and greatest influence in Rome (ἀνὴρ εὐπατρίδης μὲν ἐν τοῖς μάλιστα Ῥωμαίων καὶ δυνατός)." *summo loco natus* (again at 5.25.1) is an idiomatic expression particularly frequent with Cicero; *summus* is repeated 4x in §§1–2. **summae ... potentiae** repeats 4.1nn. The combination of adjective and genitive: 22.1n. *genus ... aptissimum*. **pari ... dispari**: descriptive ablatives usually do not depend upon a name (5.1n. *hominem*). The adjectival antonyms, commonly in antithesis (*TLL* 10.1.278.19–21), are chiastically arranged. C. again specifies age, origin, and standing, but varies the expressions and their order. **gratia** is both active and passive, signifying both "influence" and "esteem" (possibly in consequence of *beneficia* [*VL* 206]). **Diuiciaco**: an Aeduan druid and pro-Roman ruler, he stayed with Cicero in 61 when seeking help from Rome against Ariovistus (6.12.5; Cic. *Diu.* 1.90; *Introd.* 2b). He helped C. repeatedly during the first two years of the campaign; his subsequent disappearance may intimate the decline of the pro-Roman party (first and last mention at 1.3.4 and 2.14.1–15.1; Thévenot 1960: 21–25). He shares his name with a *rex Suessionum* (2.4.7; cf. *GPN* 81–83). **traditum** "introduced" (*OLD* 7); cf. *BC* 3.57.1 *Caesar ... Clodium ... ab illo traditum ... in suorum necessariorum numero habere instituerat.* **ex humili ... summam dignitatem**: Val. Max. 3.3 *ext.* 7 *ut et humili loco nati ad summam dignitatem consurgant* is similar. The advancement of pro-Roman individuals was standard Roman procedure (cf. 4.12.4; *Introd.* 2c). **in equitum numero conuenerant** "they had, as part of the group of horsemen, joined (Caesar)." **nominatim ... euocati** recurs 4x in C. The participle is technically used of those "invited by a military commander to serve under him" (*OLD*); one wonders whether they were also serving as security (5.4.2; cf. 54n.). **ab eo**: sc. *Caesare.*

39.2–3 his erat … ex his: anaphora. **principatu**: 4.1n. **illa … controuersia**: 32.2–33.4.

39.3 media fere nocte recurs thrice in Curt. (and once in Iuv.); a suitable time for dramatic developments. **orat … posset**: within the reported plea, *prauis, amicitia, deficere*, and *hostibus* represent the Roman viewpoint. **ciui- tatem … deficere**: Eporedorix here confirms what C.'s account intimated (37n.). **prauis … consiliis** recurs in Sall., Livy, and Phaedr. *prauus* ("mis- guided") is common in political discourse: Cic. *Rep.* 1.51.3 *statum prauis hominum opinionibus euersum*, Livy 5.29.8, Hor. *Carm.* 3.3.2. On the *color* of *adulescens*: 4.1n. **amicitia**: 31.5n. *amicus*. **populi Romani**: 1.3n. **futurum**: 14.7n. *laturos*. **prouideat**: with relative connectives C. uses the subjunc- tive and the infinitive (e.g. 1.31.7) indiscriminately. **coniunxerint**: the perfect subjunctive represents a future perfect in *oratio recta* (*NLS* 280). **leui momento aestimare** "deem of slight importance"; it varies *neglegere*. *momentum* occurs first here in C.

40 C. departs hurriedly with most of his troops, as if fearful of a military confrontation (§1n. *legiones*). He fails to adjust the camp's size, a near catastrophic mistake (41.2–4), for which he offers a proleptic apology by way of an emotional reference to the Aedui's special standing and empha- sis on the urgency (§§1, 2nn.). When he reaches the auxiliaries, they are quickly swayed by the appearance of the alleged murder victims, "wit- nesses" to C.'s innocence (nn. on §§ 5, 6). Given that the Gauls attack his camps during his absence (and 41.2 *summis copiis* to boot), it would seem that it was the plan all along to lure C. away, which might have succeeded, if not, once more, for C.'s speed (§4n. *passuum*, 41.5n. *ortum solis*). That speed is rendered by the rapid sequence of (mostly) short cola.

40.1 The notion of *amicitia* (39.3) seeps into the description: *affectus, sol- licitudo, indulgere*, note, too, the emphasis in *magna, semper, praecipue*, and *Haeduorum ciuitati* (cf. 1.3n. *populi*). **Magna … sollicitudine**: tellingly in first position; 3.2n. *maior … res*. **praecipue indulserat** "he had shown par- ticular regard," repeating 1.40.15, rephrasing 33.1; cf. 5.54.4; Plut. *Caes.* 26.5 τιμώμενοι διαπρεπῶς (sc. 'Εδοῦοι). **nulla interposita dubitatione** "with- out letting as much as a moment's hesitation pass." **legiones … omnem**: the size of the contingent suggests that C. feared a military confrontation.

40.2 C.'s acknowledgment of his failure to shrink his camp prepares his reader for the problems related in the next chapter (Rambaud 171–76; 45.8–9n.). Contrast his deceptive manipulation at 5.49.7. **tali tempore** "in such a critical situation"; *talis*, like *tantus* (1.2n.), often derives its spec- ificity from its context (*OLD* 1). **ad contrahenda castra** (sc. *maiora*): the phrase (already at 5.49.7) recurs in Livy 7.37.8, Flor. 1.45.22. A camp should be sized *ad quantitatem ... exercitus. nam propugnatores angusta* (sc. *castra) constipant et ultra quam conuenit latiora diffundunt* (Veg. 3.8). **quod res posita ... uidebatur** "as speed seemed of the essence"; *posita* echoes *interposita*, tightening the narrative.

40.3 C. Fabium legatum ... relinquit recurs almost verbatim at *BC* 2.24.2 (and 8.39.4). *legatum relinquere* is a standard expression (in *VII*: 5.3, 11.3, 49.1), as is *praesidio relinquere*, which occurs 9x in C. (incl. 60.2, 62.8, 68.2). A trusted legate since at least 54 (5.24.2 [with Welch 1998: 107n.44), Fabius (*RE* 17) would continue distinguishing himself in the civil war. **castris** here refers to both camps (as at 45.7, 46.3, 80.2, 83.1; cf. 68.1). **paulo ante**: highlighted by position.

40.4 adhortatus ... ne necessario ... permoueantur "he admonished (29n.) his soldiers not to mind the laborious march in this moment of urgency"; cf. *BC* 3.41.5 *militesque adhortatus ut aequo animo laborem* (sc. *itineris) ferrent.* The ordeal of the march, *qui* (sc. *labor) uel maximus est in re militari* (Cic. *Verr.* 2.5.26; cf. *qui labor quantus agminis* [*Tusc.* 2.37]), is a staple of military operations and narratives, famously mastered by C. and his men (Veg. 1.27). But this march is extraordinary even by C.'s standards (below); hence the especial encouragement. **necessario tempore** is here of greater pregnancy than at 32.2, as *necessarius* means both "critical" and "compulsory." **cupidissimis omnibus**: sc. *militibus*; the abl. absolute is used instead of a part. construction (4.1n. *conuocatis*). C.'s soldiers are characteristically eager (19.4n.). **milia passuum xxv**: this would suggest that the Aedui had marched 5 miles since Litaviccus' stage act (38.1 *milia ... xxx*), which is unlikely (39n.). A legion's typical marching speed was ca. 20 Roman miles per day, except on difficult terrain (Veg. 1.27; Goldsworthy 1996: 110). C.'s troops left after midnight (39.3 *media fere nocte*), marched 25 miles, rested for three hours, and marched back to reach camp before sunrise (41.5 *ante ortum solis*), thus covering 50 miles within 24 hours. For other speedy marches, see Ash on Tac. *Ann.* 15.16.3. **conspicatur**: C. favors the verb (*TLL* 4.498.25–26; Cic. shuns it); cf. 15.2n. *conspiciuntur*. **moratur atque impedit** is a typical *hysteron proteron*, wherein the important fact comes first (Verg.'s *moriamur et in media arma ruamus* is the classic example); cf. Miodoński-Wölfflin on *BAfr.* 21.3 *incendebant atque expugnabant*, Kenney on Lucr. 3.159–60 *propellit et icit*; *Index*, s.v. **interdicitque ... interficiant**: the repetition (a *redditio* of sorts [*HLR* 625]), supported by a chiasmus, links the prohibition with the prohibited.

40.5 False witnesses had declared the two Aeduan nobles dead; alive, they witness to C.'s innocence. **illi**: sc. *Haedui.* **interfectos** pointedly recalls Litaviccus' false claim (38.1–3n.). **inter equites**: sc. *Romanos.* **suosque**: 28.6n.

40.6 The rapid change may hint at the Gauls' fickleness (21n.). **fraude:** first here in C. **manus tendere:** its significance is spelled out in Livy 44.42.4 *manus ... tendentes suppliciter uitam orabant.* For other instances of this form of supplication (cf. 15.4–5n.), see Otto s.v. *manus* (7), Oakley on Livy 7.31.5; for other uses of the same gesture, see N-R on Hor. *Carm.* 3.23.1 *caelo ... manus.* [**deditionem significare**] is unparalleled and, as Whitte first saw, probably an interpolated gloss on *manus tendere*, whose syntax the interpolator might have intended to mimic (alternatively, a *scilicet* [*uel sim.*] was lost, or its verbal form changed from *significa[n]t*). Its nature is indicated by its awkward position and the fact that outstretched hands (and relinquished weapons) were the standard gestures of "capitulation." Holmes ad loc. adduces arguments in its favor. **proiectis armis:** as C. states (2.32.1), *deditionis nullam esse condicionem nisi armis traditis*, which was true of ancient warfare generally (Oakley on Livy 6.8.10); cf. 11.2n. *arma ... dari.*

40.7 suis clientibus: 4.1n. **quibus ... deserere:** C. identifies them at 3.22 as *soldurii*, remarking on their devotion unto death (cf. 6.19.4, where C. remarks how the dearest *serui et clientes* were cremated with their patrons; Voisin 2009). This following is a Celtic commonplace, which Tac. *Germ.* 14.1 transposes to the *Germani* (to the passages in Rives ad loc. add Strabo 3.4.18; cf. Rives on Tac. *Germ.* 13.2 "retinue"). **more Gallorum:** 2.2n. *quo more.* **nefas** "an abomination." **patronos:** first here in C. **perfugit** is preferable to *profugit* because of its connotation "to desert" (cf. 37.3n. *distineat*): escaping to Gergovia he irrevocably deserted.

41 C. makes a virtue out of necessity when he presents his refraining from punishment as an act of favor, continuing his theme of leniency (§1n.). He also continues his "proleptic apology" (40n.) in emphasizing how brief was the rest he granted his soldiers, before hurrying back to his camps. Nevertheless, about halfway he is met by messengers who, in stark, urgent, and partly reported words (nn. on *quanto, summis, crebro, isdem, permanendum*), tell of a Gallic assault on the undermanned Roman camps.

41.1 C. emphasizes his lenient treatment; but given his reluctance to provoke the Aedui before his reunion with Labienus (43n.) – what else could he have done? **nuntiis ... missis ... docerent:** the subjunctive expresses purpose. **suo beneficio** "out of personal kindness"; cf. *BC* 2.32.8 *Caesaris beneficio estis conseruati*; Sall. *Cat.* 54.2 *Caesar beneficiis ac munificentia magnus habebatur.* The emphatic possessive is indirectly reflexive (as though C. were the subject of the abl. absolute). Given Aeduan resentment of Roman patronage (37.4n. *beneficio*, 37.5n.), one hopes C. chose a different word in communication with them (as at 54.3

merita). **iure belli** is set against *suo beneficio*. Ariovistus had referred C. to *ius belli* (1.36.1), and there are many references to such a *ius/lex/*νόμος: *esse enim quaedam belli iura, quae ut facere ita pati sit fas: sata exuri, dirui tecta, praedas hominum pecorumque agi misera magis quam indigna patienti esse* (Livy 31.30.2 [with Briscoe], based on Polyb. 5.11.3–4 [with Walbank]). It is often invoked regarding the winner's behavior (cf. Cic. *Deiot.* 25 on Deiotarus' debt to C. *a quo … uel interfici belli lege potuisset*). But, as Briscoe remarks, there was "no agreement on what actions were permitted"; cf. 47.5n. *abstinerent*; Seavey 1994: 44–61. **tribusque … datis**: the motif is common; Livy 34.16.3 *paucis horis noctis ad quietem datis* is particularly close. **castra … mouet**: a common expression (8.5, 18.1, 20.1+3, 53.3; *TLL* 3.554.39–79), here synonymous with *proficisci* (as C. lacked the time to set up camp).

41.2–4 The report is a model of limpid stringency (18n.). **medio fere itinere** "about halfway"; without "in": 24.3n. *toto*. **quanto res … fuerit** is a Caesarian formula: 2.26.5, 5.48.2, 6.39.1; cf. 1.17.6 *quanto id cum periculo fecerit*. For the word order, which emphasizes *quanto*, cf. Livy 9.39.5 *quantis numquam alias ante simul copiis simul animis*, and 15.5n. *unum*. The perfect suggests the danger's discontinuation (41.4 *discessu*). **summis copiis** "in full force" (Edwards); *summus* = "greatest in amount" (*OLD* 8); its implication: 40n. **crebro** along with *assiduo labore* and *perpetuo* renders the relentless strain. **integri defessis succederent**: 25.1n. *integer* is standard military language for fresh reserves (Sall. *Cat.* 60.4 *integros pro sauciis*, Livy 9.32.9 *integri fessis*). **propter magnitudinem**: 40.2n. *ad contrahenda castra*. **isdem** "the very same people," emphatic by position. **permanendum**: the prefix underlines the duration (cf. Cic. *Red. pop.*19 *quod uiro forti adimi non potest, id ei manet et permanebit*).

41.3 multitudine … multos: the paronomasia is here (and 42.6) used emphatically. *multitudine* also echoes *magnitudinem*. On the swarm of missiles: 82.1n. **sagittarum**: 31.4n. **omnis generis telorum** recurs *BC* 1.26.1 (*BHisp.* 11.2, 13.6), grows into a Livian mannerism, and appears at Verg. *Aen.* 9.509–10, Val. Max. 1.7 *ext.* 4. The double genitives: 22.1n. *cuiusque*. **haec** refers to the last-mentioned circumstance or the assault more generally. **magno usui fuisse tormenta**: *BAfr.* 29.3 recounts a gruesome instance of their lethal and demoralizing power; Veg. 4.29 notes: *more fulminis quicquid percusserint aut dissoluere aut inrumpere consuerunt*.

41.4 Fabius is credited with circumspect action (cf. 40.3n. *Fabium*), dispatching messengers to alert C. and preparing for the next day. The infinitives form a *tricolon*, wherein, rather typically, chiastic and parallel arrangements are combined. **discessu**: 5.2n. *aduentu*. **eorum**: sc. *hostium*.

obstruere ceteras: gates were a camp's weakest part and normally secured by *stationes* (11.8, 69.7); cf. *BC* 1.27.2, Oros. 2.6.10. **pluteosque uallo**: 25.1n. *pluteos*, 70.5n. *uallo*. **similem ad casum** "for a like occurrence"; cf. 4.10n. *leuiore de causa*.

41.5 his rebus cognitis: 18.2n. **summo studio militum ante ortum solis … peruenit**: cf. 36–43n. (the Appianic parallel), 40.4nn. *cupidissimis, milia passuum*.

42 C.'s development of this phase draws on the Romans' deep cultural grammar (*Introd.* 3g): the Aedui are presented as typically credulous and excitable (§§1nn. *primis*, 2 *impellit, auaritia, temeritas, leuem*), who madly attack only to regret it (nn. on 43, 63.8), thus revealing stereotypical *infirmitas* (36–43n.). C. expounds on two stereotypes, fickleness and wrath, which he combines with the metaphorical theme of "political unrest = madness" (§4n. *sanitatem*; 43n.; Woodman 2010); this combination is facilitated by the conception of "wrath" as *insania* (§§2, 4n. *iracundia, furorem*). The account of the attack is strikingly schematic (nn. on §3, 5 *qui … constiterant*).

42.1 Dum … geruntur repeats 37.1n. **primis** and **nullum** (further stressed by its position and *sibi*) emphasize the Gauls' rashness.

42.2 The strong condemnatory language, rather uncommon in C. (but cf. 1.40.4, 2.3.5, 5.7.2, 7.77.9; *BC* 3.59.3), is in effect apologetic, as if the Aedui had but little choice. **impellit**: 1.3n. **auaritia**: sc. *Romanorum bonorum*. Such "greed for spoils" (Polyb. 2.19.3; cf. Livy 5.51.10, Dion. *Ant. Rom.* 13.9.2) is a stereotypical Gallic trait; it heightens their susceptibility to bribes, too (1.5n. *praemiis*). Within the narrative C. alludes to it frequently (e.g. 5.34.1); but he complicates it in his digression (6.17.3–5). **iracundia et temeritas** "reckless anger" (an unparalleled hendiadys, but cf. 1.31.13 *barbarum, iracundum, temerarium*) is another trait of the stereotypical Gauls, *flagrantes ira cuius impotens est gens* (Livy 5.37.4 with Ogilvie). For its comparison to "insanity," cf. Cic. *Tusc.* 3.11 *exisse ex potestate dicimus eos qui effrenati feruntur … iracundia*. **quae maxime generi … innata**: Greeks and Romans believed in congenital traits; cf. Polyb. 6.46.9 τὴν ἔμφυτον σφίσι πλεονεξίαν, "their (i.e. the Cretans') inborn greed." Wrathfulness was a consequence of the northern climactic conditions according to the anthropo-geographical theory (*Introd.* 3g). *innasci* occurs once more in *BG* (1.41.1). **leuem auditionem … re comperta**: C. varies the possibly proverbial commonplace *incerta pro certis* (Sall. *Cat.* 17.6 with Vretska; Otto 81). *leuis auditio* = "idle hearsay" (cf. 1.3n. *rumoribus*), with *leuis* suggesting the characteristic *leuitas* (43.4n.).

42.3 schematically arranges commonplace elements of formulaic phrasing in an asyndetic tricolon. **bona ... diripiunt, caedes faciunt**: 3.1n. *diripi ... interfici. caedes facere* occurs only in *VII* (67.7, 70.5, 88.3; cf. 1.4n. *interfici*); a "local repetition." **in seruitutem abstrahunt**: sc. *quosdam* (*uel sim.*). Cf. 14.10n.

42.4 rem proclinatam "the general tendency" (Edwards). This is the first attestation of the rare verb, which C. deploys similarly in addressing Cic. (*ne quo progredereris proclinata iam re quo integra etiam progrediendum tibi non existimasses* [*Att.* 10.8b.1]). Unsurprisingly, the commoner *inclinare* is found in certain MSS. **furorem**: as Lucan's famous *furor Teutonicus* (1.255) indicates, another reference to the (proverbial) trait of the Northern peoples (Perl on Tac. *Germ.* 25.1, Goodyear on *Ann.* 1.35.5). It is frequently associated with *insania* (N-H on Hor. *Carm.* 1.16.5 *non*; cf. Cic. *Har. resp.* 39 *furore atque dementia*), its abatement therefore equivalent to returning to sanity. **ad sanitatem reuerti** = 1.42.2 (and Sen. *Ben.* 7.31.1). *ad sanitatem* (common in Celsus) is a clear marker of C.'s use of the common medical metaphor; cf. Cic. *Tusc.* 4.13 *est autem quaedam animi sanitas, quae in insipientem etiam cadat, cum curatione et purgatione medicorum conturbatio mentis aufertur*, and, for a similarly political use, Livy 28.27.11–12 *origo omnis furoris penes auctores est; uos contagione insanistis.* **impellit** repeats emphatically §2.

42.5 M. Aristium: unknown (*RE* [1]). **fide data** "having given a pledge (of safe conduct)"; cf. *TLL* 6.1.669.5 *sponsio, quae ad alicuius incolumitatem pertinet*; 17.7n. *perfidia.* **Cauillono**: the *oppidum*, today Chalon-sur-Saône, was an important Aeduan port (90.7n.). This is its first mention. **qui ... constiterant** = 3.1.

42.6 continuo in itinere adorti is standard military language: 3.20.3, *BAfr.* 61.5 *in itinere ... ex improuiso adorti* (almost verbatim at Tac. *Ann.* 4.45.2), Livy 25.9.11, Amm. Marc. 18.2.13. Cf. 38.9n. *continuo.* The repetition of §5 *iter* tightens the narrative. **diem noctemque** is *apo koinou* with the participle and the verb. The common idiom (Landgraf on Cic. *Rosc. Am.* 6 *dies noctesque*) recurs at 77.11, *BC* 1.62.1. **multis ... maiorem**: an "amplifying antithesis," wherein "a positive adjective [is] trumped by ... [a] comparative" (Whitton on Pliny 2.3.1 *magna ... maior*; Wills 231–37). Cf. 41.3n. *multitudine ... multis.*

43 A double dissimulation runs through this paragraph: just as the Aedui pretend to rejoin C. but stealthily prepare for war, so C. feigns ignorance but ponders his escape out of (a rather sudden) fear of being surrounded (§5nn.). C.'s account might dissimulate, too: his fear may result from his actual topographical situation, and his plan to retreat may disguise the necessity to flee after the loss (36–56n.). He continues using medically resonant language (*purgandi, recuperandorum, contaminati, capti, sollicitant, mitissime*).

43.1 nuntio allato = 11.4. **in potestate teneri**: *BAfr.* 45.5 *in tua tenes potestate*; common. **eorum**: sc. *Haeduorum*; contrast 41.1n. *beneficio suo.* **concurrunt … demonstrant**: the first verb's initial position conveys haste (as does the asyndeton); note the chiasmus. **nihil publico factum consilio**: a common excuse; cf. Cato *FRHist* F88 *Persen publice numquam adiuuere, BG* 5.1.7 *nihil earum rerum publico factum consilio*, Frontin. *Str.* 1.4.11 *bellum iniussu populi inceptum*; Oakley on Livy 6.6.4–5.

43.2 C. projects Roman procedures onto the Aeduan proceedings (*interpretatio Romana*). In the asyndetic and paratactic tricolon, each colon renders one event with great economy. **quaestionem … decernunt** is administrative language; cf. Cic. *Mil.* 19 *num quae rogatio lata, num quae noua quaestio decreta est?* **bona publicare** is a standard expression, which C. is first to use of non-Roman peoples (5.56.3; *TLL* 10.2.2445.35–48). The confiscation of private property was a well-established penalty in political contexts; it here suggests that Litaviccus and his brothers were tried and found guilty (Tac. *Ann.* 6.29.1 *damnati publicatis bonis sepultura prohibebantur*). However, he is later presented as welcomed in Bibracte (55.4). *bona* recalls *bonis* to signify tit for tat; and *publicare* echoes *publico* to intimate that these were *now* the officially ratified measures. **sui purgandi gratia**: Apul. *Apol.* 48 (and 82) *purgandi mei gratia*. C. uses *gratia* instead of *causa* only here and *BC* 2.7.3 (3.1n.), and elsewhere writes *purgandi causa* (4.13.4, 6.9.6); Cic. uses them interchangeably (*Cael.* 3): *deformandi huius causa et detrahendae … dignitatis gratia. purgare* is frequent in medical discourse (*TLL* 10.2.2684.63–2686.10; cf. 42.4n. *sanitatem*).

43.3 The tricolon (*contaminati … capti … exterriti*) typically combines parallel and chiastic structures. **recuperandorum … causa**: 3.1n. Its use in medical contexts: *TLL* 11.2.447.24–47. **contaminati facinore** is unparalleled; it continues the medical metaphor (*OLD* 1b). **capti compendio … bonis** "taken with the profits from the plundered goods"; *capere* is also commonly used of diseases (*TLL* 3.340.15). *compendium* first here in C. **ex direptis bonis** repeats emphatically §1 *de bonis direptis*. **quod … pertinebant**: this parenthetical phrase, wherein *ea res* refers loosely to the two circumstances just mentioned, emphasizes that more people than just Litaviccus and his brothers are concerned. **ea res**: 11.5n. *quaeque … sint.* **timore … exterriti**: 26.5n. The verb first here in C. Its prefix is perfective in meaning. **consilia … incipiunt**: 1.3n. *de bello … incipiunt.* **ciuitatesque … sollicitant**: a cliché (4.5 *dimittit … legationes*). In this context the verb might also suggest illness (*OLD* 1b).

43.4 Xenophon's comment (*Ages.* 1.11–12) on how "Agesilaus, though cognizant of [Tissaphernes' treachery], held on to the treaty nonetheless," thereby to advertise the latter's faithlessness and his own rectitude, sets C.'s behavior in relief. **tametsi** is always followed by *tamen* in C. (*BC* 3.89.1 differs); cf. 8.2n. **quam mitissime potest**: 8.3n. *mitis* only here in C. For its medical use, cf. Celsus, *Med.* 4.22.3 *mitiora uulnera*. **nihil ... deminuere** is built around two antitheses and a wordplay: *leuitas* ("fickleness," but also "lightness" [*OLD* 3, 1]) must not meet with *aliquid grauius* ("anything too severe"; but also *grauis ... cui contrarius est leuis* [Isid. *Etym.* 9.4.31]); and what the *uulgus* (cf. Cic. *Planc.* 9 *non est enim consilium in uulgo*; 15.6n.) committed, the *ciuitas* must not pay for. C. continues to understate the Aeduan defection, here deploying the commonplace fickleness (20.5n. *multitudinis*) and glossing over that the uprising had started at the top (37n.). **inscientiam leuitatemque** "flighty thoughtlessness," unparalleled. *leuitas* is a frequent "party expression" (Clark on Cic. *Mil.* 22).

43.5 ipse "in fact, he" (*OLD* 9b). **maiorem ... exspectans** = 6.1.1. **ne**: *exspectare* may shade into *timere* (*TLL* 5.2.1898.83–99.50) and could be followed by a (here partly epexegetical) fear-clause: "he feared a greater ... uprising (and) that he be ...." But it more likely depends upon *consilia inibat* (cf. 53.1n. *ne ... tribuerent*). **ciuitatibus circumsisteretur, consilia**: 18.1n. *captiuis* (triple alliteration). The Aedui, to C.'s north, could block him from Labienus, and this remark may indicate that they had deserted already; to his south there were the Arverni. Then again, his position had always been precarious, what with Gondole and Corent nearby (36–53n.). **a Gergouia**: the preposition is used with cities "when not the town but the neighborhood is intended" (G-L 391R1). **omnem exercitum**: including Labienus' four legions (34.2). **profectio ... defectionis ... similis fugae**: the paronomasia is unparalleled; Wills 449–51 offers poetic instances of such "word-play in compounding combinations." C. is fond of the "flight-like departure" motif (cf. Polyb. 3.64.7 φυγῇ παραπλησίαν ποιήσασθαι τὴν ἀποχώρησιν, "making a retreat very similar to a flight"): 2.11.1 *ut consimilis fugae profectio uideretur*, 5.47.4, 6.7.8.

44–52 "A silence suffuses the story"

The reconstruction of the battle, its precise topography and purpose, is hampered by C.'s silence on his intention and typically schematic language (Keegan 1976: 62–67; Pelling 1981), the lack of conclusive archaeological evidence (Deberge *et al.* 2014), and textual uncertainties (nn. on 44.3 *hunc siluestrem*, 45.1). The following is most likely (Kagan 2006: 155–80, Luccisano n.d.; *CG* 756–67 discusses alternatives; cf. fig. 7): While inspecting his camp (on the Roche Blanche), C. notices that a hill hard by the plateau (44.1n. *collem*) has suddenly become unoccupied. Inquiry reveals that V. has commandeered those troops to fortify the hill's back (the Col des Goules [44.3n.]), where he fears an attack. C. decides to play on that fear, sending three contingents of cavalry in a westerly direction to roam around that hillside, while also advancing one legion (45.5n. *eodem iugo*) – thus prompting V. to relocate troops from his camps on the slope to that area of solicitude (45.6n. *illo*). This has been C.'s plan all along, as he intends to attack the camps: to that end, he stealthily moves troops from his larger camp to the smaller one and, after (unspecified) instructions to his men, dispatches them to charge up the slope (46.1–3n.), while sending out Aeduan cavalry along a different route (45.10n. *ab dextra parte*). After swiftly seizing several camps, C. orders retreat, but only the X legion stops; the others charge on up to the wall. Meanwhile, the Gauls regroup and rush from the hillside back to the defense of the wall; they are already gaining the upper hand, when the Aeduan cavalry appear on the Romans' right side (51.1n. *aperto … latere*) and, mistaken for the enemy, cause panic. To save his legionaries from a rout, C. positions the X legion on the slope and orders Fabius to advance with the XIII from the smaller camp onto the level ground at the slope's foot on the Gauls' right flank (49.1–2n.). Nonetheless, losses are high, and at an assembly C. reprimands his soldiers for their undisciplined *magnitudo animi* (52n.).

It has been suspected that C. planned to storm Gergovia by way of his stratagem (e.g. Stevens 1952: 17, Gelzer 1955: 992, Rambaud 117): He rules out an assault a little too categorically and employs conspicuously evasive language in talking about the operation's purpose (36.1n. *oppugnatione*, 44.1, 45.7, 47.1); one might also wonder what the Aeduan cavalry was meant to contribute (45.10n.), not to mention Fabius' brag, before any engagement, that he would climb the wall first (47.7n.). Yet Kagan disagrees, arguing on tactical grounds that C.'s preparations and movements fit a surprise attack on the camps better than an alleged assault on the town (2006: 170–74). If C.'s motive is questionable, so is his plotting, as it may well have been the loss at Gergovia that caused the Aedui to desert (Stevens 1952: 17–18). Or was it C.'s growing fear of his ally that caused him to take risks: first in storming Gergovia, then in crossing the Liger (53–56n.)? There may be more to their peculiar mistaken identity (51.1), too.

C. presents himself as "a maker of stratagems" (ποιητὴν … μηχανημάτων [Xen. *Cyr.* 1.6.38]; cf. Wheeler 1988: 29), and twice demonstrates the highly desirable ἀγχίνοια, "quick-wittedness" (45, 49; 18n.). For the undesired outcome his daredevil soldiery and the topography bear the blame (nn. on 45.8 *studio pugnandi*, 45.9 *iniquitas loci*; Richter

1977: 119; Rambaud 171 on parallels in C.'s accounts of Dyrrachium and Ilerda). Other apologetic details appear when the episode is read against Polybius' discussion of the proper use of "opportunities" (τῶν ἐν καιρῷ ... ἐνεργουμένων [9.12.3]). Defined as potentially advantageous but hazardous affairs, these "result in failure more often than success" out of "ignorance or negligence on the part of the commander." They require "(a) secrecy, (b) accurate calculation of times and distances, (c) ability to choose the right time and place, (d) attention to signals, one's collaborators, and the mode of action" (Walbank on 9.13.1–9). As if responding to these criteria, C. conceals his plan (45n.), stealthily moves troops, calculates precisely the crucial distance (46n.), defines the situation as suitable for a surprise attack (occasionis), and alerts his officers to the treacherous terrain as well as the risk of a disobedient soldiery (45.8–10) – thus taking measures for a possible failure of signaling even. Any reader inquisitive of "the cause of the [Gergovian] disaster" (τῆς περιπετείας αἴτιον [9.17.9]) will not find it in the commander's conduct (cf. BC 3.73.4 quod esset acceptum detrimenti, cuiusuis potius quam suae culpae debere tribui). C. makes sure to not be perceived as a dux temerarius (cf. Plancus [Cic.] Fam. 10.23.1 si quid acciderit mihi, a reprehensione temeritatis absim; Geist 2009). For parallels with Avaricum: nn. on 27, 47.5–6, 47.7, 52.

44 C. spots another opportunity (27n.) noticing a hill suddenly unguarded. His information handling (observation, reconnaissance, debriefing) is exemplary (cf. Veg. 3.6; Ezov 1996: 71–72). Details accord with the actual topography (Kagan 2006: 164–65).

44.1 cogitanti: cf. Cic.'s formulaic cogitanti mihi ... perbeati ... uideri solent (De or. 1.1; Landgraf on Rosc. Am. 67 saepenumero provides material). For other instances (in Greek, Thuc. 1.1.3 σκοποῦντί μοι, and Latin) of this participial dative of point of view, see Landgraf in ALL 8: 50–54; cf. 53.1n. eadem ... cogitans. **facultas bene gerendae rei** "a chance of successful action" (Edwards). The formulaic expression (e.g. 3.18.5; BC 1.28.2; BAlex. 10.3) recurs repeatedly in Livy. The nature of the opportunity is unspecified. **minora castra**: 36.7. **operis** "military works" (OLD 10b). **perspiciendi**: 36.1n. **collem ... poterat**: a cumbersome description, wherein, however, each attribute contains particular information; the imperfects are descriptive. **collem ... nudatum** recurs once, in Luc. 4.148: nudatos Caesar colles desertaque castra | conspiciens. The expression is suggestive, as nudatus is also uox propria for "to [be] expose[d] to attack" (OLD 4). The hill will have been one of the Hauteurs de Rizolles, which, to the southwest of Gergovia and to the north of the smaller camp, run "along several hills that now range from 707 to 732 meters in height [and] connect[s]

to the plateau of Gergovie along a narrow crest" (Kagan 2006: 158, 164).
qui ... tenebatur "which was under enemy control"; it may, however, be
an instance of the imperfect instead of the pluperfect (48.3n. *tendebant*).
superioribus diebus is a Caesarian mannerism (15x [incl. 58.5, 81.4];
BAlex. 16.3). **prae multitudine ... poterat**: *prae* is frequently used of "a
preventing cause" (G-L 408N4), but in classical Latin only "where a negative is expressed or implied" (Clark on Cic. *Mil.* 105). Livy 4.41.5 is close
to this passage: *nec ad tumulum, quem ipse tenuerat, prae multitudine hostium
credere perrumpi potuisse.*

44.2 ex perfugis: C. does not use *transfuga* (5x in *CC*). Cf. 18.1n *captiuis*. **magnus ... confluebat**: the verb (only here in *CC*) suggests a (steady:
cotidie) stream of sizeable (emphatic position of *magnus*) numbers from
various directions; cf. Verg. *Aen.* 2.796–77 *ingentem comitum affluxisse nouo-
rum | inuenio admirans numerum.* The theme as such is commonplace (e.g.
Livy 24.32.7 *perfugae ... agmen hostium augent*). The word order: 24.5n.
omnis ... multitudo.

44.3 V. was right to worry, as the Rizolles offered "the only other approach
to Gergovia suitable for an army" (Kagan 2006: 158). Excavations have
revealed a gate at the stronghold's southwestern corner along with remains
of a *scorpio* (Pertlwieser 2006: 16–58, Deberge *et al.* 2014: 37). **constabat
inter omnes**: the idiom occurs only here in C. **quod ... cognouerat**: the
typically well-informed general, cf. e.g. Tac. *Ann.* 2.20.1 *nihil ... Caesari
ignotum*, and 19.3n. **dorsum ... oppidi** "that the ridge of this range [i.e.
the Hauteurs de Rizolles] was almost level, but that it was wooded and
narrow where it gave access to the other [i.e. farther] side of the town."
Livy 44.4.4 may be indebted to this: *iugum montis in angustum dorsum
cuneatum uix ... patuit. ... leuis armatura etiam per anfractus iugi* (cf. 46.1)
procurrere, cf. Tac. *Ann.* 4.47.2 *montem occupat angustum et aequali dorso con-
tinuum* (with *Introd.* 3f). **hunc siluestrem et angustum**: *dorsus* (rather than
dorsum), which the demonstrative resumes, is extremely rare, but attested
in Plaut. *Mil.* 397 and discussed by Prisc. (*Inst.* II 170.4) as the form used
by *uetustissimi*; its rarity makes it likely. The pairing recurs at Hirt. 8.35.3
siluestribus angustisque itineribus, and Livy 38.40.6 *uia ... siluestris angusta
confragosa.* **ad alteram partem**: as seen from the *castra Romana*.

44.4 uehementer ... timere = 56.2 (of C.); popular with Cicero (e.g. *Cat.*
2.4, *Ad Brut.* 2.2.2), rare elsewhere. **nec iam aliter sentire ... quin** "and
had now no alternative but to believe that" (Edwards). The unparalleled
expression is formed in analogy to *non dubitare quin* (which, as a gloss,
surely, made it into *β*). Noteworthy and semantically similar are 1.4.4 *neque
abest suspicio ... quin; BC* 3.94.3 *neque uero Caesarem fefellit quin*; cf. 11.8n.

quin, H-S 678a. **uno colle ... occupato** "with one hill (36.5–7) already in Roman possession." **uiderentur**: 25.1n. *uisum.* **ad hunc muniendum**: sc. *locum.*

45 C. quick-wittedly (44–52n.) hatches the plan to play on V.'s fear by feinting an attack on the worrisome hill, only to storm the Gauls' camps. The maneuver (ψευδέφοδος [Polyaenus, *Strat.* 3.9.32; Wheeler 1988: 40]) is recommended in military treatises: "do not make it obvious where you will make the attack; rather, feint in some places ..., in order that the besieged will make mistakes in their preparations" (Philo, *Bel.* 8.D18 [Whitehead]; cf. Frontin. *Str.* 1.8 *de distringendis hostibus*). When presenting his plan to his soldiers, he identifies the enterprise rather apodictically as an *occasio* (§9n.), by nature hazardous (44–52n.), pointing in revelatory detail to the dangers involved (§8n. *ostendit*): both features help to forestall criticism from his external audience in Rome (cf. Powell 1998: 124–29).

45.1 Hac re cognita: 18.2n. **turmas**: "the *turma* was the smallest unit of cavalry in the Roman army, consisting of only twenty-two riders (Veg. 2.14)," Oakley on Livy 8.7.1. **eo de media nocte; imperat**: β's *eodem. media nocte imperat* reads oddly. With the text printed, cf. 2.7.1 *eo de media nocte Caesar ... mittit* (and Constans' Budé). The temporal specification ("immediately after midnight," *OLD de* 4b; K-S I 498) is explained in Censorinus, *DN* 24: *incipiam a nocte media quod tempus principium et postremum est diei Romani. tempus quod huic proximum est uocatur de media nocte.* **tumultuosius** sc. *quam populi Romani fert consuetudo* (6.7.8; 7.61.3). The vivid adjective (33.1n. *detrimentosum*) occurs only here in *CC*; it becomes a Livian favorite. On possible semantic implications: 60.3n. **peruagentur**: the compound verb is preferable, as, with one exception (4.4.1), C. uses *uagari* without local specification (where *peruagari* is generally preferred [*TLL* 10.1.1837.12–21]; see §45.3).

45.2 According to Livy, C.'s ploy had been devised by C. Sulpicius; *qua* (sc. *re*) *deinde multi nostri ... imperatores, nostra quoque quidam aetate, usi sunt: mulis strata detrahi iubet ... (et) agasones partim captiuis, partim aegrorum armis ornatos imponit. his fere mille effectis centum admiscet equites* (7.14.6–7, retold in Frontin. *Str.* 2.4.6; cf. 2.4.5+8, 10.40.8). But this account is "probably ... invented" (Oakley ad loc.), and Livy may have been influenced by C. in his presentation (arguably one of *nostri ... imperatores*). Several of Frontinus' stratagems involve dress-up, disguise, and make believe (cf. Wheeler 1988). **prima luce**: 36.3n. **magnum numerum iumentorum ... mulorumque** "a substantial number of pack-animals, mules, to be precise (*OLD -que* 6)," with the latter term specifying the former (19.1n. *difficilis atque impedita*). The text-critical issue is discussed by Eussner 1884: 266;

the sound pattern: 38.9n. "As a general rule ... the Romans did not use horses as pack-animals"; there may have been as many as 1,400 mules per legion (Roth 1999: 78, 83). **stramenta** "the coverings" (*OLD* 3). The noun, rarely applied to horses, is most frequently used of straw coverings. **cassidibus** only here in C. **equitum specie ac simulatione** "just like cavalry, by all appearances"; a pleonastic pair (19.3n. *inani simulatione*), similarly used in Cic. *Leg. agr.* 2.10, *Nat. D.* 1.3.2, Nep. *Eum.* 7.1. **collibus** is a local ablative (K-S I 350); cf. 45.5 *eodem iugo*. Holmes (ad loc.) speculates that those "must have been the lower slopes of the Montagne de la Serre, south of the Auzon." **circumuehi** first here in C. **iubet** varies §1 *imperat*.

45.3 qui ... uagentur: 9.2n. *ut ... peruagentur*. **ostentationis causa** "to make a show of themselves"; *BC* 3.71.4 *ostentationis ut uidebatur causa*. **uagentur** resumes *peruagentur*. It is normal practice (in Indo-European languages) for a simple verb to follow a compound without change in meaning (Adams 1992; Wills 438–43). They typically stand in closer proximity (e.g. *BAlex.* 11.2 *si quid grauius illis accidisset, merito casurum iudicabat*). **circuitu:** "*circu(m)itus* appears in the Late Republic as an alternative to *circu(m)itio*" (Dyck on Cic. *Nat. D.* 1.29; C. does not use the latter). A possible route: Kagan 2006: 165. **easdem ... regiones:** §1 *eo*, 44.5 *hunc ... locum*. The word order reflects *circuitus*. **omnes:** sc. *equites mulionesque*. **iubet petere:** 37.6n. *ciuitatem temere*.

45.4–6 For the shift of focalization and suspense, cf. Cato *FRHist* F76 *tribunus et quadringenti ad moriendum proficiscuntur. hostes eorum audaciam demirantur, quorsum ire pergant in expectando sunt;* 79.3n. Just as the Gauls are misled by appearances, so will the Romans be (50.2). **procul ... uidebantur:** *procul* may refer to the perceived ("in the distance") or the perceiver ("from a distance," *TLL* 10.2.1559.28–32). Panoramic views in siege descriptions can be traced back to Hom. *Il.* 2.457 ἔκαθεν δέ τε φαίνεται αὐγή, "the glare [of the Achaean armour] could be seen from afar." **ut erat ... despectus:** as described in 36.1–2; the same language will describe Alesia (79.3), where C. alludes (more fully) to the *teichoskopia. ut erat*: 22.1n. **neque ... poterat** "and yet (*neque* = *neque tamen*), at so great a distance, nothing of certainty could be made out"; cf. Livy 6.1.2 *quae magno ex interuallo loci uix cernuntur* (adapting Thuc.1.1.3). C.'s language bespeaks autopsy (cf. Grillo 2011, Marincola 1997: 63–86). **certi quid esset:** for the emphatic word order, cf. Cic. *Pis.* 68 *uere ut dicam* (with Nisbet).

45.5 eodem iugo "along the same (§2n. *collibus*) line of high ground," i.e. as the cavalry (Holmes ad loc.); other interpretations are possible. **inferiore ... loco:** 3.2n. *maior ... res*. No precise locations have been established for any legions in this episode. **siluisque occultat:** 18.1n. *insidiarum causa*.

45.6 omnes … copiae: 24.5n. *omnis … multitudo*. **illo** "to that area"; 44.4.
ad munitionem: *munitio = actio muniendi*; cf. 44.4, 48.1.

45.7 uacua castra hostium: the predicative adjective is emphatic. *uacuus*
may construe with the genitive; but the word order suggests that *hostium*
qualifies *castra* (a genuine plural [40.3n.]). **tectis insignibus suorum
occultatisque signis militaribus**: *insigne* is of wide application and signifies
any kind of distinguishing mark – including helmet crests, shield orna-
ments, and the *paludamentum* (88.1; Varro *Ling.* 7.37; cf. 50.2); they also
served distinction *within* the army (Tac. *Hist.* 1.38.3, with Damon). Under
normal circumstances, "the Roman army made a glittering show" (N-H on
Hor. *Carm.* 1.7.19 *fulgentia signis*). Cf. 62.6n. *signa*. **raros milites** "soldiers,
just a few at a time." **quid fieri uelit**: 16.2n.

45.8–9 In three instances, C. enlarges on his laconic formula *quid fieri uelit*:
4.24.5, here, *BC* 3.89.4. Each time, the elaboration "foreshadows what
does actually transpire in the narrative" (Mannetter 1995: 114; 40n.). It
forestalls criticism (cf. 40n.). **studio pugnandi aut spe praedae**: either or
both reappear at 46.5, 47.3+7, and C. will return to them with harsher
terms (52.1[n.] *temeritatem cupiditatemque*), blaming them as major factors
in the defeat. For the alternating alliteration, cf. Ov. *Am.* 1.2.46 *feruida
uicino flamma uapore nocet*, Tac. *Agr.* 29.3 *commune periculum concordia pro-
pulsandum*. On *praeda*: 28.3n.

45.9 quid … incommodi: 9.4n. *quid … consilii*. **iniquitas loci**: the same
expression recurs, in tellingly short sequence, at 52.2 (2x) and 53.1.
Treacherous landscape is a common excuse for defeats (Östenberg
2017); it is C.'s second major apologetic theme (44–52n.), to which he
alludes frequently (e.g. 46.1, 51n.). The importance of topographical
knowledge: 19.3n. **posse euitari**: C. does not use *euitare* elsewhere. But
Paul's conjecture appeals semantically (cf. *TLL* 5.2.1046.73) and palaeographically, as "eui-" could easily be confused with "mu-" (*mutari α*) or
deteriorate, by way of haplography, into *uitari β* (cf. 8.48.7 *malum dux equi
uelocitate euitauit* [*uitauit β*]). **una celeritate** "speed alone (*OLD* 6)." C.'s
soldiers will perform as told at first (46.5). **occasionis … non proelii** "[it
was] a question of a surprise [attack], not a battle"; an unparalleled chiastic *epiphonema* (20.3–12n.). Cic. *Off.* 1.142 defines *occasio* as *tempus actionis
opportunum* (*graece* εὐκαιρία); its dangers: 44–52n.

45.10 C.'s deployment of the Aeduan cavalry has met with surprise, given
their rebellious sentiments (54.2 [with Stevens 1952: 16]; cf. 44–52n.).
expositis varies *proponit* (cf. 43.5n. *profectio*). The prefix conveys thoroughness (19.4n. *exposcentes*). **ab dextra parte**: sc. of his main force. **alio
ascensu**: the route is unknown. C. specifies his motivation at 50.1.

46 C.'s topography (§§1–4), notably precise to forestall any charge of insufficient preparation (44–56n.), emphasizes the up-hill nature of the attack ("hill" is mentioned 4x [+ *ascensus*]). All the more admirable therefore is the legionaries' speedy advance, highlighted by *euidentia* (§5n.).

46.1–2 Livy 21.37.3 *molliuntque anfractibus modicis cliuos* is modeled on this passage. **atque:** 10.3n. **recta regione** "in a straight line" (*OLD regio* 1); also at 6.25.2. There is etymological play, as both words derive from *regere* (E-M, s.v.); Fowler on Lucr. 2.249 offers instances. **si ... intercederet** "were it not for the intervening bends"; *anfractus* only here in *CC*. **mille CC passus aberat** is in the indicative, as this apodosis expresses "a fact independent of the condition" (*NLS* 200). Klotz's palaeographic arguments in favor of *mille* (*RhM* 1909: 227–28) are ultimately inconclusive (Meusel, *J.B.* 1912: 19); and the measurements on the ground are imprecise. There is thus no reason to reject α.

46.2 quidquid hu[i]c circuitus ... accesserat "any additional winding to soften the ascent." On the position of the genitive: 9.4n. *consilii. huc* ("to this amount," *OLD* 3) was plausibly conjectured by Vascosanus: *huic* has no real referent. *circuitus*: 45.3n. The pluperf. is likely used analogously to a pluperf. in a generalizing clause (48.2n.). **ad molliendum cliuum** recurs in Livy only; the adj. *mollis* of slopes is technical (*OLD* 6b).

46.3 "The six-foot wall most likely followed a contour line across the face of the southern slope at an elevation of about 600 meters above sea level ... now marked by a footpath ..." (Kagan 2006: 166). **in longitudinem**: 23.1n. **ut natura montis ferebat** "as the mountain's contour (*OLD natura* 8b) permitted (*OLD fero* 21)." **quo** = *ut eo*. **nostrorum impetum** is preferable to *nostrum impetum*, as the former occurs 6x in C., the latter nowhere. **impetum tardarent** occurs 4x in C. (*BAfr.* 68.3 *impetum retardauit*) and twice in Livy. **praeduxerant**: the rare verb (= *ante (ob)ducere*) occurs here for the first time in Latin literature (*TLL* 10.2.590.61; again 69.5). **densissimis castris**: C. is fond of the superlative (first attested in him); it here describes the arrangement of (not in) the camps. Variations of the expression: Livy 5.19.9, Lucan 1.478.

46.4 Each narrative unit renders one event in this swift "phrase à relance" (11.5–6n.). **dato signo**: cf. 47.1n. *receptui cani.* **celeriter**: 45.9n. **eamque**: a typical resumptive demonstrative. **ad munitionem** "to the fortification" (*OLD* 2). **trinis castris**: again 66.2. The use of the distributive is common; it suggests that "generals and soldiers noted the number of times that they had captured ... enemy camps" (Oakley on Livy 6.29.8). It may have been part of a letter to the senate (*Introd.* 3a).

46.5 This lively detail emblematizes Roman speed (Kahn 1971: 253). Livy 24.40.12–13 is close: *ipse rex, sicut somno excitus erat, prope seminudus fugiens*; then again, to happen on an enemy asleep is a topos (Hardie on Verg. *Aen.* 9.189, 314–66). **tanta ... celeritas**: the hyperbaton, position of *fuit* (14.9n. *esse*), and repetition of *celeriter* all emphasize the speed. **oppressus**: 8.3n. **ut conquieuerat** "just when he had started to nap." A *meridiatio* was common among Romans (too): Varro *Rust.* 1.2, Cic. *Diu.* 2.68, Ov. *Am.* 1.5.1–2. **uix ... eriperet**: the narrow escape of a single man is another topos; cf. 1.53.2–3, 6.30.4 *his pugnantibus illum* (sc. *Ambiorigem) in equum quidam ex suis intulit: fugientem siluae texerunt*, Sall. *Iug.* 101.9, Tac. *Ann.* 3.39.2 (confirmed by an inscription). *de/e manibus eripere* is proverbial and favored by Cic. (e.g. *Dom.* 132; cf. Cassius [Cic.] *Fam.* 12.13.1). **superiore ... nuda**: C. twice comments on the scanty clothing of the Germani (4.1.10, 6.21.5), once of the Gauls (1.25.4). It is a commonplace in the historiographical tradition and visual representations such as the Hellenistic "dying Gaul" (Polyb. 2.28.8, Quadrig. *FRHist* F6, Diod. Sic. 5.29.2; Tierney 1959: 197–98). Here it wittily underlines the hurried escape. **praedantium** hints at the reason for the king's escape: the soldiers were already acting insubordinately (45.8 *spes praedae*).

47 Contrary to orders (§§ 1 *iussit*, 2 *praeceptum*; 19n.), the soldiers storm Gergovia; panic ensues among the Gauls. While C. blames his men for the defeat, his account is marked by exculpatory detail: They cannot hear the signal (but they also ignore their superiors); they believe in their *uirtus* (but get carried away); they even climb Gergovia's wall (6x *murus*; §7n.). Partly exculpatory, partly distracting are the vivid descriptions of the despairing women (*euidentia*, §§5–6n.) and the focus on (and focalization through) one soldier (§7). *BAlex.* 20.1–6 contains a similar development.

47.1 Consecutus ... animo proposuerat: 45.7n. *quid ... uelit. animo*: 9.1n. *opinione. proposuerat* = "he had planned" (*OLD* 11a). To accomplish one's purpose characterizes the ideal general (Woodman on Vell. Pat. 79.1). C. still skimps on specifics. **receptui cani** is an idiomatic expression that C. uses only here (*TLL* 3.265.58–71); the dative is predicative. The signal was given by the *tibicen*: *ad bellum uocat milites et rursum receptui canit* (Veg. 2.22). Riepl 1913: 3–90 surveys Roman signaling (which Veg. 3.5 differentiates into "words, sounds, and visuals"). **legionisque decimae**: C. rarely individuates legions, but this *legio Equestris* (possibly so named because of 1.42.7) is an exception. It was, along with the VII, VIII, and IX, most likely part of his original army (Hirt. 8.8.2 *ueterrimas legiones VII, VIII, VIIII*; Kubitschek 1924: 1206), and, more importantly, his favorite legion (*quacum erat*) since Vesontio (1.40.15). Its pivotal role is repeatedly acknowledged (1.42.6–7, 2.21–27, 4.25.3, 51.1; *BAfr.* 16); it seems to have earned it the honor of leading the right wing (*BHisp.* 30.7; Miller 1979: 139–40). When it rebelled, C. famously chastised the legionaries by addressing them as "Quirites" (Suet. *Iul.* 70, with Leeman 2001: 103). See further Miller 1979, and, on C.'s innovative role in the numbering of legions, Parker 1958: 55–57.

47.2 Military writers emphasize the importance of soldiers' attention to signaling: Onas. 10.2, Veg. 3.5 *nihil magis ad uictoriam proficit quam monitis obtemperare signorum*; cf. Polybius' concern (44–56n.). The topography supports C.'s claim (Kagan 2006: 237n.49). **at** marks the turning point (Gärtner 1975: 84). **non exaudito sono tubae**: the abl. absolute is concessive (cf. *tamen*). *exaudire* = "to hear at a distance" (Clark on Cic. *Mil.* 67), subtly re-emphasizing the topography. *tuba* is used generically of wind instruments and specifically (and in contrast to *bucina* and *cornu*) of the instrument that was characterized by "a markedly conical bore over its entire length" (Speidel 1984: 29). The sounding of the *tuba* is a literary cliché (e.g. Verg. *Aen.* 11.192 *it caelo clamorque uirum clangorque tubarum*; Miniconi 1951: 166); but Curt. 5.2.7 may have had this passage in mind: *tuba … signum dabat, cuius sonus … haud satis exaudiebatur.* **sono**: only here and *BC* 3.105.4. *clangor* is curiously mostly absent from the *BG* (Kraus 2010b). **satis** "fairly" (*OLD* 9b). **ut erat**: 22.1n. **retinebantur**: a conative imperfect.

47.3 The participle construction *elati* is coordinated (*et*) with the double ablative *fuga … proeliis* (5.6n.); the order of the ablatives and genitives is a typical mix (ABBABA). **elati spe … possent**: this psychological motivation (cf. nn. on 17.4–7, 19.4, 28.4 *incitati*) can be traced back to Thuc. 3.45.6 τῇ ἐλπίδι ἐπαιρόμενοι κινδυνεύουσι, "elated by hope they risk their lives"; cf. Lendon 1999: 290–304. Cic. *Phil.* 2.38 is close: *spe uictoriae elati.* **superiorumque … proeliis**: 17.7n. on *memoria.* The *insolentia ex secundis rebus* (Sall. *Iug.* 40.5) is a commonplace (Woodman on Vell. Pat. 2.110.2 *insolens*). **nihil … arduum … uirtute … possent**: a very Roman notion, as captured by Sall. *Cat.* 7.5 *uirtus omnia domuerat. arduus* frequently occurs in such contexts (so in Sallust: *non locus ullus asper aut arduus erat*; cf. Tac. *Agr.* 18.4 *nihil arduum*), possibly because (the path to) *uirtus* was proverbially "steep" (Otto, s.v. *arduus*, going back to Hes. *Op.* 287–92). It is here particularly apt, as its literal meaning is pertinent, too (*magna ualles*, 52.3 *altitudo montis*), just as in Hor. *Carm.* 1.3.37–38: *nil mortalibus ardui est;* | *caelum ipsum petimus.* **quod non**: *non* has a tendency to follow the relative after *nemo* (*nihil*) *est* (K-S II 269); 66.7. **consequi** pointedly echoes *consecutus.* **finem prius sequendi fecerunt**: the periphrasis is common in C. (Krebs 2018b: 115). **muro oppidi portisque**: *oppidi* is *apo koinou* with both nouns, as the word order, known as *coniunctio*, reveals (e.g. Xen. *An.* 1.6.1 ἴχνη ἵππων καὶ κόπρος, Hor. *Carm. saec.* 31–32 *et aquae salubres* | *et Iouis aurae*, *Rhet. Her.* 4.38). These gates will serve as *locus dramatis* (50.4 *portas excidere*, 50.5 *a porta … summouit*). **appropinquarunt**: a temporal *priusquam* regularly construes with the aorist-perfect indicative, if the main clause is negated (25.4; *NLS* §228a; K-S II 371; 1.6n.).

47.4 The Gauls mistake the significance of the clamor, understandably given the topos "of the shout at the capture of a city" (Oakley on Livy 10.42.2); cf. Livy 36.24.6 *clamor, index capti oppidi, est exauditus*. Other instances of panic (50.2n.): 6.40; *BC* 1.45, 3.64; 8.13. **tum uero** introduces an "action brusque d'un groupe" or an "aspect dramatique d'un combat" (C-L 524). **orto clamore**: 12.5n. **intra portas**: again *BAfr.* 82.1; then Verg. *Aen.* 10.23, Livy (often), hardly elsewhere. Panic revels in exaggeration: *portis appropinquarunt* becomes *intra portas* (cf. 48.1n. *oppidum teneri*; 15.6n. *perangustum*). **sese … eiecerunt**: 28.5n.

47.5–6 The details offered were standard features of the *urbs capta* motif (20–28n.), which drew the ire of Polybius (2.56.7), who criticizes Phylarchus for "put[ting] on women embracing, their hair disheveled, and their breasts bare (εἰσάγει περιπλοκὰς γυναικῶν καὶ κόμας διερριμμένας καὶ μαστῶν ἐκβολάς)"; further discussion: Cipriani 1986: 43–73. Similar scenes in *CC* occur: 1.51.3, 2.13.3 *pueri mulieresque ex muro passis manibus suo more pacem ab Romanis petierunt*; *BC* 2.4.3, 5.3; *BHisp.* 19. This scene more specifically looks back to Avaricum (26.3–4, with Bellemore 2016). On "female figures looking on battles": Fuhrer 2015. **matres familiae**: 26.3n. **pectore nudo**: bared breasts in Roman society typically signified mourning (Prop. 2.13.27 *nudum pectus lacerata* with Fedeli) or sexual availability (Catull. 55.11, Prop. 4.8.47). But one may in this context also be reminded of Hecuba (a *mater familiae*) exposing her breast to her son, Hector, in a plea for his pity (Hom. *Il.* 22.79–84). **prominentes** "leaning out" (*OLD* 2). This is the verb's only instance in *CC* and its first in Latin literature. **passis manibus**: Nonius (370.23) helpfully glosses this past participle of *pando* (*OLD* ²1a) in Enn. *Ann.* 343 *passis late palmis* with "*patentibus et extensis*." C. uses the same formulaic expression at 1.51.3 and 2.13.3 (and with the poetic *palma* at *BC* 3.98.2); the gesture is commonplace (cf. 40.6n. *manus tendere*), the language elevated (Horsfall on Verg. *Aen.* 3.263). **obtestabantur**: punctilious readers wonder how they communicated with the Romans. **neu … ne … quidem … infantibus abstinerent** "and that they not [do] as they had done at Avaricum (28.3), and not refrain from attacking (*OLD abstineo* 9) the women even and children (28.4n. *infantibus*)." The slight anacoluthon may express their distress. *abstinere ne quidem* recurs, in this context, in Livy: 2.16.9 *ne ab obsidibus*

quidem ... ira belli abstinuit, 2.22.4, 29.8.9, 39.25.10 *ne a legatis quidem, qui
iure gentium sancti sint, uiolandis abstinere*; hardly elsewhere. The women
may here appeal to the *ius belli* (41.1n.), as Livy's Heraclia would seem
to do (24.26.11): *puellis ut saltem parcerent orare institit, a qua aetate etiam
hostes iratos abstinere*, cf. Cic. *Off.* 1.35 *parta ... uictoria conseruandi ii qui non
crudeles, non immanes fuerunt.*

47.6 nonnullae/de muro/per manus/demissae is strikingly isocolic. *per
manus* = "to pass from hand to hand" (*OLD* 8a); a highly implausible detail
(Bellemore 2016: 905).

47.7 Fabius (*RE* 23) is commonly said to serve as a bad example, worse
than Petronius, dying, as he does, wordlessly (50.3–4). But C. honors
him with an iconic scene (cf. 25n.), atop the enemy wall, the evoca-
tiveness of which can be gauged from Alexander's famous stance on
the Mallian bulwark (Arr. *Anab.* 6.9.4–6); moreover, he ties him back
to the successful storming of Avaricum (Mutschler 1975: 176–78) and
commemorates him with the specification of his legion (below). Rather,
Fabius reflects C.'s admiration for raw *uirtus* as much as his belief in
the primacy of *disciplina* (52n.). Brown 2004: 292n.1 lists other "zealous
centurion[s]." **legionis VIII**: this identification should be compared to
"commemorative inscription[s] of imperial legionaries [that] very commonly identify the man's *centuria*" (Harris 2006: 318). **quem ... ascenderet**: why did Fabius long to reach the wall when that was not part of
C.'s plan? **Auaricensibus praemiis**: 27.2n. Such "possessive" adjectives
signify "character, nomenclature, and origin" (Löfstedt 1928: 83–99)
rather than mere possession (as does the genitive construction). **commissurum** "would [not] allow"; the categories of the *OLD* do not offer
this use a ready home (again e.g. 1.13.7, *BC* 3.46.3). **nactus** "come upon"
(*OLD* 5b). **manipulares**: first here in C. Despite the abolishment of the
maniple in favor of the cohort during the second century, *manipularis*
continued to be used in the sense of "fellow soldier" (*OLD* 2; Keppie
1998: 63–64). But its etymology (Varro *Ling.* 6.85 *a manu*) makes it per-
fectly suitable here, suggesting that they gave him a "hand" up. **murum
ascendit** confirms his stated intention *murum ascenderet*. **exceptans**: only
here (and possibly *BHisp.* 17.2) in *CC*; overall extremely rare. The verb's
intensive nature emphasizes the effort (K-H 955.3); the prefix may signify "thoroughly" (19.4n.) or "up" and "out" (*OLD excepto* 1); it does the
latter in *extulit*.

48 When news of the attack reaches those Gauls commandeered to fortify
the hillside (§1), they rush back to defend the town wall (§2), tipping the
scales in the Gauls' favor, as dramatized, once more, by the comportment

of the women (§3). The *Romani* (thrice, not *nostri*) begin to yield (§4). The narrative proceeds lucidly (cf. 18n.).

48.1 ad alteram partem oppidi: 44.3n. **ut supra demonstrauimus:** 17.1n. **munitionis causa:** 45.6n. **primo exaudito clamore, inde etiam … incitati** "first, they heard shouting in the distance, then they were aroused further …." *primo* is, as *inde* clarifies, an adverb (different from 28.5 *primo clamore audito*). The abl. absolute and the participial construction form a chiasmus. *clamorem exaudire* (again 81.3) is a Caesarian mannerism (5x, and *BAlex.* 20.5); it may have influenced Livy (5x). **oppidum … teneri** specifies the message; a panicked exaggeration (47.4n. *intra portas*). **magno cursu:** also 3.19.1 *huc … contenderunt, BC* 1.70.4 (*BAlex.* 20.5).

48.2 eorum ut quisque primus uenerat "as soon as each one of them arrived"; in the absence of a superlative (or comparative) in the main clause, *ut quisque* expresses sequentiality (K-S II 486; the second place of the indefinite *ut* is the original standard position [Courtney 1999: 10]); the pluperf. is regular in "generalizing clauses of repeated action" (*NLS* §271b). The expression recurs in Livy 23.23.5. **sub muro:** 36.5n. *sub*.

48.3 Pointed echoes invite comparison with 47.5. Differences appear: instead of *passis manibus* now *passum capillum*; and instead of *nudo pectore*, there is now mention of *liberi*. Comparison with Polyb. 9.6.3 reveals the scene's highly rhetorical nature (47.5–6n.): terror-stricken women "implored the gods, sweeping the temple grounds with their hair (cf. *passum capillum*); for this it was their custom to do (cf. *more Gallico*) …." **matres familiae:** 47.5, 26.3n. **quae … Romanis … tendebant:** 47.5n. The dative (instead of *ad Romanos* [K-S I 320]) is rare. For the imperfect serving instead of the pluperfect ("had just a moment ago extended"), see K-S I 154; it here signifies the rapid change. **suos obtestari** pointedly echoes 47.5 *obtestabantur Romanos*. **more Gallico:** 2.2n. *quo more*. **passum capillum** is already attested in Ter. *Phorm.* 106 and Quadrig. *FRHist* F16; *sparsi capilli* first occur at Prop. 2.1.7; nor is *spargere* attested (elsewhere) in *CC*. Disheveled hair expresses distress; it is a common motif in elegy and historiography (*effuso tristis captiua capillo*, Ov. *Am.* 1.7.39; note the quasi-formulaic *crinibus passis*, e.g. Verg. *Aen.* 1.479; 47.5n.). **ostentare … in conspectum proferre:** "theme and variation"; the latter phrase is itself pleonastic (*proferre* = "to put on view," *OLD* 2). **liberos:** the presentation of children in Greek and Roman courts of law and during supplications served a similar emotive purpose (cf. Cic. *De or.* 1.245; Treggiari 2005: 13–14, O'Connell 2017: 10); 26.3n.

48.4 There is a balanced series of pairings: *loco … numero, cursu … spatio, recentes … integros.* **erat**: 30.1n. *fuit.* **nec loco nec numero**: again 49.1, 50.1. *locus*: 45.9n. To credit the enemy with superior numbers is commonplace (by inversion, one's own troops are "the heroic few" [Murrin 1994: 162–67]): Hdt. 7.228, Polyb. 6.55.1, Cato *FRHist* F76 *tandem superat multitudo*, Sall. *Cat.* 7.7 *maxumas hostium copias populus Romanus parua manu*, Livy 6.13.1, Tac. *Agr.* 35.2. Gallic hordes: 21.1n. **aequa contentio** occurs, surprisingly, just once more (Cic. *Verr.* 3.177). *aequus*: 19.3n. **defatigati … sustinebant**: a commonplace of battle descriptions (esp. in sieges [25.1n. *recentes defessis*]), for which C. uses formulaic language. It is here vacuous, as the Gauls would be just as exhausted from hurrying back from the hill. **cursu**: Veg. 3.11 *multum uirium labore itineris pugnaturus amittit*; Onas. 6.9. **non facile** serves C. as adverb instead of *difficiliter/ difficulter* (only *BC* 1.62.1). **recentes atque integros** "fresh and unhurt" (Edwards); the binomial is frequent in Livy.

49 C. watches the tides turning, foresees a disaster, and, quick-wittedly once more (44–52n.), takes remedial measures. The section comprises the typical sequence of observation, reasoning, decision (27n.); narratologically, it also serves *ritardando*.

49.1 C. observes the developments (from a suitably chosen position [85.1n.]) and orchestrates his troops' actions, as a general should (87.3n. *proelio intersit*). **Caesar cum**: 12.1n. *Vercingetorix ubi.* **iniquo loco … copias**: 48.4n. *nec loco nec numero.* **praemetuens**: a rare word of poetic flavor probably owed to Lucr. (3.1017; Verg. *Aen.* 2.573; 1.2n. *addunt*). **Titum Sextium**: he probably joined C. the year before (6.1.1) and fought with him during the civil war (*RE* "Sextius" 13); 90.6. **minoribus castris**: on La Roche Blanche (36n.). **praesidio reliquerat**: 40.3n. **misit**: 9.5n. **sub infimo colle** "down at the foot of the hill," i.e. of Gergovia rather than La Roche Blanche (as 51.2 suggests). **ab … hostium**: as the attack was happening to the right (eastward) of the smaller camp.

49.2 ut … quo minus libere hostes insequerentur terreret "(and) that he scare the enemy away from pursuing [them] freely." I understand the second *ut* as asyndetically coordinate with the first, introducing another command (not a subordinate purpose clause). **uidisset**: 27.2n. *ascendissent.* The subject is Sextius, not C. (§3 *ipse*).

49.3 ex eo loco … ubi constiterat "from the place where he had halted"; 47.1 *constiterunt.* **legione**: sc. *decima*; cf. 47.1n. **euentum … exspectabat**: similarly *BC* 1.53.2. The phrase recurs Sall. *Cat.* 37.9; Livy 6.7.6, 8.11.2, 42.61.7. A general's looking at a battle unfolding is a commonplace in

classical historiography, most famously instantiated at Hdt. 7.212 where
Xerxes is "watching and leaping out of his seat thrice in fear for his army";
it is related to the *teichoscopy* (88.5n.). **pugnae** resumes §1 *pugnari* (cf.
16.3n. *itineribus*).

50 C.'s soldiers struggle, then panic when they mistake Aeduan auxiliaries for enemy troops. Amidst the mayhem one centurion saves his
subordinates.

In Valerius' discussion of Roman virtues, *fortitudo* tellingly comes first
(3.2 *init.*; Wardle 1997: 326; cf. Enn. *Ann.* 470 *fortes Romani sunt tan-
quam caelus profundus*). C. appears therein as *certissima uerae uirtutis effigies*
and *optimus uirtutis aestimator* (3.2.19+23). It is in this latter role that he
sketches Petronius as an *exemplum*, heroic in word and deed (cf. Roller
2004: 4–8 on the "exemplary" discourse). But while celebrating through
him Roman soldiers more generally, whom C. inspired "to face any danger" (Plut. *Caes.* 16.1), it allows him to distract from the defeat and excul-
pate the general (Welch 1998: 90, Rambaud 230–31): for Petronius, in
two direct speeches, confesses to recklessness, for which he atones by
self-sacrifice. Further discussion: Brown 2004: 292n.1, Bellemore 2016:
891n.15.

50.1–2 Thuc. narrates how, during the battle for Delium, the Theban
commander "sent two cavalry contingents secretly around the hill (ἐκ τοῦ
ἀφανοῦς περὶ τὸν λόφον, 4.96.6; cf. *alio ascensu*)" to relieve his troops; "by
their sudden appearance above (ὑπερφανέντων αἰφνιδίως; cf. *subito … uisi*)"
the Athenians, "believing another army to be approaching (νομίσαν …
ἐπιέναι; cf. *id ipsum … existimabant*), panicked (ἐς φόβον καταστῆναι; cf. *uehementer nostros perterruerunt*)." **acerrime … pugnaretur** is military diction (cf.
Cic. *Phil.* 8.17 *res geritur; conductae uineae sunt; pugnatur acerrime*) and freq.
in *CC*; 25.1n. *pugnaretur*, 87.1n. *uehementius pugnaretur*. **comminus** is "a
military term derived from *cum manu*" (Roche on Luc. 1.206); *eminus* is
its regular opposite. **hostes …, nostri … confiderent**: an adversative asyndeton; the brachylogy: 20.6n. *interuenerint*. **loco et numero … uirtute**: the
clichéd antithesis varies the one at 22.1n. *uirtuti. loco et numero*: 48.4n.
subito is emphasized by position and *sunt* (14.2n. *esse*); 26.3n. *repente*. **ab
latere nostris aperto**: 62.3n. *ab … cornu. nostris* is *apo koinou* with *uisi* and
aperto. ab latere aperto (7x in C. incl. 82.2; 2x in *BAlex.*) may be "a technical
military phrase" (Holmes on 1.25.6); 25.1n. *apertos*. It would have been
their right side (facing east, most likely), as the shield was carried in the
left hand. **ab dextra parte alio ascensu … miserat** = 45.10. **manus disti-
nendae causa** "to distract (or: divide [*OLD* 3a, b]) the (enemy) troops";
again *BC* 3.52.1 (*BAlex.* 17.3); *manum distinere* appears in *CC* only (*TLL*
5.1.1522.73–80).

50.2 C. is generally interested in "the aetiology of military panic" (1.39, 6.37.3–9, 7.84; *BC* 3.72.4; Lendon 2015: 7). The reaction is understandable: The appearance of enemy troops on the blind side was a time-honored stratagem to cause panic (Frontin. *Str.* 2.4); auxiliary troops were known to desert in the midst of combat (ibid. 2.7); in fact, C.'s first defeat in Gaul had been effected by deserting Aeduan cavalry (1.15, 18.10)! **dextris umeris exsertis** "their right shoulders uncovered"; an abl. of quality. The verb occurs only here in *CC*. Couissin 1931 reviews the evidence of Gallic dress concluding that the Aedui affixed the *sagum* to their left shoulder and ran it underneath their right arm, thus leaving the right shoulder free. Romans may have associated this with the ἐξωμίς, a tunic that left the right shoulder free and was often worn by laborers (Plaut. *Mil.* 1180; Sen. *Herc. Fur.* 766; Amelung in *RE* III 2.2328–30). Doubts: 44–56n. **quod insigne pactum esse consuerat** "which was the customary sign (45.7n. *insignibus*) agreed upon." Heller's conjecture has found favor, making this the only instance of *pangere/pacisci* in C. (once *BAlex.* 55).

50.3–4 It may have been a feature of the military report to acknowledge by name officers killed (Rambaud 29). C. likes (contrastive) pairings, including 1.18.1, 5.24.5, 5.44.1 *Pullo et … Vorenus*. They are a feature of classical historiography ever since Solon's encounter with Croesus (Hdt. 1.29–33). **quique** = *et ei qui*, the rel. clause standing in for the subject (31.3n.). **circumuenti atque interfecti**: again 62.7, 80.7; a Caesarian mannerism (9x and *BAfr.* 76.1), but otherwise unattested save for Livy and Frontinus. **murum ascenderant**: 47.7n. **murum … muro**: the polyptoton represents the reversal of fortune. **praecipitabantur**: *BHisp.* 15.6 identifies this as a barbaric custom; other instances include Livy 41.11.5, Val. Max. 9.2.4, Joseph. *BJ* 7.3.23.

50.4–6 The close parallels in Vergil's account of Anchises' woeful refusal to flee from Troy may bespeak C.'s influence; at the least, they document the poetic affinities of his episode: *abnegat excisa uitam producere Troia | exsiliumque pati. "uos o, quibus integer aeui | sanguis," ait, "solidaeque suo stant robore uires, | uos agitate fugam. | me si caelicolae uoluissent ducere uitam, | has mihi seruassent sedes* (*Aen.* 2.636–42). Diod. Sic. 17.63.4 is strikingly close, too: "surrounded and despairing over his situation, he ordered the other soldiers at least to hurry away and save themselves," περικατάληπτος δὲ γενόμενος καὶ τὰ καθ᾽ ἑαυτὸν ἀπογνοὺς τοῖς μὲν ἄλλοις στρατιώταις προσέταξεν ἀπιέναι τὴν ταχίστην καὶ διασώζειν αὑτούς. Within the *CC*, Sextius Baculus' deed is closest (6.38). **Petronius**, of whom nothing else is known (*RE* 90), is honored with an *aristeia*, demonstrating "defiance of death" (Cic. *Tusc.* 2.43 [quoted at 25.2n.]). His self-sacrifice may bring to mind the *piaculum*, "expiatory offering": *datum hoc … est ut luendis periculis publicis* *piacula simus* (Livy 10.28.13; Versnel 1981: 135–94; 89.2n.). One might more specifically think of Horatius Cocles or Cato's "Roman Leonidas" (Polyb. 6.55; *FRHist* F76). On solidarity in the Roman army, cf. the materials in Horsfall 1999: 111–12. **eiusdem legionis**: sc. VIII (46.7). **portas excīdere**: the verb, "cut out, hack a way through" (*OLD* 3b), first here in C. The expression is unparalleled. Most likely, Petronius was trying to break into Gergovia (47.3n. *portis*); but now sallying into enemy ranks, he cuts a path for his men. **sibi desperans**: Cic. *Mur.* 45 *sibi hic ipse desperat.* *desperare* rarely construes with the dative (once more in *CC* [3.12.3]). **multis ... uulneribus acceptis** occurs 5x in *BG* (again 82.2; cf. 81.5), and is generally quite freq. The motif is another cliché: Cato *FRHist* F76 *saucius multifariam ibi factus*, Polyb. 6.55.2 τραυμάτων πλῆθος ἀναδεχόμενος, Diod. Sic. 17.63.4. **manipularibus**: 47.7n. **inquit**: Petronius' speeches may strike us as "almost operatic in [their] nobility and implausibility" (Powell 1998: 123); but their rhetorical effectiveness for a Roman audience should not be doubted. **me una uobiscum** recurs at *BC* 2.31.8. **prospiciam uestrae quidem certe uitae** "I shall make provision for (*OLD* 6) *your* lives, at any rate"; *quidem* is both adversative and limiting in sense (Solodow 1978: 92–93). The *corona ciuica* recognized soldiers for saving a fellow soldier's life; C. had one (Suet. *Iul.* 2). **adductus ... deduxi**: similarly 6.10.2 *homines inopia cibariorum adductos ad iniquam pugnandi condicionem posse deduci.* This particular wordplay (43.5n. *profectio*) also occurs in Plaut. *Mil.* 790; Cic. *Att.* 7.15.2, *Sull.* 87 (with Berry). **cupiditate gloriae**: Petronius confesses to a very Roman fault (cf. Cic. *Cael.* 74 *uellem alio potius eum cupiditas gloriae detulisset*; Polyb. 6.55.4 on the Romans' "burning love of honor," ὁρμὴ καὶ φιλοτιμία). But it stands in tension with C.'s earlier warning of a different kind of desire (45.8 *spe praedae*); and he will be harsher still in his address (52.1n. *temeritatem cupiditatemque*). **in periculum deduxi**: the expression also occurs 5.31.1; *BC* 1.19.4; rarely elsewhere. But *BAlex.* 7.1 *ad extremum periculi ... deducti*, and esp. (given the context) Hor. *Carm.* 2.7.1–2 *O saepe mecum tempus in ultimum | deducte Bruto militiae duce*, may suggest a wider (military?) use. **uos ... uobis**: this polyptoton combines with *uobiscum* and *uestrae* in a tone of an urgent plea.

50.5 in medios hostes irrupit may be formulaic: cf. Cicero on the self-sacrifice of *Codrum qui se in medios immisit hostis* and the Decii [*quorum*] *deuota uita inmisit in armatas hostium copias* (*Tusc.* 1.116, *Paradox.* 12; Livy 8.9.9 [9.4.10] *se in medios hostes immisit*).

50.6 conantibus ... conamini: 20.12n. *recipiat.* **meae uitae ... quem**: a common reference of the relative to a possessive (K-S I 30). **sanguis uiresque deficiunt** is a commonplace: Cato *FRHist* F76 *defetigatum uulneribus atque* *quod sanguen eius defluxerat*, Livy 25.14.9 *uires et sanguis desereret*, Ov. *Met.* 7.857 *fugiunt cum sanguine uires*; Curt. 8.14.36. It can be traced back to Homer (e.g. *Il.* 5.296 λύθη ψυχή τε μένος τε). **est facultas** repeats *data facultate* for urgency. **pugnans post paulo**: the standard order is *paulo post*; this rare arrangement recurs 60.4; *BC* 1.20.4, 2.30.4, and in Hor., Sall., Livy, and Quint. (*TLL* 10.1.833.8–10). The triple alliteration: cf. 18.1n. *captiuis*. **suis saluti fuit**: an *epiphonema* typically concludes the presentation of an exemplary deed; cf. Polyb. 6.55.3 on Cocles "sacrificing his life, as he valued his country's safety higher …," Cato *FRHist* F76 *exercitum ceterum seruauit*.

51 The Romans' flight, starkly contrasting with an earlier withdrawal (12.5–6), would have descended into a rout but for C.'s interventions: The X legion, as positioned by him, slows the pursuant Gauls; and Sextius awaits the action with cohorts on higher ground and the camp at his back, just as commanded. C.'s arrangements agree with recommendations in military handbooks in case of defeat (Veg. 3.25): *nam si uicini colles fuerint, si post terga munitio, si ceteris abscedentibus fortissimi quique restiterint, se suosque seruabunt*. He thus saves his troops from their mistake despite the disadvantageous position, which is variously emphasized once more (*deiecti, aequiore, planitiem, radicibus collis*; 45.9n. *iniquitas*), and demonstrates the *consilium* he would claim for himself at the assembly (52n.). He saves his troops a second time by opting for circumlocutions instead of the ignominious term *fuga* (on Roman attitudes to which, cf. Rich 2012: 89–90).

51.1 To stand one's ground in battle was a tenet of the Greek and Roman ideology of war; hence Lysias' paradoxical praise of the Spartans who "were not worsted by their opponents but died right where they had been positioned to fight" (2.31) and Tacitus' pejorative remark on Germanic tactics: *cedere loco … consilii quam formidinis arbitrantur* (*Germ.* 6.4, with Perl). As for legionaries in particular, Polybius declares that they deemed nothing higher than "not to flee nor quit their ranks" (3.84.7, albeit an idealization). **Nostri cum**: 12.1n. *Vercingetorix ubi*. **premerentur**: an instance of the "pressing metaphor" (Lendon 1999: 286); 10.3n. *impetum*. **XLVI centurionibus amissis**: the casualties among centurions are high, just as they were at the Sambre, Dyrrachium, and Pharsalia (2.25; *BC* 3.71.1, 3.99.1). This may indicate that, by C.'s time, the role of the centurion was not just "to stand the ground" but "to lead the charge" (Lendon 2005: 218–19). On casualty figures: 28.5n. **deiecti sunt loco** "driven out from (*OLD* 8) their position," the prefix alluding to the height. **intolerantius** "rather impatiently"; adjective and adverb are rare and occur only here in *CC*. Military handbooks warn of hasty pursuit (Onas. 11.1, Frontin. *Str.* 2.3.14). **insequentes** echoes 49.2 *insequerentur*, helping the reader realize the accuracy of C.'s foresight (*Introd.* 3b). **legio decima**: 49.3n. **pro subsidio** "by way of (*OLD* 8a) support."

51.2 rursus "in its turn," *OLD* 4b. **exceperunt** "they aided them"; an unusual use (*TLL* 5.2.1251.81–83), paralleled at 5.16.4. **quae ... legato**: 49.1.

51.3 legiones ubi: 12.1n. *Vercingetorix ubi.* **infestis ... signis** "with their standards turned to attack the enemy," a military expression (*TLL* 7.1.1406.82–85); 62.6n. *signa.*

51.4 ab radicibus collis: 36.5n. **intra ... reduxit**: *BAfr.* 61.2 *exercitum intra munitiones suas reducere*, cf. *BC* 1.41.6. The construction is rare. **paulo minus septingenti**: 15.1n. *amplius.* Suet. *Iul.* 25.2 speaks of a *legio fusa.* Within the *BG*, C. specifies Roman losses once more at 4.12.3 (Richter 1977: 165; *BC*: 1.46.4–5, 3.71.1, 99.1; cf. 2.42.5). Oros. *Hist.* 7.10.4 speaks *de reticendo interfectorum numero* as a general Roman practice; the material evidence shows similar tendencies (Hölscher 1991: 288–90). On the question of how Romans counted their losses, see Peretz 2005: 131–32. **desiderati**: C. here employs the verb specifically of those fallen in war for the first time in Latin literature (*TLL* 5.1.703.21 [misunderstanding 7.11.8]; Peretz 2005: 129n.35 reviews the epigraphic evidence). He will be followed by later historians and military writers. In fact, both the euphemism (for "killed") and the use of the passive voice (instead of "the Gauls killed 700 of us") are typical of war literature (Fussell 1975: 189–94).

52 Following the defeat, C. calls an assembly, as V. had following Avaricum (29n.). Yet while the latter combined *cohortatio* and *consolatio*, C. combines *cohortatio* and *reprehensio* (§§1, 3 *reprehendere*; cf. his criticisms at 1.40 [with several parallels], *BC* 3.60, Suet. *Iul.* 66). But instead of charging his troops with insubordination – recruits took the *sacramentum*, swearing obedience to their commander – he states military tenets (Chrissanthos 2013: 321–23; McDonnell 2006: 301–04; Riggsby 83–106): that the soldiers and generals' responsibilities differ, that the former's *uirtus* be paired with *disciplina* and guided by the latter's *consilium*, as otherwise it may deteriorate into *temeritas* (cf. Polyb. 6.36.6–39.11; Harris 2006: 305–10). While thus denying his liability (44–56n.), he softens his soldiers' blame by acknowledging their *magnitudo animi* (§3n.). He proceeds similarly in his apologetic account of Curio's defeat (*BC* 2.38): *auctoribus temere credens consilium commutat ... multum ... adiuuat adulescentia, magnitudo animi, superioris temporis prouentus, fiducia rei bene gerendae* (the comparison with C.'s words after Dyrrachium [*BC* 3.73] is instructive, too). In the end, he forgoes punishment; the reasons specified at *BC* 3.60.1 apply: *Caesar neque tempus illud animaduersionis esse existimans et multa uirtuti eorum concedens.* The speech, addressed to the external audience in Rome, "rewrites" the defeat in the same way as his narrative (a mise-en-abyme; on "rewriting" defeat, cf. Clark 2014: 44–47).

52.1 Postero die: 27.1n. **contione aduocata** is a standard expression (*TLL* 1.893.12–20). For the functions of the military assembly: Pina Polo 1995. The *BG* contains four *contiones* (Murphy 1949: 126): 1.40, 7.14, 66. **temeritatem militum cupiditatemque**: this *coniunctio* (47.3n. *oppidi*), the first of several pairings, sternly resumes C.'s talk about *studio pugnandi aut spe praedae* (45.8n.) and "corrects" Petronius' appeal to *cupiditas gloriae* (50.4; cf. 15.5n. *perangustum*). On *temeritas*, tellingly in first place, cf. *Rhet. Her.* 3.3.6 *quam ille fortitudinem nominarit, eam nos gladiatoriam et inconsideratam appellauimus temeritatem*; Cic. *Rab. Post.* 2 *ut grauissimo uerbo utar: temeritatem.* Its difference from *uirtus* is a common topic (Thuc. 3.82.4 τόλμα ... ἀνδρεία ... ἐνομίσθη), esp. in philosophical discourse (where it is further contrasted to *magnitudo animi* [Dyck 1981]). In *BG*, it generally applies to the Gauls (42.2n.), only here and 5.52.6 to Romans (cf. Grillo 2012: 33n.51; Combés 1966: 278). *cupiditas*, meanwhile, oscillates between the more forgiving "passion" and the decidedly negative "greed" (Seyffert-Müller on Cic. *Amic.* 19). **quod ... uideretur**: cf. 1.40.1 *quod aut quam in partem aut quo consilio ducerentur sibi quaerendum aut cogitandum putarent* (sc. *milites*). **quod** is epexegetical, specifying the nature of their "greedy recklessness." **sibi ipsi iudicauissent quo ... uideretur** "they had presumptuously decided for themselves where it seemed ‹best› ..."; the slightly pleonastic phrasing: 25.1n. *uisum.* Any initiative on the soldiers' part required the general's confirmation, as Livy exemplifies in T. Manlius: *"iniussu tuo" inquit, "imperator, extra ordinem nunquam pugnauerim, non si certam uictoriam uideam* (Livy 7.10.2, with Oakley). **a tribunis militum legatisque retineri** repeats 47.2.

52.2 This reminder of C.'s care renders his criticism more effective; it matters "whether [the critic] is well-disposed towards [the criticized]," Phld. *De lib. dic.* Fr. 74. **iniquitas loci**: 45.9n. Repeated below, it forms an emphatic *cyclos.* **quid ... sensisset**: 19.3–5. This second (anaphoric and asyndetic) question specifies the first in a lively fashion by way of an example (which Vielhaber's *quod* simplifies). **sine ... equitatu**: 20.1. **exploratam uictoriam**: 15.2n. On C.'s confidence in victory: 19.4n. **paruum modo detrimentum** "even (*OLD modo* 1a) the smallest loss"; similarly 6.35.3 *paruam modo causam timoris* (*BAfr.* 54.1 *paruulam modo causulam*). At the time, however, C. emphasized the risk of a great loss of many lives (19.4n.).

52.3 To mix criticism with praise was recommended practice (cf. Phld. *De lib. dic.* T4.1 [Konstan] "when he first has stung by his reproach [διὰ τῆς ἐπιτ[ι]μήσεως] he will come to praise"). The different roles of soldiers and leaders are commonly discussed (Isoc. *Ep.* 2.2, *BG* 1.40, Tac. *Hist.* 3.20); cf. 19n. and *BC* 3.51.4 (partly quoted at 5.3n. *legatorum*). **quanto opere … animi magnitudinem … tanto opere … animi magnitudinem**: the carefully crafted period, which centers on the ring-compositional *magnitudo animi*, begins with admiration, mixes in criticism, and ends with a request. Whenever C. speaks of *magnitudo animi*, "high-spiritedness," a calque of *megalopsychia* popular with Cic. (who thought it characteristic of the Romans [*Off.* 1.61, with Knoche 1935]) and Sen. especially, the context suggests that it connotes more than just *fortitudo* (2.27.5, of the Nervii, *BC* 2.38.2, of Curio, with Mutschler 1975: 75–77); here the following relative clause makes it clear. **quos non … non … potuisset**: the anaphoric *non* is emphatic (28.4n.). **licentiam arrogantiamque**: the pairing is, surprisingly, unparalleled. *licentia* (first here in C.) is characterized by an act or expression lacking "restraint and moderation" (Wirszubski 1950: 7): *putabant per licentiam insolescere animum humanum* (Sall. *Cat.* 6.7). *arrogantia* is otherwise only predicated of Ariovistus in *BG* (1.33.4, 40.4). But in his criticism at Vesontio C. says (1.40.10): *facere arroganter* (sc. *milites*), *cum aut de officio imperatoris desperare aut praescribere uiderentur.*

52.4 C. concludes with an *epiphonema* (cf. 20.3–12n.). It reformulates a commonplace; cf. Cic. *Tusc.* 1.2 *in [re militari] cum uirtute nostri multum ualuerunt, tum plus etiam disciplina* (with Oakley 1985: 405n.120 on tensions). Xen. *Cyr.* 2.1.22 succinctly defines the ideal soldier as φιλοκίνδυνος μετ' εὐταξίας, "keen on danger in a disciplined fashion." **non minus … quam**: 31.1n. **modestiam et continentiam**: in this context, *modestia* (*militaris*) = "military subordination" becomes "a semi-technical term" (Goodyear on Tac. *Ann.* 1.35.1); but, as a virtue, it is also a natural check on *cupiditas* (*modestia est in animo continens moderatio cupiditatem* [*Rhet. Her.* 3.2.3]); as is *continentia*, "self-restraint" (*per quam cupiditas … regitur* [Cic. *Inv. rhet.* 2.54]). C. had previously lectured his men on *quantum haberet in se boni constantia* (1.40.6). **de uictoria atque exitu rerum**: the pairing, wherein the former is a specific outcome of the latter (45.2n. *mulorumque*), is rare but anticipated in Cic. *De or.* 2.72 *uis oratoris … exitu et uictoria iudicatur.* **uirtutem atque animi magnitudinem**: the pairing (again *BAlex.* 15.1, 32.3) is quite popular with Cicero (e.g. *Prov. cons.* 27, of Pompey). Roman commanders typically blamed defeat on the lack of *uirtus militum* (Rosenstein 1990: 92–113); C. does, in effect, the opposite.

53–56 The escape artist

After minor engagements to avoid the impression of flight (53.2n.), C. escapes from Gergovia in a northerly direction towards the Aedui (Thévenot 1960: 69); he crosses the Allier undisturbed (near Vichy, possibly [53.4n. *Eleuar*]). It is there that, hemmed in by the Allier and the Loire, he is finally abandoned by his Aeduan protégés (ending the Aeduan leitmotif [Gärtner 1975: 84]; *Introd.* 3c). They hurry on to destroy Noviodunum with its Roman goods, leaving C. deprived of supplies, barred from corn and cattle, and separated from Labienus. But then, instead of retreating in a southerly direction (towards *prouincia* [56.3n. *opinionem*, 66.3n. *fugere*]), he hurries farther up north, marching day and night to reach and cross the Loire (56.3) to reunite with Labienus (62.10n. *ad Caesarem*).

The Aedui fully desert C. at the worst time; he may have been led into a trap for a second time (nn. on 53.4 *ne ... quidem*; 36–56). Then again, C.'s by-the-skin-of-his-teeth escape has been identified as the major *peripeteia* in *VII* (Görler 1977: 321–23), and the plot builds towards it a little too neatly (cf. 55n.); further details: 44–52n.

53 To rekindle confidence, C. challenges V. to battle on level ground. After favorable engagements, he finally leaves Gergovia. The repetition of *confirmare* indicates C.'s primary concern; hints of sarcasm and scorn (*nihilo minus, Gallicam ostentationem, ne tum quidem*) intimate unease.

53.1 is a typical Caesarian period with its abl. absolutes, participial construction, subordinate clauses, and conclusive terse main clauses. **hac habita contione**: at 52.1, *contione* (which *hac* resumes) = "assembly"; so here (rather than "speech" [*TLL* 4.733.47]), as further suggested by *oratione* (though *oratio* may signify "message" [*OLD* 5a]). **ad extremum** "at the end [sc. of the assembly]"; cf. 4.4.1 *ad extremum tamen ... expulsi*; *Tursellinus* I 132. α's *extremam orationem* is a simplification. **oratione confirmatis militibus**: as a *cohortatio* was supposed to do (52n.). **ne ... tribuerent**: the *ne*-clause might depend upon *confirmatis* (Edwards; cf. Sall. *Iug.* 23.2, Livy 2.24.2) or summarize the gist of the *oratio* (43.5n. *ne*). But C. typically specifies his motivation before the action; so probably here: *ne* and *neu* introduce final clauses dependent upon *eduxit*. **ob hanc causam** "as a result of this" (*OLD causa* 9a). **animo permouerentur**: 9.1n. *opinione*; the singular: 1.5n. *capitis*. **iniquitas loci ... uirtuti hostium**: C. deploys the same antithesis as V. (50.1, 22.1n.). *iniquitas loci*: 45.9n. **eadem ... cogitans ... senserat**: the participle resumes 44.1 *cogitans* (marking off the Gergovian attack [cf. 28.6n. *misericordia*]); his thoughts: 43.5. This reiteration smacks of "protesting too much" (36–56n.). **legiones ... constituit**: §4 *tertio die*

suggests that C. offered battle on the same day as the *contio*. **aciemque idoneo loco constituit**: the favored formation (*acies triplex* [1.24.2]) consisted
of a first line of four cohorts, behind which three cohorts were staggered,
followed by a third line of three cohorts in reserve (Keppie 1998: 64–65,
173). *locus idoneus*: 35.5n.

53.2 C. knows to offer battle to rekindle his soldiers' confidence (cf.
Livy 39.30.7; Tac. *Ann.* 4.49.1 [with Woodman]; Veg. 3.10; Rosenstein
1990: 138n.91). It is here all the more important, as he must not give
the impression of flight when, momentarily, he withdraws (cf. Veg. 3.22;
Oros. 6.11.6 *uictus aufugit* perhaps echoes an alternative interpretation).
V. accepts the challenge to avoid appearing weak (cf. 19.4nn. and 3.24.5;
Polyb. 3.89.1; Tac. *Ann.* 6.34.1; on the psychology, see Goldsworthy 1996:
143–45; Lendon 2005: 200–02); but only as far as cavalry engagements.
nihilo minus: C.'s sarcasm – V. descended *even* onto level ground – has
escaped those who accept Vascosanus' suggestion of *nihilo magis* (cf. Stem
2017). **in aequum locum** contrasts (by way of *paronomasia*) with §1 *iniquitas loci* (cf. 19.3n. *aequo*); C. continues his apologetic theme (45.9n.).
leui … proelio = 36.1. **atque** "and, what is more" (*OLD* 1b, "followed by a
demonstrative").

53.3 Military writers encourage generals to ascertain their soldiers' mood
(Veg. 3.12.1). For similar reflections on morale, cf. 6.38.4; *BC* 3.65.1;
Lendon 1999: 295–304. **postero die**: 18.1n. **ad Gallicam ostentationem
minuendam**: cf. 19.3n. *inani simulatione* on "boasting" (*OLD ostentatio*
2b) "in the Gallic fashion" (47.7n. *Auaricensibus*) and C.'s reasoning at
4.16.1. **militumque**: the gen. is fronted in contrast with *Gallicam*. **animos
confirmandos**: just as V. busied his soldiers to strengthen them (29.7n.
instituerent). **in Haeduos** "in the direction of the Aedui" (*OLD in* 15). This
mention prepares for their reappearance on the dramatic scene in 54
(cf. 22n.).

53.4 ne tum quidem: C. intimates that his recent "victories" made
the Gauls indisposed to following him. He "colors" the situation to
his advantage; chances are even, they did not follow as they wanted
C. to cross (54n.). **tertio die**: sc. on the second day after the *contio*.
ad flumen Elauer: Napoleon III speculated it was at Vichy, about 35
miles away from Gergovia, and thus within a day's march (Thévenot
1960: 96–99). **reuersus**: Gertz's conjecture makes better sense than
the transmitted text (which should be compared to *BC* 1.61.6 *ad eum
locum fluminis … pontem imperant fieri*) and is palaeographically plausible, as *Elauer reuersus* might have caused the omission. **pontem refecit**:
as before (35.4).

54 C. is approached by his Aeduan protégés asking for leave in order to prevent their people from falling for Litaviccus' scheme (the timing is vicious, as C. is hemmed in by the Allier and Loire [Thévenot 1960: 97]). He obliges them, though cognizant of their treacherous intent. His reasoning identifies him as psychologically astute (§2n. *suspicionem*) and worthy of wielding the *patrocinium orbis* (10.1–2n.), as it exercises *imperium ... beneficiis ..., non iniuriis* (Cic. *Off.* 2.26; §2n. *iniuriam*, §3n. *merita*).

54.1 Haeduis ... Haeduos: the polyptoton visualizes the factions (cf. 32n.). **cum omni equitatu Litauiccus**: presumably merely the cavalry entrusted him (37.7); but the unqualified *omni* amplifies the significance (cf. 66.7n. *equites*). L. was last heard to be on his way to Gergovia (40.7, 43; 55.4n. *receptum*). **sollicitandos ... confirmandam**: cf. Plancus [Cic.] *Fam.* 10.8.3 *confirmandus erat exercitus nobis magnis saepe praemiis sollicitatus.* **ipsos** "they, in turn" (1.2n.).

54.2 C. continues his conciliatory dissimulation (cf. 43.4nn.). **perfidiam ... perspectam habet** "he had fully realized their treachery"; cf. 29.6n. *effectum.* This Roman charge of *perfidia* (17.7n.) should be related to the Aeduan experience of "*fides*" *Romana* in their war against the *Sequani* when they received no help (1.44.9; Thévenot 1960: 15–16; Scullard 1962: 178). **discessu**: 5.1n. *aduentu.* **admaturari** is a *hapax legomenon*, and editors have typically opted for β's *maturari*. But other extremely rare compound verbs with *ad-* are attested (Cic. *Rosc. Am.* 26 *appromitteret*), and its meaning suits the context beautifully: the prefix may express "towards completion" (Van Laer 2010: 43), and next we hear of the Aedui, they have, in fact, defected (59.1). **inferre iniuriam**: for the dreaded implications, cf. Cic. *Sest.* 58 *ille* (sc. *Tigranes*) *iniuriis in socios nostros inferendis bello prope nos lacessisset.* **ne ... aliquam suspicionem**: *aliqui* is used after *ne* when a vague "possibility is suggested but immediately denied" (H-S 195; cf. Nettleship 126.4; 20.6n. *alicuius*). It is a military commonplace that a fearful impression emboldens the enemy (cf. Xen. *Hell.* 3.5.22; 3.24.5 *opinione timoris hostes nostros milites alacriores ad pugnandum effecissent,* 6.7.8 *quo ... timoris det suspicionem,* Lendon 1999: 306–16).

54.3–4 Rhetorical handbooks recommend the mention of services to secure sympathy: *beniuolentiam contrahemus si nostrum officium sine arrogantia laudabimus, atque ... quales fuerimus ... in eos qui audiunt aperiemus* (*Rhet. Her.* 1.8). C. had used the device before (1.43.4). His terse language (*breuiter exposuit*) bespeaks *auctoritas* (Quint. 4.5.24–25, 6.3.30+33). **discedentibus** resumes *discessu* (7.1n. *missus*). **breuiter ... exposuit**: the verb suggests the *expositio* (*est cum res, quibus de rebus dicturi sumus, exponimus breuiter et absolute* [*Rhet. Her.* 1.10.17]; cf. 63.1n. *augetur*). It here substitutes for a

proper speech. **merita** replaces the possibly offensive *beneficia* (37.4n.).
quos ... accepisset: prior to C.'s arrival, the Aedui were dominated by the
Sequani and Arverni (5.2n. *Haeduos*). **quos** = *quales*. **et** "and, what is more"
(*OLD* 1). **humiles** "humiliated" (cf. *TLL* 6.3.3112.15–19). **compulsos ...
extortis**: the five participles, in apposition to *quos ... humiles*, detail the
humiliation. Both the coordination of predicative participles and abl.
absolutes and the mix of parallel and chiastic structures are typical of C.
The asyndetic *expositio*: 63n. The account rephrases 6.12.4 and 1.31.6–8.
compulsos in oppida: again 77.12; *BC* 1.47.3; then in Livy (e.g. 2.33.4),
but not elsewhere. *compellere in* is not attested before C., overall rare, and
likely military (*TLL* 3.2029.73–30.6). **multatos agris** "dispossessed (by
way of punishment) of fields." **sociis** rather than α's *copiis*, as indicated by
6.12.4 *ut magnam partem clientium ... traducerentur*. **ereptis** emphasizes the
violent aspect (*TLL* 5.2.789.20), as does *extortis*. **extortis**: once more in C.
at *BC* 1.9.2 and unparalleled in its application to *obsides*.

54.4 quam ... quamque ... amplitudinem "what position and, more particularly, what greatness" (*OLD* 11, *OLD* 2), loosely corresponding to
"*quos ... quam*" (above). Both nouns recur, similarly used, at Cic. *Phil.*
1.33, Vell. Pat. 2.29.2. **antecessisse**: C. plucks their word (§1) but gives
it a different meaning (cf. 20.3n. *opportunitate*). **dignitatem et gratiam**
"standing and influence." **his datis mandatis ... dimisit**: again at 71.4
(and 2.5.4). For *mandata* = "communications," cf. 17.8 *mandabant* (with
TLL 8.264.55), Cic. *De or.* 2.49 *si ... mandata sint exponenda ... in senatu ab
imperatore*. Further instances of *datis mandatis*: *BC* 1.25.1; *BAfr.* 2.4 (cf. Livy
7.31.8); there is etymological play, as *mandare* ‹ *manum dare* (E-M, s.v.).

55 C.'s protégés join and seal the rebellion (37n.): upon their arrival,
Noviodunum, an Aeduan town entrusted with the storage of Roman hostages, provisions, and possessions, is attacked and burned. The relation
between these events and those mentioned at 42.2–3 (of unspecified
location) is unclear; more generally, this episode is rather too neat and
schematic (and may reveal C.'s plotting events for dramatic effect [*Introd.*
3c]): Noviodunum resembles especially Cenabum, its incineration echoes
those V. had ordered after the loss of another Noviodunum (12.1n.), and
the leaders' measures and intentions have been heard of before.

55.1 Nouiodunum erat: 19.1n. *collis erat*. The location of this "New Town"
(12.2n.) remains unknown. The identification with Nevers lacks evidence; nor has the neighborhood of Diou (Thévenot 1960: 64–101) met
with consent. **oppidum** *dictum, quod ibi homines opes suas conferunt* (Paul.
Fest. p. 184); §§2–3 show this *oppidum* bearing out its alleged etymology.
ad ripas Ligeris: the "collective plural" refers "to various points ... taken

collectively as defining an area" (Cunningham 1949: 4). **opportuno loco**: it also enjoyed access to the Allier, the Nièvre, and even the Rhône.

55.2–4 huc … huc … eo: the anaphora is abandoned to signal the change of focalization. *huc* (*vel sim.*) often follows the traditional ekphrasis; so already in Hom. *Il.* 13.332–34 "there was a wide cavern … There Poseidon kept his horses (ἔνθ' ἵππους ἔστησε Ποσειδάων)"; cf. Williams 1968: 637–41. **huc … contulerat**: C. did not mention this, making this an instance of "the postponement of certain important details" until they cannot be ignored anymore (Fraenkel, *Agamemnon*, App. A). **omnes**, as indicated by its position and chiastic contrast to *magnam partem*, applies to all subsequent nouns. **pecuniam publicam**: a technical term, as its presence in *leges* attests (*TLL* 10.1.937.29–34; Cic. *Fam.* 2.17.4; Tac. *Ann.* 4.45.3 *pecunias e publico interceptas* is a characteristic variation). It would have comprised all the money C. handled on behalf of Rome. **suorum et exercitus impedimentorum magnam partem**: the asyndeton is slightly adversative; the double genitives: 22.1n. *cuiusque*. Of the four kinds of train that accompanied the army hauling supplies, tools, machinery, and personal effects – all four normally referred to as *impedimenta* – the "army train" carried what was common to the entire force, whereas the officers' train comprised what belonged to them alone (Roth 1999: 79–91; C. was rumored *in expeditionibus tessellata et sectilia pauimenta circumtulisse* [Suet. *Iul.* 46]). At some point, C. must have ordered part of the baggage train to be moved from Agedincum (10.4).

55.3 magnum numerum: 38.9n. **huius belli** "this [sc. Vercingetorix's] particular war (*OLD* 2)." **coemptum** "bought up" (in various places [2.3n. *collaudatis*]). No such purchases had been mentioned previously.

55.4 eo … uenissent: 6.2n. **de … cognouissent**: 1.1n. **Litauiccum … Conuictolitauem … legatos … missos**: a brief *narratio* (63n.) comprising three asyndetic acc. with infinitives, each with its subject in first position. **Litauiccum … receptum**: this contradicts the earlier statement that Litaviccus had been dispossessed (43.2, 54.1n.), possibly suggesting treacherous conduct all along (5.6n. *perfidia*; 15.5n. *perangustum*). **Bibracte**: located on Mont Beuvray, it was the political and commercial center of the Aeduan people, which, under Augustus, was to be deserted in favor of Augustodunum (Autun), down in the valley some 15 miles away; it is one of the most exciting archaeological sites in France (Guillaumet-Szabo 2005). It was, in 58, the location of C.'s victory over the Helvetii (1.23); 90.7n. **quod est oppidum … auctoritatis** is an authorial remark (hence the indicative); at 1.23.1 C. speaks of *oppidum … longe maximum et copiosissimum*. **Conuictolitauem magistratum**: 33.4n. **legatos … de pace**

et amicitia … missos is formulaic. The binomial (also at 1.3.1, 4.18.3) has a ring of officialese (cf. the "solemn prayer-formula" *pacem ueniamque rogamus* in Ov. *Am.* 1.2.22 [with McKeown]); it is particularly frequent in Livy, who employs it in his tripartite classification of treatises (34.57.7). There the second type applies *cum pares bello aequo foedere in pacem atque amicitiam uenirent* ….This may well be what C. had in mind, as he will represent the Aedui as assuming parity with the Arverni (63.3n.). Cf. 10.1n. *amicis*, 11.2n. de. **publice**, "officially" (*OLD* 1a), contrasts with 43.1n. *nihil publico factum consilio*. **non praetermittendum … commodum**: the implication of *commodum* may be gauged from the contrast at Cic. *Off.* 1.5 *qui summum bonum … suis commodis, non honestate metitur.* The expression occurs once elsewhere at Cic. *Dom.* 145 (differing in meaning). C. upholds his apologetic representation (36–43n.).

55.5 The schematic description recalls the uprising's beginnings at Cenabum (3). **itaque** frequently introduces a description of what was done upon realizing what should be done (*non praetermittendum*; cf. 56.1–3, 73.2; Rambaud 35). **quique** = *et iis qui.* **negotiandi aut itineris causa**: 3.1n. It is easier to see how *aut itineris* was omitted, as *itineris causa* = "for the sake of travel" is an unusual expression (but cf. Cic. *Att.* 3.7.1 *itineris causa ut deuerterer*), than why it should have been interpolated.

55.6–9 obsides … oppidum … frumenti: for the headings ("as for the hostages …"), 20.3–12n. **ad magistratum**: sc. *Conuictolitauem.* **deducendos** is a technical term ("to bring [before a court, magistrate, etc.]," *OLD* 10d).

55.7 oppidum … incenderunt: the Aedui thus embrace, belatedly, V.'s scorched-earth strategy (14.2–9n.).

55.8 frumenti, "as for the grain," is followed by an asyndetic and isocolic *enumeratio* (*HLR* 671): *quod … auexerunt, reliquum … corruperunt.* **subito** "at such short notice" (cf. *OLD* 2); C. may allude once more to the Gauls' stereotypical fickleness. **flumine atque incendio** resumes chiastically *incenderunt* and *nauibus* (cf. 17.2n. *alteri*); but the specificity also allows for balance with the first colon (17.3n. *aedificiorum*).

55.9 A string of clichéd actions. **ipsi** here marks the difference (1.2n.) between the Aeduan leaders' orders and actions. **copias cogere**: again 56.1; a military expression, as Syrus' parody and Pompey's triple use evince (Ter. *Haut.* 668, [Cic.] *Fam.* 8.12a–c), it occurs 13x in C. (2x *CC*) but barely elsewhere (Livy 44.7.8, Amm. Marc. 15.5.25, 21.7.6 [*TLL* 4.907.59–64]). **praesidia custodiasque** is a Ciceronian mannerism (e.g. *Cat.* 1.8) that occurs only here in *CC*. Both terms are often used interchangeably (Cic. *Vat.* 22 *ianuae praesidio et parietum custodiis*). **ad ripas**

Ligeris: the plural may here (unlike 1§n.) refer to both riverbanks. **equitatumque ... ostentare**: just as they (or other auxiliaries) had done before on behalf of C. (8.3). **iniciendi timoris causa**: the expression occurs thrice in Cic. (e.g. *Leg. agr.* 1.23 *timorem bonis iniecistis*) and twice in Nepos; nowhere else. **si ... possent**: 20.10n. *si*. The two alternatives are isocolic and marked off by homoioteleuton (*excludere – expellere*); the emphasis on the prefix is self-explanatory (4.2n. *expellitur*). The Gauls had previously expressed their hope of cutting off Roman supplies and forcing them to retreat into the province (14.2, 20.12; *Introd.* 2c). **aut**: 14.2n. **adductos inopia**: 20.10n. **in prouinciam expellere**: Nicasius' emendation makes good sense; the combination of prefix and preposition is typically concise (Xen. *An.* 1.2.24 ἐξέλιπον ... εἰς χωρίον, Nep. *Phoc.* 2.2 *in exilium erant expulsi*).

55.10 quam ad spem multum adiuuabat quod "the fact that ... greatly contributed (*OLD adiuvare* 6) to that hope"; 26.5n. *quo timore*. **ex niuibus**: 28.6n. *ex*. The correlation between melting snow and rising waters was well known (Hdt. 2.22 is an early instance [with How-Wells]). **uado ... transiri**: 35.1n. **omnino** (24.2n.) suggests typical overconfidence (1.7n. *facile*). **uideretur** opens up an ironic gap between the Gauls' expectation and Roman actualization (8.3n. *oppressis*, 56.3n. *opinionem*).

56 C. advertises his concerns for his men and *dignitas Romana* and opts for speed, skill, and decisiveness to extricate himself from an apparent impasse by crossing the Liger (cf. 35n.), thus stunning his enemy (§3n. *contra ... opinionem*) and securing provisions (§5n. *frumentum*). But his separation from Labienus may not have allowed any real alternative, and he may make a virtue out of necessity (Thévenot 1960: 99; cf. 41n.).

56.1 Quibus rebus cognitis: 18.2n. **si esset ... periclitandum, ut prius quam essent ... coactae copiae dimicaret** "so that, if he had to run into danger while rebuilding bridges, he would fight before larger troops had assembled there (i.e. at the river)." Translators typically construe *periclitari + in* ("run the risk of rebuilding"), which is rarely attested and lacks an exact parallel (*TLL* 10.1.1450.66–1451.7); and the regular absolute use makes good sense. The plural in *perficiendis pontibus* (8x in C.) is "rhetorical" (1.4n. *conciliis*). The triple alliteration: cf. 18.1n. *captiuis*. **essent ... coactae copiae**: 55.9n. The tense: 60.1n. *imperasset*. *essent* follows the focused conjunction (1.7n. *esse*).

56.2 "For to adopt a new plan and march to the Province – as no one, not then (i.e. under the circumstances mentioned at 55.9) either, thought should be done out of necessity – (this) was prevented by the shameful ignominy [sc. of the retreat] and ..., not to mention fear, since

Labienus ..." It would seem as if only one <u>change</u> were necessary to retain
the reading in α: *nam ut commutato consilio iter in prouinciam conuerteret, <u>id</u>
<u>ne</u> metu quidem necessario faciendum existimabat; cum* ... But (a) the acknowl-
edgement of fear is odd, and (b) *iter* ... *conuerteret* is the object of the
following *impediebat* (and *timebat*). Elberling's emendation of the first *ut*
(perhaps owed to *commUTato*) to *ne* addresses the latter problem; the reading of β along with the restoration of *ne* (lost to haplography) addresses
the former (cf. Cic. *Cat.* 4.4 *ut* ... *nemo ne ad deplorandum quidem populi
Romani nomen* ... *relinquatur*). Restoring this second *ne* seems preferable to
(i) Ciacconius' *non* (which I do not understand) and (ii) simply accepting
β's *nemo tunc quidem* ("no one, then especially"), as C. had been worry-
ing about the appearance of flight before (43.5). *ne* ... *quidem* "need not
introduce a climax" (Nisbet on Cic. *Pis.* 65); hence = "not ... either." **commutato consilio**: 53.1n. *eadem* ... *senserat*. **in prouinciam conuerteret** "to
turn in the direction of the province (7.2n.)," where C. had come from
(6.1, 8.2). The prefix aligns the action with <u>commutato consilio</u>. **infamia
atque <u>indignitas</u> ... difficultas <u>impediebat</u>**: 31.2n. *capere* (for the combination of different things), 37.1n. *erat* (for the singular), 4.2n. *expellitur*
(for the play on prefixes, here combining to emphasize the negation). C.
repeatedly shows concern for *dignitas Romana*, most famously at 4.17.1;
cf. 66.5n. and 30.3n. (and, on his *milites indignantes*, 17.4). **atque ... et ...
-que**: this is the standard use of the three particles of connection (again
58.4); *et* "combin[es] likes and unlikes" in an enumerative fashion (cf.
etiam, ἔτι), enclitic *-que* adds a closely related second member that "serves
to complete or extend the first," while *atque* also adds a related member
but with particular emphasis on it (G–L 475–77; Ringe 1880). But these
semantic differences are often blurred, and use differs between genres
(legal texts show a clear preference for *-que*, cf. the draft of a *senatus consultum* in Cic. *Phil.* 14.36–38; Courtney 1999: 3). **quod**: 20.3n. **abiuncto** "cut
off"; the rare verb, only here in *CC*, pertains to the legions, too. **Labieno**:
his mention here prepares for the episode of "the battle by the Seine."

56.3–5 Of the three main clauses, linked by *-que* (... *uenit, uadoque* ...
traduxit, frumentumque ... *instituit*), each renders an accomplishment (C-L
270; 11.5–6n.). The typically "cumulative-complex" sentence, with its
strings of abl. absolutes, is conspicuously propulsive. **magnis ... itineribus**:
1.38.5 *magnis nocturnis diurnisque itineribus*; cf. 7.9.4; *BC* 3.13.1. **contra
omnium opinionem**: 8.3n. *oppressis inopinantibus*. No one expected C. to
head for the river (55.10n.); he may suggest that the Gauls assumed he
would flee to the province (66.3n. *fugere*).

56.4 C. deploys a standard maneuver, which Veg. 3.7 describes in more
detail: *explorato uado duae acies equitum* ... *ordinantur interuallis competentibus*

separatae, ut per medium pedites … transeant. nam acies superior aquarum impe-
tum frangit, inferior qui rapti subuersique fuerint colligit. This makes it less
likely that Luc. 1.220–22 is modelled on our passage (as commentators
often claim). **uadoque inuento … pro rei necessitate opportuno** proves
the Gauls wrong (55.10). *pro rei necessitate* = "in consideration of the pressing circumstances"; it qualifies *opportuno*. **ut … possent** "in so far as they
could" (cf. *OLD ut* 32c). The Romans had crossed the Thames *cum capite*
solo ex aqua exstarent (5.18.5); such narrative detail is common (e.g. Xen.
An. 1.4.18). **ad sustinenda arma**: a rare expression (outside of Livy) and
only here in *CC*. **liberi** agrees with the noun closest to it (*umeri*; 37.1n.
erat). **hostibus primo aspectu perturbatis**: "at first sight" is proverbial (cf.
Verg.'s playful use at *Aen.* 1.617–18 *obstipuit primo aspectu Sidonia Dido,*
| *casu deinde uiri tanto*). The Gauls' wonder at the Romans overcoming
obstacles (which Polyaenus, *Strat.* 8.23.9 echoes – if for an earlier crossing) is typical (first at 1.13.2). **incolumem** is predicative and, by position,
emphatic.

56.5 Participial construction, abl. absolute, and finite verb neatly render
the sequence of actions (Eden 1962: 106). **frumentumque in agris et**
pecoris copiam: the grain fields suggest a date no earlier than August.
C.'s worry over supplies may have resurged (10.3n. *re frumentaria*) due to
the Aeduan desertion and loss of Noviodunum (55.2). On cattle: 17.3n.
repleto his rebus: the verb occurs only here in *CC*. *rebus*: 11.5n. *rem*. **iter**
… facere instituit: an administrative formula (11.3n. *conficeret*, 9.6n. *insti-*
tuit; Cic. *Fam.* 15.2.8 *iter in Ciliciam facere institui*). **in Senones**: 53.3n. *in*
Haeduos. Thévenot 1960: 109n.2 discusses routes.

57–62 LABIENUS' *ARISTEIA* IN THE BATTLE
BY THE SEINE

After Avaricum, C. dispatched Labienus (L.) with four legions to the
Senones and Parisii (34.2), stating neither motive nor intention. He may
have intended to capture Lutetia (57.1n.); more generally, he may have
hoped that, by returning L. to the restive region where he had wintered
(1.2n. *exercitum*), he might alleviate the supply crisis, "crush [their] rebellion" (*CG* 148) – or, at least, open another front line to divide enemy
resources (as V. had [5n.]) – and confine, to the north and south, the
Aedui. Whatever his plan, it apparently justified the dispatch of nearly
half his army. Little came of it (34.2n.); worse was averted *Labieni uirtute*.
    When L. set out from Agedincum to march northward on Lutetia, his
route downstream along the Seine was blocked by Camulogenus' troops,
who were ensconced in swamps (57.4n. *paludem*) to the south of the town.

L. reversed, seized Metiosedum (58.2n.), crossed the Seine, and moved downstream again, now on the opposite bank. Meanwhile, Lutetia was burned down by Gallic hands. His objective lost and troubled by the imminent arrival of the Bellovaci, he changed plan, now prioritizing the return to Agedincum. Having traversed the river once more by way of a stratagem (60n.), he won against Camulogenus (62), then reunited with C. (63).

C.'s topography being typically vague, the sites of neither the battle nor the Roman camp have been identified. There is disagreement about (a) on which bank L. initially marched and battled Camulogenus, (b) by which swamp he was blocked, and (c) which *maximum flumen* he had to overcome (*CG* 775–85, reviewing the scenarios, favors (a) the left bank, (b) the confluence with the Essonne, and (c) the Seine; but the right bank and other marches have continued to draw support [Roblin 1971: 106–07, Lombard-Jourdan 1985: 17–23]; cf. Morel 1985). Scant information can be gleaned from the archaeological record and the later accounts of the war in Gaul: a sling-ball of lead inscribed with "T.Labien" found near Sens attests to no more than L.'s presence there at some point (Sievers 2001: 238, nr. 727; another possible find in Paris: Poux-Guyard 1999); and of later accounts Cassius Dio alone mentions this episode (40.38.4).

L. is the only *legatus* to appear in every *commentarius*; but until *V*, his appearances are significant rather than long (esp. 2.26.4–27.1; Tyrrell 1970: c. 3); one wonders what caused the change (cf. Stringer 2017). Of the three longer episodes revolving around him (5.55–58, 6.7–8, 7.57–62; they share: phraseology, L.'s pretense of fear [60n.], and his plan's meeting with success [62n.]), this is the longest, and it amounts to an *aristeia*: he reads a perilous situation (58.2), builds a bridge, captures a settlement ready for war (58.4–5n.), changes plans to protect his army (59.3, 5), devises a textbook stratagem (60n.), and generally acts the part of the general (62.2). To have this *aristeia* compensate for the Gergovian defeat (Gärtner 1975: 90 "technique of compensation"), C. treats developments that overlapped with his events at Gergovia (57.1 *dum ... geruntur*) immediately afterwards in a separate set piece (cf. 29–35n.), which is marked off by two ring-compositional elements (62.10nn. *reuertitur Agedincum, ad Caesarem peruenit*). It is impossible "to separate ... what L. did from how C. has told it" (Tyrrell 1970: 31).

C.'s account has been scrutinized for non-Caesarian elements, as it must be based on L.'s report. A few of the "transgressions" that Petersdorff (1879: 14–17) identified are indeed most naturally explained as echoes of L.'s writing (57.4n. *transitu*, 58.2n. *confieri*, 59.4n. *cogitabat*, 62.2 *secundissumorum*, 62.3n. *primo concursu*; Krebs 2021: 95–102). But C. also continues his adaptation of the Polybian narrative, more particularly Hannibal's crossing of the Rhône (3.42–43) as detailed in the nn. on 57.2 *magnae copiae ... conuenerunt*, 57.4 *transitu prohibere*, 59.3 *longe ... capiendum*, 59.5, 60.1 *quattuor milia ... exspectari*, and 61.3 *sub lucem* (cf. 43.5n. *fugae*, Krebs 2021: 102–07). The episode of L. by the Seine – based on a report, stylized with the help of literary tools – thus emblematizes C.'s use of his two fundamental code models as well as *modus componendi* (*Introd.* 3a).

57 L. marches downstream along the Seine, when Camulogenus blocks him.

57.1 Dum haec ... geruntur: the formula (37.1n.) is used at 6.7.1 to introduce "L. against the Treueri"; cf. Rambaud 70–71 on formulaic transitions to reported episodes. *haec* covers events narrated in 34–56. **supplemento ... relicto**: it was common practice to employ recruits in this role (cf. 2.8.5). *supplementum*: 7.5n. **nuper** need not refer to recent events, as Cic. *Nat. D.* 2.126 (with Pease) memorably shows: *ea quae nuper, id est paucis ante saeclis*. **ut esset**: 22.1n. *ut est*. **impedimentis praesidio**: 7x in C. (usually in inverted order); the only other attestation outside C. is Livy 44.38.6. **IIII legionibus**: 34.2. The VII and the XII are identified at 62.3. **Lutetiam proficiscitur**: its name of uncertain etymology and here first attested (*DLG* 211), Lutetia was founded in the third century and flourished in C.'s time, as Parisian gold coins testify, not least because of the south-north trade route outside its gates (roads ran from Agedincum to Lutetia along both riverbanks [Roblin 1971: 105–15]; cf. Robin-Poux 2000). As testimony to its importance, C. had moved the *concilium Gallorum* there (6.3.4). Eventually renamed after its tribe, it became Paris. **id est oppidum ... Sequanae**: sim. 58.3. *id est oppidum* does not occur outside of this episode; a "local repetition" (cf. Krebs 2021: 100). The Seine separated the *Celtae* from the *Belgae* according to C.'s geography of *Gallia omnis* (1.1; Krebs 2018d: 96–102).

57.2 cuius aduentu ... cognito: the formulaic (18.3n.) transition recurs at 88.1, 3.20.3, 6.4.1; *BC* 1.12.2, 3.30.7 (and Curt. 6.6.22); cf. *BAlex.* 64.2 *de cuius aduentu ut cognouit*. **magnae ex finitimis ciuitatibus copiae conuenerunt**: the prepositional phrase's position (24.5n. *multitudo*) allows for the triple alliteration (18.1n.). The motif: Polyb. 3.42.4.

57.3 summa imperii traditur: 20.5n. **Camulogeno**: nothing else is known of this "son of the god of war Camulos" (*GPN* 60), though the name is attested numismatically and epigraphically. **prope confectus ... propter singularem scientiam rei militaris**: the paronomasia highlights the tension between his age (28.4n. *aetate confectis*; the part. is concessive) and "excellent (8.3n. *singulari*) knowledge in military matters," the latter being a general's virtue (Cic. *Leg. Man.* 28), and only to be expected of a man so named (C. may allude to the name's significance [cf. 1.4n. *Acconis*, 75.4n.

Aremoricae]); cf. also 29.2n. *imperiti* (sc. *scientia oppugnationis*). **ad eum est honorem euocatus**: the disjunctive order and the position of *est* emphasize *eum*.

57.4 is cum: 12.1n. *Vercingetorix ubi.* **perpetuam esse paludem**: this "continuous marsh" (26.2n.) has been identified variously as the grounds along the Essonne, Bièvre, or Orge, or, on the right bank, along a branch of the Seine (Duval 1961: 103; Roblin 1971: 106–07, Lombard-Jourdan 1985: 8–9). **quae influeret in Sequanam**: the subjunctive may result from an attraction to *impediret*, which expresses a natural consequence. Wistrand 1946 discusses the terminology and directionality in Roman geography. **locum ... impediret** is a lively variation of the common *impeditus locus*, first here attested, then limited to historical and technical writing (*TLL* 7.1.532.70–72). **consedit**: the verb is commonly used in military contexts in the sense of *castra ponere, exercitum constituere* (*TLL* 4.434.38). **nostrosque transitu prohibere**: *transitus* recurs only in the Labienian episodes (5.55.2, 6.7.5 [and *CC*]). A similar situation similarly phrased occurs in Polyb. 3.42.4: χάριν τοῦ κωλύειν τὴν τῶν Καρχηδονίων διάβασιν, "in order to prevent the Carthaginians' crossing."

58 L. demonstrates speed, decisiveness, and skill when, having failed to secure passage, he heads back upstream to Metiosedum (§2n.) on the Seine: he bridges the river, captures the settlement, then leads his army downstream again (on the opposite bank). When he reaches Lutetia, it has already been burned down, and the Gauls have set up camp.

58.1 uineas agere, ... explere atque ... munire: this type of coordination – AB&C (*OLD atque* 11c; Pinkster 1969) – is much rarer than ABC or ABC*que* and, in C., limited to words that are not on the same level (with one possible exception [*BC* 3.55.3]); hence *atque²* = "and thus." *uineas agere*: 17.1n. **cratibus atque aggere**: again at 86.5, *BC* 1.40.4; cf. 79.4n. *fossam ... explent. crates*, "bundles of brush (*fascines*)," were widely used not just to "fill up" marshes or ditches (86.5; a standard procedure [Oakley on Livy 9.14.9]), but also for cover (79.4 *integunt*) and fortifications (*BC* 1.25.9). On *agere ... aggere*: 17.1n. **iter munire** "to construct a (proper) road," either an existing or new one: the former is suggested by Nep. *Han.* 3.4 *itinera muniit, effecit ut ea elephantus ... ire posset, qua antea unus homo ... uix poterat*; the latter by Hor. *Carm. saec.* 41–43 *cui [*sc. cursui] per ardentem ... Troiam ... Aeneas ... liberum muniuit iter*, and *castra munire* (often loosely = "to set up camp").

58.2 id resumes L.'s efforts. **difficilius confieri**: the MSS all but unanimously support the rarely but securely attested verbal form, to which C. everywhere else prefers *confici* (3.28.1, 6.34.5, 7.66.5 [all without significant variants]; *TLL* 4.194.61–68). This might therefore reflect L.'s choice (57–62n.). The figura etymologica is understated (*facere, fieri*; cf. K-S I 275, Wills 243–53); the juxtaposition of the prefixes "dis-" and "cum-" seems particularly apt in this slippery context. **silentio ... egressus** = 11.7n. **tertia uigilia**: soon after midnight (3.3n.). **eodem quo** is a structure C. favors (25x: M-P 568.20–55; rare in *CC*). **Metiosedum**: the original name (probably Metlosedum [*DLG* 226]) and site of this settlement are uncertain, as is its relation to mod. Melun (Luccisano 1998–2001).

58.3 id est oppidum ... positum = 57.1n. **ut ... diximus**: 17.1n. C. prefers *supra*.

58.4–5 C. elsewhere comments disparagingly on pontoons to elevate the accomplishment of his proper Rhine bridge (4.17.1; Brown 2013: 46); but he knew of the importance of their mastery (Veg. 2.25.3, 3.7), wherein, as Arrian suggests, the Roman army had accomplished the greatest speed (*Anab.* 5.7.3; O'Connor 1993: 133–37). For instances of technical ekphrasis (23n.) of such a bridge, here omitted, see e.g. Hdt. 7.36, Polyb. 3.43.3–4, Tac. *Hist.* 2.34.2. **deprehensis ... perterritis oppidanis**: four consecutive abl. absolutes (only 3.1.4 and 6.12.6 have more); the mix of chiastic and parallel structures is typical (ABBABA). In *CC* both *deprendere* and *deprehendere* are attested (cf. Quint. *Inst.* 9.4.59 *deprehendere uel deprendere*). **eo**: sc. *nauibus coniunctis*. **impositis**: α's *iniectis* lacks a parallel. **rei nouitate** "the suddenness of the operation" (Edwards); similarly at 4.34.1, 6.39.3; *BC* 2.26.3. It subtly emphasizes Rome's technical superiority and "Gallic naïveté" (as emblematized at 2.30.3–4; cf. Tac. *Agr.* 28.2 *ut miraculum*), even though the Gauls knew of this technique (1.8.4). **sine ... potitur**: sc. L. The terse main clause expresses the seemingly logical result of the abl. abs. ("pull of necessity"). Rambaud 298 detects disparagement; I cannot see why.

58.5 superioribus diebus: 44.1n. **resciderant**: 35.2n. **secundo flumine** "downstream," again 60.1; this is its first attestation (*TLL* 6.1.960.1; 60.3n. *aduerso flumine*). It is also the first time C. provides any such detail at all, herein possibly motivated by Polybius' frequent mentions (3.42.6 [cf. 59.4n.], 46.3+[5] κατὰ [τοῦ] ποταμοῦ, 66.8 κατὰ ῥοῦν γὰρ ἐποιεῖτο τὴν πορείαν). **ad Lutetiam**: cf. 43.5 *a Gergouia*.

58.6 re cognita: 35.6n. **Lutetiam incendi pontesque eius oppidi rescindi**: the homoioteleuton reinforces the parallelism. The ponderous resumption in *eius oppidi* is not untypical. *rescindi* repeats §5 *resciderant* to underline the repetitive action; cf. 55.7n. *oppidum ... incenderunt*. **e regione**: 25.2n. **considunt**: 57.4n.

59 C. paints a dramatic vignette (§§1n. *iam*, 3n. *commutatione*; the imperfect dominates [10n.]): rumors circulating in ominous passives (*audiebatur, afferebantur*) and L.'s observations combine to detail a precarious position of poor prospects. L. wisely (§3n. *aliud consilium*) changes plan. His reasoning, possibly mentioned in his communication to C. (§4n. *cogitabat*, 57–62n.), is emphasized in C.'s write-up (*intellegebat, cogitabat, animi*).

59.1 Iam ... iam: in *CC* the sole instance of anaphoric *iam* (cf. C-L 509–12); its tone is one of heightened drama (32.2n.). **a Gergouia discessisse**: as narrated in 53. *a(b)* is used to indicate departure from a town's neighborhood (H-S 102). **Haeduorum defectione**: C. introduces the *fact* of the defection as *rumored* amongst the Gauls. The magnitude of the event is rendered by fourfold confirmation (59.2 *cognita*, 61.4, 63.1). Plut. *Caes.* 26.5 reports that the defection caused despair among C.'s troops (possibly inferred from 61.4). **secundo motu** "the successful uprising," as focalized through the Gauls, confident once more (1.7n. *facile*), but with reason. **rumores**: 1.2n. It may here disqualify the following (indeed mistaken) information. **Gallique ... confirmabant**: the Gauls present as accomplished what earlier in similar language they were said to attempt (55.9–10, 56.3–5; cf. 15.5n. *perangustum*); note how C. decided against returning to the province (56.2). **interclusum itinere et Ligeri** "blocked from his route and, more precisely (*OLD et* 11), the Loire." C.'s passage necessitated crossing the Loire, and so the second term specifies the first (45.2n. *iumentorum ... mulorumque*). The distribution of attestations of *iter/itinere intercludere* (only in Cic.'s military letters, Livy, and Tac.) suggests a military provenance. **interclusum ... coactum**: the first participle is subordinate to the second. **inopia frumenti**: 10.1n. *re frumentaria*. **in prouinciam**: 56.2n.

59.2 Bellouaci: located in *Gallia Belgica*, more specifically in the Thérain Valley, they are repeatedly characterized as foremost in war (to which their name would point Roman ears [cf. 1.4n. *Acconis*]); §5n. *uirtutis*. C. had defeated them in 57 (2.13–15), and they were long in joining V.'s revolt, and even then remained reluctant (75.5); the following year, however, they led a renewed effort against Rome (8.6–22). **autem** "moreover" (*OLD* 3). **defectione Haeduorum** rearranges §1n. **qui ante ... aperte bellum parare** is similar in thought and wording to 1.3. **per se** "on their own account" rather than "by their own efforts" (*OLD per* 11, 15b). **infideles**: only here in C.

59.3 C. renders the *peripeteia* with proper emphasis: *commutatione ... longe aliud ... neque iam ... sed ....* In Polyb. 3.42.5, "Hannibal looked [at the enemy on the banks] and concluded from the present circumstances (συλλογιζόμενος ἐκ τῶν παρόντων) that it would be impossible to cross the river even with force." **tanta rerum commutatione** "with the whole situation so thoroughly (1.2n. *tantis*) changed." *rerum commutatio* is popular with C. (8x [not *CC*]). The prefix signifies "on all sides" (2.3n. *collaudatis*) and correlates to *tanta*. **aliud … consilium**: formulaic, cf. *BC* 3.41.2, 77.3 *aliud sibi consilium capiendum existimauit* (with Rambaud 33) and 14.2n. *longe alia ratione*.

59.4 ut … reduceret cogitabat "[instead] he (now) thought out (*OLD* 3c) ways (*OLD ut* 1b) to bring back …"; other shades of meaning are possible. The only other instance of *cogitare ut/ne* (in *CC*) occurs in another L. episode (5.57.1): *ne quam occasionem … dimitteret cogitabat*. **acquireret … lacesseret**: a slight hysteron proteron. *acquirere* occurs only here in C. **incolumem exercitum**: on the general's concern for his troops, cf. 19.5n. *summae se … cariorem*.

59.5 namque, in C.'s age, stands normally (and in C.'s case, always) in first position and before vowels (*Antibarbarus* 2.119–20). If it is a "word of elevated style, [which] in ordinary prose of the late Republic … is found only rarely" (Adams 1973a: 142n.78), its nine instances in C. (+ [Cic.] *Att.* 1.8) and 28 in *CC* are noteworthy. **altera ex parte … alteram**: *pars* here perhaps hints at "cardinal direction" (cf. *TLL* 10.1.480.50–481.08), as Camulogenus might be said to have been to the south, the Bellovaci to the north. In any case, Polyb. 3.42.5 mentions Hannibal's concern "lest he should expect the enemy on all sides (μὴ πανταχόθεν προσδέξηται τοὺς ὑπεναντίους)'; cf. 57–62n. *alter … alter … tum* occurs with any kind of frequency only in Cicero (*Vat.* 3, *Arch.* 5, *Att.* 10.14.1). **quae ciuitas**: 28.6n. *quae … pars*. **maximam habet opinionem uirtutis**: cf. 2.4.5 reporting *plurimum … Bellouacos et uirtute et auctoritate et hominum numero ualere*; sim. 8.6.2, Strabo 4.4.5. The verbal hyperbaton: 3.2n. *maior. uirtutis opinio*, "a reputation for valor," which recurs at 83.4 (and twice more in C. [1x *CC*]) is popular with Cicero but otherwise rare. **instabant** "they were pressing"; cf. 51.1n. *premerent*. **parato atque instructo**: the pairing (again at 5.5.2) may be formulaic, if Lentulus' use in a letter to the senate is indicative ([Cic.] *Fam.* 12.15.2): *naues complures instructas et paratas*. It will become a Livian mannerism (Oakley on 6.6.13). **a praesidio atque impedimentis**: as mentioned in 57.1. **interclusas … distinebant** is unparalleled, but the redundancy is common in C. (2.19.5 *porrecta pertinebant*, 2.19.6 *abditi latebant*, 62.1 [n.] *praesentem adesse*). *flumen* has been variously identified; the Seine is the most natural referent (Duval 1961: 99; 57–62n.). *distinebat* recalls *tenebat*, thus highlighting the two side's different positions.

59.6 tantis subito difficultatibus obiectis "in the face of such great and sudden difficulties"; sim. 1.39.1 *tantus subito timor*, 3.15.3, 61.1 (and, differing in order, 4.28.2 *tanta tempestas subito coorta*). Adjectives of size regularly "host" adverbs (Adams 1994b: 138–39), which here shades into an adjective (cf. the Greek practice of nominalizing adverbial expressions by inserting them between article and noun [Xen. *An.* 3.5.14 τὴν κύκλῳ πᾶσαν χώραν]); Nägelsbach 1905: §75 provides instances. **ab animi uirtute auxilium** "help from strength of mind." While (*ex/ab*) *uirtute petere* is a commonplace (e.g. Verg. *Aen.* 12.913), the expression is noteworthy, as *uirtus animi* occurs only here in *CC* (cf. 77.5n. *animi ... uirtus*; 36.4n. *animi ac uirtutis*). Most translators understand "personal courage" (cf. McDonnell 2006: 305n.35). But *animus* may signify "the mind as seat of thought" (85.2 *ad animum occurrit*); as such it prepares the reader for L.'s tactics.

60 L. conducts himself exemplarily: He calls a late meeting (to minimize the risk of his plan being leaked [§1n. *uesperum*]) and proposes (in a pre-battle address [§1n. *cohortatus*]) that a few troops head upstream at night (to obscure observation) along with the baggage (for maximum effect and the pretense of panic [§3nn. *impedimentis, tumultu*]); meanwhile, the majority of troops should secretly move downstream (in order to cross the river [35n.]), with a few cohorts left behind for camp protection (as was proper [§2n. *praesidio*]). L. had previously received credit as a "maker of stratagems" when he also pretended panic (Frontin. *Str.* 2.5.20 confuses 5.57–58 with this instance; *Introd.* 3d). Details in C.'s account may once more be inspired by Polybius: nn. on *ea ... administrarent, prima ... progredi, ibique se exspectare, conquirit ... lintres*, and 57–62.

60.1 sub uesperum "towards evening," is not attested outside *CC* (Curt. 6.7.20 *sub uesperam*). The timing: cf. 6.7.7–8, 9.3–5n. **consilio conuocato cohortatus**: 29.1n. *cohortatus*. The triple alliteration: 18.1n. **imperasset ... administrarent**: the direct speech will have been *administrate quae imperauero* (the pluperfect in *oratio obliqua* represents the future perfect [*NLS* §272d]). The detail may be owed to Hannibal's men "making preparations for the imminent engagement according to order (παρασκευαζόμενοι ... κατὰ τὸ συντεταγμένον)", Polyb. 3.42.9. **diligenter industrieque** is an adverbial pairing unattested elsewhere except Suet. *Dom.* 8.1; the pairing of the equivalent nouns, however, is a Ciceronian mannerism. *industria* was a distinctly military virtue as exercised esp. in preparation for war (Moore 1989: 31), and an inscription praises a centurion *quod per gradus militiae suae tam industriae* [sic] *se administrauerit* (*CIL* XI 5693). *industrie* occurs first here in C. **singulas equitibus**: sc. *(naues) singulas singulis equitibus*. The latter are not cavalrymen, but officers of equestrian rank (as *Romanis* clarifies). **prima uigilia ... progredi**: 11.7n. *paulo ... egressi*. Pollio's crit-icism of Sallust for using *transgredi* of ships (*apud* Gell. *NA* 10.26.1) is undermined by common uses such as this one. Hannibal, too, dispatched men who "marched against the stream along the river for about 200 stades (ποιησάμενοι τὴν πορείαν ἀντίοι τῷ ῥεύματι παρὰ τὸν ποταμὸν ἐπὶ διακόσια στάδια)," 3.42.7. **ibique se exspectare**: ἐνταῦθα κατέμειναν, in Polyb.

60.2 minime firmas: 1.52.2 *partem minime firmam*, 7.84.2. There are three more instances of *minime* ("amounting to a negative," *OLD* 2) in *BG*: 1.1.3, 2.33.2, 3.19.6 (none in *BC*; five in *CC*). *firmus ad* is military lingo (*TLL* 6.1.814.43–48). **praesidio reliquit**: 40.3n. It was standard procedure "[to leave] some soldiers behind at the camp ... so that the enemy leader would not discover that it is empty and send men ... to seize the place."

60.3 reliquas ... proficisci imperat: C. normally construes *imperare* + *ut*(*ne*). This alternative construction (*fere ap*[*ud*] *poetas* [*TLL* 7.1.585.36]) recurs at 5.1.2, 7.6, *BC* 1.61.6, 3.42.2. It represents C.'s occasional deviation from his self-imposed rules (*Introd.* 2b). **de media nocte**: 45.1n. **cum ... impedimentis**: to increase the contingent's size (61.3n. *magnum*) or add an authenticating detail to the departure. **aduerso flumine** "upstream," again 61.3, *BC* 3.30.4; in contrast to 58.5n. *secundo flumine*. **magno tumultu** contrasts with *silentio* above and below. The tumult is intended to suggest panic (and will be interpreted thus by the Gauls at 61.4), a strat-agem discussed by Polyaenus under ψευδοπανικά; L. had used it before (cf. Polyaenus, Strat. 3.9.32 with Wheeler 1988: 40–41; 5.57.4, 6.7.8). **conquirit etiam lintres**: Polyb. 3.42.2 has Hannibal acquire canoes and boats (ἐξηγόρασε ... τά τε μονόξυλα πλοῖα πάντα καὶ τοὺς λέμβους). *lintres* = "small boats." The term is also used of troughs, which affords a sense of their size.

60.4 magno sonitu varies §3 *magno tumultu*. In *CC*, *sonitus* occurs only here and 61.3 (cf. 57.1n. *id est oppidum*). **post paulo silentio egressus** reiterates §1; *post paulo*: 50.6n. **appelli** "to be put ashore"; the proper technical term.

61 L.'s plan causes confusion, but Camulogenus is not duped into sending all his troops upstream after the allegedly §3 *magnum agmen*; instead he dispatches a *parua manus* (§5n.), and marches his actual army (§5 *reliquas copias*) downstream to confront L. But the scheme may have provided the latter enough time to cross the river (62.1). The episode is structured lucidly: L.'s actions (§§1–2) are followed by the reports received by the Gauls (§§3–4), their decisions, and, lastly, actions (§§4–5; cf. 7n. on the sequence). Passives dominate (but note §2 *praefecerat*), as does the final position of the verbs, which are noticeably varied: *transmittitur, transpor-tari, transire*, and *progrederetur, processissent*.

61.1 Eo ... uentum: 6.2n. This impersonal passive of *uenire* occurs 20x in C. (6x in *CC*); amongst other uses (Roche on Luc. 1.185), it had its place in military reports (Sall. *Cat.* 60.2 with Vretska, Livy 1.51.8, 6.29.1+5, Tac. *Ann.* 1.50.3; cf. 2.3n. *disceditur*). **ut ... dispositi** "stationed alongside the whole river, as they were"; cf. 35.1. **inopinantes ... opprimuntur**: 8.3n. **magna erat subito coorta tempestas**: similarly 4.28.3 and Cic. *Verr.* 2.46, Livy 1.16.1, 40.45.2, Curt. 10.1.44. *coorta*: 27.1n. C. had taken advantage of the rain at Avaricum (27.1n. *inutilem*).

61.2 exercitus equitatusque equitibus: cf. 18.1n. *captiuis* (the alliteration). *exercitus* = "infantry" (*OLD* 2b). **praefecerat**: sc. L. (60.1). **transmittitur**: 37.1n. *erat* (the singular).

61.3 Within the tricolon of news received, each item is marked off by homoioteleuton (*-ri*). The report partly echoes L.'s instructions (*tumultuari, aduerso flumine, sonitumque remorum*), thus affirming his planning (*Introd.* 3b; cf. also the verbal repetition of reports in epic and tragedy, as early as Hom. *Il.* 2.11–15 = 28–32). In addition, there are close parallels with 6.7.8 *maiore strepitu et tumultu quam populi Romani fert consuetudo castra moueri iubet. his rebus fugae similem profectionem effecit*. They may suggest "self-imitation" (Woodman 1979; but cf. *Introd.* 3c), perhaps by C. rather than L. (57–62n.). **fere**: 19.1n. **sub lucem** "just before dawn," again 83.7 (8.35.4 *sub ipsam lucem*). The first attestation of a rare expression (*TLL* 7.2.1907.61–64), it virtually translates Polyb. 3.43.1 ὑπὸ τὴν ἑωθινήν. **praeter consuetudinem tumultuari** "there was an unusual turmoil"; 60.3n. *magno tumultu*. The verb, regularly deponent, occurs only here in *CC* and in an impersonal passive (so occasionally elsewhere [Livy 24.21.2 *tumultuatum ... apud milites fuerat*]). Its choice (highlighted by *tumultus* above) might be ironic, as Romans associated *tumultus* especially with the Gauls (Livy 7.9.6 *tumultus Gallici*, with Oakley), who were also stereotypically tumultuous in their departures (2.11.1; Polyb. 3.43.12 Κελτοί ... διὰ τὴν ἀταξίαν). **magnum ire agmen**: this was the impression L. desired to create (60.3; below, §5). **aduerso flumine**: 60.3n. **sonitumque**: 60.3n. **paulo infra** "a little farther downstream (*OLD infra* 2b)"; 60.1 specified it as *IIII milia passuum*. Cf. 57.4n. *influeret*.

61.4 perturbatos: 29.1n. **defectione Haeduorum**: 59.1n. **fugam parare**: only here in *CC*.

61.5 e regione: 25.2n. **parua manu**: the first impression was one of *magnum agmen*, but Camulogenus learned about its real size (five cohorts) and deemed a *parua manus* sufficient. **progrederetur ... processissent**: the subjunctives are owed to virtual *oratio obliqua* (*NLS* §285), as this was Camulogenus' command.

62 In the earlier L. episodes, C. made a point of stating how everything unfolded as L. had willed it (5.58.4, 6.8.2; cf. 16.3n. *ratione prouideri*); here, too, his plan succeeds, against valiant resistance. The fact that victory was secured by his tribunes matters little (C. himself relied on subordinates often enough); L.'s invocation of C. matters much more (§2n. *adesse*), especially given that it repeats an earlier instance. It is most likely by C.'s hand, who desired to demonstrate unity and to remind his readers that "L. accomplished what he accomplished with the *imperator* Caesar's men" (Tyrrell 1970: 45–46).

62.1 Prima luce: 36.3n. **et … erant transportati et … cernebatur** "no sooner had all our men been led across than the enemy lines came into view." The imperfect is inchoative (11.4n. *comparabant*).

62.2 L. delivers a condensed *cohortatio* (29nn.). **cohortatus ut … retinerent memoriam**: 2.21.2 *cohortatus … uti suae pristinae uirtutis memoriam retinerent*. It is a commonplace of the *cohortatio* to recall past victories (cf. 1.8n.): cf. Thuc. 7.66.1, Sall. *Iug.* 49.2 *memores pristinae uirtutis et uictoriae*, Verg. *Aen.* 10.281–82 (with Harrison), Tac. *Ann.* 3.45.2 (with W-M). **pristinae uirtutis**: again 77.4, altogether 6x in C. (none in *CC*). Sallust will favor *pristinae uirtutis memores* (3x). **secundissumorum proeliorum**: according to Varro (*apud* Cassiod. *De orth.* 7.150.10), C. preferred "i" where usage vacillated between "i" and "u" (known as *sonus medius*); the MSS of the *BG* support this largely (Krebs 2021: 101n.27). It is noteworthy, then, that in the L. episodes for four out of six pertinent words the alternative form is attested in either one branch of the MSS tradition (5.55.3α *finitimis*, 57.1α *munitissumis*, 57.3α *finitumas*, 6.8.6α *proxumas* against 5.56.2 *nouissimus*, 58.1 *finitimarum*). This might, on balance, intimate that L. did not share C.'s morphological predilection and that some of his forms made it into C.'s version; which is why I embrace β's un-Caesarian form. The superlative occurs only here and in a Caesarian letter ([Cic.] *Att.* 10.8b.1; cf. *BAlex.* 11.4). **ipsum Caesarem … adesse**: C. comments repeatedly on witness as motivation (1.52.1 *legatos … praefecit, uti eos testes suae quisque uirtutis haberet*; cf. 80.5), esp. by his own eyes (2.25.3, 3.14.8; Goldsworthy 1996: 153–54). L. had allegedly encouraged his troops in this fashion before (6.8.4): *praestate eandem nobis ducibus uirtutem quam saepe numero imperatori praestitistis, atque illum adesse … existimate*. One wonders how C.'s second-in-command (57–62n.) felt about these demonstrations of accord (esp. in the light of his later opposition [34.2n. *Labieno*]). **cuius … superassent**: another commonplace; cf. Thuc. 2.89.2, 7.63.4 οὓς πολλάκις νενικήκατε, Polyb. 3.64.6, Sall. *Iug.* 49.2, Tac. *Ann.* 2.15.1. **ductu**: only here in C. **saepenumero**: all five instances in C. occur either in direct or indirect (6.8.4; 1.33.2, 1.39.1, 1.40.7) speech, wherein it is generally common (Adams 2005: 89). **superassent**: 17.3n. *sustentarint*. **praesentem adesse**: the pleonasm serves emphasis (19.3n. *inani simulatione*). The connotations suggested by *praesens* as *uox propria* of a god present "in a helpful manner" (*OLD* 3) may not have been unwelcome.

62.3–4 primo concursu occurs only here and 6.8.6 in *CC* (57–62n.); it will then become so frequent in Livy as to be "a military cliché" (Ogilvie on 5.32.3). **ab dextro cornu … pelluntur atque in fugam coniciuntur … ab sinistro**: there is a close parallel at 1.52.6 *cum hostium acies a sinistro cornu pulsa atque in fugam coniecta esset, a dextro cornu uehementer multitudine suorum nostram aciem premebant*. *in fugam coicere* is a Caesarian mannerism (10x [+ 2x]); among its rare attestations elsewhere are Quadrig. *FRHist* F52, Cic. *Cael.* 63. Together with *pelluntur* it is also an instance of "theme and variation." It was a commonplace of Roman battle descriptions that one wing fared better than the other (Oakley on Livy 6.8.6). **ab dextro cornu** but §6 in sinistro cornu; cf. 34.3n. *ab … parte*, 87.2 *ab tergo hostes adoriri*. Here *ab* may also be influenced by *pelluntur*.

62.4 primi ordines "front ranks" (cf. *OLD* 2); Damon on Tac. *Hist.* 1.55.1 lists other possible meanings in different contexts. **transfixi pilis concidissent**: 88.2n. on the *pila* volley. **nec … quisquam** "and not a single one," as suggested by the word order. **dabat suspicionem fugae**: 54.2 *dare timoris aliquam suspicionem*, 6.7.8 *quo … timoris det suspicionem*; nowhere else in *CC*.

62.5 ipse … aderat … cohortabatur repeats §2 in typically schematic fashion.

62.6 incerto … exitu uictoriae: its position and disjunction highlight the adjective (as contrary to expectation). For the genitive: 27.2n. The comparison with Cic. *Marcell.* 16 *incertus exitus et anceps fortuna belli* (twice more similarly) reveals how C. anticipates the ultimate victory (the expression is, in fact, unparalleled [*TLL* 5.2.1537.77]); cf. 19.4n. *uictoriam*, 80.6n. *dubia uictoria*. **legione tribunis**: it is hard to decide between the MSS, but corruption from α's *a septima legione* to β's *septimae legionis* is more likely, as the latter is a trivialization of the less clear "that the troops of the VII told their tribunes." **post tergum**: the sudden appearance of troops at the back of the enemy caused terror (Veg. 1.26 … *metu uniuersa confundi si intercisa acie ad dimicantium terga hostis accesserit*; cf. 50.2n.). It is a commonplace (cf. Sall. *Iug.* 58.4, Livy 5.13.6, Tac. *Hist.* 2.14.3) as well as recommended tactic (cf. 87.2n. *a tergo*; 88.3). **legionem ostenderunt**: sim. *BAfr.* 66.3; otherwise virtually unparalleled (*TLL* 9.2.1123.17–23; but cf. 67.1n.). **signa intulerunt** "they attacked." It was the task of the *signiferi* to provide the troops with directions (cf. Livy's playful line *signiferum manu arreptum secum in hostem rapit "Infer, miles" clamitans, "signum,"* 6.8.1). The carrying of the standards (on which see Töpfer 2011) towards the enemy signifies an attack (cf. 51.3n.); the opposite is *signa referre* (cf. Stäcker 2003: 179–86, 192–98, 205–18).

62.7 The Gauls behave exemplarily (cf. 25.3n.). **ne eo quidem tempore**: emphatic (cf. §4 *nec ... quisquam*). On *ne ... quidem*: 8.3n. **circumuenti ... interfectique**: 50.3n. The pair mimetically surrounds *omnes*.

62.8 Onas. 33.5 believed that a general should be careful of fighting in the melee (87.3n. *proelio intersit*) but "should despise death, if his army lost." **fortunam tulit**: a common expression of uncommon sense ("to meet" rather than "to endure" [*TLL* 6.1.1184.42–48]). **praesidio ... relicti**: as mentioned 61.5. The stock expression: 40.2n. **contra castra Labieni**: 61.5 *e regione castrorum*. **proelium commissum**: 34x in C. (10x in *CC*). **nostrorum militum uictorum**: 22.1n. *militum nostrorum*; 20.12n. *uictorem*. **impetum sustinere**: 10.3n.

62.9 cum suis fugientibus permixti: *permisceo* occurs first here in C. The expression, with which cf. Livy 26.44.4 *permixti fugientibus* (and 39.31.11), is colorful. **texerunt**: both "to cover" and "to shield" (*OLD* 2, 4).

62.10 Livy 23.31.8 is similarly phrased: *inde confecto quod mandatum est negotio reuertisset*. **hoc negotio confecto**: 5x in C. (none in *CC*). **reuertitur Agedincum** forms a ring with 57.1 *relicto Agedinco* to mark off the episode (cf. 15.6n. *misericordia*). **omnibus copiis** in contrast to *totius exercitus*: Strictly speaking, *totus* is used of "the fullness of one body," *omnis* is used of "a collective" (Serv. *Aen.* 1.185), which is why C. says 1.1.1 *Gallia est omnis diuisa in partes tres*. But, as Serv. also remarks, the semantic difference is often blurred (*TLL* 9.2.610.80–611.5). **ad Caesarem peruenit**: the last we heard, it was C. who was on his way to the Senones out of fear for L. (56.5). Did L. beat him to it? Two loose ends, perhaps, in an otherwise seamlessly woven double narrative. The location is unknown.

63–67 PRIDE AND SETBACK

After escaping his entrapment and reuniting with Labienus in the territory of the Senones (62.10n. *ad Caesarem*), it is assumed that C. stayed either there or among the Lingones to rest his troops and await the Germanic cavalry, newly solicited (Thévenot 1960: 111–17; cf. Rambaud 105). Thence, in September (perhaps), he headed south for the province to bring it aid, he claims, or rather withdraw from Gaul for the season; it would appear (66.3n. *fugere*; while C.'s troops remained numerous

[Carcopino 1958: 192–95], they had been battered [Jullian 1977: 213]). But en route, he was attacked by V.'s cavalry, about a day's march from Alesia (68n.). The Germanic auxiliaries won, and C. chased V. to Alesia.

In C.'s plot, V. is cast as "proud before the fall," a typical ὑβριστής (66n.), who, flush with victory and newly strengthened by the Aeduan alliance and a vote of confidence (63), recommends the attack that will rebound and send him fleeing. C. himself, meanwhile, appears first watchful, then in control, never harried. The realities are harder to discern: Not only is the battle location unknown, but the information offered by Plut. and Cass. Dio may contradict what can be gleaned from C.'s narrative; nor is there any knowing whether V. had planned to entrap C. at Alesia or was entrapped there himself (the former seems much more likely [67n.]). The last question mark behind this episode pertains to its understated tone: the stakes were high, as C. lets on in passing and later sources confirm, which surely should have made for a more emphatic celebration of this victory by the skin of his teeth?

63 The narrative returns to the Aedui, who compel their clients to join in the war. Their bid for the supreme command founders: V. is confirmed (§6n. *Vercingetorigem*), while they are left regretful – or so says C. who reassembles stock motifs (§§1n. *circummittuntur*, 3n. *territant*, 8n.) in a noticeably clipped *narratio*, the major point of which is the renewed amplification of the Gauls' war effort (as after Avaricum [29–35n.]; cf. *Introd.* 3c).

63.1–4 Events ensue swiftly, with not a connective to spare: *quae dicuntur sine coniunctione, ut plura uideantur* (Cic. *Part. or.* 54; Nägelsbach 1905: §200). The rhetorical form supports the content (*bellum augetur*). **Defectione Haeduorum cognita**: resumes 59.1n. The inserted Labienus episode separates the defection from its recognition (correlating narrative and narrated time). **bellum augetur**: only here in *CC*; *TLL* 2.1834.65 also cites Livy 5.8.4, 21.26.1. C.'s choice involves wordplay, as the following description is an instance of αὔξησις (*amplificatio* [*HLR* §§401–06]); similarly, 25.1n. *inspectantibus*, 38.10n. *permouet*, 54.3n. *exposuit*, 76.6n. *adspectum*, 77.3; 1.1.1 *est omnis diuisa* (suggesting rhetorical *diuisio* [cf. *HLR* §393]). Further on "self-reflexive expressions": Woodman on Tac. *Ann.* 4.11.1 *refutaueris*. **in omnes partes circummittuntur** is emphatic by pleonasm (19.3n. *inani simulatione*). The rare verb recurs in Livy and Frontin. The cliché: 4.5–7n.

63.2 The catalogue before Alesia includes the Segusiavi, Ambiuareti, Aulerci, and Brannovices (75.3nn.): Aeduan clients all. **quantum** "to the extent that." **gratia, auctoritate, pecunia**: this asyndetic tricolon increases in potency (*incrementum* [*HLR* §402]), wherein *gratia* signifies specifically the influence based on personal connections (i.e. *amici, clientes*; *VL* 308); cf. 30.3n. *auctoritatem*. The combination of "influence" and "money" is common in Greek and Latin (Pl. *Lach.* 187a πείθωμεν ἢ δώροις ἢ χάρισιν, "we may persuade them by gifts or personal favors," Cic. *Caecin.* 16 *gratia … pretio*, Sall. *Cat.* 49.1) and here continues the theme of Gallic bribery (1.5n. *praemiis*). **nituntur** forms a pronounced homoioteleuton with *circummittuntur*.

63.3 The language at 55.4n. *de pace et amicitia* has prepared for the Aeduan request. The sentence typically preserves the sequence of actions via clumsy pronouns. **nacti obsides**: sc. *Haedui* (rather than *legati*). These hostages (2.2n.) had served C. to secure Gallic compliance; they now serve the opposite purpose. **obsides … deposuerat**: for the pointed use of *deponere* ("to deposit" [*OLD* 7b]), cf. Verg. *Ecl.* 3.31 *ego hanc uitulam … depono: tu dic, | mecum quo pignore certes*. The expression recurs once (Livy 42.5.12). **apud eos**: sc. *Haeduos*, at Noviodunum (55.2). **dubitantes territant**: as did V. (4.9n.).

63.4 petunt "they then demanded" as suggested by its position; cf. §9n. *inuiti*. **rationesque belli gerendi** "plans for the conduct of war." The expression will become a Livian mannerism; cf. also Cic. *Att.* 9.19.3, Suet. *Tib.* 18 *cum compluribus de ratione belli communicauit*.

63.5 Internal challenges, often played out at an assembly, are a common theme in classical historiography; cf. Hdt. 8.2–3 (with Bowie). **re impetrata**: 35.6n. *re cognita*. **contendunt** "asked earnestly," *OLD* 7. **ipsis**: in emphatic contrast to V. It also stands in tension with *communicet* (cf. Isid. *Etym.* 20.2.14 *communicantes quod communiter, id est pariter, conueniant*). **summa imperii**: 20.5n. **re … deducta** "the issue turned into a dispute" (*OLD deduco* 12a). Their longstanding rivalry flared up (3.3n. *Aruernorum*). On factionalism: nn. on 4.2, 20. **totius Galliae concilium Bibracte indicitur**: C. employs *indicere* only with *concilium* (7x, starting with 1.30.4 *concilium totius Galliae in diem certam indicere*, which Görler 1977: 320 suggests this council resumes); the expression occurs 23x in Livy, and nowhere else (*TLL* 4.48.26–27). The location is specified by an accusative (6.44.1 *concilioque in eum locum Galliae indicto*). The significance of this *concilium* is controversial (Arbabe 2013: 30–50); cf. 4.1n. *Galliae*.

63.6 conueniunt undique frequentes "they came together from everywhere in great numbers"; the abundant phrasing recurs in Livy (33.1.2, 34.22.6, 39.3.4; not elsewhere). **multitudinis suffragiis** "a mass vote." *multitudo* (21.1n.), which follows *frequentes* naturally, may refer to the *plebs*

(*TLL* 8.1601.12–33, incl. *BC* 2.36.1); so probably here. **ad unum omnes** "all to a man." The idiomatic expression occurs 7x in C. (3x *BAfr.*); 9.5n. *omnes in unum.* **Vercingetorigem probant imperatorem**: V. is emphatically confirmed for the last time (4.6, 21.1, 30; *Introd.* 3g).

63.7 C. specifies the absent Gallic tribes (3x *abesse*) in the form of a *distributio* (*illi ... Treueri = hi*; *HLR* 671) of noticeably parallel structure punctuated by homoioteleuton. **Remi, Lingones, Treueri**: the Remi (< "Reims" [*DLG* 257]) lived in *Gallia Belgica*, about the departments of Marne and Ardennes, and remained supportive of C. throughout (2.3, 8.12), as did the Lingones (9.4n.). The Treveri (< "Trier" [*DLG* 301]), eastern neighbors of the Remi, loyally alerted C. to the arrival of the Suebi (1.37.3), but soon showed a more ambivalent attitude, which culminated in Indutiomarus' faction cooperating with Ambiorix (5.53; 55–58). Although they did not join V. in 52, C. found it necessary to dispatch Labienus the following year to their territory (8.25.2). Hornung 2016 reviews the archaeological evidence. **illi** "the (two) former." **amicitiam**: 31.5n. *amicus.* **sequebantur** "acted in accordance with," *OLD* 10. **aberant longius** "they were too far away." **ab Germanis premebantur**: Germanic aggression is a recurrent theme (from 1.1.4 *Heluetii ... fere cotidianis proeliis cum Germanis contendunt* to 8.25.2 *ciuitas propter Germaniae uicinitatem cotidianis exercitata bellis*); see Krebs 2006: 119–24, Johnston 2018: 87–91. Cf. 19.3n. *premerent.* **toto abessent bello**: *toto* suggests an ablative of time rather than separation.

63.8 The Aedui appear stereotypically fickle, regretting their self-inflicted change of fortune. The language is similarly clichéd: cf. 1.3–5 *dolerent ... queruntur ... fortunam.* **magno dolore** "with great indignation" (*OLD* 3); 15.2n. **deiectos principatu**: C. had mentioned his helping them to regain eminence (54.4n.). **queruntur ... et ... requirunt**: the chiastically arranged verbs form a phonetic *redditio* (40.4n. *interdicit*). **fortunae commutationem** is attested at *Rhet. Her.* 1.8, Cic. *Inu. rhet.* 1.19, *BC* 3.27.1, Tac. *Ann.* 12.47.4; cf. 59.3n. *commutatio.* **indulgentiam ... requirunt** "they felt the loss of (*OLD* 5) [C.'s] indulgence"; the expression recurs in [Ps.-Quint.] *Decl. min.* 328.15. *indulgentia* recurs once in *CC* (*BAlex.* 65.2). As 40.1[n.] *indulserat* indicates, *indulgentia* is colored by C.'s view. **suum consilium ab reliquis** = *suum consilium ab reliquorum consilio*; an instance of brachylogy, known as *comparatio compendiaria*, common in Greek and Latin (Hom. *Il.* 17.51 κόμαι Χαρίτεσσιν ὁμοῖαι, 'hair like [the hair of] the Graces'; H-S 826, Meusel on *BC* 2.39.3).

63.9 inuiti ... parent "It was therefore with great reluctance that ...." The asyndeton *conclusiuum* (H-S 830; Nägelsbach 1905: §200) and word order highlight the outcome. **summae spei** "of the highest prospects" recurs at Hirt. 8.8.2. It is a cliché of the young (Heubner on Tac. *Agr.* 9.6 *egregiae ... spei*; cf. 39.1). **parent:** C.'s sarcastic "last word" on the Aeduan defection.

64 V. requisitions additional troops, likely from the Aedui and allies, restates his intention of driving C. out by way of guerilla warfare, and resumes his attacks on the *prouincia.* The stakes are rising – or so it seems: the details provided are once more so hackneyed as to merit skepticism (nn. on §§1, 2–3, 5–7, and esp. *quorum ... resedisse;* 63).

64.1 V.'s arrangements are presented *imperatoria breuitate* (cf. 4n.). There are imprecise expressions (nn. on *reliquis, denique, ei rei, huc*) that have been suspected of corruption; but they are probably of C.'s own making. The actions are as typical as their phrasing; but the similarities with 4.7 are particularly striking. **ille:** *α*'s *ipse* is defensible ("for his own part" [*OLD* 3]; M-P 641.54–57 list similar uses) but probably owed to *imperat.* **reliquis ciuitatibus** lacks a contrastive group; the Aedui seem likely, which would make these *ciuitates* their client tribes (63.2n.). **denique,** "and then" (*OLD* 2), need not express finality. **ei rei:** 11.4n. It refers to the idea of the hostages' delivery. **huc:** sc. Bibracte (the last location mentioned). **omnes equites** may signify the sum total or the total of newly requested cavalry; V.'s following statement and 66.1 suggest the latter. **celeriter:** 4.6n.

64.2–3 V. reaffirms his guerilla strategy; his speech follows 14.2–9 closely. **peditatu:** cf. 20.3–12n. "heading." **contentum:** on "language of sufficiency" in the administrative discourse, cf. Coleman 2012: 218–19. **fortunam temptaturum:** 4.2n. **aut:** 14.2n. **in acie dimicaturum** recurs at *BAfr.* 81.2; rare elsewhere (*TLL* 5.1.1198.34–38). *β*'s *acie* is possible (*TLL* 5.1.1201.27–29). **abundet equitatu** repeats 14.3. **perfacile esse factu ... prohibere:** 1.3.6 *perfacile factu esse ... perficere* (V. shares *perfacilis* with Orgetorix only in all *CC*). Of the supines in *-u*, C. uses only *factu* (to which the inf. stands in apposition). It is here redundant and forms, with *perfacile*, a *figura etymologica* (cf. 58.2n.). Cf. nn. on 11.8 for adj. with *per-*, 1.7 for the Gauls' hollow sense of ease, and 14.2 for their efforts to deprive the Romans of supplies. **frumentationibus pabulationibusque:** 16.3n.

64.3 aequo modo animo: *modo,* "only," is to be taken with *corrumpant* and *incendant,* which in direct speech would be imperatives (K-S I 270). **sua ipsi frumenta:** cf. 1.16.1–3 *Caesar Haeduos frumentum ... flagitare. nam ... frumenta in agris matura non erant* (with Löfstedt 1928: 26). The emphasis on their own hands contrasts with the impersonal passive at 14.9n. *incendi* – suggesting greater confidence? **qua ... iactura ... uideant:** as the rel. clause provides the reason for their equanimity, the subjunctive is doubly motivated. Cf. 28.6n. *quae … pars*. V. here modifies 14.10 *grauia*. **perpetuum imperium libertatemque** "sovereign rule for all time"; the near oxymoronic hendiadys appealed to Cic. and Sall. (*Phil.* 3.37, 4.8, 5.37; *Cat.* 39.4). *perpetuum* bespeaks overconfidence (20.7n. *uictoria*). **consequi**: the present is variously used instead of the future, and esp. when the action is presented as already begun (K-S I 120; Eden 1962: 89).

64.4 his constitutis rebus: 9.3n. **Segusiauis**: 1.10.4 *ab Allobrogibus in Segusiauos … hi sunt extra prouinciam trans Rhodanum primi* (with *CG* 848 on the orthography). Identified as Aeduan clients (at 75.2), they were situated in the departments of Loire and Rhône around Feurs (cf. *TGF* 359). **qui … finitimi**: the Segusiavi alone, unless C. thinks of their neighbors, the Ambarri, *necessarii et consanguinei Haeduorum* (1.11.3), as proper Aedui. On the Aeduan territory, cf. Barrall *et al.* 2002: 275–92. **[ei] prouinciae**: the MSS interpolate *ei*; a copyist may have failed to understand that the reference was to the Roman *prouincia*. **milia peditum imperat**: he ordered them specifically for the attack on the province; there is no contradiction with §2.

64.5–7 V. renews (5n.) his attack on the *prouincia* (*Narbonensis*), dispatching three contingents to strike three Roman allies. **fratrem Eporedorigis**: nothing else is known of him. **Allobrogibus**: they lived in the north-eastern part of the Roman province, enclosed by the Rhône (1.6.2) and the Alps, with Geneva (1.6.3) and Vienne (9.3n.) as major settlements. Subjugated by Q. Fabius Maximus (Allobrogicus) in 120, they rebelled in 61 (1.44.9 with Holmes; Cic. *Prou. cons.* 32 *ortum repente bellum Allobrogum*, with Grillo; Brennan 2000: 359–64). They figured in the Catilinarian conspiracy (Sall. *Cat.* 40, with Ramsey).

64.6 proximosque pagos "neighboring communities." C. is the first to apply *pagus*, originally an administrative term for Italian districts (*CIL* I² 382 *senatus consultum de pago Montano*), to *Galli* and *Germani*, and usually to a segment of the people rather than the land (Bell 1995: 760–61). French *pays* is a distant descendant. **in Heluios … ad fines … depopulandos mittit**: the verb governs two constructions.

64.7 An *addendum* on the Allobroges is given after C. has completed the previous thought. **clandestinis**: 1.6n. **nuntiis legationibusque**: the pairing of individual messengers and delegations (also at 5.53.4; nowhere else) may suggest a flurry of activities. **nondum ab superiore bello resedisse** "had not yet calmed down (*OLD* 4b, only here in *CC*) after the previous war." C. attributes the same reasoning to the Helvetii in 58 (1.6.3

quod nondum bono animo in populum Romanum uiderentur, sc. Allobroges; cf.
Plut. *Crass.* 10.3), when it seemed more plausible, as it was in 61 that the
Allobroges had revolted (see above, §5). In fact, they did not cause C. any
trouble (cf. 3.6.5).

64.8 principibus pecunias: the plural signifies separate payments
(*Antibarbarus* 2.266). The juxtaposition is telling (37.1n. *pecunia*). **imperium totius prouinciae pollicetur**: a clichéd promise; it figures in the first
episode (*totius Galliae imperio potiri*, 1.2.2), as does the threat to the *prouincia* (*per prouinciam nostram iter facere*, 1.7.1; cf. *Introd.* 3c).

65 C. demonstrates foresight in meeting V.'s challenge once again (7n.),
now helped by the Gauls in *prouincia*: they not only enlist in the first-ever
non-Roman legionary cohorts (§1n. *prouincia*) but also fight V.'s Gauls of
their own volition, just as if they were Romans already (C. is at pains to
engender that impression: nn. on 2 *sua sponte, Gaio … filio*, 3 *magna … diligentia*; cf. 1.1n. *Italiae*). Hirt. would remark that C. had learned *quali quisque fuisset animo in totius Galliae defectione, quam sustinuerat fidelitate atque
auxiliis prouinciae illius* (8.46.5; Jullian 1909: 189–93 lists their services;
Ebel 1976 on the province's "Romanization"). C. himself recognizes the
weakness of his cavalry, to mend which he hires further Germanic troops
(§4n. *Germanos*); it is this measure that will win him the day thrice over
(67.5, 70.2–7, 80.6).

65.1 The prepositions and prefixes (underlined) combine to suggest that
the threat was kept away from the province. **Ad … casus** "in preparation
for … dangers," *OLD ad* 38, *casus* 8. **prouisa erant praesidia** recurs once in
a letter by Hirtius ([Cic.] *Att.* 15.6.2). C. had anticipated V.'s moves again
(9n.). **ex ipsa coacta prouincia**: sc. *Gallia transalpina* (6.1n.); the participle's position: 1.3n. *impulsi*. These troops may have formed the basis
of the *legio Alaudae*: *unam* (sc. *legionem*) *etiam ex Transalpinis conscriptam,
uocabulo quoque Gallico (Alaudae enim appellabatur), quam … postea uniuersam
ciuitate donauit* (Suet. *Iul.* 24.2; Keppie 1997: 90). Prior to the first century, legions were manned with citizens – except for severe crises (Brunt
1971: 428). **ab Lucio Caesare**: the middle position suggests that he was
involved in recruiting and allocating (cf. 1.2n. *Caesarem*). A cousin of C.'s
(*RE* "Iulius" 143), consul in 64, censor in 61, he joined C.'s campaign in
52 as *legatus*, and stayed on into the early phase of the civil war (*BC* 1.8.2),
when he may have changed sides. **ad omnes partes opponebantur** "were
set up in defense at all points."

65.2–3 The order of the transalpine peoples is inverted (64.5–6; cf. 14.3n.
quod). The "headings" (20.3–12n.), parallelism, and homoioteleuta *-ntur*

facilitate orientation. **sua sponte** emphasizes their loyalty to Rome. **cum finitimis** sc. *Gabalis et Aruernis* (64.6). **proelio congressi** recurs in Livy 31.34.5 and Tac. *Agr.* 28.2, who had this passage in mind (next note). **pelluntur** "defeated" (cf. Tac. *Agr.* 28.2 *saepe uictores, aliquando pulsi*). An instance of the "pressing metaphor" (10.3n. *impetum*), its literal meaning may be activated by *compelluntur.* **Gaio Valerio Donotauro, Caburi filio**: C. singles out a participant (cf. 3.1n. *Citam*). C. relied on this man's brother in his first year (1.47.4, 53.5); he mentioned their father, too, as having been enfranchised by C. Valerius Flaccus, whose *praenomen* and *gentilicium* he consequently added to his Celtic name (*RE* "Valerius" 114, 147; Badian 1958: 253; *DLG* 432). The appendix of the paternal lineage to Donotaurus' name (*DLG* 147, 291) emphasizes his hereditary citizenship, symbolizing successful acculturation. **principe**: 1.4n. **intra … compelluntur**: its first attestation; it will recur almost exclusively in historiographical texts (*TLL* 3.2030.6–11). **oppida ac muros**: at *BC* 2.25.1 *Curio castra Vari conspicit muro oppidoque coniuncta*, wherein *muro oppidoque* = "city wall"; such a hendiadys is here most likely, too. **compelluntur** echoes *pelluntur* (with change of meaning); cf. *BC* 3.46.5 *praecipites Pompeianos egerunt et terga uertere coegerunt.*

65.3 crebris "at frequent intervals" (*OLD* 1). **praesidiis** echoes §1 *praesidia.* **magna cum cura et diligentia**: the pairing (once more in *CC* at *BC* 2.13.2) is a Ciceronian mannerism (the exact phrasing at Cic. *Inu. rhet.* 1.30, 39); unlike Cicero, C. prefers *diligentia* to *cura* (21:4). *cura* may signify the honorable fulfillment of one's duties (*VL* 252–53); the phrase applies to both *dispositis* and *tuentur* and casts the Allobroges in a flattering light.

65.4 C. glosses over that, when the Aedui deserted, he lost most of his cavalry; this once again testifies to the effectiveness of V.'s strategic decisions (6.2n. *difficultatem*; 13.1n. *Germanos*; Introd. 2c). Given the distances and organization involved, C.'s plot strains credibility, as it would take about a month to recruit the forces. **Caesar quod**: 12.1n. *Vercingetorix ubi.* **hostes equitatu superiores esse**: C. echoes V.'s assessment (14.3, 64.2), indirectly acknowledging his strategy. **interclusis … itineribus**: twice more in C. (3.3.2, *BC* 1.75.2). Once again, C. validates V.'s strategy (14.2, 20.12). **et … nulla re** instead of *neque ulla re* for greater emphasis ("in absolutely nothing"; cf. Ringe 1880: 14–15). **ex prouincia atque Italia**: since C. considered *Gallia cisalpina* part of *Italia* (1.1n.), *prouincia* here once more signifies *transalpina* (§1n.). **subleuari** "to be supported/sent support" (*OLD* 2a). **trans Rhenum in Germaniam**: C. is the first to define the *Germani* as an ethnos living on the far side of the Rhine in the territory he calls *Germania* (Lund 1998; Rives 1999: 21–27). Consequently, when introducing the territory in *I*, he takes care to tie the *Germani* to "their" river (2.3, 27.4, 31.4–5+11+15, 33.3, 43.9; Krebs 2006: 119–20). Rhine depictions appeared during C.'s triumph in 46 (Flor. *Epit.* 2.88; Östenberg 2009: 215–19), indicating the lasting propagandistic value of the famous crossing (4.17–18, with Krebs 2008: 224–25). **mittit**: 9.5n. **pacauerat**: verb and noun are often used euphemistically and hyperbolically (as captured, sardonically, by Tac. at *Agr.* 30.5: *ubi solitudinem faciunt, pacem appellant*; Wölfflin 1888; Cornwell 2017: 11–15). A far cry from his later boast (*BC* 1.7.7 *omnem Galliam Germaniamque pacauerint*), C. may here allude to the tribes he had encountered in 55 (4.18.3; cf. 6.9.6). **equitesque … arcessit**: C. had recruited Germanic cavalry before (13.1n.). **leuis armaturae pedites**: "light infantry" likely "describes the more immediate tactical use of such infantry rather than the actual weight of their equipment" (Anders 2011: 130). **qui … proeliari**: 18.1n. *qui … consuessent.*

65.5 aduentu: 5.7n. *discessu.* **minus idoneis equis**: wildlife and livestock are commonly addressed in ethnographic writing (Hdt. 5.9.2 describes Scythian horses as "small and snub-nosed"). C. had described Germanic *iumenta* as *parua atque deformia* (4.2.2; Tac. *Germ.* 6.2 *equi non forma, non uelocitate conspicui*, with Rives ad loc.); but this may bespeak the Romans' high expectations (as articulated by Columella, *Rust.* 6.29.2–4) rather than anatomical differences (judging from the horse skeletons at Feddersen Wierde). **tribunis militum reliquisque [sed et] equitibus Romanis atque euocatis** "the military tribunes (17.8n.) and other Roman knights and re-enlisted veterans." Constans 1928: 133 explains *sed et* as relics of the gloss *sedentibus* (= "horsemen") on *euocatis*, not elsewhere identified as mounted. *euocati* is the technical term for re-enlisted veterans (*TLL* 5.2.1058.59–63, 70–73; it may also be attested on a sling-ball of lead [Poux-Guyard 1999]).

66 With C. retreating towards the *prouincia* (63–67n.), V. once more holds an assembly of the cavalry commanders of his newly strengthened troops. They embrace his surprising proposal to attack the legions and free Gaul for good.

   C. takes advantage of speech as structural device to mark the momentous occasion (15n.). In it, V. appears prideful before the fall, as C. assembles characteristics of the ὑβριστής, starting with the boastful exclamation (§2n. *uictoriae*; cf. Cairns 1996): Confident in his good fortune and augmented troops, he is not content with what he has but desires more (nn. on *satis … parum*; *confidat*). He mocks the Romans, whom he hopes to strip of their *dignitas* (nn. on *progredi … audeat, dignitate*), and makes the mistake Xerxes (the paradigmatic ὑβριστής [Val. Max. 9.5.2]) had been

warned of: "not to run into any … danger unnecessarily" (Hdt. 7.10.4).
V. may not have known, but many of C.'s readers did, that "pride, fully
matured, reaped bushels of ruin, ὕβρις … ἐξανθοῦσ᾽ ἐκάρπωσεν στάχυν ἄτης"
(Aesch. *Pers.* 821). Cassius Dio picked up on this, speaking of V.'s "contempt for C." (καταφρονήσας … τοῦ Καίσαρος) and his "stumbling out of
insolence" (ὑπὸ τοῦ θράσους ἔπταισε, 40.39.1+2). His pride in his cavalry is
ironic, given C.'s recent recruitments.

66.1 Interea dum haec geruntur: Cic. *Quinct.* 28 *haec dum Romae geruntur, Quinctius interea* … 5.37.2 *interim dum* is similarly pleonastic (Hellwig
1889: 21); cf. 37.1n. **hostium** is fronted as it contrasts with the allied
troops discussed before and applies to both *copiae* and *equites*. **copiae ex
Aruernis** "the troops from the Arverni": these are probably the troops
V. had relied on in defending Gergovia but left behind to visit Bibracte
(63.5). **equitesque toti Galliae erant imperati**: 64.1; 4.1n. *Galliae totius.*
conueniunt: C. fails to specify the location.

66.2–6 V. delivers his third deliberative speech (nn. on 14, 29): He excites
his audience with a declaration of victory (§2 *uenisse*), then shifts into
stating facts (*narratio*). By way of a *praemunitio* he refutes the position of
"leaving well enough alone" (*HLR* 854; §4), before introducing his proposal (*propositio*): to attack. He demonstrates its advisability (§5) and ends
on an emotive conclusion and the promise to have the infantry ready
as well (§6). **magno … consedit**: C. offers four potentially alleviating circumstances and concerns – just as he would to prepare his readers for
a defeat (Guillaumin 2009: 59–61). He may have hoped to march in a
south-easterly direction to Geneva (Jullian 1977: 215). **in Sequanos**: possibly named after their original habitat along the *Sequana* (Lambert 1994:
34), by C.'s time they lived to the north of the Helvetii in today's Franche-
Comté (1.1.5). In their power struggles with the Aedui they had first
benefitted then suffered from Ariovistus' help, until C. intervened (as *I*
narrates). They then virtually disappear – until now. Their history and C.'s
present march have suggested to some that they were friendly towards C.
(Plut. *Caes.* 26.6, but with Pelling); this appears questionable in the light
of their manifest hostility soon after (75.3; Thévenot 1960: 119–21; *pace*
Carcopino 1958: 116–18, 152–53). **per extremos … fines** "through the
border lands." **iter faceret**: 11.3n. *conficeret.* §4n. *impeditos.* **quo … ferri
posset**: C. continues to express his concern for the *prouincia* (64.4+8); V.
will offer a different interpretation momentarily. **circiter … consedit**: *BAfr.*
67.3 *ab eius castris milia passuum VI longe trinis castris dispertitis copiis consedit.*
ab Romanis "away from (*OLD* 4) the Romans." **trinis castris**: 46.4n. The
number of camps may here hint at the size of V.'s army (*magno … numero*).

conuocatisque ... demonstrat: the participial construction is an abl. absolute rather than a dative (cf. 4.1n. *conuocatis ... incendit*). **praefectis equitum** "cavalry commanders." **uenisse tempus uictoriae** is a crisp, rhythmical (molossus + cretic), and exaggerative shout-out – surprisingly unparalleled – which serves *captatio beniuolentiae: beniuolum efficiemus auditorem si nostram causam laudando extollemus* (*Rhet. Her.* 1.8). To the external audience, more than Gallic braggadocio (20.7n. *uictoria*), such "boastful reasoning" (Aesch. *Pers.* 820) bespeaks *hybris* (even if premature declarations of victory are commonplace, too [e.g. Polyb. 18.5.8; Livy 6.8.10]). There is dark irony in that the moment of victory had indeed arrived – for the Romans (Guillaumin 2009: 58).

66.3 fugere ... excedere: the artistic arrangement centers on *Romanos* (cf. 1.2n. *Caesarem*), emphatically states, in an isocolic chiasmus, the same fact twice ("theme and variation"), but leads with the most important development ("they are fleeing"); and it juxtaposes the enemy parties, soon to be separated for good (*Romanos Gallia*; for such significant juxtaposition, cf. Hom. *Il.* 6.6–7 Αἴας ..., ἕρκος Ἀχαιῶν, | Τρώων ῥῆξε φάλαγγα, "Ajax, the bulwark of the Achaians, broke the Trojans' battle line," *Bacas uir nequis adiese uelet*, *S. C. de Bacch.* 7). C. here discredits what seems to have been his actual flight as an untrue exaggeration by V. (Le Bohec 1998: 115; cf. §2 *quo ... ferri*; 20.8–9n.).

66.4 ad praesentem libertatem satis ... ad reliqui temporis pacem atque otium parum profici: V. may appear to demonstrate farsightedness; yet it was a well-known characteristic of the prideful soul "always to desire more than it has at present" (πλέον τι δίζησθαι αἰεὶ ἔχειν τοῦ παρεόντος, Hdt. 7.16.2; cf. Aesch. *Pers.* 824–26). For the antithesis between "now and in the future," here emphasized by the fronted positions of *praesentem* and *reliqui temporis*, cf. 4.16.6 *id sibi ad auxilium spemque reliqui temporis satis futurum*. The binomial pair is frequent (*TLL* 9.2.1186.40–45). 1.5n. *libertatem*; 23.5n. *ad*. **maioribus ... copiis** echoes *magno ... numero*, as if V. responded to the narrator's statement (cf. 38.6n. *consili*). **finem bellandi facturos**: 25.4n. The only other instance of this particular expression is Dict. Cret. 3.6 *finem bellandi fecit*. **proinde**: 38.8n. ‹in› **agmine impeditos**: the loss of *in* is easily explained by haplography (*proinde*) and probable in light of 3.24.2 *impeditos in agmine ... adoriri cogitabant*, not to mention that "on the march" *and* "hindered" (sc. *impedimentis*, as suggested below, §5; cf. 5.31.6 *longissimo agmine maximisque impedimentis*) makes for a stronger statement than merely "hindered by the march." Both the march – *plura in itineribus quam in ipsa acie pericula solere contingere* (Veg. 3.6.1) – and the baggage (10.4n.) put an army at a disadvantage.

66.5 V. employs another *argumentatio per complexionem* (20.6n.). **suis**: sc. those under attack. **iter confici**: 11.3n. **id quod ... confidat**: V.'s "confidence" to Romans sounds like "arrogance" (cf. *TLL* s.v. *confidentia*, 4.206.01, 205.45), all the more for suggesting that they would lose their *dignitas* rather than fight; it brings to mind other prideful character[s] "swayed by vain hopes" (Aesch. *Pers.* 804). The intended effect on C.'s readers can be gleaned from the internal audience's anger upon learning *qua arrogantia ... Ariouistus usus* (1.46.4). **relictis impedimentis**: sc. under duress (contrast 10.4n.); cf. 5.33.3–6. **rerum necessarium**: 55.2n. *impedimentorum.* **dignitate spoliatum iri**: the expression recurs Hirt. 8.50.3; Cicero favors it. It aptly suggests *dignitas* (30.3n.) as a spoil of war.

66.6 V.'s scorn rings hollow to Roman ears given C.'s recent recruitment (65.4n.). **de equitibus** "as for the cavalry" (17.2n. *de*), in position corresponding to *pedites* (cf. 20.3–12n.). **progredi modo extra agmen audeat** wittily mimics, by word order and choice and hesitant build-up, the action; such "ready wit is [the expression of] cultured pride (πεπαιδευμένη ὕβρις)" Arist. *Rh.* 1389b11–12. *progredi extra* is rare and possibly technical (*BAfr.* 24.2; *TLL* 10.2.1775.33). The present tense does not serve instead of *ausurus sit* but acerbically describes the Romans' general condition. **ne ipsos quidem**: edd. who prefer α's *et ... non debere* rob V. of his biting sarcasm (cf. 53.2n. *nihilominus*). As *praefecti equitum*, they know just as well as he does how pathetic is the Roman cavalry. **id** refers back to *proinde ... adoriantur.* **copias ... pro castris**: their position indicates readiness for battle; cf. *C. pro castris suas copias produxit ... ut, si uellet Ariouistus proelio contendere, ei potestas non deesset* (1.48.3). Hereby V. deviates from his oft-stated strategy not to engage in pitched battle (64.2n.). **terrori hostibus futurum**: 19.4n. *conspectum.* It here also bespeaks prideful confidence (cf. 76.5–6n.).

66.7 C. dramatizes the Gauls' determination by having them swear an oath (cf. *BC* 3.87). Such oaths all but once "foreshadow" peril or perjury in C. (Mannetter 1995: 129). **conclamant** "they shouted in approval that": by position pregnant, the verb signals the audience's approval (21.1n.) while also introducing the oath. **equites**: this imprecision (contrast §2 *praefectis equitum*) allows C. to insinuate that *all equites* swore the oath ("exagération par imprécision," Rambaud 182–86); cf. 54.1n. *omni.* **sanctissimo iure iurando**: the expression recurs once at Val. Max. 9.2.6 *sanctissimo Persis iure iurando obstrictus.* The superlative (only here in C.) has a histrionic ring. Cf. 2.2n. *iure iurando.* **ne tecto recipiatur, ne ... aditum habeat** "that no one be welcomed at home, no one have access": the epexegetical clauses specify the oath; they form a rising bicolon, whereof the latter part specifies the former ("theme and variation"). The anaphoric *ne* is similarly used at 6.21.3. *tecto recipere* is idiomatic (*TLL* 11.2.337.18–21), as is the metonymical use of στέγη/*tectum* (Aesch. *Eum.* 56 ἐς ἀνθρώπων στέγας, "into the homes of men"); as such, the latter seems to have been part of the traditional expression of banishment (*tecti et aquae et ignis interdictione*, Cic. *Dom.* 78; Rivière 2013). **uxorem:** 14.1on. *coniuges.* **perequitarit:** 39.3n. *coniunxerint.* The verb, extremely rare and first attested in C. (4.33.1), occurs almost exclusively in military (con)texts (*TLL* 10.1.1342.3).

67 C. is caught off guard by the attack (nn. on §§2 *nuntiata,* 3 *impedimenta*); but, contrary to V.'s prediction (66.5), the army train closes ranks, and the Germanic cavalry wins the day. A rout ensues; three Aeduan nobles are among the captives.

V.'s decision to risk battle has caused bewilderment ("Mais que s'agita-t-il dans l'esprit du chef?," Jullian 1977: 217), partly because it flew in the face of his guerilla strategy, mostly because he lost. Yet his recent success and C.'s distress make the move understandable (Cass. Dio 40.39.1; Deyber 2017: 91–93). There is also the distinct possibility that he had planned to fall back on Alesia and inveigle C. into moving between the "hammer and anvil" (68n.) – the cavalry battle being a means to that end (Stevens 1952: 17–18; Le Bohec 2012: 77–79); to believe that C. coaxed V. to hole up in the *oppidum* on the other hand (Carcopino 1958: 185–217) is to fall for C.'s plot (*Introd.* 2c). Given the dire consequences of another defeat, C.'s account appears understated; but the true state of affairs shimmers through (nn. on 66.2 *magno ... consedit,* §5 *tandem*), and Plutarch reports that C. lost his sword (*Caes.* 26.8 with Pelling; is this also when C. was briefly taken prisoner? [Serv. on Verg. *Aen.* 11.743]).

The battle site remains unidentified; suggestions have included Laignes, Baigneux-les-juifs, and Aignay-le-Duc (all roughly north of Alesia; Thévenot 1960: 133–45; Reddé 2012: 44–48; 68.2n. *altero die* is crucial). Cass. Dio's localization "among the Sequani" (40.39.1) may be inferred from 66.2; Plut. *Caes.* 26.7–8 lacks specificity (Pelling ad loc.).

67.1 A typical string of ablative absolutes. V.'s maneuver is standard and aims to attack C. on both sides (Veg. 3.20). **Probata re:** 15.1n. The missing demonstrative: 35.6n. **adactis** "bound" (*OLD* 9). **postero die**, by position, separates the voting and swearing from the action; 27.1n. **duae ... acies** "two (sc. *partes*) in battle formation." **se ... ostendunt** "they appeared," a military idiom (*TLL* 9.2.1122.51–59). **duobus** forms a polyptoton with *duae.* **ostendunt ... coepit**: an adversative asyndeton. **a primo agmine** "at the head of the (Roman) column." On the difference between *acies* and *agmen,* cf. Tac. *Ann.* 2.16.3 *ut ordo agminis in aciem adsisteret.*

67.2–3 The sequence of short, asyndetic, and (mostly) paratactic sentences evokes *imperatoria breuitas* (4n.). **qua re nuntiata:** 7.3n. This has

been read as C.'s confessing surprise (Jordan 1947: 46). C.'s reconnaissance: 11.8n. *exploratores.* **tripertito diuisum** varies §1; the rare adverb has
a technical ring. C.'s response is tactical standard (cf. Tac. *Agr.* 25.3–4).
pugnatur una omnibus in partibus recurs at 84.3. The impersonal verb
in initial position accelerates the narrative (as in 3.21.1, 4.26.1; cf. 1.1n.
cognoscit, 25.1n. *pugnaretur). una = uno tempore (OLD* 2); 9.5n. *omnes in
unum. partibus* echoes *partes* (with change of meaning).

67.3 impedimenta inter legiones recipiuntur "the baggage was drawn
back inside the legions" to protect it on all sides (Tac. *Ann.* 13.40.3 *recepta
inter ordines impedimenta). inter = intra* (which Nipperdey conjectured):
TLL 7.1.2126.50–52 (but it *is* confusing, as, frequently, the baggage train
travelled *between* legions as well [e.g. 2.17.2, 19.3]). Before the attack, C.
was not marching *quadrato agmine* (Sall. *Iug.* 100.1), i.e. with the baggage
train safely enclosed, as one should in the vicinity of an enemy (Veg. 3.6).
This also suggests surprise. But C. then defies V.'s prediction (66.4–5).

67.4 laborare aut grauius premi: "theme and variation"; *aut.* 14.2n. *premi:*
51.1n. **uidebantur** "could be seen"; the imperfect is iterative. **signa inferri:**
62.6n. **Caesar** in middle position: 1.2n. **aciem conuerti** "rearrange the
battle line." **et … tardabat et … confirmabat:** the parallelism, underlined
by homoioteleuton, bespeaks the orderly procedure. **ad insequendum:**
26.2n. **nostros spe auxilii confirmabat:** cf. *BC* 3.69.2 *legio celeris spe subsidii
confirmata.* The prospect of succor – a commonplace in ancient historiography (e.g. Livy 8.27.1 *cum … uana spe auxilii aliquamdiu sustinuissent*) –
reassured the troops. C.'s psychology: 47.3n. *elati.*

67.5 tandem suggests impatience: Cic. *Cat.* 1.1 *quo usque tandem,* Hor.
Carm. 3.15.2 (with N-R). **Germani:** their victorious intervention redounds
to C.'s credit, as he had recruited them specifically to redress the imbalance (65n.). **ab dextro latere:** 62.3n. **fugientesque:** 15.6n. *petentibus.*
flumen: the river has not been identified. It constitutes a rather natural
termination to a chase (cf. 1.53.1; Livy 1.27.10; Tac. *Ann.* 2.68.1; Thuc.
7.84). **persequerentur:** the prefix emphasizes the distance; it correlates
with *usque,* "all the way" (Cic. *Quinct.* 12 *ab atriis Liciniis … in Galliam …
usque transfertur*).

67.6 qua re animaduersa: this transition formula does not occur outside
of *CC* (11x; C-L 93–96). **fugae … caedes:** a "conventional pair" (Kraus on
Livy 6.8.7). **se fugae mandant:** C. took this choice expression (4x [2x *CC*])
from Sisenna (*FRHist* F22 [Krebs 2014]). **fit caedes:** sim. 70.5, 88.3. The
"passive periphrastic" with *fio,* attested from "early Latin onwards" (*OLS*
1.253–54), occurs first here in C. (then 70.1, 79.3, 88.6); cf. 42.3n.

67.7 C. focuses on Aeduan captives rather than the fact that their cavalry had switched sides (65n.). Elite captives would normally be entrusted to officers (Fischer 1914: 169). **nobilissimi**: of the six instances of the superlative, five occur in *I* (5x in *BAlex*.). This disproportion indicates C.'s reluctance to acknowledge *nobilitas* in the later books; it may here recur to highlight Aeduan perfidy (Barlow 1998: 141). **perducuntur**: 13.2n. **praefectus equitum**: 66.2. **proximis comitiis**: i.e. of the Aedui for chief magistrate (33.3–4). *proximus* may signify "just mentioned" (*OLD* 5c), highlighting perfidy once more. Speaking of *comitia* is a blatant instance of *interpretatio Romana*. **Cauarillus**: this is his sole attestation. **post defectionem Litauicci**: 40.7. **Eporedorix** differs from the rival of Viridomarus (38.2n.); unknown otherwise. **ante aduentum Caesaris** is used identically at 6.15.1; cf. 5.54.2 *aduentu in Galliam Caesaris*, 6.12.6; cf. *BC* 1.48.5, Amm. Marc. 16.3.1. Dating with C. suggests an epochal change. **bello contenderant**: the expression occurs once more at Verg. *Aen.* 4.105. The war: 5.2n. *Haeduos*.

68–90 THE GRAND FINALE (THAT WAS NOT)

"Alesia" occupies a special place within and without the *Gallic War*: Its longest episode, it contains a technical ekphrasis nonpareil (72–74), an epic catalogue of enemy forces, and the longest direct speech (75, 77); it is quickened first by the threat, then by the peril of Roman encirclement and two-fronted combat (74, 79–88n.), and it ends with C.'s conspicuous intervention and V.'s ultimate surrender (88, 89). The grand finale, it evokes the battles of Syracuse and Numantia and resounds increasingly loudly with the language of the military report to conclude not just *VII* but the entire *BG* (89–90n.) – although the war was to continue more or less immediately and for two years (*Introd.* 2c, 3a). It is designed to be a monument to C.'s generalship.

This literary monumentalization, in turn, has enabled modern archaeology to compare and interpret the findings around Mont-Auxois at Alise-Sainte-Reine: Following the discovery of an inscription containing ALISIIA (*CIL* XIII 2880 [Reddé-von Schnurbein 2001: 4]), Napoleon III and his aide-de-camp Stoffel unearthed fortifications matching C.'s description, along with *denarii* predating 52 and late Iron Age weaponry; yet, alternative sites continued to be proposed (Reddé 2012: 82–98, 109–24; Olivier 2019). But excavations in the 1990s not only confirmed the results (largely); they also brought to light additional aspects – including projectiles bearing Labienus' abbreviated name – and settled the question beyond doubt (Reddé-von Schnurbein 2001, Sievers 2001: 238 [nr. 727];

Le Bohec 2012: 98–107 reviews counterarguments). Aside from Alesia's significance in French history (underscored by Millet's statue of V. nearby [cf. Le Gall 1970]), the coexistence of C.'s expansive description and the extensive remains is virtually unparalleled in Greco-Roman literature.

Like "Avaricum" and "Gergovia" (nn. on 14–28, 36–56), "Alesia" is divided into two parts: the siege, the battle (68–78, 79–88). Of its four confrontations, one occurs before the support troops have arrived, three thereafter (nn. on 70, 79–88; Le Bohec 2012: 147–71). V.'s decision to ask for relief troops (71n.) *following* the first engagement is a typical dramatization and historically implausible – and all the more so if V. had planned the "hammer and anvil" tactic all along (68n.). The siege itself is modelled on Scipio's famed siege of Numantia in 134/3 (68–78n.); while the narrative of the two-fronted engagements incorporates elements of the battle in the Syracuse harbor (79–88n.). Throughout, the Gallic multitude is the dominant theme, as emblematized by the catalogue (75, 76.6n. *multitudinis*; *Introd.* 3c).

C.'s "dangers near Alesia became justly famous" (Plut. *Caes.* 27.5): they would earn him an unprecedented twenty days of thanksgiving (90.7n.), haunt the Gauls during the remainder of the campaign (Hirt. 8.14.1, 34.1), and impress later authors: Diodorus hints at their divine character (4.19.2), Velleius makes it explicit: *tantae res gestae quantas ... nullius nisi dei* (2.47.1; Le Gall *et al.* 1973 document further references). Bibaculus' epic line *hic qua ducebant uastae diuortia fossae* may or may not relate to Alesia (Frg. 16 Courtney), and the parallels with Sallust's account of Zama (esp. *Iug.* 57–61 [Martin 2001: 401–02]) lack specificity; but Tacitus would read C. carefully (*Ann.* 4.47–51; *Introd.* 3h).

68–78 Besieging "Numantia"

Alesia's topography necessitated a siege (68–69): When C.'s soldiers were working on the investment, V.'s cavalry sortied but lost; the latter then dismissed his cavalry to recruit further troops, rationing necessities for thirty days (70–71). This development compelled C. to augment his fortifications facing Alesia and duplicate them at his rear against the relief forces (72–74). These forces, meanwhile, were gathering in Aeduan territory, whence a quadrumvirate led them to Alesia (75–76). They arrived after the deadline, when the besieged had pondered cannibalism but settled for ejecting those unfit for war (77–78).

The narrative shows consummate skill: It juxtaposes the description of the fortifications with the enumeration of the forces to be kept at bay; both separate V.'s dispatching his cavalry from its return with the troops to align narrative and narrated time (71.9n. *exspectare*). Lastly, the end

of the wait is marked by the imaginary Critognatus' plea for cannibalism
(77n.), which dramatizes Gallic determination just as actual cannibalism ended narratives of the Numantians' resistance to Scipio (Val. Max.
7.6.ext.2 *Numantini ... a Scipione uallo et aggere circumdati ... humanorum
corporum dapibus usi*, App. *Hisp.* 96). Scipio's siege was famous (cf. Cic.
Rep. 1.17; 68.3n. *circumuallare*), and it appears to have inspired C. in
his siege works (72–74n.) and his write-up: there are several parallels
between his and Appian's accounts (nn. on 69, 77, 80.1, 81.4 *nostri ...
accedunt*, 83.2 *quem ... circumplecti*; cf. 71.4n. *frumentum*, 78.4n.). Appian
might have adapted C. to elaborate on Scipio's siege (cf. *Gall.* 18.3); and
both certainly draw from the same historiographical tradition – but it is
likely that both were inspired by the same narratives (Polybius' *History of
the Numantian War* and Rutilius Rufus' autobiography [Richardson 2000:
5]) and that C. evokes Scipio as *exemplum* to rival him in diligence (τῷ
Σκιπίωνι πάντα ἀκριβῶς διετέτακτο, App. *Hisp.* 92; cf. Rambaud 231n.127,
Reddé 2008: 287); tellingly, in all comparable numbers, C. outdoes him
(nn. on 69.6 *circuitus*, 69.7 *castella*, 72.4 LXXX), not to mention his doubling Scipio's circumvallation (74n.).

68 Following his defeat, V. moves to Alesia, a day's march away from the
battle site (§2), with C. in pursuit. The narrative – typically binary (1–2n.)
and schematic (C. presses on, arrives, surveys the scene, decides what to
do), and in typical style (6x abl. absolutes, repetitions of *castra*, *ducere*; nn.
on §§1, 2–3) – intimates that C. was in control (*fugato*, *secutus ... passum,
tribus milibus ... interfectis*, *perterritis*); but a closer reading reveals that V.
held the initiative (nn. on *protinus*, *impedimentis ... deductis*; 69.5).
     Alesia was an inspired choice for finally implementing "the hammer and
anvil" tactic, when one force pins down the enemy and the second force
assaults it (Deyber 1987; cf. 67n.); this may have been the Gauls' plan ever
since Avaricum (*Introd.* 2c). At 240 acres, it was one of the largest *oppida*
and topographically formidably fortified, just as C. explains (Petit 2001;
Reddé 2012: 132–37): Mont-Auxois rises 1,300 feet above sea level, its
slopes steep (Alesia's name may signify "cliff" [*DLG* 39]); it is surrounded
by hills except for the Plaine des Laumes to its west (69.3; cf. fig. 8).
Other factors may have weighed in its favor: Diod. 4.19.2 reports that the
Gauls honored the oppidum "as the hearth and mother-city (ἑστίαν καὶ
μητρόπολιν) of all of Gaul." Its religious significance is uncertain, but it
would have imbued V.'s choice with a strong symbolism (cf. 89n.).

68.1–2 The focalization shifts in typical fashion (*Introd.* 3c, g). The first
sentence presents continuative facts linked by *-que* and punctuated by
verbs in final position (cf. 11.5–6n.). **Fugato omni equitatu:** C. leads
with the surprising, characteristically totalizing fact (*fugare* only here in

C.); readers might remember V.'s confident 66.3n. *fugere*. **copias suas, ut pro castris collocauerat, reduxit** "withdrew his troops, arranged before the camps as they had been"; 40.3n. *castris*, 22.1n. *ut*, 36.2n. *collocauerat*. Another reminder of V.'s (over-)confidence (66.6n. *copias*). **protinus**, "straightaway" suggests that V. had prepared to fall back on Alesia. **quod ... oppidum**: the relative regularly agrees with the predicate (G-L 614.3b). **Mandubiorum**: this mysterious people is mentioned in *VII* and Strabo 4.2.3 (following C.); Barrall *et al.* 2002 survey the archaeological data. Given the cannibalistic proposal (77n.), their name calls forth *manduco*, "to chew" (C. S. Kraus *per litteras*), and all the more so as the Manducus, "Chewer," was a stock character of the *fabula Atellana* (Krebs 2023). **iter facere coepit**: 34.3n. **celeriter** is emphatic by position; 4.6n. **impedimenta ... iussit**: the presence of the baggage train suggests that, if victorious, V. was also prepared to chase the Romans. **subsequi**: 16.1n.

68.2–3 contain typically Caesarian sentences (27n.). **impedimentis ... deductis** suggests that C. intended further engagements (10.4n.), not a siege. By echoing *impedimenta ... educi* he brings out the parallel movements (*Introd.* 3g). **praesidio relictis**: 40.3n. **quantum ... passum** "as long as daytime allowed" (*OLD pati* 8); cf. 4.35.3 *quos tanto spatio secuti, quantum cursu et uiribus efficere potuerunt*. The position of *passum* creates a homoioteleuton (*-um*) that frames the colon (cf. 40.4n. *interdicitque*). **tribus milibus**: a standardized figure (11.2n. *sescentos*). **ex nouissimo agmine** "of the rearguard"; a technical term (freq. in C. but missing in *CC*), wherein *nouissimus = extremus*. In C.'s time, *nouissimus* served more generally as synonym for *extremus* (4.16.7 *hoc nouissimo proelio*); but Cic. avoided it (Gell. *Att.* 10.21). Attacking the rear is a recognized technique (again 88.7). **altero die** = *postero die* (11.1n.); its position: 67.1n. **castra fecit**: again at 83.2, 6x in total (6x *CC*).

68.3 perspecto urbis situ: as in 36.1n. The impressions are given in the next chapter. **equitatu** is an unparalled abl. of respect (*TLL* 10.1.1011.5; *NLS* §55). **qua ... confidebant** "the part of the army in which they had the greatest confidence"; cf. 28.6n. *quae ... pars*. **adhortatus ad laborem**: 40.4n. *adhortatus*. **circumuallare**: C. anticipates his survey's result in order to finish this line of narrative (cf. 64.7n.). This is not his first mention of circumvallation (11.1n.), but it may still evoke Scipio at Numantia, "the first ... to encircle a city (πρῶτος ... περιετείχισε πόλιν) that did not shun battle" (App. *Hisp.* 91).

69 C. sets the scene methodically and selectively, surveying first the Gallic side (§§1–4, 5), in itself divided according to the categories of *loci natura* and – as the heading *sub muro* indicates – man-made fortifications (*munitio* [14.9n.]); the topography of the *oppidum* (3x) is viewed with "the general's eye" (Cancik 1998: 120) from the summit (most importantly) to the plain and surroundings (*pars* 3x), with due attention to *colles* (4x) and *flumina*. Then ensue the Roman fortifications (§§6–7, headed by *eius munitionis*), whose scale and detail show C.'s command of the situation, just as they invite comparison with Scipio's siege.

Not only is Numantia's topography similar to Alesia's (cf. Schulten's map [Reddé-von Schnurbein 2001: 501]), the two descriptions by Appian and C. also reveal parallels (but cf. Horsfall 1985 on the *general* typicality): "Numantia was sheer / difficult of access on account of two rivers and ravines (ποταμοῖς δύο καὶ φάραγξιν ἀπόκρημνος, cf. §1), and dense woods surrounded it (ὕλαι … περιέκειντο, cf. §4 *colles … oppidum cingebant*); but there was one passage to the plain; it was filled with trenches and palisades (μία κάθοδος ἦν ἐς τὸ πεδίον, ἣ τάφρων ἐπεπλήρωτο καὶ στηλῶν, cf. §§3–5)"; cf. nn. on §7 *castra, castella, stationes*.

69.1 Cf. Cic. *Fam.* 15.4.10 [sc. *oppidum*] *cum esset altissimo … loco*, which supports C.'s (sometimes doubted) unaccompanied *erat*. **Ipsum erat oppidum** "as for the *oppidum*" (*ipse* in transition: *OLD* 3); a standard transition to a new section (cf. Thuc. 1.24 "Epidamnos is a city situated …"; 19.1n. *Collis erat*). **in … loco** "on top of a hill, a very elevated (cf. 36.1n. *altissimo*) place"; the latter abl. is an appositional attribute (cf. Hor. *Carm.* 4.4.1 *qualem ministrum fulminis alitem*). **obsidione expugnari** is unparalleled. C. implicitly rules out the *oppugnatio* (32.2n.).

69.2–4 Livy 36.24.8 is once more indebted to C. (cf. 27.2n. *fructum uictoriae*): *milites … radicibus montium* (*collis radices*) *circumduci ad rupem iussit, quae, fastigio altitudinis par* (*pari altitudinis fastigio*) *… erat.* **cuius collis**: 12.3n. *quo ex oppido*. **radices**: 36.5n. **duo duabus … flumina** "two rivers on two sides"; the polyptoton (32.5n. *pars cum parte*) here combines with a *geminatio* (before C. attested at Naev. Frg. 82 [Warmington], Accius Frg. 33, and Plaut. *Epid.* 27); the artful order is mimetic. The rivers are the Oze and the Ozerain. **subluebant** "washed." The verb occurs once more in *CC* at *BC* 3.97.4 *montem flumen subluebat*. It is exceedingly rare (rendering noteworthy Curt. 9.6.20 *mari subluitur*).

69.3 id oppidum "the said *oppidum*." **in longitudinem patebat** is a technical expression that recurs 70.1, 79.2 (and 1.2.5, 6.29.4; cf. *TLL* 10.1.665.46–58); cf. Oros. 6.10.18 *silua … Galliae … in longitudinem plus quam quinquaginta milibus passuum patet*. C. accurately describes the Plaine des Laumes (Reddé 2012: 113).

69.4 C.'s information is accurate (Petit 2001: 58b offers a geological map). **reliquis ex omnibus partibus**: except for the area described at 83.2.

colles … cingebant: Verg. *Aen.* 8.597 *colles … nigra nemus abiete cingunt* is the only comparable instance. **interiecto spatio**: 19.4n. **pari altitudinis fastigio** "of a rise equal in height"; the pleonastic *fastigio* (first here in C.) produces homoioteleuton (*-io*) and isocolon with the preceding abl. (cf. 17.3n. *aedificiorum*). The expression is used twice by Livy (above, 44.9.8), not elsewhere.

69.5 The fact that the Gauls were already installed at Alesia suggests that V. had planned to fall back on it (68n.). **sub muro**: 48.2n. **quae pars … spectabat** "on the side of the hill that faced east." The terminology is technical, geographical: 1.1.6 *spectant … orientem solem*, 5.13.1 *angulus … ad orientem solem … spectat*; *OLD* 10a. **hunc omnem locum**: the demonstrative resumes the relative clause (regularly when the relative precedes). **fossam et maceriam** is repeated at 70.5. The rare pairing occurs only in horticultural contexts (*Columella, Rust.* 5.10; *Arb.* 18), where the "garden wall" (*OLD*) belongs, too; cf. 72–73n. The archaeological evidence is discussed in Reddé-von Schnurbein 1993: 296–97. **sex … pedum**: 8.2n. **praeduxerant**: 46.3n.

69.6 eius munitionis … circuitus x milia passuum: the genitive is fronted to contrast with the Gallic fortifications. It is not unusual to specify circumferences; cf. Polyb. 10.11.4 "the city's circumference was not greater than 20 stades, though I am fully aware that many have stated …"; it was specified of Numantia, too (as 24 stades, with the investment more than doubling that number [App. *Hisp.* 90+93]). The MSS vary between *x* and *xi*; the actual circumference is 15 km (9.3 miles), or roughly 10 Roman miles (Reddé-von Schnurbein 2001: 77). There are thirteen references to Roman *munitio* in this first half of the episode, befitting its decisive importance (89.4n. *in munitione*). **instituebatur**: the verb's tense is inchoative ("to set to work" [*OLD* 5]). **tenebat** "contained" (*OLD* 4); unparalleled in conjunction with *circuitus*.

69.7 castra opportunis locis: 16.1n. (site selection). Their total is not specified (edd. have resorted to conjecture); nor has archaeology settled the question (von Schnurbein 2001: 507–13). Recent excavations have confirmed the three camps Napoleon had identified on the hilltops, including C.'s probable camp on the Montagne de Flavigny and Labienus' on the Montagne de Bussy (the latter identified by inscribed lead missiles [Sievers 2001: 238]). Of particular interest is the perhaps innovative feature of the *clauicula* (a semicircular ditch that protected the gate [Barrall *et al.* 2002: 179–84, Reddé 2001: 536]) as well as similarities with the camps before Numantia (von Schnurbein 2001: 509, 542). The five camps Napoleon located in the valley of Grésigny and the Plaine des Laumes, however, are misidentified or uncertain. **ibi** sc. *opportunis locis.* **castella ... facta**: the expression recurs *BAfr.* 26.6, 38.1; Livy 5.5.5, 19.5 (*TLL* 3.525.73–74). *a castris diminutiuo uocabulo sunt nuncupata castella* (Veg. 3.8). A standard feature of larger sieges (Reddé 2001: 491), "forts" had served Scipio at Numantia (App. *Hisp.* 90 δύο στρατόπεδα ... φρούρια δ' ἑπτὰ περιθείς); C. would use a similar number at Dyrrachium (*BC* 3.43.1–2, 44.2–3, with the comment at 47.1 on the *noua ... belli ratio*). Several such forts have been identified; their number is unknown (von Schnurbein 2001: 508). **quibus in castellis ... tenebatur**: Philo, *Bel.* 8.D94 recommends that, in a situation much like C.'s, "there be night-watches (ἐκκοιτίαι) at night, and [that] during the day [the general] be on the lookout in suitable places (σκόπει ἐν τοῖς ἐπιτηδείοις τόποις), and [that] he send out spies (κατασκόπους)." The detail provided at *BHisp.* 6.3 is similar (the text is uncertain). **quibus in castellis**: 12.3n. *quo ex oppido.* **stationes** are, normally, "pickets" stationed outside a camp to protect the gates (4.32.1 *pro portis castrorum in statione*; Livy 3.5.4 *uigiliae in urbe, stationes ante portas praesidiaque in muris disposita*; Fröhlich 1889: 234; Fischer 1914: 168–91). For a similarly aggressive use of them in a siege, cf. Tac. *Ann.* 6.34.1 [cf. 36.5–7n.], 14.8.2; Frontin. *Str.* 2.6. Curiously, Appian reports how Scipio "did *not* set up advance guards in citadels (προφυλακὰς ... ἐπὶ φρουρίων), as some do" (*Hisp.* 87). **ne qua subito eruptio fieret** recurs below (70.2); 59.6n. *subito.* The "sudden sortie" (7.2n. *eruptionem facere*), which the soundplay emphasizes, is a commonplace (Woodman on Tac. *Ann.* 4.47.3). **excubitoribus ac firmis praesidiis** "sentries and strong garrisons." *excubitor* is unprecedented (*TLL* 5.2.1288.29) and only here in *CC*. It suggests that some soldiers kept watch outside the *castella* (11.6n. *excubare*). The abl. of agent shades into the instrumental when persons "are regarded as the mere instruments in the hands of another" (*NLS* §44); that usage is facilitated by its juxtaposition with *praesidiis*.

70 A typical cavalry skirmish in the plain turns out in C.'s favor thanks to Germanic reinforcements (§3n.). With the Gauls fleeing, panic ensues, first at their defensive works, then inside their camps, lastly in Alesia itself. The developments are commonplace, parallels with 13.1–2nn. particularly dense. The narrative is clipped, asyndetic, and lively (the last-mentioned quality enhanced by glimpses of particular moments [cf. nn. on 63, 63.1–4; *nonnulli*]); its architecture is carefully balanced: the first half describing the battle (1–4), the second the panicked flight (5–7, *perturbantur, perterriti*), with close correspondences between the two: *contenditur – caedes, Germanos – nonnulli, legiones – legiones, angustioribus portis – intra munitiones, Germani – nonnulli.*

70.1 Opere instituto resumes 68.3 *circumuallare instituit* (7.1n. *missus*). **equestre proelium**: the initiatory move (13.1n.). **intermissam collibus**

"set between (17.1n.) the hills." **quam … supra demonstrauimus**: 69.3.
summa ui … contenditur: a cliché, typically phrased: Quadrig. *FRHist* F6
utrisque summo studio pugnantibus, Sall. *Hist.* 1.47, Livy 21.11.11. *summa
ui* occurs again at 73.1; its only other instance in *CC* is at 3.15.1. It will
become a Livian mannerism. **ab utrisque**: 7.2n.

70.2 legionesque pro castris constituit: when V. placed his troops thus
(66.6n.), it was an offensive gesture (cf. §5). Peculiarly, *legiones + pro castris*
occurs 5x in C. (once in *CC*) but not elsewhere. **ne qua subito irruptio**
varies 69.7n.

70.3 By stating that his showing his legions inspired his cavalry, C. perhaps
belittles the impact of the Germanic reinforcement; cf. 13.1n. **praesidio
legionum** follows naturally on *legiones pro castris* as *"praesidium" dictum qui
extra castra praesidebant … quo tutior regio esset* (Varro *Ling.* 5.90). **nostris
animus augetur** "our men's spirit rose"; an idiomatic expression (*TLL*
2.1350.13–29) with a dative of reference. **in fugam coniecti**: 13.2n. **se …
angustioribus portis** rephrases 28.3[nn.]. **multitudine**: 21.1n. **angustioribus … relictis** "with the passages left (*OLD* 11b; sc. in the *munitiones*
specified above [69.5] and below) too narrow" (sc. to accommodate the
fleeing). **coartantur** "pressed together"; only here in *CC* (cf. *BAlex.* 74.4
coartationem). The verb is the *uox propria* for the narrowing of a passage:
Livy 28.5.8 *angustae fauces coartant iter*, Plin. *Ep.* 2.17.3 *uia coartatur.*

70.4 acrius "too intensely" (sc. for the Gauls to resist). **munitiones** sc. *fossa
et maceria* (69.5).

70.5 fit magna caedes recurs at 88.3 (and slightly varied at *BHisp.* 37.2; cf.
42.3n.), then 6x in Dares. **nonnulli … nonnulli**: 24.4n. *alii* (on *euidentia*).
transire … transcendere: C. varies for greater precision (‹*scando* "to climb");
maceriam: 69.5n. **quas pro uallo constituerat** "which he had placed before
the rampart," as part of the *castra* (§2). Even though the camp's rampart
was preceded by a ditch (2.5.6 *castra … uallo fossaque … muniri*; 11.5n.),
the synecdochical expression is always *pro uallo*, never *pro fossa*. **promoueri**
"[the legions] move forward," now signaling confidence (§2n.).

70.6 ueniri ad se confestim: the adverb is common in administrative writing, esp. in conjunction with verbs of movement (Odelman 56–60). Cf.
61.1n. *uentum. ad = aduersus* (*OLD* 31). **"ad arma,"** already at 4.2, is "the
normal call 'to arms!'" (N-H on Hor. *Carm.* 1.35.15). Its contiguity with
conclamant suggests direct speech. **in oppidum irrumpunt**: the echo of §2
irruptio highlights the reversal; what C. feared now happens to V.

70.7 ne castra nudentur: sc. *defensoribus* (cf. 3.4.2 *nudata defensoribus*; 44.1n.
nudatum hominibus); similarly absolute: 2.23.4, Frontin. *Str.* 2.5.8. **multis**

... **recipiunt** is a lapidary sentence of epigraphic brevity (11.8n. *caperentur*) typical of the military bulletin; it forms a rising tricolon. **multis ... compluribus**: this *uariatio* occurs only here in C. but frequently in *CC*. Cf. Livy 7.8.2 *multi utrimque cadunt, plures uulnera accipiunt*. **equis captis**: those left behind in §5.

71 On the heels of another loss and with enclosure imminent, V. dismisses his cavalry (of greater cost than use to the besieged) requesting that all of Gaul send all men of arms (cf. 75n.). His parting words are commonplace (§§2–4 *merita ... suae salutis ... de communi libertate*), particularly closely paralleled in C.'s plea to the Aedui (nn. on §§2–3, 5), and once darkly ironic (3n. *cruciatum*); ringing repetitions provide structure and highlight V.'s typically decisive deeds (§§5–6; cf. 3on.), by which he hopes to stave off hunger for thirty days. But the distance some of the Gauls had to travel to recruit additional troops would have been impossible to cover twice within thirty days (cf. 1n.), and V. had probably planned to "trap" C. at Alesia all along (67n.). A rhetorical set-piece (cf. §1n.), this section is as improbable historically as it is effective dramatically (cf. 15n.).

71.1 The sequence in Thuc. 7.60 is similar (cf. 68–9on.): The Athenians notice their enclosure (ἀπόκλησιν ὁρῶσιν; cf. §1), discuss their supply shortage (ἀπορίαν τῶν τε ἄλλων καὶ ὅτι τὰ ἐπιτήδεια οὔτε αὐτίκα ἔτι εἶχον ...; cf. §4), and end deciding "to compel everyone of suitable age and even minimally fit for service to embark (ἀναγκάσαντες ἐσβαίνειν ὅστις καὶ ὁπωσοῦν ἐδόκει ἡλικίας μετέχων ἐπιτήδειος εἶναι; cf. §2 *omnesque ... cogant*)." Cf. also Livy 3.26.4: *quae* [sc. *munitiones*] *priusquam ... clauderent exitus, quinque equites ... emissi Romam pertulere* .... **Vercingetorix priusquam ... perficiantur** is part of V.'s reasoning; 12.1n. *Vercingetorix ubi*. **omnem ab se equitatum ... dimittere**: 8.4n. *omne ad se bellum*. The prefix suggests "in various directions," as does *discedentibus*.

71.2–3 partly repeats 54.3. V.'s rhetorical strategy: 54.3–4n. **discendentibus** sc. *equitibus* (cf. 15.6n. *petentibus*), as inferred from *equitatum* (a typical *constructio ad sensum*). It resumes *dimittere* (a varied *reduplicatio*, 7.1n. *missus*). **suam quisque eorum ciuitatem adeat**: 32.5n. *suas cuiusque eorum clientelas. adire* carries connotations of encouragement (*TLL* 1.620.61); with *ciuitatem* it may be technical, cf. Cic. *Att.* 1.19.2 *legati ... qui adirent Galliae ciuitates*. **omnesque qui ... ferre possint** recurs (almost) verbatim at *BAfr.* 36.1, Livy 3.42.6 (with Ogilvie); C. himself modifies the phrase at 2.16.1, 5.3.4 (cf. 75.1). The criterion is commonly mentioned: 1.29.1, 2; Polyb. 2.24.16, Dion. Hal. 8.64. *per aetatem*, "by reason of (*OLD per* 12) [their] age," precludes the association of the formulaic *ciues qui arma ferre possunt* as an economic qualification (Gabba 1976: 8). **ad bellum cogant** "[that]

they summon [all] to (join) the campaign"; the plural after *quisque …
adeat* is another instance of *constructio ad sensum.*

71.3 sua … merita: sim. at 54.3. **proponit** has rhetorical connotations: *propositio est per quam ostendimus summatim quid sit quod probari uolumus* (*Rhet. Her.* 2.28); cf. 54.3n. *exposuit.* **ut … habeant neu … dedant** is an instance of "theme and variation." **suae salutis rationem … se**: both reflexives refer to V. They should care for <u>his</u> wellbeing just as <u>he</u> (hence *se* in the colon's first position) had taken care of them. *ratio* appears twice more in different meanings (cf. 5.3n. *legatorum*). **optime de … meritum** is an idiomatic expression frequent in Roman politics (and esp. with Cicero); it recurs twice in *BC* (thrice in *CC*). *meritum* echoes *merita* emphatically. **communi libertate**: 4.4n. **hostibus in cruciatum dedant** "surrender to the enemy for torture"; the unparalleled expression (*TLL* 4.1219.37) pointedly suggests what surrender would amount to. C. might have anticipated, when he wrote this (89.4n.), that V. would, in fact, die under torture. *hostibus* = *Romanis* (14.4n.). **indiligentiores** "negligent, however slightly" (K-S II 475 A.19). The comparative, which C. also uses at 2.33.2, has but two further attestations (Varro *Ling.* 8.28, Plin. *HN* 18.81). **fuerint … interitura** corresponds, in *oratio recta*, to *si … fueritis, interibunt* (cf. 39.3n. *coniunxerint*). **milia … LXXX** is a typically inflated number, which the *oppidum*'s area (68n.) could not have accommodated (Henige 1998: 235n.53; cf. 28.5n.).

71.4 ratione inita "he had calculated." **frumentum se exigue dierum XXX habere** "he had grain, in short rations (*OLD exigue* 1), for thirty days." C. freq. uses the descriptive genitive to express time (cf. *NLS* §85b; 74.2, 90.2). *exigue*, derived from *exigere*, "to weigh" (E-M), fits the context well. Thirty days may have been the upper limit of supplies that soldiers could carry (Livy 43.1.8; Roth 1999: 68–69; but the duration also featured in legal stipulations: XXX DIES IVSTI SVNTO [*Lex XII* 3.1]). Scipio made the same provisions (Livy *Per.* 57), as would C. (74.2), and military writers stress the need to secure them esp. during a siege (Veg. 3.3). **longius tolerari posse parcendo** "they could last longer by economizing." *tolerare* = "to endure" "belonged to the higher genres of prose" (Adams 1973a: 133); Critognatus uses it (77.12). The word order emphasizes *parcendo* and produces a creticus + spondee.

71.5 his datis mandatis … dimittit repeats 54.4nn. *mandatis* resumes §2 *mandat* (cf. 7.1n. *missus*), rounding off V.'s communications (cf. 16.3n. *itineribus*). **qua erat nostrum opus intermissum**: 5.2n. *quorum erant. nostrum* is fronted to make a contrast with the Gallic fortifications (cf. 69.6n. *eius*). **secunda uigilia**: between 10.30am and 1pm (cf. 3.3n.). The timing is conventional: *signo secundae uigiliae conuenistis, quod tempus mortales somno altissimo premit* (Livy 7.35.11). **silentio**: 11.7n. **equitatum dimittit** repeats 71.1 to show how V. is true to his word.

71.6–8 The headings (20.3–12n.) *frumentum* ("as for the grain") … *pecus … copias* mark the measures. **capitis poenam** "the death penalty"; cf. 1.5n. (the metonymy), 4.9n. (V.'s punishments). **paruerint**: §3n. *fuerint* (as the punishment lies in the future).

71.7 pecus: 17.3n. **magna erat copia**: 14.9n. *omni sint periculo*. **a Mandubiis compulsa**: the abl. might signify separation ("wrested from," Hammond) or agency ("gathered by," cf. Edwards). **uiritim distribuit**: the adverb occurs here and *BAlex*. 65.2; the expression is unparalleled except for much later (including Dictys 2.19, 33). **frumentum … metiri**: another rare expression, used twice more by C. (1.16.5, 23.1; *metiri* does not occur elsewhere in *CC*), and twice by Cic. (*Verr*. 3.73 + 193). **parce et paulatim** "sparingly and gradually" (Edwards); unparalleled. It echoes both *exigue* and *parcendo*, suggesting once more that V. followed through.

71.8 quas … collocauerat: 69.5.

71.9 his rationibus "by these policies (*OLD* 10)." **auxilia Galliae exspectare et bellum parat administrare**: *BC* 2.37.6 *reliquas copias exspectare et bellum ducere parabat*; cf. 81.2. By thus positioning *parat* and *administrare*, C. effects homoioteleuton and isocolon (cf. 17.3n. *aedificiorum*). The reader will have to *wait* for several cc. (representing thirty days; cf. 68–78n.) until c. 77.

72–74 To guard against sorties and relief troops, C. builds complex fortifications (his taking credit: Dodington 1980: 30–31; Riggsby 197–202). He completes the inner investment (counterintuitively known as the "countervallation" since Napoleon's excavations [Reddé-von Schnurbein 2001: 31], cf. fig. 9), then adds an identical complex at his back (the "circumvallation" [74n.]).

Excavations have largely confirmed C.'s description (Reddé-von Schnurbein 2001); but there are differences (Bénard 1996, Reddé 2001: 489–506): While he provides invariable measurements for each construction and a uniform arrangement of contraptions along both sides of the entire investment, on the ground there is variety in all aspects including features not mentioned by C. (often in accordance with topographic needs [von Schnurbein 2001: 551–56]), and the multiple defensive lines are sporadic and less distinct (fig. 10). These differences result partly from C.'s penchant for uniformity and generalization (*Introd.* 3e), partly from his reliance on the poliorcetic tradition: the actual number of ditches varies (72.2n.), but three is the number recommended in a military handbook (Philo, *Bel.* 8.A69; cf. Reddé 2008: 284). Scipio's poliorcetics at Numantia (cf. 69n.) seem particularly relevant: they may have influenced the actual constructions – including the shapes and arrangements of camps and ditches (von Schnurbein 2001: 509, 542) – and they are evoked in C.'s writing (68–78n.). Just as important is the agricultural and viticultural discourse, which accounts for many of the numerical and phraseological specifics in C.'s write-up (Krebs, 2023).

The ekphrasis, *sans pareil* in republican literature (save for C. himself at *BC* 2.8–10; Dodington 1980: 80–85 offers statistics), is typically progressive and insistent on order (cf. 23n.). In addition to its retardatory and mimetic effects (the laborious detail representing the labors required), it advertizes C.'s *scientia militaris* and *prouidentia* as well as his legions' endurance (Rambaud 248, Dodington 1980: 62, Gerlinger 2008: 90; 80.1n. *munitionis*); it monumentalizes Roman values and the superiority of skill (cf. Scarola 1987; Brown 2013).

72 In alleged response to V. (cf. 68–78n.), C. expands his fortifications: he digs a ditch 20 feet wide in an advanced position to hinder further sorties (§1 *fossam*, §2 *pedes quadringentos*). As seen from the *oppidum*, he then drives two ditches into the ground, each 15 feet, one filled with water (§3 *fossas, interiorem*). Next follows a rampart 12 feet high, with palisades and battlements and tapered stakes protruding against an oncoming enemy (§4 *aggerem ac uallum, loricam pinnasque, ceruis*); turrets intervene at regular intervals (§4 *pedes LXXX*).

The typically systematic presentation, which shows signs of *uariatio* (*pateret ~ distarent, fossam pedum uiginti ~ fossas ... latas*), reveals its agricultural inspiration (§1 *fossam*, §2 *quadringentos*, §3 *ceruis*; 72–74n.) and bespeaks the knowledgeable general (nn. on §§1, 2).

72.1 It was standard procedure to dig an advance ditch to protect one's troops against sallying enemy forces (cf. App. *Hisp.* 90). **Quibus rebus cognitis ex perfugis et captiuis** repeats 5.18.4. *quibus ... cognitis*: 18.3n. *ex perfugis*: 44.2n. The pairing recurs in Livy's third decade and Tac. *Hist.* 4.23.3. **haec genera**: 23.1n. *hac ... forma*. **fossam ... distarent**: standard military ditches had at least one sloped side (Ps.-Hyg. *Mun. castr.* 49). This form occurs similarly described in a viticultural context: *rectis lateribus ... fossam educere ... ut eadem latitudo in imo reddatur quae coepta est in summo* (Columella, *Rust.* 3.13.9–10). **pedum xx**: the width (cf. 36.7n. *duodenum pedum*) is broader than standard. The ascertained measurements fall short and vary (von Schnurbein 2008: 200; Reddé 2012: 166). **derectis lateribus** "[its] sides vertical," more or less, as excavations show. **tantumdem**: first here in C. (then *BC* 3.63.1, not in *CC*); the suffix signifies "just,"

"very" (K-H 134b). **summae fossae labra** "the edges at the ditch's top."
labra are frequent in technical writing (Vitr. 9 *praef.* 11 *uas amplum ad
summa labra*); but C. may have in mind Sisenna *FRHist* F114 *in labro summo
fluminis* (Krebs 2014: 211). *summae* seems preferable to *summa* because
of the contrast between *fossae <u>solum</u>* and <u>*summa*</u> *fossa* and the parallelism
with *eius fossae.*

72.2 Philo recommends that "no fewer than three ditches be dug in all
fortifications," and that the second be "40 cubits" behind the first (*Bel.*
8.A69). Excavations have revealed a fourth ditch in the Plaine des Laumes
(von Schnurbein 2001: 333–42). **pedes quadringentos**: a standard agricultural measure (*sextula*, Columella, *Rust.* 5.1.9). In reality, the distance
was greater (Reddé 2001: 503). **reduxit** "he set back," an unparalleled
meaning (*TLL* 11.2.575.60); its choice enables the paronomasia *duxit,
reduxit, perduxit* (cf. 43.5n. *profectio*). **id hoc consilio** sc. *fecit*; again *BAfr.*
59.5, 86.1. *hoc consilio* is expounded by a negative purpose clause, whose
two parts are parallel and polysyndetic (*ne … aut noctu … aduolaret aut
interdiu … possent*); it, in turn, is preceded by a causal clause (*quoniam …
complexus nec … cingeretur*). **quoniam tantum esset necessario spatium
complexus** "since the size of the enclosed area was of necessity so very
large"; cf. 14.9n. *omni sint.* The subj. marks this as part of C.'s reasoning
(*oratio obliqua*). **corpus corona militum cingeretur**: this metaphorical sense
of *corpus* ("body [of fortifications]") recurs at *BC* 1.54.2 *corpus nauium.
corona* is commonly used of soldiers "ringing" a town or fortification (*TLL*
4.986.57; *cingere* is also technical [Fischer 1914: 25]); but this is its first
attestation. Livy 7.27.7 *cum corona militum cincta … caperetur urbs* and Verg.
Aen. 10.122 (sim. 11.475) *rara muros cinxere corona* may bespeak C.'s influence. **de improuiso** is a semi-technical expression in accounts of surprise
attacks (Wheeler 1988: 82); it occurs 7x in C. (and 8.36.3; with *ex* 4x in
BAlex.), while virtually absent from Cicero's works (Landgraf on *Rosc. Am.*
151). **aut noctu … aut interdiu** recurs at Livy 7.35.9 (and, less precisely,
44.39.7, Suet. *Iul.* 65); it is a typically polar expression (McKeown on Ovid
Am. 1.20). **multitudo aduolaret aut … possent** is an instance of *constructio
ad sensum* (*poss<u>ent</u>* corresponds to the idea of *hostium*); *multitudo*: 21.1n.
The concerns are typical; cf. Thuc. 2.75.6 μήτε … οἰστοῖς βάλλεσθαι, "that
[they] not be hit by missiles," Veg. 4.28.3 *ultra ictum teli*. **tela … conicere** is
phraseological (*TLL* 4.307.23–40) and frequent in *CC* (incl. 81.5, 85.5).
destinatos "assigned to."

72.3 hoc intermisso spatio: 23.3n. **fossas … perduxit**: Crassus dug a ditch
"from sea to sea" that was "fifteen feet in width and depth alike" (εὖρος
δὲ καὶ βάθος ἴσον πεντεκαίδεκα ποδῶν, Plut. *Crass.* 10.6). Normally, ditches
were wider than deep (Veg. 1.24). C.'s varied in number and size (von

Schnurbein 2001: 539–42; 2008: 201). **eadem altitudine** is asyndetic and coordinate with *latas* (cf. 22.1n. *aptissimum*). **perduxit** "he led all round"; 36.7n. **interiorem**: i.e. closer to Alesia. **campestribus ac demissis locis** "where the ground was level with the plain or sank below it" (Edwards); *campestris* occurs 4x in *VII*, 2x in *BC* 1 (and *BAfr.* 73.1); a "local repetition." **aqua ... compleuit**: confirmed by excavations (von Schnurbein 2008: 201).

72.4 Veg. 4.28.3 *fossam faciunt eamque non solum uallo et sudibus sed etiam turriculis instruunt ... quod opus loriculam uocant.* **aggerem ac uallum** "a palisaded rampart"; the hendiadys is corroborated by the following *huic. uallum* is originally the collective noun signifying the line of palisades (*ualli*) on top of the rampart (Veg. 3.8 *aggerem faciunt, supra quem ualli ... diguruntur*); by metonymy it also designates a palisaded rampart (e.g. 2.5.6 *castra in altitudinem pedum XII uallo fossaque ... muniri*). The pairing is common, incl. Val. Max. 7.6.*ext.*2 *Numantini autem ‹a› Scipione uallo et aggere circumdati.* Cf. Reddé 2001: 515–37 (the archaeological evidence). **loricam pinnasque** "parapet and battlement." The technical use of *lorica* ("cuirass") in the sense of *munimenta militaria* is first attested in C. and then confined to historical writing (*TLL* 7.2.1677.61–83). On *pinnae*, cf. Serv. *Aen.* 4.88 *minae: eminentiae murorum, quas pinnas dicunt.* **grandibus ceruis eminentibus** "with large fraises projecting" (Edwards). These forked branches were named after their resemblance to a stag's horns (Varro *Ling.* 5.117; this is the first instance of the rare term [*TLL* 3.954.69–79]). They were used in agricultural life and viticulture (Verg. *Ecl.* 2.29 [with Serv. ad loc.], Tert. *De anim.* 19). **ad commissuras pluteorum atque aggeris** "where the screens joined with the rampart." *commissura* occurs only here in *CC. plutei* varies *lorica*. **turres toto opere circumdedit** "all around the work he set up towers"; the abl. (without *in*: 1.1n.) is rare but recurs at 8.34.4. **pedes ... distarent**: Their actual intervals varied. Scipio's towers were 100 feet apart (App. *Hisp.* 90 διὰ πλέθρου; 68–78n.).

73 When sorties endanger C.'s troops, he builds additional contraptions, combinations of which were recommended in military handbooks (Philo, *Bel.* 8.A70 [Reddé 2001: 505]). But most of the details in his description are once again taken from Rome's agricultural discourse; and the inclusion of the soldiers' nicknames provides authenticating detail (§4n. *appellabant*) and moments of comic relief (nn. on *cippos, lilium, stimulos*; cf. Maurach 2002, Corbeill 2018), while bespeaking C.'s interest in language.

73.1 Erat eodem tempore ... necesse: the tricolon of polysyndetic infinitives suggests breathless action, its effect enhanced by the enclosing word order of *erat* and its unusually delayed complement *necesse*. Cf. 37.6n.

ciuitatem temere. **materiari et frumentari** belong to the *sermo castrensis* (Mosci Sassi 1983: 72, 77, 84; cf. 14.5n. *pabulandi*). *materiari*, "to collect timber," is very rare and here first attested, *frumentari* is less rare and first attested at 4.9.3 (*TLL* 8.467.29–37; 6.1.1409.27). **deminutis nostris ... progrediebantur** "when our forces, which had to proceed a considerable distance from camp, were reduced in number." **temptare ... conabantur** "they tried to make an attempt on (*OLD temptare* 12)"; cf. Cic. *Rab. Post.* 13 *temptare mansuetudinem ... conatus es?* **eruptionem ... facere**: the periphrasis (24.3n.) encloses all pertinent information (cf. 10.1n. *magnam ... difficultatem*) in a typical string of ablatives. **summa ui**: 70.1n.

73.2–9 C.'s traps have been uncovered, albeit partly and in mixed form; as has evidence of the turrets (von Schnurbein 2008: 201–03).

73.2–4 First comes a series of trimmed trunks and boughs, set in ditches 5 feet deep, intertwined, their projecting limbs sharpened. These *cippi* combine elements of Roman palisading (§§2 *praeacutis,* 3 *reuelli,* 4 *implicati*) and the *saeps agrestis* (Varro *Rust.* 1.14.2), which "is made either of stakes set closely and intertwined with brush (*uirgultis implicatis*) or ... of trimmed trees, lowered into the ground successively and firmly planted (*ex arboribus truncis demissis in terram deinceps constitutis*)." **rursus** "besides" (*OLD* 5a). **quo ... possent** characterizes, as the object to *addendum*, the addition; cf. Tac. *Hist.* 4.74 *id solum uobis addidimus quo pacem tueremur.* **minore numero militum munitiones**: a tongue twister, the first two words being near anagrams; cf. *BAlex.* 30.3 *non quo id minore numero militum consequi difficile factu putaret ...* The troops are "smaller" than they would be if the *munitiones* were smaller. **truncis arborum ... abscisis** "tree trunks and very strong boughs were cut down/off." The possessive genitive is *apo koinou* (47.3n. *oppidi*); *abscidere* (a tech. term in horticulture [*TLL* 1149.15–29]) strictly refers to the branches only. Cf. 14.2n. *aut.* **horum delibratis ac praeacutis cacuminibus** "and then their ends were trimmed and sharpened"; the resumptive demonstrative is typical. *delibrare,* "to take off the bark" (*OLD*), is an unprecedented and exceedingly rare agricultural term (*TLL* 5.1.442.23–29; only here in *CC*). *praeacuere* is a slightly more common agricultural term, of which C. is surprisingly fond (8x). *cacumen* (only here in C.) completes the mimetic sound pattern, for which the smashing alliteration and assonance in Enn. *Ann.* 187–91 may have provided inspiration (*fraxinus frangitur ... | pinus proceras peruortunt: omne sonabat | arbustum fremitu siluai frondosai*). To sharpen stakes was standard practice in palisading (Polyb. 18.18). **perpetuae fossae quinos pedes altae ducebantur**: cf. Cato *Agr.* 33.2 *sulcos perpetuos ducito. perpetuus* is best understood as signifying "a series of" (*TLL* 10.1.1646.20–23; cf. 23.1n.). *pedes altae:* 24.1n.

73.3 huc illi stipites demissi "these were sunk into the ditches (*huc* = *quas in fossas*) as stakes (*OLD stipes* 2)." *demittere* is common in agricultural contexts (*TLL* 5.1.490.38–53). **ab infimo reuincti ne reuelli possent** "they were tied back at the bottom (cf. *OLD ab* 16a) so that they could not be torn up (*OLD reuello* 2)." Cf. Polyb. 18.18.14 on the difficulty of "pulling up" (ἐκσπάσαι) Roman palisades as they were "held firmly in the ground" (τὴν ἐκ τῆς γῆς δύναμιν ἔχειν) and "interlaced with one another" (τὴν εἰς ἀλλήλους ἐμπλοκήν). **ab ramis eminebant** "they projected with (*OLD ab* 12) their branches," i.e. from where the branches started to spread out.

73.4 quini erant ordines "There were rows of five"; it has long been questioned whether these were five ditches or five rows of trunks (*CG* 811). But the following description applies much more naturally to the trees, which is not contradicted by the archaeological evidence of several ditches (cf. von Schnurbein 2001: 543). **coniuncti inter se atque implicati**: the emphatic pairing expresses tightness; it is unparalleled, but Polybius' characterization of Roman palisading, wherein "the stakes are interlaced and interwoven with one another" (βραχείας τὰς εἰς ἀλλήλους ἐμπλοκὰς καὶ τὰς ἐπαλλάξεις, 18.18.11), is strikingly similar. *implicare* recurs once in *CC* at *BC* 3.18.1. **intrauerant ... induebant**: a typically precise sequence of tense. **se ... acutissimis uallis induebant** "they would impale themselves on very sharp stakes"; sim. 82.1. All parallels for this meaning of *induo* are later (*TLL* 7.1.1269.38–56); Livy 44.41.9 *induissent se hastis* is close. The superlative (echoing *praeacutis*) occurs only here in C. **cippos**: commonly used in the senses of "boundary marker" of fields (*uel sim.*) or "gravestone," *cippus* is once glossed as ποδοκάκη, "stocks" (*TLL* 3.1078.66), which Heraeus substantiates further and relates to *quo qui intrauerant* (1902: 260). *cippus* would have come to mind naturally in this agricultural context and allowed for a sardonic pun: "boundary marker" = "traps" = "grave." Goodyear on Tac. *Ann.* 1.23.3 *"cedo alteram"* and Mosci Sassi 1983: 53–57 offer further instances of military nicknames. **appellabant**: the "soldiers" are here (and below) the most likely subject (cf. 89.3n. *iubet*). Their delight in colorful words – C.'s soldiers sang during the triumph of how they had subsisted on *lapsana* at Dyrrachium, which Pliny had to gloss as *cyma siluestris* (*HN* 19.144) – is documented in Horsfall 1999.

73.5-8 The second line consists of pits, 3 feet deep, each with a fire-hardened stake in its middle and hidden underneath brushwood; these pits were arranged in a quincunx pattern, which totaled eight rows. Inspiration again came from agricultural practice; and its technical writing also provides the vocabulary and the standardized measurements in C.'s write-up. Of particular relevance (for the *stimuli* below as well) was the planting of olive shoots (Cato *Agr.* 45 [Hooper, modified]): "Cut olive shoots (*taleas*

oleagineas) for planting in pits (*in scrobe*) three feet long (*tripedaneas*) …
Those which you intend to plant in the nursery should be cut one foot
long (*pedalis facito*), and they should be planted thus (*eas sic inserito*) …
If you plant in pits or furrows, plant in groups of three, and spread them
apart (*ternas taleas ponito easque diuaricato*). Do not let them project more
than four finger-widths above the ground (*supra terram ne plus IIII digi-
tos transuorsos emineant*)." **obliquis ordinibus in quincuncem dispositis** "in
slanting lines arranged in the form of a quincunx (only here in *CC*)." A
standard horticultural arrangement (described, though not *suo nomine*, at
Verg. *G.* 2.277–78): cf. Cic. *Sen.* 59 *arborum … directos in quincuncem ordines*,
Columella, *Rust.* 3.13 *uitem … in quincuncem disponunt*. **scrobes** "pits"; common in agricultural treatises, the term occurs in *VII* only (a "local repetition"). **tres in altitudinem pedes**: 8.2n. *in altitudinem*. The accusative of
extent is used loosely (cf. 24.1n. *latum pedes*). Three feet is a standard
depth of pits in agricultural treatises (above). **fodiebantur**: first here in
C. **paulatim angustiore ad infimum fastigio** "its slope gradually narrowing towards the bottom." For this unprecedented meaning of *fastigium*
(*TLL* 6.1.321.77), cf. Varro *Rust.* 1.14.2 *fossa … fastigium habet, ut exeat e
fundo* (sc. *aqua*). Ps.-Hyg. *Mun. castr.* 49 differentiates between two kinds
of military *fossae: fastigata uel punica. fastigata dicitur quae a summa latitudine
lateribus deuexis in angustiam ad solum coniuncta peruenit*.

73.6 huc … demittebantur partly repeats §3. **stipites teretes feminis crassitudine**: *teres*, "smooth and rounded" (*OLD* 1), occurs only here in *CC*. The
specification of the thickness (by an abl. of quality characterized by *femur*,
"thigh") is unparalleled; yet cf. Cato *Agr.* 49.1 *uineam ueterem … brachium
crassam*. **ab summo**, "at the top," expounds the prefixes *prae-*. **praeacuti et
praeusti** repeats 22.5. *praeurere* is a rare horticultural term; C.'s use (also
5.40.6) may have influenced Verg. *Aen.* 7.524–25 (with Horsfall) and Tac.
Ann. 4.51.1 (cf. *Introd.* 3h). **non amplius digitis quattuor ex terra eminerent**: cf. Cato §5. The ablative: 19.1n.

73.7 confirmandi et stabiliendi: within this unparalleled pairing, the latter
verb specifies the former (cf. 45.2n. *mulorumque*). **singuli … exculcabantur**
"they filled up one foot from the bottom with tamped-down soil"; the verb
is attested thrice more in all of Latin. **uiminibus ac uirgultis** "with twigs
and brushwork."

73.8 id ex similitudine … lilium: the demonstrative agrees with the predicate (cf. 68.1n. *quod … oppidum*). *ex*. 12.6n. The name bespeaks mordant
wit: lilies were associated with gravesites (cf. the epigraphic instruction
mihi lilia pone, C.E.L. 578 [Buecheler], Verg. *Aen.* 6.883 *manibus date lilia
plenis*).

73.9 The third line consists of logs: 1 foot long and tipped with an iron hook, they were sunk into the ground all over. It is inspired by the planting of olive shoots (quoted above, §5), as *talea* indicates. **taleae** "long thin pieces of wood," (*OLD* 2). **pedem longae**: a standard size (Cato, above, §5). **infodiebantur**: the agricultural term (Cato *Agr.* 37.3 *sarmenta ... infodito*) occurs only here in *CC.* **mediocribusque ... interuallis**: 36.2n. On the importance of spacing, cf. Cato, above, §5, *diuaricato.* **disserebantur**: for this rare agricultural verb ("to plant out," *OLD* 1; only here in *CC*), cf. Varro, *Rust.* 1.23.6 *seminibus dissitis*, Sueius *poet.* 1.7 *hoc genus arboris ... disseruere.* **stimulos**: a *stimulus* goads, pricks, stings, often to incite – but not here: in this set-up so suggestive of growth and life, it ends all incitement.

74 Having completed the encirclement, C. erects a second line of fortifications some 700 feet behind the former (the "circumvallation" [72–74n.]). Such double encirclement is rarely attested before Alesia (Campbell 2002: 96); it was sure to impress. For the archaeological evidence, see Brouquier-Reddé 2001.

74.1 Cf. Polyb. 1.18.3 on double ditches that "protect against sallies and outside attacks." **His rebus perfectis** recurs at *BC* 1.30.5. **regiones secutus ... natura** "following the most level areas as he could, given the nature of the place"; *regiones sequi* is unusual (*OLD sequor* 18). **quam potuit aequissimas**: sim. at 5.49.7; 9.3n. *quam ... potuit.* **pro loci natura**: *pro* = "in a degree or manner corresponding to" (*OLD* 12); cf. 14.9n. *loci natura.* This qualification prepares for the development at 83.2n. (a typical "donnée pre-explicative" [Rambaud 153]; cf. 40.2n.). **quattuordecim milia passuum** equals 13 modern miles (20.7 km), which is accurate (Petit 2001: 100). **pares eiusdem generis munitiones** "matching fortifications of the same kind"; the archaeological record is more complicated (Reddé 2001: 503, von Schnurbein 2001: 553). **diuersas ab his** "but facing away from the last-mentioned [sc. fortifications]"; *his* vaguely resumes the fortifications summed up in *rebus.* **perfecit** resumes *perfectis*, emphasizing the reduplication; cf. 20.12n. *recipiat.* **magna ... multitudine**: 21.1n. *omnis ... multitudo*; 68–78n. **si ita accidat eius discessu** "should this happen upon his departure (sc. for other locations within the fortified area)." The text's soundness has been questioned because of the imprecise meaning of *eius discessu* (cf. 5.2n. *aduentu*) and *accidat* (but such switches into the primary sequence occur elsewhere). **praesidia munitionum** "the garrisons of the fortifications."

74.2 Endangered foraging troops: 14.7n. *periculo.* ‹ne› aut‹em› cum periculo: Hand's conjecture (*Tursellinus* IV 178) makes sense of the readings *aut* and *ut*, except that *cum periculo* normally (*TLL* 10.1.1457) – and in C.

always – carries an attribute. **cogatur** "[that] it not be necessary" rather than "[that] he be forced." **dierum xxx**: as did V. (71.4n.). Still: *meminerant ad Alesiam magnam se inopiam perpessos, ... maiorem ad Auaricum* (*BC* 3.47.6). **pabulum frumentumque**: 16.3n. **habere conuectum**: 29.6n. *effectum habere.*

75 Catalogues were a set piece of epic poetry ever since Hom. *Il.* 2.484–785 (cf. Enn. *Ann.* 229, with Skutsch); thence they moved into historiography (e.g. Hdt. 7.59–100; Strasburger 1972). They serve a rhetorical and aesthetical purpose: "a subject divided into parts appears greater" (Arist. *Rh.* 1365a; cf. 24.5n. *alii*), the effect of which Polybius captures when he remarks that it conveys "how great was the power that [Hannibal] dared to oppose" (ἡλίκοις ... ἐτόλμησε πράγμασιν ἐπιθέσθαι, 2.24.1). But a list also provides pause before battle for proper appreciation (cf. 23n.). Within the Roman context, they resonate with conventions of the triumph: cf. the La Turbie inscription with its list of (curiously) forty-five names (Plin. *HN* 3.136–37; *CIL* 5.7817), and Plut. *Pomp.* 45.4 (with Heftner) on lists of enemy peoples on placards in processions; 28.5n. *numero* (on specific figures).

C.'s catalogue, the longest in the *comm.* by far, expands on the mini-catalogue at 4.6n. by adding peoples mostly from the east of *Gallia Celtica* and *Gallia Belgica*, many of whom are unmentioned before. These novelties compound the awe-inspiring effect of the total of ca. forty-five (!) peoples, as do their contributions (up to 35,000) in tandem with the Roman stereotype of "the northern hordes" (21.1n. *multitudo*) – all of which underscores the sense of the final show-down (68–90n.). Lucan (1.392–465) put this catalogue to subversive effect in a "catalogue in reverse" (Williams 1968: 222) to evoke the dangerous world C. left behind to fight Rome instead. Further on C.'s catalogues, see Mannetter 1995: 138–75.

C. provides the **P**eoples' names and their **N**umbers in descending order (the overarching organizing principle, as in Hdt. 8.1–2). The presentation strives for variation to break the monotony (Klotz 1928: 398 remarks on the absence of such finish at 2.4): its structure mixes chiasmus and parallelism (PN, NP; PN, PN, NP, NP; PN); one polysyndeton (§3) interrupts the string of overwhelming asyndeta, the length and balance of sentences and cola shift (contrast §§2+3), the vocabulary is varied (*clientibus ~ adiunctis, parem numerum ~ totidem*). But the text presents problems: (1.) The Senones and the Lemovices occur twice. The former's second occurrence has been restored to *Suessionibus*; the duplicate Lemovices, however, have not found a solution. (2.) The reading in §4 can hardly be right. (3.) Several of the peoples lack attestation elsewhere; some have been queried. (4.) The tally (35 + 35 + 6x12 + 2x10 + 4x8 + 8x5 + 1x4 + 3x3 + 30

[all in thousands] = 277,000) differs from the total (at 76.3) of 8,000 cavalry plus 250,000 infantry. No attempt at reconciliation (e.g. Klotz 1928)
has escaped the suspicion of casuistry; in fact, the error may be C.'s (it is
paralleled in Xen. *An.* 1.2.9 + 1.7.10).

75.1 Dum … geruntur: 37.1n. **concilio … indicto**: 1.4nn. *indictis … conciliis, principes.* **qui arma ferre possent** repeats 71.2n. **ut censuit Vercingetorix**
functions analogously to C.'s authorial cross-references (17.1n.). V.'s
precarious leadership: 29.7n. **certum numerum cuique ciuitati imperandum** echoes 4.7. *quisque* is usually enclitic (71.2n.); exceptions occur
(K-S 644). **tanta multitudine confusa**: *confundere* occurs only here and at
Hirt. 8.14.2 *perturbatum et confusum … agmen* in *CC*. It suggests a huge
chaotic gathering from all sides; in conjunction with *multitudo* (21.1n.) it
is paralleled once (Livy 24.32.9). This feared *multitudo* stands in playful
tension to the neat Roman catalogue; it was a concern ever since Hom. *Il.*
2.803–06. **ne … nec … nec … nec**: the litotes forcefully states the dreaded
alternatives; the polysyndeton forms a rising tricolon, whereof the final
two cola form a chiasmus. **moderari** sc. *multitudinem* (cf. 4.1n. *incendit*).
discernere suos "to distinguish their men [in their respective units]."
frumentandi rationem habere "have the means (*OLD ratio* 14) of corn
supply"; the expression recurs at 8.34.1. The Gauls had experienced the
difficulty before (2.10.4, 3.18.6; cf. 71.4); it is a clichéd concern: Polyb.
1.17.1–3 remarks how the Romans decided not to send all troops partly
out of concern over supplies.

75.2 As Rome's formerly staunchest ally, the Aedui and their clients naturally come first. Then follow, chiastically arranged (*imperant* HAEDUIS …
milia xxxv; parem numerum ARVERNIS …), their longstanding rivals with vassals
(3.3n. *Aruernorum*); both number five. **Segusiauis**: identified as Aeduan
neighbors at 64.4n. **Ambiuaretis, Aulercis Brannouicibus, Blannouiis**: the
Ambivareti recur at 90.5; nothing else is known of these peoples (except
cf. 4.6n. *Aulercos*), and the Blannovii have met with especial misgivings
(*CG* 393; Fichtl 2004: 125–26). **adiunctis … qui sub imperio … consuerunt**: the part. (which varies *atque*) and the relative clause (which varies
clientes) ring the peoples they characterize. **Eleutetis … Vellauiis**: C. proceeds counterclockwise, grouping two southern neighbors of the Arverni
(nn. on 4.6, 7.1) with the otherwise unknown Eleuteti and the Vellavii
(Trément *et al.* 2003); Strabo 4.2.2 locates the latter between the Garonne
and the Loire in *Aquitania* (around Saint-Paulien).

75.3 C. now mixes longer and shorter cola. **Sequanis … Carnutibus**: of
these six peoples – with the famous Sequani (66.2n.) first, the notori-
ous Carnutes (2.1n.) last – all had participated in the beginning of the

uprising except for the Sequani and the Santoni. The latter, located on the Atlantic coast in the south-west of Celtica (around the eponymous region Saintonge [*TGF* 157]), were the alleged destination of the Helvetii (1.10.1, 11.6); during the campaign's third year, they provided C. with ships (3.11.5). **Lemouicibus**: given their standing and role (4.6n., 8.46.4), their mention here is more likely than at §4. **Pictonibus ... Heluetiis**: the first three peoples (similarly grouped at 4.6nn.) stretch from the Atlantic coast gradually more inland. They are joined by the Helvetii, whose territory (in Switzerland) was bounded by the Rhine, the Jura, and Lake Geneva (1.2.3–4; they inhabited other places earlier: Tac. *Germ.* 28.2 with Perl). Some of their "districts" (*pagos*, 1.12.4) had joined the campaign of the Cimbri and Teutoni (in 113–101; 1.12.5). They briefly caused Rome worry in March 60, when they were "in arms and sortied into the Roman province" (Cic. *Att.* 1.19.2; but then [*Att.* 1.20.5]: *otium nuntiari e Gallia*; cf. *Att.* 2.1.11). C. uses their movements in his tendentious beginning of *BG* to justify his war outside his provinces (Walser 1998). This is their first reappearance after their defeat (1.29; ring composition: *Introd.* 3c). **Suessionibus**: located in *Gallia Belgica* in the departments of Aisne and Oise (around eponymous Soissons [*DLG* 285]), they neighbored the Bellovaci and the Remi (2.3.5, 4.6, 12.1+4; Fichtl 1994: 67–82). Defeated during the Belgic resistance (2.13.1), they were given to the Remi as vassals (8.6.2–3); unlike the latter (63.7n.), they joined V. **Ambianis**: neighbors of the Bellovaci and the Morini, this coastal Belgic tribe in Picardy (around Amiens [*DLG* 41]) had participated in the war of 57; they would continue to fight in 51 (2.4.9, 8.7.3–4; Bayard 2015). **Mediomatricis**: a people bounded by the Rhine (4.10.3), this Belgic tribe lived in the department of la Moselle (around Metz [*DLG* 220]; Demougin 1995). **Petrocoriis**: located in *Celtica* along the banks of the Duranus in the region of the eponymous Perigord (*DLG* 125), they were to the north of the Nitiobroges (Strabo 4.2.2; Pénisson *et al.* 2013). This is their only mention in *CC*. **Neruiis**: this powerful Belgic tribe brought C. to the brink of defeat at the Sambre, but was ultimately "nearly extinguished" (*prope ad internecionem*, 2.28.1). Three years later, however, they participated in Ambiorix's uprising (5.38.4; on the role of this "contradiction" in the debate about the composition of *BG*, cf. Brown 1999: 341n.21). **Morinis**: a coastal Belgic tribe in the department of Pas-de-Calais, they fought C. in 57 and 56, then served as C.'s naval basis in 55, when they seem to have been given to Commius as a vassal tribe (2.4.9, 3.9.10, 4.21.3; 76.1 *attribuerat*). **Aulercis Cenomanis**: this group of the Aulerci, whom C. mentions here alone, lived in and around eponymous Le Mans (*TGF* 153). **Atrebatibus**: a Belgic tribe located to the south-east of the Morini around eponymous Artois (*DLG* 59), they had been subjugated in 57 along with their eastern neighbors, the Nervii (2.23.1); afterwards, they seem to have maintained mostly friendly relations with the Romans (cf. 76.1–2n.). **Veliocassibus ... Aulercis Eburouicibus**: neighboring peoples in the north. The Veliocasses were a Belgic tribe in and around eponymous Le Vexin (*DLG* 109) in the department of Seine-Maritime and its southern surroundings; they had participated in the war of 57, and would continue their resistance in 51 (2.4.1, 8.7.4; cf. Fichtl 1994: 157, 173). On their western border lived the Lexovii (‹Lisieux [*DLG* 201]), who fought C. during the third year of his campaign (3.9.10, 29.3). They had been joined by the Eburovices, a sub-group of the Aulerci (4.6n.) around Evreux (*TGF* 154).

75.4 Rauracis et Bois † xxx † milia uniuersis ciuitatibus is rugged; a further problem arises from the breach of the principle of decreasing contributions (nor can a reason for their grouping together be discerned). Schneider's conjecture *Rauracis et Bois ‹bina›; x milia uniuersis ciuitatibus* remedies these issues but has failed to find favor. **Rauracis**: located in the area between the Jura mountains and the upper Rhine, they neighbored the Helvetii, whose migration in 58 they joined (1.5.4, 29.2). **Bois**: their pairing with the Rauraci is perhaps owed to their joint endeavor in 58 (1.5.4, 29.2); it does not imply a change of status as Aeduan clients (10.1n. *stipendiariis*; Barwick 1938: 104). **quae Oceanum attingunt** glosses "Aremoricae" (cf. O'Hara 2017: 73–75) and echoes 4.6. At 2.34.1, the same phrase concludes a similar list of peoples. **quae eorum consuetudine Ar‹e›moricae appelluntur**: Hirt. 8.31.4 *Oceanoque coniunctae, quae Ar‹e›moricae appellantur*; discussed in Fichtl 2004: 139–42. C. here (but not at 5.53.6) indicates – by way of *eorum consuetudine*, a "signpost" (O'Hara 2017: 75–79; cf. 22.1n. *imitanda*) – that he knows the Celtic etymology: *are-mori* = "along the sea" (*DLG* 53). **quo ... numero**: 28.6n. *quae ... pars*. **Coriosolites** always occur alongside other maritime tribes in *BG* (2.34, 3.7.4, 11.4; the declension varies). Their territory was located in and around eponymous Corseul (*TGF* 153); cf. Langouet 1988. **Redones** lived to the Curiosolites' east in the territory of Ille-et-Vilaine around eponymous Rennes (*DLG* 256; Pape 1995: 21). They are mentioned once elsewhere in *BG* at 2.34. **Ambibarii**: this is their sole attestation. **Caletes** are a Belgic people in eponymous Pays de Caux (*DLG* 98). Having fought Rome already in 57, they continued their resistance the year after (2.4.9, 8.7.3). **Osismi**: situated in the départements du Finistère (which may owe its name to them [cf. *DLG* 245]) and des Côtes-d'Armor, they participated in the Venetian resistance in 57/6 (2.34, 3.9.10). To their south-east were the Veneti. **Veneti** were a powerful seafaring tribe around eponymous Vannes (*DLG* 312); they lost at sea to D. Iunius Brutus during their uprising (3.11.5, 14–16; cf. Levick 1998, Erickson 2002). **Venelli**, located in the department of la Manche, had likewise risen with the Veneti (3.11.4, 17.1).

75.5 By segregating the Bellovaci (59.2n.), C. can introduce Commius, who receives special attention (76.1–2n.). **suum numerum** "their proper complement (*OLD numerus* 6)." **suo nomine atque arbitrio** "on their own responsibility and initiative (*OLD nomen* 14b, *arbitrium* 4c)," is an unparalleled, suitably emphatic pairing (*TLL* 2.414.11; cf. 19.3n. *inani simulatione*). **rogati tamen** "nevertheless, when it was requested of them (*OLD rogo* 6)." **pro eius hospitio** "in conformity with (*OLD pro* 14) their relationship (*OLD hospitium* 2) to him." To Roman ears, "*hospitium* involves a personal connection developing out of a guest-host experience" (Nicols 2001: 99). Gauls were renowned for hospitality (Posidon. Frg. 67, Parth. *Amat. narr.* 8.4–5, Diod. Sic. 5.28.5; cf. Dietler 1995).

76 C. ends his account of the army's gathering with commonplaces: the review of the troops, the identification of the generalship, the ominous remark on the parting troops' elation. The Atrebatean Commius is individuated to vivify this final phase (3.1n. *Citam*): a privileged ally, even he could not ignore the summons and joined the command – or so runs C.'s misdirecting version (§§1–2n.). The other generals comprised two further former protégés (38.2nn.), as well as the unknown Arvernian Vercassivellaunus. Together they lead the force to Alesia, whereto the narrative will return as well (§5 *ad Alesiam*; cf. 6n.).

76.1–2 C. instituted Commius as king of the Atrebates, after defeating them in the war against the Nervii (2.23.1, 4.21.7; client kings were part of Rome's foreign policy [Sands 1908; Braund 1984]; 32.5n. *diligentia*). Two years later, in 55, he dispatched him to serve as ambassador in Britannia (4.21.7). Once there, Commius was taken captive and freed by C., who then benefitted from his cavalry (4.27.2, 35): these were probably the *merita* mentioned below. He continued his service for two years (5.22.3, 6.6.3), but then took command in the great uprising (to lead the Belgic contingent [Cass. Dio 40.42.1]), continued his resistance into 51, and ultimately withdrew to Britannia (Hirt. 8.48.2–9; Frontin. *Str.* 2.13.11). His name appears on Atrebatean coins in Gaul, some found at Alesia, and Britannia (*GPN* 336).

As to Commius' actual role, Hirtius provides significant information (8.23.2–6): He was engaged in rebellious activities already in the winter of 53/2 (*superiore anno ... Caesare in Gallia citeriore ius dicente* [cf. 7.1.1] ... *sollicitare ciuitates et coniurationem contra Caesarem facere*); Labienus therefore authorized an assassination, which failed (*eum per simulationem colloqui ... interficiendum ... conficere hominem non potuit*; Hirt. 8.23.3 is critical; Cass. Dio 40.43.3 differs in detail). In contrast and by way of a *déformation historique*, C. mentions none of this (1–5n.); and he delays Commius' appearance until now, thus (a) insinuating that he joined V. late (which some, including Münzer 1900, have erroneously accepted) and (b) adding a blatant element to the amplification of this final phase (68–90n.).

76.1 The rewards – tax exemption, local autonomy, allotment of clients – were standard privileges Rome granted loyal subjects (Sherk 1969: 192–93). C. speaks the language of empire, too, as the comparison with contemporary *senatus consulta* reveals (*De Stratonicensibus* [Sherk 1969: n. 18], *De Aphrodisiensibus* [*SEG* 32]). Within *BG*, 5.25.1–2 is particularly close in motivation and phrasing: *Tasgetius ... huic Caesar ..., quod in omnibus bellis singulari eius opera fuerat usus, maiorum locum restituerat*. **huius ... Commii** "the said Commius" (the sole instance of *hic* in conjunction with a personal name [DKM ad loc.]). **ut antea demonstrauimus**: 4.27.2. This is the only cross-reference in *VII* that transcends the annalistic frame (Albrecht 1911: 19; 17.1n. *ut ... diximus*). **fideli atque utili**: the pairing is unparalleled. On "loyalty," see next note. **quibus ille pro meritis**: cf. 4.7n. *qua ... potestate*); 6.1n. *ille*. The *quid pro quo* is typical of administrative writing: "*Since* the people [sc. of Stratonica] have always guarded their ... goodwill to the Roman people, their loyalty, and alliance, ..." (Sherk 1969 n.18: 36–37 [much of it restored]). **ciuitatem** sc. *Atrebates*. **immunem esse iusserat iura legesque reddiderat**: cf. ... ἐλεύθεροι καὶ ἀτελεῖς ὦσιν νόμοις τε ἰδίοις π[ατρί]οις .... χρῶν[ται], "that they [sc. the Aphrodisians] be free and exempt from taxation and use their own traditional laws (...)" (*SEG* 32.61). On *iura legesque* (33.2n.), cf. νόμοις ἰδίοις πατρίοις τε καὶ ἐθισμοῖς, "their own traditional laws and customs" (*SEG* 32.70). On taxation: Lintott 1993: 70–96. **Morinos attribuerat**: cf. 75.3n. *Morinis*, 9.6n. *attribuerat*.

76.2 tanta uniuersae Galliae consensio: the unusual vocabulary (*uniuersa Gallia* and *consensio* occur only here in C.) emphatically renders Gallic unity (cf. *uniuersi tamquam in unum uersi*, *Diff. Suet.* 283.7). **libertatis ... recuperandae**: the objective genitives (complementing the subjective genitive *Galliae*) form a rising bicolon. They express commonplaces (1.5n. *in libertatem uindicent*, 1.8n. *ueterem belli gloriam*; Lendon 2015: 21). Cf. Tacitus *Agr.* 11.4: *Gallos quoque in bellis floruisse accepimus; mox segnitia cum otio intrauit, amissa uirtute pariter ac libertate*. **ut ... incumberent**: C. varies the polysyndeta and the theme. **neque beneficiis neque amicitiae memoria**: C.'s rhetorical point is neatly rendered by Cato (*FRHist* F89): *ea nunc*

derepente tanta beneficia ultro citroque, tantam amicitiam relinquemus? Litaviccus
had similarly conceded that he had benefitted from C. (37.4). Cf. 37.4n.
beneficio, 31.5n. *amicus.* **mouerentur** is a typical *constructio ad sensum* (as
though following *uniuersi Galli*). **omnesque** "but [on the contrary] all"
(*OLD -que* 6b); cf. Cic. *Tusc.* 1.71 *Socrates nec patronum quaesiuit ... nec iudici-
bus supplex fuit adhibuitque liberam contumaciam.* **incumberent** "[that] they
apply themselves vigorously"; cf. Cic. *De or.* 1.34 *in id studium ... incumbite.*
Only here in C.

76.3 coactis ... CCL: Polyaenus 8.23.11 and Oros. 6.11.8 confirm the
reading in β. This figure differs from the tally of contributions (nn. on
75, 28.5 [on inflated numbers]). **haec** sc. *milia militum*, resuming part of
the abl. absolute (27.1n. *hanc*). **recensebantur numerusque inibatur** "were
inspected and counted." These are the first attestations of both *recensere*
and *numerum inire* (*TLL* 11.2.294.35; 7.1.1298.64); the latter may be said
to specify the former (cf. 45.2n. *mulorumque*). To muster and tally troops
prior to battle is a commonplace (cf. Hdt. 7.81, Xen. *An.* 1.2.9). **praefecti constituebantur**: an instance of *interpretatio Romana* and a commonplace (e.g. Hdt. 7.81.1 "they appointed commanders of units of 1,000
and 10,000").

76.4 To individuate the generals of an army's contingents has tradition
(e.g. Hdt. 7.83, with two generals identified as Xerxes' cousins); cf.
88.4n. on named enemies in triumphs. **Vercassiuellauno**: not mentioned
outside *VII*, his name befits the occasion: "ver" = "royal, supreme," and
"Vellaunos" = "leader" (the middle part is uncertain [*DLG* s.vv.]). The
attribution of coins bearing "VERCA" is doubtful (Nieto-Pelletier 2004:
16–20). **consobrino** "a cousin," only here in *CC*; it provides an authenticating touch. **summa imperii**: 20.5n. **consilio**: 36.3n. *ad consilium.*

76.5–6 C. economically renders the portentous elation and sounds the
theme of viewing (79–88n.); cf. Thuc. on the Athenians at their departure
for Sicily: καὶ ἔρως ἐνέπεσε τοῖς <u>πᾶσιν</u> ὁμοίως ἐκπλεῦσαι, "and all alike were
seized by a strong desire to set sail" (6.24.3), and τῇ παρούσῃ <u>ῥώμῃ</u> διὰ τὸ
πλῆθος ἑκάστων ὧν ἑώρων τῇ <u>ὄψει</u> ἀνεθάρσουν, "in their present conscious-
ness of strength, they became heartened by the sight of the abundance of
everything they saw" (6.31.1; sim. 7.61.3, 77.4). Rambaud 227 reminds
us that C. was absent. **alacres et fiduciae pleni**: *alacer* expresses "keenness
for battle" (always in *CC* except *BC* 3.25.2). It combines with the noun
of doom (19.2n. *fiducia*) in dramatic irony (the outcome is indubitable).
The syntagm is rare; but cf. Curt. 9.2 *animos mihi plenos alacritatis ac fiduciae
adhibete. plenus fiduciae* occurs once more in *CC* at Hirt. 8.9.1; it is then
limited to the historiographical and philosophical traditions.

76.6 C.'s language renders the braggadocio: *neque ... quisquam qui* is emphatic, as is the polyptoton (*omnes ... omnium* [4.6n.]) and the following: **adspectum modo tantae multitudinis sustineri** "bear the mere sight of such an innumerable (1.2n. *tantis*) force"; cf. Tac. *Ann.* 3.45.1 *modo adspicerentur.* The rare expression *ad(/con)spectum sustinere* occurs first here (*TLL* 2.803.11; cf. Curt. 3.4.5 *conspectum ... hostis sustinere,* Tac. *Germ.* 43.5; 19.4n. *conspectum*): it is elegantly analogous to 10.3n. *impetum sustinere. adspectum* encourages the audience to engage in visualization (*euidentia,* note *cernerentur,* cf. 63.1n. *augetur*). **praesertim ancipiti proelio** "and especially in a battle fought on two fronts (*OLD anceps* 3)." **cum ... pugnaretur, foris ... cernerentur** expands on the *anceps proelium,* the asyndeton well capturing the two sides. By adding (the superfluous) *equitatus peditatusque* C. creates a rising bicolon (cf. 17.3n. *aedificiorum*). **eruptione pugnaretur** "there would be fighting following a sortie"; the expression, first here attested, recurs at 86.2; *BC* 2.14.5 (and *BAfr.* 82.3). Livy likes it (e.g. 23.49.9 *eruptione e castris pugnatum;* further singular instances: *TLL* 5.2.846.74–77). The abl. is of manner, analogous to *ui.* **foris** "on/ from the farther side"; only here in *CC.* For the contrast to *oppidum,* cf. Quadrig. *FRHist* F2 *eos qui foris atque qui in arce erant.*

77 After six chapters representing more than thirty days (71.9n.), the narrative returns to Alesia: its supplies depleted and support troops still missing, its situation is coming to a head, when Critognatus admonishes his fellow Gauls to hold firm. In typical fashion, C. marks the crisis with a debate (15n.), here climactically amplified by the *BG's* longest speech (Rasmussen 1963: 55; only Curio's second speech is longer [*BC* 2.32]). It vehemently foregoes an exordium (3n. *nihil; contra* Fabia 1889: 86), entering instead, by way of a *praeteritio,* upon the *argumentatio,* which switches from the *refutatio* to the *confirmatio* about halfway to end on an emotionally heightened note (nn. on 12, 16; both *partes* proceed from "logical argument" to "visible proof" [Riggsby 110]).

    This deliberative speech contains numerous rhetorical devices (Fabia 1889: 70, 86–90): *praeteritio, definitio, ratiocinatio, subiectio, comparatio, argumentatio e minore;* the imagery (8 *in ... cadaueribus,* 9 *Galliam prosternere,* 16 *securibus subiecta*), noteworthy diction (4 *residere,* 6 *praeterquam,* 9 *exspoliare, stultitia,* 8 *consanguineis,* 9 *addicere,* 11 *praesaepto*), sound effects (5 *animi ista, paulisper ... posse;* 16 *securibus ... seruitute*), and pervasive *clausulae* (Holtz 1913: 31–34; identified in selection below) further elevate the plea. Just as the style bespeaks the speaker's standing (*summo ... auctoritatis*), so do his motifs, some of which resonate through *VII*: there is the leitmotif of freedom (3 *turpissimam seruitutem,* 13 *libertatis causa*), along with honor (4 *uirtutis memoria,* 6 *dignitas*), commitment (7 *omnem Galliam,* 8 *propinquis consanguineisque*), and the famous condemnation of imperialism (15–16). But this condemnation and, ultimately, the entire speech are undercut by the proposed cannibalism (12–13), which C. highlights in his introduction. This tension has startled readers (Brown 2019: 286–89); another complication arises from C.'s sustained wit: from the etymological play in the introductory remark (§2n.) to Critognatus' preposterous claims (10n. *fide constantiaque*, 13n. *posteris ... iudicarem*) – as if C. had to release a certain imperialist unease in comforting laughter.

Both speech and speaker are products of C.'s literary imagination (§2n. *Critognati*; Krebs 2023; *pace* e.g. Raaflaub 2017: 258n.7); slight inconsistencies reveal his hand (78n.). The centerpiece, cannibalism, while a commonplace of sieges (Thuc. 2.70, Ps.-Quint. *Decl. mai.* 12 [in rhetoric]; Stramaglia 2003: 17–23), evokes two specific episodes: Scipio's siege of Numantia, where it famously emblematizes the enemy's fierceness, a desperate measure before the end (App. *Hisp.* 96; cf. Strabo's telling list of "the Celts, the Iberians [sc. Numantians], and many others," 4.5.4; §5n. *se ultro morti*, §13n. *libertatis*; 68–90n.); and Hannibal's invasion of Italy, when Monomachus failed to persuade the "cruel" Carthaginian of his cannibalistic proposal (Polyb. 9.24.5–8; §2n. *crudelitatem*; Cipriani 1986: 12). The latter evocation concludes Hannibal's presence in *VII* (cf. *Index*, s.v.).

77.1 A typical "cumulative-complex" sentence, wherein a string of abl. absolutes coordinated with a predicative adjective (*inscii*) "results" in a pithy main clause. **praeterita die**: 71.3. **auxilia ... frumento** resumes 71.8–9 *frumentum ... auxilia* chiastically. **inscii**, not *nescii* (8.3n. *inopinantibus*). **quid ... gereretur**: 76.3. **de exitu suarum fortunarum** "about the issue of their own fortunes" (Edwards); *TLL* 6.1.1189.56 offers two parallels: 3.8.3, *Cod. Iust.* 8.53.34.4ᵃ. The phrase goes with *concilio* and *consultabant* alike. *exitus* plays on the word's literal meaning.

77.2 The vocabulary evokes a Roman debate (cf. *Introd.* 3g). Several etymologies resonate with the speech's circumstances (cf. §8n. *consanguineis*, 78.3n. *Mandubii*). **dictis sententiis**: 15.1n. **quarum pars ... censebat**: for *censere*, "to recommend" (*OLD* 5; cf. Goodyear on Tac. *Ann.* 2.83.3 *censeretur* on its rare construal with a noun), cf. *quid censes* = "the formula with which the presiding magistrate invited a senator to express his opinion" (*OLD* 4c). **non praetereunda**: sim. 25.1. The echo seems significant, as there the expression introduces self-sacrifice as *uirtutis exemplum*. **oratio** intimates *os* (Varro *Ling.* 6.96 *ab ore ... oratio*) in line with several other etymologies. **Critognati**: this invented, elsewhere unattested name suggests both "high-born" (κριτός, "chosen, choice" [cf. *singularem*], *γνητος, "born" [γενέσθαι, cf. γνήσιος], as in κασίγνητος, "brother" [e.g. Hom. *Od.* 8.585]) – as such it will be glossed below – and "Barleymuncher" (κρίθη, "barley," + γνάθος, "jaw"); if the Celtic signifies "fils de la terreur" (*DLG* 129), it would have endeared the made-up name to C. all the more (cf. 75.4n. *Aremoricae*). **singularem ac nefariam crudelitatem**: *crudelitas* occurs once more in *BG* (1.32.4, of Ariovistus; cf. 38.9n. *crudeliter*, *Introd.* 3e). Its etymology suggests "raw meat" (Isid. *Etym.* 10.48); as does its equivalent in Polybius' discussion "of [Hannibal's] 'cruelty'" (περὶ τῆς ὠμότητος, 9.24.8; LSJ s.v.). *nefarius* is similarly suitable due to its alleged etymological connection to *far*, "a kind of husked wheat," "ground grain" (*OLD* 1, 3): *nefarius, ut Varro aestimat, non dignus farre* (Isid. *Diff.* 1.423); cf. *consumpto frumento*. The pairing recurs once at Cic. *Tull.* 8.

77.3 *occultatio est cum dicimus nos praeterire ... id quod nunc maxime dicimus* (*Rhet. Her.* 4.37; *HLR* 882). There exists a curious tension between Critognatus' *praeteritio/occultatio* and C.'s *praetereunda*; cf. 63.1n. *augetur*. **summo ... ortus ... habitus auctoritatis**: the bicolon is isocolic and parallelistic (incl. verbal hyperbata that emphasize *summo* and *magno*); it highlights the contrast between the high standing and the low proposal (78.1n. *descendant*). The first colon glosses "Critognatus." *ortus* is of a higher register than *natus*, and C. uses it but 3x (cf. Caes. *apud* Suet. *Iul.* 6.1: *maternum genus ab regibus ortum*); it also helps to avoid the jingle *Critognatus ... natus* (which Cicero embraced in *fortunatam natam ... Romam* at his peril [*FLP* 12; Quint. 9.4.41]). The construction *habere* + gen. of quality occurs once more in *CC* (*BC* 3.109.3). **nihil**, set off by *inquit* (20.8n.), vehemently amplifies the *praeteritio*; cf. Cic. *Mil.* 94 *o frustra, inquit, mihi suscepti labores!* **dicturus sum** "I do [not] intend to talk." The future periphrastic may express intention (K-S 160). **seruitutem deditionis nomine appellant**: A. Claudius Caecus railed he would rather be deaf *and* blind than hear of negotiations with Pyrrhus (App. *Sam.* Frg. 10.5): καὶ ταῦτά τινες εἰρήνην ἀντὶ δουλείας τολμῶσιν ὀνομάζειν, "and some dare call this peace instead of servitude." Misnaming is a common concern in ancient historiography, most famously at Thuc. 3.82.4 (Sall. *Cat.* 52.11), Tac. *Agr.* 30.5 with Woodman. *seruitus* occurs 4x in this speech, *libertas* twice. **neque hos habendos ciuium loco ... adhibendos censeo**: *ciuium loco* ("a position in society," *OLD* 17) is a creticus and iambic. *censere* + gerundive is legalese (cf. *S. C. de Bacch.* [*CIL* XII 581] 3 *de Bacanalibus ... ita exdeicendum censuere*, 4.2n. *temptandam*), so is *adhibere* (Coleman 2012: 213–14). *ciuis* sits oddly with the Gauls' ethnic multiplicity (*Introd.* 2b) and is best explained as another instance of *interpretatio Romana*, which may also account for the implied connection between citizenship and political participation (as underlined by the paronomasia *habendos ~ adhibendos*, on which cf. Wills 443–45, Courtney 1999 on Cato *Agr.* 156.1); cf. Fannius' question (*ORF* 144.3): *si Latinis ciuitatem dederitis* (sc. *Romani*), ... *existimatis uos ... in contione habituros locum?*

C. elsewhere reports (6.13.1): ... *plebes paene seruorum habetur loco, quae ... nullo adhibetur consilio.*

77.4 cum his mihi res sit "My business shall be with those"; a (perhaps colloquial) Ciceronian mannerism (e.g. *Rosc. Am.* 84, *Diu.* 2.109), as such not lost on Tac. (*Dial.* 10.5). **eruptionem probant** echoes the authorial *eruptionem censebat* (cf. 17.1n. *diximus*). **pristinae ... uirtutis memoria**: 62.2n. **residere** "to remain" (*OLD* 3; only here in *CC*).

77.5 Critognatus employs a *definitio ... quae rei alicuius proprias amplectitur potestates breuiter et absolute* (*Rhet. Her.* 4.35); his phrasing is standard, too: *"non est ista diligentia, sed auaritia, ...," "non est ista fortitudo, sed temeritas ..."* (ibid.), and Sen. *Ep.* 99.15 *inhumanitas est ista, non uirtus.* **animi (e)st ista mollitia, non uirtus**: *animi* qualifies both nouns (V. had accused the Gauls of 20.5n. *animi mollitiem*; cf. 59.6n. *ab animi uirtute*); *animus* occurs 4x, highlighting Critognatus' belief that theirs is a question of resolve (cf. 19.3n. *parati*, 25.2–4n. [his understanding of *uirtus*]; McDonnell 2006: 301). *ista* ("this proposal of yours") looks both back to the *consilium eruptionis* and forward to *paulisper ... non posse* (its agreement with its predicate *mollitia* is regular [G-L 211]; they form a creticus + resolved spondee). The sound pattern (37.6n. *ciuitatem temere*) combines with the assonance in a shriek. **paulisper inopiam ... posse**: the spitting alliteration suggests contempt (cf. Pentheus' rebuke at Ov. *Met.* 3.539: *hac Tyron, hac profugos posuistis sede penates*). **ferre ... offerant ... ferant**: the paronomasia forcefully contrasts the two approaches. **se ultro morti offerant** "fling themselves of their own volition onto death." Cic. uses the expression of gladiators and Milo (*Mil.* 92 *fortes ... et se acriter ipsos morti offerentes*, 94), Sen. *Suas.* 6.18 of Cic.'s death (pointedly, perhaps), Tac. *Agr.* 37.3 of the Britanni. "Collective suicide is regularly attributed to barbarians" (W-M on Tac. *Ann.* 3.46.4n. *sua manu*), and many Numantians preferred suicide over surrender (App. *Hisp.* 97; 68–78n.).

77.6 atque "in fact," "introducing a clause confirmatory of the preceding statement" (Wilkins *ad* Cic. *De or.* 1.13). **sententiam probarem**: 15.1n. **tantum apud me dignitas potest** "so much weight does the concern for dignity carry with me"; as it did for C. (30.3n. *dignitas*). **nullam praeterquam uitae nostrae iacturam** "no loss other than of our lives." *praeterquam* only here in C. (and perhaps 1.5.3). The singular is collective. *uitae iactura* recurs in Sen. *Breu. uit.* 9.1 (and then much later [*TLL* 7.1.65.50]).

77.7 omnem Galliam: C.'s Gaul, marking this as the final battle for (all of) Gaul (*Introd.* 2b, 3g). **respiciamus** "let us show concern for" (*OLD* 8). **ad nostrum auxilium** "to our aid" is concise: the "aid" consists of a "supporting force" (*OLD* 1, 4; cf. §1 *auxilia*).

77.8 quid ... animi: 9.4n. *quid ... consilii*. **propinquis consanguineisque**, "relations and blood relatives," virtually unparalleled (*TLL* 4.360.9–10; cf. 45.2n. *iumentorum ... mulorumque*). *consanguineus* is "of poetic origin" (Ross 1969: 62; generally, adjs. in *-eus* are of a higher register, except for those denoting "made of" [73.9 *ferreis*]). Its choice here is unfortunate, in the light of Critognatus' proposal. **in ipsis cadaueribus**: C. develops this impossible scenario in his battle against the Nervii (2.27.3–4): *coaceruatis cadaueribus qui superessent ut ex tumulo tela in nostros conicerent*. It is a topos of ancient battle descriptions (cf. Erbig 1931: 68), which lasts into modern times.

77.9 The polyptoton *uestro ... uestrae ... uestra* highlights Critognatus' disapproval of *their* proposal. **exspoliare** only here in *CC*. The common meaning of *spolia* = "spoils" resonates morbidly with *cadaueribus*. **uestro auxilio** pointedly modifies *ad nostrum auxilium*. **stultitia** only here in C. **temeritate**: 42.2n. **imbecillitate**: first here in C. In conjunction with *animi* it occurs at Cic. *Tusc.* 4.60, *Fam.* 7.18.1. It varies §5 *animi mollitia*. **perpetuae seruituti** recurs in legal writing (*TLL* 10.1.1643.28) and at Suet. *Tib.* 36; it will be repeated at §§15, 16. **addicere**, "to sentence to," is a legal expression (Varro *Ling.* 6.30; *TLL* 1.574.45–49; first here in C.), as is *in seruitutem addicere*, "to sentence to slavery" (*OLD addicere* 1b). *a*'s **subicere** is more common in C. (below, §16; cf. Livy 26.49.8 *exterasque gentes ... tristi subiectas seruitio*) and thus more likely to have replaced the less usual term.

77.10 an: 38.7n. **ad diem** "by the appointed day" (*TLL* 5.1.1039.10–35); possibly a legal idiom, it occurs 8x in C. (not in *CC*). **fide constantiaque** "steadfast dependability," a preposterous *iunctura* to Roman ears, who claimed these values for themselves (Livy 34.58.11, Tac. *Ann.* 15.20.4) and deemed Gauls lacking therein (17.7n. *perfidia*, 20.5n. *laborem ferre*, 54.3 *perfidiam Haeduorum*). **quid ergo** is, like *quid igitur*, a standard form of *ratiocinatio ... per quam ipsi a nobis rationem poscimus ...* (*Rhet. Her.* 4.23; Seyffert, *Scholae Latinae* 103–07, offers material). **animine causa** "for fun"; 5.12.6 *animi uoluptatisque causa*. The phrase is popular with Plaut. (e.g. *Rud.* 932 *animi causa mihi nauem faciam*), who also frequently delays the word emphasized by *–ne* (Adams 2016: 40–41; it normally occupies the first position [*NLS* §170]).

77.11 illorum: the advancing auxiliaries. **praesaepto** "barricaded in front" (*OLD*); a rare verb (*TLL* 10.2.809.54–69), twice more in *BC*. **his utimini testibus** "use these (i.e. the Romans) as witnesses!" **appropinquare ... aduentum** "that their arrival is imminent." The infinitive follows on the notion of speaking in *testis*; the phrase occurs only here in *CC*. **timore exterriti**: 26.5n. **diem noctemque**: 42.6n. To work night and day during a siege is a commonplace (Kraus *ad* Livy 6.4.10). **in opere uersantur** "they are hard at work"; cf. 27.1.

77.12–13 Switching from the *recusatio* to the *confirmatio*, Critognatus (a) evokes the *exemplum* of their ancestors practicing cannibalism in the (to Romans) famous war, even though, he adds (b), their stakes had been much lower (*nequaquam pari bello*), thus hinting at an *argumentatio ex minore ad maius* (Quint. 5.11.9; *HLR* 420). But instead of concluding "How much more reason, then, do we have ...," he (c) emphasizes how their current situation does not need *any* historical justification – it is its own *exemplum* (cf. Quint. 4.1.33 *res ... pertinens ad exemplum*). For the combined appeal to one's ancestry and posterity, cf. Tac. *Agr.* 32.4 *maiores uestros et posteros cogitate* (with Woodman). **quid ergo mei consilii est** "what, then (*OLD ergo* 2), in particular is my advice?" This use of *quid* with the gen. is idiomatic (*OLD* 4). The faux dialogue of question and answer is known as *subiectio* (*Rhet. Her.* 4.33). **bello Cimbrorum Teutonumque**: the classical *Teutoni* later become *Teutones*, which C. (and Vell. Pat. 2.12.4) may anticipate, unless he uses the ending "-um" instead of "-orum" (cf. Fischer 1853: 2.22; DKM on 1.33.4). He mentions Marius' war against *Cimbri Teutonique* at 1.40.5, thereby associating his war with his uncle's (as does Cic. in *Prou. cons.* 32 [with Grillo]; cf. Pascucci 1956). The two peoples are also mentioned at 1.33.4, 2.4.2, 29.4. **in oppida compulsi**: 54.3n. **aetate ad bellum inutiles**: sim. 2.16.5, 78.1n. Cf. 71.2n. *per aetatem*. **uitam tolerauerunt**: the (euphemistic) expression is unprecedented (but cf. Lucr. 2.1171 *angustis tolerarit finibus aeuom*); subsequent instances include Verg. and the Roman historians. The verb darkly echoes 71.4 *tolerari*.

77.13 Roman expressions of concern for posterity include Cic. *Fam.* 5.12 *commemoratio posteritatis*, Plin. *Ep.* 9.3.1 *certusque posteritatis cum futura gloria*, Tac. *Ann.* 3.65.1 *ex posteritate ... metus*; cf. 17n. **cuius rei ... exemplum**: Critognatus' use of the rhetorical *exemplum* is exemplary; cf. Quint. 5.11.6 *exemplum, id est rei gestae ... utilis ad persuadendum id quod intenderis commemoratio*; Van der Blom 2010: 12–18, 61–148. **libertatis causa**: cf. the Numantians' resistance exemplifying "so great a love of freedom and bravery" (τοσόσδε ἔρως ἐλευθερίας καὶ ἀνδραγαθίας, App. *Hisp.* 97; 68–78n.). But C. once again undermines the desire for freedom, this time by this Gaul's proposal (cf. 1.5n. *praemiis*). **posteris prodi pulcherrimum iudicarem**: *posteris prodere* is an idiomatic expression (*TLL* 10.2.1628.54) of a certain grandeur normally associated with positive deeds: *laudes unius cuiusque nostrum a patribus acceptas posteris prodere* (Cic. *Rep.* 6.23). Its incongruence, as applied to cannibalism, is enhanced to caricatural effect by the superlative of an adjective of strong aesthetic connotations (cf. the oxymoronic *Hyrcano in sanguine pulcher* | *ipse subit* [Stat. *Theb.* 7.69]), and rounded off by the ponderous *iudicarem.*

77.14 illi simile bello sc. *huius belli.* It resumes §12 *nequaquam pari bello.* **depopulata Gallia**: *depopulo(r)* was used both as a regular verb and a deponent (cf. 2.7.3 *agros ... depopulati*; 24.5n. *partitis*). **Cimbri**: cf. 1.4n. *indictis ... conciliis* (its position). **quidem** opposes the abl. absolute to the main clause: "it is true, they visited calamity on us; but they left eventually" (Solodow 1978: 61–62 discusses other possibilities). **iura ... libertatem**: in this asyndetic *enumeratio* the last member subsumes the preceding ones ("in a word: our freedom"). To retain one's laws implied sovereignty; cf. N-R on Hor. *Carm.* 3.3.43–44 *triumphatisque possit* | *Roma ferox dare iura Medis*, below, §16; 76.1n. *iura legesque.*

77.15–16 The critique is undermined by its contiguity with the cannibalistic proposition. For other instances of such a critique, cf. Sall. *Iug.* 81.1, *Hist.* 4.69, Tac. *Agr.* 30.5–31.4; Balsdon 1979: 161–92, Adler 2011; 38.8n. *latrones.* **Romani uero quid petunt aliud aut quid uolunt nisi ... considere** "And the Romans? (fronted again, as in §10) What do they ever seek or want other than ... to settle?" *aliud* is *apo koinou.* **inuidia** "a greedy grudge" (first here in C.); cf. Kaster 2005: 84–102; 38.8n. *latrones.* **fama nobiles potentesque bello** "of famous reputation and valor in war" might render the chiastic Latin. C. here captures the pride apparent in Verg. *Aen.* 6.853 *debellare superbos.* **aeternam ... seruitutem** recurs but once at Tac. *Ann.* 12.34, where other Caesarian echoes can be heard; it varies §9. **iniungere seruitutem** recurs Livy 5.2.8, Suet. *Tib.* 24.2; attestations in legal writing: *TLL* 7.1.1666.42–44. *iniungere* first here in C. **neque enim** "for ... not" (with Tarrant on Verg. *Aen.* 12.74). **alia condicione**: an abl. of attendant circumstance.

77.16 The *argumentatio* shades into the *peroratio*, wherein Critognatus' appeal to autopsia along with vivid imagery rouses emotions (cf. 1.4–8n.). **quod si**: 32.5n. **in longinquis nationibus**: both temporal and local. **respicite** "turn your attention to" (*OLD* 6); but the literal meaning of "to look round and see ... behind one" is active, too (*OLD* 2b). It echoes §7 *respiciamus.* **in prouinciam redacta**: 13.3n. **iure et legibus**: 33.2n. **securibus subiecta ... seruitute**: Critognatus ends with the reiterated threat of *seruitus*, here symbolized by the "axes" (of the *fasces lictorum*; cf. Livy 35.16.2, Tac. *Ann.* 1.59.4) weighing down on the personified province. The effect is enhanced by a palindromic assonance (14.6 *itineribus subsequitur*; cf. 37.6n. *ciuitatem temere*) combined with heavy alliteration.

78 The Gauls defer the measure, opting instead to expel those unfit for war and the Mandubii; C. refuses them shelter. Both measures are recommended in military handbooks (nn. on §§1, 4). Awkward inconsistencies betray C.'s invention of the Critognatus episode (nn. on *inutiles ... bello, si ... morentur*, Brown 2019: 296–300).

78.1 Veg. 4.7 *imbellis ... aetas ac sexus ... exclusa est ne penuria obprimeret armatos a quibus moenia seruabantur*, cf. *BC* 1.52.4. Livy 5.40.9 *turba ... inutilis bello urbe excedebat* resembles our passage. **sententiis dictis**: 77.2n. **constituunt ut**: a rare construction (*TLL* 4.522.20–34), occurring once more in *CC* (*BC* 3.1.2). **ualetudine aut aetate inutiles ... bello**: the dative construction only here in C. He partly echoes Critognatus at 77.12 (cf. 15.5n. *perangustum*). Appian reports that the Petilians "cast out into no man's land those of their own unfit for battle (τοὺς ἀχρείους σφῶν ἐς μάχας)," *Hann.* 29; cf. 28.5n. DCCC. But with those unfit gone, on whom would they turn, should they decide to act on Critognatus' proposal? **atque ... descendant** "and, in fact, they should ...," the subj. being jussive. This reading mitigates the change of subject (not, however, untypical [cf. 89.3n. *iubet*]), captures the sense of *atque* (*OLD* 2), and endows the statement with greater force. **omnia prius experiantur**: the expression, possibly rooted in a proverb, is formulaic (Landgraf on Cic. *Rosc. Am.* 24 *omnia audere mallet*); in C. it recurs at *BC* 3.57.2, and twice more in abbreviated form (26.1n.). **descendant**: the verb, often applied to *unworthy* proposals (*TLL* 5.1.649.36–37), expresses the Roman view (cf. 39.3n. *orat*), and contrasts with Critognatus' high standing (77.3).

78.2 **illo ... consilio** "that *proposal*, however." *consilio* (which varies *sententia*) is delayed, as if the narrator were unsure what to call it. **si ... morentur** "if compelled by circumstances – that is to say, the delay of the reinforcements" (Edwards; *atque*. 12.2n.). But these circumstances already obtained at 77.1. **aut deditionis aut pacis** "(unconditional) surrender or even a (more favorable) peace treaty"; cf. Cic. *Phil.* 13.48 *non modo ad pacem sed ne ad deditionem quidem.*

78.3–4 No reason is offered for the expulsion of the *Mandubii* specifically – except that "Gluttons" (68.1n.) would have to be the first to leave in times of famine. **qui ... receperant**: 68.1. **eos** lacks specificity. **liberis atque uxoribus**: 26.3n. *liberos*, 14.10n. *coniuges*. **exire** varies *excedant*.

78.4 Military handbooks recommend C.'s rejection: "if those of no use come to you, do not accept them (μὴ προσδέχου), in order that the food of the besieged will be consumed sooner" (Philo, *Bel.* 8.D16 [Whitehead, with parallels]; Cass. Dio 40.40.2–4 is understanding, too). Cf. Scipio's order not to kill stray enemies *quia diceret uelocius eos absumpturos frumenti quod haberent* (Livy *Per.* 57). **hi cum**: 12.1n. *Vercingetorix ubi*. In mixed groups, Latin uses the masculine gender (G-L 286). **flentes omnibus precibus orabant**: nn. on 26.3 *flentes* and *omnibus precibus petierunt*. The imperfect is "of endeavor" (G-L 233). **in seruitutem receptos**: the concise expression, unparalleled, sardonically echoes both Critognatus' fourfold threat of *seruitus* (77.3n.), now a reality, and §3 *receperant*, underscoring the outcome of the Mandubian cooperation. **recipi** resumes *receptos* (cf. 20.12n.). **prohibebat**: the imperfect expresses "resistance to pressure" (G-L 233).

79–88 The hammer and anvil

Once the relief troops had arrived and installed themselves (possibly around Mussy-la-fosse [Brouquier-Reddé 2001: 249]), their cavalry and light-armed infantry attacked the Romans in the plain (des Laumes) again; but when dusk set in, C.'s Germanic auxiliaries secured victory, before the besieged Gauls could intervene (79–80). The next day, the relief troops conducted an attack at night (aided, it has been alleged rather fancifully, by the full moon on 25 September [Carcopino 1958: 332]); they hoped to breach the Roman fortifications in the plain (Harmand 1967: 303–07). But the latter held, and while the besieged attempted a sortie to bring the hammer and anvil tactic to fruition (68n.), they failed, too (81–82). Consequently, the Gauls decided to change tactics: Vercassiuellaunus was to lead some 60,000 troops to a weak spot in the Roman defense to Alesia's north, most likely the camp under the command of C. Antistius and C. Caninius (probably located at the foot of Mont Réa [Reddé 2001: 498–99, 504; von Schnurbein 2001: 507]); the cavalry was to make another attempt on the plain, with V. leading out the besieged in full force (83–84, 86.4). On the day of the decisive battle, C. at first orchestrated the defense from a point of observation (on the Montagne de Flavigny, possibly [85.1n. *idoneum locum*]): when the Gauls stormed the camp, he sent Labienus with troops (85.6, 86.1, 87.3). C. then moved into the plain to coordinate the defense against V. (cf. 86.3–4), who suddenly veered against Roman fortifications higher up (86.4). But V. was warded off there, too, upon the personal intervention of C. (87.1–2), who then hurried to the battle site at Mont Réa, where Labienus was orchestrating the Roman efforts (87.3). C.'s appearance, and (more importantly, one assumes) the arrival of Roman cavalry dispatched on a circuitous route, decided the battle (88). For more detailed historical reconstruction, see Gelzer 1955: 1001–05, Le Bohec 2012: 147–72 (with further lit.). It is unclear what to make of the different account in Cassius Dio (40.40).

   The narrative, which is framed by two instances of teichoscopy and the leitmotif of the din of battle (79.3n. *ex oppido … despectus*, 88.5 *conspicati ex oppido*; 80.4n. *clamore et ululatu*, 88.2 *clamore … clamor*), is built around a rising tricolon (which mirrors the structure of *VII* at large [*Introd.* 3c]): the first battle after the arrival of the additional army replays the earlier engagement (70.1–4, 68–90n.), with Germanic auxiliaries saving the day again (80.6n. *Germani*); the second attack, while still focusing on the plain, involves more troops and is conducted at night (81–82), whereas the final three-pronged offensive involves fighting "everywhere all at once" (84.2). This arrangement – which comprises mostly commonplaces (esp. 83, 85 with nn.), the occasional careless repetition (82.2 + 84.1, 81.1 + 83.8, 86.1n. *laborantibus*, 88.5), and formulaic language galore – strains historical plausibility at least twice (nn. 82.3, 83; *Introd.* 3c); these two instances evince C.'s literary effort, which is yet more evident in his evocations of epic moments (79.3n. *ex oppido … despectus*, 84.1n. *ex arce*) and his engagement with Thucydides' account of the battle of Syracuse (to be used again in *BC* [Reggi 2002]), which may have been suggested to C. by the resemblance of the enclosed plain to a harbor and the two-faced battles. In addition to many details, C. borrows from Thucydides the mirroring of events in the reactions of the internal viewer (79n. and nn. on 80, 80.2 *erat … despectus*, 80.4 *suos pugna superiores* + *clamore et ululatu*, 80.5, 80.6 *dubia uictoria*, 82.1, 85.2 *unum esse illud*, 3 *de omni salute*, 86.3 *in eo die*, 88.4 *pauci ex tanto numero*). Aside from the motifs of viewing and the din of battle, he develops the theme of the Gallic multitude (nn. on 80.4, 82.1, 68–90).

At the same time, the stylistic influence of the military report is more noticeable than elsewhere (nn. on 83, 84, 86, 90 [Fraenkel 1956]). This choice to amplify the language of the general may enhance the realistic effect for a Roman reader; but it also works well with C.'s casting himself as a general whose planning and engineering pays off (esp. 82.1), who first orchestrates the battle from a distance, then joins the melee in person, and wins the day not once but twice – all of which in his conspicuous cloak to boot (88n.), for all to read about and remember (cf. 89–90n.).

79 The additional forces arrive and set up camp on a hill; some move out to do battle. The besieged, delighted, prepare for a sortie in their turn.

The standard scheme (arrival, encampment, cavalry engagement) is enlivened by an evocative allusion to the teichoscopy (§3n. *despectus*) and the "internal viewer," whom Thucydides famously used when he mirrored the military developments in Syracuse's harbor in the reactions of those looking on from ashore (esp. 7.71.2–4; Plut. *De glor. Ath.* 347; O'Connell 2017: 144n.5). C. similarly mirrors developments in the beholders' reactions (§3, 80.9; the contrast to his earlier narrative [3.14.8–9, quoted at 80.5] may be due to Thuc.'s absence there).

79.1 Interea: the standard transition (7.1n. *interim*) coolly understates the event's significance – to be rendered all the more effectively in §3. **Commius reliquique duces**: 76.4n. **summa imperii permissa erat** "[to whom] the supreme command (20.5n.) had been entrusted (*OLD* 3b)"; similarly at 5.11.8. **colle exteriore**: possibly Mussy-la-Fosse, to Alesia's south-west (Le Bohec 2012: 125). Some have objected to *exteriore* as "selbst-verständlich" and proposed *editiore* (Sydow 1898: 20). **considunt**: 57.4n.

79.2 equitatu ... educto: 70.1n. *equestre proelium*. **planitiem ... demonstrau-imus**: 69.3; 17.1n. (cross-referencing). **complent**: 12.5n. **paulum ab eo loco**: cf. 4.17.3 *tigna ... paulum ab imo praeacuta*; 6.9.3 *paulum supra eum locum ... facere pontem instituit*. On *eo loco*: 4.7n. **potestate. abditas in locis**: like Cic. (Clarke on *Mil.* 40), C. construes *abdere* preferably with *in* + acc. (18.3, 30.1) except for the perf. pass. part. (*in* + abl.); contrast 5.3.4, *BC* 2.9.3. Hidden troops: 45.5, 18.1n. *insidiarum*.

79.3 The focalization shifts markedly (cf. 45.4–6n.), and the significance of the arrival is highlighted by its perception through the eyes of the Gauls in Alesia; their elation is emphasized by the crisp, asyndetic sentences (cf. Quint. 9.3.50 recommending asyndeton *cum quid instantius dicimus*) and the three verbs in initial position (cf. 1.1n. *cognoscit*). **erat ex oppido Alesia despectus in campum** repeats 45.4n. and will be adapted at 80.2 and 88.5n. The view (and witness) from the besieged city is a commonplace since Hom. *Il.* 3.130 ἵνα θέσκελα ἔργα ἴδηαι, "that you may see the divine deeds [in the plains before Troy]" (N-R on Hor. *Carm.* 3.2.6–8 list further *loci*); there are several instances of such a rudimentary, evocative allusion to teichoscopy at Alesia (80.5, 84.1, 88.5). For the transition *erat ... despectus*, cf. 19.1n. *collis erat*. **fit gratulatio ... animi ad laetitiam excitantur** expresses similar ideas at the clause's beginning and end (a *redditio* of sorts [40.4n. *interdicitque*]) for emphasis and dramatic contrast to the doomed outcome (80.9n.). C.'s language supports this: The two nouns are frequently paired (Oakley on Livy 10.24.6), esp. in contexts of (premature) victory celebrations (*BC* 1.74.7); for the tone of the latter expression, cf. Cic. *Tusc.* 4.13 *cum autem inaniter et effuse animus exultat, tum illa laetitia gestiens uel nimia dici potest, quam ita definiunt: sine ratione animi elationem.*

79.4 productis copiis ... considunt: a standard move (66.6n.). *considere*, "to take up position [for battle]," differs from §1 *considunt*, "they set up camp"; cf. 5.3n. *legatorum*. **fossam ... explent**: 58.1n. *cratibus atque aggere. fossam explere*, which recurs at 82.3, 86.5, and Livy 9.14.9 (with Oakley), varies the commoner *fossam complere* (72.3; *TLL* 3.2090.78–80, 2091.36–9). **integunt ... explent**: a *hysteron proteron* (40.4n. *moratur*). **se ad eruptionem**

atque omnes casus comparant: sim. at 41.4; a slight syllepsis. *omnes casus =* "all possible (1.5n.) eventualities (*OLD* 11)."

80 C. allocates his troops. The fighting begins in the plain for all to see. The Gauls appear to be at an advantage, but towards day's end yield to the Germanic cavalry: both the relief troops and those from Alesia return to camp.

§§1–2 narrate the preparation and anticipation, 3–6 the battle, 7–9 the consequences (cf. 18n.); the Gallic defeat is viewed through Gallic eyes (§9n.). C. puts emphasis on seeing: *despectus, exspectabant, improuiso, uiderent, conspectu*, just like Thucydides (τὴν ἔποψιν, τῆς θέας, πάντων ... σκοπούντων, ἴδοιεν, οἱ ... βλέψαντες, τῆς ὄψεως, ἀπιδόντες [7.71.2–3]); cf. 79–88n.

80.1 The proper placing of troops, esp. in battlelines, was expected of a general (Frontin. *Str.* 2.3). References to allocations are frequent (*disponere* is a technical term [*TLL* 5.1.1423.13]), incl. Thuc. 7.70.3 "every man in the place assigned," and App. *Hisp.* 92 "everyone was assigned a position (χωρίον ... ἑκάστοις διετέτακτο) and forbidden to change it (μεταπηδᾶν) unless ordered"; cf. 81.4n. *ut cuique ... accedunt,* 68–78n. **ad utramque partem munitionis** "along both sides of the fortification"; the circum- and contravallation are here considered one *munitio* (α's *munitionum* is a *dis*improvement); 81.1n. *campestres munitiones* and other plurals differ. There are eighteen (!) references to the Caesarian *munitio* in this final episode (cf. 69.6n.), whose size (84.3, 86.4) and impenetrability (82.2, 85.3) are emphasized repeatedly: "le rampart n'avait pas donné la victoire à César, mais il lui avait évité la défaite" (Le Bohec 2012: 154); it redounds to C.'s credit. Cf. 82.1n. *interibant,* 87.3n. *neque ... sustinere,* 89.4n. *ipse in munitione.* **si usus ueniat** "should the need arise." This unusual alternative to *usus esse* occurs repeatedly in comedy (e.g. Plaut. *Cist.* 147 [= Ter. *Ad.* 891] *siquid usus uenerit*), twice in Cato's *Agr.* (4, 157), once in Catull. 98. Curiously, App. *Hisp.* 92 equally specifies: ὅτε χρεία γένοιτο. **suum quisque:** 32.5n. **locum teneat et nouerit** "should know his station and hold it"; another *hysteron proteron* (cf. 79.4n. *integunt*).

80.2 erat ... despectus echoes 79.3n. *erat ... campum* (of the Gauls): both sides are watching (as in Thuc. 7.71.1 πεζὸς ἀμφοτέρων). **summum undique iugum** "the summit of the surrounding ridge," as described in 69.4. The adverb shades into an adjective (59.6n. *subito*). **pugnae** hovers between *intenti* (the adj. frequently construes with the dative, e.g. Sall. *Cat.* 2.9; C. elsewhere prefers *ad* + acc.) and *prouentum.* For the difference between (the more abstract and general) *pugna* and (the hand-to-hand) *proelium,* cf. 3.4.3 *quod diuturnitate pugnae hostes defessi proelio excedebant;* C. maintains the difference more than others (Rosenberger 1992: 133). **prouentum exspectabant** repeats 29.3n. *exspectabant* resonates paronomastically with *despectus* (cf. 43.5n. *profectio*).

80.3 On the tactic, cf. 18.1n. *inter equites*; a variation is attested of Scipio (Frontin. *Str.* 4.7.27, Veg. 1.15). **raros** "here and there" (Edwards). **sagittarios expeditosque [leuis armaturae] interiecerant** "they had interspersed archers (36.4) and light-armed troops (18.1n. *expeditis*) [of light armament]." *sagittarii* and *expediti* are often grouped together, as they were both (along with other specialized groups) considered *leuis armatura* (*BC* 1.27.5 *expeditos ... ‹cum› sagittariis funditoribusque raros ... disponit*; Veg. 2.2.10 *leuem armaturam, hoc est ferrentarios sagittarios funditores*). *leuis armatura* is also used near synonymously with *expeditus* (*BC* 3.62.2 *numerum leuis armaturae et sagittariorum*); but this *iunctura* is unparalleled, tautological, and most probably an intrusive gloss. **auxilio succurrerent**: the expression is unparalleled, pleonastic, and emphatic – perhaps ironically so, as they will be the ones to die. **complures** sc. *Romani*. **de improuiso**: 72.2n.

80.4 cum suos pugna superiores ... confiderent: a typical mention of Gallic arrogance before defeat (15.2n. *explorata*; *Introd.* 3g). But cf. Thuc. 7.71.3 εἰ μέν τινες ἴδοιέν πη τοὺς σφετέρους ἐπικρατοῦντας, ἀνεθάρσησάν τε ἂν ... "whenever some saw their men victorious somewhere, they would regain heart and ...." **multitudine premi**: 21.1n. *multitudo*; 51.1n. *premerentur*. C. reemphasizes the leitmotif to emphasize the enemy's numerical superiority (48.4n. *numero*; 68–90n.). **ex omnibus partibus et ei ... et ei ... confirmabant**: 24.3–4nn. *toto muro, clamore, alii.* For the synopsis of the two groups, cf. Thuc. 7.71.4–5 "in the Athenian (land) forces ... one could hear ... Very much the same was suffered by those aboard (οἱ ἐπὶ τῶν νεῶν)." **clamore et ululatu** "a howling cry" corresponds to Thuc. 7.71.3 ὀλοφυρμῷ ... μετὰ βοῆς (sim. at 71.4). The onomatopoeic noun, which phonetically evokes the Greek (as C. enjoyed doing [Krebs 2018c: 518n.6]), is first attested in Catull. 63.24 *acutis ululatibus agitant* (the verb: Enn. *Ann.* 344); C. used it at 5.37.3 *suo more uictoriam conclamant atque ululatum tollunt* (nowhere else in *CC*). It is commonly applied to women and barbaric peoples (Verg. *Aen.* 4.667 *femineo ululatu* [with Pease], Livy 21.28.1 *Galli ... cum uariis ululatibus cantuque moris sui*, Tac. *Germ.* 7.2, Ps.-Quint. *Decl. mai.* 3.6). The Gauls were famed for their war cry (Oakley on Livy 7.10.8; 12.5n. *clamore*), and the din of battle figures prominently in all three engagements (81.2+3, 88.2n.). C.'s hendiadys recurs in Livy (44.47.9) and Curt. (e.g. 8.10.18).

80.5 Cf. 3.14.8–9 *reliquum erat certamen positum in uirtute, qua nostri milites facile superabant, atque eo magis quod in conspectu Caesaris atque omnis exercitus* *res gerebatur, ut nullum paulo fortius factum latere posset; omnes enim colles ac loca superiora, unde erat propinquus despectus in mare, ab exercitu tenebantur.* Thuc. 7.70.3 expresses the commonplace relation between witness and courage succinctly: ἕκαστος ἠπείγετο πρῶτος φαίνεσθαι, "everyone was eager *to be seen* as most excellent." Cf. Xen. *Hell.* 7.1.30 πάντων ... περιβλεπτότατοι, "of all the most-looked-at from all sides," Quadrig. *FRHist* F5 *in conspectu duorum exercituum* (sim. F6), Hirt. 8.42.4. **quod** "the fact that." **neque recte ac turpiter factum celari poterat** varies the theme with greater specificity (30.1n.). In the polar expression (72.2n. *aut noctu) ac*, "and ... alike," is unusual (but cf. Nep. *Pr.* 3 *honesta atque turpia*); U's *aut* is a simplification. **et laudis cupiditas et timor ignominiae:** a polysyndetic and isocolic chiasmus. 50.4n. *cupiditate gloriae*, 17.5n. *ignominiam.*

80.6 a meridie ... occasum: the duration of battle is a clichéd index of the fierceness of fighting, as Plautus knew when he included it in his imaginary battle account (*Amph.* 253 *pugna usque a mani ad uesperum*). Nightfall typically suspended a battle, as darkness rendered conditions more hazardous (Enn. *Ann.* 5.5 *bellum aequis manibus nox intempesta diremit*; cf. 81.5, 24n.). The suspension then became a commonplace (to which Pliny alludes: *actionem meam, ut proelia solet, nox diremit, Ep.* 4.9.9), and especially when the outcome hung in the balance (Oakley on Livy 7.33.15 *ni nox*) – as here. To Roman readers, the following development will therefore have appeared all the more surprising (approaching a *paraprosdokian* [19.4n. *uictoriam*]). **dubia uictoria** "with victory in the balance." A common motif (cf. Vergil's [*G.* 2.283] beautifully balanced *proelia, sed dubius mediis Mars errat in armis,* Ov. *Am.* 1.9.29 *Mars dubius* [with McKeown]; 62.6), this particular phrasing occurs first here (*TLL* 5.1.2111.67); popular with Livy (as early as 1.36.2 [*Introd.* 3h]), it is otherwise rare. Thuc. 7.71.3-4 expresses the same idea thrice (e.g. ἀντίπαλόν τι τῆς ναυμαχίας). **pugnaretur:** 25.1n. **Germani:** for the fourth time, C.'s Germanic cavalry saves the day (65n.). **confertis turmis** "they amassed squadrons (45.1n.) of cavalry"; unparalleled except for Amm. Marc. 24.6.8 *equitum turmas ... confertas.* **propulerunt** "they drove them off." The military use of *propellere* is first attested in C. at 4.25.1 (*TLL* 10.2.1968.55); cf. 10.3n. *impetum.*

80.7 quibus in fugam coniectis: 62.3n. C. is imprecise; only the cavalry (including, perhaps, *expediti*) fled (cf. 66.7n *equites*). **circumuenti interfectique:** 50.3n. Their fate contrasts darkly with their intended role (§3).

80.8 cedentes: sc. *Gallos.* **usque ad castra insecuti:** 67.5 *usque ad ... persequuntur*, 26.2n. *insequendum.* **sui colligendi facultatem:** sc. for a counterattack.

80.9 The marked contrast with 79.3–4 (*ad laetitiam, productis copiis … ante oppidum*) highlights the reversal; C. continues to mirror events in the reaction of the beholders (79n.). **uictoria desperata**: the expression, first here (*TLL* 5.1.739.80), recurs in Cic. *Fam.* 7.3.2, Vell. Pat. 2.85.4, Curt. 9.2.34, and Flor. *Epit.* Cf. Cic. *Phil.* 12.10 *desperatio uictoriae*.

81–82 After further preparations, the outer troops attack the plain again – at night. The legionaries resume and hold their positions, additional troops fortify the points of attack; assisted by the *munitiones*, they hold off the numerically superior Gauls, who withdraw at dawn, before the besieged Gauls are able to join the melee.

The second engagement is an amplified version of the previous one: this time the outer troops challenge the Romans on and around the *munitiones*, but fail to receive support from the inner troops once more (82.3n.). They also try to take advantage of the darkness (cf. nn. on 24, 27.1 *non inutilem*); but C.'s development of the motif is characteristically understated (contrast e.g. Thuc. 3.22, Tac. *Ann.* 4.50–51; *Introd.* 3c).

81.1 A typical cumulative-complex sentence comprising mostly abl. (absolutes). **uno die** "only one day," contrasting with *magno … numero* (cf. 9.5n. *omnes in unum*). **Galli**: placed like 1.4n. *principes*. **hoc spatio**: a typical resumptive demonstrative; cf. 4.7n. *qua potestate*. **magno cratium scalarum harpagonum numero**: a rising tricolon. *harpago*, "a pole fitted with a hook" (*OLD* 1), is a technical military term first here attested (*TLL* 6.3.2538.75). Cf. 38.9n. *magnum numerum*. **media nocte silentio ex castris egressi** repeats 11.7n. **campestres munitiones**: the fortifications in the plain (69.3; 72.3n. *campestribus*), detailed in 72–73.

81.2–4 Cf. Tac. *Ann.* 2.20.2 *funditores libritoresque excutere tela et proturbare hostem iubet; … quantoque conspicui magis propugnatores, tanto pluribus uulneribus deiecti*; 13.39.3 *libritoribus funditoribusque attributus locus unde eminus glandes torquerent*. **subito clamore sublato**: *subito* hovers between adjective and adverb (cf. 59.6n.). The topos: 12.5n. **qua significatione**: 28.6n. *quae … pars*. **de … cognoscere**: 1.1n. **fundis, sagittis, lapidibus**: a rising tricolon, cf. Thuc. 7.70.5 (quoted at 82.1). *funda* = "sling shot" rather than "sling" (cf. 5.35.8 *in aduersum os funda uulneratur*; *TLL* 6.1.1549.10–11), in line with the other two missiles (contrast Livy 38.20.1 *qui* [sc. *lapides*] *funda mitti possent*). **proturbare** "to upset and cause to fall forward" (cf. *TLL* 10.2.2298.16–17). **reliquaque … pertinent** repeats 19.6n. Cf. Polyb. 5.71.9 "with timber and stones and everything of that sort (παντὶ τῷ τοιούτῳ γένει)." **parant administrare**: sim. 71.9. *parare* = "to set about."

81.3 eodem temp*ore* clam*ōre* exaudito: 24.1n. *temp*ore *… frigore*, 48.1n. *exaudito clamore*. **dat … Vercingetorix … educit**: the two actions are arranged chiastically around their common subject. **tuba signum**: 47.1n. *receptui cani*. C. does not mention the formidable Celtic war trumpet, the Carnyx (Piggott 1959; 2.1n. Carnutes); its effect is captured memorably in Polyb. 2.29.6 (quoted at 88.2n. *clamore*). **educit**: sc. *eos*, as easily inferred from *suis*.

81.4 nostri … accedunt reprises 80.1n. (just as App. *Hisp.* 93 τῶν τειχομάχων … ἀναπηδώντων ἐς τὰ τείχη, "with the wall fighters leaping up to [their positions on] the wall," reprises *Hisp.* 92). **superioribus diebus**: 44.1n. **suus cuique erat locus attributus**: *quisque* naturally follows the possessive (32.5n.) serving in turn as host to the copula *erat* (cf. 5.52.2 *non decimum quemque esse reliquum militem*, 6.15.2; cf. 5.2n. *quorum erant*); *attributus* receives the emphasis of the final position. **ad munitiones**: the plural comprises the individual positions each man took (cf. ἐς τὰ τείχη, 55.1n. *ad ripas*). **fundis, librilibus, sudibusque … [ac glandibus]** "with sling shots, stones, and [sc. sharpened] stakes … [and sling shots]." This is the first attestation of the extremely rare *librilis*; if Paul. Fest. 116 is sound, it defines *librilla* (*librilia*) as *instrumenta bellica, saxa scilicet ad brachii crassitudinem in modum flagellorum loris reuincta*, which suggests the same metonymical ambiguity (launching device, launched device) as with *funda*. Some have read it as adjectival, "slings throwing large stones" (Holmes *et al.*), but Tac. (quoted above, §§2–4n.) offers a strong argument against such a reading (cf. Veg. 2.23.9 *sed et manu sola omnes milites meditabantur librialia saxa iactare*). On balance, to athetize *ac glandibus* as an intrusive gloss (on *librilibus*?) is a fairly unobtrusive intervention that makes excellent sense. *sudis* "as a weapon" (*OLD* 1b) is not attested before C. Later attestations suggest that he made it a staple of military narratives (e.g. Sall. *Cat.* 56.3 *praeacutas sudis*, Livy 23.37.3, Tac. *Ann.* 4.51.1). **proterrent**, "to frighten off," is rather rare; as a military term (already at 5.58.4), it recurs at Verg. *Aen.* 12.291.

81.5 prospectu … adempto is first attested here; it found favor with Roman historians (*TLL* 10.2.2205.74–78). *prospectus* echoes paronomastically both *conspectus* and *despectus* (43.5n. *profectio*, 80n.). **multa utrimque uulnera**: 59.6n. *tantis subito*. **complura tormentis … coniciuntur** would follow more naturally on *fundis … proterrent*, and Sydow 1898: 20–21 proposed transposing it, which would also result in the smoother transition … *uulnera accipiuntur. … at Marcus Antonius …* But the alleged displacement is hard to explain, and C.'s writing is not always as orderly and balanced as in c.18. On *tormenta*: 41.3n.

81.6 M. Antonius, the future triumvir (*RE* 30), is here mentioned for the first time by C. He had joined him in Gaul in 54, returned to Rome the following year to run for the quaestorship, then rejoined C. in 52 to serve him for the remainder of the campaign and beyond (Cic. *Phil.* 2.48–50 with Ramsey). **hae partes**: the area indicated in §1, wherein the just-narrated events (hence: *hae* [*OLD* 4]) took place. **qua ex parte**: 34.3n. *ab altera … parte.* **his** (rather than 84.2 *huc*) refers to *qua ex parte* as if C. had written *quos nostrum* (cf. 71.2n. *discedentibus*). **auxilio … summittebant**: unparalleled and pleonastic (like 80.3 *auxilio succurrerent*). **ex ulterioribus castellis deductos** "[other men] drawn from forts (69.7n.) farther away." The phrase is standard military language.

82.1 Cf. Thuc. 7.70.5: "as long as (ὅσον μὲν χρόνον) a ship was approaching to charge (προσφέροιτο), the [soldiers] on the deck employed javelins, arrows, and stones (τοῖς ἀκοντίοις καὶ τοξεύμασι καὶ λίθοις) plentiful against it (ἀφθόνως ἐπ' αὐτήν); but once they were alongside (ἐπειδὴ δὲ προσμείξειαν), the soldiers on deck moved to hand-to-hand fighting and tried to capture each other's ships." Tac. *Ann.* 4.47.3 will make the same observation (*Introd.* 3h). **plus … proficiebant** "they were rather more successful." **multitudine telorum**: the juxtaposition of *plus* and *multitudine* suggests the reason for the success. The swarm of missiles (detailed in 81.2) is a common motif: *hastati spargunt hastas. fit ferreus imber* (Enn. *Ann.* 266); it here corresponds to the "barbaric" hordes (21.1n. *multitudo*; 79–88n.) and naturally causes *multa uulnera.* Most famously, the Persians had threatened the Greeks that their missiles would block out the sun (Hdt. 7.226.2; Cic. *Tusc.* 1.42 *in umbra igitur pugnabimus*, Sen. *Constant.* 4.2 *cum stolidus ille rex multitudine telorum diem obscuraret*). C. is fond of the expression (41.3, 86.5; 7x in total; 5x in *CC*). **propius successerunt** "they came up closer"; Sisenna *FRHist* F7 *Marsi propius succedunt.* **aut se ipsi stimulis … aut in scrobes … aut … pilis muralibus interibant**: a parallelistic and polysyndetic rising tricolon. C. mentions first the *stimuli* (73.9n.) as the Gauls' first obstacle; and he foregoes mention of the *cippi*, as they lay within reach of the *pila muralia*, which held off the Gauls. The devices' proclaimed effectiveness redounds to C.'s credit. **se ipsi stimulis inopinantes induebant** rephrases 73.4. 8.3n. *inopinantibus.* **delati in scrobes transfodiebantur** "they fell down (*OLD* 3b) into the pits and were run through," cf. Verg. *Aen.* 9.543–54 *pectora duro | transfossi ligno.* This is the first (and in *CC* only) attestation of *transfodere*, perhaps chosen for its etymological play on *scrobis* (73.5): *fodere … est foueam facere* (Isid. *Etym.* 17.5.33). **pilis muralibus**: the contexts here and at 5.40.6 suggest that these were pikes hurled from the wall. But specifics are lacking, as (1) there are but two more attestations (Curt. 8.10.32, Tac. *Ann.* 4.51.1 [*Introd.* 3h]), (2) Sall. and others seem to speak simply of *pila* in identical contexts (*Iug.* 57.3 *oppidani in proximos saxa uoluere, sudis, pila ... mittere*), and (3) the archaeological evidence is doubtful (Bishop-Coulston 2006: 116–17).

82.2 is a typical cumulative-complex sentence, wherein abl. absolutes combine with a part. construction. **multis ... acceptis** modifies 81.5; cf. 50.4n. **nulla munitione perrupta** "but no part of the fortification was breached." **lux appeteret**: the verb's intransitive use of time is common, but this particular expression occurs first here, then in Livy 10.29.10, Curt. (3x), Tac. *Ann.* 4.51.3, and Amm. Marc. 20.7.6 (*TLL* 2.283.49–50). **ab latere aperto**: 50.1n. **ex superioribus castris eruptione** "in case of a sortie from the [Roman] camp(s) above them"; cf. 80.2. **se ad suos receperunt** echoes 80.9 *se in oppidum receperunt.*

82.3 The Gauls' lack of coordination contrasts sharply with the Romans' orchestration. But one wonders how long it could have taken the besieged Gauls (given the developments at 79.4), and, consequently, how plausible an explanation this is. **interiores** "those situated on the inside (i.e. of the Roman fortifications)," *OLD* 2. **quae ... praeparata** may refer back to 81.1, even if the context there does not seem to include the Gauls in Alesia. **priores fossas** causes much difficulty (and its singularity [*TLL* 10.2.1330.16] hardly helps matters): if viewed from Alesia (as *interiores* suggests), *priores*, "in a more forward position" (*OLD* 1), would rule out the 20-foot trench closest to Alesia (72.1; identified as 79.4 *proxima fossa*, and there described as being filled up). But whether it refers to (parts of) one or both of the 15-foot trenches (72.3) or any of the intervening contraptions (cf. 73.2 *perpetuae fossae* of the *cippi*, which Holmes ad loc. favors) cannot be established. **diutius** "too long." **prius ... cognouerunt quam ... appropinquarent** "they realized that their comrades [on the outside] had withdrawn before they were able to get near the [Roman] fortifications"; 1.6n. *priusquam.*

83 The outer Gauls regroup and plan an ambush where the Roman fortifications are weak. With their ambush troops lying in wait, they renew the attack in the plain (§8n. *campestres munitiones*).

The weak spot has been identified as Mont Réa: At its foot the most weapons have been excavated; evidence of the circumvallation is missing, too (Sievers 2001, Reddé 2001: 498–99, 504; cf. von Schnurbein 2001: 507; §2n. *circumplecti*, 88.2n. *pilis*). But if this attests to a historical core, the narrative also reveals a dramatizing intention: The discovery of a weakness (here improbably late) is a common device to prepare for the climactic moment of battle narratives ever since Ephialtes' guiding Persian forces on a path at Thermopylae (Hdt. 7.213–16; cf. Plut. *Cat.*

Mai. 13.1); more generally, all elements in C.'s tale are commonplace, as the comparison with Hannibal's ambush reveals (Polyb. 3.71): Hannibal "had noticed a place (συνεωρακὼς … τόπον, cf. §1 *cognoscunt*)" that was "well-suited for an ambush (εὐφυῆ δὲ πρὸς ἐνέδραν, cf. §2)." He decided to lay his ambush there and "shared his plan with his brother Mago and his council (κοινολογηθεὶς Μάγωνι τἀδελφῷ καὶ τοῖς συνέδροις, cf. §5 *occulte inter se*)"; he entrusted his brother with the command (cf. §6 *propinquum*), for which "he chose from the whole army the most valiant men (ἐξ ὅλου τοῦ στρατοπέδου σημηνάμενος τοὺς εὐρωστοτάτους, cf. §4 *ex omni numero … maximam uirtutis opinionem*). He dispatched them at night … along with guides (συστήσας ὁδηγούς, cf. §§7 *prima uigilia*, 1 *locorum peritos*), having agreed with his brother on the best time for the attack (περὶ τοῦ καιροῦ τῆς ἐπιθέσεως, cf. §5 *adeundi tempus definiunt*)."

The passage is stylistically especially indebted to the military dispatch (short *guttatim* cola, paratactically arranged, with frequent use of demonstratives; cf. 79–88n.).

83.1 The sequence – a defeat followed by a debate – is typical (cf. 14.1, 29.1, 52.1). **magno cum detrimento repulsi** "beaten back under heavy losses"; cf. Lentul. [Cic.] *Fam.* 12.15.7 *Dolabellam … conatum esse aliquotiens ui introire; repulsum semper esse cum magno suo detrimento.* **Galli … consulunt:** 15n. **locorum peritos** smacks of a technical term (*peritus* itself may signify "guide" [*TLL* 10.1.1501.24–26]); among its few attestations are *BAfr.* 50.2, Amm. Marc. 16.2.3, 18.6.21. **superiorum castrorum** is typically taken to refer to all the "elevated" camps (80.2). But *superior* may refer to "places conventionally regarded as higher" (*OLD* 2), which Mont Réa is from C.'s most likely point of view (as is Montagne de Bussy); so *superiorum* might here mean "farther north."

83.2 erat … collis: 19.1n. *collis erat.* It is the Réa. **quem … opere circumplecti non potuerant nostri:** C. did not mention this at 74.1n. *pro loci natura;* cf. 55.2n. *huc … contulerat. circumplecti* is somewhat rare (*TLL* 3.1157.21–51) and occurs only here in C. (cf. *complexus* at 72.2, 74.1). The assertion is borne out by the archaeological evidence (Joly-Barrall 2001: 468); App. *Hisp.* 90 mentions a similar circumstance (λίμνην συνάπτουσαν οὐκ ἐνὸν περιτειχίσαι). **propter magnitudinem circuitus:** as specified at 69.3 and 74.1, respectively; 45.3n. *circuitu.* **necessario:** C. emphasizes the necessity as it was a maxim *ne mons castris immineat, per quem superuenire hostes aut prospicere possint, quid in castris agatur* (Ps.-Hyg. *Mun. castr.* 57); cf. 85.5n. *tela coniciunt.* **paene iniquo loco et leniter decliui** "on basically unfavorable (19.3n. *aequo*) ground given its gentle sloping (88.1n.)"; the most important information is fronted (cf. 40.4n. *moratur*). The singular *leniter decliuis* varies 19.1n. *leniter accliuis; decliuis* is first attested in C. (2.18.1 [*TLL* 5.1.196.31]).

83.3 C. Antistius Reginus had conducted a levy the year before (6.1.1); cf. 90.6. If he is identical with the man at Cic. *Att.* 10.12.1, he would seem to have stayed with C. until 49 at least (*RE* "Antistius" 39). **C. Caninius Rebilus** would go on to serve C. for the remainder of the Gallic campaign (90.6; *VIII pass.*) and beyond to become consul for one day in 45 (*RE* "Caninius" 9).

83.4 duces hostium: those specified at 76.4, as 83.6 reveals. **ex omni numero**: 76.3. **maximam uirtutis opinionem**: 59.5n.

83.5 quid quoque pacto agi placeat "[about] what to them seemed best to do and how." The idiomatic *quo pacto*, an adverbial expression derived from *pactum*, "agreement (*OLD* 1), condition," occurs only here in C. The two questions: 4.8n. *quodque.* **occulte … constituunt**: the adverb first here in C. On the precaution of secretive planning for fear of betrayal: 9n. **adeundi tempus definiunt cum meridies esse uideatur** "as time of attack they set roughly [or: when it was seen to be] midday"; *esse uideatur*, a resolved cretic-spondee/trochee, was a known Ciceronian favorite (Berry on Cic. *Sull.* 3.9). Military writers recommend the schedule, if for different reasons: … *in aestu, ante lucem coepto itinere, ad destinata perueniant* (Veg. 3.2).

83.6 propinquum: 76.4n. *consobrino.*

83.7 prima uigilia: 3.3n. *uigiliam.* **sub lucem**: 61.3n. **montem**: called *collis* above, §2. **ex nocturno labore sese reficere**: military writers warn against entering battle right after an exhausting march (Veg. 3.11.7 *ne longo spatio fatigatum militem … ad publicum proelium cogas*).

83.8 meridies … uideretur reprises §5; cf. 61.3n. **quae … demonstrauimus**: 83.2. Cross-references: 17.1n. *diximus.* **ad campestres munitiones accedere** repeats 81.1n. **copiae pro castris**: 70.2n. *pro castris.*

84 V. finally leads his troops from Alesia to attack the Romans, who are spread thin along the fortifications and intimidated by the engulfing din of battle, at their front and rear. The strategy of "hammer and anvil" comes into effect at long last (68n.).

The reentrance of V. (in primary position for the first time since 71.1) signals the beginning of the final battle, which is also marked by an elevated register (nn. on *arce, crates … parauerat, suum periculum … aliena … uirtute*, 5); but the overall character still bears the imprint of the military bulletin (79–88n.).

84.1 ex arce Alesiae: *arx* connotes both heavy fortification (*arx ab arcendo quod is locus munitissimus urbis*, Varro *Ling.* 5.151) and elevation (*altissimum in urbe quod est arx tutissimum uocatur*, *Ling.* 7.44) – two qualities attributed to Alesia (69.1nn.); when contrasted to *oppidum*, it refers specifically to the citadel or "inner city" (*amisso oppido fugerat in arcem*, Cic. *Sen.* 11). Of a higher register, its use here in combination with the repeated evocation of the teichoscopy (79.3n. *despectus*) places Alesia in the tradition of great cities beginning with Troy (e.g. Hom. *Il.* 2.133 Ἰλίου ... πτολίεθρον; Plaut. *Bacch.* 954, Verg. *Aen.* 2.56 *Priamique arx alta*). **conspicatus**: 40.4n. Viewing: 8on. **crates ... reliquaque quae ... parauerat** varies 81.2n. *crates ... reliquaeque quae ... parant administrare* and partly repeats 82.2. The two enumerations differ in all but the first item; this one is more recherché. **longurios** "long poles"; cf. 3.14.5 *falces ... insertae affixaeque longuriis*, 4.17.8 *longuriis cratibusque consternebantur*. The only other author to use the term is Varro (*Rust.* 1.14.2, 2.7.10). **musculos** "mantelets." C. offers a detailed description at *BC* 2.10–11; Veg. 4.16.1 defines them as *minores machinas quibus protecti bellatores*; they resemble *uineae* (17.1n.). This is the first instance of the extremely rare military term (*TLL* 8.1700.23).

84.2 rephrases 67.2[nn.]+4. **pugnatur uno tempore omnibus locis atque omnia temptantur**: the verb's initial position conveys speed and urgency. The climactic motif "πανταχόθεν ἅμα," "everywhere at the same time" (Thuc. 7.70.1; cf. 79–88n.), is further highlighted by the totalizing polyptoton (4.6n. *omnium*; Wills 224–25). On the – chiastically arranged – second colon, cf. 26.1n. *omnia experti*. **minime ... firma**: 60.2n. The artistic separation (once more in *CC* at 1.1.3 *minimeque ... saepe*; contrast 60.2 *minime firmas*) highlights both parts; cf. Cic. *Fin.* 3.14 "*explicabo ..., nisi alienum putas, ... sententiam.*" "*Minime id quidem,*" inquam, "*alienum ....*"

84.3 C. had anticipated the difficulty arising from the disproportion of the size of the defensive works and the number of troops (72.2). **Romanorum**: the fronted gen. marks the changed focalization. **distinetur**: in antithesis to *concurritur*. **nec facile**: 25.1n. **occurrit** "responds" to *concurritur*.

84.4 On C.'s psychological sensitivity, cf. 17.4–7n. **multum ... ualet** "was very effective at (*OLD ualere* 7b) [scaring our men]." **clamor qui ... existit**: battle clamor at the rear normally suggested that the troops were (about to be) surrounded; cf. 62.6n. *post tergum*, 80.4n. *clamore*. **suum periculum in aliena ... uirtute constare** "[that] their personal danger depended on the courage of others." The antithetically phrased evaluation inspired Livy 7.8.1 *euentum suum in uirtute aliena ponit*; it, in turn, allows for the decision between β's *uirtute* and α's *salute* (Klotz 1941: 221–22). The observation derives additional force from its contrast to the typical assertion *uos ... libertatem atque patriam in dextris uostris portare* (Sall. *Cat.* 58.8), Sil. *Pun.* 17.198 *nunc in nostra spes ultima dextra*, Tac. *Agr.* 30.2 *spem ac subsidium in nostris manibus*.

84.5 The "horrible imaginings" is a commonplace (Publ. Syr. 12 *semper plus metuit animus ignotum malum*, Livy 9.24.8 *omnia ex incerto maiora* [with Oakley], Tac. *Ann.* 2.82.1, Cass. Dio 14.57.2), which C. will rephrase at *BC* 2.4.4 (text uncertain). It is phrased sententiously (cf. 26.4n. *timor*; Preiswerk 1945: 214).

85 On the other, Roman, side, C. takes up a position of observation to send relief forces when necessary. There is fighting in the plain and at Mont Réa, where the Gauls use sophisticated techniques (*testudine facta, agger … coniectus*) to cause duress.

Repetition of *maxime* (2x; cf. *magnum … momentum*) and polyptoton of *omnis* (2; cf. *uniuersi*) combine with the singularizing statement *unum esse illud tempus* to convey the urgency of events largely developed with the help of commonplaces (many of which recur in 86): it is striking just how schematic is the account and drained of individuating detail.

85.1 Generals regularly sought a good observation point, typically elevated and at their army's rear or front (Goldsworthy 1998: 152–54; 49.1, 87.3n. *proelio sit*). **idoneum locum nactus**: the possibly formulaic expression recurs 4x in *BC* (Odelman 1985: 181–82); 9.4n. The Mt. de Flavigny is a likely location (69.7n.); it afforded the required view (von Schnurbein 2001: 507). **quid quaque in parte geratur cognoscit**: Cic. *Inu. rhet.* 2.12 *quid quaque in parte considerari oporteat* (he favors the combination). C. tellingly emphasizes tactical intelligence at this crucial juncture (*Introd.* 3d). **laborantibus summittit**: 13.1n. (reiterated at 86.1).

85.2–3 Cf. *BC* 2.5.3 *neque erat quisquam omnium quin in eius diei casu suarum omnium fortunarum euentum consistere existimaret*. **utrisque ad animum occurrit**: an unparalleled variation of the idiomatic *animo/is occurrere* (*TLL* 9.2.396.69–80; 9.2.397.69–70). **unum esse illud tempus quo maxime** "that this was the one moment when above all," 37.3n. *unam esse*; *maxime* qualifies *quo* in analogy to e.g. *nunc cum maxime* (cf. 32.2n. *ut maxime*). The expansive pleonasm – cf. Thuc. 7.70.7 νῦν, εἴ ποτε καὶ αὖθις, "now, if ever again" – emphasizes that the moment of crisis had arrived (a commonplace soon to be reiterated by C. [86.3n. *in eo die*]). **conueniat** "it behooved."

85.3 Cf. Thuc. 7.70.7 "Amongst the Athenians (τοῖς μὲν Ἀθηναίοις) there were shouts to their men that they must force a passage (βιάζεσθαί τε τὸν ἔκπλουν) … Amongst the Syracusans and their allies (τοῖς δὲ Συρακοσίοις καὶ ξυμμάχοις) there was …" C.'s salient antithesis is further highlighted by parallelism and homoioteleuton. **perfregerint**: cf. 39.3n. *coniunxerint* (as the action is prior to any hoped-for salvation). **de omni salute**

desperant: *BC* 2.41.8 *de sua salute desperantes*; C. favors the expression (6x, incl. 88.5; 3x *CC*; cf. 1.1n. *cognoscere de*). It is a commonplace to state "the fight for survival" – "they would either escape or perish" (Thuc. 7.71.3; cf. Hom. *Il.* 15.502–03 [86.3n. *in eo die*]) – at the height of conflict. *salus* is frequently contrasted with *uictoria*: *illi celerem … uictoriam, hi salutem suam* (*BC* 3.111.6, Tac. *Agr.* 5.2 *tum de salute, mox de uictoria*); or else with *gloria*: *securi pro salute de gloria certabant* (Tac. *Agr.* 26.2, with Woodman). **rem obtinuerint** "they achieved (*OLD* 9) their goal (*OLD* 12)." **finem laborum omnium**: cf. Tac. *Agr.* 34 *imponite quinquaginta annis magnum diem*; 27.2n. *laboribus*. C. will echo the narrator again at 86.3.

85.4 ad superiores munitiones: at the troublesome camp below Mt. Réa's top (83.1 [n.] *superiorum*, 83.2). **laboratur** pointedly resumes §3 *laborum*. **quo … demonstrauimus**: 83.8. Cross-referencing: 17.1n. **exiguum loci ad decliuitatem fastigium magnum habet momentum** "though slight, the downward slope of the position was of great consequence" (cf. 82.2); *ad* = "in (a manner or way)" (*OLD* 36), specifies the downward character of *fastigium*, "slope" (73.5n.). The concessive force of *exiguum* (in relation to *magnum*) may have caused the substitution of α's *iniquum* (which would recall 83.2 *iniquo loco*). *momentum* may pun on the word's literal meaning "movement."

85.5–6 alii … alii: 24.4n. **tela coniciunt**: 72.2n. To the militarily astute reader, the remark follows the previous one naturally: *cauendum … ne ex superioribus locis missa ab hostibus … tela perueniant* (Veg. 3.8.3; cf. 83.2n. *necessario*); but the description moves on from the troubled camp to the Roman fortifications, generally. **testudine**: the "tortoise" (Varro *Ling.* 5.161) was a military formation wherein soldiers interlocked their shields at the sides and on top so as to leave no opening to weaponry (Livy 34.39.6); Cass. Dio 49.30.1–4 discusses tactical uses (one of which C. attributes to the Gauls [2.6.2]). It differs from the "tortoise with ram" (Lendle 1975). **subeunt** "move up to attack." **defatigatis … integri**: 25.1n. **in uicem** "in their turn."

85.6 ab uniuersis: the collective term is hyperbolic, adding to the climactic tenor. It may also be motivated by rhetorical habit (cf. 24.5n. *alii … alii … omnis*). **quae … occultauerant**: the *stimuli, scrobes*, etc., as described in c.73. **nec … nostris nec uires suppetunt**: the distribution of the words produces an isocolon (cf. 69.4n. *fastigio*). C. is fond of the commonplace motif of dwindling resources (20.11, 50.6, 77.2). The phrasing is perhaps echoed in Amm. Marc. 31.13.5 *cum … neque uires illis neque mentes suppeterent ad consilium*. **arma** and *tela* are often synonymous; but, strictly speaking, the former are defensive, the latter offensive (*arma his imperata* *galea, clipeum, ocreae, lorica* …: *haec ut tegumenta corporis essent; tela in hostem hastaque et gladius* [Livy 1.43.2]).

86 C. dispatches L. with relief troops (§3n. *Labienum*), then enters the fray himself (§3 *ipse*), most likely to oppose V. in the plain (with both leaders, Jullian 1909: 528 speculated, no more than a shout away from each other). But the *munitiones* (§4n.) held again, and the besieged Gauls veered to a different location higher up (unknown [Le Bohec 2012: 167]).

This passage – with its short cola, predominant parataxis, and generic features (cf. 5.1n. *ipse*) once again much indebted to the military report (79–88n.) – is clearly divided (§4n. *interiores*) into two nearly equal parts (cf. 7on.); the first of which shows C. moving from observation to more active participation in the most traditional (and ultimately epic [§3nn., 87.3n. *proelio*]) fashion.

86.1 His rebus cognitis: 18.3n. *cognitis* echoes 85.1 *cognoscit* (7.1n. *missus*). **Labienum**: his exact location is unknown, but 85.4n. *ad superiores munitiones* likely. **subsidio laborantibus mittit** varies 85.1. 5.3n. *subsidio*; 13.1n. *laborantibus*.

86.2 affects the style of the order as given *imperatoria breuitate.* **imperat** construes with a paratactic subjunctive (cf. 2.2n. *sanciatur*). **sustinere** "hold out" (*OLD* 4d). **deductis cohortibus eruptione pugnet** "[that] he draw off his cohorts (81.6n. *deductos*) and fight by way of a sortie (76.6n. *eruptione*)." **id ... ne faciat** "He should not do this"; this is a negative command in *oratio obliqua* (following *pugnet*).

86.3 adit may, in this context, suggest the approaching and addressing of separate groups prior to battle, as practiced ever since Agamemnon (Hom. *Il.* 4.231–33 ἐπεπωλεῖτο στίχας, "he walked through the ranks," θαρσύνεσκε παριστάμενος, "he stood next to and encouraged"); for echoes in the historians, incl. Thuc. 7.63, see Albertus 1908: 40–42. **reliquos** lacks precision (like 64.1n. *reliquis*); sc. *milites.* **cohortatur** signals the *cohortatio* (29n.), which was expected of generals in a moment of crisis (Onas. 1.13; cf. Thuc. 7.60.5; it can be traced back to Hom. *Il.* e.g. 15.485–500). In phrasing and content it reprises 27.2. **ne labori succumbant** "that they not surrender to the difficulties (13.1n. *laborantibus*)"; the expression (*succumbere* only here in *CC*) recurs once at Apul. *Met.* 6.17. The commonplace – Thuc. 7.63.1 χρὴ … διαμάχεσθαι ὅσον ἂν δύνησθε, "you must fight till the end with all you've got" – was memorably expressed in modern times in Churchill's "We shall never surrender." **superiorum dimicationum fructum**: another commonplace (27.2n. *pro tantis laboribus*). *dimicatio* occurs only here and *BC* 3.111.2 (10x in *CC*); *fructum*: 27.2n. **in eo die atque hora** "on that very day and hour"; for this demonstrative use of *is*, see *TLL*

7.2.480.3–11. The "now [and here]" – νῦν ἄρκιον ἢ ἀπολέσθαι ἠὲ σαωθῆναι, "now, it is certain, we shall either die or be saved" (Hom. *Il.* 15.502–03), καρτερήσατε, εἴπερ ποτέ, "now, if ever, stand firm" (Thuc. 7.64.2), "this day we fight" (Aragorn's speech) – is a commonplace of the *cohortatio* then as now; it here echoes the narrator's 85.2n. *unum esse.*

86.4 interiores: 82.3n. Its frontal position marks the change of focalization. **desperatis ... locis** "[they] gave up on the level grounds"; their attempts are mentioned at 83.3. **propter ... munitionum**: 80.1n. *munitionis.* **loca praerupta atque ex ascensu temptant** "they tried the precipitous parts, that is to say (*OLD atque* 1) by way of ascending." It is easier to explain why *atque* was omitted (α) than how it would have been added (β). The instrumental use of *ex* is common (*TLL* 5.2.1111.52–1113.43). **huc ... conferunt** is the uninspired third mention of this maneuver almost identically expressed at 82.3 and 84.1.

86.5 The asyndetic tricolon renders crowded action (63.1–4n.). **multitudine telorum**: 82.1n. **propugnantes** is somewhat unusually used instead of the readily available noun (25.4 *propugnatores*; 4.9n. *dubitantes*). *pro-* here signifies "at the front of (sc. the top of the towers)." **deturbant** "they brought tumbling down" (*OLD* 1); cf. 81.2n. *proturbare. deturbare telis* (*uel sim.*) is a military expression (*TLL* 5.1.846.53–64); for its recurrence at Sall. *Hist.* 2.87 and Tac. *Ann.* 4.51.1, cf. *Introd.* 3h. **aggere et cratibus fossas explent**: 79.4n. *fossam ... explent. uallum ac loricam rescindunt*: to tear off the rampart and parapet (72.4n. *loricam*) is another standard measure (Oakley on Livy 9.14.9 *pars fossas explerent, pars uellerent uallum*). But *scindere* is much more common with *uallum* than *rescindere*: it recurs once at Verg. *Aen.* 9.524.

87 At the latest trouble spot, C. first sends relief forces, then intervenes himself. Having fought back V.'s troops (in all likelihood – peculiarly, V. is not mentioned), he turns to helping Labienus, who was unable to secure the camp at Réa (86.1n. *Labienum*). C. gathers troops and dispatches a cavalry unit to arrive there on a circuitous route (§2n. *circumire*). Informed by Labienus of what to do, he joins the fighting.

C. seems at pains to amplify his contributions: By juxtaposing *subsidio adducit. restituto proelio* he effectively suggests that *his* intervention decided this part of the decisive battle (exemplifying how the "présentation des faits" may imply "une manière de les interpréter" [Rambaud: 363; Grillo 2012: 19]). More significantly, perhaps, he rather forcefully inserts himself into the final scene (§3 *ut proelio intersit*, cf. nn. on 88, 88.1 *proelium committunt*), which is clearly dominated by Labienus (Le Bohec 2012: 167; cf. 34.2n. *Labieno*). C. had "proven" his mettle before; but he clearly wishes to be seen possessing *fortitudo in periculis* (Cic. *Leg. Man.* 29 [of Pompey]) in these final scenes as well.

87.1 A demonstration of C.'s military orchestration (13.1n. *summittit*), the tricolon proceeds in a noticeably orderly way at this time of crisis (*primum ... post ... postremo*), ending suitably with *ipse* (5.1n.) in the longest colon. **Mittit** in initial position renders the urgency. **adulescentem:** 9.1n. **postremo ipse ... adducit:** C. here suggests, and below asserts, his participation in battle. **cum uehementius pugnaretur:** a common variation of 50.1n. *cum acerrime ... pugnaretur.*

87.2 restituto proelio: the expression occurs once more in *CC* at 1.53.1; it will become a Livian mannerism (starting at 2.47.1). **quo Labienum miserat:** 86.1. **cohortes ... iubet:** another asyndetic tricolon. **circumire ... a tergo adoriri:** C. envisions a standard maneuver; cf. Veg. 3.18.4 *aduersariorum sinistrum cornum ... circumire debet et a tergo semper urguere,* 62.6n. *post tergum.* **circumire exteriores munitiones:** a military phrase (Galba [Cic.] *Fam.* 10.30.3 *cum equites nostrum cornu circumire uellent,* TLL 3.1136.78–37.30). They were to go around the circumvallation (*CG* 818 discusses routes).

87.3 Livy 9.17.3 identifies three factors in warfare, present here: *plurimum in bello pollere uidentur militum copia et uirtus* (cf. *coactis ... cohortibus*), *ingenia imperatorum* (cf. *circumire ... a tergo ... iubet, Labienus ... existimet*), *fortuna per omnia humana maxime in res bellicas potens* (cf. *fors obtulit*). **Labienus postquam:** 12.1n. *Vercingetorix ubi. postquam* construes with the imperfect when it describes "a continuing situation" (*NLS* §217[5]). **neque ... uim hostium sustinere poterant** reprises 86.2 *sustinere non possit.* The *munitio* fails at long last (curiously, Labienus is exculpated); cf. 80.1n. *munitionis.* The physical metaphor: 10.3n. *impetum.* **coactis una de XL cohortibus** "having gathered 39 cohorts." The high number, some 15,000 troops, has met with misgivings; and all the more since *fors* is credited with their appearance. **fors obtulit:** C. respected chance (*multum ... in re militari potest fortuna,* 6.30.2; sim. 6.35.2, *BC* 3.10.6, 68.1; *BAlex.* 43.4) just as much as Polybius (e.g. 2.4.3–5 [Preiswerk 1945: 222]; Mantovanelli 2000: 221–23 offers discussion, Oakley on Livy 9.17.3 instances elsewhere). It was the general's duty to limit its reach by planning (as *BC* 1.72.2 implies). Cf. 20.6n. *Fortunae.* **Caesarem ... facit certiorem quid faciendum existimet:** Labienus' communication is written in the style of the military dispatch (1.1n. *certior factus,* 7.3n. *anteuertendum*); but it need not be "derived from Labienus' report" (Rambaud: 34; cf. 9on. and *Introd.* 3a). **accelerat** recurs once in *CC* at *BC* 2.39.6. **proelio intersit:** although the responsibilities and locations of a commander and a soldier were mostly mutually exclusive

(85.1n.), and military handbooks expound "on why a general must not fight in battle" (Onas. 33.1), the Homeric ideal of the soldier-general (*Il.* 3.179 βασιλεύς τ' ἀγαθὸς κρατερός τ' αἰχμητής) continued as a commonplace in the "rhetoric of battle" (Gerlinger 2008: 33–59; cf. Cic.'s praise of Pompey [quoted above, 87n.] and C.'s praise of *Cotta ... imperatoris et in pugna militis officia praestabat* [5.33.4]). Conspicuous instances of C. include: 1.25.1, 2.25.2 (with Plut. *Caes.* 20.8), *BC* 3.67.4; cf. 24.2n. *excubaret*, Plut. *Caes.* 56.2 (with Pelling). Suet. *Iul.* 62 credits C. with: *inclinatam aciem solus saepe restituit.* But the scene in *BAfr.* 31.4, where *Caesar ... in praetorio sedens per speculatores et nuntios imperabat quae fieri uolebat*, offers a realistic corrective (Austin-Rankov 1995: 60).

88 C.'s conspicuous appearance coincides with the culmination of battle. When the relief troops he had dispatched on a bypass appear at the Gauls' rear, they cause panic: the Gauls flee, to be pursued later by Roman cavalry. The "inner" Gauls withdraw also.

The narrative is arranged in three parts (cf. 18n.): from C.'s dramatic arrival with a Pompeian and Alexandrian flourish (§1) to the final battle (§§2–4) and its consequences (§§5–7). It uses repetition (cf. *Introd.* 3b) to mimic the engulfing din (§2n. *clamor*), to tighten the narrative (§3 *post tergum ... terga uertunt; fugientibus; caedes ... occiditur*), and to emphasize themes (*fug** occurs 5x, *caedes* and *occidere* 3x); and it brings two leitmotifs to their conclusion (§2n. *clamor*, §5n. *conspicati*; 79–88n.). The most significant part representing the actual battle is written in the terse style of the communiqué once more (Fraenkel 1956; 79–88n.). Its conventions may also be partly responsible for the schematic nature of the representation: there is little that is not commonplace (the remark on the inner Gauls [§5n.] is a particularly tired repetition). Most significantly, the arrival of the cavalry at the enemy's rear is both a recommended strategy (3n. *equitatus*) and all too neat; one may also wonder about the sudden absence of Labienus (87n.).

88.1 aduentu ex colore uestitus cognito: 9.5n. *aduentu*, 18.3n. *aduentu ... cognito*. C. alludes to the topos of the (re)invigorating effect of the general's appearance: *conspectu ducis refectus militum est animus* (Livy 9.27.13; cf. Oakley on Livy 6.8.2, 8.6 *addendum*). The garment is probably the *paludamentum*, which, strikingly purple (or white [Val. Max. 1.6.11]), was worn over the breastplate by commanders for distinction (cf. Varro *Ling.* 7.37 *quae propter quod conspiciuntur qui ea habent ac fiunt palam, paludamenta dicta*; Olson 2017: 77–79 offers *testimonia*). C.'s cloak is mentioned frequently, and his conspicuity became a topos of its own: at Val. Max. 1.8.8, Cassius is haunted by C.'s ghost *purpureo paludamento amictum*, Luc. 1.245 presents *et celsus medio conspectus in agmine Caesar* (with Roche), and Cass. Dio 42.40.5

reports how the Egyptians took aim at him in his purple (cf. Suet. *Iul.* 64, Flor. *Epit.* 2.13.59). C. perhaps emphasizes his dress out of rivalry with Pompey, who claimed inheritance of Alexander's cloak (App. *Mith.* 117). **quo insigni ... consueuerat**: 28.6n. *quae ... pars*, 45.7n. *insignibus*. This has been suspected as a gloss, since – it is argued – every Roman commander habitually wore the *paludamentum*. But this appears questionable in the light of *BAfr.* 57.3 *Scipio sagulo purpureo ante regis aduentum uti solitus*; at the very least, the latter offers support for the clause in question. **quas ... iusserat**: 87.2. **ut ... cernebantur** "as these downward slopes and depressions (sc. of Mont Réa, presumably [Le Bohec 2012: 167]) could be seen from the upper positions" (Edwards, modified). **decliuia et deuexa** is an unparalleled pairing, wherein both nouns are used as neuter substantives for the first time (*TLL* 5.1.196.60, 5.1.858.6). *deuexus* (synonymous with *decliuis* [83.2n.]) occurs only here in *CC*. **proelium committunt**: 62.8n. The battle was raging before C. arrived; the imprecise expression serves to amplify his arrival's significance (nn. on 87, 66.7 *equites*).

88.2–3 The scene aggregates commonplaces; but Sall. *Cat.* 60.2 is noticeably close: *postquam eo uentum est unde a ferentariis proelium committi posset maxumo clamore cum infestis signis concurrunt: pila omittunt, gladiis res geritur ... maxuma ui certatur.* Adcock 1956: 68 found "hardly a word that is not pure prose, but the effect is epic." **utrimque**: sc. on the Gallic and the Roman side. **clamore sublato ... clamor**: the *cyclos* mimetically places *clamor* on both sides (*utrimque*) of the phrase, with *clamor* echoing *clamore*. The din of battle commonly marks the climax: Polyb. 2.29.6 recounts how, when fighting the Gauls, "the resounding surroundings seemed to make noise all of their own (ἐξ αὐτῶν δοκεῖν προΐεσθαι φωνήν)," and App. *Hisp.* 93 mentions "trumpeters sounding from every tower." 12.5n. *clamore sublato*. **excipit rursus** "took it up (*OLD excipio* 16) in turn." **omissis pilis**: "[n]ormally the *pilum*, a heavy throwing spear, was used to fire a volley from a distance (*eminus*) as a prelude to fighting at close quarters (*comminus*) with the *gladius*, a short thrusting sword" (Ramsey on Sall. *Cat.* 60.2; more on the *pila* volley: Goldsworthy 1996: 197–201, and on the *pilum*: Bishop 2017; C. may have improved its design: 1.25.3, with Parker 1958: 44). To dispense with the spears was originally a pragmatic action, more or less motivated by spiritedness; it became a popular motif (*TLL* 10.1.2145.73–2146.6; in *CC*, however, it recurs only at 1.52.4). Its suggestive significance (which β's *emissis* misses) is well captured in Livy 9.13.2 *ne mora in concursu pilis emittendis ... esset* (cf. Oakley on 6.12.8). For *pila* found at Mont Réa, see Bishop-Coulston 2006: 51–52. **gladiis rem gerunt**: a stock phrase, which, however, recurs only at 5.44.1 in *CC*.

88.3–4 A series of briefest asyndetic phrases tersely reports the victory (Dorey 1966: 82–83 offers parallels). It may evoke a triumphal inscription (cf. *Introd.* 3c, 90n.). **equitatus**: 87.2n. *circumire.* **cohortes aliae** "cohorts as well (*OLD alius* 5)." **fugientibus**: 7.1n. *missus.* **fit magna caedes**: 70.5n. The verb in first position marks the climactic consequence.

88.4 To single out enemy leaders killed or captured is a standard feature of historical narratives (Hdt. 7.224.2, Livy 45.39.7 *Perseus rex captus, Philippus et Alexander, filii regis, tanta nomina*; cf. Tac. *Ann.* 4.32.1 on *ingentia … bella … fusos captosque reges* in republican historiography). Royal captives would be paraded in the triumph (Plut. *Pomp.* 45.4); their names might be included in triumphal inscriptions (Beard 2007: 120–21). **Sedullus**: many edd. have accepted de Saulcy's emendation based on Celtic coins bearing a name of that spelling; but it remains questionable (*GPN* 468). **dux et princeps** "war commander (62.5 *dux hostium*) and chief magistrate (1.4n. *principes*)"; cf. 1.13.2 *cuius legationis Diuico princeps fuit, qui bello Cassiano dux Heluetiorum fuerat.* **occiditur**: a standard term for killing in the administrative register, which decreases in frequency from *I* to *VII* (Opelt 1980: 110–11; cf. *Introd.* 3b). **signa militaria**: 2.2n. **LXXIIII**: Romans kept records of such numeric detail (*BHisp.* 9.3 *scuta sunt relata LXXX*; on "Roman military record-keeping," see Oakley on Livy 7.37.16, 9.45.17); military standards are especially frequently mentioned. **pauci ex tanto numero … recipiunt** resembles Thuc. 7.87.6 ὀλίγοι ἀπὸ πολλῶν ἐπ' οἴκου ἀπενόστησαν, "few out of many returned home," which concludes the Sicilian expedition (79–88n.). It is also a theme, however (Aesch. *Pers.* 800 παῦροί γε πολλῶν; *BHisp.* 4.2 *ex infinita hominum multitudine pauci in oppidum*). **se … in castra recipiunt**: 20.6n.

88.5 The battle ends as it began: with an evocative teichoscopy (79.3n. *erat … despectus*). **caedem et fugam**: this pairing recurs at *BC* 2.34.6 (and *BAlex.* 18.3); it will become a Livian mannerism. **desperata salute**: 4x in C. (4x in *CC*), rare elsewhere (but 2x in Curt.); cf. 85.3n. *de salute … desperant.*

88.6 fit … fuga: in an otherwise logical order of words, the fronted *fit* highlights the rapid development that followed the news (cf. Cic. *Verr.* 5.93 *fit ad domum eius cum clamore concursus*). **hac re audita**: 61.4n. **ex castris**: the camps of the relief troops (79.1). **quod nisi** "and if … not"; *quod* connects this sentence to its predecessor (K-S II 321.3). The counterfactual "*ni(si)* de rupture" is a common device in Roman historians (C-L 597–609).

88.7 de media nocte: 45.1n. The cavalry rested till midnight, then pursued. **nouissimum agmen**: 68.2n. **consequitur** "caught up with." **capitur atque interficitur** varies 50.3n. *circumuenti … interfecti*; cf. 11.9n. *caperentur.*

reliqui ex fuga in ciuitates discedunt "the others fled (28.6n. *ex fuga*), each making their separate ways to their peoples."

89–90 THE CODA

Instead of a lapidary remark on the conclusion of the campaign, C. dramatizes the ending with yet another speech and the staging of V.'s surrender (89n.): this makes for a conclusive ending not just of the campaign but the conquest (*Introd.* 3c; cf. Batstone-Damon 2006: 40–41). However, just as C.'s staying in Gaul for the winter and the specifics of his troop allocations suggest that he knew the campaign – let alone the conquest – to be far from over (nn. on 90.4–7, 90.7 *ipse Bibracte*; Hirt. 8.1–6 reports war activity continuing in December [*Introd.* 2c, "Timeline"]), so are the arrangements that c. 90 details in the style of the military report a well-worn closural feature (90.3n. *legiones*) and *eo ipso* suggestive of the continuation of the war. These historical facts interfere disruptively with the narrative design, leaving "the door ajar" (Grewing *et al.* 2013); meanwhile, C.'s two dominant code-models – the official register and the historiographical genre (*Introd.* 3a) – can be seen at work.

89 C. brings his account to an austere end (nn. on §§3–4, *Vercingetorix deditur*), which later sources embellish (Cass. Dio 40.41, Plut. *Caes.* 27, Flor. 1.45.26; Oros. 6.11.10–11 differs insignificantly; Guillaumin 1985; cf. *BC* 2.42.4 *proelians interficitur* on Curio's death in contrast to Luc. 4.793–810, App. *B Civ.* 2.46.1). But for all its austerity, it effectively dramatizes the "concession of defeat" variously represented in Roman literature: *qui uicit non est uictor nisi uictus fatetur* (Enn. *Ann.* 513 [with Skutsch]); *itaque se uictos confiteri; orare … ne ad ultimum supplicium progredi necesse habeat* (sc. C. [*BC* 1.84.5]); *dedi imperatorem, arma poni iubet, et fatentes uictos se esse imperio parere* (Livy 4.10.3 [with Oakley on 6.4.8]). Reinach suggested that a dramatic adaptation was performed at the *Ludi Caesaris Victoriae* (1902: 428 [cited from Guillaumin 1985: 748n.16]).

C. has V. exit – just as he entered (4.1) – with an address, i.e. *concessio* (*Rhet.* 1.24; Cipriani 2002: 61–62): He restates that he had waged war for *communis libertas* (another ring-compositional element), then cloaks the admission of defeat in "the need to concede to Fortuna" (§1n. *Fortunae*); tellingly, he foregoes the plea for mercy (the common second part of the *concessio*, i.e. *deprecatio*; cf. *BC* 1.84.5 [above]), and proudly presumes his surrender: if, by C.'s pen, V. started out as a rabble-rousing chieftain (1–5n.), he meets his end a defiant *fortis uir* (as Livy sensed [Flor. 1.45.26]). His determination to sacrifice himself for his people has religious tones (§2nn.), to which Cassius Dio and Plutarch are attuned.

But no detail in the later accounts necessitates the assumption of a source other than C. (cf. Sordi 1971: 170–71), except perhaps Dio's mention of V.'s erstwhile friendship to C. (ἐν φιλίᾳ ποτὲ τῷ Καίσαρι, 40.41.1; Gelzer 1955: 982, 1006).

89.1 Postero die … concilio conuocato repeats 29.1n. **id … bellum** "that war." **suarum necessitatum** "personal circumstances" (*OLD necessitas* 4); the possessive stands in antithesis to **communis libertatis**, which returns to the beginning, reasserting the book's theme (4.4n.). **Fortunae cedendum**: the idiomatic expression renders a sententious (26.4n. *timor … recepit*) commonplace (Eur. *Rhes.* 584 οὐ βιαστέον τύχην, [Cic.] *Fam.* 11.1.3 *dandus est locus fortunae*, Heliod. 5.6.2 εἴξωμεν τῇ τύχῃ; *TLL* 6.1.1185.19–26). To blame *fortuna* is a recommended exculpatory measure (*Rhet. Her.* 1.24); it also denies that the Romans owed their victory to *uirtus*. Yet in invoking *dea Fortuna* (20.6n.), V. links C. with the good fortune that the perfect general required, Pompey had possessed abundantly (Cic. *Leg. Man.* 28, 47, esp. … *diuinitus adiuncta fortuna. de huius* [sc. *Pompei*] *autem hominis felicitate* …), and C. repeatedly claims for himself (Grillo on Cic. *Prou. cons.* 30 *fortuna*).

89.2 offerre is commonly used of sacrifice (*TLL* 9.2.503.31–504.45), and some of C.'s ancient adaptors sensed the religious significance in V.'s conduct (Guillaumin 1985). Alesia's religious standing (68n.) offers a resonant background. **seu morte sua Romanis satisfacere seu uiuum tradere**: V.'s self-sacrifice would have resonated with the Gauls' reported belief *pro uita hominis nisi hominis uita reddatur, non posse deorum immortalium numen placari* (6.16.2); to a Roman, it would have suggested a *deuotio*: a magistrate's expiatory sacrifice of (normally) himself to placate or reconcile the gods (Versnel 1981).

89.3–4 What follows are terse notes in standard military diction (90n.) on the typical details of surrender. **mittuntur**: its frontal position suggests they were sent right away. **de**: 9.1n. **iubet**: the subject is to be inferred from *ad Caesarem*. "The lack of specification of a grammatical subject when the context is considered to make it plain … is particularly common in legal and religious prescriptions" (Courtney 1999: 2) and frequent in C. (20.11n. *posse*, 73.4n. *appellabant*, 78.1n. *descendant*). **arma tradi, principes produci**: a "brusque" asyndeton *bimembre* (Nägelsbach 1905: 704–05) stipulates in formulaic language (11.2n. *arma … dari*) the necessary surrender of arms (40.6n. *proiectis armis*; Livy 4.10.3 [above, 89n.]). The archaeological record: Poux 2008: 416–18.

89.4 in munitione "amidst the fortifications," as the symbol of Roman superiority (80.1n. *munitionis*). **consedit**: the verb is used of those sitting in judgment (*TLL* 4.433.81–434.20). **eo duces ... proiciuntur**: C. varies the expressions and inverts their order (cf. 55.8n. *flumine*). **Vercingetorix deditur**: in contrast to *duces producuntur*; it is thus unclear whether V. surrendered himself (as §2 suggests). The momentous event, emotively rendered by Plutarch and modern painters (including Lionel Royer; cf. Harmand 1985), is here barely mentioned, and in the least significant middle position (29.2n. *uicisse*) to boot – as if V. were now slotted back into insignificance. Cassius Dio reports that V. was kept prisoner for six years, then paraded in C.'s triumphal procession, and finally executed (40.41.3).

89.5 C. resumes the practice of *diuidere et imperare*. **reseruatis ... si ... posset** "He withheld (*OLD* 2) ... to see whether (20.10n. *si*) he could ...." **ciuitates**: their clients. **captiuis**: if Isidore's etymology *captiuus dicitur quasi capite deminutus* (*Etym.* 10.54) circulated at C.'s time, C.'s "of the 'headless' one 'head' each" would be a macabre pun. **toti exercitui capita singula** "one person (*OLD caput* 7) each to the whole army"; the arrangement is chiastic. **praedae nomine** "as booty" (*OLD nomen* 24); again Hirt. 8.4.1, Suet. *Iul.* 38.1, Isid. *Etym.* 15.13.5. Cf. 11.9n. *praedam.*

90 The war suspended rather than concluded (Hirt. 8.1.1 *omni Gallia deuicta ... complures ... ciuitates renouare belli consilia nuntiabantur*, cf. 89–90n.), C. makes winter arrangements. He himself stays in Bibracte and composes his year-end report for the senate (and, probably, *VII* [*Introd.* 3a]).

This chapter reads like a military dispatch. Fraenkel 1956 identified in §§2–9 (and 83.1, 86.5, 88.3–4) "the rigorous uniformity (*harte Gleichförmigkeit*) of the sentence structure, ... the monotony of terse and asyndetic paratactic main clauses, and [the fact that] the verb, with one exception, comes at the end and the object at the beginning of the sentence" as typical features (§8n. *litteris*; cf. N-R on Hor. *Carm.* 3.8.18; *Introd.* 3a). Thematically, there are parallels, too (nn. on 2–4, *legiones ... mittit*, *captiuorum*, and 4–8; Rambaud 19–43). Some have suggested that C. "copied" his report; but Fraenkel wisely suggested that C. *chose* the form with its "measured animation (*verhaltenes Pathos*)" *to emotive purpose*. It also functions as the counterpoint to the preceding chapter (cf. 3n.) and the symphonic arrangement of the book, which here returns to its generic beginnings. Yet, this is neither how the *BG* ends (Hirtius will pick up the baton) nor how the campaign comes to a close (C. will stay on for two years). Cf. Batstone-Damon 2006: 41–42 on *BC* as an "expansion" of *BG*.

90.1 His rebus confectis ... proficiscitur: a signature Caesarian sentence (cf. 1.1; nn. on 6.1, 13.3). **recipit** "he regained possession of" (*OLD* 13); cf. *BAlex.* 44 *ciuitates quae defecerant ... recipiebat.*

90.2–4 describe standard procedure in standardized language: cf. Cic. *Fam.*
15.4.10 *Pindenisso capto obsides accepi; exercitum in hiberna dimisi. Quintum fratrem negotio praeposui ut … exercitus collocaretur.* The first two sentences form
a chiasmus: *imperat … obsidum – captiuorum … reddit* (most editors accept
Kraffert's transposition). **quae imperaret se facturos pollicentur**: a military
formula used in the context of *deditio* (Timpe 1972: 282–87, Odelman
1985: 178–79); cf. 30.4n. *imperarentur*; 2.1n. *pollicentur*. **imperat magnum
numerum obsidum**: similarly at 4.22.2. *imperat* resumes *imperaret* and tightens the narrative (cf. Quadrig. *FRHist* F57 *erat consul. ei consuli*; Wills 272;
Courtney 1999: 7). Cf. 38.9n. *magnum numerum*, 2.2n. *obsidibus*.

90.3 legiones … mittit: necessary information in a report (Cic. *Att.* 5.20.5
+ *Fam.* 15.4.10 [above, §§2–4n.]; appropriated in Pollio [Cic.] *Fam.*
10.33.3 *in Lusitania legiones in hibernis collocaram*) and a commonplace
in Roman historiography (esp. frequent in Livy), the move into winter
quarters serves as closural device in all of *BG* except *V* (1.54.2, 2.35.3,
3.29.3, 4.38.4, 6.44.3; Batstone-Damon 2006: 37–39). Winter quarters
burdened the local communities (Cic. *Att.* 5.21.7; cf. *ILS* 38 [19 Crawford
II, II.6–17]). None of C.'s camps have been located (Reddé 2018: 287–
300 reviews the *status quaestionis*).

90.4–7 C.'s detailing his allocations (Hirt. 8.46.3–4 is just as detailed) may
originate in the pragmatic necessities of his reporting; but it also bespeaks
the size of his army (34.2n. *legiones*) and the scale of his operations, not
to mention *qua prudentia hiberna disposita essent*, which was "an essential
quality of the ideal general" (Vell. Pat. 2.111.4 with Woodman). Typically
(47.1n. *decimae*), C. does not individuate the legions (as Hirt. does [e.g.
8.24.3]); nor does he provide a rationale for his distribution (again, Hirt.
8.46.4 *ne qua pars Galliae uacua ab exercitu esset*). But, crescent-shaped
(from the north-eastern Remi to the south-western Ruteni), it served "to
safeguard the loyal, to overawe the disaffected, to cover the Province, and
to be ready for mutual support" (*CG* 283). C. apparently knew where the
embers would flare up again (nn. on *ne … accipiant, in Bituriges*).

90.4 Labienum: Labienus has pride of place amongst the *legati*; he had
wintered amongst the Sequani before (1.54.4). It is unclear why he
received a subordinate. One of his legions would soon be called upon
(Hirt. 8.6.3). **Marcum Sempronium Rutilum**: his first (and only) mention
in *CC*. He is probably identical with the addressee of Cic. *Fam.* 13.8 (*RE*
"Rutilius" 5, "Sempronius" 82).

90.5 Gaium Fabium: he would have to leave his winter quarters almost
as soon as he had settled in (Hirt. 8.6.3). **Lucium Minucium Basilum**:
first mentioned the year before when he almost caught Ambiorix

(6.29.4–30.3), he likely continued serving C. during the civil war but then turned assassin (Cic. *Fam.* 6.15; *RE* "Minucius" 38). **ne ... accipiant**: The Remi had remained loyal throughout (63.7n.); it was all the more incumbent upon C. to protect them (10.1–2n.). The motif of the threat in the neighborhood is common; it allegedly started the conquest of Gaul (1.2.4, 1.6). C. was right to worry about the Bellouaci (59.2n.). **quam ... calamitatem**: cf. 9.4n. *quid ... consilii.*

90.6 Bituriges would continue their resistance right away (Hirt. 8.2.2).

90.7 Quintum Tullium Ciceronem: Cicero's younger brother (*RE* "Tullius" 31) joined C.'s staff as *legatus* in 54 (first mention at 5.24.2), having honed his military and administrative skills as governor of Asia from 61–58 and *legatus* of Pompey in Sardinia (57/6). He stayed on with C. until early in 51, distinguishing himself against the Nervii (5.40–52), less so at Atuatuca (6.36–42), then helped his brother in Cilicia, before joining Pompey in the civil war. He was quickly pardoned by C. but died along with his son in the proscriptions of 43. **Publium Sulpicium**: sc. *Rufum*. He had joined C.'s staff as *legatus* in 55 (4.22.6); he played an important role during the civil war, following which he served as *censor* in 42 (*RE* "Sulpicius" 93). **Cauilloni**: 42.5n. Its access to rivers (the Rhône via the Saône) and several roads – including those leading to Bibracte, Lugdunum (Lyon), and Agedincum (10.4n.) – made it the perfect trading center (Billoin *et al.* 2009). **Matiscone**: to the south of *Cauillonum*, this oppidum also offered access to the same rivers and several roads (cf. Rebourg 1994). **ad Ararim**: the Saône, described as *flumen ... quod per fines Haeduorum et Sequanorum in Rhodanum influit* (1.12.1), was the site of C.'s (?) first victory in Gaul against the Helvetian Tigurini (Plut. *Caes.* 18.2 with Pelling). **rei frumentariae causa**: C. acknowledges his year-long concern over supplies for the last time (10.1n. *frumentaria; Introd.* 3c); the only other book to end with a reference to supplies is 6.44.3 *frumentoque exercitui prouiso.* **ipse Bibracte**: as was standard, C. mentions himself last (5.2n. *ipse*). He usually spent winters in Italy (1.1n. *Italiam*), except in 54 when a renewed outbreak necessitated his staying in Gaul (5.53.3–5, 6.1.1); he was worried, too, in 52 and rightly so: by the end of December he was out campaigning again (Hirt. 8.2.1). His choice of the Aeduan capital (55.4n.) was both strategic – centrally located and well connected, it allowed for fast movements to anywhere in Gaul (cf. 63.5; Thévenot 1969: 37–42) – and political (mixing threat and honor; cf. 5.2n. *Haeduos*).

90.8 his rebus ex litteris cognitis: C. mentions *supplicationes* at 2.35.4 *ob easque res ex litteris Caesaris dierum XV supplicatio decreta est* and 4.38.5 *his rebus gestis ex litteris Caesaris dierum XX supplicatio ... decreta est.* The formula thus mentions "events," source of information, and length of the honor. This makes α *his* (= *his rebus*) *litteris* (= *ex litteris*) more likely than β *huius anni rebus*, esp. as: *litteris* is indispensable, a scribe's eye would have leapt easily from *his* to *litteris*, and *huius anni (rebus)* reads like a gloss on *his (rebus)*. Since *his* by itself is harsh (but not impossible), and *rebus* is partly attested, it would seem that both readings preserve parts of the archetype, and *his rebus litteris cognitis* (printed in the *ed. princeps* [Meusel, *Coniecturae Caesarianae*]) is certainly possible; but not only does C. not use *litteris cognoscere* (*TLL* 3.1512.41–51), it also appears that *cognoscere ex litteris* was the standard formula in administrative contexts (e.g. Lentulus [Cic.] *Fam.* 12.14.3 *ex litteris quas publice misi cognosces*, Sall. *Iug.* 9.3 *ex litteris imperatoris … cognouit*, Livy 40.2.5 *ex litteris … propraetoris cognitum*). **litteris**: Roman leaders abroad regularly reported back to the senate (e.g. Cic. *Fam.* 15.1+2; Rambaud 19–43, Osgood 2009). They were standardized in form (Fraenkel 1956, Horsfall 1988; cf. *Introd.* 3b). The final report, at the end of the year, mattered much in discussions of whether an honor such as the *supplicatio* was merited (Cic. *Att.* 7.2.6). C.'s missives, innovative in form, were still extant in Suetonius' time (*Iul.* 56.6 [with Morello 2018: 223–24]): *epistulae … ad senatum extant, quas primum uidetur ad paginas et formam memorialis libelli conuertisse*. They will have formed the basis of the *commentarii* (Reinach 1915; *Introd.* 3a). **supplicatio redditur** is unparalleled. *reddere* = "to render (ritual offerings)" (*OLD* 9b); but the verb hints at the notion of reciprocation. A *supplicatio* (possibly related to *placare*, "to give satisfaction") was a festival in honor of select or all gods to repent in crisis (*obsecratio*) or express gratitude in success (*gratulatio*; Halkin 1953, Hickson-Hahn 2004). Originally one-day long, it lasted twelve days for Pompey, and fifteen and then twenty days for C. (2.35.4, 4.38.5).

WORKS CITED

Reviewers cited in the introduction are listed with the reviewed author, the exceptions being Badian 1990, Conte 1993, Ogilvie 1977, and Rambaud 1962.

Adams, J. N. (1971). "A type of hyperbaton in Latin prose," *PCPhS* 17: 1–16

  (1972). "Latin words for 'woman' and 'wife'," *Glotta* 50: 234–55

  (1973a). "The vocabulary of the speeches in Tacitus' historical works," *BICS* 20: 124–44

  (1973b). "The substantival present participle in Latin," *Glotta* 51: 116–36

  (1976). "A typological approach to Latin word order," *IF* 81: 70–99

  (1978). "Conventions of naming in Cicero," *CQ* 28: 145–66

  (1992). "Iteration of compound verb by its simplex in Latin prose," *Eikasmos* 3: 295–98

  (1994a). *Wackernagel's Law and the placement of the copula "esse" in classical Latin*, Cambridge

  (1994b). "Wackernagel's Law and the position of unstressed personal pronouns in classical Latin," *TPhS* 92: 103–78

  (2003). *Bilingualism and the Latin language*, Cambridge

  (2005). "The *Bellum Africum*," in: T. Reinhardt, M. Lapidge and J. N. Adams (eds.), *Aspects of the language of Latin prose*, Oxford: 73–96

  (2016). *An anthology of informal Latin, 200 BC–AD 900*, Cambridge

Adcock, F. E. (1932). "Caesar's dictatorship," in S. A. Cook, *et al.* (eds.), *The Cambridge ancient history: Vol. 9. The Roman republic 133–44 B. C.* Cambridge: 691–740

  (1956). *Caesar as man of letters*, Cambridge

Adler, E. (2011). *Valorizing the barbarians: enemy speeches in Roman historiography*, Austin

Agbayani, B. and C. Golston (2016). "Phonological constituents and their movement in Latin," *Phonology* 33: 1–42

Ahlberg, A. W. (1911). "De traiectionis figura ab antiquissimis prosae scriptoribus Latinis adhibita," *Eranos* 11: 88–106

Allen, J. (2006). *Hostages and hostage–taking in the Roman empire*, New York

Albertus, J. (1908). *Die παρακλητικοί in der griechischen und römischen Litteratur*, Strasbourg

Albrecht, Fr. (1911). *Die Rückverweisungen bei Caesar und seinen Fortsetzern*, Berndorf

Albrecht, M. von (1989). *Masters of Roman prose from Cato to Apuleius*, Leeds (1997). *A history of Roman literature. From Livius Andronicus to Boethius*, Leiden

Anders, A. (2011). *Roman light infantry and the art of combat: the nature and experience of skirmishing and non-pitched battle in Roman warfare 264 BC – AD 235*, Cardiff (Diss.)

Andrewes, M. (1937). "Caesar's use of tense sequence in ind. speech," *CR* 51: 114–16

Ankersmit, F. R. (1994). *History and tropology: the rise and fall of metaphor*, Berkeley

Arbabe, J. (2013). Du peuple à la cité: vie politique et institutions en Gaule chevelue depuis l'indépendance jusqu'à la fin des Julio–Claudiens, Paris (Diss.)

Arnold, B. (1995). "The material culture of social structure," in Arnold–Gibson: 43–52

Arnold, B. and D. B. Gibson (eds.) (1995), *Celtic chiefdom, Celtic state*, Cambridge

Ash, R. (2002). "Between Scylla and Charybdis? Historiographical commentaries on Latin historians," in Gibson–Kraus: 269–94

Audano, S. (2017). *Tacito. Agricola*, Santarcangelo di Romagna

Audouze, F. and O. Büchsenschütz (eds.) (1992). *Towns, villages and countryside of Celtic Europe: from the beginning of the second millennium to the end of the first century BC*, London

Austin, N. J. E. and N. B. Rankov (1995). Exploratio. *Military and political intelligence in the Roman world from the Second Punic War to the Battle of Adrianople*, London.

Badian, E. (1958). *Foreign clientelae (264–70 B.C.)*, Oxford
(1966). "Notes on *Provincia Gallia* in the late republic," in R. Chevallier (ed.), *Mélanges d'archéologie et d'histoire offerts à André Piganiol*, vol. 2, Paris: 901–18
(1968). *Roman imperialism in the Late Republic*, Ithaca
(1974). "The attempt to try Caesar," in J. A. S. Evans (ed.), *Polis and imperium: studies in honour of Edward Togo Salmon*, Toronto: 145–166
(1990). "Meier, Caesar," *Gnomon* 62: 22–39
(2009). "From the Iulii to Caesar," in Griffin: 11–22

Balsdon, J. P. V. D. (1939). "Consular provinces under the late republic," *JRS* 29: 57–73
(1960). "*Auctoritas, dignitas, otium*," *CQ* 54: 43–50
(1979). *Romans and aliens*, Chapel Hill

Barlow, J. (1998). "Noble Gauls and their other in Caesar's propaganda," in Welch–Powell: 139–70

Barrall, Ph. and J.-P. Guillaumet, P. Nouvel (2002). "Les territoires de la fin de l'âge du fer entre Loire et Saône: Les Eduens et leurs voisins," in: D. Garcia, F. Verdin (eds.), *Territoires Celtiques. Espaces ethniques et territoires des agglomérations protohistoriques d'Europe occidentale. Actes du XXIVe colloque international de l'AFEAF Martigues*, Paris: 271–96

Barrett, J. C. (1989). "Afterword: render unto Caesar," in J. C. Barrett, A. P. Fitzpatrick, L. Macinnes (eds.), *Barbarians and Romans in north-west Europe: from the later republic to late antiquity*, Oxford: 235–41

(1997). "Romanization: a critical comment," in D. J. Mattingly (ed.), *Dialogues in Roman imperialism: power, discourse, and discrepant experience in the Roman Empire*, Portsmouth, RI: 51–64

Barthes, R. (1968). "*L'effet de réel*," *communications* 11: 84–89

Bartsch, S. (2006). *The mirror of the self: sexuality, self-knowledge, and the gaze in the early Roman empire*, Chicago

Barwick, K. (1938). *Caesars* Commentarii *und das* Corpus Caesarianum, Leipzig

(1951). *Caesars* Bellum civile, *Tendenz, Abfassungszeit und Stil*, Berlin

Batstone, W. W. (1990). "*Etsi*: a tendentious hypotaxis in Caesar's plain style," *AJP* 111: 348–60

(2018). "Caesar constructing Caesar," in Grillo–Krebs: 43–57

Batstone, W. W. and C. Damon (2006). *Caesar's civil war*, Oxford

Bayard, D. (2015). "Amiens/Samarobriva, cité des Ambiens: aux origines de la ville romaine," *Gallia* 72: 145–60

Beard, W. M. (2007). *The Roman triumph*, Cambridge, MA

Beikircher, H. (1996). "*Princeps, terticeps* usw. Zur Argeerfrage," *MH* 53: 262–64

Bell, B. M. (1995). "The contribution of Julius Caesar to the vocabulary of ethnography," *Latomus* 54: 753–67

Bellemore, J. (2016). "Caesar's Gallic women under siege," *Latomus* 75: 888–909

Bénard, J. (1996). "Alésia: du mythe à l'archéologie," in Reddé, M. (ed.), *L'Armée romaine en Gaule*, Paris: 40–65

Berti, E. (2000). *M. Annaei Lucani Bellum civile, liber X. With introd. and comm.* Florence

Bertrand, A. C. (1997). "Stumbling through Gaul: maps, intelligence, and Caesar's *Bellum Gallicum*," *AHB* 11: 107–22

Billoin, D. *et al.* (2009). "L'agglomération de Chalon-sur-Saône de La Tène finale au début de la période gallo–romaine: un port comptoir aux origines de Cabillonum," *Rev. Arch. du Centre* Suppl. 35: 263–78

Bishop, M. C. (2017). *The* pilum: *the Roman heavy javelin*, Oxford

Bishop, M. C. and J. C. N. Coulston (2006). *Roman military equipment: from the Punic wars to the fall of Rome*, Oxford (2nd ed.)

Bömer, F. (1953). "Der *commentarius*: zur Vorgeschichte und literarischen Form der Schriften Caesars," *Hermes* 81: 210–50

Bömer, F. (1966). "Caesar und sein Glück," *Gymnasium* 73: 63–85

Braund, D. C. (1980). "The Aedui, Troy, and the Apocolocyntosis," *CQ* 30: 420–25

(1984). Rome and the friendly king: the character of the client kingship. London and Canberra: Croom Helm, and New York: St Martin's Press, 1984

Bräunlich, A. F. (1918). "The confusion of the indirect question and the relative clause in Latin," *CP* 13: 60–74

Brennan, T. C. (2000). *The praetorship in the Roman Republic*, Oxford

Brizzi, G. (2010). "Cesare soldato: strategia e imagine," in Urso: 85–103

Brown, R. D. (1999). "Two Caesarian battle-descriptions: a study in contrast," *CJ* 94: 329–57

(2004). "*Virtus consili expers*: an interpretation of the centurions' contest in Caesar, *De bello Gallico* 5.44," *Hermes* 132: 292–308

(2013). "Caesar's description of bridging the Rhine (*BG* 4.16–19): a literary analysis," *CP* 108: 41–53

(2019). "The expulsion of the Mandubii and Caesar's subversion of the speech of Critognatus (*De Bello Gallico* 7.77–8)," *CW* 112: 283–307

Brown, V. (1976). "Caesar, Gaius Julius," in F. E. Cranz, P. O. Kristeller (eds.), *Catalogus translationum et commentariorum*, vol. 3, Washington: 87–139

Brouquier-Reddé, V. (2001). "Le camp A," in: Reddé–von Schnurbein: 249–85

Bruant, J. (2017). "From excavation to restitution of the networks of Roman and pre-Roman roads: the footprints of the 2222 m and 2535 m leagues in the Carnute, Senon and Parisii territories (Gallia Lugdunensis/France)," *Open Archaeology* 3: 339–60

Brunt, P. A. (1971). *Italian manpower 225 B.C. – A.D. 14*, Oxford

(1978). "*Laus imperii*," in: P. D. A. Garnsey, C. R. Whittaker (eds.), *Imperialism in the ancient world*, Cambridge: 159–91

Brutscher, C. (1958). "Cäsar und sein Glück," *MH* 15: 75–85

Büchsenschütz, O. and I. Ralston (2014). "Nouvelles remarques sur les *Muri Gallici*," in J. Bullinger, J. Crotti, C. Huguenin (eds.), *De l'âge du Fer à l'usage du verre. Mélanges offerts à Gilbert Kaenel*, Lausanne: 101–08

Cadiou, F. (2013). "*Alia ratio*. L'armée romaine, la guérilla et l'historiographie moderne," *REA* 115: 119–45

Cagniart, P. (1992). "Studies on Caesar's use of cavalry during the Gallic War," *AW* 23: 71–85

Cairns, D. L. (1996). "Hybris, dishonour, and thinking big," *JHS* 116: 1–32

Cairns, F. and E. Fantham (eds.) (2003). *Caesar against liberty? Perspectives on his autocracy*, Cambridge

Campbell, B. (1987). "Teach yourself to be a general," *JRS* 77: 13–29
  (2012). *Rivers and the power of Ancient Rome*, Chapel Hill
Campbell, D. B. (2002). *Aspects of Roman siegecraft*, Glasgow (Diss.)
  (2019). "Siegecraft in Caesar," in Armstrong, J. and M. Trundle (eds.),
  Brill's companion to sieges in the ancient Mediterranean, Leiden: 241–64
Campi, A. (1996). "Cesare e i mercenari Germanici," *RIL* 130: 3–17
Cancik, H. (1998). "Rationalität und Militär – Caesars Kriege gegen
  Mensch und Natur," in: R. Faber *et al.* (eds.), *Hubert Cancik. Antik,
  Modern: Beiträge zur römischen und deutschen Kulturgeschichte*, Stuttgart:
  103–23
Canfora, L. (1999). *Giulio Cesare. Il dittatore democratico*, Rome [Review by
  R. Seager in *BMCR* 2007.07.24]
Carcopino, J. (1958). *Alésia et les ruses de César*, Paris
Champion, C. B. (2016). "Introduction," in V. Liotsakis, S. T. Farrington
  (eds.), *The art of history, literary perspectives on Greek and Roman histori-
  ography*, Berlin: 1–11
Champion, T. C. (1985). "Written sources and the study of the European
  Iron Age," in id. and J. V. S. Megaw (eds.), *Settlement and society. Aspects
  of West European prehistory in the first millennium BC*, Leicester: 9–22
Chassignet, M. (2018). "Caesar and Roman historiography prior to the
  Commentarii," in Grillo–Krebs: 249–62
Chausserie-Laprée, J. P. (1969). *L'expression narrative chez les historiens
  Latins*, Paris
Chevallier, R. (1997). *Les voies romaines*, Paris
Choitz, T. (2011). "Caesars Darstellung der Schlacht von Gergovia,"
  Gymnasium 118: 135–55
Chrissanthos, S. G. (2001). "Caesar and the mutiny of 47 BC," *JRS* 91:
  63–75
  (2013). "Keeping military discipline," in B. Campbell, L. A. Tritle (eds.),
  The Oxford handbook of warfare in the classical world, Oxford: 312–29
Christ, K. (1994). *Caesar: Annäherungen an einen Diktator*, Munich [Review
  by K. Bringmann in *Klio* 97 (1997): 253–55]
Cipriani, G. (1986). *Cesare e la retorica dell' assedio*, Amsterdam
  (2000). "La fine di Vercingetorige e la fine dei Commentarii cesariani:
  retorica delle parole e retorica delle immagini," in Urso: 55–89
Clark, J. H. (2014). *Triumph in defeat: military loss and the Roman republic*,
  Oxford
Coffyn, A. (1986). "Recherches sur les Aquitains," *REA* 88: 41–61
Colbert de Beaulieu, J.-B. (1962). "Les Monnaies gauloises au nom des
  chefs mentionnés dans les Commentaires de César," in Renard,
  M. (ed.), *Hommages à Albert Grenier*, Brussels-Berchem: 419–46

Colbert de Beaulieu, J.-B. and G. Lefèvre (1963). "Les monnaies de Vercingétorix," *Gallia* 21: 11–75

Coleman, K. M. (2012). "Bureaucratic language in the correspondence between Pliny and Trajan," *TAPA* 142: 189–238

Collins, J. H. (1952). *Propaganda, ethics, and psychological assumptions in Caesar's writings*, Frankfurt a.M. (Diss.)

(1972). "Caesar as political propagandist," *ANRW* 1.1: 922–66

Collis, J. (1984). Oppida: *earliest towns north of the Alps*, Sheffield

Combès, R. (1966). Imperator: *recherches sur l'emploi et la signification du titre d'*imperator *dans la Rome républicaine*, Paris

Constans, L. A. (1926). *César, guerre des Gaules*, vols. I–II, Paris

(1928). "Quelques corrections," *REL* 6: 132–33

Conte, G. B. (1993). Review of S. J. Harrison, *Vergil: Aeneid 10*, in *JRS* 83: 208–12

(2007). *The poetry of pathos: studies in Virgilian epic*, Oxford

Cooley, A. E. (2009). Res gestae Divi Augusti: *text, translation, and commentary*, Cambridge

Corbeill, A. (2018). "Wit and irony," in Grillo–Krebs: 144–56

Cornwell, H. (2017). *Pax and the politics of peace: republic to principate*, Oxford

Couissin, P. (1931). "*Dextris umeris exsertis*," *REL* 9: 320–26

Courtney, E. (1995). *Musa lapidaria: a selection of Latin verse inscriptions*, Atlanta

(1999). *Archaic Latin prose*, Atlanta

Cowan, R. H. (2007). "The clashing of weapons and silent advances in Roman battles," *Historia* 56: 114–17

Creer, T. (2019). "Ethnography in Caesar's Gallic War and its implications for composition," *CQ* 69: 246–63

Cunliffe, B. (2018). *The ancient Celts*, Oxford (orig. 1997)

Cunningham, M. P. (1949). "Some poetic uses of the singular and plural of substantives in Latin," *CP* 44: 1–14

Cupcea, G. (2017). "Timekeeping in the Roman army," *CQ* 67: 597–606

Cursi, M. F. (2013). "*Amicitia* e *societas* nei rapporti tra Roma e gli altri popoli del Mediterraneo," *Index* 41: 195–227

Dahl, B. (1882). *Die lateinische Partikel ut*, Kristiania

Damon, C. (1993). "Caesar's Practical Prose," *CJ* 89: 183–95

(2007). *Tacitus: Histories book I*. Cambridge

(2010). "Déjà vu or déjà lu? History as intertext," *PLLS* 14: 375–88

(2015). *Studies on the text of Caesar's* Bellum Civile, Oxford

Dangel, J. (1995). "Stratégies de parole dans le discours indirect (*De Bello Gallico*)," *De Vsu. Etudes de syntaxe latine offertes en hommage à Marius Lavency*, Louvain-la-Neuve: 95–113

Davies, G. (2006). *Roman siege works*, Stroud. [Review by D. B. Campbell in *BMCR* 2007.05.32]

Debal, J. (1983). *Histoire d'Orléans et de son Terroir*, Le Coteau

Deberge, Y. *et al.* (2000). "Nouvelles recherches sur les travaux césariens devant Gergovie (1995–1999)," *RACF* 39: 83–111

(2014). "Témoignages de la Guerre des Gaules dans le bassin clermontois, nouveaux apports," *RACF* 53: 1–47

Dehn, W. (1960). "Einige Bemerkungen zum *Murus Gallicus*," *Germania* 38: 43–55

De Jong, I. J. F. (2014). *Narratology and classics: a practical guide*, Oxford

Delétang, H. (2008). "En Sologne biturige, l'oppidum de Neung-sur-Beuvron (Loir-et-Cher) et les tombes aristocratiques," *Bulletin du groupe de recherches archéologiques et historiques de Sologne* 30: 13–30

Demougin, S. (1995). "À propos des Médiomatriques," *CCG* 6: 183–94

Deyber, A. (1987). "La bataille d'Alésia. Les raisons d'un choix," *R.H.A.* 167: 67–73

(2009). *Les Gaulois en guerre*, Paris

(2017). *Vercingétorix. Chef de guerre*, Chamalières

Dickey, E. (2002). *Latin forms of address: from Plautus to Apuleius*, Oxford

Dietler, M. (1995). "Early 'Celtic' socio-political relations: ideological representation and social competition in dynamic comparative perspective," in Arnold–Gibson: 64–71

Dixon, K. R. and P. Southern (1992). *The Roman cavalry*, New York

Dobesch, G. (2001). *Ausgewählte Schriften*, Cologne

Dobson, B. (1974). "The significance of the centurion and primipilaris in the Roman army and administration," *ANRW* II.1: 392–434

Dobson, M. (2013). "No holiday camp: the Roman republican army camp as a fine-tuned instrument of war," in J. De Rose Evans (ed.), *A companion to the archaeology of the Roman republic*, Oxford: 214–34

Dodington, P. M. (1980). *The function of the references to engineering in Caesar's "Commentaries,"* University of Iowa (Diss.)

Dorey, T. A. (1966). "Caesar: the 'Gallic war'," in id. (ed.), *Latin historians*, London: 65–84

Drinkwater, J. (1983). *Roman Gaul: the three provinces, 58 BC – AD 260*, London

Dunn, F. M. and T. Cole (1992). *Beginnings in classical literature*, Cambridge

Du Pontet, R. L. A. (1900). *C. Iuli Caesaris: Commentariorum, Vol. 1: Libri VII de Bello Gallico*, Oxford [Reviews by H. Meusel in *Deutsche Literaturzeitung* 49: 3109–11; T. R. Holmes in *CR* 15: 174–77]

Dupraz, J. (2004). "*Alba Helvorum*, genèse (Ardèche)," *Supplément à la Revue archéologique du centre de la France*: 219–32

Durand, R. (1930). "*Altero die*," in *Mélanges Paul Thomas*, Bruges: 214–28

352 WORKS CITED

Duval, P. M. (1961). *Paris antique des origines au troisième siècle*, Paris

Dyck, A. (1981). "On Panaetius' conception of μεγαλοψυχία," *MH* 38: 153–61

Džino, D. (2010). *Illyricum in Roman politics, 229 BC–AD 68*, Cambridge

Ebel, C. (1976). *Transalpine Gaul: the emergence of a Roman province*, Leiden

Ebert, C. (1909). *Über die Entstehung von Caesars "Bellum Gallicum,"* Nuremberg

Eden, P. T. (1962). "Caesar's style: inheritance versus intelligence," *Glotta* 40: 74–117

Edwards, C. (1993). *The politics of immorality in ancient Rome*, Cambridge

Erbig, F. E. (1931). *Topoi in den Schlachtberichten römischer Dichter*, Danzig

Erdkamp, P. (1992). "Polybius, Livy and the Fabian Strategy," *AncSoc* 23: 127–47

Erickson, B. (2002). "Falling masts, rising masters: the ethnography of virtue in Caesar's account of the Veneti," *AJP* 123: 601–22

Erskine, A. (2013). "How to rule the world: Polybius Book 6 reconsidered," in B. Gibson and T. Harrison (eds.), *Polybius and his world. Essays in memory of F. W. Walbank*. Oxford: 231–45

Eussner, A. (1884). "Adversarien," *BBG* 20: 261–70

Ezov, A. (1996). "The 'missing dimension' of C. Julius Caesar," *Historia* 45: 64–94

Fabia, P. (1889). *De orationibus quae sunt in commentariis Caesaris de Bello Gallico*, Paris (Diss.)

Falileyev, A. (2010). *Dictionary of continental Celtic place-names: a Celtic companion to the Barrington atlas of the Greek and Roman world*, Aberystwyth

Fantham, E. (1972). *Comparative studies in republican Latin imagery*, Toronto (2009). "Caesar as an intellectual," in Griffin: 141–56

Farrell, J. (2005). "Intention and intertext," *Phoenix* 59: 98–111

Ferraris, I. (1997). "Indutiomaro precursore di Vercingetorige?," *Aevum* 71: 113–22

Feldherr, A. (ed.) (2009). *The Cambridge companion to Roman historians*, Cambridge (2009b). "Introduction," in id.: 1–8

Feller, T. (1929). *Caesars Kommentarien über den Gallischen Krieg und die kunstmäßige Geschichtsschreibung*, Borna-Leipzig

Fichtl, S. (1994). *Les Gaulois du Nord de la Gaule*, Paris (2004). *Les peuples gaulois. IIIe–Ier siècles av. J.-C.*, Paris (2005). *La ville celtique. Les oppida de 150 av. J.-C. à 15 ap. J.-C*, Paris (ed.) (2010). *Murus celticus. Architecture et fonctions des remparts de l'âge du Fer*, Bibracte

(2013). "Rome en Gaule: organisation territoriale de la Gaule de l'époque de l'indépendance au début de la période romaine," in S. Hansen and M. Meyer (eds.), *Parallele Raumkonzepte*, Berlin: 291–306

Fischer, F. (1853). *Die Rectionslehre bei Caesar*, Halle (2 vols.)

Fischer, W. (1914). *Das römische Lager, insbesondere nach Livius*, Leipzig

Fitzpatrick, A. and C. Haselgrove (eds.) (2019). *Julius Caesar's battle for Gaul*, Oxford

Flaig, E. (2003). *Ritualisierte Politik: Zeichen, Gesten und Herrschaft im Alten Rom*, Göttingen

Fletcher, G. B. A. (1968). "*Lucretiana*," *Latomus* 27: 884–93

Flower, H. I. (1996). *Ancestor masks and aristocratic power in Roman culture*, Oxford

Fowler, D. P. (1990). "Deviant focalization in Vergil's *Aeneid*," *PCPhS* 36: 42–63

(1997). "Second thoughts on closure," in: D. H. Roberts, F. M. Dunn, D. Fowler, *Classical closure: reading the end in Greek and Latin literature*, Princeton: 3–23

Fraenkel, E. (1916). "Das Geschlecht von *dies*," *Glotta* 8: 24–68

(1956). "Eine Form römischer Kriegsbulletins," *Eranos* 54: 189–94

(1964). "Kolon und Satz. Beobachtungen zur Gliederung des antiken Satzes," "Nachträge," in id., *Kleine Beiträge zur klassischen Philologie* I, Rome: 73–130, 131–39

Fränkel, H. (1933). "Über philologische Interpretation am Beispiel von Caesars *Gallischem Krieg*," *NJbb* 9: 26–41

Frese, R. (1900). *Beiträge zur Beurteilung der Sprache Caesars mit besonderer Berücksichtigung des* bellum civile, Munich

Fröhlich, F. (1889). *Das Kriegswesen Caesars*, Zürich

Fuchs, H. (1938). *Der geistige Widerstand gegen Rom in der antiken Welt*, Berlin

Fuhrer, T. (2015). "Teichoskopia. Female figures looking on battles," in J. Fabre–Serris, A. Keith (eds.), *Women and war in antiquity*, Baltimore: 52–70

Fuller, J. F. C. (1965). *Julius Caesar. Man, soldier, and tyrant*, London [Review by J. P. V. D. Balsdon in *CR* 16: 217–220]

Fussell, P. (1975). *The Great War and modern memory*, New York

Gabba, E. (1976). *Republican Rome, the army, and the allies*, Oxford

Gärtner, H. A. (1975). *Beobachtungen zu Bauelementen in der antiken Historiographie*, Wiesbaden

(2006). "Synkrisis," in Cancik, H. *et al.* (eds.), *Brill's New Pauly*, Leiden

Gaertner, J. F. (2018). "Das *Corpus Caesarianum*," in Grillo–Krebs: 263–76

Gaertner, J. F. and B. Hausburg (2013). *Caesar and the Bellum Alexandrinum. An analysis of style, narrative technique, and the reception of Greek historiography*, Göttingen

Galinsky, K. (1996). *Augustan culture*, Princeton

Garcea, A. (2012). *Caesar's* De Analogia: *edition, translation, and commentary*, Oxford

Geist, S. (2009). *Der gescheiterte Feldherr (dux ferox)*. Frankfurt a.M

Gelzer, M. (1955). "Vercingetorix," in *RE* VIII A.1, Stuttgart: 981–1008

  (1968). *Caesar: politician and statesman*, Cambridge

Gerlinger, S. (2008). *Römische Schlachtenrhetorik. Unglaubwürdige Elemente in Schlachtendarstellungen, speziell bei Caesar, Sallust und Tacitus*, Heidelberg

Gerrish, J. (2013). "*Civitatem recipit*: responding to revolt in Thucydides 3 and Caesar's *Bellum Gallicum*," *New England classical journal* 40: 69–86

Gertz, M. C. (1896). *C. Iulii Caesaris Belli Gallici libri VII: A. Hirtii Belli Gallici liber octavus*, Hanover

Gesche, H. (1976). *Caesar*, Darmstadt

Gibson, R. K. (2002). "cf. e.g.: A typology of 'parallels' and the function of commentaries on Latin poetry," in Gibson–Kraus: 347–56

Gibson, R. K. and C. S. Kraus (eds.) (2002). *The classical commentary*, Leiden

Gilliver, C. M. (1996). "The Roman army and morality in war," in A. Lloyd (ed.), *Battle in antiquity*, London: 219–38

Glück, C. W. (1857). *Die bei C. J. Caesar vorkommenden keltischen Namen*, Munich

Goldsworthy, A. K. (1996). *The Roman army at war 100 BC – AD 200*, Oxford

  (1998). "'Instinctive genius': the depiction of Caesar the general," in: Welch–Powell: 193–219

Görler, W. (1976). "Die Veränderung des Erzählerstandspunktes in Caesar's *Bellum Gallicum*," *Poetica* 8: 95–119

  (1977). "Ein Darstellungsprinzip Caesars. Zur Technik der Peripetie und ihrer Vorbereitung im *Bellum Gallicum*," *Hermes* 105: 307–31

Gotoff, H. C. (1984). "Towards a practical criticism of Caesar's prose style," *ICS* 9: 1–18

Goudineau, C. (1998). *Regard sur Gaule*, Paris

  (2003). "Le gutuater gaulois: idéologie et histoire," *Gallia* 60: 383–87

Grendler, P. F. (1989). *Schooling in Renaissance Italy: literacy and learning, 1300–1600*, Baltimore

Grewing, F. F. and B. Acosta-Hughes, A. Kirichenko (eds.) (2013). *The door ajar. False closure in Greek and Roman literature and art*, Heidelberg

Griffin, M. (ed.) (2009). *A companion to Julius Caesar*, Malden

  (2009b). "Introduction," in Griffin: 1–8

Grillo, L. (2011). "*Scribam ipse de me*: The personality of the narrator in Caesar's *Bellum Civile*," *AJP* 132: 243–71

  (2012). *The art of Caesar's* Bellum Civile: *literature, ideology, and community*, Cambridge

(2015). *A commentary on Cicero's De Provinciis Consularibus,* Oxford

(2016). "Caesarian intertextualities: Cotta and Sabinus in *BG* 5.26–37," *CJ* 111: 257–79

(2018). "Speeches in the Commentarii," in Grillo–Krebs: 131–43

Grillo, L. and C. B. Krebs (eds.) (2018). *The Cambridge companion to the writings of Julius Caesar,* Cambridge

Gross, O. (1911). *De Metonymiis Sermonis Latini a Deorum Nominibus Petitis,* Halle

Gruen, E. S. (1971). "Some criminal trials of the late republic. Political and prosopographical problems," *Athenaeum* 49: 54–69

(1974). *The last generation of the Roman republic,* Berkeley

Guey, J. and A. Audin (1964). "L'amphithéatre des trois-Gaules à Lyon," *Gallia* 22: 37–61

Guillaumet, J.-P. (1996). *L'artisanat chez les Gaulois,* Paris

Guillaumet, J.-P. and M. Szabo (2005). *Études sur Bibracte,* Glux-en-Glenne

Guillaumin, J.-Y. (1985). "La reddition de Vercingétorix selon les auteurs anciens," *Latomus* 44: 743–50

(2009). "Dissimulation et aveu chez César autour du combat de cavalerie préliminaire du siège d'Alésia (BG VII.66.2)," *CEA* 46: 55–69

Halkin, L. (1953). *La supplication d'action des grâces chez les Romains,* Paris

Hall, L. (1998). "*Ratio* and *Romanitas* in the *Bellum Gallicum,*" in Welch–Powell: 11–43

Harmand, J. (1967). *Une campagne Césarienne: Alesia,* Paris

(1972). "Des Gaulois autour de César (suite)," *RSA* 2: 131–67

(1985). "Vercingétorix devant César," *Les dossiers, histoire et archéologie* 92: 24–31

(1989). "Historiographie d'un mythe. L'invention de Vercingétorix de 1865 à nos jours," *Storia della Storiografia* 15: 3–16

Harris, W. V. (1979). *War and imperialism in republican Rome: 327–70 B.C.,* Oxford

(2006). "Readings in the narrative literature of Roman courage," in S. Dillon and K. Welch (eds.), *Representations of war in ancient Rome,* Cambridge: 300–20

Haselgrove, C. (2019). "The Gallic War in the chronology of Iron Age coinage," in Fitzpatrick–Haselgrove: 241–66

Häussler, R. (1968). *Nachträge zu A. Otto Sprichwörter und sprichwörtliche Redensarten der Römer,* Hildesheim

Hellwig, P. (1889). *Über den Pleonasmus bei Cäsar,* Berlin

Henige, D. (1998). "He came, he saw, we counted: the historiography and demography of Caesar's Gallic numbers," *Annales de démographie historique* 1: 215–42

Heraeus, W. (1902). "Die römische Soldatensprache," *ALL* 12: 255–80

Hering, W. (1954/5). "Strabo über die Dreiteilung Galliens," *WZ Rostock* 4: 289–333

(1963). *Die Recensio der Caesarhandschriften*, Berlin

(1997). *C. Iulii Caesaris Commentarii rerum gestarum*: Vol. 1, *Bellum Gallicum*, Berlin (orig. 1987)

Hernández, A. M. (2009). "Bases manuscritas de la práctica conjetural en la edición aldina del *Bellum Gallicum*," *Emerita* 77: 223–45

Hickson-Hahn, F. (2004). "The politics of thanksgiving,' in C. F. Konrad (ed.), *Augusta Augurio: Rerum Humanarum et Diuinarum Commentationes*, Stuttgart: 31–51

Hölkeskamp, K.-J. (2010). *Reconstructing the Roman republic: an ancient political culture and modern research*, Princeton

Hölscher, T. (1991). "Vormarsch und Schlacht," in L. Baumer, T. Hölscher, L. Winkler, *Narrative Systematik und politisches Konzept in den Reliefs der Traianssäule. Drei Fallstudien, JDAI* 106: 261–95, 287–95

Holtz, L. J. M. (1913). "C. Iulius Caesar quo usus sit in orationibus dicendi genere," (Diss.), Jena

Hornung, S. (2016). *Siedlung und Bevölkerung in Ostgallien zwischen Gallischem Krieg und der Festigung der römischen Herrschaft*, Frankfurt a.M.

(2019). "The Hermeskeil fortress: new light on the Caesarian conquest of eastern Belgic Gaul and its aftermath," in Fitzpatrick–Haselgrove: 201–26

Horsfall, N. (1985). "Illusion and reality in Latin topographical writing," *G&R* 32: 197–208

(1988). "Stylistic observations on two neglected subliterary prose texts," in *BICS* Suppl. 51, *Vir bonus discendi peritus*: 53–56

(1999). "The legionary as his own historian," *AncHist* 29: 107–17

Horsmann, G. (1991). *Untersuchungen zur militärischen Ausbildung im republikanischen und kaiserzeitlichen Rom*, Boppard am Rhein

Hough, J. N. (1940). "*Apertos Cuniculos* (Caesar *Bellum Gallicum* vii.22.5)," *CPh* 35: 190–92

Hyart, C. (1954). *Les origines du style indirect Latin et son emploi jusqu'à l'époque de César*, Brussels

Jal, P. (1989). "Les dernières paroles de Vercingétorix," *RÉL* 67: 134–39

Jauss, H. R. (1970). "Literary history as a challenge to literary theory," *New Literary History* 2: 7–37

Jehne, M. (2006). "Methods, models, and historiography," in Rosenstein–Morstein-Marx: 3–28

Jervis, A. (2001). *Gallia Scripta: images of Gauls and Romans in Caesar's Bellum Gallicum*, Philadelphia (Diss.)

Johnston, A. C. (2018). "Nostri and 'the other(s)'," in Grillo–Krebs: 81–94

(2019). "Rewriting Caesar: Cassius Dio and an alternative ethnography of the north," *Histos* 13: 53–77

Johnston, P. D. (2008). *The military consilium in republican Rome*, Piscataway

Joly, M. and P. Barrall (2001). "Les vallées: la contrevallation et la circonvallation au pied du Pennevelle," in Reddé–von Schnurbein: 477–88

Jordan, C. (1947). *César et Attila en Gaule. 3 énigmes historiques*, Paris

Joseph, T. (2018). "Caesar, Vergil, and Lucan," in Grillo–Krebs: 289–303

Jullian, C. (1909). *Histoire de la Gaule. La conquête Romaine et les premières invasions Germaniques*, Paris (vol. 3)

(1977). *Vercingétorix*, Paris (orig. 1902)

Kaenel, G. (2019). "58 BC: The Helvetii, from the Swiss Plateau to Bibracte … and back," in Fitzpatrick–Haselgrove: 73–90

Kagan, K. (2006). *The eye of command*, Ann Arbor

Kahn, A. D. (1971). "Vercingetorix. A new play by C. Julius Caesar," *CW* 64: 249–54

Kassel, R. (1958). *Untersuchungen zur gr. und röm. Konsolationsliteratur*, Munich

Kaster, R. A. (2002). "The taxonomy of patience, or when is 'patientia' not a virtue," *CPh* 97: 131–42

(2005). *Emotion, restraint, and community in ancient Rome*, Oxford

Keegan, J. (1976). *The face of battle*, New York

Keeline, T. and T. Kirby (2019). "*Auceps syllabarum*: a digital analysis of Latin prose rhythm," *JRS* 109: 161–204

Keitel, E. (1987). "Homeric antecedents to the *Cohortatio* in the ancient historians," *CW* 80: 171–72

Kelsey, F. W. (1905). "The title of Caesar's work on the Gallic and Civil War," *TAPA* 36: 211–38

Keppie, L. (1997). "The changing face of the Roman legions (49 BC – AD 69)," *PBSR* 65: 89–102

(1998). *The making of the Roman army*, London

Klotz, A. (1910). *Cäsarstudien*, Leipzig

(1917). "Iulius (Caesar)," in *RE* X.1: 182–275

(1928). "Zu Caes. bell. Gall. VII 75," *Philologus* 83: 390–99

(1941). "Zu Caesar," *Mnemosyne* 9: 218–224

(1953). "Caesar und Livius," *RhM* 96: 62–67

Kneissl, P. (1983). "*Mercator – negotiator*: Römische Geschäftsleute und die Terminologie ihrer Berufe," *MBAH* 2: 73–90

Knoche, U. (1935). *Magnitudo Animi. Untersuchungen zur Entstehung und Entwicklung eines Römischen Wertgedankens*, Leipzig

(1951). "Caesars *Commentarii*, ihr Gegenstand und ihre Absicht," *Gymnasium* 58: 139–60

Knox, P. E. (1986). "Adjectives in -osus and Latin poetic diction," *Glotta* 64: 90–101

Kollmann, E. D. (1977). "Die Macht des Namens," *StudClas* 17: 45–60

Korpanty, J. (1997). "Syllabische Homophonie in Lateinischer Dichtung und Prosa," *Hermes* 125: 330–46

Kraus, C. S. (1994). *Livy. Ab urbe condita. Book VI*, Cambridge

(2005). "Hair, hegemony, and historiography: Caesar's style and its earliest critics," in T. Reinhardt *et al.* (eds.), *Aspects of the language of Latin prose*, Oxford: 97–115

(2007). "Caesar's account of the Battle of Massilia (*BC* 1.34–2.22): some historiographical and narratological approaches," in Marincola: 371–78

(2009). "Bellum Gallicum," in Griffin: 159–74

(2010). "Divide and conquer: Caesar, *De bello Gallico* 7," in C. S. Kraus *et al.* (eds.), *Ancient historiography and its contexts: studies in honour of A. J. Woodman*, Oxford: 40–59

(2010b). "Speech and silence in Caesar's *Bellum Gallicum*," in D. H. Berry, A. Erskine (eds.), *Form and function in Roman oratory*, Oxford: 247–63

(2018). "Caesar in Livy and Tacitus," in Grillo–Krebs: 277–88

Krausz, S. (2015). "En 52 avant J.-C., les Bituriges Cubi face à César: l'énigme de Noviodunum et de Gorgobina," *Études Celtiques* XLI: 7–30

(2019). "Julius Caesar's assault ramp at the *oppidum* of Avaricum in 52 BC," in Romankiewicz, T. *et al.* (eds.), *Enclosing space, opening new ground: Iron Age studies from Scotland to mainland Europe*, Oxford: 23–31

Krausz, S. and I. Ralston (2009). "Le siège d'Avaricum en 52 avant J.-C. ou comment les Gaulois se sont défendus contre les Romains," in O. Büchsenschütz *et al.* (eds.), *L'âge du Fer dans la boucle de la Loire*, Bourges: 145–156

Krebs, C. B. (2006). "Imaginary geography in Caesar's *Bellum Gallicum*," *AJP* 127: 111–36

(2008). "*Magni Viri*: Caesar, Alexander, and Pompey in Cat. 11," *Philologus* 152: 223–29

(2010). "*Borealism*: Caesar, Seneca, Tacitus, and the Roman discourse about the Germanic north," in E. S. Gruen (ed.), *Cultural identity and the peoples of the ancient Mediterranean*, Los Angeles: 202–21

(2013). "Caesar, Lucretius and the dates of *De Rerum Natura* and the *Commentarii*," *CQ* 63: 751–58

(2014). "Caesar's Sisenna," *CQ* 64: 207–13

(2015). "The buried tradition of programmatic titulature among republican historians: Polybius' Πραγματεία, Asellio's *Res Gestae*, and Sisenna's redefinition of *Historiae*," *AJP* 136: 503–24

(2016). "Thucydides in Gaul: the siege of Plataea as Caesar's model for his siege of Avaricum," *Histos* 10: 1–14

(2017). "Caesar the historian," in K. A. Raaflaub (ed.), *The landmark Julius Caesar: the complete works*, New York, web essay DD, 210–13

(2018a). "More than words. The *Commentarii* in their propagandistic context," in Grillo–Krebs: 29–42

(2018b). "Caesar. A style of choice," in Grillo–Krebs: 110–30

(2018c). "Greetings, Cicero! Caesar and Plato on writing and memory," *CQ* 68: 517–22

(2018d). "The world's measure: Caesar's geographies of *Gallia* and *Britannia* in their contexts and as evidence of his world map," *AJP* 139: 93–122

(2021). "'Making history': constructive wonder (aka *Quellenforschung*) and the composition of Caesar's *Gallic War* (thanks to Labienus and Polybius)," in A. D. Poulsen, A. Jönsson (eds.), *Usages of the past in ancient historiography*, Leiden: 91–114

(2023). "Blood on his words. Barley on his mind. True names in Caesar's speech for the legendary Barley-Muncher (*BG* 7.77)," *CQ* 73

(forthcoming). "Les fleurs du mal. The unsurprising origin of Caesar's siege works before Alesia (esp. *BG* 7.72–74)"

Kremer, B. (1994). *Das Bild der Kelten bis in Augusteische Zeit*, Stuttgart

Kubitschek, W. (1924). "Legio (republikanische Zeit)," *RE* XII.1: 1186–1210

Kuch, H. (1965). Φιλόλογος. *Untersuchung eines Wortes von seinem ersten Auftreten in der Tradition bis zur ersten überlieferten lexikalischen Festlegung*, Berlin

Labisch, A. (1975). Frumentum Commeatusque. *Die Nahrungsmittelversorgung der Heere Caesars*, Meisenheim

Lambert, P.-Y. (1994). *La langue gauloise*, Paris

Lamoine, L. (2003). "Préteur, vergobret, princeps en Gaule Narbonnaise et dans les Trois Gaules," in M. Cébeillac-Gervasoni, L. Lamoine (eds.), *Les élites et leur facettes*, Rome: 187–204

(2006). "La pratique du vergobret," *CCG* 17: 81–104

Landgraf, G. (1888). *Untersuchungen zu Caesar und seinen Fortsetzern: insbesondere über Autorschaft und Komposition des Bellum Alexandrinum und Africanum*, Erlangen

(1978). *Kommentar zu Ciceros Rede* Pro Sex. Roscio Amerino, Hildesheim (orig. 1913)

Langouet, L. (1988). *Les Coriosolites, un peuple armoricain*, Saint-Malo

Lau, D. (1975). *Der Lateinische Begriff* Labor, Munich

Lausberg, M. (1980). "Caesar und Cato im *Agricola* des Tacitus," *Gymnasium* 87: 411–30

Lavan, M. (2013). *Slaves to Rome*, Cambridge

Le Bohec, Y. (1998). "Vercingétorix," *Rivista Storica dell'Antichità* 28: 85–120

(2001a). "Gutuater, nom propre ou nom commun?," *Gallia* 58: 363–67

(2001b). *César chef de guerre; César stratège et tacticien*, Monaco

(2005). "Le clergé celtique et la guerre des Gaules: historiographie et politique," *Latomus* 64: 871–81

(2012). *Alésia*, Paris

Lebreton, J. (1901). *Caesariana Syntaxis quatenus a Ciceroniana differat*, Paris

Leeman, A. D. (1963). *Orationis ratio; the stylistic theories and practice of the Roman orators, historians and philosophers*, Amsterdam

(2001). "Julius Caesar, the orator of paradox," in: Cecil W. Wooten (ed.), *The orator in action and theory in Greece and Rome. Essays in honor of George A. Kennedy*, Leiden: 97–110

Le Gall, J. (1970). "Cent ans après. Un témoin méconnu de l'histoire du Second Empire, la statue de Vercingétorix sur le Mont Auxois," *Mémoires de l'Académie des Sciences, Arts et Belles-Lettres de Dijon* 117: 199–219

Le Gall, J. *et al.* (1973). *Alésia: textes littéraires antiques*, Paris 1973

Lendle, O. (1975). *Schildkröte: antike Kriegsmaschinen in poliorketischen Texten*. Wiesbaden

Lendon, J. E. (1999). "The rhetoric of combat: Greek military theory and Roman culture in Julius Caesar's battle descriptions," *CA* 18: 273–329

(2005). *Soldiers and ghosts: a history of battle in classical antiquity*, New Haven

(2015). "Julius Caesar, thinking about battle and foreign relations," *Histos* 9: 1–28

(2017a). "Battle description in the ancient historians, part I: structure, array, and fighting," *Greece and Rome* 64: 39–64

(2017b). "Battle description in the ancient historians, part II: speeches, results, and sea battles," *Greece and Rome* 64: 145–67

Lenoir, M. (1996). "La littérature de *re militari*," in C. Nicolet (ed.), *Les littératures techniques dans l'antiquité romaine*, Geneva: 77–108

Leonhardt, J. (2013). *Latin: story of a world language*, Cambridge

Levene, D. S. (2005). "The late republican/triumviral period: 90–40 BC," in Harrison, S. (ed.), *A companion to Latin literature*, Malden: 31–43

Levick, B. (1998). "The Veneti revisited: C. E. Stevens and the tradition on Caesar the propagandist," in Welch–Powell: 61–85

Levithan, J. (2013). *Roman siege warfare*, Ann Arbor

Lind, L. R. (1979). "The tradition of Roman moral conservatism," in Deroux, C. (ed.), *Studies in Latin literature and Roman history*, Brussels: 7–58

Lindholm, E. (1931). *Stilistische Studien zur Erweiterung der Satzglieder im Lateinischen*, Lund

Lintott, A. W. (1972). "Imperial expansion and moral decline in the Roman Republic," *Historia* 21: 626–38

(1993). *Imperium Romanum: politics and administration*, New York

Litwan, P. (2011). "Caesars Beschreibung des *murus Gallicus* (*BG* 7.23) und die Eisennägel," *MH* 68: 148–53

Löfstedt, E. (1928/1935). *Syntactica. Studien und Beiträge zur historischen Syntax des Latein*, vols. 1/2, Lund

Lohmann, D. (1990). "Leserlenkung im *Bellum Helveticum*. Eine 'kriminologische Studie' zu Caesar, *BG* 1.15–18," *AU* 33: 56–73

Lombard-Jourdan, A. (1985). *Aux origines de Paris: la genèse de la rive droite jusqu'en 1223*, Paris

Loreto, L. (1993). "Pensare la Guerra in Cesare," in Poli: 239–343

Lowrie, M. (1995). "A parade of lyric predecessors: Horace *C.* 1.12–1.18," *Phoenix* 49: 33–48

Luccisano, S. (1998–2001). "A propos de l'*oppidum* sénon de Metlosedum," *Bulletin du Groupement archéologique de Seine-et-Marne* 39–42: 43–50

(n. y.). "La bataille de Gergovie en quelques cartes," www.gergovie.net/bataille-de-gergovie

Luce, T. J. (1971). "Design and structure in Livy: 5.32–55," *TAPA* 102: 265–302

Lund, A. A. (1998). *Die ersten Germanen*, Heidelberg

Luttwak, E. N. (2016), *The grand strategy of the Roman Empire*, Baltimore [orig. 1976]

Mack, S. (1978). *Patterns of time in Vergil*, Hamden

Macmullen, R. (1963). *Soldier and civilian in the later Roman Empire*, Cambridge

Maier, U. (1978). *Caesars Feldzüge in Gallien (58–51 v. Chr.) in ihrem Zusammenhang mit der stadtrömischen Politik*, Bonn

Malitz, J. (1987). "Die Kanzlei Caesars – Herrschaftsorganisation zwischen Republik und Prinzipat," *Historia* 36: 51–72

Mannetter, D. A. (1995). *Narratology in Caesar*, Univ. of Wisconsin-Madison (Diss.)

Mantovanelli, P. (2000). "Cesare et la fortuna," in Urso: 211–30

Marciniak, K. (2008). "Cicero und Caesar. Ein Dialog der Dichter," *Philologus* 152: 212–22

Marincola, J. (1997). *Authority and tradition in ancient historiography*, Cambridge

(ed.) (2007a). *A companion to Greek and Roman historiography*, Malden

(2007b). "Speeches in classical historiography," in Marincola: 118–32

Marouzeau, J. (1922–49). *L'ordre des mots dans la phrase latine*, 3 vols. Paris (1970). *Traité de stylistique latine*, Paris (5th ed.)

Marsden, E. W. (1969). *Greek and Roman artillery: historical development*, Oxford

(1971). *Greek and Roman artillery. Technical treatises*, Oxford

Martin, P. M. (2001). "Salluste a-t-il voulu rivaliser avec César?," in C. Hamdoune (ed.), *Ubique amici*, Montpelliers: 389–402

Maurach, G. (2002). "Caesars humor," *WJA* 26: 53–60

Maxfield, V. A. (1981). *The military decorations of the Roman army*, Berkeley

McCone, K. (2006). "Greek Κελτός and Γαλάτης, Latin *Gallus* 'Gaul'," *Sprache* 46: 94–111

McCutcheon, R. (2013). *An archaeology of Cicero's letters: a study of late republican textual culture*, [Diss.] Toronto

McDonnell, M. (2006). *Roman manliness: virtus and the Roman republic*, Cambridge

McDougall, I. (1991). "Dio and his sources for Caesar's campaigns in Gaul," *Latomus* 50: 616–38

Meier, C. (1980). Res publica amissa. *Eine Studie zu Verfassung und Geschichte der späten römischen Republik*, Wiesbaden [orig. 1966]

(1996). *Caesar: a biography*, New York

Menge, P. (1905). "Eine List des Vercingetorix," *Neue Jahrbücher* 15: 520–23

Mennessier-Jouannet, C. and Y. Deberge (eds.) (2007). *L'archéologie de l'âge du Fer en Auvergne*, Lattes

Mensching, E. (1988). *Caesars* Bellum Gallicum: *Eine Einführung*, Frankfurt a.M

Micunco, G. (1995). "Il ponte sul Reno (Caes. Gall. 4, 16–19)," *InvLuc* 17: 97–120

Miller, M. C. J. (1979). "*Legio Decima Equitata*. The Tenth Legion after Caesar and the colonists of Patrae," *AncW* 2: 139–144

Milnor, K. (2009). "Women and history," in Feldherr: 276–87

Miniconi, P.-J. (1951). *Étude des thèmes "guerriers" de la poésie épique gréco-romaine*, Paris

Moles, J. L. (1989). *Plutarch: the life of Cicero*, Oxford

Mommsen, T. (1895–1905). *History of Rome*, vols. 4–5, New York

Moore, R. (2013). "Generalship: leadership and command," in B. Campbell, L. A. Tritle (eds.), *The Oxford handbook of warfare in the classical world*, Oxford: 457–73

Moore, T. (2017). "Alternatives to urbanism? Reconsidering *Oppida* and the urban question in Late Iron Age Europe," *Journal of world prehistory* 30: 281–300

Moore, T. J. (1989). *Artistry and ideology. Livy's vocabulary of virtue*, Frankfurt a.M.

Morel, D. (1985). "La bataille de Lutece (52)," in: *Lutece: Paris de Cesar à Clovis*. La société des amis du Musée Carnavalet, Paris: 75–78

Morello, R. (2018). "Innovation and cliché: the letters of Caesar," in Grillo–Krebs: 223–34

Morrell, K. (2017). *Pompey, Cato, and the governance of the Roman empire*, Oxford

Morrison, J. (2006). *Reading Thucydides*. Columbus

Morstein-Marx, R. (2000). "*Dignitas* and *res publica*: Caesar and republican legitimacy," in K.-J. Hölkeskamp (ed.), *Eine politische Kultur (in) der Krise? Die "letzte Generation" der römischen Republik*, Munich: 15–140

(2004). *Mass oratory and political power in the late Roman republic*, Cambridge

(2021). *Julius Caesar and the Roman people*, Cambridge

Mosci Sassi, M. G. (1983). *Il sermo castrensis*, Bologna

Mouritsen, H. (2017). *Politics in the Roman republic*, Cambridge

Münzer, F. (1900). "Commius," *RE* 4.1: 770–71

Murphy, C. T. (1949). "The use of speeches in Caesar's *Gallic War*," *CJ* 45: 120–27

Murphy, P. R. (1977). "Themes of Caesar's *Gallic War*," *CJ* 72: 234–43

Murrin, M. (1994). *History and warfare in Renaissance epic*, Chicago

Mutschler, F.-H. (1975). *Erzählstil und Propaganda in Caesars Kommentarien*, Heidelberg. [Review by M. Rambaud, in *REL* 55: 54–60]

Nägelsbach, K. F. von (1905). *Lateinische Stilistik*, Nuremberg (9th ed.)

Naiden, F. S. (2006). *Ancient supplication*, Oxford

Nenninger, M. (2001). *Die Römer und der Wald*, Stuttgart

Nicolet, C. (2009). "Caesar and the two Napoleons," in Griffin: 410–17

Nicols, J. (2001). "*Hospitium* and political friendship in the late republic," M. Peachin (ed.), *Aspects of friendship in the Graeco-Roman world, JRA*: 99–108

Nieto-Pelletier, S. (2004). "Monnaies arvernes (Vercingétorix, Cas) en orichalque," *RN* 160: 5–25

(2012). "Le portrait monétaire gaulois. Les monnayages du Centre de la Gaule (IIIe–Ier siècles a. C.)," *CEA* 49: 235–58

Nipperdey, C. (1847). *C. Iulii Caesaris commentarii cum supplementis A. Hirtii et aliorum. Caesaris Hirtiique fragmenta*, Leipzig

Nisbet, R. G. M. (1995). "Aeneas Imperator," in *Collected papers*, Oxford: 132–43

Norden, E. (1920). *Die germanische Urgeschichte in Tacitus' Germania*, Leipzig

Nörr, D. (1989). *Aspekte des römischen Völkerrechts: Die Bronzetafel von Alcantara*, Munich

North, J. A. (2006). "The constitution of the Roman republic," in Rosenstein–Morstein-Marx: 256–77

Oakley, S. P. (1985). "Single combat in the Roman republic," *CQ* 35: 392–410

(1997). *A commentary on Livy, books VI–X, volume I: introduction and book VI*, Oxford

(2005). *A commentary on Livy, books VI–X, volume III: book IX*, Oxford

Oberhelman, S. M. (2003). *Prose rhythm in Latin literature of the Roman empire*, Lewiston

O'Connell, P. (2017). *The rhetoric of seeing in Attic forensic oratory*, Austin

O'Connor, C. (1993). *Roman bridges*, Cambridge

Odelman, E. (1985). "Aspects du vocabulaire de César," *Eranos* 83: 147–53

Ogilvie, R. M. (1977). "Mutschler, *Erzählstil und Propaganda in Caesars Kommentarien; Gärtner, Beobachtungen zu Bauelementen in der antiken Historiographie besonders bei Livius und Caesar*," *CR* 27: 185–87

O'Hara, J. J. (2017). *True names: Vergil and the Alexandrian tradition of etymological wordplay*, Ann Arbor (orig. 1996)

Olivier, L. (2019). "The second battle of Alesia: the 19th-century investigations at Alise-Sainte-Reine and international recognition of the Gallic period of the late Iron Age," in Fitzpatrick–Haselgrove: 285–309

Olson, K. (2017). *Masculinity and dress in Roman antiquity*, New York

Opelt, I. (1980). "'Töten' und 'Sterben' in Caesars Sprache," *Glotta* 58: 103–19

Oppermann, H. (1933). *Caesar: Der Schriftsteller und sein Werk*, Leipzig

(1974). "Probleme und heutiger Stand der Caesarforschung," in D. Rasmussen (ed.), *Caesar*, Darmstadt (2nd ed.): 485–522

Osgood, J. (2009). "The pen and the sword. Writing and conquest in Caesar's Gaul," *CA* 28: 328–58

(2010). "Caesar and the pirates: or how to make (and break) an ancient life," *G&R* 57: 319–36

Östenberg, I. (2009). *Staging the world: spoils, captives, and representations in the Roman triumphal procession*, Oxford

(2017). "Defeated by the forest, the pass, the wind: nature as an enemy of Rome," in J. H. Clark, B. Turner (eds.), *Brill's companion to military defeat in ancient Mediterranean society*, Leiden: 240–61

Pagán, V. E. (2005). *Conspiracy narratives in Roman history*, Austin

Pallavisini, A. (1972). "Tradizione e novità nel giudizio di Cesare sui barbari nel *De bello Galllico*," *CISA* 1: 98–107

Pape, L. (1995). *La Bretagne romaine*, Rennes

Parker, H. M. D. (1958). *The Roman legions*, New York

Pascucci, G. (1956). "Cimbri et Teutoni in Cesare," *SIFC* 27/28: 361–73

(1973). "Interpretazione linguistica e stilistica del Cesare autentico," *ANRW*I.3: 488–522

Paul, G. M. (1982). "*Urbs capta*: sketch of an ancient literary motif," *Phoenix* 36: 144–55

Paul, W. (1878). "Kritische Bemerkungen zu Caesars *Bellum Gallicum*," *Zeitschrift für das Gymnasialwesen* 32: 161–99

Pausch, D. (2011). *Livius und der Leser: Narrative Strukturen in* ab urbe condita, Munich

Pelling, C. B. R. (1981). "Caesar's battle-descriptions and the defeat of Ariovistus," *Latomus* 40: 741–66

(2011). *Plutarch Caesar: translated with introduction and commentary*, Oxford

(2013). "Xenophon's and Caesar's third-person narratives – or are they?," in A. Marmodoro, J. Hill (eds.), *The author's voice in classical and late antiquity*, Oxford: 39–75

Pénisson, P. *et al.* (2013). *Quoi de neuf chez les Pétrucores? Dix ans d'archéologie en Périgord gallo-romain*, Périgueux

Peretz, D. (2005). "Military burial and the identification of the Roman fallen soldiers," *Klio* 87: 123–38

Pertlwieser, T. (2006). *Gergovie 2006. Recherches sur les fortifications de l'oppidum. Fouille du rempart sud et de le Porte Ouest*, Auvergne

Petersdorff, R. (1879). *C. J. Caesar num in bello gallico enarrando nonnulla e fontibus transscripserit*, Belgard

Petit, C. (2001). "L'environnement du site d'Alésia," in Reddé–von Schnurbein: 55–103

Pezzini, G. (2018). "Caesar the linguist: the debate about the Latin language," in Grillo–Krebs: 173–92

Phang, S. E. (2004). "Intimate conquests: Roman soldiers' slave women and freedwomen," *AW* 35: 207–37

(2008). *Roman military service: ideologies of discipline in the late republic and early principate*, New York

Pickering, P. E. (2003). "Did the Greek ear detect 'careless' verbal repetitions?," *CQ* 53: 490–99

Piggott, S. (1959). "The carnyx in Early Iron Age Britain," *AntJ* 39: 19–32

Pina Polo, F. (1995). "Procedures and functions of civil and military *contiones* in Rome," *Klio* 77: 203–16

Pinkster, H. (1969). "AB & C-coordination in Latin authors," *Mnemosyne* 22: 258–67

(1992). "The Latin impersonal passive," *Mnemosyne* 45: 159–77

Pitcher, L. (2018). "Caesar and Greek historians," in Grillo–Krebs: 237–48

Pizzani, U. (1993). "La cultura filosofica di Cesare," in Poli: 163–89

Poli, D. (ed.) (1993). *La cultura in Cesare*, Rome

Poux, M. (2008). "L'empreinte du militaire tardo-républicain dans les faciès mobiliers de La Tène finale," in M. Poux (ed.), *Sur les traces de César*, Bibracte: 299–432

(2012). *Corent: Voyage au cœur d'une ville gauloise*, Paris

Poux, M. and L. Guyard (1999). "Un moule à balles de fronde inscrit d'époque tardo-républicaine à Paris (rue Saint-Martin)," *Instrumentum* 9: 29–30

Powell, A. (1998). "Julius Caesar and the presentation of massacre," in Powell–Welch: 111–39

Power, T. (2014). "The originality of Suetonius," in Power, T. and R. K. Gibson (eds.), *Suetonius the biographer. Studies in Roman lives*, Oxford: 1–20

Preiswerk, R. (1945). "*Sententiae* in Caesars Commentarien," *MH* 2: 213–26

Premerstein, A. von (1900). "Commentarii," *RE* 4.1: 726–59

Raaflaub, K. A. (ed., trans.) (2017). *The landmark Julius Caesar. The complete works: Gallic War, Civil War, Alexandrian War, African War, and Spanish War*. Pp. xcii + 804, ills., colour maps, New York

(2018). "Caesar, literature, and politics at the end of the Republic," in Grillo–Krebs: 13–28

Raaflaub, K. A. and J. T. Ramsey (2017). "Reconstructing the chronology of Caesar's Gallic Wars," *Histos* 11: 1–74, 162–217

Radin, M. (1918). "The date of composition of Caesar's *Gallic War*," *CP* 13: 283–300

Ralston, I. (2006). *Celtic fortifications*, Gloucestershire

(2019). "The Gauls on the eve of the Roman conquest," in Fitzpatrick–Haselgrove: 19–47

Ramage, E. S. (1987). *The nature and purpose of Augustus' Res Gestae*, Stuttgart

(2003). "Aspects of propaganda in the *De Bello Gallico*: Caesar's virtues and attributes," *Athenaeum* 91: 331–72

Rambaud, M. (1958). "L'ordre de bataille de l'armée des Gaules d'après les Commentaires de César," *REA* 60: 87–130

(1962). "Thévenot (Emile). Les Éduens n'ont pas trahi," *RBPh* 40: 438–40

(1968). "César à travers les Commentaires," *Latomus* 92: 46–75

(1979). "César et la rhétorique. À propos de Cicéron (*Brut.* 261–2)," *Caesarodonum* 14: 19–39

Ramsey, J. T. (2009). "The proconsular years: politics at a distance," in Griffin: 37–57

Rasmussen, D. (1963). *Caesars Commentarii. Stil und Stilwandel am Beispiel der direkten Rede*, Göttingen. [Review by A. Maniet, in *AC* 34: 250–51, 1965]

Rawlings, L. (1998). "Caesar's portrayal of Gauls as warriors," in Welch–Powell: 171–92

Rawson, E. (1975). "Caesar's heritage: Hellenistic kings and their Roman equals," *JRS* 65: 148–59

Rebourg, A. (1994). *Saône-et-Loire (71/4). Carte Arch. de la Gaule*, Paris

Reddé, M. (ed.) (1996). *L'armée Romaine en Gaule*, Paris

(2008). "Alésia du Texte de César aux vestiges archéologiques," in Reddé–von Schnurbein: 277–89

(2012). *Alésia: l'archéologie face à l'imaginaire*, Paris (2nd ed.) [C. Haselgrove, in *Germania* 83: 426–30]

(ed.) (2018). *L'armée Romaine en Gaule à l'époque républicaine. Nouveaux témoignages archéologiques*, Bibracte

(2019). "Recent archaeological research on Roman military engineering works of the Gallic War," Fitzpatrick–Haselgrove: 91–112

Reddé M. and S. von Schnurbein (1993). "Fouilles et recherches nouvelles sur les travaux du siège d'Alésia," *CRAI* 137:281–314

(eds.) (2001). *Alésia. Fouilles et recherches franco-allemandes sur les travaux militaires romains autour du Mont-Auxois (1991–1997)*, 3 vols., Paris

(eds.) (2008). *Alésia et la bataille du Teutoburg*, Paris

Reggi, G. (2002). "Cesare e il racconto delle battaglie navali sotto Marsiglia," *RIL* 136: 71–108

Reinach, S. (1915). "Les communiqués de César," *Revue de philologie* 39: 29–49

Reijgwart, E. (1993). "Zur Erzählung in Caesars *Commentarii*," *Philologus* 137: 18–37

Rey, S. (2015). "Roman tears and their impact: a question of gender?," *Clio* 41: 243–64

Rich, J. W. (1986). "*Siluae Callesque*," *Latomus* 45: 505–21

(2011). "Structuring Roman history: the consular year and the Roman historical tradition," *Histos* 5: 1–43

(2012). "Roman attitudes to defeat in battle under the Republic," in M. Simón *et al.* (eds.), *Vae victis! Perdedores en el mundo antiguo*, Barcelona: 83–111

Richardson, J. S. (2000). *Wars of the Romans in Iberia: Iberike*, Warminster

(2008). *The language of empire*, Cambridge

Rickman, G. E. (1971). *Roman granaries and storebuildings*, Cambridge

Richter, W. (1977). *Caesar als Darsteller seiner Taten: Eine Einführung*, Heidelberg

Riepl, W. (1913). *Das Nachrichtenwesen des Altertums*, Leipzig 1913

Ringe, C. (1880). *Zum Sprachgebrauch des Caesar I (et, que, atque/ac)*, Göttingen

Rives, J. B. (1999). *Cornelius Tacitus: Germania*, Oxford

Rivière, Y. (2013). "L'interdiction de l'eau, du feu … et du toit (sens et origine de la désignation du bannissement chez les romains)," *RPh* 87: 125–55

Robin, S. and M. Poux (2000). "Les origines de Lutece," *Gallia* 57: 181–225

Roblin, M. (1971). *Le terroir de Paris*, Paris (2nd ed.)

Roller, M. (2004). "Exemplarity in Roman culture: the cases of Horatius Cocles and Cloelia," *CP* 99: 1–56

Roloff, K.-H. (1952). "*caerimonia*," *Glotta* 32: 101–38

Rosenberger, V. (1992). Bella et expeditiones: *die antike Terminologie der Kriege Roms*, Stuttgart

Rosenstein, N. (1990). *Imperatores victi. Military defeat and aristocratic competition in the middle and late republic*, Los Angeles

Rosenstein, N. and R. Morstein–Marx (eds.) (2006). *A companion to the Roman republic*, Malden

Ross, D. O. (1969). *Style and tradition in Catullus*, Cambridge

Rosset, C. (1954). "Frontin, auteur des stratagèmes, a-t-il lu le *Bellum Gallicum?*," *REL* 32: 275–84

Rossi, A. (2003). *Contexts of war: manipulation of genre in Virgilian battle narrative*, Ann Arbor

Roth, J. P. (1999). *The logistics of the Roman army at war (264 B.C.–A.D. 235)*, Leiden

Rowe, G. O. (1967). "Dramatic structures in Caesar's *Bellum Civile*," *TAPA* 98: 399–414

Roymans, N. (2019). "Caesar's conquest and the archaeology of mass violence in the Germanic frontier zone," in Fitzpatrick–Haselgrove: 113–35

Rüpke, J. (1990). *Domi militiae: Die religiöse Konstruktion des Krieges in Rom*, Stuttgart

(1992). "Wer las Caesars *bella* as *commentarii?*," *Gymnasium* 99: 201–26.

(2018). "Priesthoods, gods, and stars," in Grillo–Krebs: 58–67

Sands, P. C. (1908). *The client princes of the Roman empire under the republic*, Cambridge

Santangelo, F. (2012). "*Sullanus* and *Sullani*," *Arctos* 46: 187–91

Saulcy, F. de (1865). "Letters sur la numismatique gauloise XX," *Revue numismatique* 3: 133–52

Scarola, M. (1987). "Il muro di Avaricum: Lettura di Cesare, *B.G.* 7, 23," *MD* 18: 183–204

Schadee, H. (2008). "Caesar's construction of northern Europe: inquiry, contact, and corruption in *De Bello Gallico*," *CQ* 58: 158–80

(2018). "Writing war with Caesar: the *Commentarii*'s afterlife in military memoirs," in Grillo–Krebs: 318–32

Scheidel, W. (1996). "Finances, figures and fiction," *CQ* 46: 222–38
Schiesaro, A. (2010). "Cesare, la cultura di un dittatore," in Urso: 241–49
Schmalz, J. H. (1907). "Zu Claudius Quadrigarius," *PhW* 27: 925–26
Schneider, C. E. C. (1855). *Commentarii de bellis C. Iulii Caesaris*, Halle
Schnurbein, S. von (2001). "La plaine des Laumes. La contrevallation," "Camps et *Castella*," "Les Fossés et les Pièges," "Topographie, système défensif et armament antique," in Reddé–von Schnurbein: 311–49, 507–14, 539–50, 551–56
   (2008). "Alise-Sainte-Reine. Die Spuren der Belagerungswerke," in Reddé–von Schnurbein: 195–208
Seager, R. (2003). "Caesar and Gaul: some perspectives on the *Bellum Gallicum*," in Cairns–Fantham: 19–34
Seavey, W. D. (1994). *Ius belli: Roman ideology and the rights of war*, Chapel Hill (Diss.)
Seel, O. (1977). *C. Iulii Caesaris Commentarii rerum gestarum*, Leipzig
Shackleton Bailey, D. R. (1965). *Cicero's letters to Atticus, Vol. I*, Cambridge
   (1992). *Onomasticon to Cicero's speeches*, Stuttgart (2nd ed.)
Sherk, R. K. (1969). *Roman documents from the Greek east*, Baltimore
Sherwin-White, A. N. (1957). "Caesar as an imperialist," *G&R* 4: 36–45
Sievers, S. (2001). "Les armes d'Alésia," in Reddé–von Schnurbein: 121–293
Slotty, F. (1927). "Der soziative und der affektische Plural der ersten Person im Lateinischen," in *Indogermanische Forschungen* 44: 264–305
Solodow, J. B. (1978). *The Latin particle quidem*, Oxford
Sordi, M. (1971). "Cassio Dione e il VII libro del *de Bello Gallico* di Cesare," in: *Studi di storiografia antica. In memoria di Leonardo Ferrero*, Turin: 167–82
Speidel, M. P. (1984). "Eagle-Bearer and trumpeter," in: id., *Roman army studies* I, Amsterdam: 3–43 (orig. 1976)
   (1994). *Riding for Caesar: the Roman emperors' horse guards*, Cambridge
Spilman, M. (1932). *Cumulative sentence building in Latin historical narrative*, Berkeley
Stäcker, J. (2003). *Princeps und miles: Studien zum Bindungs- und Nahverhältnis von Kaiser und Soldat im 1. und 2. Jahrhundert n. Chr.*, Hildesheim
Steel, C. and H. van der Blom (eds.) (2013). *Community and communication: oratory and politics in republican Rome*, Oxford
Stem, R. (2017). "Irony and the text of Caesar, *Bellum Gallicum* 5.31.5," *CQ* 67: 307–10
Stevens, C. E. (1947). "55 BC and 54 BC," *Antiquity* 21:3–9
   (1952). "The *Bellum Gallicum* as a work of propaganda," *Latomus* 11: 3–18, 165–79

(1980). "North-west Europe and Roman politics," in C. Deroux (ed.), *Studies in Latin literature and Roman history*, Brussels: 71–97

Stramaglia, A. (2002). *[Quintiliano]: La città che si cibò dei suoi cadaveri (Declamazioni maggiori, 12)*, Cassino

Strasburger, H. (1938). *Caesars Eintritt in die Geschichte*, Munich

(1968). *Caesar im Urteil seiner Zeitgenossen*, Darmstadt (orig. 1953) [Review by J. P. V. D. Balsdon, in *JRS* 59: 276–77]

(1972). *Homer und die Geschichtsschreibung*, Heidelberg

Stringer, G. P. (2017). "Caesar and Labienus: a reevaluation of Caesar's most important relationship in *De Bello Gallico*," *NECN* 44: 228–46

Suolahti, J. (1955). *The junior officers of the Roman army in the republican period*, Helsinki

Sydow, R. (1898). *Kritische Beiträge zu Cäsars* Bellum Gallicum, Berlin

Tatum, W. J. (1999). *The patrician tribune: Publius Clodius Pulcher*, Chapel Hill

Thévenot, E. (1960). *Les Éduens n'ont pas trahi*, Brussels (rev. by H. H. Scullard (1962), *CR* 12: 177–78)

(1962). "L'*oppidum* éduen de Decize-sur-Loire: la position et le rôle de cette place dans la campagne de 52 avant J.-C.," *RACF* 1: 195–200

(1969). *Les voies romaines de la cité des Éduens*, Brussels

Thomas, R. (2000). *Herodotus in context: ethnography, science and the art of persuasion*, Cambridge

Thomasson, B. E. (1991). Legatus: *Beiträge zur römischen Verwaltungsgeschichte*, Stockholm

Thome, G. (2000). *Zentrale Wertvorstellungen der Römer*. Bamberg

Thorne, J. (2007). "The chronology of the campaign against the Helvetii: a clue to Caesar's intentions?," *Historia* 56: 27–36

(2018). "Narrating the Gallic and Civil wars with and beyond Caesar," in Grillo–Krebs: 304–17

Tierney, J. J. (1959/1960). "The Celtic ethnography of Posidonius," *PRIA* 60: 189–275

Timpe, D. (1972). "Rechtsformen der römischen Außenpolitik bei Caesar," *Chiron* 2: 277–96

Töpfer, K. (2011). Signa Militaria – *Die römischen Feldzeichen in der Republik und im Prinzipat*, Mainz

Torigian, C. (1998). "The Λόγος of Caesar's *Bellum Gallicum*," in Welch–Powell: 45–60

Travilian, T. T. (2013). "Figuring fear in the Roman historians," *NECN* 40: 87–122

Treggiari, S. (2005). "Putting the family across: Cicero on natural affection," in M. George (ed.), *The Roman family in the empire*, Oxford: 9–35

Trément, F. *et al.* (2003). "Le territoire des Arvernes: limites de cité, tropismes et centralité," in Mennessier-Jouannet–Deberge: 99–110

Troadec, J. (2006). "L'Avaricum de César: une ville?," in I. Chol (ed.), *La memoire des lieux: hommage à Robert Périchon (1928–1999)*, Clermont-Ferrand: 120–32

Tyrell, W. M. (1970). *Biography of Titus Labienus, Caesar's lieutenant in Gaul.* Accessed at https://msu.edu/~tyrrell/labienus.htm

Ulrich, R. B. (1993). "Julius Caesar and the creation of the *Forum Iulium*," *AJA* 97: 49–80

Urso, G. (ed.) (2000). *L'ultimo Cesare: scritti, riforme, progetti, congiure*, Atti del convegno internazionale (Cividale del Friuli, 16–18 settembre 1999), L'Erma di Bretschneider, Rome: 55–87

(2010). *Cesare: Precursore o visionario*, Florence

Usener, H. (1903). "Dreiheit (Fortsetzung)," *RhM* 58: 321–62

Utard, R. (2004). *Le discours indirect chez les historiens latins, écriture ou oralité? Histoire d'un style*, Louvain

Van der Blom, H. (2010). *Cicero's role models. The political strategy of a new-comer*, Oxford

(2018). "Caesar's orations," in Grillo–Krebs: 193–205

Vanggaard, J. H. (1988). *The Flamen: a study in the history and sociology of Roman religion*, Copenhagen

Van Laer, S. (2010). *La préverbation en latin: étude des préverbes ad-, in-, ob- et per- dans la poésie républicaine et augustéenne*, Brussels

Vasaly, A. (1993). *Representations: images of the world in Ciceronian oratory*, Berkeley

Versnel, H. S. (1981). "Self-sacrifice, compensation, and the anonymous gods," in *Le sacrifice dans l'antiquité*, Geneva: 135–94

Vogt, J. (1960). "Caesar und seine Soldaten," *Orbis* 89–109 [orig. 1940]

Voisin, J.-L. (2009). "La mort volontaire du vaincu chez les Celtes," *MEFRA* 121: 395–405

Wagner, O. (1924). "Zu Caesar, *De Bello Gallico*," *Philologische Wochenschrift* 44: 1085–87

Walbank, F. W. (1974). "Polybius between Greece and Rome" in E. Gabba (ed.), *Polybe: neuf exposés suivis de discussions*, Geneva: 3–38

Walser, G. (1998). Bellum Helveticum: *Studien zum Beginn der caesarischen Eroberung von Gallien*, Stuttgart

Walsh, P. G. (1954). "The literary techniques of Livy," *RhM* 97: 97–114

Waquet, F. (1998). *Le Latin ou l'empire d'un signe: XVIe–XXe siècle*, Paris

Wardle, D. (1997). "'The sainted Julius': Valerius Maximus and the Dictator," *CP* 92: 323–45

Watson, G. R. (1969). *The Roman soldier*, Ithaca

Webb, R. (2016). *Ekphrasis, imagination and persuasion in ancient rhetorical theory and practice*, New York

Welch, K. (1998). "Caesar and his officers in the Gallic War commentaries," in Welch–Powell: 85–110

Welch, K. and A. Powell (eds.) (1998). *Julius Caesar as artful reporter: the war commentaries as political instruments*, Bristol [Review by A. Riggsby, in *BMCR* 1999: n.p.]

Wheeler, E. L. (1988). *Stratagem and the vocabulary of military trickery*, Leiden

(2010). "Polyaenus: *scriptor militaris*," in K. Broderson (ed.), *Polyaenus – Neue Studien*, Berlin: 7–54

Whitehead, D. (1979). "Tacitus and the loaded alternative," *Latomus* 38: 474–95

Whitehead, D. (2002). *Aineias the tactician: How to survive under siege*, London

Will, W. (1992). *Julius Caesar – eine Bilanz*, Stuttgart

Willi, A. (2010). "Campaigning for *utilitas*: style, grammar and philosophy in C. Iulius Caesar," in E. Dickey, A. Chahoud (eds.), *Colloquial and literary Latin*, Cambridge: 229–42

Williams, G. (1968). *Tradition and originality in Roman poetry*, Oxford

Williams, J. H. C. (2001). *Beyond the Rubicon: Romans and Gauls in republican Italy*, Oxford

Wimmel, W. (1974). *Die technische Seite von Caesars Unternehmen gegen Avaricum (B.G. 7.13ff.)*, Wiesbaden

Winkler, L. (1995). *Salus: vom Staatskult zur politischen Idee*, Heidelberg

Winterbottom, M. (1983). "Caesar," in Reynolds, L. and N. Wilson (eds.), *Texts and transmission: a survey of the Latin classics*, Oxford: 35–36

Wirszubski, C. (1950). *Libertas as a political idea at Rome*, Cambridge

(1961). "*Audaces*: a study in political phraseology," *JRS* 51: 12–22

Wiseman, T. P. (1974). "Legendary genealogies in late-republican Rome," *G&R* 21: 153–64

(1979). *Clio's cosmetics: three studies in Greco-Roman literature*, Leicester

(1985). "Competition and cooperation," in id., *Roman political life*, Exeter: 3–20

(1998). "The publication of *De bello Gallico*," in Welch–Powell: 1–9

(2009). *Remembering the Roman people*, Oxford

Wistrand, E. (1946). "Nach Innen Oder Nach Aussen? Zum geographischen Sprachgebrauch der Römer," *Göteborgs Högskolas Årsskrift* 52: 1–55

(1978). *Caesar and contemporary society*, Gothenburg

Witte, K. (1910). "Über die Form der Darstellung in Livius' Geschichtswerk," *RhM* 65: 270–305, 359–419

Wölfflin, E. (1888). "Der euphemistische Gebrauch von *pacare*," *ALL* 5: 581

(1893). *"Elegantia Caesaris," ALL* 8: 142–43

(1977). *Ausgewählte Schriften*, Hildesheim

Woodman, A. J. (1979). "Self-imitation and the substance of history: Tacitus, *Annals* 1.61–5 and *Histories* 2.70, 5.14–15," in D. West and A. J. Woodman (eds.), *Creative imitation and Latin literature*, Cambridge: 143–55

(1988). *Rhetoric in classical historiography: four studies*, Portland

(2010). "Community health: metaphors in Latin historiography," in F. Cairns, M. Griffin (eds.), *Papers of the Langford Latin Seminar, fourteenth volume: health and sickness in ancient Rome; Greek and Roman poetry and historiography*: 43–62

(2014). *Tacitus: Agricola*, with C. S. Kraus, Cambridge

Woolf, G. (1993). "Rethinking the *Oppida,*" *Oxford journal of archaeology* 12: 223–34

(2019). "The Gallic Wars in Roman history," in Fitzpatrick–Haselgrove: 9–19

Wylie, G. (1989). "Why did Labienus defect from Caesar in 49 BC?," *AHB* 3: 123–27

Yakobson, A. (2016). "*Optimates, populares*," in *Oxford research encyclopedia in classics*, New York

Zecchini, G. (1978). *Cassio Dione e la guerra gallica di Cesare*, Milan [Review by C. B. R. Pelling in *CR* 32 (1982): 146–48]

(2001). *Cesare et il mos maiorum*, Stuttgart

Ziolkowski, A. (1993). "*Urbs direpta*, or how the Romans sacked cities," in: J. Rich, G. Shipley (eds.), *War and society in the Roman world*, London: 69–91

Zoido, J. C. I. (2007). "The battle exhortation in ancient rhetoric," *Rhetorica* 25: 141–58

INDEX LOCORUM, GENTIUM
PERSONARUMQUE

Only names in the Latin text are included. "!" indicates names not mentioned before VII; "*" precedes towns. An explanatory note will accompany the first instance of each name unless otherwise noted below (n.).

Acco: 1.4
* Agedincum: 10.4; 57.1; 59.4; 62.10
!* Alesia: (68n.); 68.1, 2, 3; 75.1; 76.5; 77.1; 79.1, 3; 80.9; 84.1
Allobroges (*gens*): 64.5, 7; 65.3
Ambiani (*gens*): 75.3
! Ambibarii (*gens*): 75.4
! Ambiuareti (*gens*): 75.2; 90.6
Andes (*gens*): 4.6
! M. Antonius: 81.6
Aquitania: 31.5
Arar (*flumen*): 90.7
Arecomici: see Volcae
Aremoricae (*gens*): 75.4
! M. Aristius: 42.5; 43.1
Aruerni (*gens*), <u>Aruernus</u>: 3.3; <u>4.1</u>; 5.5; 7; 7.1, 5; 8.2 (*bis*), 4, 5; 9.5; 34.2; 37.1; 38.5, 6; 64.6; 66.1; 75.2 (*bis*); <u>76.4</u>; 77.3; <u>83.6</u>; <u>88.4</u>; 89.5; 90.2, 3
Atrebates (*gens*): 75.3; 76.4
Aulerci (*gens*), <u>Aulercus</u>: 4.6; <u>57.3</u>
  ! A. Brannouices: 75.2
  ! A. Cenomani: 75.3
  A. Eburouices: 75.3
!* Auaricum: (14–28n.); 13.3; 15.3; 16.1, 2; 18.1; 20.4; 30.3; 31.3, 4; 32.1; 47.5 (7); 52.2

L. Minucius Basilus: 90.5
Bellouaci (*gens*): 59.2, 5; 75.3, 5; 90.5
* Bibracte: 55.4, 6; 63.5; 90.7
Bituriges (*gens*): 5.1, 2, 3, 4, 5, 7; 8.5; 9.6; 11.9; 12.2; 13.3 (*bis*); 15.1, 4; 21.3; 29.4; 75.3; 90.6
! Blannouii (*gens*): 75.2
Boii (*gens*): 9.6; 10.3, 4; 17.2, 3; 75.3
Brannouices (*gens*): see Aulerci
Britannia: 76.1
D. Brutus: 9.1; 87.1

Caburus: 65.2
! Cadurci (*gens*), <u>Cadurcus</u>: 4.6; <u>5.1</u>; <u>7.1</u>; 64.6; 75.2

! L. Caesar: 65.1
G. Iulius Caesar: *passim*
Caletes (*gens*): 75.4
! Camulogenus: 57.3; 59.5; 62.5, 8
Carnutes (*gens*): 2.1, 3; 3.1; 11.3; 75.3
! Cauarillus: 67.7
!* Cauillonum: 42.5; 90.7
! Celtillus: 4.1
! Cenabensis (*gens*): 11.7; 28.4
!* Cenabum: 3.1, 3; 11.3, 4, 6; 14.1; 17.7
Cenomani (*gens*): see Aulerci
Ceuenna (*mons*): 8.2, 3; 56.2
Q. Tullius Cicero: 90.7
Cimbri (*gens*): 77.12, 14
! P. Clodius (Pulcher): 1.1
Commius: (1–5n.); 75.5; 76.1 [n.], 4; 79.1.
! Conconnetodumnus: 3.1
! Conuictolitauis: 32.4; 33.4; 37.1; 39.2; 42.4; 55.4; 67.7
Coriosolites (*gens*): 75.4
! Cotuatus (?): (3.1n. *Gutuatro*)
! Cotus: 32.4; 33.3; 39.2; 67.7
! "Critognatus:" 77.2; 78.1

!* Decetia: 33.2
Diuiciacus: 39.1
! G. Valerius Donotaurus: 65.2

Eburouices: see Aulerci
! Elauar (*flumen*): 34.2; 35.1; 53.4;
! Eleuteti (*gens*): 75.2
! Eporedorix: 38.2; 39.1, 3; 40.5; 54.1; 55.4; 63.9; 64.5; 67.7; 76.4

G. Fabius: 40.3; 41.2, 4; 87.1; 90.5
! L. Fabius: 47.7; 50.3
! G. Fufius Cita: 3.1

! Gabali (*gens*): 7.2; 64.6; 75.2
Galli, <u>Gallus</u>: 1.2; 12.6; 13.2; 15.4; 17.7; 19.2; 20.7; 22.1; <u>25.2</u>; 26.1, 5; 29.6; 30.1, 4; 40.7; 45.6; 46.3;

INDEX

(It includes Greek and Roman authors if Caesar engaged with them repeatedly [or they with his work], and other individuals as they seem relevant to *VII*. References to {P} are to the introduction, otherwise to the notes. A lemma typically includes references to those instances that receive a definition/explanation or are otherwise significant [unless frequency matters, as s.v. "topoi"]; in longer lists of instances, the particularly pertinent notes are in bold.)

377